JOHNNY

R.S. ROSE AND GORDON D. SCOTT

JOHNNY

A SPY'S LIFE

THE PENNSYLVANIA STATE UNIVERSITY PRESS
UNIVERSITY PARK, PENNSYLVANIA

Excerpts in chapters 12, 13, and 15 from R. S. Rose, *One of the Forgotten Things: Getúlio Vargas and Brazilian Social Control, 1930–1954*. Copyright © 2000 by Greenwood Press. All rights reserved. Reproduced with permission of Greenwood Publishing Group, Inc., Westport, Connecticut.

Library of Congress Cataloging-in-Publication Data
Rose, R. S., 1943– .
Johnny : a spy's life / R. S. Rose and Gordon D. Scott.
p. cm.
Summary: "The life and career of a spy, the German-born Johann Heinrich Amadeus "Johnny" de Graaf (1894–1980), who was a double agent for the British against the Soviets before the Second World War, and worked for Canada against Canadian Fascists during the war"—Provided by publisher.
Includes bibliographical references and index.
ISBN 978-0-271-03569-7 (cloth : alk. paper)
1. Graaf, Johnny de, 1894–1980.
2. Spies—Great Britain—Biography.
3. Intelligence officers—Great Britain—Biography.
4. Germans—Great Britain—Biography.
5. Espionage, British—History—20th century.
6. Great Britain—Relations—Soviet Union.
7. Soviet Union—Relations—Great Britain.
8. Spies—Canada—Biography.
9. Anti-fascist movements—Canada—History—20th century.
10. World War, 1939–1945—Canada.
I. Scott, Gordon D., 1935– .
II. Title.
UB271.G72G69   2009
327.12410092—dc22
[B]
2009023603

Copyright © 2010 The Pennsylvania State University
All rights reserved
Printed in the United States of America
Published by The Pennsylvania State University Press,
University Park, PA 16802-1003

The Pennsylvania State University Press is a member of the Association of American University Presses.

It is the policy of
The Pennsylvania State University Press to use acid-free paper. Publications on uncoated stock satisfy the minimum requirements of American National Standard for Information Sciences—Permanence of Paper for Printed Library Material, ANSI Z39.48–1992.

This book is printed on Natures Natural, which contains 50% post-consumer waste.

In memory of
VIOLET LILLY SCOTT

CONTENTS

List of Illustrations   ix
Acknowledgments   xii
Abbreviations   xiv
Explanatory Note   xvii

Introduction   1

1 | Wilhelmshaven   3

2 | Merchant Marine   16

3 | Conscripted   33

4 | Osowiec   50

5 | Germany in Chaos   62

6 | *Die* KPD   86

7 | The Moscow Student   101

8 | Assignment Romania   139

9 | British Missions   151

10 | Berlin and Prague   165

11 | Manchuria and China   178

12 | Brazil One   194

13 | Argentina   213

14 | The Return to Moscow   225

15 | Brazil Two   259

16 | The War's First Years   290

17 | The Montreal Nests   305

18 | A Man from the Sea   321

19 | To Catch a Submarine   343

20 | The Control Commission   358

21 | Home   372

Epilogue   386

. . . and the others   389

Aliases   391

Notes   393
Bibliography   427
Index   437

ILLUSTRATIONS

1. Mitscherlich Straße about the time that Johnny left home. Photo: Stadtarchiv Wilhelmshaven.
2. The *Niobe* under sail. Photo: WZ-Bilddienst.
3. A probable photograph of Johnny de Graaf in 1914 in the Kaiserliche Marine. Photo: Deutsches Marinemuseum Wilhelmshaven.
4. The battleship *Westfalen* before the Great War. Photo: Deutsches Marinemuseum Wilhelmshaven.
5. Part of the Osowiec Fortress. Photo: Alain Lecomte.
6. Willy de Graaf, Albert Funk, and Johnny de Graaf. Photo courtesy of Johnny de Graaf III.
7. The mines in Ahlen.
8. Ruth Fischer. Photo: Hermann Weber/Andreas Herbst.
9. Karl Radek in 1923. Photo: http://www.havelshouseofhistory.com/.
10. Arthur Ernst Ewert. Photo: Deutsche Post der DDR.
11. Maria de Graaf, Oscar de Graaf, and other comrades at a KPD rally in 1929. Photo courtesy of Johnny de Graaf III.
12. Horst Wessel depicted on the cover of the sheet music to "Die Fahne Hoch." Photo: To-Ma Edition.
13. Tuure Lehén, alias Alfred Langner, in a Soviet army uniform, during the early 1940s. Photo: Kansan Arkisto/The People's Archives.
14. Peteris Kuzis, alias Ian Karlovich Berzin. Photo: Олма Медиа Групп.
15. Dmitri Manuilski. Photo: Linea Rossa-Genova.
16. Johnny de Graaf, sometime between 1930 and 1932. Photo: FBI.
17. Johnny de Graaf, sometime between 1930 and 1934. Photo: FBI.
18. Johnny de Graaf in 1932 on his mission to the United Kingdom. Photo courtesy of Gordon D. Scott.
19. Béla Kun. Photo: Marxist Internet Archive.
20. Harry Pollitt. Photo: Communist Party of Britain.
21. George Aitken in 1944. Photo: People's History Museum/Communist Party of Britain.
22. Marianne and Oscar de Graaf with Helena Krüger during Helena's June 1933 trip to Ahlen. Photo courtesy of Johnny de Graaf III.
23. Frank Foley's August 1939 passport photograph. Photo: United Kingdom, Foreign and Commonwealth Office.

24. Valentine Patrick Terrell Vivian at the races on March 21, 1930. Photo: Hulton Getty Picture Collection.
25. Manfred Stern in 1932. Photo: Verlag Dr. Wolfgang Weist.
26. Eugene Dennis, alias Comrade Milton, in May 1950. Photo: Steve Trussel.
27. Luís Carlos Prestes in 1934, before leaving Moscow for Brazil. Photo: Anita Prestes.
28. Getúlio Vargas with his police chief, Filinto Müller, on July 27, 1940. Photo: CPDOC/FGV—Arquivo Souza Costa.
29. Alfred Hutt in 1937. Photo: Arquivo Nacional.
30. Johnny de Graaf in 1935. Photo: Arquivo Público do Estado do Rio de Janeiro.
31. Helena Krüger in early 1936. Photo: Arquivo Público do Estado do Rio de Janeiro.
32. The bomb that did not explode in the house on Rua Barão da Torre. Photo: Arquivo Público do Estado do Rio de Janeiro.
33. Johnny's bomb factory in Grajaú after it was discovered by the police. Photo: Arquivo Público do Estado do Rio de Janeiro.
34. The last known photograph of Helena Krüger, taken in San Martín in 1937. Photo courtesy of Waltraud Krüger.
35. The house at Calle Florida 246, and the upstairs bedroom where Helena Krüger died. Photo: R. S. Rose.
36. Stella Blagoeva. Photo: *Jurnalul National.*
37. Vyacheslav Molotov. Photo: Navajo.CZ.
38. Kliment Voroshilov. Photo: Hugo S. Cunningham.
39. Johnny de Graaf Jr. as an adult. Photo: Gordon D. Scott.
40. Oscar de Graaf in his Wehrmacht uniform on October 28, 1940. Photo courtesy of Johnny de Graaf III.
41. Marianne Oberschild (nee de Graaf). Photo courtesy of Johnny de Graaf III.
42. Johnny de Graaf in 1938. Photo: Arquivo Nacional.
43. Gertrude Krüger in 1938. Photo: Arquivo Nacional.
44. DESPS in Rio de Janeiro in the late 1930s. Photo: Arquivo Público do Estado do Rio de Janeiro.
45. The house at Avenida Rainha Elisabeth 219. Photo courtesy of Waltraud Krüger.
46. To the right of Johnny and Gerti are her parents, Emilie and Gustav Krüger, in 1938 or 1939. Photo courtesy of Waltraud Krüger.
47. Johnny's 1937 Ford, before it was wrecked, in a photo taken by Ernst Krüger. Photo courtesy of Waltraud Krüger.
48. Ernst Krüger in the Spreewald Forest, south of Berlin, after returning from Brazil. Photo courtesy of Waltraud Krüger.
49. The scuttling of the *Graf Spee*. Photo: Dave Page Collection.
50. Franz Gruber's DESPS archive photo. Photo: Arquivo Público do Estado do Rio de Janeiro.

51. De Graaf relaxing on the back veranda at Rainha Elisabeth. Photo courtesy of Gordon D. Scott.
52. Cecil Borer in 1939. Photo: *O Mundo*/Biblioteca Nacional.
53. The Polícia Central in the 1930s. Photo: Arquivo Público do Estado do Rio de Janeiro.
54. The Fortress of Santa Cruz. Photo: R. S. Rose.
55. Cliff Harvison. Photo: RCMP Museum, Regina.
56. Palmerston Avenue 49 in Montreal's Mount Royal suburb. Photo: R. S. Rose.
57. Werner von Janowski's RCMP mug shot. Photo: Library and Archives Canada.
58. Adrien Arcand in 1933. Photo: Canada Wide Media.
59. Tim Buck. Photo: Communist Party of Canada/Parti communiste du Canada.
60. The Wilberforce apartments in London. Photo: R. S. Rose.
61. Johnny at the end of the war in 1945. Photo: FBI.
62. De Graff in the uniform of a British army officer. Photo courtesy of Johnny de Graaf III.
63. The boardinghouse at 1863 Dorchester Street West (now called Boulevard René-Lévesque Ouest) in Montreal. Photo courtesy of E. Kefalidis.
64. Oscar and his wife, Leni, visiting Johnny on the steps of the Montreal boardinghouse during either their 1952 or 1953 trip. Photo courtesy of Johnny de Graaf III.
65. Wedding day. Sári and Johnny on June 14, 1952. Photo courtesy of Johnny de Graaf III.
66. Going swimming during the visit of Oscar and his wife, Leni (taking the picture), to Montreal in 1953. Photo courtesy of Johnny de Graaf III.
67. At the wheel of his car. Photo courtesy of Johnny de Graaf III.
68. Harry Gold. Photo: FBI.
69. Thomas L. Black on July 14, 1950. Photo: FBI.
70. The main house at Horningtoft. Photo: Brockville Museum, Brockville, Ontario.
71. Tourist cabin proprietor. Photo courtesy of Gordon D. Scott.
72. In old age. Photo courtesy of Gordon D. Scott.
73. All that remained of Horningtoft when visited by one of the authors in 1995. Photo courtesy of R. S. Rose/Jack Armitage.

ACKNOWLEDGMENTS

At the outset, R. S. Rose wishes to express a word of appreciation to Knut Sveri in Stockholm *fordi du ga meg ønske*. Second, but they rightly deserve to be first, are Ernst Krüger, his wife, Waltraud, as well as Oscar and Leni de Graaf, plus their son Johann de Graaf III. Without their help this partial biography would never have been written.

Originally, it was Rodolph de Graaf's approval of Rose's emerging interest in his cousin that got his side of things going. He gave the family's permission to see restricted political police documents in Rio de Janeiro. Without William Waack in Berlin, and later in Rio, the journey to those documents, and to ones in Germany and Russia, would have been much slower. In that respect, Yuri Ribeiro Prestes was a tireless asset and a truly generous individual. John W. F. Dulles in Austin and Wilhelm Mensing in Bonn were such help that R. S. Rose can never express his total gratitude. After learning that the de Graafs had made it back to London in 1940, a whole host of Canadians came into play, the most important of whom was Gordon Scott.

During his youth in Montreal, Scott knew both Johnny and Gerti. As an eight-year-old boy, he remembers them returning to his home late at night, where they were staying briefly. Johnny would tiptoe to his bedside and deposit a coin or two into a wooden bank, which he had given Gordon. Gerti would lean over and kiss Gordon's forehead. Johnny, Gerti, and Gordon's parents would later visit one another's homes frequently, for chats, meals, and games of bridge. None of the Scott children, however, were allowed to visit their house, on the pretext that they worked at night and slept during the day. The true facts were revealed a year or so later, when they learned of Johnny's unique occupation and of the guarded guest who resided in his basement. Gordon vowed then that someday he would write Johnny's life story.

This project had a larger group of people from around the world helping from time to time. Besides the Canadians, there were Americans, Argentines, Austrians, Belorussians, Brazilians, Danes, English, French, Germans, Hungarians, Norwegians, Poles, Romanians, Russians, Swedes, and Ukrainians, all offering their expertise in understanding the man behind the whispers of Johnny de Graaf. So thank you, Valtair Almeida, Кирилл Михайлович Андерсон, Stefan Antheck, Jack and Audrey Armitage, Candy Ashbridge, Nilo Batista, Dean Beeby, Gus Begalki, Gilles Bengle, Lars-Erik Björlin, Cecil Borer, Shirley Brawn, Roger Chartrand, Andy and Leona Chatwood, Stanley Clark, Blake Clarke,

Андрей Доронин, Marcel Douek, Edward Duffy, Peter Erler, Sándor and Angela Fegyverneky, Bill Flores, Paulo Apulcro de Fonseca, Peter Gabrielsson, Arch Getty, Yelena Gogolieyn, Frances Grandbois, J. Barry Gurdin, Norm and Odette Harder, Gusztáv Harsányi, Gusztáv Harsányi Jr., Joe Hartman, Stanley Hilton, Kurt Jacobsen, Andrzej Kawczynski, E. Kefalidis, Endre Kovács, Tadeusz Krawczak, Joachim Krüger, Lieselotte Krüger, Leslie Laczko, Alan Lecomte, Luiz Cláudio and Cecília Marigo, Jack McClelland, Licia Mendeiros, Eliana Furtado de Mendonça, Myriam Mensing, Lisa Meranger, Joseph Naszady, Bogdan Oźlański, Waldecy Catharina Magalhães Pedreria, Elina Pessanha, Neil Pollock, Jorge Posse, Pedro Posse, Gerhard Schrempp, Eleanor Scott, Howard Scott, Ron Scott, Violet Scott, Michael Smith, Joanne Stanbridge, N. Leslie Sterritt, Ron Stewart, Don Swayne, Anja Teymourian, Andrew Thorpe, Vladimir Tismaneanu, Jim Warren, Selena Williams, Nancy Winder, Artur Wiśniewski, Ingrid Woods, Miroslaw Worona, Glenn Wright, and Wilmont Young. Ned Root was the bridge that brought the two authors together.

A special word of thanks goes to Donna Scott for the continuous support and encouragement shown to her husband, Gordon, over the years. Likewise, R. S. Rose is deeply indebted to his mother, Juanita Vertresse Rose, for lending him enough money to go to Canada before she died. She was one of the few who believed in what he was doing in 1995 when he came up to California from Brazil without a dime, but with dreams of finding Gerti alive in Montreal.

The authors are grateful for permission to use parts of the following works by R. S. Rose: "Johnny's Two Trips to Brazil," *Luso-Brazilian Review* 38, no. 1 (2001); and *One of the Forgotten Things: Getúlio Vargas and Brazilian Social Control, 1930–1954* (Westport, Conn.: Greenwood Press, 2000).

ABBREVIATIONS

AHI	Arquivo Histórico do Itamarati (Historical Archive of the Itamarati)
AHPBA	Archivo Histórico de la Provincia de Buenos Aires (Historical Archive of the Province of Buenos Aires, La Plata)
ANL	Aliança Nacional Libertadora (National Liberation Alliance)
APERJ	Arquivo Público do Estado do Rio de Janeiro (Public Archive of the State of Rio de Janeiro)
BAN	Brazil, Arquivo Nacional (National Archive)
CNA	Canada, National Archives
"C" Division	Royal Canadian Mounted Police, Quebec Branch
CIA	Central Intelligence Agency
CIC	Citizenship and Immigration Canada—Citoyenneté et Immigration Canada
Comintern	Communist International. The Comintern existed from 1919 to 1943 for the sole purpose of exporting Soviet-style revolutions to other countries. China and Brazil were two of the main targets.
CPC	Communist Party of Canada
CPGB	Communist Party of Great Britain
CSIS	Canadian Security Intelligence Service—Service canadien du renseignement de sécurité
DESPS	Delegacia Especial de Segurança Política e Social (Special Police for Political and Social Security). The Brazilian political police in Rio de Janeiro and other cities from January 10, 1933, to March 28, 1944.
FBI	Federal Bureau of Investigation
GBB	Germany, Bundesarchiv (Federal Archive), Berlin
GBF	Germany, Bundesarchiv (Federal Archive), Freiburg
GHD	Germany, Hauptstaatsarchiv (Main State Archive), Düsseldorf
GSA	Germany, Stadt (City), Ahlen
GSH	Germany, Staatsarchiv (State Archive), Hamburg
ИККИ (IKKI)	Исполнительный комитет коммунистического интернационала (Ispolnitelnii Komitet Kommunisticheskovo

	Internatsionala—Executive Committee [of the Communist] International)
KPD	Kommunistische Partei Deutschlands (German [Communist] Party)
M4	Soviet Army Intelligence
MI5	Military Intelligence 5 (British). Areas of operation in 1930–1940 were domestic intelligence and counterespionage; the MI5 was renamed the Security Service in 1931, but "MI5" or simply "5" is still used.
MI6	Military Intelligence 6 (British). Areas of operation in 1930–1940 were foreign intelligence and counterespionage. The correct name is the Secret Intelligence Service, or SIS, but "MI6" or simply "6" is still used.
НКВД (NKVD)	Народный комиссариат внутренних дел (Narodnij kommisariat vnutrennih del—the People's Commissariat of Internal Affairs). The Soviet secret police from 1934 to 1946.
"O" Division	Royal Canadian Mounted Police, Ontario branch
ОГПУ (OGPU)	Объединенное государственное политическое управление (Ob'edinennoe gosudarstvennoe politicheskoe upravlenie—Combined State Political Directorate, also translated as All Union State Political Board). The Soviet secret police from 1923 to 1934.
OMC (OMS)	Отдел международных связей (Otdel mezdunarodnoj svjazi—Department of International Contacts, also translated as Department of International Connections). The section of the Comintern responsible for links with Communist parties outside the Soviet Union. It was later renamed the Communication Department.
PCA	Partido Comunista de la Argentina (Argentine Communist Party)
PCB	Partido Comunista Brasileiro (Brazilian Communist Party)
PCR	Partidul Comunist Român (Romanian Communist Party)
QPP	Quebec Provincial Police
RA	Revolutionärer Ausschuß (Revolutionary Committee)
RCMP	Royal Canadian Mounted Police
RFB	Roter Frontkämpferbund (Red Front Fighter Organization)
РГАСПИ	Российский государственный архив социально-политической истории (Rossiiskii gosudarstvennyi arkhiv sotsial'no-politicheskoi istorii—Russian State Archive of Socio-political History)
SA	Sturmabteilung (Storm Division). The Nazi Brownshirts.
SIS	Secret Intelligence Service (see MI6)

ABBREVIATIONS

...che Partei Deutschlands (German Social
...)
..., Control Commission for Germany
..., Foreign and Commonwealth Office
..., National Archives
... of State
...hives
...aldemokratische Partei Deutschlands (Inde-
...Social Democratic Party)
...мунистическая партия (большев-
...) (vsesoiuznaia kommunisticheskaia partiia [bolshe-
vikov]—All-Union Communist Party [Bolsheviks]). The
Communist Party in the USSR from 1925 to 1952.

ZK   Zentral Komitee (the Central Committee of the KPD)

EXPLANATORY NOTE

All material within quotation marks that has no endnote reference is the actual comments of Johnny de Graaf or of someone he was quoting. Most of these remarks were recorded by Gordon Scott and transcribed later. In those instances where de Graaf's observations were taped elsewhere, they have been given an endnote identifying the source. De Graaf left no diary. To do so could have meant a death sentence had the pages fallen into the wrong hands. All quotations and other items mentioned by Johnny were corroborated where possible. Only a limited number of instances were at odds with secondary sources, and each is mentioned in a corresponding endnote. The other endnotes relate specifically to a word, if following a word in a sentence; generally to a sentence, if following a sentence; or to a paragraph, if at the end of a paragraph. They *do not* relate to all information between any given pair of endnote numbers.

In 1940, in an attempt to provide some cover for Johnny, the English suggested, and he agreed to, a name change from de Graaf to de Graff. That praxis is followed in part of chapter 16, once it was decided, and in all subsequent chapters.

Additionally, the material released by the U.S. Federal Bureau of Investigation, from the 101-page interview made by the FBI of de Graff in Montreal in 1952, had numerous names censored by functionaries at the U.S. Department of Justice. A copy of this crucial document was given to the Royal Canadian Mounted Police, probably as one of the conditions for granting the interview, and was kindly released to the authors by the Canadian Security Intelligence Service—without any redacted words. The FBI account will be the default version here except in those situations where the censored name is revealed in the RCMP copy and used in the text. Thank you, Canada! Merci, Canada!

INTRODUCTION

The tale you are about to read is an incredible one. It is the adventure of a man considered a hero by some and an adversary by others. Certainly, in the champion's role he was no ideal protagonist. He was far from perfect. He was guarded against Jews, he could be vindictive, and he probably murdered one of his common-law wives. He was also stubborn and often unbending. These shortcomings might rightly excuse our attention of lesser men. In the case of Johnny de Graaf, however, what he did for His Majesty's government and later for the Allies outshines his faults and supports his story being told.

Different from many biographies, *Johnny* is largely taken from the subject's own words. It has been edited and added to with fourteen years' worth of research in thirteen countries by R. S. Rose. The project originally began with Gordon Scott's series of interviews, which started in February 1975. Almost instantly, this resulted in his home phone being bugged by parties unknown. For a year he traveled from Ottawa to Brockville, Ontario, Canada, to stay at Johnny's tourist lodge, Horningtoft, and record the conversations with his longtime acquaintance. When concluded, on January 31, 1976, there was a small mountain of tapes. As the interviews were being made, Scott would transcribe them in longhand and finally write them up on a typewriter after he returned to Ottawa or otherwise had time to do so. In this way he created a working manuscript. The tapes themselves were later discarded, but the typed, and some of the longhand, versions survived. Herein can be found several of the problems that caused havoc with the manuscript. At the time of the interviews, de Graaf was in his early eighties and either slowly becoming senile, forgetting names, or purposefully misrepresenting them to conceal or glorify some unknown fact. Johnny also spoke English with a pronounced German accent, which did not help. Scott speaks no German. Errors, therefore, entered the research as Scott listened to and wrote down what was being said on the tapes, as, for example, in the case of

Arthur Ewert, who was listed originally as Avid Eban. In other situations, Johnny left out entire details, such as the death of Helena Krüger in Buenos Aires.

R. S. Rose began his investigation of de Graaf after becoming the first academic to be allowed an extensive look at the Brazilian political police files in Rio de Janeiro in 1991. He subsequently brought his own kind of expertise to the project, namely, that of books, of knowing where to find facts and how to confirm statements. He also tracked down and extensively interviewed what was left of Johnny's family in Germany, as well as the Krüger family in Brazil.

Johnny de Graaf worked for years for Britain's Secret Intelligence Service, or SIS, commonly known as MI6. The British and the Argentines were the only major players to refuse all queries—save two by the English—for information about de Graaf. Even with permission from Johnny's family, the mighty English bulldog remained steadfast and unwilling to let the truth be told about one of their key operatives during the period just prior to World War II and for the duration of the war itself. They claimed that revealing such information would endanger their abilities to conduct contemporary intelligence work, or that it would endanger national security. The Argentines refused to provide anything except the death certificate of Helena Krüger. Even with the help of the American Embassy, government bureaucrats in Buenos Aires declined to reveal what they have in their files from 1936 on Francisco Gruber (Johnny's alias there). Because these two sources of information have been withheld, this annotated biography is in reality an incomplete one.

Refusing to give up, Rose obtained his information from American, Brazilian, Canadian, German, and Russian government archives and intelligence services. He spoke with anyone who knew anything about the man, including his surviving Canadian case handlers. One of the concessions by the British government, by the way, was an important piece of the puzzle. Until receiving a letter in 1994 from M. T. Murray of the United Kingdom Foreign and Commonwealth Office,[1] Rose believed that Johnny and Gerti had perished at sea in 1940 while on their way to England, ironically torpedoed by a German U-boat. Murray's letter and newspaper clipping confirmed that such was not the case. The English yielded on only one other group of documents. Rose discovered a file on de Graaf at the National Archives outside London that is too sensitive for the public to see until January 1, 2047. The items in this file cover the period in Johnny's life from 1940 to 1946. Following a two-year battle to have the ban lifted, fourteen pages were released. They contained little that was new.

1

WILHELMSHAVEN

Many things are set in motion close to the sea. There is something almost magnetic about its changing beauty, about its power. There is equally something that draws one into this saga of a man who did so much, but was never caught or found out. Even he was amazed in later years that he had gotten away with it all.[1] The journey of Johann Heinrich Amadeus de Graaf began by the water where the Weser River empties into the North Sea and eventually the Atlantic Ocean. The place was Nordenham, Germany, on May 11, 1894.[2]

At the end of the nineteenth century, Nordenham was a sleepy kind of a town a short ferry ride from Bremerhaven, one of Germany's major ports. The de Graaf bloodline came to the Fatherland generations earlier through the porous border with Holland. Johnny,[3] as he was called all his life, was the oldest of seven children. He had two sisters and four brothers. Following Johnny came Sophie, Willy, Oscar, Waldemar, Paula, and the last of his siblings, Walter, on May 3, 1908.[4]

Of medium build with shining blue eyes, Johann Wilhelm Ludwig de Graaf was a little shorter than his future wife. Known by his second name, Wilhelm occasionally wore gold-trimmed pince-nez glasses, which he was forever losing. He was a gentle man, loving, circumspect, and seldom angry. Born on July 22, 1868, in Geestemünde or Geestendorf, both now part of Bremerhaven, Wilhelm must have had a very happy childhood, for he was devoted to his parents.[5]

Wilhelm de Graaf lived for music, and from his youth surrounded himself with melodies and compositions. Life was hard, however, for many musicians in Germany of the late nineteenth century. A pianist, Wilhelm lived off the earnings of one musical performance until another came along. Wilhelm met Amanda while performing at a concert in Bremen, fell in love, and married her on March 2, 1892, in the same city.[6] Smitten with his bride, his feelings for her would grow in the years to come, blinding him to reality.

Anna Louise Henriette Amanda de Graaf, nee Schulte, known simply as Amanda, was twenty-three years old at the time of Johnny's birth. She was five foot four (1.63 meters) tall with jet-black hair. Considered attractive by many, Amanda was born on August 30, 1871, into a middle-class family in Hamm, which is to the south of Nordenham in the province of Westfalen. Her father died during her youth and her mother and sister remained in Hamm. Wherever the couple lived in the years to come, they never visited Amanda, her husband, or her children, even at Christmas.[7]

As Wilhelm's career progressed, his wages did not increase by much. The family's standard of living continued at the subsistence level. This was indicative of the low esteem suffered by musicians in general at that time.[8] He and the family arrived in Hamburg on September 16, 1912. Wilhelm felt that the big city would offer him more chances to find engagements. In a stroke of luck, he eventually did land a temporary position playing the piano with the Hamburg Philharmonic Orchestra. But things did not go all that well. In fact, the family moved from one working-class residence to another in Germany's second city. In all, there would be thirty-three apartments and houses between November 11, 1912, and July 17, 1918. Where he could, Wilhelm rigged up a place to practice, which may have provoked the ire of his less artistic neighbors and added to his reasons for moving so often. Yet the main reason for so many changes of address, which could have only added to the instability of the family, was poverty.[9]

Before giving Hamburg a try, and when Johnny was still living at home, the family lived in Wilhelmshaven. Between 1900 and 1912 they moved eight times in that city.[10] The life of a professional musician on the hunt for a gig, moreover, consumed more and more of Wilhelm's time. Paris, Copenhagen, Berlin, and lesser places all took possession of him for long periods. Whenever he could break free and return home, it was a joyous occasion, even if it was only for a weekend or a few days. Although Wilhelm de Graaf nearly lived out of his suitcase, he was the kind of person who always found a moment to send messages to his family from ship, train, or hotel.

Despite her husband's absences, Amanda was apparently not lonely. She kept whatever home they were in spotless, her children well fed and well clothed, and managed the family purse as best she could under the circumstances. Returning from a tour, Wilhelm would give her his entire salary, and often that same day ask her for some meager amount to get a shave or purchase a cigar. He once gave her four hundred marks, which was a very good wage at the turn of the century.

As Johnny was the oldest and strongest, his mother expected him to be her number one helper. Whether looking after his brothers and sisters or doing all the heavy work meant for a man, his chores were demanding and never ending. Slowly, more and more was placed on his shoulders under the threat of a spanking if he failed in carrying out everything to perfection. Except for Sophie, the two girls helped little. From time to time she offered to assist her brother against their mother's objections.

Johnny loved to visit his father's parents. Before leaving home, however, Amanda would always demand that he wear his shabbiest attire. He hated doing this because he had several nice things to wear, but Amanda was adamant. At first, his grandparents fell for the deception. Over and over again, with limited funds, they bought whichever child was visiting some new item of clothing, and then loaded him or her down with food to take home. The escapade was enacted in reverse if her husband was away and the grandparents were the ones doing the visiting. As they entered, their gaze took in what they thought to be Wilhelm's poor family, nearly in rags, hungry, the cupboard bare. Feeling bad about what they saw, they dug deep into their pockets or brought things for the children. When they left, no sooner would the door close behind the little drama, than Amanda would grab each new item and squirrel it away in one of her numerous hiding places. She made sure her little actors were well coached in the proper response to any question, under threat of the usual alternative. Over several years this swindle drained her father and mother-in-law dry. The time must have come when Johnny's grandparents questioned the endless mooching. Out of family pride, however, they hesitated to ask their son about his financial situation. The sham ran on love fired by the twin forces of deception and greed.

When he was seven, Johnny rebelled and exposed the poor-family swindle to his grandmother. Shortly afterward, the visits and gifts declined, much to Amanda's frustration. Johnny still got new clothes from his grandparents on his solitary trips, but they insisted that the new things remain at their house. When Johnny returned home still wearing his old outfit, he was met by an angry woman who beat him, hoping to find out why the well had run dry. Again and again he would answer with, "Had they given me new clothes, wouldn't I be wearing them?" Bruised and aching from blows administered by anything handy—broomstick, fire poker, pot, or pan—young Johnny refused to admit that he had revealed his mother's charade. Amanda, though, was certain something was amiss, and she suspected that he was behind it. But despite all her bullying, her son remained silent. Sophie and Johnny agreed that they would keep everything from their father whenever he was home, and the family atmosphere was light and merry. They wanted to spare him the pain and also doubted whether he would even believe them. A romantic, music, dreams of love, and pleasure were his escapes. Anything that dealt with reality, particularly with the certainty of womanhood gone astray, was avoided.

School should have afforded Johnny an island away from the madness at home. Perhaps it did at times. But the breathing space and stimulation that school provided were short lived. By 1900, Wilhelmshaven had a large military training base for the army and navy. As youthful spectators, de Graaf and his childhood pals spent much of their spare time at one or the other facility, eagerly watching the comings and goings of soldiers and ships. Sometimes underfoot, they would be shooed away from the all-military harbor area around the Kaiserliche Werft,[11] only to reappear at another location. They were generally fascinated by all the armed muscle on display, and they often chattered about how men were treated by the Prussian system of strict discipline and rigid regimentation.

Military instruction was compulsory at school on a much reduced scale. One might have expected that Johnny would fit right in with this curriculum owing to his curiosity about the soldiers and sailors in training. Part of the curriculum involved the usual drills and exercises, and there were lectures on the glorious German armed forces. But Johnny quickly learned to hate these lessons and came to view the giant military machine with contempt. For him, the nationalistic dogma was too hard to swallow. In its place, and as a refuge, he began drifting down to the Wilhelmshaven waterfront, transferring his awe to the large cargo and passenger liners preparing to sail to exotic-sounding places in different parts of the world.

Johnny sat on the pilings and observed the goings-on, or built little rafts and paddled out to the ships at anchor around Handelshafen and Neuer Hafen.[12] During Johnny's youth, these two inner harbor areas had some of their activity diverted to the interim Handelshafen, which was really an inlet off the Jade Busen. The reason for the detour was the construction of the Kaiser Wilhelm Bridge, cutting the Handelshafen and Neuer Hafen in half. The bridge would become a symbol of the city. But since Johnny was really interested in the sea, he probably paid little mind to the emerging span. Instead, he busied himself memorizing the types of vessels, country flags, and merchant navy ranks. Conversations with dockside sailors opened up a panorama of great adventure and excitement. "So you want to go to sea, little pup?" they would laughingly remark. "It is a hard life but a life of men. Eat well and grow strong and maybe someday, if you are up to it, you'll sail with us."

For a while, Johnny's mother eased up on him, and he began coming straight home from school more often. His daily tasks included taking the little ones out for air in a carriage or going on some errand. When he finished, with a couple of *Pfennige* (one *Pfennig* equals one one-hundredth of a mark) for his effort, he grabbed a tram to the docks. His mother never gave him the coins before he completed his chores, despite his repeated pleading. Johnny had no other way to earn money, so he either worked for her for loose change or walked from whatever apartment they lived in to the harbor. Every chance he got, he went down to the port to look at all the big sailing ships and daydream. Johnny imagined himself on one of these vessels, saying farewell forever to Wilhelmshaven and his difficult home. He vowed to himself that he would make it all happen one day.

An added boost to Johnny's mounting interest in the sea came from his aunt

Johanna, his father's sister. She had married a sea captain, Dietrich Gerkins. The couple produced a son, Walter, who was about the same age as Johnny. Sometimes Johnny would be invited to the Gerkinses' home in Bremerhaven. When that happened, if the two boys were lucky, Uncle Dietrich would take his nephew and son aboard his ship, the *Niobe,* down at the waterfront. The wooden sailing vessel weighed 505 tons. She was more than 212 feet (nearly 65 meters) long and had been built in 1863 in Glasgow.[13] Captain Gerkins showed the two youngsters around the three-masted ship and patiently answered their questions. He was an excellent sailor, becoming captain of the *Niobe* when he was just twenty-four. The boson's mate taught both lads all about the ship's three thousand ropes, each with a different purpose. He let them climb high into the rigging, then down again, to learn more about knots, tides, winds, and the various sails. Johnny's aunt and uncle were very kind to him during this period and showered him with warmth. By now, Johnny yearned for the sea, the waves, the salt air, and a rolling deck under his feet—and his relatives knew it. At the same time, his life at home took another turn and became more distasteful than ever.

When her husband was away one Saturday afternoon, Johnny's mother gave him some *Pfennige* and urged him to go down to the harbor for a swim. Astonished, her son asked himself, "How come?" She had never offered him money before without some kind of catch. Amanda's pleasant smile and insistence focused his reservations. Another odd thing had happened the week before, when she had him place an ad down at the newspaper office. Years later, he learned that her classified read, "Whoever lends a young woman 100 marks, will be given back by agreement." It would eventually all make sense, and would only add to his endless questioning of authority.

Johnny accepted the money and set out for the harbor, telling his mother goodbye. "Spend the afternoon and enjoy yourself," she called out, as her son strode down the walk. "Something is rotten in the state of Denmark," Johnny mused to himself. He proceeded at a leisurely pace to the street and walked a few blocks for good measure. Fifteen minutes of slow meandering passed, and then he turned around and doubled back, still at an unhurried pace.

Entering his backyard from the street behind his home, he made straight for the small balcony above the kitchen porch. He hopped up and sat on the surrounding fence before climbing a column to the safety of the balcony above. Crossing the terrace, he could reach up and grab the rain gutter at the roof's edge. Slowly he moved, hand over hand, grasping the thin strip of metal until he reached the other balcony, facing his parents' bedroom. It was one of those foolish things of youth. Had he lost his grip, he would have plunged three stories, broken numerous bones, or even been killed.

As soon as his feet touched the balcony railing he lowered himself without a sound onto the solid flooring. Hugging the sidewall beside the large pane-glass doors, and shielded by the inside drapery, he glanced in nervously. There she was, completely naked, lying on her back in bed, while in motion above her was a smiling stranger, stark naked, thrusting his body in and out between her open legs. Stunned, Johnny pulled back, his face red, his body shaking with anger. Somehow he quickly made it across the roof, gripping at anything, until he was down on the ground. Then he raced across the lawn and dove into a clump of cool trees, so thick one could barely see through their foliage.

With his face nearly buried in the moist earth, Johnny quietly sobbed his heart out and beat his fists in the dirt. How long he flailed away in his nightmare he could not say, but the sun was setting when he regained his composure and made his way, unseen, to the front door.

"You're late!" his mother barked as he entered. "And look at your clothes! Go upstairs and wash before you come down to dinner!"[14] Johnny said nothing. Her face was a blur, her words meaningless, as he bounded up to the second floor to escape from the sight of her. Dinner progressed with Amanda de Graaf believing her firstborn was ill. He was sullen and quiet. Her probing questions received no response, ceased as fast as they had commenced, and climaxed in exasperated looks. When the dishes were cleared, Johnny hastily retreated to his room once more, locking the door behind him. Sitting there, he again contemplated the meaning of his discovery. He tried not to think about his father, and when he couldn't help it, the thought brought a lump to his throat. That night he tossed and turned in bed, sleeping little, until at last he came up with a plan of action.

Johnny left for school early the next morning and stopped off at the telegraph office on the way. Sophie had lent him a little money without explanation of what it was for, and he carefully printed out a wire to their father's hotel in Berlin. "Urgent you come home at once, Johnny." He said a silent prayer that the orchestra had not moved on to another city.

Two days later Wilhelm de Graaf arrived, much to his wife's surprise. Quickly, he called Johnny outside for a private explanation. Johnny's knees shook and his voice trembled as he recounted what he had witnessed, knowing full well that in doing so he was searing his father's heart. Wilhelm de Graaf's expression went blank. For several minutes he remained silent. Thanking his son, he finally strode into the house. His cool composure must have given way to anger, for he and his wife got into a big argument. The children could hear them screaming at each other. Amanda steadfastly denied everything and repeatedly leveled accusations against their son, calling him a "dirty liar," "troublemaker," and "unruly brat!"

Wilhelm's last words were, "Yes, I have learned by now that there is a big difference between some men and some women." The house, of course, was spotless, as Amanda made very certain that no telltale clues would expose what she had been up to with her visitor. Johnny could only guess that his mother worked her usual magic on his father, as all was calm between them an hour later. Wilhelm departed that evening to join the orchestra, which was about to leave Berlin for London. Amanda was the incarnation of kindness and love as she kissed him goodbye at the door. "Look after your mother and do what she tells you, Johnny," his father murmured as he patted his son on the shoulder. "She has convinced him," Johnny thought, as he watched his father stroll out of sight.

Wilhelm de Graaf's departure swept in a wave of terror and retaliation for Johnny as his mother attempted to break her little tormentor. Johnny was made to write letters to his grandparents that she dictated, full of lies about his constant acting up. They apparently believed what was in them, because on his next visit they scolded him for this or that misbehavior, in spite of his vigorous protests that it was all just another ruse, forced on him and on them by his mother. Then again, not much convincing was really needed. They had long realized the devil at work in their daughter-in-law, and they began to avoid her.

The other children, the ones old enough to understand what was going on, sided with their mother. Sophie tried to keep peace in the family. In so doing, however, Sophie was usually accused of being on Johnny's side in the endless bickering that took place. Amanda generally won these disputes, and Johnny's life became more of a living hell than at any time in his childhood, which was rapidly coming to an end. There were only a few acquaintances he could talk to, including his closest friend, Nose, but he never burdened any of them. His troubles were too personal. Tribulations were discussed only with his grandmother in Wilhelmshaven. She was his one real confidante.

Even with the pressure at home, Johnny received good grades in many subjects at the Kaiser Wilhelm[15] Gymnasium (high school). However, the Prussian approach and lack of freedom to question took their toll. De Graaf became an iconoclast without knowing what the word meant. His rebelliousness was most notable with teachers who pounded into their pupils the glories of the German state and the necessity of iron discipline. Rapt attention was the rule, and history classes were the worst. Courses that should have opened curious minds to the wonders of the past were run like boot camps. German unity, from 1871 to the period following the war with France, all the battles, and all the victories were covered and memorized. At the end of the hour, everyone had to stand and honor the Kaiser by singing "Heil Dir im Siegerkranz" (We Hail You, Crowned Victor).[16]

Doubting more and more that he was being told the truth, Johnny began asking questions like, "How come we Germans are the good ones while those on the other side of the border are always the scum of the earth?" Of course, such blunt inquiries were not what his teachers wanted. They would reply with comments like, "It's not for you to ask. You have to follow your instructors and their wisdom." Johnny would answer, "Sir, are you able to prove to me that the people who live in Holland, France, and Switzerland are really good-for-nothings? I believe that they are as fine a people as those in our country." This outspokenness merely prompted heavier doses of disapproval from his instructors. Young Johnny soon developed a hatred for nationalism wherever he found it. He would later learn that it was not confined to Germany but could be found in all countries at all times. Only the level and intensity varied.

De Graaf was not alone in finding it hard to make sense of his history books. A friend, Fritz Frimmer, was having the same problem. So Fritz took Johnny to visit his father, the editor of the local Social Democratic newspaper. Herr Frimmer gave his son and Johnny a condensed German history book and told them, "Study it, for it was written by a German who wound into its pages a limited degree of nationalism. When you've finished, and if you don't understand some parts, come and see me and I will lend a hand." They completed the book with no trouble, and then he lent them one on France, because Germany always seemed to be war with the French. A longtime Social Democrat, Frimmer pointed out many informative things for the two boys. They asked him questions not permitted in school, and he gave them answers. The more they read, the more opposed they became to the Germany of the Kaisers.

Every year, a big event at school was Kaiser Wilhelm II's birthday. Students went to class for an hour and then were free to take part in the festivities. On this special day, Johnny and his classmates sang the usual "Heil Dir im Siegerkranz" plus one other song, "Der Kaiser ist ein lieber Mann" (The Kaiser Is a Dear Man). It began, "Our Kaiser is a dear man who lives in Berlin, and if he wasn't so far away from here, I would go right to him." Through all of this, de Graaf continued to probe his teachers; and the more he probed, the harder his teachers made things for him. Some instructors may have noticed that inside this youth a great battle was taking place, and they did not like what they saw. In those days in Germany, the usual answer to such unmanageable pupils was physical punishment. The routine called for two additional boys, one on each arm, to hold the troublemaker over a bench while he was being caned. Johnny suffered through this humiliation again and again. But as time passed this kind of reprimand became harder because de Graaf grew considerably during his teenage years and could wiggle free nearly at will. On one such occasion, four boys had to hold him down. Johnny maneuvered his toes for leverage, however, and plunged forward, knocking the young men down. His head finally rammed into the teacher's stomach, and he also went flying, books and all. Ten extra whacks with the cane in the principal's office and a long lecture were his reward. Despite this outcome, several classmates did swing to his side after seeing his open defiance. They knew from experience that the boys were all treated in the same way. On the other side of the classroom, the girls seldom had conflicts with the teachers; but as onlookers to these little battles, they must have been very frightened.

Johnny's science class covered thunder, lightning, and the tides, which interested him greatly. On the other hand, Albert Giesler,[17] who sat in front of de Graaf, was one of the biggest cheaters in school. He always tried to sit in the teacher's chair before the instructor arrived. He would make note of what everyone was doing and write it on the blackboard for the teacher to see when he entered the room. The little plagiarizer would also tattle on his classmates, telling the teacher, for example, "Fritz had his breakfast in class," which was against the rules. De Graaf could not stand Giesler, nor could most of the other students.

One day, the pupils were working on a project dealing with electrical storms. Johnny had finished his work, which was nicely written and ready for a quick check by the teacher. Suddenly, Albert Giesler turned around. Just as quickly, Johnny told him to mind his own business, as this was one of the many ways in which Albert copied for his own benefit. Giesler's response was to spit on Johnny's book and shove his ink so that all of the neat pages got wet and smeared. Johnny then grabbed the inkpot from his own desk and dumped it all over Albert and his papers. The teacher, Herr Feilder, was livid and ordered de Graaf to go to his second-grade homeroom and wait for him there.

A former noncommissioned officer, Feilder soon stomped into the classroom, which also contained one of Johnny's younger brothers. Grabbing a stick, he told Johnny to raise his fingers with the tips pointed up. Feilder slammed the rod down on the exposed digits, hurting Johnny terribly. Johnny took it in silence as the teacher told him to raise his fingers again. He frowned at the man, took hold of a slate from a nearby desk, and slapped it down on Feilder's head, leaving him framed and causing the other children to burst into laughter. The teacher then seized Johnny's elbows and slammed them onto the desktop over and over again, until blood streamed from his arms onto his pants and down onto the floor. Johnny reeled under the pain, feeling weak from this episode, which left him with lifetime scars.

Feilder told his victim to wash off the blood in a small sink at the back of the room. After cleaning himself as best he could, Johnny returned, grabbed another slate, and whacked his tormentor with it in the same manner as before. He then ran across the classroom, opened a window, and jumped out, knowing that he would land in a sandbox below. Landing easily, he picked himself up and ran home. He rushed into the apartment, where his mother asked him what had happened. He told her he had fallen down during gym. At home between engagements, Wilhelm took his son to a doctor, who cleaned the wounds, stitched the broken skin, and bandaged Johnny's elbows. Later that afternoon, Johnny got to his little brother, who had witnessed everything, and told him that if he ever said anything, he would beat the life out of him. He never said a word.

Following the doctor's orders, Johnny stayed out of school for six weeks. The physician had asked him how it happened. Johnny replied, "It's a question of someone hurting me, and believe me, I hurt them back." The doctor knew there was a lot his young patient was not telling him. One thing was for sure: the damage had not been caused by any accident in a physical education class.

When de Graaf returned to school, Feilder called him out into the hall. He asked Johnny if his father planned to go to court over the incident.

"Herr Feilder, I am not Albert Giesler!" Johnny replied.

Feilder was speechless, amazed—and also frightened. Then he turned and said to Johnny, "You're an adult already, Johnny, aren't you?"

"If you ever touch me again, I will kill you!"

"And your father?" Feilder mumbled.

"My father," de Graaf answered, "sent me to the doctor because I lied to him."

"You did?"

"Yes," Johnny said, "I told him I was exercising during gym and fell down."

"You've grown up much too fast," said Feilder. He never touched the oldest de Graaf boy again.

Puppy love entered Johnny's life in 1908 in the form of a very pretty brown-haired classmate named Emma Todicain. They often played together, and they relished their mutual secrets and dreams at the end of school each day. Johnny often carried Emma's books home after class, and he now and then went out with her alone or together with other students. Johnny remembered fondly that he and Emma used to pool their few coins to buy a bar of chocolate. Emma's parents were very nice people, especially her father, who worked in the shipyard. One day he said, "Well Johnny, how are you coming along with my daughter? You play together, go dancing and all that."

"Yes," Johnny nodded.

"Never take anything extra from her," Herr Todicain commanded.

"I have never asked for anything extra," de Graaf responded.

"I know; you are a good boy, Johnny," he went on. "I don't want you or Emma to make youthful mistakes, even though I know in my heart you won't."

Johnny was very fond of this man. He respected him and his beautiful daughter too much to try anything foolish beyond the odd kiss.

Along with his little romance, Johnny was avoiding his mother as much as possible in order to avoid any new conflicts with her. He had already landed his first small jobs in the real world, carrying suitcases at the train station in Wilhelmshaven and collecting empty bottles in a wooden wagon he had constructed. Any money he scraped together his mother took, with the help of Sophie and Waldemar. They would hold Johnny's arms behind his back while she went through his pockets. He soon decided that any change he earned could not be brought home. Johnny gave Nose the money he earned, along with any new clothes, which his friend kept hidden at his house. In the event that Johnny needed something and asked his mother for the money, she would always refuse. Shoes and clothes he bought for himself by the age of twelve. He even had his own coat and watch, all earned and paid for with his own small income.

Another turning point arrived abruptly. Johnny was surprised when told to take two iron pots of food to a worker at the port—another of his mother's lovers? When Johnny stormed, "I won't do it!" his mother grabbed the fire poker. He yanked it from her hand and shouted, "If you use this once more, I'll hit you!" Then he threw it out the window, while she bellowed that she would tell his father. To this Johnny responded, "Tell him!" When Wilhelm came home that night, his wife revealed what had happened. Johnny's father was soon confronting him.

"Did you lift your hand against your mother?"

Young Johnny replied, "I did, Daddy, and if you lift your hand against me, the same story goes for you. I am not willing to take any more beatings from anyone."

Poor Wilhelm still believed nearly everything Amanda told him about their son. While he had never struck his own children, this latest exchange perhaps underlined what would happen if he suddenly got the urge. Johnny went on, "Against *her,* I'll resist with everything in my power." His father noted sadly that his son had started to refer to his mother in the third person.

Even as Johnny became more alienated from his teachers and the woman who bore him, Christmas was a very special time. Amid all the joy and preparation for the holiday, his brothers and sisters would write out their wishes and put them into a stocking. Wilhelm de Graaf always waited until his little ones were fast asleep on December 24 before leaving to buy the presents. As one Christmas approached, probably during a period when Wilhelm was out of work, Johnny wrote just one item on his piece of paper, a little electric train. When Christmas morning arrived, however, there was no toy engine under the tree. His father looked at him and said nothing, knowing full well how downhearted his son was. Then he remarked, "The *Christkind* [Christ Child] was sold out, Johnny."[18] The next day, Johnny asked him to go for a walk around the town, and during their stroll they passed a shop window display of trains. Johnny said to his father, "Daddy, if you have no money, don't lie to me. I know there is no Christkind. You are our Christkind." Wilhelm put his arms around his son and started crying.

By 1908 Johnny had almost completed his second year in high school, when he made up his mind to go to sea.[19] He was barely fourteen and working harder than ever at his studies, since he knew he would need them as a sailor. One teacher asked de Graaf what he wanted to be when he got out of school. Johnny blurted out that he was going to become the captain of a ship on the high seas. "Oh," the instructor said, "you're such a wild one already." When school ended that term, he asked Johnny again, and again Johnny replied, "Yes, I have more desire than ever." The teacher nodded his solemn approval and wished the budding young man good luck.

When Johnny told his father he wanted to be a sailor, Wilhelm replied that he should wait. "Go back to school for two more years, Johnny, and then go to sea," he advised. "When you have had enough of the ocean, you can go to a university and have everything you need to be a good musician. I will help you."

"No, father," Johnny responded. "If it were just you and me at home, maybe I'd stay, but I can't hang about any longer with that woman in the house."

Eventually, the senior de Graaf gave the future seaman his blessing and signed the necessary permission papers. Owing to his age, the Polizei (police) required parental approval. But when Amanda learned that her husband had given in, she promptly took possession of the forms and said that that would be the end of it. Making matters worse, she refused to give Johnny any money, as she doubtless feared he might use it to go to sea.

Amanda kept her money on the night table between the twin beds in the master bedroom of the family's apartment at the time, at Mitscherlich Straße 10.[20] Next to the cash were the permission papers. When he was alone one day, Johnny saw several marks lying on the nightstand that she had taken from him the previous evening. He still had another seven marks concealed at Nose's. Then he hesitated. Also on the nightstand were some four hundred marks he knew he really could use. He picked up the notes and held them in his hand, along with the permission documents. For a long time he stood there fighting with his conscience. One voice said, "Take all the money!" Another urged him, "Take only the authorization paper and the seven marks that belong to you!" Making his decision, he took what he needed and left. No one saw him go; there were no goodbyes.

Johnny traveled from Wilhelmshaven to Bremerhaven, where he walked to the home of his aunt and uncle, in the hope of getting a berth on the *Niobe*. He felt quite proud of himself for having passed up the temptation of the four hundred marks on his mother's nightstand. Surely he could sail with his uncle, given their good relationship and the warm welcome he had always experienced in their house. When he arrived, Aunt Johanna said, "Did your mother give you her consent to be a sailor, Johnny?"

"Auntie, she did not, and I took only the money that belonged to me. I don't want anything else from her."

"Well, perhaps I should send you home," Johanna Gerkins replied.

"If you decide to do that, Auntie, I will throw you out of the window, and that's that!" She smiled warmly at her nephew's determination.

"Have no fear, Johnny," she continued. "You may not know this, but none of us ever liked your mother very much."

"I know that," Johnny replied, "and I understand the reason. You have good cause not to be fond of her."

"Well, my boy, let's see what we can do for you," she said, as she led Johnny into the warm kitchen, knowing he had not eaten for some time.

Fortunately for de Graaf, his uncle kept in the attic all kinds of odds and ends, including soap, shoes, and waterproof clothing, all necessary equipment for a novice sailor. Johanna took him upstairs and fitted him with everything he needed. Johnny was now ready, lacking only a sailor's hammock. And after a short while, his kind aunt arranged even that. The next morning, following a big breakfast and many hugs and farewells, Johnny made his way to his uncle's ship. By nightfall the *Niobe* was at full sail on the North Sea. Onboard, a fourteen-year-old apprentice had embarked on the first leg of an adventure that would span five decades.

2

MERCHANT MARINE

The *Niobe* sailed south for the African coast. The trip would later take her across the South Atlantic, around Cape Horn to the Pacific side of South America, then north to various ports in Mexico. On the way back, the *Niobe* would venture farther into the Pacific and stop in Australia to load wool for the fur markets in England. There was great competition among ships for the fleecy cargo, particularly those that could deliver it on time. The rage for British woolens in Europe required a steady flow of the product if the trade was to be profitable.

The *Niobe* was a three-masted merchant schooner. Iron ships were just starting to appear on the seas, initiating the competition of sail versus steam power for key trade routes. There were crafts of all descriptions, including passenger liners, freighters, and vessels powered by a combination of sail and steam. A deluge of companies advertised their international destinations and timetables in the major newspapers of the day. The *Niobe* was a part of this parade. She was manned by Captain Gerkins, a chief officer, third and fourth officers, a boatswain, a petty officer, a carpenter, a sailmaker, and seventeen able-bodied seamen. At the bottom of the list were the apprentices, Johnny and his cousin, Walter Gerkins. Walter had also decided to sign on in Bremerhaven.

The two novices began their education at sea by hauling food supplies from storage to the galley. Other chores found them oiling sailors' boots, cleaning the mess hall and toilets, and carrying out all the other tedious tasks that those more senior did not want to do. They also stood watch from 8:00 A.M. to 6:00 P.M. Johnny and Walter liked the schedule, for it gave them a sound night's sleep. But at the piercing clang of the watch bell, one of the crew would come in and shake them awake, shouting, "Get up, you silly bastards, time to do your duty! It's raining." The prevailing weather conditions were always included in this wake-up call.

The boys performed many drills high up in the rigging, before the watchful eyes of the chief mate. He yelled this or that instruction to them about the ropes or the canvas. At first, most of the adjustments had to be practiced on deck. Their training also included lessons in reading the compass. They had to know it backward and forward, even how to repair it. Mastering this key navigational device was very difficult in the beginning.

The food was not fancy by any stretch of the imagination, but it was solid and edible. All the meat was salted and kept in barrels, as the *Niobe* had no refrigeration. Potatoes and cabbage were rare, as they did not keep long. Fresh fruit, which could not be obtained unless they were in port, would quickly rot at sea. In a short while, all of the provisions became very monotonous. The men were served beans, lots of beans. In fact, because his crew ate them so often, Captain Gerkins was known as "the Bean Captain." There was a lot of flatulence on the *Niobe*.

Early in the voyage, Walter began to complain. He whined to his father about a sailor who slapped his face. Captain Gerkins then called the whole ship's company to the upper deck. Looking out over the men, he said, "This greenhorn is my son. If he believes he has any privileges because of who he is, he's badly mistaken. You men are to make sailors out of both these lads." Then, turning to Johnny, he pointed out that although he was his nephew, he was hardworking and a fast learner. "Should these two boys ever register a complaint against any of you, I will throw them out of my cabin. You make sailors out of them, not me."

This was a big thing; the crew was pleased and respected the captain's stand, leaving poor Walter seething with anger and embarrassment. Generally, the hands onboard the *Niobe* were reasonable but rough men. Despite their size and tough exteriors, they showed understanding and great tolerance. De Graaf had no doubt that he and his cousin often tried their patience. Then again, no one could say that the two boys were not becoming sailors. The crew took pride in the accomplishments of the apprentices and reprimanded them for their failures. It was a tough life, yet Johnny loved it, and he picked up more and more from his rugged instructors. The language of sailors, too, was as coarse as their exteriors and gushed forth in daily salvos until it became commonplace in the ears of the new recruits. Narratives of all kinds filled the spraying mist and churning seas before Johnny and Walter. Johnny, fortunately, found himself being increasingly accepted by the crew. Walter, in contrast, still smarted from his dashed pride. He made progress as well but had a difficult time forgetting his imagined status, often judging others with contempt. He had one leg on board and the other over the side, as Johnny would tell him, much to his annoyance.

Under a steady breeze, with smooth seas and at full sail, the *Niobe* soon made her way down the African coast. Two days on shore, tied up at Matadi,[1] in what became the Belgian Congo,[2] gave the crew time to stretch their sea legs. Coming ashore, they witnessed one of the last relics of man's inhumanity to man on the west coast of Africa—still active slave markets. In 1908 Africans continued to be captured occasionally in the interior and sold at auction in the Atlantic ports.[3] Many years before, the Germans had been the first to forbid the transporting of slaves on their ships. Britain followed, for not entirely altruistic reasons,[4] leaving France, Portugal, and the others to fight it out for dominance in the transportation of indentured servants to the New World. Johnny said that all his life he reeled in horror from this disgrace before God. He avowed that it was a bitter experience for a youth of his impressionable age—though he would soon observe that this was not all that was happening to Africans at the mercy of Europeans.

The Belgians were building a railway from the mouth of the Congo River to Leopoldville (now Kinshasa) some 480 miles (750 km) long. The countryside abounded with mosquitoes and disease. White foremen went into the bush and caught hundreds of blacks. Many died from the effects of the savage labor routine or from insect bites while working the line. Johnny spoke to a German-speaking slave from Cameroon who told him that under each wooden tie lay five dead bodies. They succumbed while laying track, a hole was dug, and the remains were dumped in, covered with earth, and capped by a tie. The process of putting down track proceeded uninterrupted. Johnny took this as visible proof of the power of colonialism and the exploitation of indigenous peoples. Whenever he thought about this story, it made his blood boil. If he remembered it while at sea, he became quiet and less sullen. He claimed that international pressure brought a lot of publicity and disgrace to the Belgians for their involvement with slavery.

Pushing south, the *Niobe* arrived in Cape Town, discharged its cargo, took on new cargo, and added to its galleys. Within forty-eight hours she was out to sea again, this time heading west across the South Atlantic. The trip around Cape Horn was a vivid nature experience for the young de Graaf. Storms raged and the weather turned icy cold. It required several attempts before Captain Gerkins entered the Strait of Magellan and swung past Punta Arenas. Johnny saw his first glaciers on the peaks the ship passed in the calmer currents of the channel. Finally through to the Pacific, the ship headed north for Chile, where many small industries flourished. Few were of any magnitude. They did run into a German brewer who made beer for distribution along the western seaboard. But all in all, the people were poor and miserable, forced to obey rulers who controlled the coast right up to Peru. The scene was virtually unchanged from there to Mexico.

Soft winds and medium seas propelled the *Niobe* west, across the Pacific to Australia. Entering Melbourne harbor, she dropped anchor and the men proceeded to discharge her cargo. Australian workers, many of whom were former inmates of British prisons, did much of the loading and unloading. There were even some, both men and women, who were merely undesirables sent by English courts to Australia. Walter and Johnny soon learned all about it. The deportees were hastily thrown on ships and transported to Britain's Australian colony to work more or less as dock slaves. The women toiled away as cooks or maids for the colonial bureaucrats and military officers. If they performed well, they were eventually freed. While working on the *Niobe,* the indentured stevedores were ordered by their guards not to talk to the crew.

The police had a nice little business in place when a sailor deserted his ship in Melbourne. Any policeman could earn an extra £20 by returning the runaway to the abandoned vessel. The sailor would then have to pay back the reward, replenishing the ship's funds with the given amount. Seafarers were free from apprehension, on the other hand, if their ships departed without them.

Johnny studied the British system of exploitation and found that it differed little from that practiced by other nations. But the English did do better in one respect; they included a small measure of civilization in their brand of control rather than nothing at all. Even so, de Graaf rebelled against the injustices he observed everywhere the *Niobe* touched port. His preconceived hopes and opinions about the world vanished from his thinking. He was cast adrift in the stark reality of life in the age of imperialism. Each shock added to his growing awareness of nations and their leaders. During this first voyage, his distaste and defiance mushroomed rather than mellowed. The rebellion he had experienced in childhood, at school, and now at sea gained momentum. Johnny wept inwardly for the underdog and the downtrodden, shackled like beasts to ill-gotten wealth.

The *Niobe*'s wool cargo filled the holds, baled in sacking below decks. Melbourne faded from view as the schooner set sail once again. This time the destination was England. It was fine by de Graaf. He longed for the open ocean. Swaying decks, salt air, and billowing sails were known to soothe the troubled spirit.

Captain Gerkins ordered all hands to make for the river Thames and the English capital as fast as possible. The quicker the ship could reach London, the more money the captain would make as a premium. He forced his crew to work like Trojans, cramming on every piece of linen the ship could carry. The overworked sailmaker was kept busy supplying the vessel with more fabric, which was quickly added in somewhere. It was the start of a race against time on the ocean.

The *Niobe* made such speed that she passed several steamers on the way, ships that were supposed to be much faster than any craft under sail. They ran into some bad storms in the Indian and Atlantic Oceans, yet the captain said that if his schooner lost any canvas, it was of little concern. They carried plenty of replacement fabric. True skill was required, not just to sail the *Niobe* under such conditions but to react quickly to the constant commands from the bridge. The only real loss was one small sail amidships. The journey from Melbourne to Plymouth, England, took fifty-three days, three or four days fewer than normally required. All on board were justly proud of the feat.

Unfortunately, Johnny and Walter ended up having several clashes during the voyage.

"Walter, if you think you can rule me or anyone else on the ship, I will throw you overboard!" the youthful de Graaf snapped at his relative.

"I'm doing it," Walter laughed. Captain Gerkins's boy carried on in this way until Johnny started ignoring him. After unloading at London, the *Niobe* slid across the North Sea to Rotterdam to pick up cargo for the return trip to Australia. Walter became so haughty during this short crossing to Holland that Johnny decided to talk to his uncle.

"Uncle Dietrich, will you please pay me off?" de Graaf asked.

"What's wrong, Johnny?" the surprised captain replied.

"To put it bluntly," Johnny remarked, "if I make another trip with your son, I'll likely throw him overboard."

"Um hum," Gerkins said. "I was afraid of this. If you leave the ship, Johnny, then I'll demand that he leave it too."

De Graaf explained that he did not wish for Walter to be forced to leave the *Niobe*.

"That's justice!" Captain Gerkins sternly replied. "Walter has to grow up!"

The pair of budding seamen signed off the *Niobe* in Rotterdam and located separate berths on two of the many ships in port. Two years later, much to Johnny's torment, Walter and his ship were lost at sea in the Indian Ocean. The craft disappeared without a trace. No bodies or wreckage were ever found. The news would touch Johnny deeply; and since he had gotten Walter kicked off the *Niobe*, he felt responsible. Out of guilt, he stopped writing to his aunt and uncle.

Johnny's new ship was an Italian merchantman, the SS *Caterina Acalo*. The situation on some European ships was not the best in those years, as conflicts seemed to break out among the mixed crews at the drop of a hat. De Graaf avoided many a fracas by not taking sides and sticking to his assigned duties. He had a quick ear for languages and really began picking them up on the *Caterina Acalo*, as the *Niobe* had been an almost all-German crew. His new ship traveled to many countries, and shore leave gave him the opportunity to talk to various officials and continue his education through firsthand experience.

One voyage brought the *Caterina Acalo* up the south coast of China to Hong Kong. After docking, Johnny noticed Chinese coolies lugging coal up swaying planks, where they discharged their burden into the coal bunkers of an array of steamships. Over and over, like ants, they clambered up the boards. They received one "coppa," as they called it, a piece of tin, for each bucket of coal they dumped in the ship's bunkers. A full pail, when Johnny lifted one, weighed approximately forty pounds (or just over eighteen kilos). Some pails were heavier. The mistreatment of people only trying to make a meager living moved him—and they were the individuals who had the good jobs.

As for the bad jobs, in those days many seafaring nations had their steamships' boilers scaled in Chinese ports. This was a maintenance procedure in which a vessel had sediment chipped off the inside of its boiler. It was labor-intensive, dangerous work, especially because the Chinese began on the boiler almost immediately after a ship entered port, when the boiler was still very hot. So severe was the need for a job, and so low was the pay, that a death or an injury here and there did not matter to the owners and managers of these vessels. No one really cared. The rich lived magnificently in the name of law and order, while ordinary Chinese slept on the ground like dogs.[5]

The *Caterina Acalo* went further up the coast to Shanghai, where the British and Germans controlled Chinese workers with Gurkhas, the fierce warriors from northern Nepal. The British and French were smart. They seldom used their own forces. They wanted the Chinese to see the police as Satan's own special brigades, not directly associated with Britain or France. Through it all, a coolie would receive about four cents a day for fourteen hours work, with a herd of uniformed brutes bellowing at him to move faster and carry more.

The *Caterina Acalo* sailed on to the German colony of Kiautschou (now called Qingdao), where abuse was dispensed with ethnocentric abandon. Chinese farmers with buckets of pears sold them for a penny per pear in street stalls. Some of the fruit was about the same size as a half-grown turnip. Johnny bought one beautiful pear from a farmer who was flanked by the two buckets of his labor. A group of rowdy German sailors arrived at this outdoor enterprise and grabbed up all the pears, throwing the man five *Pfennigs,* an amount then worth about three pence in English currency. The Chinese man said, "money, please, money." His insistence on a fair price enraged the seamen, who picked up the proprietor and threw him into the street. Observing this were sixteen men off the *Caterina Acalo,* one of whom was de Graaf. Despite being outnumbered, they took offense at the condescending Germans and decided to teach them a lesson.

Johnny and his companions completely dominated the exchange and chased many of the bloodied German crew back to their ship, lying in port. Even so, once the fisticuffs ended, Johnny's side was arrested and thrown in jail. It was de Graaf's first arrest. There would be many more. The *Caterina Acalo*'s captain bailed his men out and gave them a stern warning. Johnny protested, but this only resulted in orders to go back to the ship and stay there.

At last the *Caterina Acalo* upped anchor and headed across the Pacific to Valparaiso, Chile, with a load of saltpeter, to be used in making ammunition. There were no wharves at Valparaiso, so the cargo had to be off-loaded into small boats in Valparaiso Bay and taken ashore. Ships at anchor would help each other, so that once one was unloaded, the crews would start on another vessel. Johnny noticed that his uncle's schooner, the *Niobe,* was also in the harbor. The *Caterina Acalo*'s captain ordered some of his men over to the *Niobe* to give her a hand. Johnny asked his captain if he could pick someone else, as he did not want to face Dietrich Gerkins. But the *Acalo*'s captain would have none of it. "I said, you go with them!" he shouted. Orders are orders, so seaman de Graaf had no choice but to go with the *Caterina Acalo*'s party. His uncle stood at the rail of the *Niobe* as they rowed alongside. As soon as Johnny was on deck, Dietrich grabbed him, put his arm around his shoulder, and said, "What's wrong with you, Johnny?"

"Well," de Graaf said, "I heard Walter was lost at sea, and I feel miserable about it."

"No, Johnny," Gerkins explained. "You shouldn't, that's life. It could have been you, and I would have felt as bad about it. I knew he would have a very hard time at sea with his attitude. Now, if you don't visit us the next time we're in port, I'll have you arrested by the police, you young devil. You're our son now and we want you to know our home is always yours. Your aunt and I want you to be our boy by adoption."

De Graaf embraced his uncle with tears in his eyes. Johnny returned to his ship feeling that a big load of guilt had disappeared, knowing that his uncle had never held him responsible for his cousin's death. Both he and his wife wanted him as their son, God bless them. What a fool he felt he had been, blaming himself.

When the voyage ended, de Graaf changed ships and set sail for Australia on the steamer SS *Furth* of the German-Australian Line. The sailors called the *Furth* a "whore ship" because of the rations. She was a cargo tub where the crew seldom saw a piece of bread. Some of the men came down with scurvy and lost their teeth. The captain and officers were brutes, real German nationalists, who walked around with handcuffs hanging over their belts, ready for use.

One day, one of the sailors on Johnny's watch took sick. Johnny reported this to the bridge when he came on duty. They said, "Send him up here."

"Sir, it is impossible for him to come to the bridge," Johnny answered.

"What are you talking about?" they shouted. "It's none of your business! Now send him here!"

The captain then called up the boatswain, who nervously remarked that the sailor was indeed very sick. The skipper commanded de Graaf to take the helm, while his chief, another tyrant, always blaming the sailors for everything, went down to see the ailing man. There were no doctors aboard many ships, and the chief officers had little medical knowledge beyond first-aid training. Lying deathly ill on deck, the poor seaman received a couple of aspirin, and that was it.

Johnny stayed at the helm for two hours and then asked a superior to arrange for a replacement. "When my watch is over I will have you relieved!" he spat. The man must have felt provoked, for the next minute he lunged at Johnny. Fortunately, de Graaf saw him coming, dodged to one side, and let him brush past. Johnny walked over to the man, smacked him on each side of his head, and forced one of his arms behind his back until he screamed in pain. Finally, he released the officer.

According to the law of the sea, the blow was considered mutiny. Thereafter, the officer chuckled to himself, repeatedly telling Johnny that he would face the music when the ship reached Newcastle, New South Wales.

"We'll have you arrested by the German consul!" he smirked.

Johnny looked at him and said, "Why don't you try me for a few rounds here?"

"You would like that?" he answered.

"Yes," Johnny replied, "I would like that very much!" Johnny felt he would have killed the man if given a chance. But before they could resolve the matter, half of the crew, including stokers and firemen, went on strike. They demanded baked white bread once a week rather than saltwater biscuits all the time. The captain and his officers gave in to the demands. After that, they dared not arrest or confine any of the crew until they made Australia, even if trying to set an example.

De Graaf realized that he would have to jump ship before the *Furth* tied up in Newcastle. He also knew from earlier voyages that under Australian law the police would round up deserters. A £20 reward was a real enticement in those times. Not only would he have to flee the vessel before she landed, he would have to beat a hasty retreat from the port area until the *Furth* departed. As the ship eased into the harbor at Newcastle, de Graaf dove overboard. He swam ashore unseen, sloshed up to the North Coast Highway (now the Pacific Highway), and began walking south.

Before long he was many miles from the coast, sitting by the roadside, when a local drew up in his farm wagon. He asked the young man if he was a sailor, to which Johnny replied that he was.

"Well," he said, "one end of my flagpole line has come down and I have nobody to climb up the pole to put it back. How about giving a hand, son?" Johnny agreed, if the farmer would give him something to eat before he started the work. The farmer agreed. De Graaf climbed into the wagon and was taken to the small farm, where he was served a heaping platter of bacon, eggs, toast, and coffee, a meal he had dreamed of while aboard the *Furth*.

Once finished, he shimmied up the flagpole and brought the loose rope down in his teeth. The farmer handed de Graaf a pound note and served him another good meal at noontime.

"Would you like a full-time job on my farm?" he asked. Johnny politely declined, explaining that he was a sailor and not really disposed to life on a ranch.

"The way you climbed that pole, there is no doubt you're not a farmer," he answered. The man gave Johnny a glass of beer and they parted company.

De Graaf returned to the North Coast Highway. He soon came to a little town, keeping well away from the port. Skirting the community, he met a man resting on the curb. As it turned out, the man was as hungry as Johnny. Johnny told him to stay put while he found another farm and bought something to eat. When he returned, the two men feasted on bread, sausage, and milk, and then agreed to look for work together the next day. Late that evening they found a place to sleep in a field off the road. The following morning de Graaf discovered that his new acquaintance had robbed him and disappeared. Johnny had always been a sound sleeper. The thief must have observed where Johnny kept his money, feigned sleep, and lifted the cash during the night.

It dawned on de Graaf that the man would probably head for the nearest town and spend his new windfall, so he walked to the nearest village. Entering the only bar, he spotted the robber. Johnny silently crept up behind his quick-fingered companion and grabbed him. Holding the thief firmly by his arms, Johnny said, "I would have given you half the money I had, which would have been ten shillings, but you wanted everything for doing nothing." At that point, everyone in the bar shouted, "Throw him out of here!" Johnny obliged, tossing the thief out the door. He then removed his belt and gave the man one hell of a whipping before a small crowd of onlookers. When the guy had suffered enough, Johnny took ten shillings off him, kicked him in the rear, and went on his way.

He continued his southward journey toward Sydney and Melbourne, calculating as he walked that his former ship should have left Newcastle by then and that he was a free man. Johnny had with him all his possessions except his sailor's book, which was still in the captain's cabin of the *Furth,* along with his Union of Sailors and Firemen card. Still, the realization that if he had a run-in with the authorities he would not be returned to the *Furth* was an enjoyable feeling, causing him to slacken his pace as he moved down the coast. He held a number of odd jobs as he traveled, mostly in restaurants, where he could get meals as well as a little money for washing dishes and sweeping up. In Sydney, de Graaf worked as a waterfront laborer and slept in harbor sheds. Slowly he saved up what he needed for another union card. But when he went around to the federation's headquarters, he was told that he could not see an official until he passed a sailing exam. He passed the exam, and soon all the necessary documents were in his hands. He could look for a new ship.

In the Port of Jackson, Sydney's harbor, lay a German ship, the SS *Tübingen,* named after the southern German city. As de Graaf looked her over, the captain, standing at the vessel's rail, called down to ask if he was looking for a ship. Eighteen-year-old Johnny replied that he was. In 1912 he was not yet a full seaman, as it took novices four years in the merchant marine to get their able-bodied seaman papers, or A.B.'s. De Graaf signed on with the *Tübingen* as an ordinary seaman. One of the ship's cadet officers had broken his leg and they needed a replacement.[6] This ship's captain was a Mr. Krenick, and the *Tübingen*'s destination was Bremerhaven. Another cadet officer became ill and had to remain on shore, so yet one more stray, like Johnny, was signed on before they left Australia.

International regulations required that a certain number of A and B's be on each ship. Captain Krenick asked Johnny how long he had to go before he would be an A.B. De Graaf answered, "Sir, that's entirely up to you. I have the qualifications and am willing to prove it." Another seaman also felt qualified, so the captain told both men to go to opposite ends of the bridge. Then he told them what tasks to complete, using sailors' techniques. First on the list was splicing. During this test, Krenick hopped back and forth between his two candidates to see how they were doing.

After an hour of commands and tasks, he called a halt.

"You had one year to go," he told Johnny, "stand up. Have you heard in the old days that they took a sword and laid it on your hand? Well, I don't have a sword, but from today on, you are an A.B. seaman." The other fellow was only about halfway through his tasks, but the captain was kind and told him in a nice way that he would have to spend another year as an ordinary seamen before he could qualify as an A.B.

When the *Tübingen* arrived in Bremerhaven, Johnny was paid off, with no papers other than the replacements he had been able to obtain in Sydney. They were not the same as his originals, which were probably sitting in the office of the German consul in Australia. Captain Krenick paid de Graaf thirty marks, and he checked into Bremerhaven's sailors' home, a kind of inn for sailors where one could sleep and eat between voyages.

Johnny opted to join the SPD (Sozialdemokratische Partei Deutschlands, or German Social Democratic Party) while he was in Germany in 1912. It was the only time he set foot on his native soil that year, and 1912 was the year of his affiliation.[7] He also decided to visit his uncle, although the *Niobe* was not in port. He went to the house, and fortunately Uncle Dietrich and Aunt Johanna were at home. Both were happy to see him. Johanna scolded Johnny for not coming sooner, and for blaming himself for Walter's death. Then Captain Gerkins reminded him of his offer.

"That speaks for Johnny, doesn't it? Now we have no children, you will be our son."

De Graaf's mind wandered back to his youth in Wilhelmshaven. With a lump in his throat, he replied, "Yes, I love you both dearly."

Before he returned to the docks in search of a ship, Johnny promised to write his aunt and uncle. He could have signed on with Dietrich's vessel, but he did not want to sail with him, for reasons he could not articulate, perhaps because he still had thoughts about his dead cousin. Returning to the *Niobe* certainly would have been a constant reminder of Walter. A new berth was what he needed, and a rolling deck under his feet.

De Graaf signed on with a German ship that had been sold to a British company, the SS *Bremerhaven*. He and another lad had just signed the log when the captain informed them that his ship would be sailing against regulations. The seacocks had all been stolen. He pointed out that his two new sailors had better know how to swim, should the ship be swamped and go down without these safety valves.

Under cover of darkness, the *Bremerhaven* was able to glide illegally out of port and was soon knifing through the waters of the North Sea, then south through the English Channel. They hit a bad storm later that night. It was a terrible experience. Water sloshed below decks into the holds, and the cargo floated and shifted in a nightmare of work. As the *Bremerhaven* turned toward land, the crew manned her pumps. Somehow they remained afloat and eventually made it to the Welsh port of Swansea. There de Graaf quietly left the ship. He did not want to remain on the *Bremerhaven*, as she was certainly not seaworthy. The total voyage had lasted only two days, but they had been the two worst days of his life at sea.

Johnny lodged at the sailors' inn in Swansea, where he remained until the *Catilina A. Walmen,* a three-masted Italian ship, came into view and docked. Five sailors—two Germans, including de Graaf, two Belgians, and one Scot—signed on, replacing five who decided to leave the vessel. The majority of the crew was Italian and was very poorly trained, with little knowledge of sailing. The new men faced their own first taste of bad weather on the way to Genoa. Following one watch, fresh recruits had gone below decks, where they tried to stay warm, when they were ordered back on deck again. As they emerged through a hatch, they were horrorstricken to see the Italian crew slashing the sails with knives. At that instant it was obvious that the vessel would founder. How could she continue without sails? The *Catilina A. Walmen* would certainly end up on the rocks in no time.

Johnny and his four colleagues raced below decks, grabbed some large sticks from the carpenter's locker, and went up on the forecastle. The five of them would have to take on thirty-five enraged crew members. The Italian captain just stood on the bridge and watched. The ship's cook translated for the crew what Johnny and the others had to say. They told the foolish sailors that they were committing a crime against everyone on the ship as well as the ship herself. A few drew their knives and started for the five defenders, but they were stopped by the clubs. In a matter of minutes, the Italians were stripped of their knives and lay on the deck, nursing their battered heads. All the while the captain had stayed where he was, looking down on everything, never uttering a word.

Afterward, when the sails had been repaired and the storm had passed, the captain invited the *Catilina A. Walmen*'s rescuers to his cabin for a glass of wine. There he told them that the crew had acted the way they did because they were jealous over being paid less than half of what the new men earned. "That is their problem," Johnny remarked. The others informed the captain that if they felt they should be paid more, they should organize and join a union, like they had. "Oh!" he replied, "they'd never do that." Fair enough, but de Graaf and his group asked that they be allowed to set the mainsail. Although it was a job requiring ten men, they would do it alone. "Keep the rest of the crew from that sail, because if there's any interference, we'll do the same as we did before," they advised. The captain agreed and kept his word, the five protectors looked after the mainsail, and the Italian crew stayed out of reach, having learned their lesson.

As soon as the *Walmen* tied up in Genoa, the ship's company announced that they were signing off. The captain was very upset, but Johnny told him he could not expect the best from any crew not properly paid. He and the other four seamen likewise signed off, as none of them wanted anything more to do with the ship. Merchant seamen were a suspicious lot, and what had happened on the *Walmen* only increased their skepticism. Johnny would encounter the *Catilina A. Walmen* again in the Indian Ocean, but he could not tell if she had the same men on board or not.

Johnny was now stranded in Italy, and the only vessel looking for new sailors was a North German Lloyd craft, the SS *Barbarossa*. She was a big, twin-stacked passenger liner that sailed between Germany and the United States and was currently filled with immigrants. Since they all got along well, the group of five from the *Walmen* made a pact to stay together if possible. But the *Barbarossa* only needed two sailors, so Johnny and another seaman signed on, while their three shipmates hid in the lifeboats. The stowaways were kept supplied with food and water and remained undetected for the entire voyage. There were a few close calls, but calmness and fast thinking enabled the little group to skirt all obstacles. The *Barbarossa*'s first port of call, Algiers, took only a few hours. Then it was a dash to the other side of the Atlantic and the United States. Arriving at the North German Lloyd's rebuilt docks in Hoboken, New Jersey,[8] across the Hudson River from Manhattan, the two official seamen signed off and were able to land the other three without being spotted.

There was a strike in progress at the port, and the sailors' union asked all seamen not to sign on to any new ships, as they were in dispute with the shipping companies. The five men pooled the little money they had, which in the Hoboken of 1913 went a long way. One could buy a pitcher of beer and a meal for five cents.[9] Hoboken was a sailors' town with some 280 saloons within half a mile of the docks and a large German-speaking community.[10] The North German Lloyd lines were located at the pier near 4th Street. Most of the bars were situated from 5th Street west on River to Newark Street. Sailors could sleep upstairs at any number of taverns for another nickel or take advantage of the German-run *Heilsarmee* (Salvation Army), where beds rented for ten cents a night a decade earlier. Johnny and his four shipmates enjoyed the area to the fullest. If they caught the ferry across the Hudson to New York, it was another five cents each way.[11]

When the strike ended, the five men signed on with the Red Funnel Line's SS *Cayo Manzanillo*, a Cuban-owned single-screwed vessel destined for her homeport of London, under Captain McL. Hunter.[12] Once they had crossed the Atlantic and arrived in the English metropolis, Johnny stayed on board the ship. The *Cayo Manzanillo* soon sailed on to Kristiania (renamed Oslo in 1925), and then to Antwerp. They arrived on Christmas Eve, and a local pastor arranged a little yuletide celebration for the sailors. At the end of the party, the clergyman spotted de Graaf leaving the hall and asked the young man how much money he planned to spend that night.

"Oh," Johnny replied, "about a hundred Norwegian *Kroner*" (US$18.18 at the fixed rate of exchange then prevailing).[13] It was a nice bit of change for the years before the Great War.

The pastor asked Johnny if there was someone at home he could make happy. De Graaf's hesitation prompted the cleric to ask what was wrong. Johnny broke down and told him the story of his family, in all its ugliness. Johnny knew that the pastor wanted him to send the money home. The man explained how one could send funds by cable and be guaranteed that they would reach the person most loved and missed. So Johnny gave him the Norwegian currency. The minister arranged delivery somehow on Christmas Eve, despite the heavy flow of wires on the telegraph lines that evening.

When the money arrived, Wilhelm de Graaf cabled back to the pastor, "Where's my son?" The preacher told him the port and the name of the ship. Fortunately, the *Cayo Manzanillo* remained in Antwerp for several weeks, discharging and loading cargo and undergoing some necessary repair work. As a result, it was not long before a letter from Johnny's father arrived. Sitting down on a cargo hatch, the young man who had left home for a life at sea at age fourteen opened the envelope and learned of the tragedies back in Germany. His father explained that while he was on tour, the family had been living in a second-floor flat at Breitergang 43, located in what was essentially a Hamburg slum. Amanda decided that she had had enough and sold all the musical instruments and all the furniture, right down to the bare walls. She then placed newspapers on the floor for Sophie, Willy, and Oscar to sit on and deserted the family on April 2, 1914, taking her three youngest children with her.[14] She took all the family's money and left a lover. Amanda later turned up in Hamm, staying with the widower of her sister. She must have known that her husband was due home soon. When he arrived, he was heartbroken. He briefly placed his remaining offspring in a children's home,[15] found a new place to live, and hired a housekeeper. Johnny's father and older sister Sophie decided to bring up the two boys between them until each was grown and married.

Johnny was stunned as he read the account, and from then on often wrote his father when he could. All of his childhood animosity toward his mother resurfaced, and he cursed her anew. Johnny could only imagine the despair and struggle his father was enduring in trying to keep everyone together. He enclosed what money he could spare to ease their financial burden.

Strangely, it was not long before he received a letter from the very person who had caused all this trouble, Amanda de Graaf. He deduced that she could only have obtained his address by contacting the International Sailors' Information Office. The German consul gave de Graaf her sealed note, addressed in her usual beautiful handwriting. He wondered what she wanted.

Sitting in a restaurant called the Green Doggy, a little place on an Antwerp side street where many sailors went to enjoy themselves, Johnny opened the letter. It read, "My dear son, I know I did you terrible wrongs, but sometimes we do things we regret later. I know this now and feel very sorry about it. You have chosen to be a sailor and travel the high seas. It is well known sailors are very loose with their money. Look ahead and send some of your money home [here she gave her address] and I will take it to the bank for you so you can build up your savings. Love, Mother."

Johnny was with a very lovely French girl at the time, who asked him, "What's the matter with you? You have a cynical smile on your face." Before he could reply, a photographer approached and asked if he could take a picture of de Graaf and his lady at the table with their bottle of champagne. The man took two pictures. When they were developed, Johnny wrote on the back of one and slid it into an envelope addressed to his mother. His inscription read: "Received your letter, and trust you can see where my money goes. Johnny."

During this shore leave, Johnny had a likeness either of this mademoiselle's head or that of another tattooed on his upper right arm. The same forearm bore a tattoo of an eagle with a snake in its talons. His other arm, just below the elbow, would come to be forever decorated with a prominent anchor.[16]

Finally, in April, the *Cayo Manzanillo* left Antwerp for the Mexican port of Veracruz. Her cargo manifest said that she carried machinery, but she was really carrying machine guns, rifles, handguns, and ammunition. During the Mexican Revolution (1910–20), Veracruz received numerous German and other foreign ships off-loading weapons for the forces of Mexico's autocratic president, Victoriano Huerta. But once the *Cayo Manzanillo* reached Mexico's Caribbean coast, the U.S. Navy stopped her at the entrance to Veracruz Bay. A battleship commanded her to drop anchor while the Americans bombarded the city on April 21, 1914, leaving hundreds dead. This was the so-called Tampico Incident, in which U.S. gunboat diplomacy throttled an often drunken dictator.[17] When the naval shelling subsided, the American warships seized the *Cayo Manzanillo*'s cargo. The craft was eventually released and sailed immediately up to Wilmington, Delaware, where she took on a load of freight before preceding back to Antwerp.

On July 18, 1914, the *Barbarossa* slid out of Bremen for her last run to New

York. Somewhere in the Atlantic, she slowly passed the *Cayo Manzanillo* with Johnny at the helm. Captain Hunter shouted, "War between England and Germany!" and a lot more that was not understood. The first mate then took the wheel so de Graaf could yell his captain's message over to the *Barbarossa* in German. They shouted, "Lots of luck to you!" and Johnny hollered the same back to them as the *Barbarossa* headed for an uncertain fate in America.[18]

Once the *Cayo Manzanillo* tied up in Antwerp, she discharged her payload and loaded coal for the trip back to Wilmington. From Delaware, the vessel headed for Savannah, Georgia. Before reaching port, Johnny tried to learn from the captain whether he would be interned when they reached Savannah, since he was still a German national by birth. He did not have quite enough years of British employment to apply for British citizenship. Captain Hunter informed him that in Savannah, unlike Wilmington, he was likely to be detained.

"Will we be staying on the coast or going on to Britain?" Johnny asked him.

"Back to Britain," Hunter replied sternly. De Graaf was in a real bind, for he had no intention of being interned in England as a civilian, or any desire to be forced to join the German armed forces. He had been a seaman for six years, but he was still too inexperienced to have become acquainted with the duplicity of American morality in action.

After docking in Savannah in early September 1914,[19] Johnny asked Captain Hunter if he would pay him off, as he had just done with two crewmates, a Russian and a Belgian. Hunter refused, despite de Graaf's repeated requests. Johnny then went to the local home for sailors, where he explained his problem to a pastor. Ultimately a lawyer was summoned, who agreed to handle the case. Proceeding to the ship, the trio pressed the captain for de Graaf's sailor's book and earnings, which amounted to US$200.[20] The Savannah harbor authority checked the ship's log and backed up Johnny's claim. The Russian and the Belgian had been paid, so why not de Graaf?

The three men told Hunter to pay Johnny "or else," but he still refused. Taking de Graaf aside, the lawyer told him he would eventually get his wages but that it would take time. He suggested that his client leave the ship before it set sail again while he referred the case to higher authorities. Johnny agreed, and when darkness cloaked the *Cayo Manzanillo*, he dove off the ship and swam to shore. The waters around Savannah were known for sharks. Johnny had US$100 in his pocket, the clothes on his back, and a small bundle of personal items. Once he reached the beach, he made straight for the railway lines to the west of town. Drying off and tidying himself up, de Graaf waited on one of the last suburban platforms out of Savannah. He boarded the first train that stopped, bought his ticket from the conductor, and was soon speeding north. After a nearly eight-hundred-mile train ride, Johnny arrived once again in Wilmington.

When not at sea, a sailor's place is down at the shore among the ships. De Graaf went straight to the harbor and began surveying each vessel at the docks as well as those at anchor out in the Delaware River. "Well, you have to do something. Soon the Americans will be involved in this war, which will mushroom into a wider conflict," he thought to himself as he stood alongside an American cruiser in his sailor's garb. His daydream was interrupted by an officer's command from somewhere above, and a man came down the gangplank. He asked if Johnny was looking for a ship, to which Johnny replied that he was.

"You like her lines, son?" the officer asked. De Graaf nodded. "Come along and I'll show you around," he said warmly, leading the way.

The craft was spotless, very modern, with everything in its place and battle ready. He invited Johnny into the officer's mess for dinner. Johnny thanked him but declined.

"Lieutenant," he said, "I would much prefer to eat with the able seamen in their mess, if you don't mind."

"Oh, I guess you want to know what you'll get to eat if you come on this ship," the officer replied. "I don't blame you."

Johnny then mentioned that he had seen a lot already and was very impressed, but wanted to get a glimpse of how the ratings lived.

The ship was a wonder, with excellent food and fine accommodations, a sailor's joy. De Graaf agreed to sign on and the next day was processed through the medical inspection. He was declared A-1, a prime candidate. But the bubble burst the following morning after an immigration official appeared out of nowhere. He complained that de Graaf could not be signed on because he was not an American citizen; moreover, the official claimed, "he is a deserter." Captain Hunter had evidently spread the word.

Quickly put back on shore, Johnny's sudden sadness ended rapidly when the papers from his lawyer arrived as he was thinking about what to do next. It was the first American intention certificate ever given to a runaway. Eventually he could use it to become an American citizen. The paper stated that he did not support Germany and would never bear arms against the United States. Along with this welcome news was a check for his *Cayo Manzanillo* wages, minus the lawyer's fee. De Graaf was elated. Now things would get better for sure.

Johnny soon found, however, that no ship would take him, as Hunter's ill will had spread to nearly every vessel in port. He reckoned there must have been some kind of blacklist floating around with his name on it. Wandering around the harbor, he finally met Captain Marquis Square. Since he had sailed with Square before, he was offered a berth. His ship was steaming for Britain and then Rotterdam. Square suggested that Johnny sign on as a Swede to avoid being detained in England. He could also stay on board in Rotterdam because he would be taking a big chance if he set foot on soil where his German nationality could cause conscription into the German armed forces. The captain assured him that the arrangement was strictly between the two of them and that he would keep it secret.

Sleek and trim, the SS *Sondike* was of Dutch registry. She left Wilmington and made good speed over a smooth sea. Approaching the Scilly Islands, southwest of Cornwall, a British cruiser rode alongside and escorted her into Plymouth. There, the military and immigration officers asked the captain if there were any individuals on board other than Dutchmen. Square replied that there was one Swede, and they requested to see him.

"Are you Swedish?" they asked, to which de Graaf replied that he was.

"Where are your parents?"

"My parents are dead," Johnny responded.

"Do you have a sweetheart?"

"I have a sweetheart in every port," was the reply.

This seemed to satisfy then until one officer said, "Go into that other room and we will see you again in a few minutes." Ten minutes passed while Johnny waited, when suddenly the door was flung open by a smallish, wavering Irishman more intoxicated than sober. He commenced to address de Graaf in slurred Swedish, beginning with "hej" (hello). This was followed with several questions, to which Johnny replied with sufficient fluency to fool the drunkard. Finally the Irishman staggered to an officer in the other room and said, "Oh, he's a bloody Swede all right, sir." Johnny was released and allowed to return to the ship, which shortly set out for Rotterdam.

During the voyage from Delaware, Johnny had grown uneasy about Captain Square. He had heard tell of Dutch who were pro-German, and he hoped, despite his agreement with Square, that he was not one of them. Yet his suspicions lingered. As the *Sondike* eased past Hoek van Holland, on her way up the Maas River to the Port of Rotterdam, he decided he could not take the chance. When the shore lights began to glisten on the dark water, he dove off the ship, taking with him the clothes he was wearing, some money, a knife, and his U.S. intention papers, rolled up in a waterproof skin.

As soon as Johnny touched the shore, he climbed the bank and headed for a small clump of dark woods at the edge a field. There he could dry off, rest up, and perhaps pay a visit the next day to the union hall. Before entering the shadow of the trees, he paused, glanced back, and saw the *Sondike*'s aft lights disappear down a bend in the Maas in deathly quiet. Johnny had turned twenty that May. He had grown into a man just half an inch short of six feet (nearly 182 cm) tall and weighed some 185 pounds (84 kg). He was big-boned, with strong hands. His father's light blue eyes, intelligence, and composed demeanor, especially when choosing his words, gave him a certain charisma. It was October 16, 1914.[21] The conflict in Europe had been raging for just over ten weeks.

3

CONSCRIPTED

The weak October sun warmed Johnny's back as he zigzagged through Rotterdam's side streets to the office of the Seafarers' International. He had slept soundly in the forest and awoke pleasantly refreshed. A quick wash of his upper body in a nearby stream prepared him for the meeting ahead. By timing his entrance into the city for midmorning, Johnny felt the bustle of people and traffic would give him cover.[1]

He arrived at the union hall, proceeded up two flights of stairs, and swung open the boldly lettered glass door. A matronly receptionist handled his inquiry briskly and indicated that he should take a seat while she went down the hall to locate the union secretary. In a matter of seconds she was back to say that the secretary would see him, and gave him directions to the correct office. De Graaf proceeded down the hall, passed through another door, and was greeted by a familiar face. Before him stood an old school chum from Wilhelmshaven, Wilhelm Johansen.

"Hey, Johnny, where have you been?" Johansen inquired happily. De Graaf shook his acquaintance's hand warmly.

"I've been all over, while you've been working your way up, landlubber style, to finally arrive here as Seafarers' secretary," de Graaf replied.

"Great to see you, Johnny. You know, as a Dutchman, you could come home for good and settle down," Johansen informed his guest. He was referring to Johnny's family name being of Dutch heritage.

The conversation was just starting when the door opened and in walked Marquis Square. The captain of the *Sondike* was just as surprised to see Johnny as Johnny was to see him. De Graaf explained his sudden disappearance as an effort not to get him into trouble by having a German national on board in port, which he understandingly accepted. Square seemed to relax. The details were explained to Johansen, who nodded his head in support.

"You should have no trouble here, Johnny, for the pro-German element in the city would think twice before tackling a neutral Seafarers' International Union member," he assured de Graaf. Captain Square agreed.

"Politically," he continued, "are you for Karl Liebknecht and Rosa Luxemburg?" Liebknecht was an Independent Social Democratic member of the Reichstag (parliament) and an orator who came out against appropriations for World War I; Luxemburg was a left-of-center activist. After the war, on January 15, 1919, they would be murdered by members of the reactionary Freikorps (Free Corps), a ragtag band of demobilized soldiers and others loyal to former or situational commanders and essentially opposed to communism taking hold in Germany.[2]

Johnny told them he would not discuss his politics, to which Johansen replied, "Why not?" for it was safe to do so.

"Then you are a coward, Johnny, for one has nothing to fear here," he retorted. "If you are not willing to stand up for your principles like me, then by definition, you have to be a coward."

De Graaf got very angry, shouting that no one had ever called him a coward in his life, and that he would tell Johansen how he felt politically but that he might regret what would be said. The Kaiser, the Imperial German war machine, and all of Johnny's views and hatreds soon filled the room to overflowing. He carried on for several minutes, only vaguely aware that Captain Square mumbled something about crew lists, excused himself, and left the room halfway through this outpouring. Exhausted, Johnny finally concluded and slumped into a chair.

"You have lived and seen much," Johansen said softly. "Had I known or experienced what you have, I would never have asked you to give your views. Please forgive me." After a moment of quiet, the two men proceeded to discuss Johnny's desire for a new ship from Rotterdam. They parted a short while later, agreeing to meet the following day, when a new berth list would be available, as many ships were expected in port. Johnny shook Johansen's hand, completely unaware that their second meeting would never take place.

De Graaf did not see Captain Square in the outer office as he passed through, so he continued on to the street, content with the hopeful assurances of a ship. He had walked only a block when a car drew up beside him, the door was flung open, and out of nowhere two men appeared. They grabbed Johnny and threw him into the back seat of the vehicle. It all happened so fast that Johnny did not realize he had been arrested. With Johnny wedged between two burly traveling companions in the cramped back seat, the car sped through the traffic like a slippery eel. Handcuffs were hastily snapped onto de Graaf's wrists once his arms had been forced behind his back and out of the way.

When Johnny's initial surprise wore off, he demanded angrily, "What the hell is this all about?"

"You are under arrest as a German citizen and are being deported back to

Germany," came a stern voice from the front seat. Johnny shouted, protesting his innocence, but to no avail. All his yelling fell on deaf ears. Stunned, he finally slumped into a quiet state of disbelief, staring straight ahead.[3]

The car zoomed to the Dutch border not far from Emmerich, Germany. When it pulled to a stop, his captors alighted from the vehicle and enthusiastically greeted the German border guards. "Another Square special for you," they told the grinning soldiers, as Johnny was yanked out of the car and literally thrust into their arms.

"Germany thanks the captain!" came the cheery reply. The doors slammed shut and the car turned around, speeding in a cloud of dust back to Rotterdam.

Johnny was taken to a wooden office and remained standing beside two armed guards while a third phoned for transport. He fumed at his own stupidity to have ever trusted that snake, Square, in the first place.[4] "How well I played into his hands, only to escape, but then to arrive in his clutches again through a lack of caution," Johnny reflected.

Marquis Square must have been delighted to listen to part of Johnny's rambling against the government, and then to excitedly phone for his arrest from the neutral ground of the union office. Johnny could picture it all. What a fool he had been. He had actually added to Square's wealth as an informer. "Well, poor Wilhelm," Johnny thought. "Don't wait for me tomorrow. I'll have left your life just as I blew in." On his own he had found a ship, Wilhelm would conclude, and without much more thought would proceed with the day's business.

A small van rolled up, breaking Johnny's thoughts. He was shoved into the vehicle and joined by two armed soldiers, who sat beside him on the long wooden bench. Instructions were given to the driver, who set out for Wesel, the headquarters of the district army commander.

The officer in charge of the Wesel bastion was a graying all-military man who eyed Johnny closely as he stood before him. De Graaf still clutched his sailor's bag, covered with several flags of the world. His hands were swollen but now free of handcuffs. The stout officer listened intently as Johnny told his story, occasionally glancing at a colleague who stood beside his shiny desk.

"You will now join the Fatherland's armed forces," he announced when Johnny had exhausted his tale.

"I will not, and you cannot make me. I demand my rights in accordance with this American citizenship paper." Johnny withdrew the U.S. intention document, complete with gold-leaf seal, from his bag and tossed it onto the officer's desk. De Graaf's escorts moved to restrain him, but the commandant waved them off as he glanced at the official parchment.

"A lousy piece of paper, quite worthless here," he sputtered sarcastically. "You will serve the country of your birth, young fellow, or be shot. Look out that window and you will see a post where we tie rebels against Germany, and execute them if they persist in being stubborn."

Johnny glanced out the window and, sure enough, saw a post that appeared well worn and splintered in places. There was no doubt the man meant what he said. Johnny's mind worked feverishly as he sorted out what to do. If he was to be shot, it had to be for something more worthwhile than this. Little choice remained.

"All right," Johnny indicated, he would sign up. His opponent grinned a wicked smile. "May I visit my father in Hamburg first, whom I have not seen for six years?"

"No, you cannot," the officer shouted. "We know who you are, and the sooner you are in the military, the better and safer for us. We will, however, inform your father by wire of your present whereabouts and he no doubt will be pleased you are under discipline and now serving the Fatherland. Which branch of the military do you choose?" The choice was not difficult.

Five days after jumping ship in Rotterdam, Johnny was made a new conscript in the Imperial German Navy, the Kaiserliche Marine.[5] Once the paperwork was finished, they gave him his transportation orders and a military ticket for the train. He was to travel at once to the Second Naval Artillery Division at the base in Wilhelmshaven. There he would start his *Grundausbildung,* or basic training. It was the very place where as a boy he and his buddies had watched the preparation of new recruits from afar. Now he was to be one of them, and other young boys would probably observe him through the holes in fences.

No doubt was left in his mind about attempts to escape or not appearing on the ordered date in Wilhelmshaven. In wartime, if caught, he would receive a long prison term—if he was lucky. But more than likely, he would face a firing squad for being absent without leave. Disgusted with his luck, Johnny made his way to the train station and displayed his third-class ticket, but was probably moved to a second-class carriage owing to a lack of third-class carriages during the war. He flung his sea bag into the rack above the seat and settled down for the journey ahead. "One day from today," he mused, "I will be in their damn uniform. They may think they have me now, but they do not have me! They will have to kill me before I knuckle under! Damn Germany! Damn them all!"

Bursts of steam, shouts of departure, and hasty goodbyes interrupted Johnny's defiant thoughts. A gust of oil fumes and muffled sound streamed into the cloistered compartment as its door opened to usher in a gentleman and his wife. Ramrod straight, the man was decidedly middle-aged, tall and slender with graying temples. His companion appeared near the same age and pleasant. She had a smiling face and clung to the man's arm firmly as he secured the cushioned seat across from de Graaf.

The train suddenly lurched forward amid more deafening noise. Fixed objects outside began moving, indicating the train's departure. Soon the station vanished in a dirty window and was replaced by a rocking motion and clicking monotony.

"You are a merchant marine?" inquired the stranger. Johnny glanced at him, sitting so correct in his civilian clothes.

"Yes, I am," Johnny replied.

"Do you like being in the navy?"

De Graaf could not help himself. "The navy I know is the merchant navy, not the Kaiserliche Marine. Those sons of bitches wouldn't even give me time to see my family, who I haven't seen for six years," he spewed out in contempt.

The prudish man looked intently at Johnny's colorfully decorated sea bag on the rack above. "Yes, people don't always know what to do, so they follow rules to the letter," he continued, "most unfortunately!" They chatted for a while and Johnny slowly came out of his foul mood, just as the city of Bremen eased into view. The proper man was very interested in Johnny's ship postings and travels as the two men bantered back and forth. A few minutes later the train rolled into Bremen's Hauptbahnhof (main train station) and screeched to a halt.

"Now, sailor, take it easy. It's no good to be rebellious. Easy does it. Then you'll come out in one piece," he soothingly advised. Scribbling something on the back of a card he produced, he rose and handed it to Johnny. It was a military pass for the naval base. On the back he had written, "Three days from this date, report for duty. Use this pass as proof." The words were followed by a signature that Johnny could not make out. Young de Graaf's delight was unbounded. "Sir, who are you?" Johnny inquired suspiciously.

The man did not reply at first, for he was busy pulling his cases from the rack and helping his companion prepare for their departure. Turning to de Graaf before he exited, he smiled and said, "Good luck. We have had a fine discussion, which I am sure benefited us both. Please take my advice and learn to stomach the new experiences you will encounter in the military." With a wave of his hand he disappeared into the throng on the platform. Perplexed by the encounter, Johnny toyed with the card in his hand, lost in thought. Finally he realized that the train was once again in motion.

"Hamburg, here I come!" he thought. Johnny would soon see his father again, and Sophie and the rest of his brothers and sisters. Once in Hamburg, he found his family's new home, turned up the walkway, and knocked on the front door. Wilhelm de Graaf must have been near the entrance because he quickly opened the door, hardly allowing his son time to view anything of the family's new home.

"Johnny, it's you!" he shouted in amazement as Wilhelm's firstborn stood grinning on the threshold. Their spontaneous embrace brought tears to both men's eyes as they stood clinging to each other. Sophie and the others, all talking nonstop, came running, as kisses and bedlam ensued. Sophie had grown into a very attractive young woman. She and her brothers, except for Waldemar, were also transformed.

His father recounted Amanda's departure, his struggles to keep things going with Sophie's assistance, and how the occasional money from Johnny had helped. Wilhelm eased his troubled mind as Johnny listened, and his heart went out to his gentle father. Gifts Johnny had purchased for them after leaving the train included food as well as something special for each one. It was like Christmas, with exclamations of delightful surprise, bear hugs, and more kisses amid a wrapping-strewn floor. The few days he had were delightful, as he again got to know each of them.

Wilhelm, Sophie, and Johnny discussed the German situation and the current war, with all of its negative aspects for the German people. They could see no sense in the conflict and, like many Germans at the time, hated the government's military machine, with its insatiable appetite. It left only death and destruction in its wake. The Kaiser, supported by the SPD, wanted Germany to be a world power. Bullying and land grabbing were the cornerstones of his foreign policy.

A splinter group left the Social Democrats in April 1917 and called itself the USPD (Unabhängige Sozialdemokratische Partei Deutschlands, or Independent German Social Democratic Party). The faction actually began to take shape just before Christmas 1915, from a core of twenty SPD members in the Reichstag who voted against additional funding for the war. They advocated peace without victors but were overpowered by the mainline SPD nationalists. The USPD nonetheless continued to gain public support for its outspoken and defiant stand. Wilhelm Dittmann, Georg Ladebour, and Hugo Haase were the strong voices of the new party.[6]

Rebels and antinationalists made up a good portion of the membership of the USPD. There was also a sprinkling of ordinary Germans who opposed the war and the Kaiser. Persecution, beatings, and scorn walked with these nonconformists, forcing them to work underground. Miniature rallies produced fights and bloodshed as rivals gathered both inside and outside USPD meetings. Pro-government parties planted browbeaters at key points to spark altercations. In coordinated attacks, and with superior numbers, they would rush in and crush the dissident assemblies. No meeting was safe unless it was held in secret. Even then, moles infiltrated the movement, forcing the dissenters into more closely knit, smaller, and more trusted groups.

Johnny believed in the Independent Social Democrats. Not only did they oppose the war, but they disavowed the nationalist views of "Germany the Great" he had come to loathe in his youth. Johnny had already dropped out of the larger SPD over the war issue in 1914. Three years later, he would side formally with those who were building the USPD.[7] His father shared his convictions, but only to the degree of telling his son; otherwise he kept his own counsel.

The interlude, nice as it was, soon ended, as the day of Johnny's departure arrived. Amid displays of affection and promises to write, he left his family clustered on the station platform. Despite his father's objections, Johnny pressed several banknotes into his hands in one final act before boarding the train. With his face pressed against the glass, he could still see his family waving on the platform as the train pulled slowly out of Hamburg.

Wilhelmshaven was larger than the North Sea base Johnny remembered from his childhood. He could see a good portion of it through the twin arches of the main gate on Göker Straße, where the sergeant on duty demanded his papers.[8] The day had arrived all too soon, but his 8:00 A.M. appearance proved that Johnny was a man of his word. The short, stocky guard viewed all of this with suspicion, particularly when Johnny produced the small card, which contradicted what was stated on his travel orders.

"Hey," he hollered like a little elephant, noticing the counterorder.

"Take it easy, Sergeant," de Graaf eased in. "It's official, so would you please inform Captain Friker that I am here?"

The sergeant was clearly annoyed. De Graaf was nothing but a lousy merchant marine to him, and one with the nerve to tell him what to do. Turning angrily, he made a call and was instructed to show the new recruit to the main office. Mumbling and cursing to himself, the sergeant strode rapidly ahead, forcing Johnny almost to run to keep up with him. Arriving at the captain's headquarters, de Graaf hardly recognized the man in civilian clothes from the train. Now he stood before Johnny in his full uniform, with the four stripes of an admiral on his sleeve.

"So, you managed to get here on time, I see," he smiled warmly.

"Yes sir," Johnny replied, "and proud of it."

"Do your best for us, son, for we need sailors like you in our profession," he counseled.

Johnny was then processed through the records division, medical facility, and on to the quartermaster's section. Among thirty new recruits for the Sixth Company, Johnny was issued his clothing, uniform, and kit, including a toothbrush. He lumbered under armloads of gear as he wobbled to the barracks on the far side of a large parade ground. Entering the building, each man dumped his load on long tables in the center of the room. With bunks lining both sides of the hall, the thirty newcomers began labeling all their belongings with numbers and names. A uniformed sailor everyone began calling "Scoopies"[9] took it upon himself to issue commands, perhaps feeling that he had just inherited a fresh class of nitwits. Glancing up from his writing, Johnny recognized a fellow merchant marine he had sailed with on several voyages. He was at the far end of the table, and amid everyone's chatter de Graaf shouted to him in Italian, bringing a look of delighted surprise to his face.

The Kaisiserliche Marine seaman looked at them both, irritation coloring his stern expression. "Oh, now I'm going to teach you a lesson, you bunch of international vagabonds," he sputtered. "You smart guys don't think I know what you're saying, but I'll show you."

"If you did understand what I said, "Johnny informed him, "you would know we only said hello while we were doing our work."

"Shut up!" Scoopies retorted in a rage. "Get your rifle and top coat and come here!"

The last week of October was cold both inside and outdoors, as chilling gusts heralded the coming winter. Scoopies picked up a three-legged stool, turned it upside down on the floor, and commanded de Graaf to sit on one of the upturned legs and then twirl his heavy rifle. Johnny refused the order, adding fuel to the man's frenzy. Shaking uncontrollably, he screamed in a piercing voice, "You merchant marine scum! Bums, the lot of you! You rotten bastards should be pleased and thankful to eat the Kaiser's bread, and proud to wear his uniforms!"

That was too much! De Graaf swung his rifle in a wide arc, butt first, stopping only when it connected with his tormentor's head. A guttural shout vibrated through the room as Scoopies dropped unconscious to the floor. Whistles and shouts came from somewhere, doors opened, people grabbed Johnny in a blur. Shackles were slammed on his wrists and legs as he was rudely dragged to the guardhouse cells. He did not recall being struck down, but he was certainly manhandled by the naval police who responded to the barracks turmoil.

Morning found both Scoopies and de Graaf standing before the commanding officer of the company in his office. Poor Scoopies was adorned with a wrapping of gauze bandage covering some three-quarters of his head. He looked like a spent bullet after hitting a brick wall. The officer was very familiar, and it dawned on Johnny that he had sailed with him. Johnny remembered the man as the youngest officer, indeed the youngest crew member, on the SS *Seiten*. The man studied the report on the desk before him, questioning de Graaf's accuser as he read. Then, turning in Johnny's direction, he inquired, "Is this report correct as stated here that you knocked Scoopies out?"

"Yes sir," Johnny answered promptly, "but there is something left out. I knocked him down because he called us dirty, stinking scum of the earth; and we should be pleased to eat the Kaiser's bread and wear his uniforms."

"What?" the officer exclaimed.

"In that case, sir," Johnny continued, "you are also scum of the earth, having been a merchant marine officer."

"Did you say these things, Scoopies?" he demanded.

Johnny interrupted. "Don't ask him, sir; call the thirty witnesses from our barracks and they will tell you who is right."

"Take it easy, sailor," he commanded with annoyance. "We don't need that. Scoopies, did you say these things?" Head down, the able seaman mumbled that he had.

"Fourteen days' arrest, sailor, now get out!" he barked at Scoopies' throbbing, bandaged head.

Turning to de Graaf after Scoopie had departed, he said kindly, "Listen, sonny, I remember you as a very fine, capable seaman without once showing fear. I am confining you to three days in the brig. Pick up six bundles of bread to go with you." He smiled and shook his head as Johnny left. Johnny polished off all the bread on the first day. He felt that it was the most comfortable stretch of confinement he had ever spent, and he was indeed fortunate to have gotten off so lightly.

De Graaf soon rejoined his mates, who all felt very much as he did about Germany and its imperialist aims. Fresh faces had been added to the group, but they were all merchantmen, drafted as he had been, with brooding defiance for their captors. Scoopies' replacement was a bullheaded petty officer, another Kaiser man all the way. The stand-in and a clique of other petty officers vowed to fix the new recruits. They swore, condescended, and treated the conscripts like dirt at every opportunity. Then again, their support must have been tenuous, since they did not venture anywhere alone. They could be seen in a group of three or four at all times. Hostility virtually shimmered in waves anytime the two sides met.

One day they picked on Johnny, mustering him outside in the freezing cold without benefit of a coat. He was made to crawl on his knees and elbows with a rifle gripped between his teeth like a bone. "Now, you bum, crawl to the gym!" they commanded amid shouts, jeers, and the odd kick. The base gym happened to be a mile and a half (2.42 km) away, over a cinder path, the parade ground, a stone walkway, and a steep embankment. Johnny's companions could not help him because they had been locked in the barracks, and two bullies stood guard outside.

As de Graaf started to move, small pebbles dug deep into his elbows and knees. "Faster!" the petty officers shouted as he hobbled forward. The movement slowly tore his skin into a pulpy mash of bloody flesh. In excruciating pain, he covered the terrain. Johnny's lumbering pace slowed and then stopped completely when he reached the gym and collapsed. Well-aimed kicks landed on his blood-soaked arms and legs as he was ordered, "Now, go back!"

The hatred Johnny had when he started now combined with his determination not to be overcome by what they dished out. "Can't you get up?" a shrill voice inquired.

"No sir," Johnny mumbled vaguely. He remembered being lifted up by many hands, then passing out. When he came to, he was in great pain in the spotless Marine Lazarett (hospital) examination room on Kaiser Straße. How ironic, he must have thought, to be just one block away from his old high school, the Kaiser Wilhelm Gymnasium. Who would ever have thought that this young man, who had quit his formal education at age fourteen to join the merchant marine, would one day be lying in a hospital, all busted up, just meters away?

A ghost of a doctor hovered over him, checking his elbows, knees, and raw flesh, torn to the bone in some places and dripping with blood. The physician's angry words penetrated Johnny's haze. "How did this happen?" he demanded of the accompanying petty officer. "This man will need several operations."

"He was injured during drill, sir," came the weak reply.

"Injured during drill? What kind of drill?" the doctor demanded. "He did not fall—his wounds are those of some kind of inhuman punishment that even a dog could not endure."

"It was a discipline matter, sir," came the wobbling reply. "He's a troublemaker and had to learn a lesson for himself and his pals."

"Discipline does not tear away a man's flesh like raw meat, you fool!" shouted the doctor. "From now on you will stop this kind of treatment, understood? You should be well aware that you'll be in very serious trouble when I complete my report. Now get out of my sight, you sadist!"

Muttering to himself, the doctor cleaned and dressed Johnny's wounds and administered a tetanus injection. He instructed an aide to see that Johnny was ready for an operation the next morning and to inform him that he would remain in their care for at least two weeks while the wounds healed. Before departing that evening, he leaned over his patient's bed and said he was sorry to see what had happened. He counseled de Graaf that in the military one is not asked to think or express himself openly. Obey and carry out orders: that was the rule. Questioning and free discussion, as in civilian life, did not exist. Johnny was told to listen carefully. "If you want to remain alive, knuckle under, whether you believe it right or wrong. Follow my advice, and you will see it is correct. Disregard it, and the punishment you have experienced will be just a scratch compared to what man is capable of meting out to his fellow man." There was no place for rebels in the Kaiser's system. "You are young and unaware of these things. Think free if you must, but keep it to yourself, so that when the war is over you can practice what you believe. I hope you live a long life."

Although Johnny said he always remembered the physician's words, his spirit remained unbroken. The following morning, a number of skin grafts were performed. In short order the wounds healed. The medical care and excellent food enabled him to return to duty in two weeks, still limping. His fellow conscripts rejoiced at his return. They told him that they had been informed that he had gotten what he deserved, and that the same awaited others who did not give in to the authority of the group of noncoms. This approach only served to unite the draftees further. From that moment on, they plotted their strategy and defiance with meticulous care, seeking every means at their disposal to disrupt the hated military training. Where they could undermine, sever, or destroy, they would, without regard to their personal safety. They came to think of themselves as the "Group of 42," men who were strong willed and had a burning common purpose.

Instruction progressed rapidly in weapons, drills, physical education, and seamanship. Because of their merchant marine experience, Johnny and his mates were far more knowledgeable than the usual inductees. When several weeks' instruction came to an end, assignments were posted and the forty-two men were split up. One could see that the base commandant was no fool in the way he passed these rebels on to the ten ships in port, from support vessels to battleships. By dividing the troublemakers, scattering them far and wide, the port's chief officer aimed at control and submission. His theory was "divided they fall."

But it was a mistake. In fact, the mutual bond and belief among the group had became so well defined that splitting them up only sowed more seeds of unrest, on a now much wider field. The forty-two agreed to continue their efforts, each one as a leader who would develop a following. Meeting places and communication methods were arranged before they took their postings. Johnny and two others were assigned to a minesweeper with destination orders for the North Sea. The vessel was to blow a hole in the British sea net off the German coast, enabling ships from the Kaiserliche Marine to slip through the barrier. The warships would then steam closer to the heart of Britain and inflict losses on British shipping.

The operation unfolded on a night that was frigid cold by the time they reached their coordinates in the open ocean. High seas and strong winds made the ship sway to and fro almost unbearably under a moon that remained conveniently hidden in the clouds. On the tumbling aft deck, five sailors and Johnny, all in life preservers, gathered with a lieutenant who commanded them to jump into the icy water and swim to the nets. Reaching the barriers, they were to attach timed explosives that would split the webbing. The men argued with the officer that in such seas they could not make it to the nets. "Would it not be better to draw in closer, attach the explosives, and set them off electrically?" they asked. The officer became livid and would not hear of it. Despite the chorus of protests and pleading for reason, he was adamant.

With great difficulty the six men eased themselves over the side, laden with explosives in backpacks on top of their bulky live preservers. The seas immediately threw them back. They swam with all their might, only to have wave after wave roll down on them. The ship rocked uncontrollably despite its bow facing the heaving water. The vessel shuddered as each wave that crashed against her split into gusts of salty spray. Following many futile attempts, Johnny and his fellows could do no more. They were totally exhausted and numb with cold. One after the other, they crawled aboard from starboard as one large roller swept them against the deck.

The officer was furious. With the help of a few protesters ordered up out of the bowels of the ship, he literally kicked and pushed the tired sailors back into the sea. By this time, Johnny and his shipmates did not care if they lived or died. Their six bobbing heads could not be counted collectively, as some were climbing a wave, others on the crest of one, still others in a trough between swells. Hypothermia was imminent. The cold numbed each swimmer to the marrow. Their frozen arms and legs would not move. The men hung like dead fish on the surface, held above the water only by their life preservers. The weight of their satchels of explosives tipped their precarious balance as more waves crashed over them. The burden became unbearable. With phenomenal effort, man after man forced his unfeeling hands up to his shoulders and unhooked the packs of explosives. As the charges sank from sight, the relief was instantaneous. Five swimmers made it back to the ship. Hans, the sixth, was never seen again. He obtained peace in death after four hours in the bitter sea.

Over their soaked and coughing bodies, crumpled on deck, the officer who had ordered them into the water ranted and raved. He kicked the five survivors as he swore, but the men beneath his feet did not seem to care. The biting cold and exhaustion were interrupted with a painful thud to Johnny's head. The lieutenant's boot had connected, bringing with it realization and consciousness. Johnny remembered rising up on his knees and then standing. Vaguely he saw a face before him. Lashing out with all the energy he could muster, he swung a frozen fist into the object. The officer reeled on impact, and if not for the crew who caught him as he fell back, he would have hit the rolling deck and been washed overboard. As it was, he took the full impact of the blow in the face, which cut his lip and released a few teeth, which became souvenirs for the crew.

Spitting and spraying blood, the lieutenant blathered like a madman, delivering another kick to Johnny's limp form, as de Graaf had immediately dropped after delivering his personal message of protest. "To the brig with him," the lieutenant shouted over the howling wind, despite protests from the crew. Five sailors carried de Graaf to confinement below. Ten minutes later, through swollen eyes and reeling brain, Johnny saw the door open. He was carried out. The officer, disheveled and soaked in blood running from his open mouth, was thrown into the cell and the door was slammed shut behind him.

Johnny learned that after taking him below, the crew members returned to the aft deck to find the lieutenant kicking and swearing at the remaining prostrate forms. That did it. They grabbed him and administered a few well-placed blows to his groin, midsection, and head. Tying his hands and legs, they lugged him down to take Johnny's place.

The result of all this was a group session with the captain. When informed of what had gone on and where his first officer was, he placed the five seamen in their quarters under guard. He had blankets, hot coffee, and brandy sent in, followed by hot soup and sandwiches. The lieutenant remained in the brig, and his duties were filled by a petty officer who had sided with the crew. Later, the captain visited the five survivors and patiently listened to their story. He then proceeded to give each a severe scolding about following orders, despite the elements and their personal thoughts. He acknowledged that the officer had no right to kick anyone. He would be dealt with once the ship reached base.

The return voyage was indeed speedy, for the captain realized he had trouble on board. The base command considered it the safest course given stormy seas and the stormy crew. The lieutenant was released from the brig on orders from the captain the day before they arrived back at Wilhelmshaven. No one saw him because he was relieved of duty and remained in seclusion in his cabin until the ship tied up.

The party awaiting the ship's arrival at dockside consisted of several high-ranking officers, a few lesser ratings, and a detachment of naval police. The rebels were marched off and confined in the base brig on bread and water until the court-martial a few days later. They did not see the vessel's captain and first officer before the testimony. The court-martial itself was quick and expedient, as delay is not to one's advantage during wartime. All gave their accounts. The poor captain was demoted for failing to carry out his mission and was never seen again. The lieutenant was reduced in rank and received time in the brig. Johnny was given thirty days in the stockade and a verbal reprimand. Regardless, he felt that he had been justified in doing what he did. His stay in the base stockade passed without incident. Several members of the Group of 42 were also there, having caused disruptions on their vessels. Hans was written up as a hero and his family was told that he had died during a dangerous mission at sea, having served his Kaiser well. Hans would have turned over in his watery grave if he had known this, for he was not comfortable with the whole business of serving Germany. The rest of the crew from the minesweeper was split up and assigned to other ships.

Dittmann, Ladebour, and Haase, the three USPD politicians, made themselves known to some of the Group of 42. Having heard of their exploits from the start, they met with various members, usually alone and always off base. Financial aid was offered, as was full support from their political party. Leaflets and pamphlets critical of the Kaiser soon inundated Germany's military bases. In the months that followed, the USPD continued meeting with the "42" to replenish propaganda supplies, discuss plans for a mutiny, and obtain equipment to assist in breaking the Kaiserliche Marine. The movement began to be called the Revolutionärer Ausschuß (Revolutionary Committee), or RA. It rapidly grew in strength, with new cells popping up on ships and at naval bases. The original group of forty-two men soon grew to more than two thousand at Wilhelmshaven alone.

Each small unit of three or four expanded and divided like an amoeba, until literally hundreds of cells existed in the German navy. There was even a small presence in the brig, a place where many new converts joined the cause. Under threat of death, the names of each supporter and the details of all RA meetings were kept secret. For a long time, the underground society was a well-guarded mystery, despite the constant military probes and spies attempting to ferret out information. Try as it might, the navy could not stop the RA. Every so often a ship's gun would jam, sand would grind machinery to a halt, or a key replacement part would go astray. The plots grew larger and bolder as the RA's power and daring increased.

On his release from the brig, Johnny was assigned base guard duty. He was ordered to keep watch on a bridge adjacent to the naval complex. During his first patrol he met Emma Todicain again. As his old school sweetheart attempted to cross the viaduct, he recognized her despite the eight years that had slipped away since their last meeting in 1908. She did not immediately remember him. The young woman presented de Graaf with a pass, but stamped on the back were the words "No Admittance."

"Emma," he said, "I am so pleased to see you."

"How dare you," she snapped, not knowing the speaker. Then she stood back, amazement dawning on her face as she exclaimed in surprise, "My God! It's you, Johnny!" They embraced, plying each other with questions and answers at the same time. She was happily married, and her parents still lived in Wilhelmshaven.

After this joyous reunion, Johnny allowed Emma to cross the bridge so that she could get her groceries on the other side. One needed a special pass to cross over, owing to the close proximity of this bridge to the base, despite its being a well-used thoroughfare. "How come you are in the navy, Johnny, when you wanted the high seas, but no part of the military?" she inquired on parting.

"Circumstances, Emma, but I'll still beat them," Johnny replied with determination.

"I'm sure you will, Johnny," she smiled. "You always were one to rebel at things others would accept without question. Good luck. I'll be thinking of you."

On reaching the far end of the bridge, she waved, as did Johnny. "Dear Emma," he thought, "how you captured my heart when you were young." The next day de Graaf was not given bridge duty, so he guessed that the guards, who obeyed rules to the letter as only Germans can do, would turn her back if she returned.

Assignment to a battleship, the SMS *Westfalen* under Captain Johannes Redlich,[10] soon followed. A prominent vessel in Germany's emerging Hochseeflotte, or High Sea's Fleet, the *Westfalen,* and Johann de Graaf, played a significant role in the Battle of Jutland at the end of May 1916.[11] This was the only major naval battle of World War I, and both sides claimed victory. Actually, the Germans sank more ships and lost fewer men. Yet it was only a paper victory, because the ratio of warships between the two navies remained about the same.[12] The British continued to have more of everything.

Johnny had been promoted to chief warrant officer, or *Bootsmann,* in charge of one of the *Westfalen*'s gun turrets. The *Westfalen* led the German line at one point during the Jutland encounter and was responsible, entirely or in part, for sinking five British destroyers, the HMS *Ardent, Fortune, Sparrowhawk, Tipperary,* and *Turbulent*. Another five were damaged, the HMS *Broke, Contest, Petard, Porpoise,* and *Spitfire*.[13] De Graaf was awarded the Iron Cross first class for bravery during the fight and was given a depiction of the battle signed by the Kaiser. Only Germans who had been in the clash were awarded such pictures. Johnny refused the medal, taking it off his tunic and throwing it on the deck. For this act of insubordination he was placed in the brig for twenty-eight days and was later told to accept the citation—or else.[14]

Germany, by this time, had a navy of sixty thousand sailors, a large number of whom were convinced that the German way was not their way. The command at Wilhelmshaven asked many of these men to volunteer as officer trainees, but the majority, including Johnny, refused. Some did come forward, those, unlike like the larger group of malcontents, whose convictions were not set in stone. Perhaps they felt as the physician did who had attended to Johnny's elbow and knee wounds. Since they were in the navy, they might as well live as best they could and try to get through the war in one piece.

As for de Graaf, an officer gave him another stern warning—cooperate or suffer the consequences. This time the lecturer was Lieutenant Commander Wolf, as he walked down the rigid line of rebellious sailors presenting themselves for inspection on the *Westfalen*'s quarterdeck. Wolf doled out caustic comments to each man. When he reached de Graaf, he stopped and eyed him from head to toe. Without warning his hand streaked out, striking de Graaf's cap from his head. "Your hat was crooked. Pick it up and put it on properly, you bum," he shouted.

The words had barely left his mouth when Johnny, as if reaching for his cap on the deck, grasped a metal utility box beside his left leg. Bringing it swiftly up and forward with great force, de Graaf slammed it into Wolf's startled face. The officer staggered back from the blow, bellowed, and could only watch as his blood began spurting everywhere. As when he had leveled able seaman Scoopies, there followed angry orders and a scuffle. Johnny was seized and escorted into the bowels of the ship under guard. He was tossed into the brig, this time for five days. Wolf, like Scoopies, did not fare as well. For more than a week he sported assorted bandages, provoking comments behind his back and snickering from the crew.

Otto Klutzka, a member of the mutinous group, kept Johnny posted on the various base happenings during his confinement.[15] De Graaf told him to contact the group leaders and step up the activities of the RA in protest. A day later, Johnny heard a loud explosion when an ammo dump was blown up. No one was injured, but the explosion did cause a great deal of chaos in Wilhelmshaven. The authorities never learned that Johnny was the reason for the explosion. When released from confinement, he was transferred to another vessel, and together with four other seamen soon met with Dittmann and Haase in the city. It was an encounter at which they laid out plans for continued action and were brought up to speed on other happenings in the military. Johnny and his four colleagues were told that every naval base in Germany had become a hotbed of rebellion. Even some army and air units were involved.

The Revolutionärer Ausschuß decided to increase its efforts and set a tentative date for an overall naval mutiny. Meanwhile, the German high command, constantly frustrated by opposition to the war among the ratings, had put together an effective spy network. This resulted in several arrests and in four death sentences for sailors on the *Westfalen*. The turncoat there was a seaman named Adams.[16] Nonetheless, by then the RA's sabotage and propaganda had begun to show dramatic results. Nothing moved smoothly in the navy anymore. Equipment failures and general disrespect became commonplace. RA cells continued to grow, and the Imperial German Hochseeflotte fell into a state of inactivity. What missions there were, were usually less than successful. Incompetence combined with daily rumblings of possible sedition made successful sorties unusual. The administration in Berlin was beside itself and shouted more and more loudly for sterner measures in the ranks.

The silent force was effectively disrupting the Kaiser's great dream and sapping his strength. Fights among officers and men occurred more and more often, as the turmoil raged from lavatories to crow's nests. A massive meeting was about to take place. It would be the beginning of the final assault. The RA had been a small group of dissenters in March 1915, but more than two years later they were on the verge of overthrowing the government.

Without warning, on August 17, 1917, a sizable number of RA members, including the original "42," were arrested. The base had turned into an armed camp, and more than two thousand naval crewmen were awakened from their sleep at bayonet point, rounded up, and carted off. Some members were hastily transported to various prisons in other parts of Germany. Johnny was among those put under heavy guard in a place he knew well, the Wilhelmshaven base brig. Through its spies and agents provocateurs, the admirals had finally obtained the names of the mutiny's entire inner circle.[17]

All of the insurgents on the *Westfalen* were court-martialed, as were those on the other battleships. They had to wear their uniforms, complete with medals. Johnny wore his service ribbons and Iron Cross.[18] Poor Otto Klutzka, the friend who had kept Johnny informed in the brig, was terrified. He was an innocent lad from a Ruhr coal miner's family who had largely been coerced into joining the founding group. Johnny assured Otto that he would speak on his behalf at their trial and attest that he had been compelled to join the "42" against his will. Johnny kept his word, but Klutzka was given a five-year prison term anyway. On hearing the sentence, Johnny stood up and shouted, "Is this your justice for this man?" His remarks must have shaken the military magistrates, because they conferred for a while and then reversed their sentence. Otto Klutzka was released.

Some of the others were found guilty of leading the rebellion and sentenced to death. Two innocent men, Max Reichpietsch and Albin Köbis, were eventually shot. The navy believed they were instigators rather than the followers they actually were. Johnny, too, was to face the firing squad, but owing to the intercession of his one of his captains, his sentence was reduced, on October 13, 1917, to one year and nine months at hard labor.[19] De Graaf would be taken to a special facility in eastern Poland, the Osowiec Fortress, to begin his prison term. The Osowiec stronghold had once been in Russian territory but in 1917 was controlled by Germany.

Following their hearings, the Group of 42, now reduced by one member, was conducted from Wilhelmshaven to Kiel. There they were hustled onto a waiting ship watched over by eighty-four armed guards and two noncommissioned officers.[20] As the steamer plied its way east, Johnny felt pleased when he thought of Otto. Klutzka was one man who would not be suffering. Little did de Graaf know that of the forty remaining core members chained to him, thirty-three from the *Westfalen*,[21] only seven would still be alive nine months later.

4

OSOWIEC

The train carrying the mutineers from the coast rolled to a stop at the platform that served as the Osowiec station. Awaiting them in early December 1917[1] was a blistering cold day of minus 28 degrees Centigrade (or minus 18.4 Fahrenheit). Everyone was quickly loaded into a truck and transported to the Polish bastion, perched not a kilometer away in a setting of picturesque woods and hills. Snow lay deep on the ground, cloaking the entire landscape in a mantle of soft whiteness. The new arrivals' clothing on that winter day consisted only of their lightweight navy uniforms and shoes. They did not have overcoats, caps, or gloves to provide any protection from the elements.[2]

Between 1880 and 1890, Russia constructed the Osowiec complex in stages as the centerpiece of its web of defense against Germany. Located near a bog of the Biebrza River, the four-fortress stronghold closed the only passage across the vast marshes of the Biebrza. Consisting of a great number of canals, moats, and ramparts, it fell to the German army in 1915 as a result of a strategic evacuation by Russian troops. The Kaiser's forces put part of it to use as a prison.[3]

The installation was impressive. It had high walls in some places and a drawbridge across a sharp, stony creek that gushed with water when not frozen over. Rifles poked in the prisoners' direction from secure lookout positions cut into the surrounding granite cliffs. The manmade portion ran off into the horizon on both sides of the bridge. The transporting guards unloaded the prisoners, releasing them to their new captors, who were armed with rifles and sidearms.

Lining up in twos, the convicts were marched over the bridge, along a road for some two hundred meters (about 218 yards), to an assembly area approximately a hundred meters square (nearly 109 yards square). The parade of clanking chains was finally given the snarling order "Halt!" by several of the guards. They had arrived at their destination. The rebels from the Kaiserliche Marine stood in front of a long administration building awaiting inspection.[4] Everywhere the new prisoners looked, guards were posted, trigger-ready and menacing. As they mumbled to themselves about the slim chances of escape, snowflakes swirled everywhere, depositing more moisture on their thin clothing and freezing, sodden shoes. The sting of biting cold dug deep into their bodies.

An order for silence was suddenly issued. A sharp whistle burst brought everyone to rigid attention as the prison commander made his appearance. Captain Hoffman Bermann was a strict disciplinarian, six feet (1.83 m) tall, of slim build, decked out in a crisp army uniform. He wore a peaked Prussian helmet with cloth earflaps underneath, a big, wide-collared winter greatcoat, high boots, and gloves. Bermann was an immaculate dresser, his uniform always trim and neat. He and officers like him were the pride and joy of the Kaiser. He was also a brutal man who delighted in breaking spirits and bodies at the same time. Johnny and his forty companions later discovered that Bermann had once been in charge of a town in Alsace-Lorraine, but owing to the numerous scandals he created he was replaced and reassigned to Osowiec.

Captain Bermann swaggered before the assembled inmates, deriving an unnatural delight from the plight of each man standing before him. His arrogance showed in every move as he surveyed the shivering prisoners. With an armed guard on each side, he began his opening address in German, "Not one of you dirty traitors will leave this fortification alive. You have no country, you conspirators who wanted the Fatherland to lose the war."

He repeated himself over and over again while the captives began to freeze in earnest, standing in four inches of fresh snow. "Not one of you subhuman beasts will leave here alive," he screamed. Bermann ranted on like this for more than an hour, calling the new prisoners every name he could think of. Some men soon keeled over into the ankle-deep snow, where they lay unconscious. When they could hold it no longer, others added to their misery by urinating in their light trousers. More bodies fell face down in the snow-encrusted courtyard, as swirling winds played a deathlike whisper over their collapsed forms.

At last Bermann's tirade was over and he barked orders to the guards. Those still standing were commanded to retrieve their fallen comrades and then march double-time to the building facing them. Somehow they accomplished this, the semifrozen carrying the frozen, prodded on by kicks and blows from rifle butts. Inside, they were processed, then led outside again to one of the holes used to store ammunition when the fortress was in Russian hands. The light nearly ceased as they entered and were forced down wet, rough-hewn stone steps to a lower floor where they were shoved into a black dungeon. Their catacomb was one of several closeted amid cold water and mildew. Small splinters of wooden ammo cases lay rotting in the swill. Pungent smells of decay and ruin greeted their already shocked senses.

It was soon learned that other dungeons at Osowiec contained more prisoners, sixty to a cell. Johnny and his forty colleagues were jammed into a confinement area that held one wet, soiled mattress and blanket for every five men. Those who had fainted in the outer courtyard were eventually revived with help from the more able, who rubbed the circulation back into their blanched skin. All of the prisoners had frostbite, the scars of which would last a lifetime. Their sleeping space did nothing to ease their discomfort or aid their blackened fingers and toes. The men were forced to take turns standing and sleeping on the mattresses and threadbare blankets. Packed tightly, they rotated from the inside out, pressing close and sharing precious body heat. Wolfgang, the first of the forty-one to collapse in the courtyard, regained consciousness, but his sickly pallor and overall weakness was troubling. His small frame was bathed in beads of perspiration he could ill afford. He lapsed in and out of delirium throughout the night.

The dimly lit outside corridor rang with the nailed boots of patrolling guards. Occasionally these guards would stop before the thick wooden door of some cell to peer through the small grillwork of solid bars. Their curses and spit showered the pitiful men huddled beyond in the darkness. The prisoners had no doubt that the guards had been chosen for their ability at dispensing rough treatment. Screams of torture and madness continually broke the stillness. Each thud and groan told the prisoners that a rifle butt had again clubbed someone in the head.

The first night of terror at Osowiec strengthened the bond between the men of the defunct RA. They pledged to watch out for each other, no matter what might unfold in the time ahead. They had just made this pact when a guard announced sarcastically outside the cell that the current temperature had risen to 10°C (50°F). Standing in his storm coat before the barred door, he also took a morbid delight in revealing how many prisoners had died up to that point. But his callousness only made the men in Johnny's cell more determined to survive. Morning brought a ration of moldy bread and a little water with ice forming on the top. Then nothing, and then another night, the wet stone floors again serving as beds for those who could not stand.

Unshaven and in rags, the forty-one men were marched upstairs and over to the administration building to be interrogated. To speed up the process, the guards made full use of clubs, whips, and chains. The men were returned to their cells, broken and bleeding, to nurse their injuries for a short while before being taken upstairs again and again. Under this kind of torment, the body weight of the convicts from Wilhelmshaven quickly dropped, reducing once strong sailors to vestiges of their former selves. Johnny too lost weight, and his back was torn into and severely scarred by repeated thrashings. So unsightly were his wounds when they healed that he rarely went without a shirt in public.[5]

Posted everywhere throughout the slimy corridors were signs informing guards that should they capture or kill an escapee they would be compensated with three weeks paid vacation. Four from de Graaf's group died from beatings during the first week. Their bodies remained in the cell with the rest of the men for several days. Then Wolfgang coughed nonstop one night. The cries and pleas for aid for him went unheeded. By morning, he too had passed away. At first, sorrow and anger for their fallen friends was tough on everyone. As the months passed, however, the group's sensibilities hardened. By then, death had become a daily companion.

At six o'clock one morning a policy change was announced. The prisoners received their usual soggy ration of bread. Then they were lined up and marched into the white world outside the fortress. The same rail line that had brought them to Osowiec meandered northwest through the forested landscape to the community of Grajewo.[6] For the balance of the bitter winter months, their job was to keep this line cleared and operating. Repair work on embankments, ties, and the roadbed never ceased, as the line had been allowed to fall into disrepair. To complete the task, each man was issued a pair of wooden clogs with no socks. No further articles of clothing were provided. Rags were the sole shield against the ever-present winter gusts and snowfall. In groups of eight, the prisoners worked the line. A well-armed guard was responsible for each group, positioning themselves in their warm, full-length coats on every flank. Yet it was the winter's chill and dampness, not the guards, that forced the prisoners to keep working with their picks and shovels. This was the only way to keep from freezing to death. Bareheaded and barehanded, the inmates mustered what energy they had to keep their blood flowing. Hands touching metal came away without flesh. A face in the wind iced up, as did feet that went too long without movement. Biting winds tore through their nearly cheesecloth clothes until their skin tingled a pulsating red.

Running away was impossible, as a guard's bullet could travel faster than any man who attempted to make for the tree line. The jailers were forever on the alert, keen on earning a vacation bonus away from the frozen hell. Anyone who did reach the trees unscathed would be tracked down and shot if he did not die of exposure first. The waist-deep snow in the woods and the constant foul weather provided an inferno of their own instead of a refuge. Escape was sheer suicide from any angle. Those from the other groups who did attempt it never survived.

Hans, the youngest and gloomiest member of the Wilhelmshaven group, nevertheless felt he had to try. A Berliner, he was tall, slender, and married. His despondency caused the group great concern. Day after day, night after night, Hans talked of nothing but escape. He too had seen the original forty-one members dwindle after they reached Osowiec. Each new week saw more of his companions freeze to death. All the same, breaking out continued to be his sole obsession, and no amount of reasoning made any impact. "It's suicide, there's no possibility of making it alive," he was told over and over, but these appeals failed to change his mind.

Things went reasonably well for the following two weeks. Thereafter, Hans became sullen and moody at a pace that corresponded with the ebb and flow of his dreams of a successful escape. Despite everyone's pitiful condition and own thoughts of hopelessness, they attempted to make their conversation positive and cheery when dealing with Hans. The group even shared its little bread ration with him when his mental and physical condition deteriorated. Then one morning he was suddenly happy. The others were so delighted that they immediately gave him more of their own rations, hopeful that his constant hunger, like theirs, would be somewhat appeased by these additional gestures.

In an upbeat way the day progressed, with only a light snow falling as the group hammered, picked, and shoveled along the rail line. A bright sun glowed warmly from above, and there was no breeze to chill the glorious rays of delicious warmth. The guards appeared less wicked, even speaking without contempt, an unprecedented respite. A forest wall glistened like a million jewels spread out on drooping boughs in wondrous winter splendor.

Without warning, the magic was shattered. "Hey, Wolf, there goes your holiday," rang out, as the prisoners raised their heads to witness Hans dashing for the woods, having dropped his pick a split second earlier. There followed a pause, almost as if people were stunned; then Sergeant Wolf turned, took aim, and fired. Spellbound, the prisoners heard the deadly shot and saw the distant form drop into the cushioning snow. "Oh, he'll live and have a nice little memory for himself," Wolf assured the shocked onlookers. In unison, the prisoners raced to the fallen body, panting from the long run as they reached him. But there was no hope. Hans was dead. A bullet hole through his back had ended his race for freedom. In the seconds that followed, his blood had gushed out of his weak frame, turning the snow around him a sickening red.

Johnny and the rest of the men gazed at the sprawled, youthful man in sorrow and prayer. Sergeant Wolf viewed his downed game with great delight, amid a chorus of backslapping and praise for his marksmanship from his armed colleagues. Hatred crept into the condemned Germans as they looked from their dead companion to the jubilant faces of his killer and tormenters. Had they followed their immediate impulse, they would have thrown themselves on the guards and murdered a few of them before being subdued. The clenched fists at their sides, however, tipped off the sentries, who quickly took aim at the prisoners and screamed at them to return to their assigned duties. Four men were detailed to carry Hans's body back to the fortress.

Two more months of filth, hunger, and bereavement slowly passed. By February 1918, twenty-seven men remained of the original forty-one. With each new week the number was reduced still further. Morning revealed unresponsive forms, barely alive from the night before. Some men could not even manage to stand. The daily march to the rail line claimed others. Falling during a work detail brought a torrent of rifle butts to defenseless bodies. Those fortunate enough to be taken to the fort infirmary often died anyway, despite the medical aid. Prisoners who were deemed to have recovered were soon returned to the horrible cells and freezing work.

Sergeant Wolf swelled in his reputation as a vile killer. Where other guards exercised restraint, Wolf charged into each situation with maximum force. Refreshed from his three-week holiday, he returned with increased gusto, looking for his next reward. Wolf's name soon made all the inmates at Osowiec shudder in fear. His acts of unhindered savagery reverberated in the thoughts of new victims yet unselected.

Added to the daily work gangs was a platoon of German soldiers. They labored on the rail line, too, and were generally appalled by what they witnessed in the treatment of prisoners. Occasionally, at the risk of joining the prisoners in their cells, they slipped the captives the odd piece of black bread or leftover scrap from a meal. On a particular March day in 1918, a soldier working beside Johnny mumbled softly, "I'll give you some fish tomorrow." De Graaf was delighted and whispered a reply of thanks. "How can I get it to you?" the soldier continued, not looking Johnny's way but continuing his blows with a sledgehammer. Johnny told him he could not hand it to him directly, since this would be noticed. A little way up the line, however, was an uneven spot under a rail. He could place it there, near a refuse barrel, where de Graaf would retrieve it. Toward nightfall, before he left for the dungeon, he pointed out the spot to the soldier.

Johnny's excitement was pretty high the next day as he worked his way up to the agreed place. Under the rail, covered in snow, were several herring wrapped in paper. Thinking that the coast was clear, Johnny stooped over, lifted the little package, and hastily stuffed it under his jacket. "Wolf," a petty officer guard shouted, "here comes another holiday!" Johnny froze in place, not daring to move, knowing that Wolf without hesitation would fire a round his way. Wolf called de Graaf forward as he dropped his rifle to the crook of his arm. Johnny walked through the crunchy snow toward him, never taking his eyes off Wolf's rifle. "What did you pick up there?" he inquired sternly, while a twisted smile played at the corners of his mouth. "I saw someone throw something in the garbage barrel," he lied, "so I went over and picked it up." All work stopped as the rest of the road gang looked on with fear in their eyes. Wolf swung his rifle, knocking the package out of Johnny's frozen hands, whereupon he stomped the little fish into the snow with his heavy boots. Johnny looked down only for a second. Then, without warning, Wolf swung his rifle butt, giving his victim a glancing blow to the head. Johnny recalled the searing whack, then blackness, as he fell unconscious to the snow.

When he awoke, he was in the prison infirmary with his head wrapped in gauze, pulsating in pain. A doctor stood over him. "Is this Sergeant Wolf's handiwork?" he inquired. Johnny nodded. The doctor sighed in disgust. He kept de Graaf under observation in the infirmary for two weeks while treating the head gash and pain. Extra food rations were provided, which Johnny eagerly devoured. Not only was the additional chow welcomed by the ravenous patient, it was also a form of insurance, since it was intended to keep Johnny silent about the incident. When he felt better, he was released and once again went back to work on the railway line. His cellmates were glad to see him. They believed that he had died, as six others had done during his stay in sickbay.

Sergeant Wolf rejoiced in seeing that his quarry had returned for another round. Johnny met the doctor several weeks later, when he was called out of his cell for morning inspection. Believing the physician to be a kindly man, revolted by Wolf's deeds, Johnny was shocked when the doctor turned to Wolf and said, "This one is still strong; it will take more." A short time later, Wolf was transferred. None of the prisoners ever learned where he went, but they were overjoyed when they were told that he was finally gone.

Milder weather and daily sunshine at long last resulted in melting snow. The creek under the drawbridge gushed, trees put out buds, and soft warm breezes mixed with scents of moist earth lifted the convicts' spirits. The group was soon reassigned to farm detail, aiding the Polish peasants with their planting and fieldwork. Following morning roll call, they were marched under guard down country roads to their new work areas. Most of the farmers were kind, and when they could spare it without being seen, they gave the men small bits of food. This was not as easy as it might sound, since the guards continued to hover around like brood hens, suspicious of everything, regardless of the prisoners' weakened condition. Although under threat of death by the occupying forces, the Polish locals never stopped taking chances to assist the Osowiec inmates. Many of them hated the German army and felt sympathy for the outcasts—a situation not too unlike their own.

November 1917 was a momentous month in human history owing to the start of the Russian Revolution. By the spring of 1918 Johnny and his colleagues had heard about the event through the prison grapevine and hoped for a Russian invasion. When this failed to occur, the prisoners at the fortress in eastern Poland concluded that a big battle was going on somewhere in Russia. They felt that in time fighting would break out in Poland, too, and result in their release. Late that summer the Poles whispered to the prisoners that the German army had buckled, and that Russian forces could be expected on Polish soil in the months ahead. Everyone in the cells eagerly awaited this development.

Johnny continued to work in the fields, watching his contemporaries die, although not at the same rate as during the winter. Many times these deaths came when someone took a chance and grasped a stalk of wheat or some berries. The better weather did not bring better treatment from Bermann's guards. To grab a piece of harvestable crop was strictly forbidden, but so great was the prisoners' hunger that some no longer cared about the blows they would receive. In each evening's coolness, as the smaller and smaller group began its march back to the fortress, and despite Wolf's absence, the scene was the same. Sick men fell to the ground, weak men fell to the ground, and rifle butts continued to thud into the heads of inmates on the ground.

September 1, 1918, began in an unusual way. Normally, each morning after the one daily meal, the prisoners would go out to work. On this day, however, they were not ordered to their jobs. At 6:00 A.M. the meal was suddenly given a boost. Extra bread rations were allocated and washed down with coffee, not water. Something was up. Adding further mystery, a passing cook announced, "Good food today—you get pea soup with bacon in it." More surprises were in store, as new blankets and mattresses suddenly arrived for each man. The old ones were carted away. Pails of warm water, soap, and mops were placed before each confine and orders were issued to clean up the filthy, reeking cells. After doing the best job possible with these luxuries, the men watched teams arrive and spray all the catacombs with lice and tick insecticide. The prisoners mumbled among themselves in amazement about this perplexing burst of activity.

Finally, a guard informed them in a whisper that Major General Luiz Freiherr von Liliencron, inspector of military penal institutions, was soon to arrive for an examination of Osowiec.[7] Now it all made sense. Von Liliencron was a nationally respected and very powerful man on the German General Staff in Berlin. The bustle the prisoners were witnessing was a coat of stage paint. The veneer would last only as long as his visit. The inmates knew then that the clean blankets and mattresses would shortly disappear and be replaced by the sweat-stained and decaying bedding they knew so well.

Officers strode by for an advance check before von Liliencron's arrival. They sternly warned everyone that if addressed by General von Liliencron, he was to be referred to as "Your Excellency." To all of his questions concerning food or conditions, the only permissible reply was, "Good, Your Excellency." Each prisoner lined up outside the cells in the clammy corridor, as von Liliencron's approach was signaled. He was a tall man of military bearing with kindly features. As he stopped before the inmates, his entourage, following at his sides and in his wake, clustered in close, displaying forced smiles.

Pausing to speak a few words to each prisoner, he soon came to de Graaf. Johnny was in a devilish mood. In response to von Liliencron's compassionate gaze and inquiry as to how he was, Johnny cried out, "Your Excellency, you really don't have to ask us how we are, for certainly you can tell, can't you?"

Von Liliencron looked de Graaf straight in the eye. "Yes, I can," he replied solemnly. Anger and contempt lit the faces of the camp commandant and the other officers. "Just look around us here, Your Excellency," Johnny continued, by then having his undivided attention. "Look around at the conditions we live in and that will give you the whole story."

By this time several petty officers had moved in close beside the general. As they did, von Liliencron placed his hand on Johnny's shoulder and said, "We will change that, my son." At these words de Graaf felt his German blood boil. Turning away, von Liliencron moved on to the next set of corridor doors and the cells beyond. As he disappeared, the last door clanging behind his party, Johnny received his reward.

A blanket was quickly thrown over his head as a group of guards tossed the sarcastic jailbird to the floor. Johnny fought this unexpected force as best he could but made no progress against the rifle butts and vicious kicks raining down on him. It did not take them long to pound him into limp unconsciousness. His drooping carcass was hauled to a special cell outside the building but still within the fortification. Chains were snapped on his legs and arms, then looped around his neck. A twenty-one-day sentence in the hole had begun.

In the morning, still shackled, his entire body wracked with pain, he was told to come out of his cell with his toilet pot. The effort required was considerable. Hunched over in his chains, he had to hop, and then lower his head in order to allow his hands enough slack chain to reach the pot. Finally he stumbled out into the passageway, but did not move fast enough and a guard gave him a swift kick in his hindquarters. Johnny was sent flying down the hall, but the pot slipped from his chained grasp and soared into the air, releasing its contents on the jailer before crashing to the floor. De Graaf had just regained his feet when the guard kicked him again, throwing him on his back. After that, the man grabbed a handful of chain and dragged de Graaf back into his cell. The metal door slammed shut, and Johnny could hear the jailer's curses as he ranted to his two assistants. The cell was freezing cold, its poured cement walls and floor covered with ice crystals. Tied in his shackles, Johnny sat bunched up in a corner, his teeth chattering with the cold and his body aching with new wounds.

Twenty-four hours later the guard reappeared, but Johnny was ready for him this time. During the night, he had managed to slip from under the loose chain over his neck, giving him extra slack for his hands down to his shackled ankles. He bunched up some surplus chain in one hand. The guard entered Johnny's cell, mocking him, as de Graaf sat crouched in one corner. As he turned to leave, commanding his prisoner to follow, Johnny seized his opportunity. With his fist full of steel, he lashed out and caught the guard in the small of the back. In agony and surprise, the guard fell forward, colliding with the cell door and bringing his two assistants running. All three men jumped de Graaf, delivering pounding blows that soon brought him to his knees. Once he had been subdued, the slackened coils were tightened to the point that he had to hop, humped over, to the door slot each morning and extend one chained hand in order to pass out his toilet pot and pick up his meager slice of bread. Another three weeks were added to his solitary confinement.

The day came when Johnny was returned to his cellmates. After eleven months at Osowiec, only seven of the original group remained, and these seven were more dead than alive, mere walking ghosts left behind to suffer a while longer. What they had been through showed in everyone's weight. De Graaf's robust 190 pounds (86 kilos) had dropped to 104 pounds (47 kilos) by November 1918, and he was losing a little more each day as he looked for crumbs to eat. All of his leather possessions had long since been sucked to a dry bone white for their nourishment. His hollow, dull eyes shone from their deep sockets. Shriveled skin, once full and healthy, stretched on nearly exposed bones and ribs. Lice and ticks were his constant companions. As expected, the delousing of the cells had ceased after von Liliencron's visit.

On November 3, 1918, a second naval revolt erupted back in Germany. On the ninth, the Kaiser abdicated and fled to Holland. November 9 was a day like no other for Johnny and the men still alive in the bastion near the Biebrza marshes.[8] They awoke to deathly quiet. Silence replaced the normal shouts to get up, curses from the guards, marching feet, and the smacks of rifle butts. Their cell doors, always bolted, swung open at their touch. Slowly the prisoners emptied out into the corridor, amazed to find no guards or any sign whatever of their existence. With hearts pounding, they followed the well-known trail down the corridor, then step by step up to the floor above. Their frequent pauses were greeted with eerie silence, which provided the group of unbelievers the courage to venture on. Everywhere they looked it was the same, no sign of German uniforms. "What had taken place during the night to cause this mass evacuation?" they asked themselves. Could the Russians have made it to Poland and forced the German army to flee?

Propelled by excitement, their voices rising, they soon arrived at the mouth of the former ammunition storehouse to find one corridor gate still locked. No matter how they pushed and pulled, it would not budge. Using two discarded spoons, they started digging out the cemented-in bolt that fastened one side of the door. In a few hours it dropped sideways from its moorings. So laborious was the work for the weakened men that they had to rest often, taking turns, two at a time, for ten-minute spells. Once they had removed the bolt, they headed for the gate of the main building. Much to their sorrow, they found it also solidly barred. From this new position, however, they could see into the compound's courtyard. Each man was nervous with the taste of freedom.

Attacking the main building's barrier, the prisoners started their rotation again, digging with their spoons at the cement-encased hinges. While two men worked, the other five sat on the floor peering through the grill. Suddenly a feeble shout interrupted the effort. Everyone turned to see Kurt pointing with his emaciated arm. They strained to see what had caught his attention. Yes, they saw movement; a form appeared, then another. Exhilarated, the inmates watched as the little shapes ran in their direction.

The prisoners shouted as best they could, waving their arms up and down as more figures headed their way. Soon a horde of farmers and peasants were attacking the gate with their shoulders and crowbars. In no time they had forced the grill open and rushed in to help the men they had just liberated. The joy on both sides could not be expressed in words. The Poles were free of the German army. Johnny and what was left of his group had been emancipated. The weakened and battered were hastily wrapped in warm blankets, carried across the courtyard to waiting carts, and wheeled across the drawbridge. The wagons were laden with hay, bundles of blankets, and old coats for added softness.

The freed prisoners were given food in small quantities at first, to keep their shrunken stomachs from rejecting a gulped-down meal. All the peasants had, from their meager stock of clothing and provisions, they gave to their new friends. In the small village nearby, they proceeded to answer the former inmates' many questions. They were told that the entire garrison had pulled out overnight and left for Germany. Russian forces were now only a two-day march away, putting the fear of God into any German caught outside his country. The area annexed by Germany was only kilometers away. Eastern Prussia was just beyond. The fleeing troops were soon across the border and on home ground.

The farmers fed, bathed, and, with limited medical supplies, cleaned and dressed the wounds of the former captives. The men basked in the attention, but they knew that to remain there for any length of time could place everyone in grave danger. Behind the open arms and smiles, the peasants worried about being caught giving aid to Germans of any kind: it could mean a firing squad for both Pole and prisoner. Thus it was that following their brief day of food and rest, the outcast Germans decided to leave. Their hosts protested only weakly, for both sides knew it was best. A few Polish veterans provided the group with several old rifles for the trip. They were an odd assortment of weapons of various ages. Each came with a few rounds of ammunition, and all were in working order. In a final gesture of friendship, the Poles gave the men warm clothing, maps, more food, and transport west to Germany.

Nightfall came early as the last of the prisoners set out in two wagons. Their escorts led them to the frontier along an unguarded path. The two groups parted with firm handshakes and whispered goodbyes. Those going to Germany crossed the border and melted into the shadows. Soon they were crouched under the branches of a wide fir tree already heavy with an early snow. They decided to separate, each man going his own way, to reduce the chances of being caught together in a group. They made a pact before parting never to reveal to anyone the identities of the others, even under torture. Then the men who had been through so much together said a collective "auf Wiedersehen" and vanished into the woods. Johnny recalled saying a silent prayer as the forest mantle claimed them, one after the other.

De Graaf knew that he wanted to return to Hamburg. It was a good distance away, more than 550 miles (some 885 km), but by hitchhiking and getting a couple of long rides, he managed to get there in just two days. He soon learned, though, that his family had moved to Bremen the previous July.[9] By mid-November 1918, after the announcement of the armistice, he was approaching Bremen's outskirts. He could not help thinking that three years had passed since he had seen his brothers, sisters, and father. He arrived at their home on a cold and breezy night, but he did not feel the wind's bite. Warmly clad in his borrowed boots and thick, high-collared coat, and with a full stomach, Johnny's anticipation let him ignore the winter's chill as snow particles fell from the sky. A light was on in the living room, so he reasoned that the hour was not too late. Just to be on the safe side, he slowly skirted the house and emerged from the thick shrubbery beside the front door minutes later. Hastily he knocked, stepping back immediately into the shadows.

Seconds passed, though it seemed like an eternity, before the door opened, revealing Sophie, outlined in a flood of light. Johnny stood and gazed at her, restraining his tears. With weighty feeling in his voice, he said, "Don't be afraid, all I want is a little bread." She took a step back, looking her uninvited guest over from head to toe. Fear showed in her eyes as she absorbed the old clothes, the thin face and hollow eyes, of the figure before her. Regaining her composure, she said softly, "My good man, we don't have much." "A little," Johnny replied, "I would be most grateful." She then ushered him into the small hallway, whereupon his father appeared, having heard the door shut.

Sophie went to the kitchen while Wilhelm de Graaf stood and stared at Johnny. The senior de Graaf drew back at first, then with courage and curiosity took a step forward, peering closely into his firstborn's eyes. Wilhelm's face turned white as he stepped back again, and his hands came up to his now open mouth. "My son, my boy, it is you? What have they done to you?" he exclaimed in amazement. At that, Johnny's heart burst, and the two men fell into a tight embrace. Returning with a crust of black bread in her hand, Sophie dropped it, stood aghast, then rushed forward. Tears coursed down her soft cheeks as she threw her arms around Johnny, sobbing uncontrollably.

The reunion was soon complete, and the three sat before the warmth of the living room's bright fireplace. Between mouthfuls of food that Sophie forced into her brother, Johnny managed to tell them a little of his recent past. Soon his voice trailed away and he fell into a deep, peaceful sleep in a soft chair before the healing fire. Such contented slumber he had long forgotten. Gone were the cold, the torture, and the starvation.

5

GERMANY IN CHAOS

The Fatherland was a mess. Johnny had learned as much by word of mouth in Osowiec. During his convalescence, he read alarming news stories printed under sensational headlines. Some of the propositions made in these stories might have worked; others were the work of crackpots. The USPD had lost its hold on youth groups, which in September 1916 had coalesced into a breakaway organization called the Spartacus Bund (or Spartacus League).[1] Illegally organized by Karl Liebknecht and Rosa Luxemburg and trained by navy deserters, this band of rebels met secretly in basements and attics to plan attacks and provoke disorder. With its general hatred of the rich, the Spartacus Bund encouraged the poor to rise up and fight the government. Their tactics included the upsetting of nationalistic meetings with stink bombs, raiding collections of items for the war effort, and tossing dead rats into police stations. One act that provoked the unending ire of conservatives was the hanging of the Kaiser in effigy. This took place in countless places. Printed copies of the image were also made and passed around from hand to hand.

The two strongest parties in power in late 1918, the SPD and the Catholic Center Party (known as Zentrum), supported the Kaiser's forces and his family, the Hollenzollerns. Liebknecht and Luxemburg fought a ceaseless battle to be heard but found that they had little influence in the German Reichstag. Opposition to Liebknecht and Luxemburg by members of the other parties grew, if only because of their outspokenness. Moralizing for a more humane society, their words fell on the deaf ears of traditionalists seasoned for several generations in the cauldron of patriotism, expansionism, and militarism. Also newly released from prison, Liebknecht and Luxemburg provided an uncomfortable alternative to the powerful in Germany. Johnny admired them both, especially Rosa.[2]

Unrest in the navy, momentarily set back the year before with the arrest and imprisonment of the "42," was far from stamped out. Other dissidents took their places. Ernst Friedrich Wollweber, a stocky seaman from the battleship SMS *Helgoland,* kept the cause alive with support from naval ratings, as well as from Wilhelm Dittmann of the USPD and several of his colleagues. Resentment and hatred continued in the Kaiserliche Marine. Hundreds of sailors still went hungry, lived in cramped quarters, and suffered dreadful punishments. Their superiors often lived in a veritable lap of luxury, eating and drinking the best of foods and wines. The fleet's enlisted men wanted more than merely an end to the war. They sought revenge for all the degradations of the past. Action committees met in shipyard latrines, the center for clandestine revolutionary get-togethers. Desertions also increased as sailors bolted for parts unknown, selling their uniforms to buy food. In Munich and Berlin, in the provinces of Saxony and Silesia, armed runaways blended into the civilian population, forming and training new recruits to the movement. Court-martials increased as more ringleaders were arrested, tried, and shot by firing squads.

On October 28, 1918, while Johnny and the last of his colleagues were rotting away in Poland, the Hochseeflotte received sailing orders for a suicide assault on the English flotilla. True to their class, German naval officers spoke with excitement of the armada's "death voyage." Attempting to discourage feelings that the war was about over, they informed the crews that all hands were expected to go down with their ships. Somehow the officers felt that group stoicism in the face of death would win German respect and honor for those who had created the navy. In fact, the Hochseeflotte was preparing to sail in larger numbers than the force that met the British at Jutland.[3] The people of Kiel, Bremen, Hamburg, and lesser ports waited uneasily. Would the warships really leave for the open seas with crews that were so full of bad feeling? The moment of reckoning finally arrived. On November 3, just as they left their moorings, Kiel exploded in mutiny.

Aboard the battleship SMS *Thüringen,* the enlisted men seized the vessel. They dropped anchor and disarmed the officers. Choruses of "Down with the Kaiser! Down with the war! We want peace!" rang out from ship to ship and port to port, supported by tearful families waiting beyond the gates. The battleship *Helgoland* was brought to a standstill as stokers doused fires in the boilers. A total of 580 mutineers on board the *Thüringen* were arrested and locked in their quarters to await court-marshals. With help from the public, rebels rescued them hours later and regained control of the ship. Seaman Wollweber rushed to the rear mast of the *Helgoland* and hauled down the Kaiser's flag. He tore it to shreds and hoisted up the first red flag over the fleet.

All night long sailors commandeered trucks, some of which were promptly mounted with machine guns. In caravans flying the flags of revolution, the vehicles were driven into Bremen and other cities. People lined the streets to cheer as the lorries passed. Workers joined the revolt, arming themselves with guns, bayonets, and hammers. Sailors stormed the Oslebshausen Prison on the outskirts of Bremen and released scores of inmates, who threw commandeered great coats over their jail-issued garb and merged with the throngs in the streets. Officers in the military and the police were roughed up if they refused to transfer their weapons. Meanwhile, mutineers paraded with their naval cap bands turned inside out and rifles slung over their shoulders, butts up. The city capitulated without a fight when residents joined the protest. Standing on the balcony of the city hall, Wollweber declared, "We stripped the Kaiser of his boots; now let us finish off the capitalists. Long live the German Soviet Republic."

Hamburg, traditionally the reddest town in Germany, followed Bremen, as Soviets came to power there too. Revolt followed revolt when sailors spearheaded the drive south to anti-Kaiser territory. The Prussian government gave way, and Bavaria was proclaimed a republic. Loyalists attempted to restore order when field-gray army regiments 75 and 213 returned from the front, hungry and covered in mud. Entering Bremen from the northwest, the officers from both contingents marched with their sabers drawn. Although they were quickly disarmed by revolutionary troops, some units refused to give up and retreated. They made their way back to Kaiser-held cities in the east. For a couple of nights, horses abandoned by the army roamed the streets. They were rounded up and slaughtered by the locals to supplement meager food stocks.

With the end of World War I, Johnny could travel as a free man, as military demobilization followed the end of hostilities. When he was feeling stronger, he made his way to Bremen in hopes of obtaining aid from the USPD.[4] Much to his surprise, however, the USPD turned its back and refused his request for employment or any kind of financial help. They even ignored his connection with the RA, Dittmann, and associates from his earlier posting at Wilhelmshaven naval base. The Independent Social Democratic Party seemed to be of the opinion that Johnny's usefulness was a thing of the past.

Disillusioned, de Graaf made contact with elements in the Spartacus Bund and rapidly met many members he had known as sailors in the Kaiserliche Marine. For several weeks Johnny attended Spartacus meetings and took an active role in the debates and discussions. But the Spartacus Bund too had a problem with funding and was in no position to render aid or employment. Each night he attended their gatherings, believing in the cause against the former Kaiser, the Hollenzollerns, and their allies, the SPD and Zentrum. Combined, these groups advocated homage in nationalism. The SPD was the worst. It had forsaken working-class hopes in favor of its own ambitions.

Penniless and out of work, Johnny set out for the local military office in Hamburg to seek unemployment relief. At the registration counter, the unfriendly faces of noncommissioned officers greeted him. He did not inform them of his horrifying experience in eastern Poland, just that he was down and out and looking for work. They gave him a note for six marks per week (less than US$1.50) to live on, and a promise to try to find him a job.

For two more weeks he stayed at home, giving the six marks to his father so that the family could have a little more to eat. Each night Johnny attended party meetings. During the day he helped out with pamphlet work. A notice soon arrived instructing him to report again to the military office. When he arrived, along with eleven other seamen, he was informed that work was available digging coal in the mines of the Ruhrgebiet, or Ruhr area. In fact, these mines were in the northern part of the Ruhr at this time.[5] "If you don't go, you will not collect anything more," they sternly informed the group. Work there or starve was the message.

Johnny raced home, said goodbye to his family, and with one mark plus a ticket supplied by the military office boarded a train for the trip south to Ahlen, Westfalen. Entering the Ruhrgebiet, he apparently stopped for a time in the city of Münster. Normally the run to the Ruhr was an eleven-hour ride. On this day, probably December 11, 1918,[6] it took twenty-four hours because of commotion caused by the revolutionary forces. Insurgents had pulled up rails, played havoc with rolling stock, and damaged bridges. Although only twelve sailors were on the train with him, many had gone before, and others would follow, until more than two thousand rebel seamen ended up in collieries of the Ruhr.

Ahlen is situated at the northeastern apex of the Ruhr Valley, and before the construction of later decades the platform of the train station afforded a panoramic view of the area. Alighting from the train, the group of sailors proceeded down a flight of steps and through a short tunnel to the village itself, which was divided east from west by the rail line, the former area occupied by miners, the latter by the wealthier middle class. All the homes were built of brick. At the office of Westfalen Coal Mines Numbers One and Two, Johnny and the others signed in and inquired about lodgings. Directed to homes taking in boarders, de Graaf saw to it that all of the naval personnel from the train were accommodated somewhere.

He recalled en route to Ahlen that Otto Klutzka, the friend from Wilhelmshaven he had stood up for at the court-martial, lived in the city. Johnny knew that Otto came from a mining family, and on numerous occasions during their navy days, Otto had asked Johnny to join him on family visits while on shore leave. Johnny had never taken him up on the invitation, but he felt that he already knew the Klutzka family from their many conversations.

When Johnny arrived at the Klutzkas' door, the family welcomed their guest like an old friend. Evidently Otto had told them of Johnny's help at their trial. Otto arrived an hour later, and when he saw Johnny the two men immediately embraced. Otto's father, Anton, was a tall, sturdy man with thick black hair.[7] He talked excitedly as he introduced the others members of the household. Margarete Klutzka, unlike her Polish husband, had been born in central Germany.[8] Her plump, medium-height features were reflected in a round, creased face, a face that openly displayed a life of hard work and constant demands. Margarete was very religious, a homebody who was anything but a housekeeper, as Johnny would soon learn. Otto himself was on the short side and had blond hair. He was a physical specimen indeed, owing to his strenuous occupation. An only son, Otto was a fine, bright, hardworking fellow of whom any family would be rightly proud.

Emma, the oldest daughter, worked at a factory in Ahlen that made pots and pans.[9] She was in her midtwenties, tall, overweight, with jet-black hair. Emma appeared forceful in manner and speech. Unmarried, she had a three-year-old daughter born out of wedlock. Her child required a great deal of attention. Johnny found another sister, Maria, age eighteen, a shy, quiet young lady with a very pleasing personality. Dark brown hair bordered her smiling face, short stature of five foot three (1.60 m), and 110-pound (50 kg) frame. She worked at the same factory as Emma, both of them on the day shift. She was called Maria, Mia, or Maria-Mia. Two younger sisters, Anna and Dora, were both of school age, one blond, the other brunette, and both forever active inside and outside the house.

The Klutzka dwelling was a standard brick structure of two floors. It had a large wash area on the ground level in the rear that contained a couple of big tubs and wall hooks for dust-covered work clothes. Next to this room was a good-sized kitchen and eating area. The living room contained assorted worn furniture and a coal stove, and led to a small bedroom of 6 × 8 feet (1.83 × 2.44 m). It had a single bed and built-in cupboard. Two large bedrooms filled the top floor, separated by a well-used bathroom. The girls and baby slept in one room. The other was the larger master bedroom, nicely paneled, containing a double bed and two dressers.

At first, Johnny was allotted the small room next to the living room, but once he started at the mine, and on shifts different from Otto and his father, they took turns sleeping there while Anton and Margarete Klutzka slept undisturbed upstairs. Later on, Otto would arrive at all hours. So it was easier for one man to roll in and claim the bed while the other rolled out and headed for work. Perhaps this was just as well, because one thing that bothered Johnny, from the day of his arrival, was the constant disarray of the Klutzka household. It showed an utter disregard for basic cleanliness and order. Anton was a neat and tidy man, and was constantly on his wife to keep their abode the same way. But Margarete and their daughters paid him little mind, much to his frustration.

Following a sparse but filling meal the first evening, Otto and Johnny got into a long discussion about de Graaf's starting work the next day in the mine. A *Hauer*, or novice miner, was the lowest-paid individual underground and got the poorest and most strenuous job assignments. He was quite literally at the bottom rung of the ladder. Johnny had no knowledge of mine work whatsoever, but he certainly had no plans to start as a *Hauer*. The two friends agreed that he should pose as an experienced miner from Australia, and with any luck he would join Otto and Anton on their shift. If they could get him assigned as their third man, they could show him the ropes while covering for him. He would be ranked and paid as an experienced mine worker.

Promptly at 6:00 A.M. they arrived at the dispatcher's office, where de Graaf filled out an application for employment, stating that he had worked in a mine in Newcastle, Australia. His deception would take a long while to check out, should anyone be disposed to do so. An engineer entered, looked at his completed card, and nodded to the clerk. "So," he said, "you state you have experience?"

"Yes, in Australia," de Graaf answered.

"Well, we'll find out in two or three weeks whether you're a first-class miner or not, when our inspectors check out your work," he stated firmly. With that, the engineer turned to a clerk, mumbled a few words, and within the hour Johnny was deep in a mineshaft working between Otto and his father.

Initially the work was backbreaking, as he could swing his pick only once to their five or six strokes. The two men showed Johnny how to work safely and quickly using the least effort and energy. They handled the security work of beams and reinforcements while answering all his questions. Two better, more experienced teachers he could not have had; they provided a crash course in three weeks, night and day. What was discussed at home was applied at work, as Johnny's mind boggled to keep harmony with his aching muscles and tired body. He was still on the thin side from his prison ordeal, not in fit physical condition. Maria, who had taken a shine to the new man in the house, scrounged from local farms enough food to supplement his daily rations. Slowly Johnny's strength and weight returned.

One day, after three weeks working in the mine between the Klutzkas, an engineer and two inspectors appeared in the shaft. "Gentlemen, here is our Australian coal miner," the engineer informed them, pointing to Johnny, who continued working. Using all the shortcuts Johnny had learned, he carried on nonstop while his examiners observed. They watched for a time, saw how he worked, and left convinced that he was an experienced miner. That day Johnny jumped to the highest pay grade. They had pulled it off.

Soon thereafter he was assigned to another team and shift, regretfully leaving Otto and Anton. Thanks to them, he never had to start at the bottom and could continue elsewhere as a miner with a confirmed classification. They all rejoiced as one in their little victory. Maria continued to do everything in her power to please Johnny, from obtaining additional food to packing his lunches. Without letup, she strove to capture his attention and interest. He felt she was falling in love with him, but he had given her no encouragement. Johnny did not want to be bound at this time in his life. He did not feel love for her, only sympathy for her plight and unending effort.

Emma approached Johnny on his return from the pit one day. In her soft-spoken manner and without hesitation, she said they could be far more than friends. Johnny had no great fondness for Emma and quickly told her as much. "I plan to get attached to no one, and certainly not to you," he said. She understood Johnny's feelings and thereafter gave him up as a lost cause, much to his delight. A few days later, as he lay on his bed after a grueling day in the mine, he overheard a few words of conversation in the kitchen between Mia and Emma. Mia was protesting as Emma responded, "Don't be silly, crawl into bed with him and he will take you. Then you'll have your man."

"I cannot do that!" Mia angrily replied. It was a brief exchange, but enough for him to know full well that he was the suggested candidate.

On January 15, 1919, Johnny formally joined the renamed Spartacus Bund and started a chapter in Ahlen. About two weeks earlier, at the end of December, and following tedious discussions, the Spartacus Bund had reconstituted itself as the official Communist Party of Germany, the KPD, or Kommunistische Partei Deutschlands. The action was an open secret, yet every free moment de Graaf had, he traveled around the Ruhr, looking up fellow sailors who might feel sympathetic to the Bund's ideals. Other Spartacus units were thus established.[10] Spartacus tactics and demonstrations continued as before in the streets of Berlin, Bremen, Hamburg, and elsewhere.

Indeed, dissatisfaction led to conflict in Berlin in January 1919. The new prime minister, Friedrich Ebert (1919–25), moved his government to Weimar. He also handed the defense of Berlin over to Gustav Noske, who used the Freikorps, and what was left of the troops under western front officers, to head off Spartacus's attempts at seizing national power. On being given his new job, Noske made a remark that followed him for the rest of his life: "Someone will have to be the bloodhound."[11] "The bloodhound," Noske, meant that, if captured, each armed rebel was to be executed immediately; anyone breaking curfew was to be executed immediately; and all unarmed prisoners taken to Berlin's Moabit Prison were to be executed immediately. Freikorps soldiers followed his orders to the letter. Let loose in the capital, they blew some suburbs to pieces in fights with the Spartacus Bund. They likewise executed hundreds of civilians, including Karl Liebknecht and Rosa Luxemburg. On January 15, Rosa, like Karl, was murdered by a group of officers headed by Captain Waldemar Pabst. Luxemburg was shot and her body flung into a city waterway, the Landwehr Canal. Her remains were discovered five months later, bloated, putrid, and weighted down with stones.[12]

In Bremen, sailors shouted, "As long as we have a machine gun, a loaf of mutton bread, and a liverwurst, we have no cause to worry!" Street fighting in

Munich, Hamburg, and Silesia continued unabated. On January 27, the Kaiser's birthday—until then a national holiday—bedlam occurred as the opposing groups collided. Hurling bottles and stones, sailors with red armbands and their allies tried to destroy any form of commemoration of the Hollenzollern bloodline.

In February the devastation heaped on Berlin was repeated in other cities. Reichswehr (the Weimar Republic's army) and Freikorps troops, under the command of war minister Noske, crushed revolutionary soldiers in their path. Word spread that Berlin was sending forces to suppress the Soviets in Bremen. On February 3, workers in Bremen armed themselves, as rumor had it that Colonel Wilhelm Gerstenberg's thirty-five-hundred-man force was on its way.[13] Using their bicycles, Spartacus youth were mobilized to serve as dispatch riders. They were commanded by the Revolutionary Defense Committee and were not likely to be suspected and halted by advancing loyalist forces.

Gunfire, shelling, and hand-to-hand, street-to-street fighting took place as the Kaiser-friendly forces stormed into Bremen to capture its bridges. Workers and sailors fired at the loyalists from doorways, windows, and rooftop gun nests. As the trained divisions took over the city, wresting it from Soviet control in only two days, blood trickled through the gutters. When defeat was certain, several KPD leaders made their escape in disguise. Anti-Kaiser towns gave refuge to the retreating Reds, strengthening local rebels in their own defenses as opposition troops continued to advance. Wave after wave of violence followed. The arrested and apprehended were tortured, summarily shot, or hanged.

All on the Left keenly felt the loss of Liebknecht and Luxemburg. More determined than ever to reject the Kaiser's replacement government, Johnny and his comrades established teams of support and discontent throughout the Ruhr.[14] Gradually the membership grew. De Graaf became so involved in his duties of assisting in planning that the weeks and months skipped by unnoticed. Between his shifts in the mine, party activities, and Mia asking for various things, he was caught up in a never-ending deluge of activity.

One tragic day, Mia's shift at the factory ended when a chunk of her hair was pulled out by the roots. She had caught it in a machine on the assembly line. Painful as it was, the shock and embarrassment were worse, sending Mia into a depression. Johnny felt sorry for her, remembering her many kindnesses to him. She loved him, but he could still muster only feelings of sympathy for her in return. Feeling guilty about their unmatched feelings, he stole away for a lonely walk to think it all over. Johnny knew he would be stuck in the Ruhr for a long while. Mia had done all in her power to kindle his affections for her. Yet he remained the love object, not the lover, a feeling that made him uncomfortable. In his pity for Mia, and determined to make the best of things, he made a rash decision.

Returning home, Johnny asked Maria to marry him, much to her surprise and the delight of her family. Great excitement shook the household as preparations for the union began. Two weeks later, on February 20, 1919, they were wed in a simple ceremony.[15] Half of Ahlen turned out to watch the couple take their vows and wish them well. Maria's father and mother beamed, as only proud parents can do, pleased to no end that Johnny was finally an official family member. Otto and his sisters showered the bride and groom with good wishes when the ceremony was over. Then friends and guests joined in a small banquet followed by a rousing round of dancing.

Unfortunately for Johnny and Mia, they could not immediately find a home for themselves and had to remain where they were until something became available. Maria continued to work at the factory, Johnny in the mine. They only saw each other when their hours coincided. She doted on him, trying to fulfill his every wish, even accepting his refusal to go to church with understanding tolerance. He never attended church. Johnny doubted the existence of God, an opinion based on the cruelties he had seen and experienced. Murder, starvation, torture, and slave labor did not add up to a creator who really cared, in his view. But Maria would not go to church without him, even though he repeatedly told her to go anyway. So they both stayed away, much to her mother's annoyance. When Johnny's mind was set, however, no amount of talk or threats would change it. It was a lifelong trait.

Maria and Johnny got along well at first, but that slowly changed. One day he came across many boxes of blouses and skirts stored in the attic. Johnny called Maria up to the loft and showed her the apparel still fit for wear, which she said were hers. "Take them out, mend them, wash them, and make use of them," he suggested. She agreed, but days later he found them back in the attic. Evidently, the effort to clean the garments was just too much. His anger swelled at this waste of good clothes that his new family hoarded but refused to use out of sheer laziness to wash. This way of living was far from his idea of caring about oneself and one's surroundings. It infuriated him. It also eased his guilt over the work he was doing for the party. His political responsibilities were taking him further and further from Ahlen, as he visited other mines to cultivate pockets of united opposition. Johnny followed the news outside the Ruhr, too, and along with other activist leaders he attended several meetings in secret places and small towns outside the valley. He often rode his motorcycle to these gatherings.[16]

The original group of five recruiters, including Albert Funk and de Graaf, had grown by leaps and bounds since its formation early in 1919.[17] Two thousand sailors became involved with little prompting. In turn, they formed more cells of support from area workers. Political discussion groups of a few people increased rapidly, requiring ever more space for meetings with the new supporters. They received pamphlets and propaganda printed in cobwebbed basements on underground presses that had been smuggled in from outside the Ruhr.

With two other local leftists, Johnny attended a meeting in Unna, a small town east of Dortmund, where a member of the SPD in charge of coal production gave a speech. The man talked and talked, never really touching on the misery that existed but relying instead on a popular complaint. "Turnips in the morning, turnips at midday, turnips at night. Let's get away from all this turnip business!" he shouted. He then praised the glorious things the Social Democrat Party had accomplished for the people. Not able to control his pent-up feelings any longer, Johnny got to his feet and tore up his prepared statement. Then he questioned the SPD representative before the suddenly attentive audience. De Graaf shouted to the spectators, "What have he and his group really done for the German people?" Undoing the man's deceptions, Johnny gave his listeners a volley of facts that exposed the utter incompetence of the SPD, as the speaker glared in his direction from the stage.

When Johnny left the hall, police lying in wait abruptly arrested him. The SPD orator had arranged it. Friends informed de Graaf afterward that he continued telling those left in the auditorium what a miserable soul Johnny was and that everything he said was a lie. "Let not what that swine said linger in your minds," the SPD adherent shouted. At the same time, outside, six police subdued de Graaf, forcing him to the ground with punches, kicks, and thumps from their nightsticks. Handcuffed, he was tossed into an armed police van half-unconscious and driven to a mental institution.

For a week he remained in confinement while his keepers endeavored to prove him insane. They made a great effort to make him grab a red-hot poker. When that failed, he was served human waste made to look like a steak dinner. Time and again they tried, and time and again they failed. Johnny got little sleep and ate little real food during this new nightmare. His initial demands for a doctor were ignored. After a week, one was produced who questioned him at great length while reading the institution report. He checked de Graaf over, commenting with some shock, "It's a wonder you are still alive, boy; you must have an iron constitution. There is nothing whatever wrong with your mind. I have no idea who would send you to such a place as this." It turned out that the physician was a member of the Independent Social Democratic Party and hated the SPD and the Kaiser as much as Johnny did.

On November 28, 1919, Maria gave birth to her first child, a large, chubby-cheeked lad of nine pounds, two ounces (4,173 grams), much to Johnny and Maria's delight.[18] They named him Johnny Junior, and as he grew, he would prove to be aptly named. At nearly the same time, a place to live became available at Schuckertstraße 20. It was a small apartment in a building containing three other dwellings. Johnny and his new family settled into their street-level flat of one bedroom, a bathroom, a little living room, and an adjoining kitchen. It was not spacious, but it was theirs. Donations of discarded furnishings in good repair soon filled the beige-colored residence.

Maria had quit her job before little Johnny arrived so that she could care for him full time. Much to Johnny's revulsion, however, their orderly nest soon took on the appearance of Maria's parental home, in permanent disarray, with clothes, food, and surplus boxes piled everywhere. Johnny maintained that he talked to Maria in a kindly way, repeatedly explaining the need to keep the place clean and uncluttered. Maria promised to try, but day after day, week after week, little progress was made, and the rooms continued to appear shell struck. Johnny became so exasperated that he would clean the house himself, showing Maria how to dust, sweep, and wash. Yet nothing really helped. Days passed with dirty dishes littering the kitchen, beds unmade, and clutter strewn from wall to wall. It became such a sore point that Johnny mentioned it to her father. Anton suggested that Johnny give her a good beating with his belt. "That sorts the lazy ones out in a hurry," he remarked. Perhaps, but the approach of his father-in-law was too drastic in Johnny's view. He felt that talking and showing was better. However, things never did get better. As little Johnny grew, the organization of their home became worse. Maria also started putting on weight, lazily doing nothing to burn it off. It was clear to her husband that she wished to live like a pig, so he stayed away from home more and more as the political demands on his free time increased. Resentment for his wife and the Kaiser made him bitter.

The year 1920 was one that de Graaf would never forget. In February, Prime Minister Ebert demanded that miners work overtime for the benefit of the nation. More coal was needed. Yet the men in the mines did not have enough food to keep them working for even an eight-hour shift without collapsing from lack of strength. Miners' wages were not high, and food costs were escalating. Also at this time, Johnny's youngest brother, Oscar, who had been working on a farm, unexpectedly appeared in Ahlen. He wanted to join Johnny working in the mines. Oscar was a clean-cut lad of sixteen. Johnny and Maria were happy to have him in their home.

The government's overtime order, in its entirety, was relayed by the KPD's Berlin branch to party headquarters in Essen, which in turn passed it on to the Hamm area general branch. All along the line, comrades agreed to hold community meetings and enlist support for opposing this directive from Ebert. In Ahlen a gathering was called, and Johnny was one of those who spoke to the packed hall. "Comrades," he began, "I know Germany needs coal as well as do our own families, widows, and invalids. However, we miners also know full well we cannot work longer hours without more to eat. We demand the government give those who are asked to work overtime more food; otherwise we will not produce more coal."

To cheering applause, all of the workers stood united. Throughout the Ruhr similar assemblies took place. Funk and even Oscar assisted Johnny at these get-togethers. The feeling was that the miners had spoken. It was up to the administration in Berlin to make the next move. When the government refused to do anything, the entire Ruhr area went on strike. But there was little if any violence from the strikers, as they did not want to antagonize local police. The protesters had nothing against them. Many were their friends and neighbors. If the demonstrators wanted police support for the cause, they could not battle them at the same time. This carefully planned strategy of peaceful protest was largely followed, winning numerous sympathizers from the ranks of the police.

Forty-eight hours later the Ruhr was paralyzed, and the government relented. Additional supplies of bread, sausage, and American lard were distributed to the overtime workers. The labor stoppage was called off and all miners returned to work. The strike committee, however, continued to feel that the government would eventually use force to wipe out the mineworkers' gains. The KPD began setting aside special funds for families who could not help themselves. Should the breadwinner go on the lam, get arrested, or be killed because of his involvement in some street action, the KPD's Rote Hilfe Deutschland (German Red Assistance) was there.

By this time Johnny had become known throughout the Ruhr, from Hamm to Duisburg, as the "sailor miner." It was the rebel hero treatment, and it caused problems. When children, for example, greeted him on the street with "General Johnny!" it made him wonder just who was listening. Government informants were, for one. He was quietly placed on the wanted lists. Nonetheless, the Ahlen police did not want to risk picking him up. They were conscious of the fact that to do so could provoke a fresh backlash from the miners.

Work stoppages occurred so often that the government finally decided to assemble one hundred troops from the provincial military headquarters in Münster and send them to Ahlen.[19] Aware of the advancing force, Johnny and his comrades were ready. Südstraße, the narrow main street into Ahlen, soon began to tremble with the sound of marching boots approaching. But just as the soldiers moved in strength onto the constricted thoroughfare, a large group of Ahlen's women surrounded them. The city's men appeared on rooftops armed with sticks, bottles, rocks, and the odd rifle. With the soldiers totally surrounded and bewildered, the women proceeded to sweet-talk them into laying down their weapons. As they spoke, de Graaf shouted for them to surrender and return to Münster in one piece. A nervous young lieutenant led the soldiers. He followed his orders for a few minutes before turning over his sidearm. Then the women gently disarmed those under his command as the men on the roofs stood poised, ready for any opposition. Stripped of everything but their uniforms, the soldiers watched while the townspeople stacked up the arms. Couriers were dispatched to Essen and Hamm to inform the KPD of the victory. The emasculated troops trudged back to their barracks in Münster. The senior military commanders were livid.

Meanwhile, additional strikes were called, further infuriating the government, since each walkout augmented the nationwide loss of coal. Through their intelligence network, the KPD soon learned that a second contingent of three hundred heavily armed soldiers had been dispatched and was coming Ahlen's way.[20] Again the miners armed themselves before taking to the familiar rooftops and windows above Schuckertstraßa. This time the women were told to remain indoors with the children. The men and teenage boys crouched down and waited, equipped with the weapons taken from the first group of soldiers.

When the detachment advanced into Ahlen, no sign of the town's inhabitants was to be seen. Then, unexpectedly, Johnny shouted from the top of one of the buildings, "Soldiers, we don't want anything from you but the right to live. We have no cause to fight you, but if you do not retreat, you will be cut down like dogs! We are all Germans. So let's not take each other's lives. This would certainly result in all your deaths. We do not even ask you to disarm; merely turn around and go home." They did.

Between these two displays, Prussian interior minister Carl Severing came to town to plead with the inhabitants to lay down their arms and return to work. When his speech failed to produce the results he was after, he ordered the second show of force. Police vigilance was likewise tightened up. Elements of regional law enforcement began to keep selected mineworkers under surveillance around the clock. Across the street from his home on Schuckertstraßa, de Graaf could see the guard assigned to him almost daily.

About a week after the last soldiers from Münster were turned away, Johnny was awakened in the middle of the night by a knock on his back door. It opened into a rear garden. A neighbor from down the street wanted to speak with him. He was a police official but was warmly sympathetic to the KPD. "Johnny, get out now!" came his voice from the darkness. "They have orders to arrest you and the other leaders. Contact them, get away fast, I can tell you no more." His voice trailed off as he melted away.

De Graaf knew that to stay would cause bloodshed for his family and comrades. Quickly throwing a few things into a bag, he kissed Maria and little Johnny goodbye, telling Oscar to look after them. Grabbing his bike from the backyard, he crossed to a rear street and cautiously contacted three others. By morning they were many kilometers away, riding as fast as their feet could peddle. The group of bicyclists reached the Rhine close to the Dutch border within a few days. Knowing that they would be arrested if recognized, traveling was done on side roads. They slept in fields. Their families and supporters back in the Ruhr would never reveal their whereabouts. They would also see that all the arms and ammunition were rounded up and hidden deep in the surrounding mines.

The four fugitives stopped for a while in the Niederrhein region, the picturesque area of the lower Rhine River. In a stroke of luck, a resident *Schlotbaron* (a "canal baron," or power broker on the river) named Karl Haniel, whom Johnny called "von" Haniel out of respect, was in need of some men at one of his mines. Haniel was a wealthy man who had his assistants keep the questions to a minimum. He also owned a fleet of ships that sailed up and down the Rhine River. The mine was a light coal, surface variety, with shafts going only to a depth of ten to twenty feet (3.05 to 6.1 meters). Safety, however, left a lot to be desired, since there was no lighting in the tunnels. Instead, the miners had to use single carbon lanterns. The constant flame of these lamps in places where black powder was used for blasting, not to mention underground gas, was a deadly hazard. Joined by a Russian miner, they filled half-ton wagons called *Loren* for eight marks per load. The five-man group worked hard and long, living out of a dormitory-type shed close by.

The fugitive Germans kept in touch with the KPD, issuing instructions to colleagues and reassurances to wives and children back home. This was done through the local party's excellent courier service. Everything began to go smoothly again. The local police even abandoned the hunt for the wanted miners. Strikes still continued in their absence, but each man's family was well provided for by party funds.

One day Haniel began a conversation with de Graaf. "Johnny, I need more coal for my ships. Would you fellows mind working longer hours in order to dig more?" he inquired.

"No problem," Johnny replied, "if you pay us more."

"That I can't do," Haniel answered, "because I am not allowed to pay higher than union rates."

"We do not work under union conditions in your mine," Johnny replied, "so you are not bound to their rates. You are well aware of the unsafe conditions here that only men like us would work under." Haniel then offered another eight marks for each additional *Lore*.

"Twenty," countered Johnny, which, after long thought, Haniel finally agreed to.

Suddenly the men's wages skyrocketed to two or three hundred marks a day, as the little team turned out additional loads with gusto. They remained at the mine for several months. Finally, Interior Minister Severing offered a general pardon to all Communist leaders. Johnny and his comrades were able to return home without being arrested. Their families and friends rejoiced at the news. The men went back to work at the Westfalen mines with no opposition or loss of seniority. Spartacus membership expanded, and party gatherings became much larger with the amnesty. The strikes had ended, and the Ruhr area was peaceful for a time. Life became pleasant and had a semblance of normalcy.

But it was not without personal tragedy. Early one morning in 1920, Oscar asked his brother if he could take the noon to 6:00 P.M. shift. Usually he worked 6:00 P.M. to midnight, but he had a girlfriend and wanted to take her to the last showing of a movie that evening. De Graaf cleared it with the other foreman, and an elderly neighbor with a family of five switched places with Oscar. At the 6:00 P.M. shift change, Johnny and his men were at the mine head as the earlier shift was about to surface. The cables above squeaked and groaned as the large wicker basket containing Oscar and fifty-seven others surfaced from the depths. Before they could open the gate, a whirring noise sounded and the cables snapped, plunging the human load two thousand feet (nearly 610 meters) to their deaths. Johnny's younger brother Oscar was gone at just seventeen.

De Graaf was numb with grief. Oscar had been a good friend and brother, and he mourned his loss for a long while. The entire village turned out for the burials, everyone deeply saddened by this tragedy that had snatched loved ones from their midst. Three weeks later, nine more lives were lost down in the holes where men gave their all to support their families.

In 1921 Johnny obtained the lifelong badge of a coal miner. Working bare to the waist, he fell while swinging a pick and slightly lacerated his face. Coal dust entered the wound, and de Graaf had a one-inch blue-black scar just above his right cheek for the rest of his days.[21] The back of his left hand also had an irregularity. It had been burned at one time, producing a surface that was very smooth with white scar tissue. These areas stood out from normal coloring, underlining veins and bones that looked somewhat different.

Following World War I, many men from the former Imperial German armed forces found themselves unemployed. The Versailles peace treaty in 1919 stipulated that Germany had to reduce the number of men in uniform to one hundred thousand. Cobbled to this was the feeling that Woodrow Wilson's Fourteen Points were nothing more than a trick to get Germany, not the rest of the world, to comply with the Versailles accords. The mood in the country grew morose with the announcement of each round in the military downsizing. War reparations would cause additional problems for Germany in the 1920s, when a commission finally agreed to pay £6,600,000. In addition, Germany lost all of its colonies to the other imperialist powers; was forbidden to form a single German-speaking state with Austria; had to cede territory in Europe; was forced to build ships for the former Allies; and had to admit its responsibility for starting the war. British economist John Maynard Keynes astutely predicted that all of this would be too much for the Germans to take and they would eventually seek revenge.[22]

How could things have gotten this bad? many Germans asked themselves. The summer before the armistice, it looked as if the Central Powers were winning the war. As one unit after another was deactivated, rumors spread across Germany that Communists, Jews, and other no-goods—people interested only in pacifism and profits—had stabbed the nearly victorious western front troops in the back. In the winter of 1918–19, the Allies allowed Germany to keep a large number of soldiers in the Baltics to help those states in their quest for independence from the Bolsheviks in Russia. By the end of 1919, and by then a Freikorp, the Baltic units were withdrawn and restationed at Dallgow-Döberitz, just to the west of the Berlin city limits.

Into this cauldron Captain Waldemar Pabst placed Wolfgang Kapp, one of the founders of the right-wing Fatherland Party, to exploit the coalition government of Gustav Bauer and his vice chancellor and finance minister, Matthias Erzberger. Erzberger was a member of the Zentrum and had led the German delegation that signed the Versailles treaty. Pabst, Kapp, and their co-conspirator General Walther Freiherr von Lüttwitz, together with behind-the-scenes support from General Erich Ludendorff, wanted a regime change in Berlin. There were hints that Kapp really desired a return of the monarchy. Then again, Wolfgang Kapp was too open about his less obvious intentions and wound up being arrested. This prompted Lieutenant Commander Hermann Ehrhardt, from one of the two Baltic marine brigades at Dallgow-Döberitz, at the urging of Lüttwitz, to issue an ultimatum on March 12, 1920, for Kapp's release and the installation of a new national administration. The government discussed the options most of the night before rejecting Ehrhardt's demands at dawn on March 13. By then, however, Ehrhardt's force of more than five thousand troops had marched into the capital. Many of Ehrhardt's men wore swastikas on their helmets for identification, the first time the capital was awash with the symbol that would come to signify such evil.

Defense Minister Noske asked the chief of the General Staff, General Hans von Seeckt, to use his two thousand available soldiers to defend the government.[23] Von Seeckt, referred to as "the sphinx with a monocle," refused.[24] Bauer and his cabinet quickly left by car for Dresden and then Stuttgart. Before driving off, they issued orders for a general strike—effective immediately.

By 7:00 A.M. Germany had a new government, with Wolfgang Kapp at its head and General von Lüttwitz as minister of defense. For the next five days the Kapp administration tried to bring order to Berlin. But these efforts were doomed, because Ebert's general strike nearly paralyzed the entire country. Gas, electricity, newspaper, and water services were completely interrupted. Laws were ignored and looting became common, especially in Berlin. To the south, in Stuttgart, when Ebert agreed to hold elections, Kapp said that his demands had been met. He then resigned and lit out for exile in Sweden.

During Kapp's short reign, fighting erupted in the Ruhr. On March 14, 1920, at his headquarters in Münster, the district's military commander, Lieutenant General Oskar Baron von Watter, ordered a number of his Freikorps and regular Reichswehr soldiers to key points in the province. Their assignment was to reestablish order. The Westfalen region was aflame with USPD, SPD, KPD, radical Communist, Syndicalist, and Anarchist-leaning groups—all of them opposed to the Kapp Putsch (coup). For the next three weeks the two sides, composed of about sixty thousand loyalist troops and some fifty thousand leftist-idealist irregulars, calling themselves the Red Army of the Ruhr, met head on. The Red Army was under the leadership of a former Kaiser-era officer, Karl Stemmer. Good fighters, the Red Army of the Ruhr at first pushed the government's forces out of the valley in seemingly endless battles.[25]

The section Johnny was with held a round-the-clock conference in Essen that lasted three days. They had already defeated the Weißenstein Freikorps and the local police and had taken over the city.[26] As word spread that more putsch troops were coming nearer, Johnny traveled back to Ahlen. Alighting from a train, he and his supporters formed the seven-hundred-man Rosa Luxemburg Battalion and swarmed around the train station complex. Johnny was made the battalion leader by a voice vote. The group sewed together a red flag emblazoned with the name of their dead martyr. Together with other party leaders, de Graaf went into the mines to get the hidden dynamite, weapons, and tools, much of it taken off the army units from Münster. It was a small stash, but it was brought to the surface and distributed. The train station was renamed the Workers and Soldiers Commission and was made the Rosa Luxemburg's headquarters.

Throughout the length of the Ruhr, each town formed similar fighting units ready to move when called. Word reached the Workers and Soldiers Commission that initial forward units of the putsch had been spotted ten to twelve kilometers (6.2 to 7.5 miles) away between Ahlen and Hamm. The defenders contacted the nerve center in Essen and were told to take up their positions. Insufficiently armed, they soon drew battle lines with the approaching force and fought them tenaciously before being forced to give ground. Johnny got in touch with Essen again and told the leadership there that if they did not send reinforcements, the surge of well-armed putsch soldiers could not be held in check.

He was ordered to retreat to the Lippe River, a small tributary of the Rhine near Hamm. Arriving on March 18, 1920,[27] the Rosa Luxemburg Battalion secured an area outside the city, including a large dance hall. De Graaf placed his men at key spots and posted lookouts around the hall. Two nights later, putsch soldiers moved into the city without resistance from Hamm's twenty thousand residents. They took the community's elected representatives aside and gave them a talk on how things would be, which really meant how the Hollenzollerns would be brought back to run the country. Some of the politicians fell for it, and later that night, in a small group, they walked to the river that separated the two sides. The lookouts reported their arrival and the Red Army of the Ruhr began cocking its weapons.

Each of the delegates carried a white flag. Advancing as far as they dared, they shouted across the Lippe that the Red Army of the Ruhr could not win. "What you're trying to do is crazy! Give up your arms and return to your families in peace!" Then they asked that those rebels who were not diehard leftists be allowed to drop out and go home. His men watched nervously as de Graaf stood up and told the emissaries that the offer was a first-class fairy tale. His key fighters stood on all sides of the hall while this exchange took place. The balance of Johnny's contingent sat on the floor. "Your group marched with the Kaiser and now you march with the putsch."

"I refuse," Johnny shouted back in the direction of the fluttering white flags. Turning to the assembled troops in the auditorium, he explained what they had just heard. But he could sense the hesitation of some of those sitting on the baseboards. He reasoned that they must have been thinking of leaving and speculated that most were SPD adherents.

In a firm tone he told the gathering, "All the Spartacus form up in this corner, SPD and independents in that corner, and Roman Catholics who are in our forces in the other corner." Once settled in their designated positions, Johnny told the men to choose the course they would follow. Those who really wished to go could do so, but they would have to leave all their arms at the door on their way out. Any attempt to leave with a weapon would be met with gunfire.

De Graaf's diehards faced down the others as some of those wishing to march out slowly got to their feet. They dropped their guns at the door in a pile and left, filing out one by one with hands raised. Surveying the scene, Johnny saw that he had lost half his men. But at least those who remained were in possession of all the arms. They later learned that General von Watter had imprisoned the political delegates he had sent to plead his case.

Late that evening the Rosa Luxemburg Battalion crossed the bridge outside Hamm and encountered heavy machine gun fire. The bulk of the putsch forces were now ten kilometers to the rear, but they had some companies along the Lippe near Hamm. It is reported that the Freikorps units entering Hamm fooled the residents into thinking all was well. They even staged a musical performance in the town's main square. The next day, however, Freikorps soldiers began rounding up and executing people indiscriminately.[28]

The Rosa Luxemburg Battalion fought bravely as it worked its way toward the small village of Pelkum. Weeks before, some one hundred of their supporters had been killed there. This included nurses in uniform.[29] Fighting a pitched battle all the way, they lost another ninety-three men by the time they reached Pelkum. The Red Army of the Ruhr's headquarters in Essen was only about twenty-eight miles (almost forty-five km) away. As they had depleted their numbers badly, and still had not received reinforcements, de Graaf borrowed the only transportation at hand. A Pelkum farmer and former soldier lent him a large white horse and saddle that he used to gallop to Essen.

In Essen itself everything was in disarray as the city prepared to meet the advancing nationalist force. Johnny failed to obtain any additional assistance from the KPD, but its leaders assured him that all the Ruhr miner battalions had been mobilized. He was told to proceed to Dortmund, which was facing a pitched battle at that very hour. De Graaf made it back to his men just in time to learn that the enemy had advanced to a point just a few kilometers down the road. He moved his units to Dortmund and fought hand to hand alongside the community's own defenders. It was a nearly hopeless struggle that ultimately ended in retreat. The exodus moved in a northeasterly direction, joined by a number of dispersed units and local people who increased their size to some twelve thousand men. But the ranks of the putsch were also being transformed; they had jumped to about eighty thousand in number, a superiority of more than six to one.

De Graaf called everyone together and announced to those who wanted to leave that the time had arrived. For those who stayed the course, he said, "We will fight until we lose the last man. If we attack and have to go against the city of Hamm, you'll likely all die!" It was an ominous warning, but no one left the ranks. The clash that followed came to be called the Battle of Pelkum. At one point in the struggle, Johnny blew up the sides of a gorge, killing a number of loyalist troops.[30] His ability with explosives caught the attention of the few Soviets Moscow had sent to lend support. But it was too little too late.

The augmented Rosa Luxemburg Battalion suffered a host of new casualties before reaching the canal gates, nearly four miles (6.4 km) outside Essen, with little ammunition remaining. Carl Severing then appeared as if by magic and asked for a meeting to work out a truce. Again Berlin was trying to split the insurgents' forces with the offer of an amnesty in return for disarming. Severing talked as if he was neutral, not backing the putsch, but few if any believed him.

The troops under de Graaf settled in to hold the canal at all costs. It was not long before a major appeared from the other side waving a white flag as he walked to the center of a bridge. "Boys, you have put up an excellent fight, but don't you realize it's hopeless?" he shouted. "Your few against our many cannot hope to win. Why don't you drop your arms and go home to your loved ones, alive?"

"Major, will those higher-ups of yours agree to what you ask of us?" Johnny shouted back. The major said something about not being able to promise.

"Well," Johnny remarked, "surely you know we won't give in, then, but will continue fighting."

The officer dropped his white flag and walked back to his forward lines. The next day de Graaf sent a courier to Essen for ammo. When the man returned, he was shaking slightly and had a blank expression. The young messenger reported with tears in his eyes that the city of Essen had fallen. "Impossible!" de Graaf growled. But he was wrong. Desertions and internal squabbles in the face of the mounting atrocities by von Watter and those in his command had finished off Essen as the leftist stronghold during the first week of April 1920.[31]

Calling the group leaders together, Johnny gave them the bad news and an idea of the Rosa Luxemburg's situation. "One possibility is to fight through to the older part of Essen, where the metal workers have sympathy for our cause. Then we could continue east to the city of Hattingen and try to obtain more support. In Hattingen, we can stay to see if our general forces can meet up with us."

The men quickly decided to follow this course, finding light resistance as they proceeded. Slowly, with Freikorps pressing close behind, they entered Alten-Essen (Old Essen). Clearing the way was a large moving van mounted with machine guns. As the Rosa Luxemburg's soldiers made their way down the people-lined streets, they were greeted with welcome shouts of "Bravo! Bravo! Viel Glück!" (Bravo! Bravo! Good luck!). Worker support was evident as women handed out the little food they could spare to the passing rebels. Old men and young boys cheered and saluted as the bedraggled procession passed through the town.

Reaching Hattingen, they again met friendly crowds that applauded their entry into that city. There was no opposition. Not a single shot was fired. The battalion continued. Some of its troops looked exhausted, walking in ripped clothing stained with blood and the mud of battle.

"Don't you think we should surrender, Johnny?" a tired and dirt-caked group of men asked.

"You can leave if you wish," de Graaf replied. "And, although I need you, the other side has very little mercy." The men thought for a moment, then turned back the way they had come, tears running down their cheeks, and left. Several hundred followed, war weary, tired, hungry, and sick of it all. Johnny could not blame them. Neither would he make an attempt to stop anyone, since the group as a whole had fought well.

All that remained were about nine thousand devoted Spartacus fighters, divided into groups of a hundred. Johnny called a meeting with his own unit's leaders while the men rested in a nearby meadow. They discussed their position, disappointed that the larger body of men had yet to make contact. "Johnny, we'll take over the Wupper Valley and win yet!" they stated enthusiastically.

Annoyed by this suggestion, de Graaf told them he had never been a robber and was not going to become one. They had not reached such a low point that they were going to steal from poor farmers—the very people they were fighting for. He did not want to promote the opportunity for those less convinced to do so either. The few that contemplated running amok in the Wupper obviously felt remorse despite the fact that the battalion was in a very bad spot.[32] The Rosa Luxemburg's ammunition was spent, its troops were in deplorable condition, and just kilometers back, Freikorps forces were on their trail. The situation looked bleak, but they would not become bandits in the Wupper to survive.

Scanning the hilly terrain with binoculars, Johnny was surprised to see a British flag flying from a high bluff. Suddenly it dawned on him that they had stopped to rest in an international zone close to the British-controlled sector of occupied Germany. To enforce the terms of the Versailles treaty, in early March 1921, the

French, Belgians, and English had all moved their forces into parts of the Ruhr over German objections. Britain had been allocated vast areas north of Cologne. De Graaf was suddenly excited. He and his colleagues felt that they had stumbled across a refuge.

Calling the men to attention, Johnny announced that the British occupation forces were above them and that he had sailed on several British ships. The justice on those vessels was more pronounced than in Germany itself. He then mentioned that he would pay the British troops a personal visit to see what he could arrange. He asked his men to be patient.

They all shouted their approval. Each individual knew that what was needed now was time, which was rapidly running out. Turning to one of his lieutenants, Johnny handed him his pistol and told him to keep it until his return. Holding a large white flag, de Graaf then walked to the far bluffs as fields of men watched, slowly getting up to form ranks and follow. They halted at a barbed-wire fence, where Johnny commanded them to discard any article not belonging to them. "I know the British," Johnny shouted. "Should they find any such goods in your possession you will be treated as thieves; but if you have only what is yours, they will help you. We will not be treated as prisoners of war but as internees of a civil war."

As de Graaf left the formation, a British noncommissioned officer greeted him at the gate. Coming to attention, Johnny said, "What you see below us are nine thousand fighters who have fought against Germany. We have just battled the putsch forces that outnumbered us ten to one. I request permission to see your officers." The young, smartly uniformed solider saluted and hurried to a field phone. Shortly afterward, a major and a few combat troops appeared. Johnny repeated his statement to the officer.

"Yes, we know of your forces," the major stated. "You have lost control of what cities you had."

"Certainly, that is correct, sir," de Graaf replied. "But we stood and fought against a hundred thousand men that you and the other Allied powers allowed the other side to have. I am only asking for sanctuary for my officers and men." The English officer smiled and told de Graaf to wait while he contacted headquarters in Cologne by phone.

Ten minutes passed before he returned. "You can enter, but tell your men they must disarm prior to entry," he commanded. "That includes all ammunition and grenades," he added. Johnny then asked him if he could bury his revolver, for he thought he might need it after internment. The major consented, adding, "You are a daredevil. Hide it where you can locate it later."

Returning to his troops, Johnny explained what had been said, telling them to leave their arms and ammunition to the left and right in piles beside the gate, as they filed into the compound. No one disobeyed the order. The major asked if he could search de Graaf's men once they had assembled, explaining that it was his right to do so, for they had made it a condition of entry. A careful search of the large formation turned up not one gun or round of ammo. Johnny was rightly proud.

De Graaf learned later that the putsch forces had demanded that the British shove the rebels back outside the barrier, or let them come in and take them out, but the English refused. Had the Freikorps gotten near the Allied occupation lines, the agreement of occupation would have been violated and all hell would have descended on the German government.

What was left of the Rosa Luxemburg Battalion was soon transported by rail to Grevenbroich, near the city of Cologne. Pulling into this community, they noticed another train on an adjoining track getting ready to go in the opposite direction. In order to make room for the remnants of the Rosa Luxemburg internees, the British had disgorged several thousand German security police who were already in custody. These men had been the law when the Kaiser was in power. They were on their way to a camp farther south.

"There's some nice work for you to do," the major said, pointing to the full carriages beside the ones with Johnny and his men. "They're your friends of yesterday, are they not?" he asked, a coy smile spreading across his face.

"Would you permit us?" Johnny asked.

"Yes, but only for thirty minutes, and then stop," the major answered with beaming anticipation.

The Rosa Luxemburg group jumped from their train and swarmed en masse toward the train on the adjacent track. They leaped aboard and dove into an instant slugfest with the former police. Johnny and his men did themselves proud. The Kaiser's police were given a veritable thrashing. Meanwhile, the British soldiers rested easy, watching the bloody melee go on in front of them for half an hour. A whistle finally signaled the end of the skirmish, as the train full of police prepared to pull out, now laden with a battered human cargo.

The Grevenbroich internment camp was a large facility of long gray barracks, surrounded by kilometers of barbed-wire fencing and high sentry towers capped with floodlights. The battalion marched past the guards at the main gate and selected their quarters in groups of one hundred, as directed. Shortly afterward, Colonel Elbrick, the camp commandant, and the major called Johnny and his leaders together for a discussion. Speaking in fluent German, the colonel opened the meeting. "Gentlemen, you put up a wonderful battle against the so-called enemies of your country. A truly great battle. How would you like to give it another try?"

"I beg your pardon, sir?" Johnny asked, thinking he had misheard him. "Would you like to fight the Freikorps again?"

"That would be impossible," de Graaf replied. "We cannot hope to win against all the forces they have."

Johnny then asked permission to break off the discussion for the moment. He wanted to see that his men were settled with hot drinks and food, which they badly needed. When he returned later that day to continue the conversation, Johnny brought along ten of his officers. Elbrick explained that they would release the battalion to tackle the putsch soldiers, while the British would follow up behind and occupy all the newly acquired territory wrested from the enemy.

Several of Johnny's men greeted the idea with enthusiasm, but he remained silent, his mind trying to figure out the British reasoning. "You will have my answer as soon as you have told me everything," he said finally, noticing that Elbrick's eyes had never left his the entire time. The colonel went on, explaining that the British would supply them with all the captured German booty they had—guns, ammo, and transport—to fight the putsch. That would mean declaring war on them, Johnny thought, while the British remained neutral, suppliers of the battalion's equipment and the beneficiaries of its gains.

Coldly returning Elbrick's stare, Johnny countered that he and his men would not become brigands for British imperialists. He then pointed out that the English troops had the numbers and the equipment to defeat the putsch forces. If his Britannic Majesty's army wanted more territory, they would have to win it themselves.

Elbrick looked at the Germans before him sternly and then smiled, saying quietly, "You have made your point and I admire you." Later that day the British asked the Rosa Luxemburg Battalion to supply one man from each thousand of their number to work with their English counterparts in supplying food, clothing, and other items. All would be under Johnny's and a senior British officer's command. Eventually, Johnny and three others were allowed to go twice a week into Cologne, without escort, to purchase supplies for the camp.

Several months later, Interior Minister Severing gave a radio address informing all of Germany that the government had proclaimed an amnesty. "Everyone who fought past battles is to be treated as a free man, able to return home and settle in peace, unhindered," he proclaimed. "The exception," he continued, "will be the leaders and commanders of the forces against the government. These criminals and reactionaries will be hunted down and arrested." Colonel Elbrick soon came into the Rosa Luxemburg's quarters to ask if they had heard the proclamation. If not, it had been recorded and he could broadcast it over the camp's public address system. That was not necessary, as Johnny's men were aware of the broadcast. Nonetheless, the entire camp was called together, and over the facility's loudspeakers Johnny explained what the news from Berlin meant. "With the exception of officers, you can now go home without fear of arrest. For the leaders, the guarantee of safety is not there. Go home now with the compliments of Herr Severing."

Gathering his eight officers together, Johnny told them that the British had given the men forty-eight hours to leave. The officers were also free to go, he said, but he did not recommend that they take the chance.[33] He felt that the putsch troops would kill them if they simply walked out or were captured. The officers agreed, but the rank and file wanted to know who would lead them. Johnny said that he might regret it, but he would take them only as far as the Hamm city limits. From there, they could get rail transportation and fend for themselves.

With the British offering their farewells, and with advance scouts leaving first, the core of the Rosa Luxemburg Battalion marched out of the English sanctuary and into German-held territory. The battalion advanced right through the middle of putsch-controlled areas without challenge. Leaving his troops outside Hamm, de Graaf and eight officers took off in another direction.

The nine men traversed swamps, stumbled over fallen trees, and sloshed through waist-deep mud. After weeks of hiding in forests and farmers' fields, a Spartacus courier from Hamburg located them. All nine were tired and hungry. They had eaten only what could be successfully foraged. The courier explained that they must split up and continue to live underground. It seemed easy enough to say, but the total time spent in hiding would stretch to more than six months.[34] Near the end of this period de Graaf was moved into Germany's second city. In a Hamburg safe house, he enjoyed his first real meal and his first real sleep in a bed in months. Not in the arms of his father, sisters, and brothers, as after Osowiec, but he was able to relax again for a luxurious moment.

6

DIE KPD

The KPD sent one of the Osowiec seven to pick him up. For safety's sake, the party had decided that Johnny's new destination would be the Baltic Sea. His contact was Willy Hazor. Cleaned up and in fresh clothes, Johnny went to a café near the Hamburg Hauptbahnhof, where Willy was waiting with two tickets to Kiel. He approached Hazor's table as Willy glanced up without a sign of recognition and asked, "What can I do for you, sir?"

"I want the rat from Osowiec," Johnny replied, as Hazor looked at de Graaf closely. Hazor did not recognize the intruder's face at first, as Johnny had filled out quite a bit since their Polish days. Yet the mere mention of their ordeal was enough for Hazor to casually get up, collect his things, and walk de Graaf to the station.

Entering the Hauptbahnhof, they were about to descend one of the long stairways to the platforms below when a voice rang out that chilled them both to the bone. "In a short while the tunic will fit you!" came a shrill shout from the crowd. Hazor and Johnny froze as they recognized the voice of Sergeant Wolf, the guard from Poland. He was shouting and pointing at Johnny as bewildered passers-by watched. Willy Hazor murmured, "For heaven's sake, Johnny, lets get out of here! Walk next to me!" People gathered around, asking, "What did the man do?" Hazor explained how Wolf killed fellow Germans back at Osowiec. As Wolf was making his way through the crowd toward the two men, people turned toward the former guard and shouted, "Kill the bastard! The swine!" They surrounded Wolf, punching and kicking him to the ground in a fury.

The public address speakers announced that the train was leaving as the two men rushed down the steps and boarded a car while it slowly moved away. They heard whistles blowing and watched police rushing past the windows, racing for the level above to investigate the ruckus. Johnny could only bless the leftists in

Hamburg and Hazor's quick thinking for their narrow escape. It had all happened so fast—the shout, the scuffle, the getaway, and then the police—that their hearts pounded furiously for minutes afterward.

Leaving the train at Kiel, de Graaf was moved by many people from one city to another via train, car, and taxi. He stayed in the city only long enough to try to board a ship, a ploy that did not work. Hustled away by more dissidents, he entered a whirlwind of endless travel punctuated with a stop in an isolated town bordering the North Sea. There Johnny kept in touch with the party while working as a miner for more than a year. Three other rebel leaders joined him. All four finally left the area and traveled to Bremen.

West of Bremen, in the city of Oldenburg, Johnny was arrested in July 1920 for not having the proper papers to hold a job. It is not known what kind of position he was seeking or held at the time. De Graaf did, however, work for the KPD's Rote Hilfe Deutschland during this period. The government took his past activities into account and gave him an eighteen-month sentence. He was incarcerated until that November, when a second amnesty was proclaimed. This one covered all the leftists from the Ruhr.[1]

Johnny returned to Ahlen without being bothered by the authorities, but there was a catch. He was informed that the mines could no longer use him. A "Do Not Hire" mark was stamped in his workbook, a document that all Germans had to show their employers before they could begin any kind of legal employment.[2] Fellow miners wanted to strike over his ban, but at a party meeting Johnny told them it would serve no purpose and just cause unnecessary bloodshed. De Graaf traveled to Hamm and Essen looking for work, but none of the mines there would touch him. He had no choice but to draw on unemployment until he could find a job, even as his party work continued and intensified. At such places as the Saxon mine near Hamm, the authorities began following Johnny. Eventually, they tailed him everywhere in the Ruhr. At one point, in 1922, he and Albert Funk were arrested for their involvement in the armed clashes between small groups of workers and the French and Belgians around Düsseldorf and Duisburg. He received another eighteen-month term but apparently was granted a pardon.[3]

It should be pointed out here that the available literature on two KPD conferences is inconclusive with respect to Johnny's contribution. He is mentioned as having attended the Eighth National KPD Conference in Leipzig[4] from January 28 to February 1, 1923,[5] and only briefly commented on at the one-day district affair (the Bezirkskonferenz) in Essen on March 23, 1923.[6] The respected Hermann Weber places Johnny at Essen, but he may be confused.[7] It can be assumed that Johnny did attend the Essen meeting because of his party activities in the area. What is known is that Johnny decidedly opposed the efforts of Ruth Fischer and her followers at one or both conferences. His comments below about Leipzig could possibly represent a breakthrough in what transpired there. Obviously, this is a subject for additional research.

In 1923 the Red Front Fighter Organization (or RFB, the Roter Frontkämpferbund) boasted two million members. The RFB was the KPD's wing of street combatants during the Weimar Republic. Many marched through the streets of Berlin and Leipzig in platoons, waving red flags and wearing red armbands. More than two thousand KPD members attended the affair in Leipzig. The main meeting was held in a well-decorated union hall. Clara Zetkin, a personal friend of Lenin's, was the most senior woman participant.[8] Once a member of the SPD, she opened the conference. Those from the powerful Berlin party, including Ruth Fischer (the alias of Elfriede Eisler), followed Zetkin to the lectern. Comrade Fischer made no bones about her intentions to lead the German Communists. She urged the gathering to "ease up," especially the Hamburg-Hamm group, which she said was rocking the political boat. Fischer and the others wanted the KPD to continue with its "peaceful demonstrations" approach. This drew great applause from the bulk of the representatives. "March through the damned streets wearing red ties, red caps, and beat the hell out of drums, all the way to the gates of the bloody Reichstag!" she shouted. "Make noise and we shall be heard!"

Johnny felt that he had never listened to so much bunk in his entire life. Fischer also used too many profanities for his taste. He and a number of others wanted the Berlin people replaced by workers who demonstrated more sense. Those taking this path banded together and insisted that Fischer and August Thalheimer be replaced. Their plea, which was contrary to the majority opinion, caused a heated debate. But they held firm.

A Berlin delegate buttonholed de Graaf, asking, "Johnny, what are you doing?" Perhaps the questioner was not ready for a blunt reply.

"I cannot believe, and will not believe, that children's trumpets, toy drums, red ties, and hats are anything but a pile of crap!" Johnny exclaimed. "We can organize the working class in an adult way to fight for the cause without resorting to kid's play and childish politics." The startled delegate mumbled something and excused himself.

Another member stood up and said, "Go home, Fischer! Go home with your children, back to Berlin. We know what we will do!" As these comments stirred murmurs on stage, several delegations bunched around de Graaf. "What do we do now?" they asked in nervous voices.

"We'll send a note to the Zentral Komitee [the ZK, or Central Committee] or a delegation, if necessary, asking them to iron out this mess," Johnny responded.

When they reassembled the next day, de Graaf was the only delegate who voted against another party resolution. A couple of delegates close by attempted to raise his hand in agreement, but he shook them off and angrily stood up to say that he voted against the measure. This upset a number of powerful hardliners, who again cornered Johnny and tried to change his mind, without success. They accused de Graaf of attempting to split the party, but he could not have cared less. In his view, nitwits controlled the KPD. He felt that its chairman, Heinrich Brandler, fit this mold perfectly. Brandler would become part of the "right opposition" following the death of Lenin in 1924.[9]

Representing the Comintern (Communist International),[10] Arthur Ernst Ewert, "a tall drink of water with a soft brain," took offense at Johnny's meddling and berated him before the other delegates. It was a dangerous move. De Graaf countered, giving birth to a battle that would last for years. A representative from Berlin, Willy Leow, tried to cajole Johnny into pulling their way, but he was told to get out of de Graaf's face. Leow scurried back to Fischer and her group, trembling like a leaf, and pointed his bony finger Johnny's way, telling her what he had just been told to do.

On the third day Fischer and her supporters played their ace. They had been in contact with Moscow before the conference. Comrade Karl Radek, then editor of the newspaper *Pravda* (Truth), was accordingly instructed to come to Leipzig and offer his support if necessary. Radek (whose real family name was Sobelson),[11] was a little man with thick glasses and a sharp tongue. When he arrived, he addressed the conference and then held a special meeting with the dissenters. This new gathering took place on the top floor of the Leipzig Trade Union Building, where Radek accused the nonconformists of trying to divide party policy. Turning to Johnny, he said angrily, "You are the most outspoken delegate against the election of Ruth Fischer. What are you trying to accomplish, a split in the whole party, for what?"

Heatedly, de Graaf answered, "Yes, I oppose her election and will fight against those in the majority who are for it. We do not want to split the party, only to clean the party. We want people with purpose, workers that can provide leadership and who are able to achieve what the party sets out to do." This only provoked hours of debate with Radek, who tried his usual approach of being witty. Johnny finally told him point blank that the political leaders from Berlin needed to be straightened out and that Radek could tell Moscow exactly that.

Radek soon realized that humor was not going to work and that Johnny's eight allies all commanded a solid majority within their home parties. So he suggested that the nine dissidents become members of the Central Committee of the KPD. This he arranged much to their delight, since this gave them a stronger voice. When the big day finally arrived to reelect Ruth Fischer, one of the delegates from the Ruhr voted for her selection. Johnny raised his hand against this motion, as once more some of those in the opposition tried to keep his arm down. Forcing his way to his feet, he slapped the faces of those who were trying to restrain him and shouted, "If any of you try to stop my vote during this free election, there will be trouble." The haggling went on for some time until the main vote came. With the results, to the rejoicing of Johnny's faction, Fischer and her colleagues were removed from the ZK. De Graaf was overjoyed in victory. The conventions over, the delegates headed home to give reports to their local branches.

Johnny remained in the Ruhr, still unemployed and still unhappy at home. He sought some kind of escape in work as life with Maria became even more volatile. His wife, well cared for during his absences, had become lazier than ever. She disregarded all housework while gaining rings of unsightly fat. One morning, bouncing the nearly three-year-old Johnny Junior on his knee, de Graaf's neck and back started to itch. Closely checking his playful little son, he found that the boy had lice. Johnny exploded at Maria. She cried, promising repeatedly to clean things up. Johnny found the windows so black he marked a "Z" on one, meaning "swine," and told her to have all the windows clean by the time he returned. That evening, after an unsuccessful day looking for work, he found the window he had marked clean but the others still dirty and untouched. Johnny threatened to walk out if this kept up, despite Maria's begging. She did tidy up that time, but it was not long before the place was back in its usual pigsty state.

By a stroke of luck, de Graaf obtained a job with Heinrich Layman, a member of the German Stahlhelm (German Steel Helmet, or Soldiers of the Front Association). The Stahlhelm was the largest Freikorps group during the Weimar Republic. Much later, in 1934, they were assimilated into the Sturmabteilung (Storm Division, or SA), the Nazi Brownshirts.[12] Layman ran a large grocery store outside Ahlen. He asked de Graaf to sell soap in the mining communities of the Ruhr, retaining whatever he could make over the retail price. Loading a large wagon with boxes of bar soap, Johnny began canvassing miners' homes. They kidded him about his new job but bought his products in abundance anyway. Business was so good during these months that some days he sold more than a thousand bars and made a good profit for himself.

At night he would attend party meetings, arriving home at all hours to then trudge off with his cart early the next morning. So delighted was Layman that he asked Johnny to work in the store itself as his assistant. De Graaf accepted the new assignment and enjoyed working with this plump, balding, pleasant man who always had a kind word and time to chat with his customers, mainly miners, and their families.

Layman had a large dog that followed Johnny everywhere. When de Graaf worked late, the animal would often remain with him. Soon, noticing his pet's switch of allegiance, Layman gave Johnny the dog. Elated, de Graaf walked his new friend along the side of the highway back to Ahlen that night. Several vehicles passed them from the rear, projecting long shadows of Johnny and the dog in their headlights that would get shorter and shorter until the automobile or truck passed in a whoosh. Without warning, the lights of one car seemed out of place. The speeding vehicle suddenly struck the dog and hurled him across the road. Broken and whimpering, Johnny raced home with his pet over his shoulders. He cleaned him and touched up his wounds, thinking he would take the animal to a veterinarian in the morning. He carefully putting the dog to bed on a blanket under the kitchen table, and the dog gave Johnny a wet lick before the lights were turned out. The following morning, Johnny found him dead. Very upset about this loss, he explained what had happened to Layman, who gently consoled his employee. "He was always your dog, Johnny," he said, "in life and now in death."

Heinrich Layman's mother, a staunch Social Democrat, was not pleased that her son had hired Johnny. The woman hated anyone who was not a member or sympathizer of the party she preferred. Her son withstood her sharp demands to fire de Graaf, which often resulted in heated words' passing between Heinrich and his mother. Despite the woman's bitterness, Layman and Johnny became good friends and soon decided to solicit grocery orders door to door in Ahlen and the neighboring towns. It proved to be a great idea. Before long they were taking daily requests, which Johnny would write out in his order book for delivery the following week. The prices were the same as elsewhere, but Layman's selection was far wider, and home delivery was a plus. He also allowed purchases on credit. Layman would be pleased in the months ahead when Johnny got word to him that he had a new son. The lad was born on April 4, 1924,[13] and Johnny named him Oscar after his younger brother, killed in the mine accident four years earlier.

About the time he was working with Layman, Johnny's wariness toward Jews became more visible. This behavior grew out of two principal causes. He felt that Jews had cheated him while he was delivering groceries, and he ate up the propaganda that they had contributed greatly to the economic collapse of Germany following World War I.[14] Of the two rationalizations, the former was probably the more important. He used to say, "Most people will give to those in need. The Jews will sell it to you." This faulty thinking was partially a product of its time. Anti-Semitic diatribe was rampant in Europe long before the advent of the Nazis. Hitler and his followers only threw gasoline on an already smoldering fire. But one might rightly have expected more from de Graaf, who despised those who confused morality and truth. Truth was something he valued highly, whether from a Jew or a Gentile. There must have been moments when he questioned his own bigotry, for at times he overcame it. Some people close to him were Jews. All who were acquainted with the man, however, knew that his word was his bond.[15] Needless to add, he expected the same in others. He would bend over backward for a friend, but if anyone crossed Johnny de Graaf, that person had made an enemy forever.

One of the results of the 1923 Leipzig conference was an effort that came to be rated a top priority as time passed. Not only was there a new attempt to increase membership and organize workers for an eventual overthrow of the government, but arms as well as brainpower came to be imported. The KPD was sent Soviet agents and M4 intelligence officers (Soviet Army Intelligence) who assisted in training and the supplying of cash to buy munitions. Johnny's region's Soviet contact was a soft-spoken M4 agent with a crew cut named Ian Karlovich Berzin (actually Peteris Kuzis).[16] The two men liked each other almost from the start. As with his colleagues scattered throughout Germany, Berzin provided funds and instruction. Johnny's people used the money to buy rifles, grenades, and machine guns from British, French, and American occupation forces who wanted to make extra cash clandestinely by selling their equipment. De Graaf remembered getting four rifles for a few dollars apiece, machine guns for US$15 to $20 each, and boxes of grenades for a dollar a box from the Allied troops.

Since many French soldiers had Communist sympathies, they were the best suppliers of military hardware by the start of 1923. It was thus probably no surprise when the occupation forces discovered that some of their soldiers were making large profits from these illegal sales. The end product was a relentless policy to hunt down the buyers. Allied military police attempted to capture Johnny's group after infiltrating some of the cells and making a limited number of arms purchases. Near Dortmund in May 1923, the French picked Johnny up for antimilitary agitation. They already had a warrant for his arrest but did not know what he looked like. Sent to the Steinwache police station, he managed to escape the following month to an area of Germany not under Allied occupation. In so doing, however, he got into an altercation with a German policeman and knocked him out.[17] For gunrunning, propagandizing, and assaulting the constable, Johnny was now on the French and German wanted lists. Headquarters instructed him to get away for a while until things cooled off.

Johnny was ferreted across the border to Belgium that June and once again became a sailor. His vessel was a small barge, the *Onn 6,* out of Strasbourg that plied the Rhine carrying assorted cargo. On one trip he jumped into the river and saved a woman who was trying to commit suicide. Bringing her ashore, he revived her, only to be met with a torrent of her best verbal abuse. She wanted to die and he had fouled up her nearly successful endeavor. Irritated, de Graaf turned the woman over his knee and spanked her, trying to wake her up to what she had wanted to do.[18] There is no information as to whether she attempted to end her life at a later date.

Hidden securely on board the *Onn 6* were more arms, purchased at safe ports of call along the river. Johnny sailed under his correct name but without a passport, which he knew would cause problems if not remedied before long. Arriving in Duisburg, he went to the KPD office and was dismayed to learn that the party would not help in arranging some kind of documents, either genuine or forged. They wished him luck. Then it occurred to de Graaf that he should try the city commandant, a French officer. Going to the man's office, Johnny told his story in German and broken French. He told the official that he was a sailor and asked if he could obtain a berth on a French merchantman.

"Yes," the officer replied, "you can sail, but you have to have a passport." Johnny answered by saying that he also was a revolutionary fighter who had recently fought the German fascists, who wanted another war. At that moment they were looking for him. "Oh," he said, "*la Bouché*" (blockheads, or, in this case, blockheads high up in an administration). The man then gave Johnny a note to take to the city consul's office and request a passport. Johnny did as he was told and got a passport without difficulty. Armed with the safety of his new identification, he continued sailing the Rhine, buying arms, and shipping them inland to hidden caches.

October 1923 approached with rumblings of a Communist uprising. Training for an insurrection had been going on in major cities across Germany. Detachments of Red sailors (in both the navy and the merchant marine), stevedores, and union workers had been in contact with underground sources for months to obtain arms. For days on end they awaited Moscow's decision on a general uprising. Courier after courier arrived in Berlin from Moscow. The Kremlin ordered a revolution, countermanded the order, and reissued it again. In Berlin, the ZK was undecided. Local leaders were immersed in their own factional squabbles and confused over the inconsistent commands from the Soviet Union. The ZK was composed of "right-wingers" such as Heinrich Brandler, August Thalheimer, Gerhard Eisler, Wilhelm Pieck, Walter Ulbricht, and Arthur Ewert. Opposed to them, the "left-wingers" consisted of Ernst Thälmann, Ruth Fischer, Fischer's boyfriend, Arkadi Maslow, and Willy Schwan.[19]

The USDP was split over the issue of autonomy versus unification with the KDP. When the left fringe refused to join the KPD and the planned revolt, Thälmann threw a tantrum and dispatched couriers to key points in Germany with the order for the rising. At this, the other members of the Central Committee leaped from their seats, staring at one another in disbelief. Brandler was first to regain his composure. He sent his men to stop the messengers. But the courier for Hamburg had a good head start. Brandler's confidant rushed to the station. "Too late!" he was told. "There goes the train." For a while the individual stared at the lights in the last car of the train as it rolled out of the station toward Hamburg. Then he went home.

On the eve of October 23, 1923, the Hamburg group attacked. Unaware that they were alone and unsupported, they began a rampage of revolutionary action. Police stations were raked with gunfire, trains and trucks were torched, and barricades were thrown up, as armed bands of Hamburg leftists followed previously laid plans. Large numbers of Reichwehr troops and police rushed to the city to assist its besieged defenders. Retreating street by street, the Reds slowly caved in to the overwhelming government force. Some escaped, but most paid with their lives, still believing that parallel battles were going on elsewhere in Germany. That night the Hamburg party was obliterated by the unfortunate error of one leader and one courier. Marxists in the Ruhr were warned, like others in Germany, to cancel the uprising. Word went out to each cell to stay quiet until calm returned, as the KPD had been dealt a major setback that would take years to repair.

In February 1924, French river authorities picked up de Graaf in Mannheim aboard the *Onn 6*. They turned him over to the Germans to face the charge of assault against a member of the police department and for being the organizer of a weapons-smuggling ring. Given a sentence of two years, he was taken to the Hechingen Work Prison, only to be released after ten months, in late November 1924.[20] Arriving back in Ahlen on November 24, he was thoroughly dismayed with revolutionary life. Still, the party provided for de Graaf through Rote Hilfe while he sought work as a seaman. But no vessel would sign him on, so he returned to the Ruhr to try again to find a job as a miner. This too failed to produce anything. Following seven months of unemployment, in June 1925, the KPD sent him to Hamm with orders to organize the city's Red Front. It was the first time Johnny was directly on the payroll of the KPD.[21]

Toward the middle of 1926, he attended a three-month course in economics and politics in Dresden. Nearly a hundred students from all over Germany attended the classes. The KPD paid for everything. That Easter, under the auspices of the Red Front, Johnny organized a commemoration march for the victims of the insurrections that had taken place in the Ruhr. Hermann Schmans from Wiescherhöfen and Albert Funk assisted him. The protesters were made to agree not to walk with sticks, truncheons, metal weapons, or firearms. More than a thousand people took part. It was peaceful, and Johnny's contingent from Ahlen was the largest.[22]

De Graaf was arrested again in June 1926 on charges of disturbing the peace and for being an organizer/leader of an RFB unit that had fought with rightist Steel Helmet thugs. This time the sentence was twenty-one months.[23] His incarceration meant that he missed the birth of his next child. On September 4, 1926, Maria had a daughter.[24] They named her Marianne, and she was the last of their children. Over the coming years, Johnny Jr., Oscar, and Marianne would nearly become strangers to their father. It was also painfully apparent that the de Graaf marital situation had become hopeless. Johnny felt that his home environment was not conducive to bringing up children, let alone conceiving them. When he was home, never a day went by that he and Maria were not at each other's throats. Their arguments were always over the lack of housekeeping and cleanliness. Maria's laziness, excessive weight, and total disregard for tidiness caused such friction and ignited such anger that after repeated threats Johnny walked out. Thereafter he lived apart from his wife and children but continued to give them financial support to the best of his ability. There was no doubt that this arrangement caused great hardship for parents and children alike, yet all attempts to save the marriage had failed. Johnny, Maria, and the three children had no choice but to handle life as best they could, with regret, certainly, but hopefully without hostility. Johnny's intermittent periods of employment and party activities at night only lightly masked his unhappy marital situation. Johnny always felt guilty about the problems his split from Maria caused his children. They were surely the innocent and blameless victims of the unsuccessful union.

In January 1927 the ZK managed to arrange the release of forty prisoners, including Johnny.[25] The KPD's Wilhelm Florin put Johnny to work delivering the district's Communist newspaper, the *Ruhr Echo*.[26] His route was Essen, Dortmund, and Hamm, a one-way journey of slightly more than forty miles (64.4 kilometers). He was paid 120 marks a month for working fifteen hours a day at the newspaper and nine hours organizing the veterans. He only slept, and not well at that, on the trains between the three cities. Additionally, in 1927, Thälmann, who had become head of the KPD two years earlier,[27] offered Johnny the job of RFB leader in Hamburg. De Graaf refused, however, explaining that he wanted to stay in the Ruhr. Johnny finally found regular work that May in the Ahlen-Hamm area as a hot asphalt layer on a road gang. This allowed him to quit the newspaper-delivery job, since Florin had fallen under the KPD's right-leaning wing, led by Heinrich Brandler.[28]

Nineteen twenty-seven was a significant year owing to another event. At a Whitsunday KPD rally in Berlin on June 5, with his estranged wife and at least two of his children among the group from Ahlen, Johnny caught sight of nine-year-old Helena Erma Krüger. Through a political connection, he arranged lodgings for himself with the Krügers at their apartment whenever he was in the capital. This was no small feat, since leftists in Berlin were often swamped with requests to put up visiting KPD members when the assemblies were large. At the time the Krügers, Gustav Ernst Karl and his wife, Pauline Emilie, had a flat at Pappellallee 32 in the Prenzlauer Berg district. They had three children. The oldest was Helena (nicknamed Elena, Lena, and Lee); then came Gertrude (or Gerti), and finally Ernst.[29]

Johnny was attracted to Helena at first. Her mother, Emilie (people always called Frau Krüger by her middle name), even encouraged the relationship. While staying in the Krüger home, Johnny also met their younger daughter, Gertrude Erika. Petite and rosy-cheeked, she struck de Graaf as a miniature princess with ringlet hair. There was some kind of instant bond between Gerti and Johnny, despite their ages. At one point Emilie remarked, "It appears that our other daughter, Gerti, has fallen for you, Johnny, and that's most unusual for she's quite shy among strangers." While relationships with both Helena and Gerti would have to wait, it should be noted that the process by the lower classes of palming their underage daughters off on men who might be able to provide a steady income to the child's parents was not uncommon in the inflation-wracked Weimar Republic. To Emilie Krüger, Johnny appeared to be an influential member of the party. She must have thought there was cash there somewhere.[30]

Back from the rally in Berlin, a courier arrived at Johnny's street job and informed him that he was wanted at party headquarters in Essen right away. He received permission from his foreman to leave and took off on his motorcycle, wondering why he had been summoned. Reaching Essen, he made his way to the dingy gray stone party building, parked his vehicle, and descended into the basement. An official there told him that he had been elected by the Ruhr workers to the post of secretary of the party for the Hamm district.[31] This was indeed a great honor. Johnny was also aware that five men had held the post in a little more than a year and been replaced, one after the other, because of their ineffectiveness.

At first he refused, saying that he had a job as well as a little peace and wanted things to stay that way for a while. A Berlin KPD representative who was present, however, informed him that he could not say no. It was a party order. The new job paid two hundred marks, which he still turned down, pointing out that he was making double that as an asphalt worker. De Graaf haggled for an hour, until they raised the offer to 350 marks. He accepted on the promise of more money later. His district was nearly fifty-six miles (ninety km) to the east and almost seventy-five miles (120 km) to the west of Hamm. The area stretched from Gronau near the Dutch border to the Catholic district in Münster.

Putting in long hours, Johnny and his comrades were able within two years to significantly increase the regional KPD membership. They held many organizational meetings and printed pamphlets with a small duplicating machine. Johnny was assisted by his comrades in Hamm, and each cell was kept posted throughout the area. Propaganda was distributed to the German armed forces as well, which put Johnny's group on a collision course with the police. There was so much to do, so little money to do it with, and so little time to do it in, that the job became a pressure-packed nightmare.

Pleased with the results nonetheless, the party asked de Graaf to take over the western section of Gronau as well. This was a substantial textile region that Johnny felt was impossible to add to his already bulging portfolio of responsibility. The party promised it would send speakers to assist him and continued to badger him until he agreed. He enlisted the assistance of twenty members, plus seventy comrades from the RFB in Hamm. With the combined help, he was able to mobilize successful antiwar demonstrations in Gronau. The party then urged that he speak more on political life, as there were unrealistic expectations that the whole city could be converted in a matter of months. They assured him that their most skillful agitators would lend a hand. Word soon arrived that the Berlin

KPD was sending a speaker and member of the Reichstag. Johnny and his team were instructed to rent a hall and print pamphlets announcing the meeting.

Prior to the speeches, de Graaf informed the guest orator that they had packed halls in the past by speaking on the workers' level and not on an abstract political level. "Talk in their language, not yours," Johnny told him. Much to everyone's disappointment, however, only fifteen people showed up. The guest began his delivery, but the audience shouted him down. They wanted to hear Johnny. De Graaf took his place, informing his listeners that this man represented them in the Reichstag and urging them to hear him out. "He is a political man, and even though he does not talk like you and I, listen to him, for he has a message," Johnny shouted.

"No, no," they shouted back. "We don't want him. You talk, Johnny."

The meeting was a flop because de Graaf refused to upstage his guest and even announced to the audience that he would not speak. The listeners then got up and walked out, leaving Johnny with a large rental bill for the evening.

A month later Berlin sent a message to the effect that the party was sending a second speaker. They wanted Johnny to prepare an assembly and hire another hall. He told them he wished them well but that this time his chapter would not pay for the auditorium; it could not afford the loss. Berlin asked for a compromise. Johnny eventually agreed but told them he would rent a movie theater and that they could show social films they had from all over the world. "We would advertise 'Speaker: Johnny de Graaf,'" he told them. "I would open the session but then bow out, saying I had laryngitis, and thereby turn the meeting over to the Berlin man."

That evening the theater was packed. De Graaf took the podium and said, "Comrades, I am sorry but I have a terrible cold tonight and cannot speak. So I'll ask our friend from Berlin here to take my place." They let him talk for fifteen minutes and then bellowed for him to sit down. "We want Johnny!" they chanted. "He is the only one who understands us!" At this, de Graaf got to his feet, said a few words, and then started a beautiful film called *The Mother of Maxim Gorky*. It painted a rosy picture of how the Russian people lived. Party headquarters was annoyed that its top speakers were unsuccessful, but the local speakers packed the halls. Johnny too was irritated because, as a so-called party executive, he was forbidden to march in demonstrations, a rule he nearly always ignored.

Arthur Ewert and other party officials still could not get it through their heads: people in the Ruhr wanted leadership from their own kind. One had to toil alongside the workers at their level rather than talk above them with words and supercilious pronouncements they did not understand. They accepted and related to the Communists but would not tolerate high-sounding political blowhards. Johnny had many clashes with Ewert on this point. It did not help their already blooming animosity.

In Essen, de Graaf set up a small party office and began propaganda work under the guise of a legal business. When night fell, he printed outlawed newssheets that were distributed in the streets, especially to soldiers of the Reichwehr. Everything seemed to be going smoothly. Then, like lightning, all was turned upside down again. Two members of the political police, one nicknamed "Pigeon Willy," paid Johnny an unexpected visit at the party office in November 1929.[32] Willy was a most curious individual. Of small stature and with shriveled features, his hawk-like eyes took in everything. "I have to look around, Johnny," he said with a cocky smile. "Just routine." Johnny was suspicious of Pigeon Willy's intentions almost immediately. Poking through the rows of papers and checking shelves, he and his lanky assistant missed nothing. Johnny became anxious and wondered if it showed. Well hidden in the basement were more than two thousand recently completed handbills. At last, to Johnny's relief, Willy said, "Well, there's nothing here."[33] De Graaf smiled and began to regain his composure.

"Willy," he said, extending a hand that contained a small bank, "here's a collection box for prisoners on our side, which could hold another donation." Pigeon Willy grinned, put five marks in the box and said, "Johnny you just want to keep me here."

"No," de Graaf replied, "I was just asking for your support for a worthy cause."

Waving Johnny off, and followed by his slim assistant, he opened the door and walked out. Everyone breathed a sigh of relief. Two days later Pigeon Willy, along with police from the district office, greeted de Graaf without warning as he opened the office one morning. Johnny was placed under arrest and bundled to a waiting car. Willy said, "I put five marks into this little box the other day, Johnny, but now in order to get it back, I have to take you with it."[34]

Hurriedly, they drove to the provincial prison at Münster, where Johnny was informed of the preliminary charge, treason against the German state. In his case, this was punishable by a sentence of seven to eight years. He was slapped into a small cell in the massive stone building and left to languish for more than a week before being taken before a judge. Food was black bread and water, but he was not ill treated by the guards. Probably this was because many of them seemed drawn to the KPD.

In front of the magistrate and a board of military officers, Johnny was read the full charges, which had been increased to high treason, illegal publications, and disturbing the peace.[35] He was amazed that they had a thick dossier on him containing everything he had done for years. One officer remarked that the police had admired the strategy and tactics of Johnny's group during the strikes of 1920. He was informed that he could ask questions and obtain defense counsel. Thanking them, Johnny said that he would defend himself when his trial came up in three weeks' time. Back in his cell, a guard whispered that he liked Johnny's fighting spirit, as did the others, but could not say so openly for fear of losing his job.

Several days later the KPD sent over two lawyers, Dr. Horstman and Dr. Obuch,[36] both former members of the Reichstag. They said they could arrange for de Graaf's discharge. They got him out on pretrial release in January 1930, after his lawyers convinced the court that Johnny was a family man with children and was not going anywhere. The prosecution wanted to sentence him to six months' imprisonment, but Johnny felt that it could actually have been seven to ten years.[37] His decision to flee was thus an easy one, but it may have been aided by another event.

Throughout the two and a half years following his return from the Whitsunday rally, Johnny had kept in touch with the Krügers. He even took his firstborn to live with them. Emilie and Ernst, at least, did not like the idea, and Johnny Junior left with his father after a few days.[38] Authoritarian with their own children,[39] the Krüger family and Johnny had long discussions, walking as a group through the Tiergarten and other Berlin parks. De Graaf would combine this delightful pastime with party trips to Berlin. Journeys to the capital needed some kind of diversion, as Berlin had become a hellish place in the closing years of the 1920s. More and more, Nazi Brownshirts battled Communists, Socialists, and idealists in the streets. On one of these occasions, a belligerent member of the SA, Horst Wessel, organized an attack on the regional Communist Party headquarters in Friedrichshain, seriously injuring four KPD comrades. He was also known in other Red areas of Berlin, such as Prenzlauer Berg, where the Krügers lived.

A marked man, Wessel and his landlady, Frau Salm, started arguing over his rent on January 14, 1930. Residing with Wessel was either a current or former prostitute, Erna Jaenicke, a fact that could have resulted in the landlady's losing her lease on the apartment. Frau Salm had let the flat to Wessel secondhand, and she was the widow of a Communist. For that reason alone, Wessel did not like her. She claimed that he threatened to beat her. Rather than contact the police and risk being kicked out of the flat, the widow went to a nearby bar for help. The tavern had a large number of KPD members among its usual patrons. Johnny de Graaf was either at the establishment or somewhere else in town, and he was contacted to help organize a response to Horst Wessel's arrogance. Two men, Ali Höhler and Erwin Rückert, were chosen. They walked to Wessel's apartment and knocked on the door. When the Nazi opened it, Höhler shot him in the mouth. Wessel died in a hospital on February 23. Joseph Goebbels, the future Nazi propaganda minister, turned one of the poems found in Wessel's apartment into a song, the "Horst Wessel Lied" (Horst Wessel Song). It became the Nazi Party's official anthem, second only in importance in Germany to "Deutschland, Deutschland über Alles."[40]

Johnny gave the likely murder weapon, a 9mm Parabellum, to Gustav Krüger, who kept it hidden when his family moved from Pappellallee 32 to 75. The Krügers always lived in Prenzlauer Berg. When they relocated to Sonnenburger Straße 22, Gustav buried the gun, sealed in oilcloth and covered over by sand, at the bottom of their home aquarium. Later, when the family moved to Bornholmer Straße 81, he hid the pistol under one section of the apartment's parquet floor. It is unknown but probable that Gustav Krüger took the weapon with him to the family's last residence in Berlin, a fourth-floor flat at Gleim Straße 10.[41]

Soon Johnny was on a train speeding south out of Germany to Switzerland. Walter Ulbricht and Wilhelm Pieck had provided the funds and given him his first false passport.[42] Staring out the train window, he somehow knew he was leaving behind his home—never again to see it in the same way.

7

THE MOSCOW STUDENT

A bright winter sun lifted Johnny's spirits as the train arrived in Bern, Switzerland.[1] Alfred Langner (the alias of Tuure Lehén)[2], a Finn working in his county's embassy, was de Graaf's new contact. Langner was reported to be "an expert on revolutionary warfare [and] a member of the Fourth Department of the Red Army."[3] Johnny later learned that he was also the permanent secretary of the War and Anti-Militarism Department of the Comintern. The ZK supplied Langner's name and arranged a convenient rendezvous for their first meeting.

In 1930 Langner was between thirty-five and forty years old. He was six feet (1.83 m) tall and had a slim build, with rosy cheeks and straight, dark blond hair, cleanly parted, above a rather prominent nose.[4] The two men met in a park area of the Marzili, right in the heart of Bern and south of the Hauptbahnhof. After identifying themselves, they strolled along snowy paths, where Johnny learned that Langner was a Soviet military officer. Covered by his diplomatic duties, he headed recruitment for trainees.

Already informed of Johnny's past history, he quickly turned to the troubles and actions within the Ruhr Valley that de Graaf knew so well. "Had you remained in Germany, Johnny, you would be cooling your heels with a long imprisonment in Münster's cells," he calmly stated.

"I am well aware of that," Johnny replied, "and greatly appreciate all the aid the party has given me, in coming to my rescue and escape." Langner smiled and nodded his head in agreement.

"With your knowledge and experience, you could be most valuable to your benefactors and to yourself if you would join us in the USSR," he quietly commented. "How would you like to study in the University of Lenin at our expense?" Johnny's pulse quickened at the thought, as he had longed for a university education, and now it was being offered to him on a platter. Langner must have noticed Johnny's delight, for in his smooth fashion he turned up the volume.

"Come to Russia, my friend, and all you have ever yearned for in our progressive way will be made available to you," he expounded with dedicated gusto. "You will be enrolled in many courses, from economics to politics, and be assisted by the finest brains in the Soviet university system. Students from many countries, including Germany, are there right now, broadening their knowledge." His picture thrilled Johnny beyond his wildest dreams, as Langner opened greater vistas with each carefully chosen word. De Graaf's heart thumped wildly as he hung on to each agreeable morsel, knowing that his appetite for knowledge was insatiable. All lectures would be given in one's native language. His room on campus would be provided, along with all meals, clothes, and expenses, including monthly pocket money, by the Soviet state.

De Graaf quickly agreed to go, much to Langner's delight and praise. Certainly Johnny could not return to Germany to starve and risk arrest again as a hunted man. Had he been even remotely aware of what lay ahead, however, and of his disillusionment, he would have declined Langner's offer. Then again, he was proud and reveled in the tribute bestowed on him by this new mentor. He would be an older student, at thirty-six years of age, but who really cared?

They concluded their final arrangements for Johnny's departure, a day later, once again meeting in the Marzili. Langner explained that de Graaf was to enter Russia posing as a wool buyer, hastily producing the necessary documents and passes to substantiate the story. Other instructions followed, which Johnny repeated back to him until Langner was satisfied. Once he had it all correctly memorized, a warm smile and handshake completed the last encounter. The two men parted, each going his separate way.

The train ride from Bern to Moscow sped past new frontiers and countryside. Johnny had never seen most of it. He skirted Germany, bubbling to the brim with an adventuresome spirit. Everything had happened so fast that he could barely eat, as foreign sights and sounds took his mind off his stomach. He had to change trains along the way, with the route taking him through Italy, Austria, Czechoslovakia, and Poland before entering the Soviet Union. Only the area between Warsaw and Bialystok looked somewhat familiar. The cold outside and the Polish language brought with them thoughts of Osowiec and his lost comrades, as the train continued east. As Johnny sat locked in thought, time passed quickly until, on February 14, 1930, the interspaced signs, all reading "MOCKBA," slowly presented themselves through the window at Belorusskaya Station as the train stopped.[5]

Following his instructions, Johnny paced up and down the long, uncovered platform, raising and lowering to his chest a small red handkerchief held in his left hand. In a few moments a man approached and said, "Comrade Johnny, follow me," as he strode past. De Graaf turned and trailed along, keeping his eyes on the man's back. The two-person procession moved through the station crowds to the open backseat door of a car waiting outside. The mysterious greeter, who Johnny would later learn was Comrade Leibovitch,[6] jumped into the driver's seat and said nothing. He then drove to the main office of Отдел международных связей (Department of International Contacts), commonly known in the West as OMS. The OMS was responsible for relations with foreign Communist parties. This included providing them with secret funding, propaganda, and the various items used by agents when abroad—money, passports, and documents relevant to foreign assignments.

De Graaf was ushered into the office of the vice chief, Alexander Lazarovich Abramov. Comrade Abramov was suspicious of Johnny and grilled him on what he was doing in the Soviet Union. Satisfied, he sent the new arrival to a hotel and ordered him to stay there. Perhaps unbeknownst to Abramov, Johnny had only seven rubles in his pocket. He was also famished and could not speak Russian. Once checked in, and following some thirty-six hours alone in the room, he remembered that he had a friend from Germany named Gerhart Fuchs working at Comintern headquarters. Johnny left a sign in German on his door reading, "Gone for cigarettes," walked out of the hotel, and located Fuchs, who took him to a restaurant. Although it is not known when he began, Johnny smoked cigarettes and came to use a small holder whenever possible.[7]

After the meal, he returned to the hotel and discovered that someone had been there looking for him. The visitor was named General Alex, a man Johnny would come to know better later. When the general returned, he wanted to know where Johnny had been, since he was told not to leave the premises. Alex was then between five foot nine and five ten (1.75 and 1.78 m) in height, with a weight of around 180 pounds (81.8 kg) and not older than forty-five years of age. He had a flat Slavic nose and gold caps on his front teeth. Originally he had been a Polish army officer who had joined the Soviet Red Army in 1917.[8]

General Alex greeted de Graaf with a burst of caustic rebuke. Amid the general's hoarse ravings for leaving the hotel against explicit orders, the man somehow managed to introduce himself. Still, it was most apparent that he felt highly slighted, since Johnny could barely offer a defense to his tirade of pent-up hostility. General Alex made it quite plain; Johnny's hunger was secondary to breaking a command. No explanation or rebuttal was acceptable, and he continued to heap verbal abuse on the fresh arrival from Germany for a solid half-hour.

Taking Johnny with him, the general had his driver deliver them both to the Residence Reception Center at the International Lenin University. General Alex then escorted de Graaf inside and roared instructions to the bewildered individual on duty. Seconds later he abruptly turned on his civilian-clad heel and exited. After a moment, the stunned clerk regained his composure and muttered something to himself about "damned military bastards!" Then he proceeded to familiarize Johnny with the numerous forms requiring his signature. That done, he called another man, who showed de Graaf to his new quarters.

They walked down corridors and up several staircases until finally stopping before a brown oak door numbered 809. The room inside revealed a most attractive setting. Johnny's new billet was about nine by twelve feet in size (2.74 × 3.66 m) and newly painted in a light green. This generated a warm hue of gold as sunlight streamed in from the large window overlooking the well-manicured grounds below. A ready-made bed was positioned in the middle of the room, its headboard touching the far wall. There was a desk with a lamp beside the window and a chest of drawers against the wall near a built-in cupboard. Everything was complemented by a light brown scatter rug. Before departing, Johnny's guide showed him the large communal lavatory with showers at the end of the long hallway.

The new guest had barely acquainted himself with his new surroundings when a knock on the door ushered in a uniformed official from the secret police, the OGPU (or ОГПУ, Объединенное государственное политическое управление—the Combined State Political Directorate, also translated as the All Union State Political Board). Each residence hall contained an administrator from the OGPU whose responsibility it was to watch the students, report on them, and act as an information host to the newcomers. He or she was an ombudsman and was there to settle complaints and to bring university infractions to a student's attention. The OGPU kept tabs on everyone, civilians, the military, and foreigners.

The man introduced himself as Comrade Pavel Vasiliev, a simple student advisor.[9] Johnny momentarily surveyed this man with an outstretched hand and friendly smile. Massive would be the best word to describe him. He was huge, at least six feet tall (1.83 m), with a large head topped with bushy black hair, grasping bear-paw hands, and a solidly built, well-maintained frame hovering over size thirteen shoes. His rough exterior at first took de Graaf aback. But after Johnny learned Russian, he would admire Comrade Vasiliev's beautiful use of the language, and even on that first day, when they spoke in German, Vasiliev had a soothing voice. Moreover, he was more than just a student advisor. Vasiliev was Alfred Langner's immediate superior. He was similarly in charge of Орготдел, or Orgotdel, the Organization Bureau of the Comintern.[10]

After asking Johnny if he was comfortable in his new room, Vasiliev began informing him of the rules and regulations for foreign students. They were to sign in and out at the foyer desk each time they went out of the residence. They would abide by the curfew hours and always inform the desk clerk of their destination and their expected date and time due back. The Russian language was never to be spoken outside the building, only one's native language. Liquor was forbidden in school and on the school grounds. Finally, there was to be no contact with the opposite sex. He told Johnny to see him and no one else regarding special requests or wishes and said he would take care of it. Should de Graaf notice or hear of any student abuse of rules, wild talk, or antistate dissension, it was his duty to report it to Vasiliev at once. Outside contact with the Soviet populace was forbidden except for service needs. Infractions were to be reported. Again he emphasized that Johnny was to speak in German off campus.

Johnny listened to every word, as he was shown through the building, from lecture rooms, library, staff offices, and gym, to the spacious cafeteria, which was crisp, clean, and well lighted, with seating for many hundreds. Johnny would discover that the dining hall food was bland but abundant and well prepared. The fifty rubles a month he got in spending money was ample for outside expenses and cigarettes, which could be purchased in the cafeteria. During a coffee break, Comrade Vasiliev introduced him to several German students, who appeared most friendly.

Returning to his room after his lengthy Saturday tour with the OGPU officer, Johnny was pleasantly surprised to find his desk laden with many textbooks in German and abundant supplies of notebooks, pens, and pencils. Within a few days his sparse clothing was to be refurbished in this same unobtrusive way, while he was off attending lectures. The weekend passed quickly as Johnny walked around the sprawling facility and all its buildings, from auditoriums to the campus hospital. Female residences were separated from male residences, foreign students from Soviet students, in a great master plan of "divided they are uncontaminated, hence conquered."

Monday morning came briskly with the 6:00 A.M. call to fall out for thirty minutes of calisthenics led by a Red Army instructor. Breakfast was at 7:00 A.M. in the cafeteria. Classes began at 8:00 A.M. and lasted until 6:00 P.M., with an hour for lunch. Saturday was a school day too, but only until 3:00 P.M. True to their word, the Soviets lectured in the languages of their foreign guests. The professors were extremely well versed in their subjects and would encourage questions and group discussion in a highly educational atmosphere. As time passed, graduate students from other countries added to the lectures in conjunction with the university faculty. These senior students would often answer questions that stumped the professors, but never in an uncomplimentary way. The approach was very popular among the rest of the student body since it allowed everyone to express their knowledge and experiences. The courses of study lasted six months, one year, and three years. After three months, only those felt to be qualified or talented were allowed to continue. The subjects included Leninism, party structure, Marxian economics, history of the Soviet Union, agriculture, labor-union organization, front organizations, and military training. Many important Communists, including Stalin, were occasional guest speakers.[11]

Weeks slipped by in such haste that Johnny was not aware of their passing, owing to the demanding schedule. His free time was usually spent in preparation for the week's work ahead. This left little opportunity to seek out the sights and new experiences away from campus. He did manage, however, after first obtaining permission from the OGPU officer, to visit a number of *dachas* (summer cottages) around Moscow. These were special houses reserved for intelligence personnel who had completed missions and were awaiting their next assignments, often in their native countries. After returning home, they would continue as Soviet operatives in deep cover. Some of these sleeper agents attained such influential positions that their value to the Soviet state was immeasurable. Johnny enjoyed chatting for hours with these people about their past missions. There was a secondary reason, however, for his interest: he was developing a desire to leave the Soviet Union.

"Workers come first!" the system proclaimed, yet almost everywhere he saw facts to the contrary. "No rich class, everyone is equal!" But this was not so. Disparities shouted from the rooftops as the well-dressed party hierarchy limousined past ragged peasants with pushcarts. Basic freedoms of speech, choice, and expression, in which de Graaf believed so deeply, were nonexistent. The state and its political police saw to it through an omnipresent network of informers that prisons and Siberian work camps were always brimming with dissidents. Trials were a mockery of justice. The innocent along with the guilty were prejudged without recourse. A slip of the tongue, even among friends, could well result in someone's vanishing from the face of the earth. Dogma preached was not dogma practiced. It was a soul-searching process, and Johnny could really find no justifications. The corruption and the deception of it all were his nagging companions. Night after night he tossed in his sleep, until at last a plan unfolded. He had been in the Soviet Union just three months.[12]

The idea flashed into Johnny's head when he realized that armies traveled outside their own borders. The Red Army was forever on the move, sometimes in other lands, where soldiers could desert. As the thought took root, Johnny began spending long hours in the vast university library. This was in addition to his normal course of studies. A helpful librarian kept him supplied with volumes on war, strategy, and tactics from many countries. Each book was devoured. Battles, maneuvers, and warfare buzzed in de Graaf's tired head for weeks on end. Needless to say, this extra activity did not go unnoticed. One day he was called to the office of the OGPU advisor. As he hastened to this appointment, he could not overcome the feeling that his diligent fishing had brought him his first nibble.

Vasiliev greeted de Graaf warmly as he was ushered into his brightly lit but confined gray office. The officer's great bulk literally dwarfed his polished miniature desk. "Please sit down, Comrade." Vasiliev gestured to a well-worn wooden chair before Johnny. Once seated bolt upright, Johnny met Vasiliev's piercing, watchful gaze.

"I have been informed by many sources that you have virtually camped out in the library," he told Johnny. De Graaf nodded. "All the books you take out are military volumes, which you study late into the evening." Vasiliev was swollen with pride in his efficient system of intelligence gathering. "I am well informed of your scholastic achievements here, as well as your background. Your efforts in the Ruhr Valley and the problems you created for the Kaiser we have in your OGPU file. So, as you can see, Comrade Johnny, we know you well," he smiled. "You are interested in warfare, my friend?"

"Yes," Johnny replied. "I am indeed deeply fascinated with it. However, I am also aware I have to know politics and many other subjects as well, Comrade Vasiliev."

Vasiliev smiled in agreement as he told de Graaf to continue to pursue the learning that could lead to important opportunities in the future. A firm, crushing handshake was extended and the brief chat was concluded. Johnny was elated, for it was not hard to understand the workings of the OGPU system of relaying information, good and bad, to key state officials. The fish had risen to the bait without knowing the hook had been set. "Swim around, swim around," he mused. "Soon I'll reel you in."

Two weeks later, Johnny was surprised when he was ordered to Vasiliev's office once more. He was informed that he was being transferred to the Frunze Military Academy. Outwardly humble but inwardly ecstatic, he thanked his superior for the opportunity. Johnny was to begin training as an officer cadet in the Red Army. Both men were noticeably proud, as the model student set out on phase two of his plot to extricate himself from the Soviet Union.

Vine-covered redbrick buildings sprawled across untold acres of a parklike setting on the northern edge of Moscow. This was Frunze, with its countless parade grounds, gyms, military garages, and parallel row upon row of elongated classrooms and residences. Operated by M4 and watched over by Alfred Langner's section of the Comintern,[13] the central administration building squatted amid a never-ending circle of activity. Trucks and tanks rumbled over one training area while rigid columns of cadets drilled in others. A high mesh fence encompassed this vast military operation, sprinkled liberally with gates and armed checkpoints.

Here was felt the great might of the future marshal of the Soviet General Staff, Semyon Mikhailovich Budenny, a close friend of Stalin and a man whom Johnny would meet in due time. De Graaf was not alone this first day as he was issued his kit and complete military gear. There were forty-two others (thirty-five Germans and seven Czechs), all lined up at the quartermaster's office. Their dark trousers were a cavalry-type issue adjoined with battledress tunics in a light shade of brown, later to be adorned with rank insignia and other patches.

The quarters for officer candidates were barracklike long dormitories with fifteen metal beds down each side of a gray-painted room. A solid wooden clothes box stood rigid before each bed, opposite wall hooks for coats and caps. The far end of de Graaf's new accommodations contained neatly placed study tables, adorned with lamps abutting the dull walls. Smartly uniformed officers carefully went over the rigid academy rules, from saluting officers to avoiding Soviet females when away from base. The whole operation was enforced with strict discipline.

In short order Johnny and his dorm mates struck up an affinity, aided greatly by the usual segregation by nationality and native language. The day commenced with a 7:00 A.M. bugle call and mess from 8:00 to 9:00 A.M., after which the men marched to classes. The academy commandant turned out to be none other than General Alex, the angry officer whom Johnny had met at the hotel in Moscow. Johnny hoped that he had forgotten the incident as he now stood before the class introducing, by way of a German translator, the instructors one by one. Some of these people Johnny would forever know by their first names alone.

Major Max, the arms and explosives instructor, was a short, stout, good-looking officer. He had been a prisoner of war in Germany during World War I. Max was a very pleasant man with a great sense of humor and a fair command of the German language. General Manfred Stern,[14] a tall, distinguished-looking officer with red glowing cheeks and round face, was the field-training specialist. An Austrian, he also had been captive in Germany. Other officers followed, all of them authorities in their chosen fields. There was General Tony, an expert in radio transmissions, and Colonel Petrov, who taught sabotage. Major Waldemar explained codes, ciphers, photography, invisible inks, and microfilming. Alfred Langner instructed in printing and distributing banned ideas in the capitalist West. Captain Werner gave classes in military strategy along with Lieutenant Colonels Kurt Fischer and Otto Braun.[15] Werner had been a former captain in the Kaiser's army. Countless lesser instructors filled in areas of mechanized armament and transport, Russian history, physical education, first aid, politics, and other subjects.

General Alex, not familiar with languages other than Russian, was never without his female translator. She was called Maria and was extremely attractive and highly proficient in her field. Since all of the lectures and training were given in German, the subjects were easier to understand with the accompanying texts. In no time Johnny felt much at home in his new world, diligently applying himself to learning all he could. He and the other aspirants marched or quick-marched from classroom to classroom. Drill with and without arms, judo, karate, and commando attack and defense hardened their bodies and gave them self-confidence. Evenings saw them intently occupied with their books. Nursing sore muscles, they joined in discussions, only to fall exhausted into bed when the order was given for lights out.

No one complained about the meals, which by then tasted better because of all the exercise. Countless field maneuvers, led by General Stern, had the officer hopefuls scaling walls, swinging from ropes, and swimming streams with full backpacks. Their training also included crawling over rough terrain while live machine gun fire blazed above their heads. Language classes added humor as the men struggled to become more fluent in the many tongues each had acquired before arriving at Frunze. They greatly enjoyed Major Max's classes in arms and explosives; Max was a born teacher who added light dashes of humor in fumbling German. One day he greeted the cadets with a mound of international small arms parts lying at his feet. "You have studied the workings and handled the known small arms from all major countries," he coyly remarked. "Now prove to me you know what you have learned," came the command. With a flourish of his hand, he gave each man a small card, each bearing a different photo of a small arm. "At the count of five, you are to find in this mess the parts for your gun. Assemble it in working order and present it to me," he announced. "Before you begin, I would like to inform you smart fellows that you have ten minutes to accomplish this simple task."

The men lunged for the metal heap at his count of five, grabbing screws, spring pins, and barrels in mad haste. A chaotic chorus of "This is too short!" "I need a spring!" "Hey, that's my butt!" resounded in the room as everyone browsed, sorted, and traded as quickly as possible to complete their weapons. It seemed like the chore had barely commenced when Major Max blew his whistle. "Time's up, and not one gun finished," he exclaimed without annoyance. "Would you say you have a lot to learn?" he inquired. Disappointed, the students nodded in agreement.

Within a week Max had his charges able to assemble a gun from the pile of parts within five minutes. Not content, a week later they could do it in the dark and blindfolded in record time. Their expertise soon reached the point that they could assemble these guns in less than a minute, in all kinds of conditions. In time, they graduated to larger weapons, going through the same process until Major Max was satisfied.

One day Max stood before the cadets with a light machine gun in his hands, his finger resting on the trigger. He began to grope around for a word, but try as he might he could not remember how to say the object his finger was touching in German. He swore in Russian as his frustration turned into anger. The students roared with laughter, watching the weapon bounce up and down in his thick hands, his foul language and annoyance mounting. "Auslöser," the cadets shouted between uncontrollable giggles. If he heard the word, he gave no such indication. Another barrage of choice Russian followed, as he shouted above the din. "Don't laugh. I'll find it. You know the word I mean for this thing, like a man does with a woman!"

The students hooted, joined now by Max himself, in a tearful laughing throng. For all Max's primitive ways, he always found a method of expressing himself somehow. To a man, the students felt he was one of them. His great humanity and kindness won him respect as an outstanding person and superb arms expert.

Despite finding this new life highly interesting, de Graaf never lost sight of his objective. He did not accept the Soviet system with its so-called new visionary ways, ways that did not solve the problem of what Johnny said was 84 percent illiteracy within its borders. He realized that the spotlessly clean Soviet cities faced basic problems that were still unresolved. From the many books he read, he was aware that the Kaiser's government he hated so much had arranged for and transported Lenin from Switzerland to Russia to organize the Revolution of 1917. He abhorred the methods applied by the Bolsheviks, and never desired in any way to become part of their legacy.

A fellow Communist miner from the Ruhr Valley whom Johnny knew well, Karl Franserra, was also at the academy. Karl was specializing in wireless and codes, and he later become an instructor in the Red Army Intelligence Radio Section.[16] They saw each other often and formed a friendship that lasted many years. One weekend, while on leave, Karl confirmed Johnny's suspicions that trained female agents were part of the academy network. "These girls you sometimes see around the base who are fluent in many languages will give you their bodies if necessary in order to pick your innermost thoughts," he stated. "A real trap, Johnny." Karl went on, "Several fellows who dated some of these gals found out too late they were informers enhancing their own careers. Within hours they had turned in their starry-eyed dates, who were promptly expelled as dissidents against the state without a hearing." De Graaf had steered clear of these women, feeling that even the odd German-speaking Soviet female would be just what Karl said she was. No one could trust anyone in the Soviet Union. Informers were everywhere, hidden in every walk of life.

General Alex bore the brunt of many heated discussions with the students. Often, a great deal was lost in rendering General Alex's Russian into German. This caused a fair amount of confusion. Once, getting Maria off by herself, Johnny mentioned that her translations were poor and that she should stay in bed with Alex where she belonged. Maria's irritation with the comment matched her shining red hair as she stomped off in a huff, not realizing that Johnny had been joking. An hour later General Alex summoned de Graaf and several other students to his office. A stormy tirade followed, which resulted in extra guard duty for Johnny and the other provocateurs. Alex and Johnny were never to see eye to eye. This resulted in numerous small clashes and widened the rift between them.

The general's unpopularity was not limited to Johnny. Several others disliked his caustic ways and annoying impatience. All of this snowballed, propelling General Alex into even worse behavior. De Graaf recalled one of his infrequent lectures, this one entitled "How the Bolshevik Party Established the Three-Zone Intelligence Underground System." Maria translated his every word perfectly as he read parts of his text from a volume on Russian history. The subject matter concerned cell formation, propaganda, and underground printing. He spoke of how terrorists in Russia, more than a hundred years before, worked and plotted for the government's overthrow. Alex paused to unveil the rudimentary printing press they had used. "You should do the same thing, using the same equipment handled by these comrades of the past," he emphatically concluded.

Johnny got to his feet and said politely, "Comrade Alex, what one could do in the wide open spaces in the Soviet Union could not be done in well-organized police-controlled countries such as Germany, Poland, or just about wherever one went, without metal for the type. Locating metal to be used for this purpose would be almost impossible in such societies." Glaring at de Graaf, the general swore, turned around abruptly, and walked out, slamming the door behind him and leaving the comment unanswered. No doubt Johnny had incurred his distaste with such outspokenness. Later, when Johnny discussed the incident with General Manfred Stern, Stern assured him that he was correct but that Alex would never admit being wrong.

General Stern, a knowledgeable officer in revolution and government overthrow in addition to being a well-seasoned veteran, was eventually transferred from the Frunze Military Academy to M4 under command of the General Staff. De Graaf and Manfred Stern would work closely on an important mission soon enough. In the meantime, Johnny missed his counseling and friendship, as did many others.

General Alex returned two weeks later to continue his sessions on intelligence and the role of open and covert agents. He shouted scornfully at those who ever broke the cardinal rule of espionage: never acknowledge or converse in any way, if you unexpectedly meet a fellow intelligence officer in the street or on some form of public transportation. "Pretend you don't know each other, for it could mean your death and the death of a mission, if ever-watchful enemy spies have you under observation," he resolutely commanded. That made a good deal of sense, because in intelligence work you could never reveal your existence to everyone. So powerful and frightening was his observation that no student would ever forget the great importance of this life-and-death rule. From that point on, Johnny told his USSR acquaintances and others not to greet him, should they ever meet somewhere in the world.[17]

Training intensified as it became more apparent that Johnny's unit was being prepared for Red Army intelligence work in other countries. Major Max soon showed the group his playground, much to their amazement. Stretched out before them were several meadows, cluttered beyond imagination. The first was a broad field, strewn with literally every form of transportation available. Trains stood on sidings. Tanks, cars, trucks, and planes were everywhere. Another fenced-in field held an astonishing number of field guns. Far to the left, a good distance away, rusting stacks and decks of ships sat sprinkled throughout the high lush grass. The cadets' awe was short-lived, as the men began studying the use of explosives. One concoction, a black powder that became highly dangerous when lightly brushed with moisture and sugar, rose to an inside temperature of five to six thousand degrees Centigrade (9,032 to 10,832 degrees Fahrenheit). A little package of this stuff placed on a ship's bulkhead would explode as it absorbed natural moisture. The effect was devastating. The real beauty of the powder, however, was that it allowed the agent ample time to be several miles away when it went off. In addition to training and the practical use of explosive devices, the men learned to fire rifles without using the sights. Major Max was very good at this. He could discharge a weapon from a moving locomotive with deadly accuracy. Even after weeks of constant practice, no student could beat his score.

The men were taught how to damage artillery, rendering it useless to the enemy. These same weapons they then learned to repair. This was because their lives could one day depend on the use of destroyed arms left by a retreating enemy. The experiences in these unbelievable meadows enabled each cadet to perfect his ability to such a point that he completed assigned tasks virtually in his sleep. Finally came the wireless classes, coding and decoding, and the study of papers, inks, and documents and their forging. Understanding dyes and chemicals, developing contacts, and learning how to use covers and fronts left the students little free time.

They spent weeks on every aspect of intelligence work and became versed in using ordinary items to their advantage. That was the fascinating and dangerous contradiction in it all. For example, they were shown how an ordinary camera could be used to photograph key documents, places, or people, and then, while one was engaged in light conversation, become a deadly weapon of attack or defense. In the final analysis, de Graaf came to feel that Soviet methods in intelligence training, even in the 1930s, were second to none.

Graduation night arrived, and all the cadets' efforts of the past months culminated in this exciting evening in June 1930. De Graaf's class of forty-two sat in their well-tailored uniforms at long tables placed horizontal, in the Russian seating style, to the colorfully decorated head table. The guest of honor was Joseph Stalin himself, heavily mustached and smiling to all in an immaculate and amply decorated uniform. Sitting with Stalin was a group of officers composed of generals Voroshilov, Alex, Stern, Berzin, and Yagoda,[18] future head of the НКВД or NKVD.[19] Major Max, Alfred Langner, and assorted aides to Stalin were likewise present.

Speech after speech filled the hall to resounding applause. Stalin praised everyone's efforts and glorified the victories to come. He then sat down to an overwhelming ovation. There followed a meal of special food and drink. The generals treated the graduates like princes. Toasts, awards, and presentations followed, each cadet getting a chance to shake Stalin's hand as he received his commission. That evening Johann de Graaf became a major in the Red Army.

Not to be outdone, the students had several awards of their own to make.

Eight men formed a unit at arms and made a grand presentation to General Alex. Much to Stalin's delight, Comrade Alex was presented with a massive, red-painted plywood Soviet star attached to a rusty chain. Across the star's face was written, "To General Alex, forgiven for not keeping promises." Alex was greatly embarrassed and annoyed but smothered his true feelings with a waxen smile. Stalin, on the other hand, found it all hilarious, as did his entourage, thinking it a superb joke. A more solemn moment followed, as with great respect and affection the class stood and presented Major Max with an engraved silver cigarette lighter. Tears sprang to his eyes as he read the inscription, "To our teacher, beloved Max." The new graduates shared in joy and sorrow in his deeply felt reaction to the gift. He touched everyone deeply as his emotion-filled voice humbly acknowledged his spoken feelings. It was truly a night to remember.

The next morning brought a command to report to General Staff headquarters in Moscow. Johnny could hardly contain his excitement as he hastened to his appointment. When he arrived, he was ushered into General Berzin's spacious office by an aide. A smiling face topped by a military-style brush cut greeted de Graaf from behind a marble desk. Coming to attention, Johnny smartly saluted the familiar officer seated before him. Ian Berzin gestured to a chair, as Johnny absorbed the thick pile carpet, book-lined shelves, numerous cabinets, and colorful paintings adorning clean beige walls. "Forgive me, General, but have we not met before last night?" de Graaf politely inquired. A gentle nod of Berzin's head and soft gray eyes assured the man in front of him that they had. Johnny continued, as the pieces fell together. "Germany, Ruhr Valley, Berlin," he stated with certainty.

"Yes," Berzin replied. "You have a good memory, for I was the agent who gave you instructions and money to purchase arms in organizing your revolution."

The two warriors had a very enjoyable discussion, ending when the general informed the new major that he was to be attached to the International Division in the Far East under General V. V. Blücher (real surname: Galem). For the time being, however, he would work for M4 and be under Berzin's command.[20] Likewise, Johnny would be enrolled in a special course on advanced intelligence in European strategy and tactics. The class was to be given in the very building in which they were speaking.

There were twenty-four students in the course, which took up a detailed analysis of European nations and M4's methods of infiltrating them. At the end of the class, everyone felt more aware of the opposition each new agent would face during international assignments. Several instructors spoke of their personal experience with this new world of foreign-station espionage. Completion of the class brought Johnny's assignment as an intelligence operative with the Red Army, Far East command, attached to the General Staff in Moscow and reporting to M4.

Johnny's new residence was one of the agent hotels run by the OGPU not far from Red Square. There were several of these hotels, where operatives waited for calls to duty or rested upon completion of a mission after returning to the Soviet Union. An agent's free time was his or her own, excluding the varied and restricted hours each day when they had to be in their rooms if headquarters wish to contact them. Messages either awaited agents at the desk in the foyer or were communicated in brief phone calls made to their rooms, giving an appointment date and time. No discussion was allowed on these OGPU taped calls. Agents were to present themselves at the command center at the indicated hour. After arriving, detailed instructions were provided. Whenever possible, de Graaf dressed sharply when in civilian clothes.[21] He was not ordered to do this. It was just his style. For a week he enjoyed sightseeing in Moscow decked out in his finest. As he was lounging about his room one morning, waiting for a call from M4 and thinking about what he would do when he left the hotel, he was startled when the phone actually rang, summoning him to headquarters. Simple and brief, an unknown voice said, "One P.M. tomorrow," and abruptly hung up.

The following day, seated in Langner's office, Johnny was surprised to learn that an unexpected change of events had altered his anticipated first mission. With Langner were Fritz Heckert, a representative of the KPD, and Dmitri Manuilski, one of the powers in the ИККИ (IKKI, or Executive Committee of the Communist International). Meeting Manuilski would prove beneficial to de Graaf near the end of the decade.[22]

Langner explained that the Comintern needed someone for a position it could not fill. He noted that it was true that M4 and the Comintern worked on some projects independently and together on others. For this venture the Comintern needed a coordinator who knew all about mining coal, since coal was the lifeblood of the growing Soviet economy. The individual selected was to head up a mining camp in the Donbass area of the Ukraine. The world economic crisis, coupled with massive German unemployment, made this an urgent need. In the summer months of 1930, between four and five thousand Germans would take special trains to the USSR, many leaving from Essen. Members of the KPD, or Germans sympathetic to the party, would be brought into the Soviet Union to work in mines, in construction, and in the steel industry.[23]

One of the initial groups of approved individuals reached several hundred in number.[24] They would soon be on their way to the USSR. Johnny was told that he would meet them as one of Moscow's new field representatives. It was the first big mission for his superiors. His job would be to ensure that the proletarian guest workers were provided with food and shelter. Schools had to be arranged for their children. The housing, planning, and construction heads of the Comintern were to coordinate this assignment with Johnny and provide him with all appropriate aid. He would be lent to the Comintern from July to December 1930,[25] while they learned to manage the operation themselves, then would be recalled to Moscow. Langner realized that Johnny was disappointed by all of this, as he thought he was being summoned for a mission out of the country. That would have to wait, since the General Staff had agreed to lend the Comintern the benefit of Johnny's talent and experience in this matter.

Despite his feelings, Johnny realized that protest would be fruitless. He was to be kept in Mother Russia with no hope of escaping through Soviet-occupied Poland. Langner was only carrying out his instructions. Johnny could not blame him. Langner no doubt felt for his agent, knowing that Johnny wanted a foreign assignment. Johnny thanked his superior on departing as Langner wished him well, stating his belief that de Graaf would obtain an intelligence mission next time.

Long discussion sessions with Comintern headquarters project officials followed in order to look over the operation's requirements. Housing construction was already under way, as they examined numerous plans and blueprints of the entire undertaking. The main location of Johnny's mission would be the Juny Commune in Kharkov. It was one of six ventures under development at that time. The others were scattered all over this valuable region, known as the Donbass. There were a few around Moscow but more in southwestern Siberia and spread about the Kuznetsk Basin.[26] The Kuznetsk held the largest reserve of coal in the world. Around Kharkov, mine shafts and equipment were already in full use. Johnny's first task was to accelerate the building of structures to accommodate the new arrivals. It was a liaison position, one to ease the settlement of imported German-speaking workers. Everything appeared great on paper, but de Graaf had doubts as to what he would find once he got there. The Germans had been told that after they arrived, should they want to return home, they could do so by application to the German consul without opposition from the Soviets. Moscow would regret this gesture in time. There were likewise recruitment issues back in the Fatherland. Some of the workers were sick or crippled from wounds received in World War I. Others were unfamiliar with mining.[27]

Traveling day and night by rail and truck, de Graaf soon found himself at the Juny Commune's Camp No. 6 facility, not nineteen miles (30.6 km) outside Kharkov.[28] Forty Soviets worked the mines, living in newly constructed homes that outwardly appeared most attractive. Thick forests of towering fir trees, interrupted occasionally by sheer rock cliffs, ringed the lowland valley location. Deep, rutted dirt roads weaved in and out of the virgin wilderness. Mineshafts and sinkholes, amid a cluster of administration buildings, littered the basin floor. Johnny admired the great effort that was clearly evident. Long months of hard work had gone into the formation of this place. From the sheltered, leveled habitation area, sharp, rock-cut paths chewed their way down jagged inclines to the mine head. So steep was the rise from the pit area that conveyer belts twisted upward to cleared plateaus, where waiting trucks received the chopped black fill.

Drivers with more skill than brains traveled up and down shambling lanes, bearing their burden to a rail stop fifty miles (80.5 km) away. Steep inclines and narrow roads with hairpin turns could spell instant death for any gambling driver. In the gorges below one could see the smashed miniatures of wrecked trucks in total stillness.

Andrei Milov, a chunky, round-faced, squat individual sporting a half-digested stump of a cigar, was the construction manager. He greeted Johnny enthusiastically as they both stood ankle deep in mud, surveying the town. The veteran's heavy growth of black beard complemented his disheveled hair and rough general appearance. "Welcome, Comrade, to Camp 6," he remarked between gusts of rising cigar smoke. "You no doubt like the new homes you see completed or under way?" he continued, as Johnny assured him that he did. Each residence was made of bricks and wood and contained many large rooms. The roofs, stretching to high peaks, were built to withstand snowfall.

"Do not be deceived by the wrapping until you've seen the gift," Andrei said, as they crossed the road to enter the first unoccupied house. Stepping into the structure, Johnny exclaimed in distress, "My God!" The shoddy workmanship was beyond belief. "Now you understand, Comrade. What I say is true," the foreman added, following his guest's initial gasp of surprise. "Crooked walls, Comrade, doors off center, bent beams, knotted floor boards, and walls that don't come flush with the roof," he continued. "This is only a part of what I have to live with daily."

Johnny studied a window frame, crooked as a dog's hind leg. It gradually sloped from one tight base corner to the other, with a one-inch gap between the sill and the casing. He slipped his fingers through the opening to the outside with ease. "This is finished?" Johnny queried, amazed and angered by the other's matter-of-fact attitude of complacency and unconcern.

"Yes," came Andrei's glum reply. "It's finished and so are many more like this." Johnny looked at the man, feeling surely that he spoke in jest, for no reputable construction foreman would ever stamp his approval on such a blatant mess as this. It was an amateurish attempt at building.

"Damn it, man!" Johnny shouted. He asked how such a thing could happen right under the foreman's very nose. Then came his order to call the men back to work, rip down the place, and start again. Calling the man a nitwit, Johnny stated that children could do a better job. He then wanted to know if he was going to have to show him the proper way to build homes that people could live in.

Andrei's eyes narrowed as he looked Johnny full in the face, his gloved hands now clenched. "I know construction like the back of my hand, Comrade, and no, I do not tolerate sloppy work or poor construction." De Graaf and Andrei Milov contemplated each other through clenched teeth. Andrei continued, "Comrade, here things do not proceed as in Moscow. We are given a specific lumber allotment, by board size, for each home. We try to make green boards straight, to stretch five-foot planks to six feet [1.52 to 1.83 m] and cut out bad knots to make solid boards. The plans have to be followed, but the materials are short, inferior, and green. Besides, they are not enough to complete even the basic work required. I've complained to the state lumber camp, Comintern people in Moscow, and everyone else but have gotten nowhere," Andrei said. "They all shift the blame, and the Comintern says we must be wasting materials, for they have it all worked out to the last board in their budget. We've installed heating pipes but have no furnaces. Plumbing gets connected to nothing. They say they shipped toilets, sinks, and tubs, but they sure never came this way. Comrade, you're new here. You'll see what I mean."

Johnny capped his anger as they went from room to room, house to house, witnessing the stark facts, the bureaucratic bumbling, and the effort at local salvage. Both men remained silent after the tour. They continued to Andrei's wooden bunkhouse, desperately seeking to get warm before the glowing pot-bellied stove in the center of his sparse surroundings. The foreman showed Johnny to a room of his own where a battered spring bed joined a roughly made three-drawer dresser and cigarette-burned night table boasting a dusty oil lamp. A little, ill-fitting window crying to be cleaned looked out between dingy curtains to the mud, rock, and forest beyond. The weather had turned foul.

Over a meal of black bread, gruel, and cucumber, tossed down with gulps of vodka, de Graaf quizzed his host well into the evening. It was a personal, almost tearful, conversation, in which Andrei revealed his innermost frustrations with the bureaucracy that kept him in a straightjacket. Upset and troubled by it all, Johnny had problems sleeping that night. The incompetence of the situation made up his mind for him. He would raise hell like never before and shake up a few idiot officials about this inherited mess.

The following morning both men set out for the whistle-stop on two saddled horses. They could have taken a truck from the mine except that the two trucks due in never appeared. A third truck, fully loaded with coal, had broken down with a bent axle not far from the camp. This meant that horses were the only way out. Most of the day was thus spent in the saddle, the animals tiring but patient as they surefootedly held the road and avoided the pitfalls. Darkness smoked in as the animals and men reached the rail station out in the middle of nowhere. Once the horses had been fed and quartered in a shed, Johnny and Andrei entered the station to await the train's late arrival. A solitary railroad worker joined them before the stove as the travelers munched on bread and small sausages.

Hours later they were aboard the slow freight train, heading to the nearest city, the community where the wood shipments originated. Daybreak found them walking the deserted streets, waiting for the lumberyard to open. When the gates were unlocked, a two-hour encounter with the lumber agent did not solve the camp's building predicament. Demands only resulted in his requisitions, showing that he had shipped as per the Moscow instructions. When Johnny and Andrei showed him the blueprints of the homes he shook his head, acknowledging that his supplies came nowhere near the actual material needs. The man hid behind his orders, and although he was sympathetic to the problem in Kharkov, he could offer no assistance more than to say that he would take the case to those who issued him his guidelines. The men got the same story at the plumbing and heating supply yard, where a thin, malnourished manager regretted the delay in toilets and basins but stated that he could not ship what he did not have. His trouble lay with the manufacturing works in Stalingrad, from which he often waited for up to a year for needed items.

Andrei and Johnny left, fed up, and caught a truck back to the rail stop. There, de Graaf wired Comintern headquarters in Moscow, asking them to send a committee planner down so he could obtain action from his end. They hopped the first freight train and at dawn lurched into the station where their horses were quartered. Alighting from a boxcar, both men ate something at the station and then saddled the horses for the long trip back to Camp 6. In their absence, a cold rain had fallen, adding to the construction problems by turning the rough roads into slippery quagmires. Because of the weather, construction slowed to a snail's pace, as essential supplies could only be brought in at increased risk. In a matter of days, work came to a standstill.

A week later a few trucks rumbled in, two with supplies and several loaded with new German residents who were not expected until everything was complete. "Comrade, we are not halfway ready to house these workers," de Graaf complained to the transport leader. "See for yourself; you were not due until all was ready."

"That's not my problem," he retorted. "I just follow orders, like you, and when they said, come here with these people, I came." Johnny scribbled a wire to Moscow, explaining the situation, which the man agreed to send from the railhead.

They hastily set up a temporary command center with the assistance of Andrei, some of his workers, and Igor, the mine manager. In this way they started to bring a little order to the bundle-laden Germans. The new arrivals were dispatched in groups to the so-called completed homes in order to get them out of the cold. Several families would have to bunk together until the remaining homes could be completed. After that, Johnny, Andrei, and the assistants entered the lightly stocked storehouse and began emptying it of blankets and other critical supplies. Each item was dispersed as fairly as possible. Johnny felt sorry for these uprooted volunteers, who now realized that the place in which they had been deposited was far from the worker's paradise they had been promised. All day and well into the evening, everyone in the camp's administration toiled to somehow feed, house, and help the Germans. Exhausted, the managers finally fell asleep, one after the other, fully clothed beside the stove in Andrei's quarters, while outside swirled the first snowflakes of the Russian winter.

Not unexpectedly, the morning brought additional problems, as the mine foremen rounded up the new workers and trudged them down the glossy slopes to the white-draped pits. Andrei disappeared to supervise his builders while de Graaf remained to deal with a horde of angry housewives. The women had long lists of complaints, which were the same as those that angered him on his own arrival. Making note of each difficulty, he traveled through the mud and snow from home to home, cooling tempers with assurances that they were working on the various problems. That evening Andrei and Johnny pored over the grievances, trying to find short-term solutions until Moscow got off the pot. Despite the specifications, they ultimately agreed to build the remaining dwellings properly, forsaking numbers for fewer, smaller, but better-built homes.

The following day, the village children collected forest moss for chinking the gaps and holes in the finished structures. This helped to keep out the cold winds and drafts. A week later, everyone was ecstatic over the arrival of a truck with two dozen pot-bellied stoves. The driver had somehow scrounged them from an army supply depot 150 miles (241.4 km) from Kharkov. Johnny did not ask how he accomplished this feat but gave him a bottle of vodka for his efforts. Andrei's men quickly assembled the black iron units, using plumbing pipes from the unfinished buildings as stacks and flues. The loss of these pipes was not viewed as a tragedy, since there were no tubs or toilets to which they could be connected. Several more trucks soon got through. They carried additional lumber, food, and handheld metal washbasins. All the same, Johnny's delight turned to anger as he read a Comintern telegram handed to him by one of the drivers. It read, "All construction supplies according to our specifications should be on site. Assured plumbing was sent months ago. See no new need for further assistance at this end." Johnny swore at this blind stupidity, immediately dispatching another, more strongly worded cable to the capital. There they sat in Moscow, warm, well fed, and comfortable, pushing paper, while their ineptness caused chaos. He cursed them and the Soviet system that had created them.

In the meantime, construction of the outhouses commenced with lumber meant for new homes. Slowly the workers built their own version of new family dwellings, which relieved some of the congestion but did little to ease low morale among the German workers. A few mothers who had been schoolteachers were located, and, with the limited number of textbooks the children brought with them, a school was started in one of the houses.

Igor complained to Johnny one day that his new workers were certainly not the best from the Ruhr Valley. He felt that the Comintern in Berlin had sent all its dissidents and problems to the Donbass. Igor found most of the men unskilled and troublesome, clashing often without cause with their Soviet counterparts. Two nights passed, and a fight developed outside the administration facility.

Johnny watched the number of onlookers growing. Before a riot developed, he went out among the Soviets and Germans and told them to drop their clubs and go to their lodgings. A large German miner, pick in hand, came forward to meet him, promising he would flatten de Graaf. When he was about six feet (1.83 m) away, Johnny took out his revolver and commanded him to let go of the pick or he would not hesitate to put a bullet between his eyes. The man stopped in his tracks, swore, let the tool fall, and turned around and headed home. The others followed. Johnny was the only armed person at Camp 6. He made sure his gun was with him at all times. That was the first and last time he had to draw the weapon. Thereafter, his presence alone quelled fights. Opponents knew the odds were in the man from Moscow's favor.

Objections about food were a continual problem, as Russian black bread and cucumbers for breakfast did not agree with German tastes. German palates were accustomed to German bread and thick sausage. Several months passed before a Comintern official arrived and de Graaf had the opportunity to argue this point rather than just send telegrams. Johnny elaborated for the individual that all this should have been taken into account before the project began. The representative met this criticism with a tirade. "Those bloody no-good Germans can eat our food or starve!" he expounded in a temper tantrum. Andrei bore the brunt of the next harangue, which occurred when the bureaucrat took a look at the attempts at makeshift housing. Despite the efforts to explain their problems with materials and lack of equipment, the man would not listen, sputtering, "The plans laid down have not been followed."

For two days, a heated discussion took place, as the official from the capital toured the Juny Commune. Johnny and his crew defended their actions. But the official continued to block out explanations. He repeatedly shouted, "You did not follow the plan!" He was informed that the plan was wrong, but this too made no impact on his thinking. Finally, leaving in a huff, he caught a truck back to the railroad, conveying to those he left behind that they were in big trouble. Johnny and the others hoped his report would be so damning that they would be relieved and sent home. They had had enough.

As the summer passed, Johnny was ordered to travel some 350 kilometers (roughly 217 miles) past Kiev to Shepetovka. This was a Ukrainian train station near the border with Poland. His task was to head the welcoming committee for German families coming into the USSR to work on one-year contracts. It was a festive affair, with music and flags waving in the breeze as the special train pulled in from the west. It took a while for all the people on board to leave the carriages and assemble for further instructions. Johnny's welcoming remarks were short and to the point. "Perhaps some of you will not find what you imagined. But everyone must cooperate in the realization of the five-year plan."[29] On another trip to Shepetovka, he told a smaller group, "Don't think that roast fowl will fly into your mouths, but rather that you came to cooperate in the larger goal of construction."[30] Then the trains and trucks would leave with the workers and their families for the assigned mines. The journey to the Donbass usually took a day, while those traveling on to the Kuzbass region might need more than a week.

On August 2, 1930, Maria, Johnny Jr., Oscar, and Marianne all arrived at Shepetovka to be met by Johnny. They traveled together back to the Juny Commune.[31] The arrival of de Graaf's family, however, had no effect on the problems at Juny. Johnny could not afford to spend much time with them, since things continued to be done in a slipshod manner. Johnny trekked from one camp to the other, attempting to improve the lot of the workers and what they were producing. As if this was not enough, the electric current would go out at unexpected times, hygiene was spotty, and there were cases of typhoid fever.[32] Sometimes miners had only cold-water showers after coming up out of the ground following a shift. Oscar de Graaf remembered that his father ran around so much that he only saw him twice while he was there. On the first occasion, Johnny arrived to make sure the showers had hot water. The second time was a visit. Whenever possible, Oscar's father ate with the workers and their families. Laborers ribbed Johnny about this more than once. One tongue-in-cheek joke went, "Okay, now you eat cucumbers with us, but we don't know what you eat in Moscow."[33]

It was but another of the endless food complaints. In fact, the grumbling never really ended. Even with Johnny trying to be fair by presiding as judge over personal disputes at the local Comradeship Court, the criticism continued.[34] Many Germans, at least half of the original four or five thousand, applied to the German consul and received permission to return to Germany because of bad living conditions in the USSR. Others left because they heard rumors that things had gotten better under Hitler. Those who stayed but who later returned to Germany usually did so once the Stalinist Terror got under way in the spring of 1937. The last stragglers were expelled by the NKVD just before the start of the German invasion of the USSR in June 1941. Some Germans stayed throughout the war, working as virtual slave laborers.[35]

Johnny learned that in other such camps, the bulk of the newcomers stayed only a short time and then turned around and headed back to Germany. Maria was tougher. She was also married to Johnny. But once her year's contract was up, with little sight of her husband, she too packed up and left. Maria and the children stayed with Gustav and Emilie Krüger in Berlin for a month before arriving back in Ahlen on October 3, 1931. Johnny had asked the Krügers to take care of his family on their return. He felt bad that they had been party to another disaster.[36]

Given the periodic exoduses, the camp had too few people, but it limped along, waiting for key supplies that never arrived. Late one afternoon in the third week of February 1931, a truck stopped de Graaf as he rode a gray mare down the main village road in Kharkov.[37] "Here, Comrade Johnny," the weary driver shouted, leaning out his cab window. "I hope it's good news." He handed Johnny a telegram and sat gazing at him from behind the wheel as de Graaf tore the envelope open. Excitedly, he scanned the brief message, which read, "Eleven o'clock Friday" and was signed by Berzin in Moscow. "Good news, Comrade?" the driver asked.

"Excellent news, my friend," de Graaf replied. "I leave today for Moscow."

"I'm glad for you, Comrade Johnny," the driver said with delight. "You have worked hard here and deserve a long rest."

Andrei, Igor, and other friends wished Johnny well as he hurriedly got his things together. Soon the Juny Commune disappeared as a truck sped him to the rail stop to catch a train. De Graaf was to learn later that one year later only six Germans remained at the mine villages of the nine hundred who had first arrived. The Soviets could only blame themselves for the failure. Johnny would long remember the experience. It taught him to make do with nothing but determination and ingenuity. Afterward, an engineer with whom Johnny had battled in connection with the camp was executed by a firing squad. It was dubiously said that the man had been involved with the first Comintern director, Gregory Zinoviev, and Moscow party chief Lev Kamenev in a plot against Stalin.[38]

General Berzin laughed when he heard about de Graaf's clashes with the Comintern. "We knew it wouldn't be easy, Johnny," he explained. It was perhaps at this point that Berzin informed Johnny that he had been transferred from the KPD to the Всесоюзная Коммунистическая партия (большевиков) (that is, the ВКП[б], or VKP[b] in Roman letters). This honor was not bestowed lightly. Johnny had been made a member of the All-Union Communist Party (Bolsheviks), the Communist Party in the USSR, as member no. 2173673.[39] Berzin undoubtedly congratulated de Graaf, and Johnny must have feigned delight. Following the pleasantries, he was again assigned to Langner over at the Comintern. This time, de Graaf was sure, things would be different.

For the next six weeks Johnny was educated in the ways of the Comintern. He was even given a new Comintern code name, "Comrade August." Especially important in his schooling was how the Comintern tried to organize cells within the military in capitalist nations and demoralize the soldiers they could not organize. As part of his responsibilities, de Graaf examined Langner's files and estimated that there were approximately two hundred agents in the field. These operatives were not identified in the records. Some were "legals," or covered by diplomatic immunity, such as Langner had been in Bern, while others were "illegals," that is, operatives without any protection at all.

Finally, Langner summoned Major de Graaf to his office through an official phone call. "At last," Johnny thought, "the promised foreign assignment!" If his hunch was right, he would be able to escape the Soviet system once and for all.

FIG. 1 Mitscherlich Straße about the time that Johnny left home. The de Graafs' apartment building is the second from the corner on the left side of the street, with an awning shielding the entrance. The group on the left might well be made up of Johnny (the tallest youth), his sisters, all of his brothers except the recently born Walter, and their father. The adult male, after image enhancement, appears to be wearing pince-nez glasses.

FIG. 2 The *Niobe* under sail.

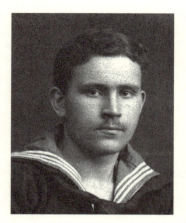

FIG. 3 A probable photograph of Johnny de Graaf in 1914 in the Kaiserliche Marine.

FIG. 4 The battleship *Westfalen* before the Great War.

FIG. 5 Part of the Osowiec Fortress.

FIG. 6 Willy de Graaf, Albert Funk, and Johnny de Graaf (left to right) in a photograph taken on August 13, 1921, in Ahlen. It has the following inscription on the back: "Dedicated to the three Spartanists." Willy eventually became a Nazi. Albert was murdered by the Gestapo at Recklinghausen in the 1930s.

FIG. 7 The mines in Ahlen.

FIG. 8 Ruth Fischer.

FIG. 9 Karl Radek in 1923.

FIG. 10 Arthur Ernst Ewert.

FIG. 11 Maria de Graaf (standing, second from the left), wearing a white collar and gray dress, in a partially damaged photograph. She is together with her son, Oscar de Graaf (kneeling on the left). Along with other comrades, they are at a KPD rally in 1929.

FIG. 12 Horst Wessel depicted on the cover of the sheet music to "Die Fahne Hoch," or "Horst Wessel Lied."

FIG. 13 Tuure Lehén, alias Alfred Langner, in a Soviet army uniform in the early 1940s.

FIG. 14 Peteris Ķuzis, alias Ian Karlovich Berzin.

FIG. 15 Dmitri Manuilski.

FIG. 17 Johnny de Graaf, sometime between 1930 and 1934.

FIG. 16 Johnny de Graaf, sometime between 1930 and 1932.

FIG. 18 Johnny de Graaf in 1932 on his mission to the United Kingdom.

FIG. 19 Béla Kun.   FIG. 20 Harry Pollitt.   FIG. 21 George Aitken in 1944.

FIG. 22 From left to right, Marianne and Oscar de Graaf with Helena Krüger, during Helena's June 1933 trip to Ahlen.

FIG. 23 Frank Foley's August 1939 passport photograph.

FIG. 24 Valentine Terrell Patrick Vivian at the races on March 21, 1930.

FIG. 25 Manfred Stern in 1932.

FIG. 26 Eugene Dennis, alias Comrade Milton, in May 1950.

FIG. 27   Luís Carlos Prestes in 1934, before leaving Moscow for Brazil.

FIG. 28   Getúlio Vargas (foreground), with his police chief, Filinto Müller, on July 27, 1940.

FIG. 29   Alfred Hutt in 1937.

FIG. 30   Johnny de Graaf in 1935.

FIG. 31   Helena Krüger in early 1936.

FIG. 32 The bomb that did not explode in the house on Rua Barão da Torre.

FIG. 33 Johnny's bomb factory in Grajaú, after it was discovered by the police.

FIG. 34 The last known photograph of Helena Krüger, taken in San Martín in 1937.

FIG. 35 The house at Calle Florida 246, and the upstairs bedroom where Helena Krüger died.

FIG. 36   Stella Blagoeva.

FIG. 37   Vyacheslav Molotov.

FIG. 38   Kliment Voroshilov.

8

ASSIGNMENT ROMANIA

Langner informed Johnny that his first foreign mission would be in the Balkans.[1] He was to leave in early April 1931. Berzin added that for M4, his job was to organize Communist cells against the Romanian army. In addition, he was to obtain an outline of the pipelines at the Ploesti refinery, some thirty-five miles (56.3 km) north of Bucharest.

Johnny was given half a year's salary, US$1,200, plus another US$500 by Abramov (or a total of US$23,277 in 2009 dollars),[2] and told to pick up twenty thousand Austrian shillings in Vienna. The Soviets always paid him inside the USSR in American currency. Langner likewise handed Johnny the typed details of a fake German passport and told him to memorize the particulars of his new identity and then return the notice to OMC. He would pick up the passport when he got to Berlin. The name on his new travel documents was Ludwig Dinkelmeyer, a mining engineer. He left Moscow on a train bound for the German capital using a different Swiss passport.[3]

Secure in his compartment for two days, Johnny had lots of time to think as the vast fields of western Russia and then Poland flashed past the window. His Москва-Брлин (Moscow-Berlin) train had the usual corridor down one side of the coach opposite the various compartments in each car. Soon tired of sitting, he slid open the door to his compartment and went for a stroll in the outside walkway. As de Graaf passed a man who stood staring out the window, the individual suddenly turned and said, "Have a good time, Johnny." Startled, de Graaf froze momentarily, then looked back to see the grinning face of General Alex. It was the unpopular instructor who had told his classes never to break the iron rule of espionage—on no account recognize or speak to a fellow agent in the field as if you know them. Flashing surprise, an inner voice in Johnny's mind rang out, "Nail him!" Alex was fortunate that Johnny usually made fast decisions.

Calm replaced his irritation as he replied in German, "I'm terribly sorry, sir. I don't understand you. What are you talking about?"

If he was shocked by Johnny's reply to his stupid greeting, it was impossible to tell, because General Alex shut up tight, gave his former pupil an angry glance, and abruptly walked off. He had a compartment in the same car, where he remained until he got off somewhere along the way. Johnny never saw him again during the rest of the trip. He knew that Alex would report him.[4] He could only hope that the general's account would contain a semblance of truth, or else some lie that his own version would expose. Of course, the incident could have been a test of his loyalty, whether to the USSR, to what he had been taught, or both.

In Berlin he sought out his connection, Paul Wilhelm,[5] at a tobacco store in the Wedding suburb. At a nearby café, Johnny exchanged his Swiss passport for the German one in the name of Dinkelmeyer and proceeded to secure the necessary visa from the Romanian Embassy. As soon as it was issued, he took a train to Vienna and met his new contact, identified only as "Alois." This get-together took place at Alois's home, where de Graaf picked up the Austrian currency in a sealed envelope. The next day at first light, Johnny was on the platform in the cold waiting for his train to Bucharest.[6]

Easing into the Romanian capital the following morning, he left the Gară train station, followed his memorized instructions, and checked into the designated hotel in downtown Bucharest. His Romanian party contact appeared an hour later with a light knock on Johnny's hotel room door. No doubt he had watched the VKP(b) man's arrival and followed him far enough to realize that he had the right individual by comparing a photo provided by the Comintern. On opening the door, Johnny was greeted by a bald, middle-aged, tubby individual.

"You stay for a long while?" the man inquired.

"Only for nightfall, minutes away," de Graaf replied. This coded exchange confirmed the contact, and Johnny let him in. He recited two phone numbers, one that Johnny should call in a week's time; the other would be available twenty-four hours a day in case of an emergency. After a brief rundown on the military situation, code words for the phone, and a handshake, the man left. The visitor knew nothing of Johnny, and Johnny knew nothing of him. In this way, if either man was arrested, he could not turn in the other.

Johnny waited two hours after his contact's departure and then checked out, informing the front desk that he had a sudden change of plans due to a family illness. Bag in hand, he walked the side streets until a "room for rent" sign in a window caught his attention. The owner of the home was an elderly Austrian widow, very kind and pleasant, who showed Johnny a comfortable bed/sitting room upstairs, which suited his needs perfectly. He explained that he was a mining engineer from Germany on vacation, in between sentences of her own informing him that her late husband had been a military officer killed during

World War I. She was a frail, gray-haired lady of medium height and proved to be noninquisitive. The room she rented Johnny had a large window overlooking the street below that let in the light in warm rays. Johnny would eat all his meals in cafés and restaurants, as the arrangement with the woman was for a room only.

In the morning, Johnny presented himself before the *Siguranza,* the seedy Romanian political police. They required that all foreigners register with them within twenty-four hours of arrival. De Graaf fed them the mining engineer story and produced documents to back it up. They could also tell he was a miner because of his slight blue blemish above his right cheek. It was all rather perfunctory. Duly registered, Johnny proceeded on his way.

A week passed during which he contacted no one. He usually read in his room or ventured out to eat or stroll around the city, taking in the sights. Soldiers passed by in shabby, frayed uniforms and dilapidated boots. Poorly paid and ridiculed in public by their superior officers, these excuses for a fighting force were ripe for revolution. At one point Johnny was sitting on a bench in downtown Cişmigiu Gardens,[7] noted for its beauty, when he saw an officer stop a passing soldier. Whatever was said between them he could not hear, but out of the blue the officer struck the enlisted man across the face, knocking him to the ground. Johnny immediately jumped to his feet, went over, and unleashed his temper on the officer. He informed him that his treatment of the recruit would be published in the *Manchester Guardian* in Britain. The man of rank and responsibility swore at de Graaf and gave him a filthy look before quickly leaving the park. The recruit on the ground got up and ran off. Further down the pathway, three soldiers were arguing about some picture with a photographer. It appeared that one of the men did not have enough cash for a picture that had just been taken. Johnny approached the irate photographer and told him to take three pictures in duplicate and he would pay for them. An officer passed by while this was taking place. Across his face was clearly written contempt for this interloper who was helping enlisted men. But Johnny could not help but feel sorry for these poor devils. They were only ordinary soldiers, as he had been years before in the Kaiserliche Marine.

One day, de Graaf traveled to a villa near Bucharest to meet a man who assisted the Comintern from time to time. The Comintern called such a person "the man between." Following a recognition signal, Johnny introduced himself to this middleman as "Julius." He was subsequently taken to a chap de Graaf remembered only as "Junescu" (probably an alias for Eugen Iacobovici), acting general secretary of the Partidul Comunist Român, the PCR, or Romanian Communist Party.[8] A couple of days later, appointments were made for de Graaf to meet in public places with two members of the undersized and illegal PCR, which had been forced to go underground in 1924. These two comrades would assist Johnny in carrying out his mission.

Not trusting indoor phones, de Graaf placed a call one evening from an outdoor telephone to the first of the PCR contacts.[9] On hearing a female voice, he spoke in German. "The weather is nice for a swim in the Black Sea if you're free," he said.

"The sun will be the warmest at noon tomorrow," came her soft reply. They hung up. From then on both Johnny and his contact could never be fooled. They remembered each other's voice, and code words were not necessary. To the best of his knowledge the Romanian police did not tap phones then, but later he did have his suspicions. Johnny played it safe in any case. It could have been this night or another, but one evening as he was walking in the streets of Bucharest, he heard someone say something directly to him as he passed—in Russian. He continued without looking in the person's direction. It could have been one more test, if indeed General Alex had been testing him on the train. He felt that had he looked in the direction of the voice this time, the Comintern would have killed him for revealing his identity.[10]

Johnny and his new contact met the following noon at Constanța on the Black Sea, some two and a half hours by rail from Bucharest. Johnny knew her as Paulina, but Cornelia was almost certainly her real name. Like the first Romanian contact, she was aware of Johnny's features and spotted him easily. Speaking to de Graaf in a casual way, and hearing his reply, Paulina understood that she had the right person. She was a slender, attractive girl in her early twenties, with dark brown hair and nicely proportioned. But unfortunately she was run down physically and at about five foot two or five foot three (1.58 or 1.60 m) appeared to weigh slightly less than one hundred pounds (45.5 kg).[11] Johnny plunged into the water and swam quite a distance from shore. Finally he flipped over and proceeded to float on his back. Paulina edged away from the crowded beach and swam out and joined him, well away from prying ears and informers. Bobbing alongside Johnny, she began relating all the military and political information in her possession on Romania's current state of unrest.

As a result of his own observations and from what Paulina told him, de Graaf came to the conclusion that the PCR needed a large number of improvements. Comrade Béla Kun,[12] party secretary for the Balkans, appeared to be the main problem. He concentrated too much on the prestige of his office and his own power designs. A Hungarian, Kun neglected internal grassroots improvements in the countries that were his responsibility. The result was a lack of direction, a great number of squabbles, and stifled growth. In Romania this produced discontent among the PCR's rank and file, along with possible informers—all spelling trouble. Good local leadership was there, but it lay dormant and without purpose through neglect and a restrictive chain of command. In addition, US$500 in party funds, sent from the Comintern in Moscow for donation to local schools for equipment purchases, somehow disappeared. Béla Kun was a disgrace to the PCR and to the Communist movement in general. Johnny reasoned that something had to be done.

Paulina had a fantastic memory for details and events. This highly intelligent woman never ceased to amaze de Graaf with her knowledge, purpose, and drive. Yet she still retained her femininity. He could see why she had been selected as his local agent, for without doubt she must have been trained in Moscow. After they reached shore, she gave him a secret copy of a party booklet soon to be distributed at military bases. His replica was in German. He was told that he could add, delete, or revise the propaganda in it as he saw fit, in order to make it more effective prior to release.

Johnny and Paulina agreed to meet again at the beach in Constanţa three days later. He would arrive first and swim out as before, and she would join him. Johnny returned to his room and began to work on the booklet. Days later, following their second swimming rendezvous, they met at a small, safe restaurant close to the beach. Over lunch de Graaf slipped Paulina the revised booklet. Presently, Junescu brought a man Johnny knew only as Saul to meet him. Saul would organize Communist cells within the Romanian armed forces.[13]

Johnny was introduced as Hans to this Romanian World War I veteran. At the time of their meeting, Saul was a spinner in a wool mill in Kišin'ov, Bessarabia. The Romanian Central Committee had evidently decided that he was the person for the job because of his wartime experience. Johnny took him to Constanţa. Renting a skiff, he told Saul to travel by land to Eforie Sud, a village farther south along the coast. He would then sail down and meet him. At the appointed rendezvous, de Graaf picked Saul up and instructed him for a period of about three days in the art of forming Communist cells. They split up and returned separately to Bucharest but continued to meet on an almost weekly basis. About three months later, the Romanian had five or six Communist cells functioning in the army barracks outside the capital.

Junescu also sent Johnny two additional men to be trained in espionage activities. Evidently they were not known as Communists to the secret police. De Graaf was introduced to them both, at different times, as Comrade Julius. This was a mistake, which would be pointed out to him when he returned to Moscow. Normal routine called for a different name with each man.

Both men were taken to the village where King Carol II had a summer resort. The PCR arranged in advance for their accommodations in a farmhouse. For twelve days Johnny instructed the two novice agents in the organization of an elementary espionage apparatus, in the use of codes, and in the necessity of methods for maintaining rigorous security measures. At the conclusion of the instruction, he gave each individual five thousand shillings. He was later told that one of them had succeeded in acquiring the blueprints to the Ploeşti oil fields;

the other, through a contact in a print shop, managed to obtain copies of the directives issued by the Romanian General Staff, hot off the presses. This gave the Soviets a duplicate version of the country's highest military orders even before most Romanian officers received them. Both men were eventually found out and picked up by the secret police. One ended up committing suicide by jumping from a fourth-story window after being threatened with torture. The other did not have even that option. He was beaten to death for his involvement. Johnny was also informed that both agents were eventually declared heroes of the Romanian working class. He never knew their real names. The source of the blueprints for the Ploesti complex was a Communist sympathizer, the director of the facility.[14]

Paulina and her counterpart from Moscow met five days later on the Black Sea. As he had done with Saul, on this occasion, too, de Graaf rented a boat, but this time Paulina swam out and joined him. Johnny continued to be captivated by this highly efficient Romanian. He saw her as a valued agent whose worth to the local party as a translator was immeasurable. Their rendezvous had to be limited, because paid informers often reported to the secret police meetings that took place in parks, shops, and restaurants within city limits. No one was certain who could be trusted. Discussions in seclusion were the only safe policy to follow, and even they had to be brief. During one such meeting, Johnny gave Paulina money for a new dress. This unexpected gift delighted her.

Returning to his rooming house, Johnny discovered that the proprietor had a surprise for Herr Dinkelmeyer as well. She told him that while he was out, two mining engineers had come looking for him and had asked her if she knew where he was. She told them no, but that he was a very nice gentleman who was there on a holiday and was very interested in coal mining. She knew little about de Graaf other than what he had told her. "Does he receive letters?" they had inquired. "No" she replied, "but he writes them." "Do you know to whom?" they probed. She said she had seen only one letter, which her tenant had left unfinished. She thought that it was to a lady. This short letter was, in fact, to one of the Krüger sisters back in Berlin, containing nothing but Johnny's best wishes to them and their family. The visitors asked that she inform de Graaf that they would pay him a visit the following day at 2:00 P.M. Johnny knew they were from the *Siguranza*.

Johnny thanked the lady for her information and went upstairs to his room, which he found undisturbed. This abrupt development bothered him, and he considered the question whether he should move. But he rapidly rejected this idea; the *Siguranza* no doubt had the house under surveillance. Even if they were not waiting outside, by suddenly bolting he would only increase their suspicions. Ludwig Dinkelmeyer stayed put.

Promptly at 2:00 P.M. the next day, two well-dressed men in business suits, both speaking German, knocked on Johnny's door and presented themselves. To their first question, as to how the man they had come to see liked Romania, he replied that he liked some things and disliked others, which was about the same reaction he had in every country. They discussed mining, and Johnny expressed an interest in seeing one of their coal mines. Astonished, they enthusiastically asked him to join them on a two-day visit to a large mine in Florety (now part of the Russian Federation), a community where the family of one of the agents lived. It was a good car ride to the north of Bucharest. "We would like to have your advice and opinion on how to improve production and cut down the mine's overhead," they told their guest.

Leaving in the morning by car, they made it to the mining city just as the sun was setting. The two agents offered to put Johnny up in a hotel, but he refused, stating that he preferred to take a room, like the workers. De Graaf had to be extremely careful in rejecting a hotel offer that a tourist normally would accept. He felt, however, that the hotel room would probably be bugged and under close observation. Johnny told them, "You don't have to spend any money on me in those big hotels. If you want to put me anywhere there's a bed, where I could get a good night's rest, it would be fine with me and save you money." They bought this explanation, and one of the agents drove him to his own home. He was put up in a very comfortable upstairs bedroom. Johnny met the man's pleasant wife and two little girls.

After dinner, while his wife tidied up and put the young ones to bed, Johnny and the Romanian political police agent chatted. They discussed the coal industry, the political situation in Europe, and many general topics. The policeman relaxed, as did de Graaf, both enjoying each other's conversation. Two days of touring followed, the men decked out in hardhats, boots, and coveralls. At the end of the tour, Johnny suggested several steps and shortcuts that would cut costs and increase production. Thanking the agent's wife for an agreeable stay, he was then driven back to his room in Bucharest. Both of the men from the *Siguranza* seemed to be convinced that he was only an informed, able mining engineer.

A short while later, Johnny received a note requesting that he visit the local police office to have his passport stamped. All the police personnel were most congenial as they greeted him. He received instant attention, as they speedily processed his papers and told him to check in again in two weeks. Before parting, Johnny was told that should he have any trouble with the law, locally or anywhere in the country, to let them know and they would take care of it. Johnny's mining escorts must have written him up in glowing terms, he concluded. Paulina, Johnny, and the two military men continued their collaboration. Johnny provided the armed services operatives with guidance in greater cell expansion, arms use, and the preparation and distribution of propaganda.

In the first years of Carol II's reign, strife had increased in the ranks at Romania's army bases. Officers, politicians, and the wealthy led luxurious lives, exactly the opposite of the nation's potential frontline troops. All of this was tempered on the anvil of European fascism, hammered home by Corneliu Zelea Codreanu and his anti-Semitic legionnaires. In 1930 Codreanu put together a group of paramilitary legionnaire units called the Iron Guards to fight Romania's fifteen-hundred-member Communist Party.[15] It was very ripe ground for planting the seeds of discontent and an eventual uprising.

By arrangement, Johnny met the political secretary and chief organizer of the PCR, a heavyset middle-aged man with a large scar above his right ankle. He traveled again to the beach to seek him out. Locating the man, de Graaf had him raise his pant leg, just to be sure. Satisfied, they rented a sailboat and headed a good distance out into the Black Sea. Over a picnic lunch they moved along in a gentle breeze. Johnny told the PCR representative what had been accomplished to date. All of this the man would later relate to Béla Kun. The relationship Johnny's sailing partner had developed with Béla Kun was awkward because neither man could agree on what Johnny was doing or on how they should go about organizing cells in the army.[16]

On top of everything else, de Graaf suspected that within his own group there was at least one spy. Countless times the *Siguranza* had been informed of PCR activities and rendezvous points, things known only to party members. Closely guarded secrets had leaked out. Johnny was even jailed briefly in early August 1931 on unknown charges, but a Russian managed to get him released.[17] A female party member was the main suspect. Johnny made arrangements for her to be closely shadowed by two trusted PCR associates, a man and a woman. These two agents were told to report only to de Graaf and he would pass on their findings to the PCR's Central Committee. A week later they provided concrete proof of this woman's contacts with the Romanian secret police.

Johnny presented the findings to a closed session of the Central Committee. The leadership decided to have her picked up, taken up into the mountains, and shot. Her body would be dropped off a cliff into the sea. The committee asked Johnny to handle this assignment, but he refused, saying, "Comrades, you are well aware I am not a coward, but I cannot bring myself to kill a woman. Please take this order off my hands and give it to another if you want it carried out." Because he was an M4 General Staff agent, they could not compel him to carry out a PCR command. Others were chosen who apprehended the girl, shot her, and tied her up with wire. Her body was then weighted with stone, so it would be a long while in surfacing from the deep. De Graaf wanted no part of it, nor did he witness the execution or burial at sea.

Two days remained of Johnny's stay in Bucharest, wrapping up various items of a military and political nature. His next stop would be a side trip, apparently to the community of Hunedoara. Arriving at the city's train station, he proceeded to look for accommodations, while obliquely checking out the area's military situation—the real purpose of his visit. Scanning the local newspaper, he ran across an interesting ad for a room for rent by an artillery major's wife. Hurrying to the address, he briefly chatted with the woman, saw the room, and took it on the spot, board included.

The major, a large, strapping, arrogant man, took a liking to Johnny, with the result that, throughout his stay, he was able to pick up much worthwhile information. He soon learned that, like many Romanian military officers, the major was supplied with two soldiers who acted as houseboys. These two men washed, cleaned, cooked, did the laundry, and performed every other household task imaginable. Johnny asked the major's wife, shortly after moving in, if she could direct him to a laundry. "Give it to me," she replied in excellent German. "The soldiers will wash and iron everything for you." De Graaf protested, but she insisted. That evening he had the opportunity to chat with the two conscripts, who informed him that the regiment provided officers with "chore aides." They received food and a very small salary for their efforts. Each man was under orders from the woman of the house as well as her officer-husband.

The amount of military information he obtained in this home was amazing. The aides and the family simply accepted him as a tourist. Then too, the major's wife was one of those people who talked nonstop—and de Graaf listened to every word. By asking harmless, carefully chosen questions he was able to gain quite a picture of the Romanian army.

The new PCR cells were working well and required limited advice. A short while later Johnny returned to Bucharest and made contact with Paulina so as to pass on his latest intelligence prior to departure. All information was conveyed to her, and to the party's district secretary, verbally. They repeated it back until they had it memorized. Later, the PCR typed out two copies, sending one to Béla Kun and the other to the Comintern in Moscow via courier. The Comintern, in turn, passed on a report to General Berzin.

Whenever de Graaf felt a mission was complete, he could just pack up and leave without any instructions to do so. Once he was released from jail that August, Johnny informed a few Romanian party officials that before long he was going on to Turkey. This was a signal. The PCR would convey Johnny's Turkish trip to the Comintern in Berlin. They would know he was really on his way back to Moscow via the German capital.

Dark, overcast skies and a light rain greeted Johnny on the day of his departure at Gară Station. He was about to board his train when someone came running down the platform, calling out in a loud voice for Dinkelmeyer. Without looking back, Johnny quickly boarded a carriage, ducked into the car's bathroom, and locked the door just as the train began to pull out. He never did find out what it was all about, thinking upon hearing his cover name shouted out that his assignment was about to go up in smoke. The problem could have been that he had mentioned to someone not in the PCR that he was in the oil business.[18] If they checked with the *Siguranza,* suspicions would have been raised immediately.

Leaving Bucharest, Johnny traveled first to Vienna for a short four-day vacation. Journeying on to Berlin, he contacted the Comintern's West European Bureau and exchanged his Dinkelmeyer passport for another. This highly efficient center made contact with all agents passing through Berlin. They provided operatives with all necessary documents and additional cash, and also received verbal reports for forwarding. They sent Johnny's duplicated mission report directly to M4, so that the verbal and written accounts acted as crosschecks.

Sometime after leaving the Berlin office, he went to the Polish consulate for a travel visa. A "clean contact," a German trained in the Soviet Union, was the sleeper agent there. The man served Moscow's infrequent and informal needs in his position as one of Warsaw's formal representatives. Not wanting to overstay his precarious welcome in Germany, Johnny boarded another train for Moscow the same evening, mailing a postcard to the Krügers before departure. He apparently did not visit them on this trip, but he knew they liked to be remembered. Without risk to them or himself, it was the best way, as he was still a wanted man in the Weimar Republic.

Reaching Belorusskaya Station in the second half of August 1931, de Graaf inserted a white handkerchief into his jacket pocket and was soon approached by another agent, who drove him directly to M4 headquarters and a meeting with Ian Berzin. Coming into Moscow by train, signals were always prearranged prior to a mission. Sometimes he would wear a flower or have a colored handkerchief, while on other occasions a piece of paper would be carried in his left hand. No introduction was necessary, for the transporting envoy was well versed in his role, as was the returning agent in his or hers. Because this had been a dual mission, M4 would see de Graaf first, followed by the Comintern, each for their debriefing and written report.

"So, Johnny, you netted a friend, or should I say a man you had a row with long ago, on this operation?" Berzin asked knowingly.

"Who?" Johnny asked, since he not had mentioned meeting General Alex on the train to anyone.

"You tell me," Berzin replied, smiling all the while. Somehow he had learned of the blabbing general. Johnny decided to put all his cards on the table, and he related the encounter without mentioning Alex by name.

"He calls himself an instructor for illegal work," Johnny said contemptuously. Berzin asked de Graaf the man's name, but Johnny replied that he would not say more. Berzin persisted, but Johnny continued to refuse, knowing that his superior could uncover the information easily through his many senior contacts in numerous departments. Johnny was certain that Ian had already discovered what he wanted and everything else General Alex had said on the matter prior to his own appearance in Moscow. Berzin and de Graaf left it at that for the moment.

As an M4 agent, Johnny would normally have checked in to the Novo Moskovskaya, across from Red Square, but following this trip he stayed at the Hotel Passage.[19] The day after his arrival, and following Berzin's orders, Johnny reported to Moscow's Comintern headquarters, where he talked with, among others, Pavel Vasiliev, the Comintern organizer. He was ushered into a large boardroom and seated across a table from all of the highest functionaries of Comintern, including Béla Kun. They were discussing de Graaf's report when Béla Kun abruptly got to his feet and began calling Johnny names, accusing him of being a thief. He claimed that the missing US$500 for school equipment had been sent to de Graaf. Béla Kun swore that he himself had remitted the money.

Irritation consumed Johnny. He told Béla Kun off, calling him a blatant liar. Johnny explained to the committee that his report was accurate, a document exposing graft, bribes, corruption, and misuse of party funds. Béla Kun jumped up and down until Johnny silenced him by paraphrasing Lenin to the effect that in Béla Kun's face one saw the ass of a Kulak, or middle-class farmer.[20] The party leaders were extremely annoyed by their Hungarian representative and the damning report. Johnny was fed up, too. He got up and walked out, going upstairs to Langner's office to wait for him to return. Silently fuming, Johnny's disgust was unexpectedly interrupted. Pavel Vasiliev had followed him.[21] Getting Johnny's attention, he said, "What you did below is understandable, but you cannot talk to the party secretaries that way."

"I can't?" Johnny shot back. "I just did, because I cannot sit and listen to lies when Béla Kun accuses party members of things that he did."

As Vasiliev tried to calm Johnny down, the men below were having quite a discussion. They sent word for Johnny to join them again. When he returned, he warned that one more insult out of Béla Kun, and he would leave. "You can present your complaint about me to the General Staff," he angrily told the Hungarian. Béla Kun stood up and apologized to Johnny, but he continued to maintain that he had sent the money. He was told to sit down by the committee chairman. Johnny often saw party members called up and accused of all sorts of things in this way. The leaders used such people as scapegoats to protect their power and control, thus eliminating the exposure of their own incompetence.

Years later, after completing another mission, the secretary of Agi-Prop, the Agitation and Propaganda Department, told Johnny about the fate of the two men he had met in Bucharest. These were the two who had been declared heroes of the Romanian working class. Johnny asked him if Béla Kun had had a hand in it. The Agi-Prop man looked at de Graaf solemnly but did not reply. Béla Kun was removed from power on September 4, 1936, arrested on June 28, 1937, and shot on August 29, 1938, for having worked for the Hungarian secret police and for disseminating propaganda contrary to the party line. It was said that he had also insulted Stalin.[22]

De Graaf had an enjoyable rest at the Hotel Passage while waiting for his next assignment. He visited the countryside and went to museums. One day Berzin called him to his office for a chat. "Are you satisfied, Comrade?" he asked.

"Satisfied with what?" Johnny replied.

Still playing tongue in cheek, Berzin went on, "Well, the man you liked so much, who broke the iron rule, has been dismissed from his post," he explained.

"That should result in saving agents' lives," de Graaf remarked without remorse, but he knew inside that it would be a while before General Alex would bother anyone again. When the two men finished talking, Johnny returned to his room at the Passage and to his sightseeing in the Soviet capital.

9

BRITISH MISSIONS

At the end of August 1931 a smiling Langner informed de Graaf of his next assignment. He would be sent to England. "A new experience for you, Johnny, and of major importance to us," said Langner, as de Graaf listened, all ears. "I've asked Comrade Pavel Vasiliev to join us today, since his people have a stake in this assignment as well." He gestured to Vasiliev, evidently unaware that he and Johnny had met several times before. Vasiliev, who was seated on one side of the office, nodded to Johnny in recognition. Also in the room was Dmitri Manuilski.[1]

For two solid hours the four men discussed the planned operation. Moscow felt that what was happening in Britain presented a golden opportunity. The government of Prime Minister J. Ramsay MacDonald was trying to deal with the debts run up during World War I by returing the country to the gold standard. Beginning in 1925, this produced a number of reductions in public spending. But with the stock market crash of 1929, which first helped the English pound and then hampered it as the American market dried up, more draconian belt tightening was scheduled for 1931. Higher taxes, reduced unemployment benefits, and wage reductions for civil servants—including the military—were part of the new proposal. As this pertained to the country's armed forces in the rigidly class-based society that was the United Kingdom in the 1930s, officers would suffer less of a pay cut than ordinary enlistees. In the Royal Navy, for example, a lieutenant commander would see a 3.7 percent reduction, whereas common seamen were scheduled to lose 25 percent of their already paltry wages. Sailors from the rank of petty officer on down aggressively opposed these parliamentary measures. Passage would mean a nightmare for sailors whose families already had to live on thin earnings.[2]

While Moscow was not yet aware of the proposed pay cuts, the "May Report," named after committee chairman Sir George May, had been out since July 31, 1931. In no uncertain terms it stated that to regain the confidence of foreign bankers and prop up the gold standard, the English government would have to save £120 million. The report ignored the fact that unemployment had shot up during the Great Depression, from 1.2 million in 1929 to 2.7 million by the fall of 1931. Implementing the measure outlined in the May Report was a recipe for disaster.[3]

Johnny's assignment was to assist George Aitken,[4] a leading member of the Communist Party of Great Britain, or CPGB. Using propaganda and agitation, their job would be to demoralize sailors in the Royal Navy to the point where they would start a mutiny. Aitken was taking a special course in Moscow at the time. Johnny would meet him prior to departure, and Aitken would follow Johnny to England a week later. De Graaf's cover name was Johanssen; he was to pose as a wine merchant of Swiss/Danish background but travel on a British passport. Berzin asked if Johnny would take the risk of traveling through Germany en route. Johnny had no apprehension about doing so and in fact thought this would add to his new cover. His route would take him from Moscow to Berlin and on to Hamburg. Herman Schubert, the general secretary of the Hamburg district KPD, would be his German contact. Schubert was instructed to provide Johnny with a sample case of wine and with business documents.[5] Vasiliev also knew of Schubert and said he could be most useful. Johnny was likewise warned that Harry Pollitt, the general secretary of the CPGB, was sending stories back to the USSR about the British party's antimilitary efforts in the United Kingdom. Moscow suspected that these stories were false; de Graaf was to evaluate their veracity.[6]

The next day, by prearrangement, Johnny met George Aitken and took an immediate liking for this red-faced, slightly portly man who knew Britain like the back of his hand. George was a member of the CPGB's Central Committee and gave every impression that his feet were solidly on the ground. He would later proudly fight with the International Brigade in Spain. Under the alias Alfred Mattern, Johnny would contact Aitken's wife after arriving in London, and she would assist him in locating safe accommodations.[7]

The following afternoon Johnny boarded a train for Berlin.[8] He got off in the German capital and stayed with the Krügers at their apartment at Papelallee 32 in Prenzlauer Berg. Gustav and Emilie Krüger persuaded Johnny to take their eldest daughter with him to England before he departed for Hamburg.[9] Even though he cared for her at first,[10] during the rest of the trip to London Johnny's mind could not leave the subject of escape from the Soviet Union. Here was a supreme opportunity, yet, as with the Romanian mission, he came away without his VKP(b) and former KPD identity cards. M4 made sure that all passes, identification, and documents were handed in before an agent left the USSR. It was an effective way to keep people from jumping ship. Johnny realized that he would have to build his bridges beforehand much more carefully.

Arriving in Hamburg, he quickly made contact with Herman Schubert, the police acquaintance he had known back in the Ruhr Valley, now the KPD district secretary. They met at a restaurant west of the Hauptbahnhof in the St. Pauli district, where Schubert advised Johnny that new passports would be ready in two days. Johnny and Helena stayed at the home of a local Communist Party member during the wait. Without asking any probing questions, a party courier arrived and delivered the false passport in the name of Herman Schneider. De Graaf was similarly given a wine sample case, business cards, and papers with a Hamburg company letterhead. Special documents attesting to his being a wine importer and exporter were also arranged.[11] From Hamburg they traveled by train to Copenhagen, then to Esbjerg on Denmark's west coast, where they boarded one of the ships that sailed each weekday to Harwich, England.[12] This was an easy way to leave Germany, and British customs presented no difficulty, barely glancing at his Soviet-fabricated English passport giving Johnny's name as Johanssen. De Graaf also had with him two German passports (one for Herman Schneider and another), a Finnish passport, and one from Switzerland.

Taking a cab from dockside, Johnny and Helena were driven the seventy-plus miles (112 km) into London to an appointed rooming house in Charing Cross. There Johnny called the newly arrived Aitken, who met him in a restaurant and took the couple on the Bakerloo tube line to a room with a Communist couple in Kenton known only as Milly and Billy. To ensure that they were safe, Johnny and Helena remained there overnight without venturing outside. Milly worked for Amtorg, the Soviet trade board in London. She spoke Russian and knew Johnny's name as well as his purpose for being in Britain. This indicated to de Graaf that the CPGB lacked sufficient security procedures, since she should not have known any of this. He later learned that she was disappointed in the entire Communist movement in the United Kingdom.[13] It was a potentially dangerous situation, especially if Milly had decided to turn in a comrade or if she had been arrested and grilled. Milly's change of heart was unknown to de Graaf when he and Helena first arrived.

Two days after settling in with the couple, Johnny accompanied Billy by tube to a physician's office near the Waterloo railroad station. De Graaf had to travel with Billy everywhere he went in London on orders from Aitken. Waiting for them at the doctor's office was William Rust, editor of the *Daily Worker,* Aitken, and the general secretary of the CPGB, Harry Pollitt. They gave Johnny a radiant account of the antimilitary work that had been going on in Britain. Aitken may have been only spouting the party line. Johnny thought Pollitt and Rust appeared nervous. Their collective report seemed exaggerated.[14]

Johnny wanted to see for himself. So Aitken took him to a basement below a cobbler's shop on Junction Road near Tufnell Park, where the *Soldier's Voice* was being printed.[15] The location had its own convenient entrance and exit from an unused alley. The shop could not have been better situated, as the business on the floor above constantly hummed with machinery that drowned out the sound of the press. When the noise upstairs stopped, the printing operation one flight down followed suit, only to start up again when the upstairs machines came back to life.

There was a young man present who worked the press. The youth advised Johnny that around five hundred copies of the *Soldier's Voice* were printed with each edition. This was a far cry from the figure of five thousand that Harry Pollitt assured Moscow were being produced. The freshly printed newssheets were bundled together and were often distributed by Aitken himself. Army and naval installations were his favorite targets, owing to contacts stationed within several barracks. Johnny personally went to the base at Aldershot. He managed to get copies to a hundred or so soldiers outside the post who were either party members or supporters. At other military facilities the CPGB threw bundles of the *Soldier's Voice* over the high-walled enclosures, hoping they would be scattered by the wind. Of course, the next morning, squads with fixed bayonets quickly cleaned up the papered grounds. A lot of the newspapers were destroyed in this way, but some were kept and passed around from hand to hand within the barracks and ports. Pollitt claimed that twenty-five hundred got through. De Graaf, however, counted only one or two newssheets as reaching the soldiers. In the Royal Navy, as well, Johnny found just one or two Communists but around forty sympathizers.[16]

Over the next three months, Johnny completely reorganized the distribution of the *Soldier's Voice*. Working for hours on end, Johnny, George, and some helpers at the printing press turned out mounds of literature. They soon had three fresh circulars coming out each week, the *Red Army,* the *Red Soldier,* and the most popular, the *Red Gun.*[17] These flyers carried editorials with banner headlines that took issue with various decisions at Westminster and in the military. Rust, over at the *Daily Worker,* contributed monthly articles. Readers were informed of progressive views and possible actions they could take on each critiqued situation—including the possibility of mutiny. The new tabloids were given to Communist dockworkers and placed in the lavatories aboard British naval vessels in Plymouth, Portsmouth, and Chatham. All of these attempts to promote working-class unrest, however, later led to the promulgation of the Incitement to Disaffection Act of 1934, which prohibited attempts to promote sedition in the military.[18]

Pollitt was receiving £30,000 a year from Moscow, and he was asking for another £5,000 for publication expenses. Johnny could tell that the CPGB leadership was keeping a fair amount of this money in reserve. At another meeting in the doctor's office, Pollitt insinuated that de Graaf would smear him once he returned to Moscow. Johnny denied this, saying that he would only tell the truth. To make his job more difficult, Johnny was in a motorcycle accident, apparently during this period of intense activity, requiring that he be hospitalized.[19]

Even before the medical center permitted his release, the CPGB was grappling with the membership issue. It stated that it had around forty-five hundred members by the end of the year,[20] but Johnny estimated only about two thousand weakly organized comrades. This changed later with a concerted effort. By the eve of World War II, the British party would reach a total of 17,539 adherents—and the dues they brought with them.[21] In the early 1930s, however, the party was miniscule and almost totally dependent on Moscow for funds. A few years earlier, when the Conservatives were in power and the country was in the throes of the 1926 general strike, Soviet labor unions supported the action with a £60,000 donation. The funds were accepted and likewise disappeared into the CPGB's coffers with nothing more than a word of thanks. That was all Moscow got out of it. They gained nothing then for the big donation, nor were they at the moment, in Johnny's opinion.

To let their officers and the admiralty know how difficult the proposed pay reductions would be in their branch of the military, sailors called a go-slow strike on the warships at anchor in the Cromarty Firth, in the northwest highlands of Scotland. These vessels made up the bulk of Britain's Atlantic fleet. The action lasted from September 11, 1931, until the order was given to disperse all ships to their home ports on September 16. The press was effectively muzzled, which caused the Invergordon Mutiny, as the disturbance came to be called, to seem larger to outsiders than it really was.[22] The naval unrest had been organized not by the British Communist Party but by the unhappy enlisted men. Johnny reiterated this to his English comrades. They were not to speak out in favor of any labor effort lest they be connected with it.

Harry Pollitt became nearly impossible to locate. This ghost of a general secretary and his associates were not in favor of the tactics suggested by Johnny and agreed to by Aitken. They wanted a full-scale mutiny. The CPGB's "class versus class" road to socialism was what Pollitt advocated. The only problem with this approach was that it had not previously won the CPGB many new members or supporters. The party was thus cognizant that it could never pull off a large-scale military uprising. When de Graaf finally did see Pollitt again, Britain's top Red remarked, "Johnny, we cannot carry out what Moscow would like, but we are able to assist in this strike." It was then arranged for a prominent retired naval officer to hold a special meeting with some key parliamentarians. A well-respected officer and excellent speaker, he told the assembled politicians, "Our military do not want to fight against their own country, but will be forced to if their wages are cut and their families' lives hang in the balance." He was well applauded.

"Three cheers for the King!" someone at the gathering shouted after his speech. They all bellowed out the homage to George V together.

In the meantime, the KPD was delighted with the events in Britain. They sent a congratulatory telegram to the mutineers of the Atlantic fleet. The American Communist Party also sent a telegram. Of course, the Communists were aware that the admiralty in London would not simply cave in to the demands of enlisted men. To save face, heads would roll—the heads of participants in the Invergordon Mutiny. The American Communists protested in advance against the punishments they knew were coming.[23]

Despite clamoring from conservative elements, the government eventually decided against the wage cuts. The authorities went on the radio with the announcement, prompting ships in ports around the country to fly extra flags in gratitude. It was a great victory for ordinary seamen and was widely celebrated. With the defeat of the bill, the strike ceased within twenty-four hours, but not the ill feeling. Crews were promised that there would be no pay reductions for the rest of the year and no arrests of the mutiny's leadership. Soon enough, however, two court-marshals took place, and thirty-six sailors were dismissed from the Royal Navy.[24] The atmosphere was tense for months.

Johnny knew the continuing unhappiness was partially a result of lack of trust in the government. People thought the MacDonald administration might sneak the pay reductions through Parliament later. After all, the prime minister himself had switched sides in Parliament, the month before the Invergordon slowdown, so as to stay in office.[25] The man had an aura of suspicion about him. De Graaf also realized that the seamen were British to the core and proud of their branch of the service. It would take more for them to pick up arms against their officers. The insufficient wages they were receiving barely kept their families alive. A further cut would be madness, but still not enough to cause any mass revolutionary reaction.

Throughout the protests, Johnny tried to stay in the shadows wherever possible. At one point, however, he almost lost it. He marched boldly into an unnamed government office and was directed to an individual in charge of policy. Relating to the bureaucrat that he had been a seafaring man living in Britain for many years, he expounded on the poor treatment of British military men. "It is a disgrace, this turmoil caused by powers in Parliament," Johnny ranted. "If this decision is not reversed you'll have quite an unpleasant rebellion to deal with, which will play right into enemy hands."

"You are quite a politician," the functionary remarked.

"Yes," Johnny said, "and if I had power like those in Parliament, I would settle this unrest before the nation lived to regret it." De Graaf did not tell him anything more about himself. Had he given the bureaucrat an inkling of his identity, he would have been in very serious trouble both in London and in

Moscow. The public servant doubtlessly wrote the whole thing off as the tirade of an irate crank.

As the pay dispute died down, the CPGB continued to try to win over more members with additional propaganda. Johnny was informed that a Conservative member of Parliament, Walter Sidney Liddall, had mentioned in connection with a pending export of Soviet oil to Britain that Soviet oil refinery workers were paid far less than their British counterparts.[26] Milly asked Johnny if it were so. He told her that he doubted it but would inform the Comintern in Moscow. De Graaf realized that his superiors in the Soviet Union would consider such a statement from a British legislator embarrassing, but valuable intelligence nonetheless.

One day Harry Pollitt handed Johnny a note instructing him to return to Moscow. It was good news since his funds were low and his mission was essentially done. De Graaf was soon bidding George Aitken and the others farewell as he set sail for France.[27] Helena was left in London, since Johnny had other plans. They were risky, but it was a chance he was determined to take. Concealed among his things were his old U.S. intention papers, which M4 had not asked for prior to his departure from Moscow. In fact, the Soviets never knew about them. Johnny had not one additional item of proof as to who he was. Without any Soviet identification, he could not verify that he was an M4 agent or a member of the VKP(b). Proof of his cover name and occupation was plentiful but worthless. Would the Americans offer him asylum on the basis of their gold seal papers alone? That was the question he kept asking himself.

Not wanting the risky exposure of walking into the U.S. Embassy in Paris, he chose instead to travel by bus to Germany and try the consulate in territory he knew well, much quieter Cologne, in the Ruhr. Arriving in the city, he went to the brown two-story building at Kaiser-Friedrich-Ufer 83 (now called Konrad-Adenauer-Ufer) on the left bank of the Rhine. It looked forbidding, despite the warmth of its American flag flying in a light breeze. Mustering up his courage, Johnny strode past the eagle-emblazoned main doors and asked the attendant for directions to an official. There was a short wait, and then he was summoned to a small, well-lit office where he introduced himself to Edward S. Parker, the puny-looking vice consul. Parker listened to Johnny's story and offer of services with a bland expression of complete boredom. Slipping a pair of glasses over his button nose, the consul's gray eyes quickly absorbed the intention papers before him. Without comment, he phoned two colleagues and asked them to join him. Before the three Americans, Johnny recounted his tale a second time. "What proof of identity do you have, other than this?" an official with a darker complexion asked, pointing a thick finger at the intention papers.

"None," de Graaf replied. "I explained that." The man glared at de Graaf with contempt.

"Don't bother us!" the frail Parker interjected. "You have given us no proof whatsoever as to your true identity, and besides, you say you served in an enemy army."

"I beg your pardon!" Johnny responded with defiance. "Doesn't that paper tell you I was not against the U.S. throughout my days and experiences in Germany?"

"It doesn't tell us a damned thing other than you have this paper, which might not even be yours!" shouted the tall third man, who had stood off to one side, silent up to that point. "We don't even know if you're the person registered on this document. You can't prove to us in any way who you really are other than by what you say!" he remarked angrily.

Johnny started to reply, but Parker held up his hand. "Why don't you tell your Soviet superiors, or German or whoever they are, that this ploy didn't work," he stated coldly, with his eyes fastened onto Johnny's. The swarthy man took over, grabbing de Graaf firmly by the arm. "Don't bother us!" he repeated. "And take your carcass the hell out of here, understand?" Johnny met their glares, shoved the hand off his arm, and briskly left, steaming mad. "The stupid fools!" he muttered to himself.

Fed up with the Americans, Johnny checked to be sure he had slipped any shadow Consul Parker might have decided to put on his tail. He skirted here and there and doubled back. He then made a hasty train connection to Berlin. Finding a seat on the train, Johnny clenched his teeth in determination that he would not give up his plan to escape. Somehow, some way, he would find a means to prove his identity and get out of the Soviet Union. There had to be a way, and by God, he promised himself, "I will find it!"

Arriving at Berlin's old Lehrter Bahnhof (station), he went to the Comintern's West European Bureau and obtained several new passports and enough cash to see him back to Moscow. His next stop was the Krügers' flat. The Berlin city works department employed Gustav Krüger laying gas pipes and water mains. It was a well-paid job. He opened the door in surprise to de Graaf's knock. The Krügers were happy to see Johnny and thanked him for his letters and postcards. He thought up some excuse to explain why Helena was still in London. Gerti now was almost a teenager,[28] still a princess, and one who loved to wrestle with her uncle Johnny on the carpet. He was very much the apple of her eye.

With a few hours to spare before catching the train, Johnny took Gerti to the local ice-cream parlor, chatting all the way. The afternoon was crisp and bright, an early snow making the air invigorating. They had a wonderful time, but it was all too short. Before saying goodbye, Emilie Kruger told Johnny that Gerti had horded all the coffee beans she could find while he was away. This was so she could serve him fresh-ground coffee instead of store-mixed on his infrequent visits. Johnny was amused by this secret and also deeply touched. With farewells, hugs, kisses, and promises to write, de Graaf sadly left for the train station.

No one met Johnny's train in Moscow, which was most odd. Without waiting, he reported to M4 headquarters. Comrade Abramov of OMS was surprised to see de Graaf as he was turning in his travel documents at his office. "What are you doing home, Johnny?" he asked gruffly.

"I was called back, so here I am," Johnny replied with annoyance. Abramov and Johnny were not always on the best of terms.

"Who ordered you back?" he asked.

"Harry Pollitt, in Britain, gave me a note to return, which I didn't question since he's the secretary-general of the CPGB," Johnny explained, trying his best to contain his irritation.

"There is something damn funny here!" Abramov went on, puzzlement evident in his tone. "We didn't expect you back yet, nor did we summon you. So what gives?"

"I have no idea," de Graaf replied, somewhat confused at this point. "If you recalled me, it would have gone through Pollitt. He gave me the note to return. I was short of funds by then and would have come back on my own within a week anyway if they could not have provided additional expenses."

"What did Berlin say when you arrived there?" Abramov snapped.

"Nothing whatsoever. They gave me money and documents and said to continue on to Moscow," Johnny explained.

"They weren't surprised at seeing you unannounced?" Abramov asked.

"No, or if they were they didn't question me on it."

"Well, did they not suggest to you it was odd, your showing up, and tell you to return to Britain after giving you funds?"

"No, they said nothing, I told you. They just gave me money and items for Moscow."

"Damn it!" Abramov shouted. "Something stinks and we'll get to the bottom of it, believe me!"

It is unclear from the Soviet records what Abramov did, though de Graaf was reprimanded for violating the overall plan. This could have been for not carrying out to the letter Moscow's directives on the hoped-for mutiny, for coming back early, or simply because Abramov had made a report. Nothing was done to de Graaf more than an entry in his file.[29] An investigation, however, was started on Pollitt and the Berlin bureau. Both Pollitt and Aitken were eventually ordered to Moscow.

After leaving Abramov, Johnny shrugged and proceeded upstairs to General Berzin's office, his mind boggled by this weird disclosure. Ian Berzin, too, was surprised to see his agent. While he filed his mission report, de Graaf explained all the details he had given Abramov. "Johnny, I wonder if Harry Pollitt planned this little caper to get you out of his area and save expense funds?" he thought out loud. "When you got to Berlin, why didn't they question your return and why didn't they advise us you were corning in?" he mused. Unfortunately,

Johnny could not enlighten him. Had he decided to return on his own, the procedure would have been to inform Pollitt, who would relay the information to Berlin. Berlin in turn would contact M4 and Comintern Central. If Moscow disagreed, de Graaf would be advised within hours, prior to departure. Conversely, a call back would have originated in M4 offices in Moscow, been passed on to the Comintern's West European Bureau, and been forwarded to Pollitt in London to hand to Johnny. In isolated cases, a more direct approach would have been used. An M4 order would have been transported via Comintern courier or another M4 agent directly to the operative on location. This method could be used if Johnny had been on assignment to check out Pollitt or others. In such a scenario, de Graaf would have been covertly landed in Britain and then recalled without anyone's ever being aware of his presence in the country.

Berzin was pleased with what had been accomplished in Britain, playing down the fact that it had not been a total success. Of value was the tidbit about the M.P.'s remark, the general assured Johnny. "The Comintern will like that." Perhaps this one fact, passed on to Johnny by the Amtorg woman, Milly, helped to soothe the appearance of an incomplete mission, although de Graaf could not understand why. It seemed like such a trivial point.

When the discussion with Berzin finished later that evening, de Graaf left the M4 building and made his way to the Metropole Hotel. The Metropole was another agents' hotel. As he walked in its direction, the ground lay deep in snow, and gusty winds ripped across Red Square. Unexpectedly, outside the Metropole stood a friend from Germany, Albert Schmidt, lightly clad and shivering. Johnny recognized him as a first officer under Karl Herltz, who was active in the German uprising of 1923. Herltz, a Communist blabbermouth, had somehow arranged for the Hamburg uprising to be named after him. He was only a lower-level organizer, but he was a big bluffer and thereby able to reap unjustified acclaim for his minimal efforts. So well did Herltz convince others of his great heroic deeds that many party meetings in Germany were held in his honor.

"Hey, Johnny, am I glad to see you!" a trembling Schmidt exclaimed, his teeth chattering with the chill. De Graaf took in his tall, underfed form at a glance, noticing that all he wore was light clothing without a coat. Falling snowflakes draped him in a ghostly white from his head to his summer-shoed feet. "Where is Herltz?" Johnny inquired, while shaking the poor man's ice-cold hand.

"Hmm, that swine! He's here in Moscow. A guest of the Soviets for propaganda use," he spat contemptuously. "He's a big hero now and Moscow is sending him around on propaganda and publicity tours as a big-time speaker," he added. "He's living in the lap of luxury while I try to get by with the threadbare clothing on my back."

"Did you not see him and ask for some winter clothes?" Johnny asked. All the while he kept an oblique eye on the trembling form before him.

"Oh, I sure did!" he responded. "He showed me his cupboard, overflowing with over a dozen military greatcoats. As he pulled each winter coat out, he told me why he couldn't just give them away. A different officer had presented him with each one. The bastard gave me nothing!"

Johnny felt very sorry for Schmidt and saw to it that he went away warmly clad, fed, and with a few rubles in his pocket. Months later, after returning from another mission, he was informed that Herltz was dead. "How did he die?" Johnny asked his contact.

"I don't know," came the reply with a smile, "but one day his body was discovered floating in the Volga River in Siberia. He was out in a boat, blind drunk, when the boat capsized. We didn't bother to help him."

Johnny shook the man's hand and said, "Good work!" He winked and walked off. Herltz had received his reward.

Something had bothered Johnny since coming to Soviet Union in 1930, leaving behind his wife and children back in Ahlen. He had offered her a divorce, yet she refused. They had not been in close touch, but Johnny was aware she was reasonably well cared for by the KPD. He had likewise sent her funds from time to time. Johnny saw no point in their being bound together by law when she could be released to remarry. Certainly there was no chance they would ever be together again. He had contacted a Soviet notary and had him draw up legal papers that would give Maria grounds, with unopposed release, to effect a divorce. She could have been free. He had mailed this bulky envelope off to her. Months later he received a reply. On opening the envelope, the legal papers he had mailed fell to the floor, ripped up in pieces. A note inside read, "Dear Johnny, I thank you for the gesture, but I do not want a divorce. I know I was at fault for our separation. Even though I tried to keep tidy, I did fail. I won't change you, and I know that. All I ask is that, when I die, I pass on as your wife. A small request but meaningful to me. Love, Maria." Johnny had attempted to let Maria out of their marriage. Little else could be done except to comply with her wishes. He always wished it could have been otherwise.

Two and a half weeks passed, and Harry Pollitt arrived in Moscow. A couple of days later, George Aitken's train pulled in. Pollitt was put up at the Hotel Lux, another agents' hotel, while Aitken was given a room at the Metropole. De Graaf was told to make sure they were kept apart. After the two British members were comfortable, Manuilski called a small conference of the ИККИ. General Berzin told de Graaf that the Comintern had asked that he attend as an observer. Also present were Marcel Cachin, one of the founders of the Communist Party of France, plus representatives from the KPD, the Italian Communist Party, and two persons from the Polish Communist Party. From the IKKI were Manuilski, Osip Piatnitski, and Langner, among others.[30] Vasiliev was also in attendance.

With Dmitri Manuilski chairing the event, the massive hall was full to capacity. Johnny watched it all from an overlooking balcony. A special one-way glass surrounded the viewers' area, allowing him to look down and see those below without being observed. Manuilski asked de Graaf to follow the speeches by special phone beside his chair, paying particular attention to Harry Pollitt's report on the British naval strike. By switching dials beside the phone, Johnny could pick up the translation of any speech in one of the several languages spoken by the various participants. At the same time, another phone allowed him to hear all of Manuilski's comments even as the speeches were in progress. The conference started with an introduction by Manuilski. From there, the representatives stood up one by one and gave their reports amid criticisms of not having done enough in the area of antimilitary propaganda.[31]

When it was Harry Pollitt's turn, he stood up and proceeded to detail the CPGB's accomplishments. When Pollitt too was criticized for the CPGB's lack of results, he tried to make excuses, then blamed it all on George Aitken. Johnny listened with fascination as Pollitt lied in response to each query. As he began talking about the £30,000 for expenses, a red light flashed on Johnny's direct phone. "Watch this," came Manuilski's whispered voice to de Graaf. Manuilski questioned Pollitt on the British dockworker situation. Pollitt tried to bluff his way through the questions, claiming that great strides were being made with the dockworkers. He stated, however, that it was crucial to obtain more financial support in order to expand propaganda, education, and deeper penetration of the stevedores. Johnny listened to falsehood after falsehood as Pollitt presented his case. George Aitken was allowed a chance to defend himself and gave truthful answers. Without doubt, the CPGB under Pollitt had made no attempt whatsoever to solicit membership on the docks. He was lying through his teeth.[32]

After the conference ended for the day, Manuilski asked Harry Pollitt and Johnny to join him in his office. Addressing de Graaf by his VKP(b) name, he began. "Comrade Mattern, you have just come back from Britain, having done some excellent work there. From your knowledge of the British situation, do you concur with Comrade Pollitt's statements that they need an additional £30,000?"

"In my opinion," Johnny replied, "there is work enough to justify that expense, but I am also aware of great waste within their party. Should you decide to cut that amount, cut first a bit from the salary budget, where there is a lot of fat." Poor Harry began to blush, finally protesting Johnny's statements and presence in the room.

Manuilski glared at him and made it very plain that he had invited de Graaf to the conference and the present meeting. "What Mattern says is true," he snarled at Pollitt. "We know what is going on and value this man's opinion." Pollitt frowned at Johnny in hostile silence.

"Don't you think it would be better to spend the additional funds in organizing a special secretariat that would develop a new newspaper solely for the dockworkers?" he asked, glancing Johnny's way first. A pause in Pollitt's continued stare, as he turned back to Manuilski. Johnny seized the opportunity to explain that he could not comment further on the dockworkers, since he had no contact with them. Nonetheless, he was well aware of the tough job they performed on the servicing of merchantmen and Royal Navy vessels. Johnny went on to point out that he had a good knowledge of docks around the world and felt that no effort had been made in Britain to date to develop this area.

Shouting in anger, Pollitt protested, but Johnny held firm. "Have you done anything at all with dockside distribution of our three papers in Britain?" Johnny asked Pollitt.

"No," he replied, now caught up in his own lies.

"That does it," Manuilski exclaimed. "Not one effort in that area, eh, Comrade? Quite different from what you stated today before me and the Congress." Harry Pollitt looked down at his feet, his face now flushed with embarrassment at having been found out.

Manuilski then asked how the progressives in Germany had worked in that country's ports. Johnny explained how the party's infiltration had been successful there. The CPGB was awarded only £15,000 after the little chat, and it was all to be spent on infiltration. To make sure this project got off the ground, the Comintern contacted M4. General Berzin then ordered Johnny to return to Britain as an advisor on the new project.[33]

Back in Britain, Johnny again used the cover of the wine merchant from Hamburg, and stayed at the same place in Kenton.[34] This time, Pollitt wanted nothing to do with de Graaf, and made sure after their first meeting, a week later, that George Aitken was appointed Johnny's co-worker and British party contact. Pollitt likewise avoided any personal involvement in the dock project like the plague. But of course he was kept informed by his CPGB comrades, if only to turn on Johnny should the effort with the stevedores fail. This arrangement was fine by Johnny, for he and George got along marvelously. They had very similar views on Pollitt and his diminishing control.

A new paper was started, politically in tune with the dockworkers, with honest editorials rather than deceptive ones. The power of the stevedores' union, support, and influence made this a prerequisite. Johnny gave local party members instructions for handling labor questions but did not get involved in carrying out a particular strategy. All progress reports came directly to him, showing inroads made and work yet to be done. The waterfront was already well organized by a union that espoused strong Socialist views, which aided the cause and the propaganda. The dockworkers were loyal to the Crown, but they sought higher wages and socialized benefits for the workforce and their families.

Posing as a merchant seaman, Johnny traveled to a number of ports, from Edinburgh to Plymouth. His common tactic in each city was to frequent the harbor pubs and engage stevedores in conversation over pints of ale. This allowed him to obtain their honest opinions. Subjects and complaints, discussed and overheard, he relayed back to the waiting presses. A week later these topics became widely distributed dockside editorials. The stevedores had their paper.

By November 1932, all was running well.[35] People were trained and effective. Johnny then made contact with Berlin, informing headquarters there that he was on his way back. In leaving the British operation in capable hands, de Graaf felt another girder had been added to his escape plans. He hoped that the apparent success of the mission would lull the Comintern and M4 into a false sense of security. Johnny crossed his fingers.

After landing on the Continent, Johnny took Helena and made straight for Berlin. This side trip really had but one purpose. He left her with her parents and continued alone to the USSR by way of Copenhagen, Stockholm, and Helsinki. He wanted to end the relationship with the eldest of the Krüger sisters. In Copenhagen he met a representative of the West European Bureau. The envoy collected his wine merchant documents and provided him with a Dutch passport in the name of Herman van Heussen. In Stockholm he checked into a hotel and was soon contacted by a Swede who took the van Heussen passport. In exchange, he was given Swiss papers in the name of Bruno Zimmermann. If the Swedish or Finnish authorities questioned him, Johnny was a lumber dealer who bought wood products in the Soviet Union. His new passport already had a Soviet visa in it, ready for use.[36]

In Moscow, M4 greeted de Graaf with a booming "Well done!" as Berzin read Johnny's mission report. "Take a few weeks' rest, Johnny," he generously suggested, "you've earned it." Comrade Mattern did, enjoying the sights and sounds away from the Soviet capital, all the while hoping that the big leap had gotten closer and was now within his reach.

10

BERLIN AND PRAGUE

"I'll take the chance and go to Germany this time. For, as you say, the assignment is crucial." With that, de Graaf accepted Alfred Langner's request to travel to Berlin and organize the nervous RFB. He hoped he would find Berlin's Communist street fighters in better shape than what he had witnessed in the Ural Mountains. Not long after Johnny's final British assignment, he had been sent east to the Urals to check on Polish miners and their morale. He pointed out to Langner that the same state of affairs existed among the Poles that he had observed in 1930 among German political immigrants to the Ukraine.[1] It was not a good situation for the Comintern.

In discussions of his new assignment with Berzin, Vasiliev, and Manuilski, it was made clear that Moscow wanted to know what strength the German Communist Party still had. Elections were pending in the Reichstag, as Germany reeled from the political battle between the contenders, in particular those on the left and the right. Hitler and his Nazis, the SPD, and the KPD all fought the country and each other for supreme reign. An on-site appraisal was urgently needed.

Already twenty thousand German refugees, many of them followers of the KPD and the KPD's Central Committee, had fled the Fatherland for the Soviet Union and several other countries. Germany wallowed in apprehension and hope of who would rule. Popular unrest and confusion were everywhere. How many members of the Red Front organizations lingered on after the mass exodus? Could the remaining leftist forces be united to oppose the growing Nazi movement? Would the SPD regain power, and if so, would they lash out at other political elements? These were the questions Moscow wanted answered. Fortunately, on this mission Johnny had been able by stealth and loan to smuggle out a large number of Soviet identification papers, and not all of them were his own.

He had concealed his Russian Communist Party book, General Staff passage cards, and various other tidbits, including meal passes to the General Staff dining room. Should luck come his way, he was ready to make another move.[2]

Heavy rain was falling when de Graaf arrived at Berlin's Schlesischer Bahnhof (now called the Ostbahnhof) bearing a forged German passport in the name of Herman Schneider on the evening of January 6, 1933. The passport was about to expire. He was carrying only US$200 to tide him over for a month. Once his travel documents lapsed, he was to make contact again with Walter Ulbricht. Wilhelm Pieck was his backup if it proved impossible to reach Ulbricht.[3]

Well disguised to avoid police recognition, de Graaf made his way to the headquarters of the ZK near Bülow Platz. Congestion was everywhere. A huge demonstration bloated the streets and sidewalks as a never-ending stream of people marched in a cold rain. Shoulder to shoulder, sixteen abreast, they rolled by, shouting, blowing horns, beating drums, and waving banners. They were protesting against the Nazis.[4]

Pressed into the moist throng of sidewalk onlookers, Johnny unexpectedly noticed Dr. Friedrich Stampfer standing beside him. Stampfer was the editor of the SPD newspaper *Vorwärts* (Forward).[5] He did not recognize de Graaf, so intent was he on watching the procession. Turning toward him, Johnny remarked, "Dr. Stampfer, do you believe all the people marching by are Communists? Or do you feel they are Social Democrats unwilling to do something about Hitler, and just let him take over?" Stampfer's face whitened as he turned and sputtered nervously, "Do not think such a thing. We don't want trouble or bloodshed." With that he pushed away from Johnny, getting lost among the wet coats and bodies beyond. Johnny realized that these SPD types were willing to accept sugar, candy, and dreams that they would eventually pay for with their lives.

De Graaf looked for various contacts he had known but managed to locate only Jakob Göbel, a regional functionary of the RFB. Göbel told Johnny that although he had reported the strength of the RFB to be a quarter-million it was actually a mere two thousand or so. The group had gone to pieces under the corrupt leadership of Willy Leow, a man next to KPD leader Thälmann. Leow was not to be found anywhere. Johnny distrusted him. He had considered Leow corrupt since first speaking with him at the Leipzig conference in 1923, as well as at other meetings that followed over the years. He held a fairly high position but did little for the party with the power and money he commanded. He was an individual who played all sides for personal gain only. Johnny finally found him and asked for a new passport and some living expenses. Leow turned him down flat, saying that he did not have any cash and that de Graaf should seek funds from some other source.[6] No suggestion was made as to which source Johnny might try.

Arthur Ewert was around at headquarters, but he too was one de Graaf could do without. Their numerous disputes in the past, when Comrade Ewert was high in the Berlin party, still burned deep in Johnny's soul. The current situation was made to order for Ewert. Should the KPD leaders be occupied or absent, without delay Ewert would haughtily take charge. Johnny recalled that Ewert once came to the Ruhr from Berlin to set the local party straight. Brandishing a long declaration, he commanded that the delegation accept and sign a ZK resolution condemning Leon Trotsky. But the Ruhr Communists refused. Johnny asked Ewert to explain what was behind it. "It was a party pronouncement that required total support," he snapped. The demand for an explanation remained. "Why, suddenly, was this man an outcast?" de Graaf wanted to know, and so did many of the other Ruhr comrades. Ewert was always a party stooge, in Johnny's opinion. Arthur played to the top, forever striving to control others beneath his station. He called for a vote on the resolution from the entire seven-city Ruhr party. The proclamation was defeated and a livid Ewert was sent packing.

Another man arrived following Ewert's hasty departure. But again the Ruhr party refused to sign until he provided the delegates with the reason for the turnabout on Trotsky. Why was Lenin's best organizer suddenly to be called a traitor? The second envoy as well left without support. Then Ernst Thälmann himself visited the Ruhr holdouts, thanking everyone for not signing, as he too wanted a reason to disown Trotsky. They knew Leon Trotsky only by his writings and as a founder of the Red Army. Time would reveal what none of them knew or perhaps only suspected of the Stalin-Trotsky conflict.

Luckily, Johnny located two Ruhr comrades in downtown Berlin. They informed him that delegations from all over the country were going to gather the next day at a special party meeting. The Central Committee of the KPD had called in its top functionaries and activists for an open assembly at the Schützenhalle near the Zoologischer Garten railway station. Johnny made note of the time and date to make sure that he would be in attendance. When the meeting opened, there was a fair-sized number of people amid rumors and uneasy anticipation. Central Committee member Wilhelm Florin brought the representatives to attention. As he rose to speak, a hush of doom filled the hall.

Florin began by observing that everyone there appeared nervous. He told them to calm their fears, for Hitler would never become chancellor. Minister without portfolio Franz Bracht, in the government of Franz von Papen, would be given the job.[7] They could count on it, he said. Ringing applause and joyful comments greeted his soothing words. Florin continued, bandaging the now closing wounds of fear and tempest. Other speakers became more and more positive, layer upon layer of them, cementing a solid belief that Hitler could not attain the ultimate prize. The issue of the Nazi leader's ascendancy was a big question mark in Johnny's mind, too. Heinz Neumann, a leading politician of the day, made a slip of the tongue at a conference discussing Hitlerism, and de Graaf now and again remembered his words at such moments. "In my opinion the best that can happen to the German people is to go through this mess, then become Communist." It was quite a statement from a leading figure, and it made Johnny so angry he could have done Neumann harm then and there.

As he sat listening to Florin, Ewert, and the others, he recalled Neumann. He found himself thinking, "You don't believe that! You cannot say the truth for it would be against the rules of your office." Florin and the party were as one, sending innocent people to their deaths—people who trusted and believed in them and the Communist cause. Forty men, some from the Ruhr, all members of the RFB, were seated at the table next to Johnny. De Graaf whispered to the closest man, "Pass the word on, we'll have a meeting tonight at midnight in the Grunewald Forest [between Berlin and Potsdam]. If possible, bring arms." Without looking around, he nodded.

Checking his watch, it was approaching 12:00 A.M. Johnny awaited the arrival of his Red Front comrades in a small clearing in the wooded area, shielded by the cover of a hazy moon. One by one they appeared, persons of responsibility and close friends, until all were present. Standing in their midst, he began by informing them that no one could call him a liar. Each person knew that Johnny was a man of his word. He then continued with his view of Florin's comments by pointing out that those who thought Franz Bracht would be Germany's next chancellor were foolish. "Adolf Hitler will become the nation's leader." When that happened, the Gestapo would be after all members of the KPD. He urged each comrade to get word to their families and friends to leave the country immediately.

With little need for discussion, the group murmured agreement and melted into the darkness. If they remained in Germany, they would have been ground to pulp under Nazi rule. As it turned out, days later, when Hitler did take power, thousands of people on the SS lists were promptly arrested. Holes had already been dug in preparation for the mass killings of known enemies from years past.

After issuing the Grunewald warning, Johnny went to work trying to locate stray party members who remained in Germany. Out of the thousands of Red Front members, he could find only a few hundred still in Berlin. "Get away! Flee!" he told those he came across, "or your life will soon be over!" Whenever he could, he provided assistance, escape routes, and a little financial help, which quickly drained his funds.

Hitler's appointment as chancellor of Germany was announced on a freezing day near the end of the month, January 30, 1933. That evening, while the eerie torchlight parade of Nazis marched by the Reich Chancellery and the new German chancellor, other Nazis were out in abundance. Aware that they would be hunting him, too, de Graaf sought his own safe haven. He began sleeping in dark cellars that offered protection from the elements, both natural and human. He spent nearly seven months underground, at times unshaven and hungry, doing what he could. He even published anti-Nazi propaganda from a small printing press he kept in a crypt in a Berlin cemetery. In late February 1933, Walter Ulbricht wanted Johnny to fight in the streets, blow up railway bridges, and commit sabotage against the Nazis.[8] De Graaf refused, insisting that disruptions without a strategic purpose would go against the principles of Leninism.

But the National Socialists had a strategic purpose. On March 18, through what was left of the party, Johnny learned that Maria had died in Ahlen. He decided, however, not to go to her funeral because the Gestapo would be there in force waiting for him. Two months later he stumbled across a flyer offering a one-hundred-thousand-mark reward for his capture. There was no picture on the wanted poster (he was number eleven on the list), though one description matched him perfectly, right down to the coal scar on his upper right cheek.[9] As distressing as these two events were, an even more pressing problem growled for attention in de Graaf's gut. Hunger was at his door.

When he was out of the country, Johnny's Soviet salary was carefully allotted and closely calculated. Most of the time expenses were extremely tight, allowing for no real extras over the bare minimum. No doubt, by Moscow's calculations, the party believed he still had ample money. What he had given to others for aid had not been much, yet it was enough to wipe him out much sooner than expected. The solution: together with Willy Leow and another KPD member, Hans Rogalla, Johnny dipped into the ten thousand marks in party funds in Leow's possession. The expropriation would prove fatal to Leow and Rogalla. De Graaf would receive a sentence of two years without an important position, perhaps saved from the executioner only by Vasiliev and Manuilski.[10]

Yet what awaited all three men in Moscow was still months away. Willy Leow lived in a fancy downtown apartment. Johnny was aware that he had a girlfriend, an attractive woman in her midtwenties who resided with her parents in a basement apartment in a working-class area. Willy's error lay in his stinginess in aiding KPD members who needed food, clothing, or assistance in escaping. He also sat on large pile of emergency funds without using them. De Graaf wanted to fix him.

After obtaining the necessary clothing from another comrade, whom Johnny also urged to flee the city, he proceeded through backstreets to the girl's home. Cleaned up and wearing a dark green felt hat, heavy winter coat with collar up, and glasses, he looked like a government official. Knocking briskly on her door, he waited, then rapped again until the girl's parents awoke and sleepily answered the intrusion into their night's slumbers. Johnny flashed some kind of badge rapidly and snapped, "Criminal Commissar." The couple began trembling in fear at what they thought was a member of the Gestapo. Backing away nervously, they allowed de Graaf to enter. "Don't worry," Johnny said to the trembling couple. "I am not a Nazi but a Social Democrat." They regained some color as he continued, but their bodies continued to quiver uneasily. "I'm here to help you. Do you know Willy Leow?"

"Yes," they nodded.

"Is your daughter with him?"

"We don't know," they whispered, dry mouthed, their eyes wide as saucers.

"Tell your daughter to stay away from Willy or she will be arrested with him by the Gestapo!" Johnny commanded. They mumbled something, trying their best to smile in appreciation as de Graaf quickly opened the door and left.

Hours later, Johnny watched from across the street from Willy's apartment building as Leow hastily bundled his suitcases into a nearby car. The girl's parents had tipped him off, as he knew they would. Leow rocketed out of Germany to Paris with the rest of the party money as if being pursued by the devil himself. Moscow received a wire from Johnny that very day advising them of Willy's disappearance with party assets.

By June 1933, choosing the right time to escape the Soviet system was what drove Johnny de Graaf. He decided to approach the American Embassy in Berlin, feeling that with proof of his identity he could ask to become a political refugee. Johnny had to be extremely careful, because pandemonium reigned in Germany and the Nazi net was closing fast. Death seemed to be searching for him everywhere. It had to be now or never.

Presenting himself to U.S. ambassador, William Edward Dodd, Johnny related his story. De Graaf's judge, a distinguished gray-haired man, read all his documents and listened intently without interruption. Finally he told Johnny that he was sorry but that U.S. law prohibited the acceptance of other countries' agents. "I deeply regret this, but those are our regulations, which I have no alternative but to abide by," Dodd stated dourly.

"Certainly you can see I fought against Germany and every dictatorship," Johnny pleaded. "I have always battled for justice, democratic justice. Now I come to you to offer my services and you say no!"

"I am sorry," the ambassador replied firmly. "It is our law. Good day, and good luck."

Johnny left in dejection, feeling he had lost his life's biggest contest. Hungry and tired but unwilling to give up, he decided on a whim to visit the British Embassy at Tiergartenstraße 17. Hugging the early evening shadows, he tried to push out of his mind the thought of what would happen to him if caught with his false German passport. He cautiously walked the back alleys and poorly lit side streets until he reached the embassy of His Majesty's government. Perhaps they would believe his story.

Once admitted, he was introduced to Frank Foley,[11] the first secretary and passport control officer. Foley was a slim, clean-cut man of medium height and weight, with a small sparkling face and straight, carefully parted but graying hair. Later in the decade, he would begin wearing glasses and his hair would thin, but in 1933 Johnny was unaware that he was standing in front of the second-highest-ranking officer of SIS (the Secret Intelligence Service) in Germany. Sometimes referred to as MI6, Military Intelligence 6, the SIS was Britain's foreign intelligence and counterespionage arm. Covered by his position as first secretary, Foley carried out his real assignments under diplomatic immunity, free from the danger of arrest and from all travel restrictions. Nonetheless, the SIS had been allowed to become less imposing than MI5 (British domestic intelligence) in the years between the wars. The global conflict would change that. As things heated up, the two agencies did not always remain within their assigned spheres of activity. They often bickered, cooperated, or operated on each other's turf.[12]

"Mr. Foley," de Graaf began, "I will make my story short, and afterwards, if you have no place for me, say so, forget what I have said, and let me go my way." Foley nodded, calmly relaxed behind his large polished desk. Johnny told his life story once more, putting everything out in the open. He spoke for more than an hour, showing the secretary documents and relating incidents while Foley, without much comment, took it all in. "I want to break and battle this system," Johnny concluded.

Then Foley began asking question after piercing question, each carefully worded to set traps and expose deceptions. Johnny gave him his real name, going over every detail and record, until Foley had compiled several sheets of written facts. "May I keep these documents for twenty-four hours?" he inquired, gesturing to Johnny's smuggled Soviet identification and assorted passes.

"Yes," Johnny replied. "All I ask, should you decide not to accept me, is that you'll forget this meeting, don't report anything, and let me escape from Berlin," he said nervously, somewhat repeating himself.

"Agreed," Foley stated with a sincere smile of honesty and firmness.

Foley approved Johnny's suggestion that he would contact him the next day by placing a telephone call at a specified time to the public phone in a safe restaurant. Johnny knew that Foley could easily check out his story through the countless sources at his disposal. Within hours they could have a whole dossier of information.[13]

A few minutes before the scheduled call, Johnny entered the dingy restaurant via a side door, unobserved, and lingered by the darkened wall phone. He had used this spot before to make and receive calls. The phone rang once. He pounced on it. "Johnny," came Foley's whispered voice. "Wrong number," Johnny replied. "Dial once again." De Graaf continued to hold the receiver to his ear. "Come now," came his reply. Johnny hung up.

Aided by another mantel of night fog Johnny reached the embassy, entered through an unlocked alley door, and was taken straight to the first secretary's office. Foley rose, greeted de Graaf warmly, smiling all the while, and shook Johnny's hand. Then, both seated, he began.

"Do you know a member of the Reichstag named Dittmann?" he inquired.

"Yes," Johnny replied.

"Haase?"

"Yes, him also. When the Labor Party split from the SPD, they were the leaders of the USPD."

"Did you know a member of the Reichstag named Ladebour?" Johnny answered that he did. "You were one of his organizers, were you not?" he asked.

"Yes, that's correct," de Graaf asserted.

"We know of you, Johnny, and now at last we have the honor to meet you personally," he smiled emphatically. De Graaf stared at him in complete surprise. "The three leaders were in our employ, and the USPD, whom we financed, was all part of it," he explained. "Congratulations, Johnny, you worked for us daily, receiving money and information from our office, which you got to the battleships during the mutiny."

"Wow!" de Graaf exclaimed in utter astonishment. "So I was working for you all that time without knowing it?"

Foley grinned and nodded his head. He then explained how the British had bankrolled the movement. "In the beginning, everything started out well," he said, "but somewhere there was a leak and the whole plot failed. It would have succeeded, too, since the navy was all set to go, but the army did not move as planned."

Johnny was stunned, at a loss for words. Finally he drew a deep breath, regained his composure, and said, "Had I known at the time that you people had aided, financed, and supported Dittmann and the others of the Independent Party, I wouldn't have done it. At that moment, I was certainly not willing to fight for one capitalistic power against another, of that you can be sure."

"Damn it, man! I like you, Johnny," Foley retorted. "Here you stand before me fighting for your life and then have the nerve to tell me had you known, you wouldn't have been part of the mutiny plot."

"That's right," Johnny snapped. "I would not have been a party to it." Their eyes met in mutual determination.

"Whom do you want to fight now?" he coyly asked, regaining his composure.

"The Nazis," de Graaf responded without hesitation, "dead or alive."

They talked for another hour, during which time Johnny requested political asylum. No decision was reached on that question, but they did agree to meet again the following day. Foley provided de Graaf with a little money for food, and Johnny took his leave.

The following evening, Foley had a surprise. "How would you like to continue working for the Soviets," he asked, "while at the same time informing us of all your moves and missions for them? In that way you can be of the greatest advantage to us."

De Graaf refused point blank. "Mr. Foley, all I want is political asylum," Johnny stated. "I would be agreeable to working for you, but not as a double agent. I want to leave the Soviet Union and communism once and for all." Looking him straight in the eye, Johnny continued, "I can't conceive of what you ask of me, although I do see the necessity of it. You really want to know what is cooking in the Soviet Union and what they are up to abroad, don't you?" Foley nodded, his eyes never leaving Johnny's. They then discussed the proposal in greater detail. Finally, hours later, Johnny agreed. "All right, I'm your man. I'd rather work for Great Britain than for the Soviets," de Graaf told him. There was, however, one condition, "Never ask me to put my hand on a Communist worker, for one does not become a Communist out of the blue moon," de Graaf said. "They paid a terrible price during World War I, the Depression, and now all this. However, I will not hesitate to fight against their leaders."

Johnny and Frank shook hands in agreement, their evening discussions ending on a firm note; another get-together was planned for the following evening. That night, walking home through the mist, de Graaf thought about how odd it was. Fate seemed to bring the enemy of yesterday into the confidence of today. He liked Foley. Approaching his basement hiding place, he was startled to bump into a West European Bureau courier, following the same shadowed path but coming from the opposite direction. On recognizing Johnny, he said excitedly, "Thank heaven I found you, Johnny, I've looked high and low for you. Moscow got through to us yesterday with the last message. They said to tell you to leave Berlin at once for Moscow, via Prague.[14] All that can be done for the Red Front has been done. Moscow wants you out of Germany fast, now that Hitler is in power."

Johnny thanked the man, who told him he would have been out of Germany the day before, had he been able to locate de Graaf and pass on the message. They wished each other well, and the messenger made an about-face and vanished the same way he had come. Johnny next contacted Jakob Göbel and ordered the ex-organizer of the RFB to Moscow. The purpose of this was to get someone there who could testify against Leow.[15]

This new development certainly fit right into Foley's plans. Johnny made an urgent call to him at the embassy well before sunup. Foley was delighted by the news. He also expressed no surprise when informed that de Graaf did not have a *Pfennig* in his pocket. Assuring Johnny that this could be fixed, they proceeded to discuss money and methods of contact for the new counterintelligence agent. Johnny's British salary would be deposited in London. He could draw on it anytime, plus expenses, through Frank. Whenever he left the Soviet Union he was to make contact with the British via Copenhagen. Prior to reentry, contact would also be made.

Foley, through his diplomatic cover, could meet Johnny anywhere in the world. All that was needed was to get word to him. At no time was de Graaf assigned an agent number.[16] Foley insisted that he was never to phone or have direct contact with any British diplomatic mission or institution unless Foley instructed by him to do so. All names, aliases, and phone numbers were to be memorized, not committed to paper. Should Johnny ever be arrested, in no way could he be connected with the British, nor could he count on their intervention. To them, officially, he did not exist; their relationship could at no time be acknowledged.

Frank supplied Johnny with funds for the trip to Prague and even Moscow. Once in Czechoslovakia, he was to contact him in Berlin using the code name "August," the first and last time a code name was used. At all other times he would be called Johnny. Once notified, Foley would meet his new agent at a prearranged Prague restaurant prior to his return to Moscow.

That evening de Graaf cautiously made his way to the Krügers' apartment. They had moved to Sonnenburger Straße 22.[17] The Krügers were pleased by the surprise visit, but it was a short one, just long enough for Johnny to ask Helena to travel to Ahlen and check on his children. A few hours later he made for the Polish border in the company of a fellow party member. Paul Wilhelm of the West European Bureau, who was also fleeing separately, made the arrangements. Johnny's travel partner owned a small truck. The two drove all night and entered Poland the next morning without incident, just as the June sun was about to rise.

Later that day they arrived in Prague,[18] where Johnny got out and headed for the Soviet Embassy. He gave the officials there the name of his M4 contact in Moscow, General Berzin, and told them he had to report back. The minor Czech functionary who was dealing with de Graaf urged him to volunteer to take two comrades from Berlin back with him to the USSR. Johnny saw no problem in this, but he was startled when the Czech told him that he knew some information on Johnny's next mission. How he was aware of this Johnny could never determine, for not even he himself knew what his next assignment would be. The bureaucrat felt that, as a good Communist, Johnny should know. "You will be sent to Manchuria first, then to China," he said. Johnny thanked him for the tip, seriously doubting its veracity.

Back in Berlin in June 1933, Helena traveled across Germany to Ahlen to look in on Johnny's children. Oscar and Marianne were living with Emma Klutzka, Maria's sister. Helena did not stay long, fearing that the Nazis might arrest her as they were already doing to others on the left in Ahlen. She brought money, new clothes, and a letter from Johnny. Johnny said he would send more funds later. The children called her Lena. Strangely, none of them spoke of Maria, who had died just three months earlier. Johnny asked for pictures of Oscar, Marianne, and his namesake, but Johnny Jr. was not there. He had gone to Berlin to stay with the Krügers. Given that the boy came from a broken family and had no real funds of his own, the Berlin KPD had arranged everything. He was not yet fourteen, but he would soon be on his way east.

When Maria had returned from Kharkov to Germany, her husband's superiors had made him contact her and tell her that he wanted both of their sons to return to the USSR and live with him. Moscow was grooming Johnny to be an international agent, and this was their way of making sure that he would return at the conclusion of any assignment abroad. Maria refused at first, prompting a threat from Johnny to end his financial support for the family. Evidently the warning did the trick. Maria told her estranged husband he could have the oldest child.[19]

After some two months in Prague, the local Communist Central Committee gave Johnny and the two Germans money and travel papers for the train trip to Moscow, more than one week away. At the request of Vasiliev, Johnny was provided with a Soviet passport. The group was free to do as it wished until departure time. The first chance he got, Johnny bought a postcard, scribbled a message, and mailed it to Foley in Berlin. It read, "Having a jolly good time on my holiday," and was signed "August." Foley would know that everything was okay and would board a train for Prague.

De Graaf was renting a small room from Adolf Resnicek on the fourth floor of the cross street at Jecná 1, not far from Karl Square. He had used his spare time in Czechoslovakia to take in the sights—when suddenly and without warning Helena arrived, bags in hand. Nearly hysterical, she showed Johnny a letter from her parents asking that he allow her to stay because she had been exceedingly despondent over their separation. He felt he had no choice but to take her back. When told that he was heading for Moscow, Helena willingly agreed to travel with him to the USSR.[20]

Once Frank Foley's train arrived and Foley made contact, he and Johnny met in a secure restaurant not far from Prague's British Embassy. When de Graaf informed him of the possible Manchuria and China trip, Foley appeared perplexed. "How would that fellow know what's next, and what would they have in mind for you there, Johnny?" he asked, a deep frown appearing on his brow.

"I don't know how the man could know, Frank, for he's not in a position to know," Johnny returned. "Unless," he paused, "it's a dual Comintern-M4 mission and he overheard someone from Comintern mention it. He told me nothing more, but I will see him again tomorrow and try to find out if he knows additional facts." The two men talked for a while longer, then left separately, as they had arrived, agreeing to meet the following night in the waiting room of the busy downtown railway station.

The following morning Johnny paid another visit to the Soviet Embassy. He located his tipster and over a cup of coffee in the nearly deserted cafeteria tried to pump him. The man could furnish only a few more details, far from what Johnny had hoped. De Graaf refrained from pressing him too hard.

"They are suspicious of a resident Soviet agent in Manchuria," Johnny told Frank that night, standing in the large, bustling station. "That's all he could tell me on it. On China, all he knew was it was a joint mission of a military nature. Not much to go on, Frank, but he did seem to be reliable and sincere. He would not say, however, where he picked this info up. I guess he's scared."

Frank nodded in agreement, sucking on his black pipe. "When do you leave for Moscow, Johnny, tomorrow night?" Frank inquired.

"Nine o'clock tomorrow night," Johnny confirmed.

"Let's see if more develops between now and then," Foley mumbled, almost in a whisper, feigning interest in the newspaper he held before him. De Graaf stood to one side with his back to Foley, looking at the train board and lifting a handkerchief to his nose whenever he spoke. They moved to a restaurant with only a slight variation. Frank took a back booth, facing the rear wall. Johnny sat in the adjoining booth with his back to Frank's. Their conversation went on unnoticed. A shrill public address announcement of a train arrival vibrated through the arched glass façade of the main building. Getting up, Foley murmured, "Seven P.M. here," as he brushed past and went to pay his bill. De Graaf wandered around for half an hour, buying a magazine and having a coffee, before he left the station and joined the bustling crowds outside.

On the day of his departure, Johnny contacted the Soviet Embassy late in the afternoon to ascertain whether Moscow had wired any change to his plans. Confirmation of his departure from Prague and arrival time in Moscow had been sent to M4 headquarters; no modifications were requested. Johnny did not see his informant, nor did he seek him out, as this could have triggered the man's suspicions. Johnny told Helena to meet him later, and with his bag took a cab to the railway station for his final rendezvous with Foley.

He checked his suitcase at the left-luggage office at 6:30 P.M. and strolled to an open food bar, where he ate a light meal. Half an hour later he was gazing at wall posters in the slightly congested waiting room. Within minutes, Frank was at his side. "Any change, anything new?" came Foley's resonant voice. Staring ahead at the wall before him, Johnny replied, "No." Foley gave his agent instructions and contacts in both Manchuria and China should he actually be sent there. "Good luck, Johnny. Keep in touch," he murmured, then disappeared into the crowd. Johnny continued looking at the travel posters on the big wall, then turned and went over to the hardwood benches and sat down, taking out his newspaper. Helena and the two fellow travelers arrived separately. The last man had just made his departure for Moscow,[21] feeling none the worse for having had too many beers in the city.

It was in the first half of September 1933 when Helena and Johnny's train reached Moscow.[22] They were met and driven to M4 headquarters. There Johnny gave his full mission report to Ian Berzin. "You did your best, Johnny," Berzin remarked. "It was a hell of a mess, and we had no choice but to get you out fast. The party is shot to hell there now with Hitler in power, and it will be a long while before we patch up our shambles. No Communist's life is worth anything under the Nazis, especially yours."

Willy Leow's departure came up; the Communist hunt for him was in full swing. "You provided a valuable service by informing us of his absconding with the funds," Berzin said warmly. "We'll nail that fellow no matter where he goes." Johnny nodded in agreement. It could not happen to a nicer guy, de Graaf thought, his hostile feelings toward the man still near the surface. Johnny had no regrets about setting him up and no doubts about his pending doom.

Later that night Johnny and Helena checked into the Hotel Passage and were given room 17.[23] De Graaf was dead tired from the trip and all the mental activity. At the desk in the foyer he was given a letter postmarked Ahlen, Germany, and addressed to him care of a Moscow box number. In their room he opened the envelope while seated on the bed. He read the first few lines and relived what he had learned in Berlin, and what Helena had explained when she arrived at the Prague boardinghouse. His sister-in-law, Emma, informed him that his wife, Maria, had passed away on March 18, 1933. She was overweight and had succumbed to a heart attack. Maria was not yet thirty-four years old when she died, and their daughter, Marianne, would always feel that her father was somewhat responsible.[24]

Although he had been in Berlin, it was a good thing that Johnny had decided not to go to the funeral. Hitler's police and troops were waiting in Ahlen. An estimated three thousand people filled the streets from the hospital where she died to the cemetery. Some were there to pay their respects, others to see if her husband would make an appearance at his wife's last journey. There were mixed feelings about the couple. All through those years their children were shunned for being the offspring of a famous Communist.[25] But that night, more than twelve hundred miles (more than 1,930 km) to the east, Johnny sat numb on his Moscow bed, as thoughts and memories of his past life and failed marriage rolled before his eyes.

11

MANCHURIA AND CHINA

The shrill ring of the bedside phone woke de Graaf from a short night's fitful sleep. He lifted the receiver to hear a distant voice say, "eleven A.M.," followed by an ominous click. Quickly glancing at his bedside clock, Johnny saw to his shock that it was already 10:00 A.M. A fast shower, a shave, and quick snack downstairs followed, before making the appointment with General Berzin.

Arriving at his superior's office, Johnny gave the general Emma's letter, which he read silently. Then, looking up at Johnny, he said respectfully, "I am sorry your wife passed on, Johnny," extending his hand. De Graaf thanked him, a little annoyed that M4 regulations required him to report all personal matters. Over cups of coffee that Ian had sent in, Berzin explained that Willy Leow had been apprehended in Paris. In his possession were most of the party's funds. Leow told Comintern officials that he had not embezzled the money but had bolted to avoid arrest.

"The Comintern is holding a hearing on this affair now," said Berzin. "Would you like to appear as a witness in the case?" Johnny agreed, and a half-hour later found the two men seated in a small committee room at Comintern headquarters. Little sneak Willy was there, waiting in front of a panel of officials, and he glanced nervously in Berzin and de Graaf's direction as they entered the room. Vehemently denying that he was a thief who had deserted his post without permission, Willy angrily called the whole episode a frame-up.

"Why did you not send us word of your exit, and why did you not contact the party when you arrived in Paris?" the investigating board asked.

"There was no time," Willy answered. "I had to leave Germany in hours once I got word of my impending arrest." They bantered back and forth, as Willy tried to explain his avoidance of the French Communist Party. His one thought, he pleaded, was to get to Moscow as fast as he could.

Leow suddenly stood up, shaking with rage, and pointed his dancing finger at de Graaf, shouting, "He set me up! He is the one who should be tried!" The chairman pounded his gavel, forcing Willy to slump back into his chair. Johnny then took the stand and testified to Willy's departure, his advising Moscow of his flight, and the hardships endured by party members in Berlin through Leow's miserliness and the lack of funds. Willy rose again, ranting that Johnny was behind it and was out to get him.

He was sternly called to order and made to sit down while the board explained to him that de Graaf was a good Communist for reporting his flight from Berlin. "Mattern did the right thing in immediately advising us, so you have no cause whatsoever to attack this true party member, who actually did you a favor," they responded. The climax came when the board ruled to discharge Willy Leow for grave misconduct. He was banished to the city of Engels/Pokrovsk, the capital of the Volga Republic, to work in a lowly position as an editor at a German publishing house. Johnny was later told that Leow was so angry to find that he had no power in Engels that he eventually walked into the center of the main street, pulled down his pants, and defecated in full view of onlookers. On February 26, 1936, he was picked up by the NKVD in Engels and charged with organizing a group of Trotskyite terrorists. In early October 1937 he was found guilty and shot.[1]

During the Comintern process against Leow that September in 1933, comrades who knew Johnny came to his and Helena's room at the Hotel Passage. During one visit they all got into a discussion about Rogalla and Leow. Johnny described Hans Rogalla as the "shame of the VKP(b)."[2] They agreed that their job was to fight against Rogalla and Leow, and that in the Comintern "rotten elements cover each other up."[3] Johnny later accused A. I. Gekker of being removed from investigating the Leow case, defending Rogalla, acts of terrorism, and covering up in the process. This prompted Gekker to call Johnny a pig.[4] De Graaf put this comment in his back pocket to use against Gekker later, if the opportunity presented itself. Rogalla was ultimately found guilty of participating in fascist counterrevolutionary propaganda among German emigrants and sentenced to five years in the gulag. He was shipped off to Magadan in the Far East. In March 1938 he was arrested there on a charge of sabotage and was executed that May.[5]

The morning following the board's decision on Leow, de Graaf was again called to M4 headquarters, where Berzin and Langner greeted him.[6] They exchanged a few views regarding the Leow ruling and then got down to business. De Graaf's new mission would be short and sweet—the two years without an important position were evidently overlooked. As he had been told in Prague, he was being sent to Manchuria. The Soviet apparatus there was mostly Comintern, but there were some General Staff people, and a particular officer had been one of Johnny's instructors at the Frunze Military Academy, Captain Werner. He had built up an outstanding international intelligence and espionage network that served the USSR. What got the attention of Moscow, however, was that it was financially self-sufficient. They wanted to know how this excellent and reliable apparatus functioned and how it could operate without financial aid when all other networks could not. "This man has yet to ask for a ruble," Berzin stated. "Find out how he does it." The ex-captain was proud of his autonomy. Self-sufficiency, however, ran counter to Soviet policy, which was to control the purse strings and thereby the people and the operations. It bothered Moscow to have a successful independent running loose.

Werner was a Comintern agent; hence, the General Staff of M4 had no business or permission to carry out an investigation. Internal bickering played a continuous part in the relationship between these two organizations. In their own way, both mistrusted the other's role in jobs that often overlapped. It was essential that the Comintern not get word of Johnny's new assignment. This would be unofficial in every way, done in the guise of an agent just passing through who had heard of this fabulous operation and wanted some tips on setting up the same elsewhere. If the Comintern knew the General Staff was poking around in its units, there would be hell to pay, right up to Stalin.

Probably in the latter part of August 1933,[7] and traveling alone, de Graaf took the Trans-Siberian Railway all the way across the Soviet Union to Chabarovsk, then the connection train down to Vladivostok. Provided with funds by Abramov,[8] he hitchhiked from Vladivostok to Mukden, the capital of Manchukuo,[9] Japanese-controlled Manchuria, where Werner was located. In Mukden he was handed along to a Polish agent who provided him with a new passport and the necessary papers.

Late that first night, after settling into his Mukden hotel, Johnny mailed a postcard to Frank Foley in Berlin. It stated briefly, "On my way home, J." Foley would know by this that his agent was in Manchuria, but only for a short while. For two days Johnny lay low, not making any contact with Werner. On the third day Johnny phoned him, explaining he was in the area, now an M4 agent, and wanted to see his old instructor. "Would you care to pay me a visit," de Graaf asked, "and share a bottle of vodka in my hotel room?" Werner agreed, but asked for crème wine instead.

Werner arrived not long thereafter, a jovial, round-faced, short, stocky man who made himself comfortable almost as soon as he entered the room. Over a few drinks, de Graaf told him he was on his way to Hong Kong, Shanghai, and then Singapore, and would greatly appreciate any advice or knowledge he could pass along on setting up units of the same high quality. "I'm a novice at this," Johnny said, "and could sure use some expert guidance and help. If you have any doubts that what I say is not so, please contact Moscow and they will confirm it," Johnny told him. Werner shook his head—"That won't be necessary"—

content in his verbal and personal appraisal. Had he contacted M4, Berzin would have backed up Johnny's story. Had he decided to go by way of Comintern, however, the officials there would have been greatly surprised and rudely enlightened. Fortunately, he had no communication with either. Werner was most obliging, stating that he would arrange for Johnny to see his operation, books, and methods in order to help him get started. Not only did he do this, but later he also provided Johnny with contacts in each city he planned to visit.

Next stop was Werner's headquarters at Dairen (now called Dalian), some 230 miles (or just over 370 km) southeast on the coast. Near the city of Port Arthur, Dairen was a bustling town on the Liaodong peninsula sticking out into the Yellow Sea. Werner was really good at his subterfuge of intelligence gathering at no cost to Moscow. De Graaf had complete exposure to his setup, and marveled at its compactness and efficiency. To his disbelief, however, he learned that Werner's financing came from selling Ford automobiles and trucks. Three other Communists worked with him, all running Ford dealerships that sold Fords to the Chinese and to Chiang Kai-shek's Kuomintang Army. Through their outlets they were able to amass great profits and run their intelligence web without Moscow's aid. They imported, sold, and exported these vehicles while maintaining a highly skilled and wide-ranging spy network. Johnny was able to verify all they said, and he departed after two weeks, amazed and full of praise for such an arrangement.[10]

De Graaf traveled on to Hong Kong using the itinerary he had mentioned to his former Frunze Academy teacher. This was done in case Werner decided after all to verify de Graaf's movements. In Shanghai he made contact with the British consul general's visa officer, George Vernon Kitson,[11] at his home. Frank had passed on his name during the Prague meeting and told Johnny to go ahead and contact him despite earlier orders. Besides his diplomatic duties, the visa officer was an intelligence contact who forwarded de Graaf's findings back to Foley in Berlin.

In Hong Kong Johnny quietly caught a steamer up to Vladivostok, the train to Chabarovsk, and the Trans-Siberian Railway back to Moscow.[12] When he walked into Berzin's office, in October 1933,[13] his chief almost fell over on being presented with the written and verbal reports of the Manchuria assignment. "A car dealership! Those fellows should be giving us advice here in Moscow," he said, chuckling heartily. Much later, when Foley was informed in person, he too exploded in laughter. "Smart devils, they take the cake!" he said.

De Graaf was given a brief two-day vacation in Moscow, which came to an abrupt end when he was told to report to M4 headquarters. There, General Berzin informed him that he was to leave for China. "This mission is organized by the Comintern, but we too have a great stake and interest in it," he explained. "Your job will be to train the west Chinese army under General Zhu De in guerrilla tactics and strategy, developing his troops in order to attack Chiang Kai-shek and the Japanese deployment on the coast."

Much to Johnny's delight, he was told that his supervisor, who was already in Shanghai, would be General Manfred Stern, the Frunze Academy instructor whom he greatly admired. Shanghai had become one of the most vital centers of the proletarian struggle in China.[14] Johnny's old enemy, Arthur Ernst Ewert, led the Comintern's efforts. While he welcomed the thought of working with Stern, he detested the idea of having anything to do with Ewert. General Berzin, with the other assembled General Staff officers, cautioned de Graaf. "Be careful. The one similarity between the Comintern and us is that what we both seek is to bring forces through Chiang's army to northern China."

In addition, the British and Chiang Kai-shek's people were still reflecting on raids they had made against the Comintern's Far Eastern Bureau in Shanghai in late 1931, netting several important Comintern leaders in the city. They had already apprehended Joseph Ducroux (alias Serge Lefranc and Dupont) on June 1, 1931. Under intense questioning, Ducroux revealed enough information for the police to pick up Ho Chi Minh in Hong Kong and Hsiang Chung-fa, general secretary of the Chinese Communist Party (CCP), in Shanghai. Finally, the documents on Ducroux linked him with Hilaire Noulens. Actually a Soviet Comintern operative, Yakov (or Yacob) Rudnik, Noulens arrived in the city in March 1930. His job was to revamp all OMS activity in Shanghai and provide support to Comintern agents. When he and his wife were suddenly picked up on June 15, 1931, an information windfall fell into the hands of the authorities. The recent history, the extensiveness of the material in the possession of the police, and the trials of Noulens in August 1932 contributed to a tricky and dangerous environment for anyone Moscow sent to China.[15]

Johnny hurriedly packed his bags. He was given US$3,000 in salary, plus another $1,000 for expenses along with five passports, before boarding a train for Helsinki. Helena was again left behind. Johnny used a Swiss passport from Moscow to Helsinki and across the Baltic Sea by ship to Sweden, a Belgian one by rail from Stockholm down to Copenhagen, and another Swiss passport from Copenhagen through Germany to France. In Paris he was given a fake American passport in the name of Harry Wickman, a rich cattle rancher from Texas.

Along the way he contacted Frank Foley, who joined him in Paris. They met before de Graaf left for Venice to board the Italian liner SS *Congo Russo* bound for Shanghai. While still in Europe, Johnny had also been presented with a check drawn on the Bank of Hong Kong in the amount of US$30,000 for Arthur Ewert but made out to Harry Wickman.[16] Johnny advised Frank of the operation and the money he was carrying, and agreed to keep in touch through the British visa officer in Shanghai. Frank informed him that the Krügers were well. This was delightful news, and Johnny arranged for them to receive additional funds through Foley.

The twenty-one-day sea voyage was uneventful, allowing Johnny ample time to fully study the work before docking in Shanghai in early November 1933. He checked into the city's first Western-style hotel, the Astor (now called the Pujiang). He would later move into a rooming house run by Frau Walter, a German Nazi who had lived all her life in Shanghai.[17] Comrade Milton, an agent from Profintern, the Soviet Trade Union International, and subordinate to the Comintern, soon contacted de Graaf at the Astor and took him by rickshaw to the home of Arthur Ewert at the Foncim Apartments, Route Frelupt 643, flat 34D, in the French Concession.[18] Arthur and his wife, Elise, or "Sabo," had arrived in Shanghai using fake American passports on September 13, 1932. Arthur's cover was that of a businessman working for an American firm called the Construction Supplies Company.[19]

"So, we meet again, Mattern," he began, a conceited smile playing across his thin lips. Looking down at Ewert's five-eight frame,[20] but straight into his eyes, Johnny replied, "I have never cared for you, Ewert, and will be against you for as long as you live."

"All right, have it your way," Arthur replied, slightly deflated.

"You also had better know now that I am under the command of General Stern of the General Staff and not under your control," Johnny continued.

"Oh, you are, eh?" he retorted. "You're a friend of General Stern?"

"Yes, he is my commander and an excellent officer," de Graaf responded firmly. Ewert looked at Johnny with contempt and then walked into another room, shutting the door behind him, ignoring de Graaf. It was the first time the two men had met since Germany.

Ewert had been born into poverty in eastern Prussia on November 13, 1890.[21] He joined the SPD when he was eighteen and worked in his uncle's saddle business, then in a steel mill. Blessed with intelligence and a voracious love of reading, but hampered by his self-important ways, Arthur met his future wife, Elise Szaborowski, through Arthur's sister, Minna, at a dance organized by the SPD youth movement. She was four years and one day older than Arthur.[22] The SPD sent them to Toronto in May 1914 to make contact with groups holding similar views. During the following four years, Arthur and Sabo were active in various Socialist groups in Canada and, to a lesser degree, in the United States. Professional activists, they had no time for children. When Sabo became pregnant in Canada, she terminated it. The couple was arrested in Toronto in March 1918 for their political activities. Arthur was deported to Germany, and Sabo followed in February 1920.

Back in Germany, Arthur became deeply involved with the Spartacus groups and then the KPD. He worked for the German electrical firm AEG during the postwar years. Sabo and Arthur finally married on September 28, 1922.[23] The KPD sent him back to the United States five years later, in August 1927, as the only Comintern delegate to the convention of the American Workers Party. He let himself be swayed by the minority faction of American Communists, headed by Jay Lovestone, over the majority bloc, led by William Z. Foster. Unfortunately for Ewert, his absence helped Ernst Thälmann consolidate his bid, instead of Ewert's, for the KPD leadership. Likewise, a part of Thälmann's success was his compliance with Moscow's preference for Foster over Lovestone.

Ewert was elected to the German Reichstag and served as a KPD delegate from 1928 to 1930. Also in 1928, he went to Moscow for the Comintern's Sixth Congress in 1928, where he was admonished for rightist tendencies. That is, he was rebuked for his long-held view on a consolatory approach to leftist members of the SPD—a view opposed by Stalin, who personally scolded Ewert, calling the German SPD a bunch of "social fascists." Stalin backed Thälmann. This partiality would ultimately drive Ewert out of the KPD, despite his confession of his errant ways, and into the cadre of individuals still thought to be useful enough to be given foreign assignments by the Comintern.

In 1929 Arthur was told to prepare for a transfer to Latin America. While learning Spanish, his knowledge of the English language resulted in another posting to the United States in 1930. Moscow wanted to know how the Foster faction, by then victorious, was doing vis-à-vis the expelled followers of Lovestone. Moscow also wanted to know how Ewert would do, considering his previous loyalties. As it turned out, he was well aware that he was being watched and tailored his actions to Soviet wishes. The Fosterites happily reported their satisfaction with Ewert to the USSR.[24]

Following his final North American posting, in 1931, Arthur was sent to Uruguay to head the Comintern's South American Bureau. While in Montevideo, Ewert became involved in events that would shape not only the remainder of his life but also those of one of the most important Brazilians of the twentieth century, Luís Carlos Prestes.[25]

Using an interpreter and calling himself Comrade Chung, Johnny gave a class in Shanghai for fifteen soldiers from the Eighth Route Army. He later taught a second group of twenty soldiers from the same force. Both courses were designed to train the Chinese Communists in guerrilla warfare. At the conclusion of each class, the soldiers returned to their units in Jiangxi (also called Kiangsi).[26]

Johnny had always held a very high opinion of Manfred Stern, a man of vast field experience but without strong political leanings. A Jew,[27] Stern was a fighter in true soldier fashion. Concerning field maneuvers he was highly competent; concerning guerrilla tactics he knew nothing. Stern was without question a soldier's soldier and a valued friend. Arriving at Johnny's door he greeted de Graaf with a booming "Thank heaven it's you, Johnny! I'm sure glad to see you! I need a fighter to whip that damned . . ."

"What's the trouble, Fred [General Stern's nickname]?" Johnny interrupted.

"Ewert!" Stern concluded. "That rat wants to run the whole show, always poking around and being a bloody irritation! He's constantly delaying me in our work, which he knows nothing about, but thinks he does." Fred eventually showed Johnny a large-scale wall map depicting the eastern part of China. In the region around Jiangxi, the Communist Chinese Army of a hundred thousand poorly armed but well-trained troops were up against Chiang Kai-shek's forces. The former chief of the German General Staff, General Hans von Seeckt, was advising Chiang's army.[28] Along the southern coast, the Japanese waited. De Graaf studied the map closely, noting how Stern had outlined the zone plans in typical General Staff style. Certainly it was not an outline of guerrilla-battle zoning for offensive aggression.

"Can I have the map, Fred, and would you do me a favor?" Johnny asked. Stern nodded as Johnny propped the diagram against the other wall. "You are an excellent field officer, Fred, but not a hit-and-run fighter," de Graaf commented.

"You're darn right!" Stern replied. "I'm no guerrilla strategist."

"Here we need guerrilla warfare to fulfill the General Staff mission expected of us, Fred," Johnny remarked. "How about going out for a coffee and giving me three uninterrupted hours to work on this chart?"

"No, don't be a nut, Johnny," said Stern. "This is our only copy, which the Comintern is supposed to get."

"Let me worry about that, Fred," de Graaf replied. "Have no fear, just let me work up a new map, and Ewert won't know the difference." Fred Stern hesitated, then threw up his hands and walked out.

As soon as he had left, Johnny hung up a fresh map and corrected the entire outline, re-marking it for a guerrilla offensive. He completed it just before Fred returned a couple of hours later. Stern looked over the new chart, compared it to an older sketch he had made, and noted the numerous changes. After a pause, he turned to de Graaf and said, "Johnny, in my opinion, you should be the general, and I should be the little major."

"But you are the little major," Johnny jokingly told him. Both men laughed. Looking at the map again, Stern said enthusiastically, "Say this is great, just what the doctor ordered." The modified plan aimed at taking the city of Nanchang and forcing Chiang Kai-shek's soldiers into a corridor between the provinces of Jiangxi, Fujian (also know as Fukien), and Zhejiang.[29]

They agreed to present the revised map to Ewert and the staff of the Comintern for their information only. Here Stern and de Graaf gambled that Ewert and his associates, being politically inclined, would have little knowledge of military forces anyway. Johnny asked Fred to sign the map but Stern refused, saying that it was Johnny's work and that his initials should be on it.

"I want you to have the honors, so please sign," Johnny told him. "Should the General Staff ask you, knowing your qualifications, it'd be up to you if you say it's mine."

"Johnny, you're going to be more trouble around here than the darned devil himself named Ewert!" Stern joked. Fred and Johnny often bantered like this, a luxury allowed between friends.

They arranged a meeting with the Comintern that night. Stern would point out the revisions in the map and say, "Comrades, here is the plan of attack and placement of troops." Arthur Ewert would then show how little he understood. At the appointed time, Ewert and the others arrived. Ewert hardly glanced at the map. "It won't be accepted," he announced. Johnny thanked him and said, "That map and all other papers will be sent by air to the General Staff in Moscow. Furthermore," he went on, "I can predict that their answer to this rejection will result in you being forced from your post here and recalled." There was far more power in the General Staff than in the Comintern, which it would not hesitate to demonstrate. "That's the way we'll proceed," Johnny informed his shaken Comintern colleagues. "Our own wireless station will soon be set up, so we'll have no further need of your facilities of communication," de Graaf added. Ewert stood up, gave Johnny a cold stare, and left the room, slamming the door behind him.

Otto Braun (the alias of Karl Wagner),[30] the Comintern's military advisor in Shanghai, attended this meeting and naturally was in Ewert's corner. Braun had arrived in China as part of a two-man team, each with US$20,000 to give to Richard Sorge, who was in Shanghai to purchase the freedom of Noulens. Braun either ignored or refused to follow Manfred Stern's directives, or he carried them out, but too late for them to be effective. Johnny thought the man was egotistical and lacked patience. He was not alone in this assessment. Braun did not get along with General Zhu De. The two men argued, and Zhu De dismissed Braun from his staff.[31]

The modified map, with full outline of the plans and strategy, was dispatched to Moscow that night and approved the following day. Months later Ewert would be removed from office and called back to Moscow. The accompanying report would make him look like a fool who could not understand a good military campaign map when he saw one. Among the items mentioned to their superiors in the USSR was Ewert's shoddiness at a number of things. Arthur had several irritating habits, some of them lethal for a spy. Of paramount concern was his practice of leaving compromising documents lying around his living quarters. He was warned time and again to keep this material well hidden. On one occasion Ewert's Foncim apartment was broken into and robbed of a single US$500 bill, apparently left lying in the open. Arthur claimed that there were three additional $500 bills in the same spot. Comrade Milton, together with Stern, Johnny, and another comrade, thought the break-in was the work of the Shanghai municipal police. De Graaf sent details of the affair back to Vasiliev in Moscow.

The questionable incident of the $500 bill dovetailed into another matter: a visit to the widow of Sun Yat-sen. Sun, the spiritual father of the Kuomintang, had married Soong Ching-ling, who disliked Chiang Kai-shek. Following her husband's death, Soong lived for a while in Berlin before returning to Shanghai, where she resided on Rue Molière in the French Concession. Chiang's police kept her house under constant observation, duly observing all who came and went. The arrest of a number of Chinese Communists, particularly those with whom Ewert had contact, was plausibly tied to either the robbery of the $500 or the meeting(s) with Soong.[32] Then there was the issue of Arthur's passport. Ewert used the same bogus American passport, no. 542115, bearing the name of Harry Berger, during his previous South American mission and the present one in China.[33]

In addition to these careless mistakes, another event came to cloud Arthur's reputation in China. About ten days after the disagreement between Stern, de Graaf, and Ewert over the revised military plan, Ewert asked Johnny to train Milton in sabotage. During a trip of some forty kilometers (nearly twenty-five miles) out of Shanghai to test a waterproof fuse, Johnny discovered that Comrade Milton was trying to kill him—at Ewert's urging. The new fuse had been attached to a bomb that mysteriously went off too soon. De Graaf immediately suspected Milton, and he managed to get him to confess, give up the assassination attempt, and begin reporting to Johnny on Ewert's movements. Johnny suffered a leg injury in the explosion, which required a trip to the hospital when the group returned to Shanghai.[34]

Comrade Milton was actually Eugene Dennis. From the end of World War II until 1957, Dennis would serve as the general secretary, and from 1959 to 1961 as the national chairman, of the Communist Party of the United States of America, the CPUSA.[35] His botched murder attempt in 1934 undoubtedly convinced de Graaf that the hostility between himself and Ewert had been bumped up to a higher level. He would have to take care of Ewert, if he got the chance. Otherwise, his nemesis might beat him to it.

When Johnny's leg healed, he prepared to travel west to begin training General Zhu De's troops. Fred would remain in Shanghai to run the command post. One evening, prior to departure, Johnny, disguised as a door-to-door peddler, made his way to the home of the British visa officer. George Kitson recognized de Graaf from his previous Shanghai visit. After exchanging passwords and a cordial greeting, the two men got down to the details of the current undertaking, which the Englishman said he would relay to Foley in Berlin. Later, unnoticed, and following a change of clothes, de Graaf struck out for the front by rail. Along the way General Zhu De and his staff, who boarded the train midway in the journey, introduced Johnny to Zhou Enlai. Zhou, then the vice chairman of the Central Revolutionary Military Commission, which controlled the Red Army,[36] appeared most amiable and was very interested in the offensive plans about to unfold. Zhu De, a short, lightweight man, had a winning way with Zhou, leaving no question in Johnny's mind as to his high capabilities.

Arriving at their destination in Huangshi, they proceeded by truck to the field headquarters. De Graaf was assigned a private billet and taken on a field tour, which ended later that night in a long briefing. He was impressed with General Zhu De's officers and soldiers, who were already a good guerrilla force. They would battle Chiang Kai-shek's far larger and far superior army for years.[37] Johnny's assignment was to teach the troops about plots, strategy, and the maneuvers of insurrectionary battle. The morale of the hundred thousand fighters was very high under Zhu De, a natural leader and born optimist. Zhu took his hat off when talking with his men.[38] Surveying their firearms, however, de Graaf was appalled to find that they had a large array of assorted foreign rifles of different calibers, but hardly any ammunition.

They began by sorting out all the arms and bullets so that each man and each unit had the correct ammo for the corresponding weapon. In this way they formed companies, some made up solely of British guns, some of French, and yet others of American arms. The troops were eager to learn. After dispersing the available weaponry, Johnny found that they were still short of arms and began to look for other providers. He bought a fair number of military supplies from southern troops who were trying to remain neutral but were willing to aid General Zhu De's fighters if the price was right. Once purchased, these arms were smuggled through a neutral province to the hands of Mao Zedong in the Communist territory of Jiangxi.[39]

Even as the weaponry roundup was in progress, Johnny began tutoring group leaders and their troops in the use of explosives. He stuck to the basics, taking a lot of time with training before permitting anyone to handle black powder. One had to become familiar with the explosive when it was dry. No one should mess with the stuff once it got hot. So deeply was this drummed into these men that before long they could set explosives in their sleep. In battle, they blew up barracks, equipment, and the odd ship from a safe distance of several miles.

Finally, after a detailed briefing, it appeared that everything was ready. Johnny wired Fred Stern at Shanghai command to keep him informed. The offensive imminent, Zhu De's officers delivered strict orders to the troops that any man caught robbing or plundering farmers along the way would face a sentence of death by firing squad. "If the peasants can sell you food or supplies of any kind, pay them for it," they commanded. In the battles that followed, Johnny believed that only two men were executed for disobeying this order.

The march to the northwest began. The goal was to circle around Chiang's forces and attack the Japanese first. Succeeding in that mission, they would engage the Kuomintang army of two million men. Zhu De's troops were greatly outnumbered, but the leftist tactics of "Bite here, fight there" paid great dividends. When it was Chiang's turn, his troops never knew when or where Zhu De's units would strike or what their strength was at any given moment. Soon Zhu De's original force of a hundred thousand men gained size and momentum, increasing by half a million followers. Armed farmers had swollen the ranks. They trusted the soldiers who paid for goods, as opposed to Chiang's troops, who robbed, raped, and murdered.

In the interim, Stern had been having discussions with representatives of Cai Tingkai, leader of the Nineteenth Route Army located on the coast near Fujian. Cai was not for Chiang Kai-shek or the Communists, but he agreed to help Zhu De keep Chiang's troops from overriding his positions. Zhu De could then attack Chang Kai-shek from two sides, using the Nineteenth Route Army as his ally. In return, Zhu De guaranteed the Fujian full independence later. If all went well, Chiang would be caught in a classic pincers movement.

Arthur Ewert was informed of this agreement, reached after weeks of bartering with Cai Tingkai, but he dealt it a deathblow. Against the express wishes of General Stern, he granted a three-page interview to the Shanghai weekly *China Forum* at the end of November 1933, in which he revealed, and essentially condemned, the alliance. Other newspapers picked up his remarks, with disastrous consequences. Ewert also called the Fujian leaders bourgeois who were only interested in preserving military rule against the wishes of the CCP. He even said that Cai Tingkai and the Nineteenth Route Army had pro-American leanings.[40] The reaction was predictable. Thanks to Ewert, Cai Tingkai backed out of the agreement and remained truly neutral thereafter.

The ramifications of Arthur Ewert's exposé, however, were probably not what he intended. Johnny and Stern were incensed after all the work they had done to obtain Cai Tingkai's help. At one point Stern and Ewert even faced each other with drawn revolvers over Ewert's betrayal.[41] Even so, the rebel forces under Mao and Zhu De scored several more victories. Indeed, Johnny would later report that the Red revolutionaries had destroyed seventy-six aircraft at the Nanjing military airport without sustaining a single loss.[42] But the opportunity to smash the Kuomintang army, following a year of Chiang's final "extermination campaign," eluded them.

Johnny denounced the entire Communist organization at Jiangxi to London via the British visa officer in Shanghai, who probably informed the Kuomintang. Following a series of meetings, Mao was demoted to the role of figurehead. Those who did not fall to Chiang's forces, perhaps as many as 120,000 troops and 30,000 civilians, began leaving the area in October 1934. The escape plan was Zhou Enlai's; Mao had wanted to stay and fight. Their journey to the west would be the start of the famous Long March.[43]

Months before the exodus, Chang Kai-shek turned up the heat on the hunt for Communists in Shanghai.[44] General Stern and Johnny kept abreast of the military situation from the safer confines of the international settlement. Comrade Milton stripped Ewert of his political responsibilities. Arthur took refuge in his wife's apartment at Bubbling Well Road 941, in the former American Concession.[45] Finally, General Stern was recalled to Moscow, ending his part in the Chinese mission and separating the two colleagues. Johnny wished him well as they embraced prior to his departure, probably in April 1934.[46]

The evening Stern left, Johnny made his way to the home of his British contact, dressed again in peddler's clothes. They discussed the mission's accomplishments and de Graaf's unsupervised time ahead until Moscow cabled. Kitson, comfortably relaxed in his living room, began to speak on one particular British problem of long standing. It appeared that a foreign spy had been obtaining English industrial secrets, undetected, over a span of some thirty years. Try as they might, British businesses could not ferret him out. Several industries worked on British production contracts, most in the armaments field. Someone in management must have been passing on the plans in a way not yet understood. Those officials, none in senior positions, had been put under surveillance, but nothing tangible had surfaced.

"These men are passing on information, Johnny. We know it, but how they do it and to whom they give it, we can't pin down," he said gravely.

"If I were running this intelligence setup," Johnny replied, "I would use a Chinese laundry as the drop and cover. Such businesses have lots of people going in and out all day without creating suspicions. Have you considered that possibility?"

"No, we haven't," Kitson replied thoughtfully. "But it sure would be logical, now that you mention it. The city is full of such establishments."

For the rest of the evening they discussed the problem and possible solutions until a plan of action unfolded. Besides Johnny, there were eight foreign intelligence agents from SIS in Shanghai. One member of this nine-man squad, or one of those who selected the nine operatives, might well have been the British vice consul in Shanghai, and SIS agent Harry Steptoe. Steptoe had had a hand in the arrest of Hilaire Noulens.[47] What was needed was something he knew how to do. The group put tails on the six individuals when each suspect was away from work. Over a period of time they would look for any common denominators. Johnny and two others began checking out nearby Chinese laundries. The agents assembled the following morning in a deserted warehouse basement. For the entire day they mapped out their strategy of surveillance and reporting until each man was totally familiar with the tactics to be used. They narrowed down the thousands of laundry establishments in Shanghai to the twenty or so closest to each suspect's home. Then they checked the background of every laundry proprietor in the net. After just two weeks they had zeroed in on a shop that two suspects had visited separately, once each, during the preceding fortnight. The laundry was owned by a Japanese national and located outside those so far investigated. The building was put under round-the-clock surveillance from a rented room across the street. Three agents maintained a vigil from this spot, while colleagues continued to keep the suspects under observation.

Two more weeks passed. Nothing unusual took place, but each customer was observed through binoculars and photographed. The snapshots were passed on to Kitson for comparison with the pictures of midlevel bureaucrats working for firms that did business with the British. During the third week, one of the suspects photographed turned out to be a chief engineer for a British company who until then had not even been under suspicion. He picked up a shadow, reducing the shop surveillance team to two. Around noon the following day, another photo, of a similarly unsuspected person, was taken. As he began to be tailed, Johnny was left alone in the rented apartment. He managed to get some rest on a small cot in the back of the room. Late at night, when the shop closed, its proprietor would leave and Johnny could sleep. He and his fellow agents felt certain that they were on to something, because the suspects dropped off their laundry but never returned to pick it up.

For a solid month Johnny remained at this post, night and day, checking periodically for word from Moscow, which never arrived. The boredom of this surveillance assignment got to him; but his gut feeling that the key lay across the street gave him the motivation to continue. Finally, on a Tuesday night, the breakthrough came. The eight suspects arrived that evening, one by one, left their parcels, and then exited the laundry separately—all of them empty-handed. As each man came and went, Johnny was in contact with his team, who phoned in as they pursued their suspects.

Having watched the second customer arrive, tailed by his shadow, Johnny knew that this would be the night. He quickly instructed the other agents to return to the rented room after seeing their charges home. By the time the last customer departed, four of his men had returned to the surveillance room. When the final agent arrived, the group raced across the street and surrounded all of the laundry's exits. Three men then pounded on the front door. When the door opened a hair, the agents, with guns drawn, threw their combined weight against it, throwing the shop owner to the floor.

Hastily they lifted the proprietor to his feet, forcing him past the dimly lit counter and assorted packages to a back room. In this work area, stacked on a well-used worktable, lay the special laundry parcels. Beyond them, unwrapped, were the British secret manufacturing blueprints and a miniature camera.

The captured spy suddenly lunged for a small ceremonial sword hanging on the wall. Johnny's cohorts held the man firmly as he pleaded to be allowed to take his own life. De Graaf agreed, but only after he was questioned. His round face nodded, and he began to relate how he had worked undetected for years, obtaining from his informants countless military documents that he photographed and sent to Japan. The originals were mailed unobtrusively to the informants' homes the same night. They then returned the documents to their companies' files. All of these statements were taken down. Exhausted, the man finally asked for the sword, which he was allowed to take down from the wall. Then, kneeling on a small rug, he grasped the weapon in both hands, mumbled a prayer, and before everyone's astonished eyes, plunged the sword deep into his bloated belly. By committing hara-kiri he was able to go to his death without disgrace. Johnny had witnessed the virtual suicide of prisoners at Osowiec, but he had never before seen a Japanese ritual suicide. It was shocking!

They posted a guard on the premises. A team relieved him the next morning and went over everything. At the same time, other agents rounded up the collaborators at their homes and places of business. All were arrested, brought to trial, and convicted.

At the end of August 1934, Johnny, Comrade Milton, the Ewerts, and Ewert's radio operator received a cable instructing them to return to Moscow. De Graaf made contact with the British prior to departure and then boarded the ship with the others. The vessel skirted the Korean peninsula and docked in Vladivostok. The five Communists then took a train up to Chabarovsk and from there the Trans-Siberian Express for the six-day rail passage back to Moscow.[48] When Johnny stepped from his carriage in the Soviet capital, he was driven to M4 headquarters, where General Berzin was waiting. The general was all smiles and congratulations. Had he even suspected the dual life his agent was leading, he would probably have executed de Graaf on the spot himself. It was an unceasingly precarious role for de Graaf. One small slipup would literally be his last.

Once, discussing the China mission, Berzin remarked, "General Stern and I feel that perhaps we should keep you or another General Staff agent in China in order to see that our efforts to date do not go astray."

"Sir, that is not necessary," Johnny replied confidently, "for those troops are the finest. Right now they are teaching Chiang a lesson he won't forget. They have such determination. They certainly don't need a watchful, prodding eye to guarantee there is no letup until Chiang is whipped."

"You should know, Johnny. I'm convinced," Berzin responded, a warm smile spreading across his face.

A short while later Johnny was informed that General Stern had signed the China battle-plan map he had sent by air to Moscow. He used his own initials but underneath wrote Johnny's M4 agent number, "X-502."[49] Berzin knew this and said, "Thank you for helping one of our best field commanders." On meeting Fred Stern afterward, Johnny complained. Stern countered, "Come on Johnny, you made the maps, and it was only right your signature belonged on them, and full credit given." Johnny considered Manfred Stern a fine and honorable officer. He was also a loyal friend. Little did he know that in years to come, Americans agents would question him about General Stern. Unbeknownst to Johnny, his friend would be in a gulag by then. But at that moment, in Moscow, he was determined not to let Fred down.

12

BRAZIL ONE

"How would you like to go on a mission to Spain with me?" General Stern asked Johnny over lunch at an agents' hotel in Moscow. De Graaf looked at him curiously.

"Fred, I know Spain, the good and the bad," he replied. "I also know you. Either they will kill you, the sons-of-bitches called Legionnaires [led by Francisco Franco], or they will make life completely unbearable for you. Either way, it's a good country to avoid."

"I've just come back from Spain," Stern replied, watching surprise hit Johnny's face.

"When were you there, Fred?" Johnny asked, still somewhat stunned.

"While you were in China and thought I was back in Moscow," the general stated serenely, amused by Johnny's reaction to his news.

Gradually Stern enlightened his dining companion, stating that Spain had few trained soldiers. The balance were from the Mediterranean but were not good material. He had developed numerous plans yet had trouble realizing them. Fed up and frustrated in Spain, he had asked to be recalled. Stern returned to Moscow via the Ukraine.

"Do you think you could have changed things and succeeded with the China mission, Johnny?" he asked.

"That would have been doubtful, Fred," de Graaf soothed him, "for one can't control a riot with a loaded gun at your back."

Johnny was well aware of the problems in Spain, having read numerous reports. The Spanish military made all decisions, and whoever disagreed would be placed in a corner and have his eyes shot out. De Graaf had seen accounts of men who had died this way. Moreover, the international powers were not interested in forcing Spain into a democratic way of life.

"It was a living hell, I can tell you," Fred continued. "I barely escaped with my life."

"Should you go back," Johnny said, looking Stern straight in the face, "and I am ordered to go along, I will state categorically that I will never stay. If they ask you, Fred, turn it down, for a dead agent is no agent." Stern sighed thoughtfully, nodding in agreement.

Several weeks passed as Johnny enjoyed himself with visits to national monuments. He toured the landmarks around the Kremlin and for the first time viewed the numerous markers embedded in the wall behind the Lenin Mausoleum in Red Square. While Lenin's beard still grew and required daily care, de Graaf was flabbergasted to see plaques in honor of several cutthroats buried outside in the barrier surrounding the Kremlin. One was for Karl Herltz, the late showoff, Béla Kun, the thieving former Balkan party secretary, and others equally renowned for their wickedness. As he read their markers, he spat. A sentry approached and asked why de Graaf showed such revulsion for national heroes. "They're mostly rats!" Johnny told him. "Are there not other places to put dirty swine like these?"

"You know these two?" the soldier inquired.

"Yes," Johnny answered. "I knew them and couldn't stand them." The sentry expressed his agreement. "Maybe, for us in Russia, such skunks are required for propaganda," Johnny informed him. "But they sure as blazes don't deserve to be anywhere near Lenin!"

"My opinion too," the guard whispered. "However, they are placed there by the state and we just follow orders." Johnny cursed and walked off. "The stupidity of it all!" he muttered to himself, still fuming at his revolting discovery.

De Graaf busied himself with lecturing trainee agents and taking more intelligence courses at M4 headquarters, until one morning Alfred Langner called him to his office. Also present were Piatnitski, Manuilski, and Pavel Vasiliev. "Johnny, two alternatives for you, one, a return to China, and two, a mission to Brazil to organize a revolution," Langner began, seated behind his polished desk.[1]

"Comrade Langner," Johnny replied, "I believed this before and even more so now: China can run well by itself with what we began and set rolling. All those rebels now fighting will win without our supervision. However, Brazil is an entirely different story. As there is a choice, I would like to hear more about Brazil."

"Are you aware, Johnny, that some of your dear friends from the Comintern will also be on this Brazilian mission?" Langner modestly remarked.

"Who, for instance?" Johnny asked.

"Arthur Ernst Ewert," came the smooth reply.

"What?" said Johnny, sputtering in annoyance. "I won't take one single step for that bastard!"

"I know all about him," Langner laughed. "In fact, we knew the problem you and Manfred Stern had with him long before the Comintern called their boy home."

How Langner had received the advance information even before Stern's maps were sent to Moscow, Johnny never discovered. The thought of what else he knew made icy shivers run down his spine. He braced himself for further revelations. Manuilski then added that despite de Graaf's insistence that Ewert was difficult to work with in a group, there would be a collective to decide things in Brazil.[2] "The mission," Langner continued, "is to send down a highly specialized group, you being the only General Staff member, to cultivate, recruit, and develop cells within and outside of the military. The armed forces are in the throes of unrest. With proper fanning, a massive uprising, then a revolt, can be ignited, resulting in the ousting of the Brazilian government.

"Your task," he went on, "will be mainly involved in the training of guerrilla groups and offering advice in military strategy and tactics. A newly acquired Comintern specialist will head the actual arranging of this overthrow . . . Luís Carlos Prestes. Your assignment will be to assist him."

Prestes was a former Brazilian officer and rebel. Well liked, and highly influential in many quarters, he caught the attention and imagination of Soviet officials. In him they saw a chance to get rid of the Brazilian head of state, Getúlio Vargas, and put Prestes in his place. The Comintern had located Prestes in Buenos Aires, converted him to communism through the efforts of Abraham Guralski (the alias of Boris Heifetz) and Arthur Ewert, and sent him to the Soviet Union.[3] In Moscow, his politically training was intensified. "Prestes is a natural born leader," Langner informed Johnny, "and highly knowledgeable of his country and people."

"All right, I will go," Johnny said. "I hope this man is all you say he is."

A select group composed of Prestes, Ewert, Johnny, the head of the Argentine Communist Party, Rodolfo José Ghioldi, two other Argentines,[4] one Italian, one American, five members of the Brazilian party, including the head of the revolutionary committee from Rio de Janeiro, and Pavel Vladimirovich Stuchevski, would all travel to Rio de Janeiro. Stuchevski was a Soviet citizen and a member of the ominous NKVD. Ewert's, Ghioldi's, and Stuchevski's real wives would accompany their spouses. Johnny would bring Helena Krüger, masquerading as his wife. When de Graaf returned from China, he discovered that Helena, who was described as exceedingly attractive, had been involved with a number of men. This further cooled what was left of their relationship. Nonetheless, it was recommended that he take her with him to afford the cover of traveling as husband and wife.[5]

A bodyguard who became his lover, Olga Benário, traveled with Prestes. She walked out on B. P. Nikitin, her husband of about a year, to do it.[6] Olga was a fugitive from her hometown, Munich, where she was wanted for assisting in the escape of Otto Braun from the Moabit Prison. However, a report from Gestapo agent and former Communist Franz Grybowski, in the files of Stasi, the former East German secret police, points out that the authorities claimed that Olga was not among the activists who actually sprang Braun—but they blamed her for it anyway.[7] Following a period in a number of safe houses, the pair traveled separately to Moscow. In part, this was because she was weak from an induced abortion.[8]

Olga was the Jewish daughter of a middle-class Social Democratic lawyer who had rejected her father's politics to become a Communist at age fifteen.[9] By the time she left Moscow with Prestes, she was fluent in four languages, a markswoman, a pilot, and knew how to use a parachute. She too worked for Berzin at M4 and had already been on assignments in England and France. Manuilski personally placed Olga in charge of Prestes's safety. As the couple left Moscow on December 29, 1934, she was nearly always at his side, armed with an automatic pistol.

Traveling on poor-quality documents to western Europe, Prestes and Olga finally obtained a Portuguese passport from the left-leaning Israel Abrahão Anahory, the Portuguese consul general in Rouen, France. The passport was issued to businessman Antonio Vilar and his wife, Maria Bergner Vilar, and was valid for travel to South America. In charge of planning the trip, Olga decided on a *pièce de la resistance* to their new passport, U.S. entry and exit stamps. Since the Vilars were supposedly a rich couple on their honeymoon, there was no trouble obtaining an American visa and boarding the SS *Ville de Paris,* which arrived in New York on March 26, 1935.

In those days, passenger aircraft did not fly at night to Latin America. This meant that visas were necessary for all the stops along the way. The route took them south from Miami to Cuba, Panama, Ecuador, Peru, Chile, Argentina, and Uruguay. Finally, in Montevideo, they luckily caught a French mail hydroplane up the Atlantic coast to a beach near Florianópolis in the Brazilian state of Paraná. The craft stopped only momentarily, but it was long enough for the pair to deplane. Olga had convinced the pilot that she had relatives in the state and that by hopping off there they could save a lot of travel time. He gave his approval, and the two passengers stepped ashore without having to encounter any snooping customs officials. On April 15, 1935, still a fugitive in his home country, Luís Carlos Prestes was back. Soon, though, British diplomatic circles informed the Brazilians that Prestes had landed in the country and was using the name Antonio Vilar. The Americans followed by telling the Vargas administration that he was not simply in Brazil but in Rio de Janeiro.[10]

Prestes was more than just a wanted man. He was "O Cavalheiro da Esperança" (the Knight of Hope) to some, a dangerous dissenter to others. In 1924, a captain in the Brazilian army, he had been among those who took up arms against one of the most corrupt presidents of the Old Republic (1889–1930), Artur Bernardes (1922–26). In partial command of the military forces opposed to Bernardes, but actually the de facto leader from October 29, 1924, until February 3, 1927, the Coluna Prestes (Prestes Column) battled its way all over the interior of Brazil. The goal was to stir up the repressed peasants. The journey covered twenty-five thousand kilometers, and because they never lost a battle to the pursuing loyalist troops, they were often called the Coluna Invicta (or Undefeated Column). After running out of ammunition, most of the rebels left for exile in neighboring countries. Their revolution of the poor never caught on, but morally many Brazilians admired Prestes for what he stood up to and tried to accomplish.[11]

The rest of the core group of revolutionaries continued to land or were already in place. In March 1935, Arthur Ernst Ewert and Sabo had arrived from Montevideo. Ewert was still using his Harry Berger passport. Likewise, in March, two Soviets disguised as Belgians, Leon Jules Vallée (really Pavel Stuchevski) and his wife, Alphonsine (Sofia Semionova Stuchevskaya), touched port in Rio. Not only was Pavel the NKVD's representative, he was also delegated to be the local head of OMS. Sofia was assigned to M4.

In April, disembarking from the SS *Western World* under the alias of Luciano Busteros was Rodolfo Ghioldi and his wife, Carmen de Alfaya Ghioldi. Next to arrive, in June, was the only American, sick with tuberculosis and syphilis, Victor Allen Barron. His job was to build a radio transmitter. This was no easy task, as the pieces had to be bought separately to avoid suspicion. An Italian, Amleto Locatelli, was delegated to conduct training in street fighting, particularly in São Paulo. Reaching Rio in the second week of November, he was the last to land in Brazil. The first to arrive, aboard the French vessel SS *Florida* on January 4, 1935, nearly three months before any of the others, were Johnny de Graaf and Helena Krüger.[12]

Prior to his departure from the USSR, de Graaf was introduced to Prestes at a Moscow planning session. No one could help but be impressed by Prestes's charm, suave manners, and commanding voice. He was short, slender, and extremely good-looking, with shiny black hair and sparkling eyes. Johnny could see why he would be a highly popular hero type in Latin America. On the other hand, de Graaf questioned Prestes's knowledge when he stated that 90 percent of their work had already been done. He made no bones about the fact that he had most of the military in the palm of his hand, and that it would take little encouragement to start an uprising within the armed forces. Johnny doubted Prestes's assertions but did not get into a disagreement with him regarding his views. "Without a doubt," Johnny thought, "he's considered a godlike leader, a savior to the Brazilian people. He displays confidence enough for ten men."

Leaving the meeting, Johnny had already formed a strong impression. "This man has his head in the clouds; reality and sound logic at times escape him." Johnny was now convinced that his biggest battle would not be with the Brazilian government but with Luís Carlos Prestes and his fellow Communists, individuals like Ewert. They appeared to be caught in Prestes's spell of delusions, power, and victory with ease. In Johnny's mind, this first notion would prove to be correct. De Graaf avoided Ewert while Arthur, no doubt, did likewise.

Johnny and Helena had left Moscow under assumed names in November 1934, first by rail to Finland, then by sea to Sweden on either the SS *Svea* or the SS *Primula,* and from there by train and ferry to Denmark.[13] En route, Johnny wired Foley in Berlin. The cable read, "Dear Friend, I'm on a long trip and looking forward to seeing you in Copenhagen." Frank timed his move on receipt of the message. Arriving at København H, Copenhagen's Central Station, Johnny checked Helena into a hotel and then proceeded back to the train station to meet an express coming up from Berlin. Standing well back from the crowd, he saw Frank Foley alight. Certain that Frank had spotted him, de Graaf ambled down the road away from the station with Foley following at a safe distance. Nearing the hotel, he stopped, and as Foley passed by Johnny whispered, "ten," his room number. Johnny then crossed the street and proceeded directly to his hotel room. Frank walked on and then doubled back. Some minutes later he knocked softly on Johnny's door.

Excusing himself from Helena, Johnny accompanied Folly to another part of the hotel. Finding a place to sit, Foley inquired, "What's up, Johnny?" A lengthy account followed in which Johnny filled Frank in on his stay in Moscow and the new mission to Brazil. De Graaf told Foley that Arthur Ewert was also being sent to Rio and that his days were numbered if he could arrange it. Frank laughed a deep rumble, aware of Johnny's past encounters with Ewert. Foley was extremely interested in the Brazilian plot and felt that he should get in touch with the head of Section V (counterespionage) of SIS. That meant contacting Major Valentine Patrick Terrell Vivian, or "Vee-Vee," as he was called.[14] Foley hastily disappeared, returning in an hour with Vivian's instructions.

London wanted to be closely informed by someone inside Brazil. Johnny was told to make contact with Alfred Hutt, who was the general assistant superintendent of Light, the Canadian-owned electric company in Rio. Hutt was the second-leading SIS agent in the Brazilian capital, succeeded in importance only by the British ambassador, Sir Hugh Gurney.[15] Hutt would be Johnny's resident manager, and would transfer secret cables and messages to the British Embassy. The embassy in turn would relay everything to London. All messages would be sent and received in code that the telegraphers could not understand. When he heard that Vee-Vee was apparently Foley's boss, Johnny knew he wanted to meet him. Foley must have observed this and communicated it to his superior. Back in Moscow, de Graaf and his classmates at Frunze had been taught that Vivian was the best of the English undercover agents and that they should stay clear of him when on assignment.[16] He was said to have had a near voluminous knowledge of both the Comintern and Marxism.[17] Later, however, when Johnny got to know Vivian, he found his ways irritating. After bringing de Graaf up to date on the Krügers in Berlin, Foley departed. It was late November 1934.

The next day, Johnny and Helena flew over Germany to Brussels, then took a train to Paris and applied for Brazilian visas. Afterward, Johnny met with Vivian, who had come to Paris especially to size up the SIS's new recruit. Vee-Vee was a frail, mustached man, five foot ten (177.8 cm), who could not drink alcoholic beverages because of a stomach ulcer.[18] The two men discussed all aspects of the Comintern's efforts in Brazil. Vivian was noticeably impressed and instructed de Graaf to relay to Hutt the plans as they developed, especially if he felt they were feasible. He stated that His Majesty's government would take care of the rest.

When their visas were issued, on December 6, Johnny and Helena took a train to Basel, Switzerland, and then another to Genoa, Italy, to catch the 5,515-ton French liner SS *Florida*. They boarded as a married Austrian couple, Franz Paul and Erna Gruber,[19] and booked passage in first class, a common Comintern ploy. Gruber was supposed to be a businessman. Erna had no profession (i.e., she was a housewife). The *Florida* reached Rio late on January 4, so no one went ashore until the following day. At dockside, waiting for the Grubers to clear customs on the fifth, was Dr. Ilvo Meireles of the PCB (Partido Comunista Brasileiro—Brazilian Communist Party). Dr. Meireles took Johnny and Helena to the Hotel Flamengo in the suburb of the same name. Soon relaxing in their room, Ilvo brought "Martins" (Honório de Freitas Guimarães) to the hotel to meet Johnny. Martins was the organizer of the PCB. He took de Graaf around to meet to Antônio Maciel Bonfim, known as "Miranda" and "Fernandes," the gregarious leader of the Brazilian Communists.[20] Martins also set up the times and place to make contact: every fifteen days in downtown Rio on the sidewalks of the main thoroughfare, Avenida Rio Branco.[21]

Three months passed while Johnny waited for the rest of the team to alight. In April, Vivian arrived and met him at the Copacabana Palace Hotel. They again went over the proposed plan to overthrow Getúlio Vargas. Vivian introduced Johnny to Alfred Hutt not long afterward.[22] Johnny and Helena also found some new dwellings in a pleasant Copacabana boardinghouse near the beach. At the time, Copacabana was the most popular of Rio's South Zone beaches. Johnny's cover was to pose as a retired businessman on his honeymoon with his much younger bride.[23]

It was not until May, around the time of de Graaf's forty-first birthday, that he bumped into Arthur Ewert and Sabo. Actually, Johnny saw the couple earlier when he was looking out of his boardinghouse window and observed them sitting on the sand. Once Ewert's vessel had reached port, he eventually rented a small cottage just behind Johnny's new quarters. Knowing that Johnny was a former sailor, Arthur must have figured that de Graaf would hold up close to the sea, which proved correct. Their brief encounter, between Postos 5 and 6 on the famous mosaic sidewalks flanking Avenida Atlântica, was cold but cordial. Each suppressed his antagonism with strained effort. Johnny told Ewert to start calling him "Pedro." Arthur too had a new moniker, "Apple," which he decided to use in Brazil. The name came from Ewert's pale skin and naturally red cheeks.[24]

Ewert invited Johnny to lunch with him at the Restaurant Alvear. When de Graaf arrived for the meal, Ewert introduced him to Rodolfo Ghioldi. The Ghioldis were staying in a hotel in Botafogo located on Rua Marquês Abrantes. They soon located lodgings in Copacabana. The Ewerts had stayed at the same inn when they first disembarked in Rio. Next to occupy the Marquês Abrantes hotel, in April, were Olga Benário and Luís Carlos Prestes. The couple arrived from São Paulo by taxi. Prestes did not like to go out on the streets for fear of being recognized. That left the job of finding a more permanent place to Olga. She located a furnished home for rent at Rua Barão da Torre 636 in Ipanema. It was leased to a German working for the Bayer Company who was returning to Berlin. Olga arranged to have the lease simply transferred. Most of the household items were included.[25]

Two days after meeting in Copacabana, Ewert escorted Johnny and Ghioldi to the address on Barão da Torre for their first strategy session in Brazil.[26] Right from the beginning, the internal battles began. Prestes stood up and proclaimed that their work was almost complete owing to all the support he had already obtained. In Johnny's view, "so great was his obsession, that he literally dreamt of becoming the president overnight. The others were caught up in his ranting of easy victory, with the exception of Rodolfo Ghioldi and his wife, Carmen, who stayed level headed and reasonably rational." Arthur Ewert and his spouse supported Prestes to the hilt. Arthur brought Sabo along to all the discussions, where she always sat next to Olga. Johnny mentioned that one of the unknown Argentines attended from time to time as well. The man remained uninvolved, sitting quietly to one side as an observer. He must have felt he was witnessing a circus.[27]

At this second meeting, Prestes explained how the revolution would begin in the northeast and that they would need the help of the ANL (Aliança Nacional Libertadora—National Liberation Alliance) to pull it off. The ANL had been formed in early 1935 as a reaction to Brazil's fascist party, the Integralists, or AIB (Ação Integralista Brasileira—the Brazilian Integralist Movement). By this time Stalin saw the value of a broad coalition of forces against the rise of international fascism. These were the heady days of "united fronts" in several parts of the world. Many of these progressive groups lasted until the signing of the Non-

Aggression Pact with Hitler in 1939. The intention was to slowly radicalize each front organization. Prestes was correct in assuming that they would support him in Brazil. The ANL mushroomed in size, particularly in the major urban areas. The only real problem the ANL faced was the virulent antileftism of most persons in positions of power, especially those responsible for the press, the national legislature, and the administration of Getúlio Vargas. Brazil had never had diplomatic relations with the USSR up to that point in the mid-1930s. Vargas closed the ANL in July 1935.[28]

Even so, Prestes was convinced he could win. Looking at Prestes's companion, Olga Benário, Johnny mused that "she was a German girl twice his size, who took on his airs and beliefs, totally convinced of their ultimate victory." Prestes began with a speech on how close they were to a rebellion, from which Johnny could only surmise, "He was nuts! All his gibbering and plans just didn't make sense." "All the Communists in Brazil will join our conquest," Prestes proclaimed. Johnny looked at the man "strutting before the group like a well-oiled peacock" and almost broke out laughing. By then he knew that the PCB barely existed on the level required for a revolution. When Prestes paused, Johnny cut in, "Do I hear you right when you say we are almost ready?"

"Yes we are!" Prestes beamed. Johnny could see "his little chest thrust forward in supreme confidence."

"Luís Carlos," Johnny countered, "to my knowledge you are not even 50 percent ready. As a guerrilla fighter, I say you are neither fully organized nor ready to win over the officers and men of the Third Regiment from the main military camp. Have you forgotten that the military base in Praia Vermelha looks out on the [entrance to the] bay on one side, and has a mountain immediately behind it on another? Do you not know that every Brazilian military base has a Polícia Militar[29] garrison at its doorstep, all dedicated, well paid, well armed, and totally loyal to the president? The Polícia Militar stronghold in Botafogo contains the elite of government forces, greatly outnumbering the soldiers and officers in the fort."

"Oh," Prestes replied, "just you wait and see. They'll all come over to our side when the uprising begins." He made it sound like a declaration, to which the others nodded in agreement. At this, Johnny exploded.

"Can't you realize they are pro-government and will crush the Third Regiment in ten minutes?" he asked in disbelief. "These police regiments can close up any fortification so fast, any revolt would soon be ended."

De Graaf had done his homework and felt positive in his assessment of the situation as it stood. Successive Brazilian administrations, well aware that their army spawned revolts, took the precaution of placing police units not far away from military installations. They knew they could count on these troops and the air force, but outside of that, all others were treated with suspicion, hence the watchful control. Arthur Ewert chirped in, "You're wrong, Johnny," but was told by de Graaf to shut up. The group finally calmed down and instructed Johnny to go about his training of guerrilla teams. When this was done, the feeling was that they would be far better able to win a total victory. Johnny agreed to keep them posted. In return they promised to supply him with capable men, able to survive rigorous training. He left them arguing among themselves.

Johnny quickly telephoned Al Hutt at the Light Company. "Alfred, right now I am not sure what to do," he told him. "Will London let this thing go on and explode, or should we defuse it beforehand for safety's sake?"

"I'll check it out and get back," he replied. Hutt went to the embassy to cable London. Within hours he returned de Graaf's call. "London wants to know if you can give us a revolt date?" he relayed.

"Tell them I cannot say as yet, since it is not firmly set, but likely a few months from now, the seventh of June or July," Johnny replied. The next cable said, "Hold tight and advise progress in developments."

Martins took Johnny to a house in the Cascadura suburb to begin training urban street fighters in sabotage and bomb making. The first group had five students. As his classes continued, so too did the meetings in the South Zone at the homes of Prestes, Ewert, and Ghioldi. These latter get-togethers permitted Johnny to get to know some of the other players. An Argentine named Margarita, or Marga, acted as secretary for Ewert and Ghioldi. She visited both of their residences on an almost daily basis. Pavel Stuchevski, and later Amleto Locatelli, would prove crucial back in Moscow. In 1935, Stuchevski was described as being forty-five years old, five foot eight (1.73 m), 160 pounds (72.7 kg), and of medium build, with fire-red hair and blue eyes. He spoke Russian, German, French, and English. He rarely took part in the group meetings and was totally under Ewert's control. Locatelli came from the north of Italy near Bergamo. Johnny described him as about six feet (1.83 m) tall, probably age thirty-five or so, with blond hair and a very erect bearing.[30]

At another gathering, Johnny was asked to rig a closet in Prestes's house so that it would blow up if someone tried to break in. He also made him an exploding flashlight. Remembering how Ewert had lived in Shanghai, de Graaf asked him if he wanted his documents secured in the same way, but Comrade Apple refused. Things were dangerous, especially because Prestes, Ewert, Ghioldi, the Stuchevskis, plus Johnny and Helena all lived relatively close to one another in Ipanema. The revolutionaries were jumpy. Everyone except Prestes and Ewert moved a number of times. When Ghioldi thought the police were looking for him, he asked Johnny if he and his wife could reside with them. Johnny did not like the idea but acquiesced, and the two couples began sharing Johnny and Helena's new hillside apartment at Travessa Acaraí 49 in Flamengo.[31]

Johnny continued to alienate himself from Prestes with his endless questioning. He was amazed that the PCB, which should have been involved in the undertaking and the nucleus of the committee now planning everything, was barely represented. Their political leaders and organizers went along with it all despite not being properly informed. Prestes still insisted that the main force to be counted on were the young officers and men under them who would feel it an honor to take part in an uprising. He maintained that they would gain local acclaim and be proclaimed heroes. Johnny told the group that this was a foolish assumption. "This is not a force to depend on; this is just gambling with a handful of green officers. So far as the recruits you sent me are concerned, half of them I cannot use. The balance may develop in time to a very small attack unit. Even with these bodies added to those you think you can be sure of, they are still ridiculously outnumbered and will be defeated eleven to one."

De Graaf also insisted again that the Polícia Militar stronghold on Rua São Clemente in Botafogo had been overlooked. It might well put up a fight, blocking the unification of rebel forces in Rio once the shooting began. Following this observation, and the counterargument by Prestes that his forces would sweep by the barrack, de Graaf was excluded from most of the future meetings. Helena Krüger, however, was not. She was accepted within the group owing to her friendship with Olga and her good looks. In fact, they often called her "Alemazinha" (dear German girl), Lena, or even Gruber's wife. She would come to know where each member of the conspiracy lived.

At one of the meetings, Ewert, Ghioldi, Stuchevski, and Prestes decided that the best place for Prestes to hold clandestine encounters with officials and officers sympathetic to the ANL, and to the pending revolution, was in the back of a car. Helena was offered the job of being Prestes's chauffeur, and Johnny was told to buy a vehicle for that purpose. He provided his own car instead, a 1932 "Baby Ford." Helena did not want the work because she did not like Prestes, but Johnny insisted that she accept the opportunity. It was one of the turning points of the attempted overthrow.

Whenever they left the Barão da Torre house for a meeting, Helena, with Olga in the front seat next to her and Prestes hunkered down in back, would pick up Prestes's guest and drive around. Helena pretended not to understand the two men in the back seat, who usually spoke in French, the educated language of the day. French was used to minimize their remarks' being understood by the uninvited ear. It is unknown whether Prestes or Olga knew it, but Helena's French was good enough to comprehend the main points of what was being said. At night, Johnny got her to fill him in. In the morning, de Graaf passed the contents of the rendezvous on to Hutt, who informed English ambassador Gurney, who had the material put into code and telegraphed to London. The British intelligence community then selectively forwarded pieces of information back to Foreign Minister Oswaldo Aranha at the Itamarati, Brazil's Foreign Office. The Itamarati in turn informed Vargas and Filinto Müller. Müller was Rio de Janeiro's chief of the Polícia Civil (Detective Bureau) and director of DESPS (Delegacia Especial de Segurança Política e Social—the Special Police for Political and Social Security).[32]

Johnny began looking for a guerrilla training ground and soon located a well hidden out-of-the-way farmhouse in an old orange orchard in Bangú, deep in the backcountry to the west of the city. There he began educating a group of thirty Brazilians, which he termed "motley," in arms, explosives, and other abilities needed for civil revolution. The class took ten days. Martins had sent him the students. The course consisted of techniques for making bombs and hand grenades.[33] In his free time, Johnny found a nearby cave, where he made up his analysis of events and reports for the British. He used Brazil nuts as candles, since they can be cracked open at the tip and lit. This secrecy was in part to keep information from Helena, who did not know that Johnny was a double agent.

Despite the language problems, the training of his tiny guerrilla unit was about complete when Prestes arrived and took the students off to some unknown location. Another meeting in Ipanema began a day later. This time the date of the revolt was set for either December or the first part of January. Johnny pointed out again that they were not ready, but his protest fell on deaf ears. Al Hutt received a call from de Graaf an hour after the gathering broke up. Johnny gave him the dates and details, which were wired to London.

Martins sent a new group of thirty pupils to a different house for another two weeks of tutoring by Comrade Gruber. The course consisted of methods of street and barricade fighting. De Graaf selected six of the best students to assist him. The place had been rented by one of the faster learners, Francisco Romero. It was located at Rua Borda do Mato 187 in Grajaú. The group was taught the art of bomb making and by the end of November 1935 had assembled 245 grenades. Still not satisfied, Johnny continued to feel that he was being given the rabble off the street and expected to develop a solid team. He noted in each class that will power and leadership were lacking. Surmising what he had observed and accomplished during these lessons, he came to the opinion that the PCB was unquestionably not ready for an uprising. He contacted Ewert about this and urged that the core group discuss the matter of preparedness. In Johnny's view, they were headed for a military revolt only, nothing more, which went against Lenin's ideas on how to start a revolution. A meeting was grudgingly arranged, and Johnny was voted down 10 to 1.[34]

Perhaps the lopsided results also got him reassigned to the northeast. Ewert had flown up to Recife on an inspection tour in June. Locatelli was planning to fly to Recife on November 23 until later events unfolded.[35] Obviously, the leadership was ferrying people to Pernambuco to enhance the northeastern end of its conspiracy.

On orders from Prestes, and once Ewert left, Johnny traveled to the city in late July 1935. He stayed in Recife until early September, training two different groups of party members. The initial class was educated in street fighting, the other in ways to construct hand grenades and carry out sabotage. With his language ability, he had picked up enough Portuguese by that time to use it as the lingua franca in his courses.[36] While in Recife, Johnny made some kind of contact, either directly or through second parties, probably with the secretary for public security, Malvino Reis Neto. He explained what was being planned down in Rio for the northeast, and a code was set up whereby he would telegraph Malvino with the two words "Della ligou" (Della called) to alert him when the Communists were about to strike. Moreover, the place of their attack was also known. It would come at the largest army installation in the northeast,[37] the Twenty-Ninth Infantry Battalion of 385 men at Vila Militar Floriano Peixoto, in the suburb of Socorro, some 11.2 miles (18 km) southwest of Recife.[38] The secretary for public security, for his part, spoke with Lieutenant Colonel Afonso de Albuquerque, second in command at Vila Militar,[39] to see to it that left-leaning soldiers were slowly moved into the Second Company barracks, a building to the left of a plaza at the rear of the main post buildings.

Associates along the chain of command who were sympathetic to Moscow learned that someone had been in contact with Malvino, alerting him to the revolutionaries' plans. Already on July 31, the Soviets were telegramming Rio that individuals with access to "police correspondence in Pernambuco"[40] had discovered that the English were aware of their efforts. They were ordered to try to discover who the mole was and to revamp their security operations.[41]

Returning to Rio, de Graaf was informed that the revolution would now begin in January 1936. General conferences took place about twice a week during the next three months. Most of the individuals sent by Moscow, plus a few others, attended. Johnny continued to complain about the role of the PCB. He pointed out that none of the students he had been instructing knew that an uprising was coming. All he told them was to be ready for action. These points were gone over again and again, particularly with the general secretary of the party, Antônio Bonfim, who attended the gatherings. Johnny not only emphasized Lenin's rules for starting a revolution but elaborated on the points that Prestes and Ewert seemed to have forgotten from Lenin's thinking: (1) a united party is the vanguard of rebellion, (2) the middle class should be neutralized, and (3) cooperation should be obtained from the military forces. Again Johnny pleaded with Prestes for the creation of special units to cut off the Polícia Militar facility in Botafogo. Again Prestes adamantly refused, believing that his anticipated military forces in larger Rio de Janeiro could easily take care of anything in the Zona Sul suburb. Among the troops he was counting on was the entire Third Infantry Regiment in Praia Vermelha.[42]

The only bright, yet troublesome, spot between these episodes was when de

Graaf received a photo of beautiful Gerti from her mother in Germany, with three eligible young men standing in the background. On the card she asked, "Which will Gerti choose?" Johnny reflected for a moment and then thought, "No one!" He realized at that instant that he was falling for her.

As November 1935 approached, the conspirators' conferences continued. Johnny was still largely on the outside looking in, with Helena keeping him informed of the latest planning. He never wavered in his assessment that "the organization of the Brazilian Communist Party never changed. [It] . . . was still disorganized and generally not prepared for a revolution."[43] As a safeguard, he cabled Moscow via Paris, relaying Prestes's plan, discounting any chance of its success. At least he would be on record there, which he might need later.

Such was not the view, however, among some sections of the PCB in that part of Brazil he had left not three months earlier. The northeast had become a bomb needing only a match to go off. For generations, boss rule, known as *coronelismo,* promoted poverty, a lack of justice for ordinary people, and the *cangaço* (or rural banditry) as the area's backlash. In 1935 the death of the last great rural bandit, Lampião (Virgulino Ferreira da Silva), was still three years away.[44] The military was one of the few places where the semblance of a job was sometimes available. When one could rationalize changing sides, or when one's protector became more powerful, the state's police was another chance at a legal living. Still, grumbling by ordinary soldiers over pay and living conditions was rampant. The ANL, proselytizing among the poor and the military, had produced converts, but living with poverty was quite another issue, and something about which most of insurgents down in Rio knew little.

That October, in one more display of strongman politics, the semblance of elections returned a favored clan member, Rafael Fernandes of the Partido Popular (Popular Party), to power in Rio Grande do Norte's capital city, Natal. In accordance with the traditions of rural *coronelismo,* Fernandes promptly removed those loyal to the previous administration and replaced them with his own appointees. This included bureaucrats all the way down to the police level—none of whom were disarmed. The ranks of the unemployed and the dissatisfied grew to precipitous levels.[45]

There are several versions of how the shooting started in Natal. Some blame the outlawed ANL, others the PCB, still others the unemployed but not weaponless police.[46] The Twenty-First Infantry Battalion stationed in Natal was the linchpin. It had been cut down in size and moved to the city from Recife, with a stop near the border with Venezuela, for taking up arms against the Pernambuco *interventor* (or appointed governor), Carlos Lima Cavalcante, in 1931. The unit lacked a full complement of officers and the corresponding discipline. To correct this, in the first part of November, Vargas sent Lieutenant Colonel José Otaviano Pinto

Soares to Natal to restore order. Once installing himself, Soares discharged twenty-eight soldiers on the morning of Saturday, November 23, 1935, for possibly having taken part in a streetcar robbery. More dismissals were likely the following week. In so doing, the colonel was endangering the success of the PCB to win converts in the barracks. The removals by Soares apparently prompted local party members to act without consulting the Central Committee.[47] The opening barrage of the revolution would go off just after 7:30 P.M. on the night of November 23, 1935.[48]

Aware of what was happening before the authorities, Johnny sent his telegram to Malvino Reis Neto. Sometime near 10:00 P.M., a courier from Malvino arrived at the home of Captain Frederico Mindelo Carneiro Monteiro in the officer's compound outside of the Vila Militar in Socorro. The captain was not at home, and the messenger could only speak with Mindelo's wife. He gave her a message about the events in Natal and left an order for the captain to return to the barracks and get ready. At 11:00 P.M. on the twenty-third, Malvino ordered Wandenkolk Wanderley, head of the investigation section of the Recife police, to travel out to the Vila Militar[49] and warn them that Communists would start shooting sometime after midnight. The three-man Communist leadership, Silo Meireles, José Caetano Machado, and Wilson Sousa Fonseca, called the Secretariado do Nordeste (Northeastern Secretariat), actually began a meeting in a civilian's home at midnight. They decided to issue the call for a start to hostilities at nine o'clock the following morning. Back at the Vila Militar in Socorro, all soldiers were allowed into the base that night, but leaving was prohibited. This was to prevent them from learning about the events in Natal from the public.[50] The power was likewise cut to keep them from listening to their radios.[51]

The time factor was decisive, since it allowed the authorities to prepare their defenses and call in military reinforcements from two neighboring states. They easily defeated the rebels in Recife and then turned their attention to Natal. The rebels there had taken control of the state capital. Three small aircraft from the loyalist forces in Recife flew over Natal, dropping leaflets. The city was threatened with bombing if it failed to surrender. It did the trick. The Communists gave up or left for parts unknown.[52]

Once the leftists in Recife took up arms in sympathy with the events in Natal, the hand of the group in Rio was forced. They decided to start the Rio de Janeiro side of the rebellion on November 27 at 2:00 A.M. Meanwhile, Johnny advised Hutt of the developments. Within an hour Light's assistant superintendent had London's reply: "Let it break out." During the ensuing confusion, the British ambassador informed President Vargas of the possible danger. Vargas then personally telephoned Johnny's SIS handler to ask if the Communists could win. Hutt immediately got hold of Johnny for his read on the situation. De Graaf told Hutt to tell Vargas, "Not a chance!" The prediction rang true. Leftists in strategic southern cities were not ready to do battle. In São Paulo, it never even broke out. The most reported and most photographed part of the skirmishing took place in Rio de Janeiro. At their Praia Vermelha stronghold, the Third Infantry Regiment did most of the fighting, hemmed in by the Polícia Militar in Botafogo and then by army detachments ordered to seal them off. Two military aircraft flew overhead, strafing and dropping bombs. Finally, the Third Infantry rebels, more than one thousand strong, surrendered at around 2:00 P.M., marching out of their shot-up confine arm in arm—the officers in the lead—all smiling and singing the national anthem. Other pockets of resistance throughout the city were soon subdued. The Revolução Social (Social Revolution) or Intentona Comunista (Communist Conspiracy) was over in a preemptive four-day fiasco.[53]

Johnny later explained in Moscow that "Prestes became nearly panic-stricken as the disaster unfolded." Those who were familiar with the Cavalheiro da Esperança, however, totally disregard this suggestion and consider it something Johnny concocted.[54] De Graaf also stated that he was commanded by Prestes to "go to Grajaú and make two thousand grenades in forty-eight hours."[55] This was a physical impossibility, given the number of people he had to carry out the order. Compounding each claim are two additional points that cloud the veracity of Johnny's assertions. He was a man with a long memory for those who slighted him, and in Moscow he may well have been ascribing things to Prestes in his own defense.

The Brazilian authorities promptly arrested a few hundred soldiers and a number of conspiring politicians. Vargas gave the go-ahead for a reign of terror, which up until its conclusion was the largest such operation in Brazilian history. It lasted until June 1937 and began with a bang when leftists clamored that a number of apprehended officers were taken to the wooded area behind Rio and shot.[56] The overall slaughter, however, was more pronounced in Pernambuco, where Major Higino Belarmino summarily executed anyone his troops captured, regardless of their rank.[57]

By the end of the red scare inquisition, the total number of persons brought in for questioning, many for torturing, is estimated at between seven and thirty-five thousand. The large gap in the numbers depended on the source consulted and the politics of the reader.[58] The significance, however, was apparent enough. Getúlio Vargas was not about to forgive and forget those on the left of the political spectrum. Brazil's elite, both in and out of the military, would say "we told you so" about the Communists for generations to come.

A portion of the explosives at the rented home in Grajaú suggestively blew up on December 22, 1935; the police were called and Francisco Romero was arrested. Actually a Spanish house painter, under torture Romero gave away enough information for the authorities to discover the alias of one of the leaders of the attempted revolution, a tall foreigner who spoke English with the nickname Negro. Among the items that failed to detonate were 480 sticks of dynamite, forty-eight pieces of iron pipe loaded with the explosive, a thousand small arms cartridges, and a number of hand grenades. The authorities also uncovered radio sending and receiving equipment, acids, nitro benzine, potassium nitrate, fulminate, iron oxide, saltpeter, and a host of Communist literature. Filinto Müller's DESPS then had the Itamarati contact London for help. In the SIS files the *nom de guerre* Negro was one of those used by Arthur Ernst Ewert.[59] The British security service had been provided the information by Johnny de Graaf.

The day after Christmas in 1935, the Polícia Civil pulled up to the Ewerts' rented home at Rua Paulo Redfern 33 in Ipanema and arrested Arthur and his wife. Accompanying the authorities was a pale blond who took personal charge of the former KPD Reichstag representative. Placing him in the back of a paddy wagon, the blond secured his prisoner's hands to a crossbeam, then took out a nutcracker and calmly used it to break one of Ewert's thumbs. Harry Berger began to sweat profusely, but he did not utter a sound. Irritated, his torturer snarled at his victim in native German, "Kommunist Sohn von einer Hure!" (Communist son of a bitch!). The Gestapo was assisting Filinto Müller.[60]

As in China, Ewert left a lot of incriminating documents for the police at his newly departed home. While the physical evidence was devastating, Ewert would admit to nothing, resulting in torture sessions for the couple that continued for weeks on end. The Brazilian press had a field day branding him a Jew, but he was not Jewish. He received a sentence of thirteen years and four months and disappeared from Johnny's life forever. Eventually, Arthur was placed under the stairwell at the much-feared Polícia Especial (Special Police) for more than two years. During that time, he was forced to hear the tramping of feet going up and down the overhead steps. The confine did not permit him to stand upright. He never shaved or had a bath. Having lost his mind, Ewert was released after the war and returned to Germany, where he passed away in East Berlin in 1959. Grotesquely tortured, Sabo was also deported to Germany, where she probably died in a concentration camp sometime before the end of 1941.

After the arrest of the Ewerts, Marga was sent back to Argentina. Leon Jules Vallée, or Pavel Stuchevski, and his wife, Sofia, escaped to Buenos Aires. On a tip from Johnny, Antônio Bonfim and his girlfriend, Elza Fernandes, were arrested and roughed up. She was later released but was executed by the Communists, who thought she was the traitor informing Müller's police. Rodolfo Ghioldi identified Victor Allen Barron on the street. The police arrested Barron and most probably murdered him, calling it a suicide once the American Embassy turned a blind eye. Amleto Locatelli too fled to Buenos Aires but was never known to have been part of the plot until 1993.

Prestes and Olga scampered around Rio for a while after the capture of the

Ewerts. The bomb that Johnny placed in their closet in Ipanema, as well as the flashlight, failed to explode. They were caught after sunup on the morning of March 5, 1936, in the working-class district of Méier. Olga probably saved Prestes's life by instantly jumping between him and the revolvers of the at-the-ready police. They may well have had orders from Filinto Müller not to bring Prestes in alive. From the house at Rua Honório 279 where they were apprehended, the couple was taken to the Polícia Central (Central Police Station) in downtown Rio. They were separated and never saw each other again, despite Olga's being noticeably pregnant with Prestes's child. Prestes was given a prison sentence of sixteen years and six months, with another thirty years added later for his part in approving the murder of Elza Fernandes. Following his trial, he was kept in solitary confinement for almost nine years. He was released in 1945 as part of a general amnesty following World War II.

Olga Bernário, a Jewess, a Communist, and a fugitive from fascist law enforcement in the country of her birth, was deported along with Sabo to the Nazis in Hamburg. Vargas and his government knew full well that they were sending two women and an unborn child to their deaths. Fortunately, however, the family of Luís Carlos Prestes was able to get the baby, Anita Leocádia, out of Germany to Mexico. Olga was worked to a skeleton at the Ravensbrück Concentration Camp for women north of Berlin and then gassed to death in Bernburg, a former mental institution, in March 1942.[61]

It is said by one of the investigators of the case that Johnny gave up everyone except Prestes, but he did mention that the leader of the revolution was in Méier.[62] This would conform to de Graaf's own comments: "Promptly after the revolution's demise, I asked Hutt to have Arthur Ewert, Luís Carlos Prestes, Olga, Sabo, and all the others picked up by the Brazilian Police and arrested." Yet evidently the British still wanted the Brazilians to either ask them or do the work entirely on their own. The resulting slow going at locating suspects annoyed de Graaf to the point where he went against MI6 orders and contacted the police directly. The link may well have been with DESPS/Quadro Movel inspector Francisco de Menezes Julien. Unbeknownst to the other members of DESPS, the Quadro Movel (or Mobile Team) was answerable only to Filinto Müller. It was composed of about thirty agents and led by Filinto's nephew, Civis Müller. At a minimum, de Graaf could have told the police the whereabouts of numerous persons whose addresses he obtained from Helena.[63] Johnny stated as well that Filinto Müller knew of him "and his role in Brazil through Al Hutt and the British contacts."

It could be that Müller was just fishing for more information, or maybe it was all part of a ruse to throw off the other revolutionaries and provide Johnny with an alibi. Johnny used the first option back in Moscow. As the story goes, at around 8:00 P.M. on January 5, 1936, the police arrived at the Grubers' residence and searched it. Johnny and Helena were then taken to the Polícia Central and questioned. They were allowed to drive their own car to the station house. Coming face to face with Müller, the chief of police informed Johnny that Willi de Souza, a Berlitz language teacher he had once had in common with Arthur Ewert, had turned them in.[64] Soon Alfred Hutt appeared and, in the presence of DESPS captain Affonso Henrique de Miranda Corrêa, identified Johnny as an agent of Britain's Intelligence Service.[65] De Graaf's cover story was expanded. It was said that the police asked him questions about what he was doing in Brazil, and how he supported himself and his wife. Müller is reported to have called in the language teacher. They mentioned that this man had given a confusing story, was scolded by Filinto, and was sent away. Then, following words of support from their neighbors, the Grubers were told they could go the next day. Helena slept on a couch in one of the offices and Johnny was put into the same holding cell with Pavel, who was in custody for questioning. Neither man could acknowledge the other, as Müller's police were watching.

In the morning, Johnny and Helena walked out of Polícia Central after Müller's personal apologies for having had to spend the night. They had been in police custody for eight hours. Müller promised to help in the future if they ever needed the assistance of the Brazilian authorities. Johnny is reputed to have taken the chief of police up on his offer by stopping back by the station to have him sign his exit and reentry visas.[66]

After obtaining these official authorizations, Johnny met Rodolfo Ghioldi and warned him. Ghioldi passed the message on to Moscow. He and Carmen eventually tried to escape to Argentina but were captured in São Paulo on January 23.[67] Before leaving Rio, Rodolfo told Johnny to go to Buenos Aires and report to the Central Committee. He was to train local rebels in explosives and guerrilla tactics. Johnny conveyed this to Al Hutt, and, using his Franz Gruber passport, he and Helena boarded the SS *Highland Princess* late in the evening of Monday, January 20, 1936, for their early-morning departure to Buenos Aires.[68] It would be a short voyage down the coast to unknown prospects. The thought was unsettling, since he could not be certain Moscow had not been tipped off about him by the events in Brazil.

13

ARGENTINA

Buenos Aires had changed greatly from what de Graaf remembered from his merchant marine days. Walking down the gangplank of the *Highland Princess,* he and Helena stood at dockside surveying the skyline. The bustling metropolis and massive buildings that had altered the city's entire face astounded Johnny. Part of the reason for all the commotion could not be seen from the harbor. Just up the hill that ran parallel to the port stands Avenida 9 de Julio. It would be expanded three years later to become the widest street in the world. There would be six lanes in each direction and a long narrow park down the middle. Part of the project was already under way. The symbol of the city, a huge white obelisk, was being readied in the middle of the park at the intersection of Avenidas 9 de Julio and Corrientes. The slab of stone would be dedicated that May to honor the four-hundredth anniversary of Buenos Aires as the country's capital. The monument measured 221 feet six inches in height (67.5 meters) and was being constructed on the exact spot where the first Argentine flag had been raised in the city.

It was in the middle of summer, January 21, 1936, as Johnny and Helena began walking away from the docks to a taxi stand. As they made their way through the crush of the crowd, a Comintern courier slipped a thick envelope into de Graaf's hand as he brushed past. The split-second encounter was a display of how rarely Johnny would see the Argentine party. He had no idea how they knew he and Helena were arriving by ship on that date, nor did he try to find out.

The envelope contained ample funds and a message on one bill that said simply, "No contact." Evidently, the Partido Comunista de la Argentina felt that Johnny and Helena were still too hot after the calamity in Brazil. Ignoring this advice, Johnny went to his PCA connection, a shoe repair shop on Avenida Santa Fe, one of Buenos Aires's main thoroughfares, where the proprietor put him in touch with his link to the PCA. The operative was a man known to de Graaf only by a first name, Felix.[1]

Over the course of 1936, Johnny taught just two urban guerrilla classes in Argentina. Felix supplied the students. He was married and had a mistress, and sometimes his paramour would bring messages to Johnny.[2] The first class consisted of five individuals from different provinces. It lasted two weeks. The second course had sixteen students, mostly from Buenos Aires. Although everything was taught in Spanish, Johnny complained that his trainees could hardly read or write. Even so, he tried to teach them how to construct Communist cells and start a printing press, along with various techniques of spreading antimilitary misinformation. Because of their semiliteracy, he felt he accomplished little, as no cells were formed and no printing press was established. The PCA told him it could not help more since it lacked funding and was under too much pressure from the police.[3] The arrangement allowed de Graaf a lot personal freedom and latitude as an agent.

Using one of his former code names, Walter, Johnny knew that contact with Moscow was still to be carried out by cable via Paris. In June and again in August, he walked to a telegraph office and sent messages to the City of Light, stating in code that he was doing everything in his power to accomplish the Argentine mission. These were the only wires de Graaf sent the Soviets during his stay in Buenos Aires. At the end of February, through the PCA, he set up a meeting with Amleto Locatelli for the following month. Locatelli managed to escape Brazil by taking an English steamer to Buenos Aires on January 13, 1936.[4] When they finally met, the Italian told Johnny that he had to return to Moscow. Locatelli was convinced that a full report had to be made of the Brazilian disaster, and since he was not doing anything, he wanted to go. Johnny, Helena, and Amleto discussed what Locatelli should say when he arrived back in the USSR. He was of the opinion that de Graaf had been correct in his analysis of the situation they had just faced. That is, the PCB was not ready and Prestes was not ready. Locatelli left for Europe in June.

Coming down the gangplank the same month, on a steamer from Santos, was Pavel Stuchevski. His wife, Sofia Stuchevskaya, had arrived before him on May 2, 1936, via Uruguay. Without doubt, Johnny's situation was unique, for he was the sole suspect in Pavel's eyes, while at the same time the unknown senior MI6 agent in Argentina. Even though Stuchevski now felt Johnny was right for his constant warnings about the Brazilian Communists not being prepared for a revolution, and about the overall unsoundness of Prestes's military strategy, Pavel was still suspicious of Johnny. He believed de Graaf was a spy—for the White Russians.[5]

De Graaf was an intelligence operative, but he hid in plain sight. In Argentina he posed as a wool salesman in his travels about the country. His main sponsor in this was Britain's MI6, not anti-Soviet elements from the Russian Civil War.

Thirty British operatives were eventually placed under his command, spread out across Argentina as far away as Chile. Prior to his departure from Rio de Janeiro, Alfred Hutt provided Johnny with relay contacts in Argentina. British agents posing as embassy drivers, secretaries, or military attachés under cover of diplomatic immunity were the go-betweens. Whenever Johnny wished to contact one of these operatives, he merely telephoned a number at the embassy and left a callback phone number. A special room was selected for the meetings. There, Johnny would hand in the coded outbound reports and receive all incoming communications addressed to him. This carefully arranged method worked well and provided sufficient security.

In June 1936 Johnny turned in the entire PCA Central Committee to the Buenos Aires police. Following formal arrest procedures, the group was held briefly and released.[6] Since de Graaf had had minimal contact with them, his excuse for not being picked up was the obvious one. Toward the end of the month, Stuchevski telegraphed Moscow that the PCA considered Franz Gruber's stay in the country too dangerous. Pavel stated that Johnny had been compromised in Brazil. He also asked for instructions about paying Johnny the ten thousand Argentine pesos (then worth about US$7,187) that de Graaf wanted to buy a house.[7] There is no record of what Moscow did with Stuchevski's request. But Johnny and Helena did begin living in a smallish two-floor house at Calle Florida 246, in the San Martín district just northwest of the city limits. In July the Stuchevskis were ordered back to Moscow and an uncertain fate.[8]

Likewise in July 1936, Johnny's PCA contact instructed him to go to the Garden Restaurant in Buenos Aires. Someone would meet him there and identify himself in the proper way. The individual who eventually showed up was not from the PCA's Central Committee, and Johnny assumed he must be Stuchevski's OMS replacement. After their initial exchange of recognition signals, de Graaf saw the man once a month to be paid his M4 salary, US$200.

Between August and November 1936, Johnny and the new OMS man were involved in a very delicate deal to try to free Luís Carlos Prestes. Owing to his experience in Brazil and his belief that most Brazilians could be bought, de Graaf felt there was a distinct possibility to arrange Prestes's release. Through its OMS agent, Moscow was willing to spend US$1,000,000 to spring the Knight of Hope from the confines of his Polícia Especial cell in Rio de Janeiro. The plan called for Johnny to meet Prestes at a predetermined place on the frontier between Uruguay and Brazil. The plot failed because the responsible Brazilians wanted all the money in advance before releasing their prisoner. The Soviets were willing to pay half down, followed by the second half on delivery of Prestes. Moscow informed the Brazilians that they would even provide a fake passport and funds for Prestes to use as he traveled down to the Uruguayan border.[9]

On one less humid day, de Graaf received word from London that they were sending him an additional agent. London said he was a man with a good military record and some knowledge of intelligence. Johnny's thirty operatives were working well, and he saw no need for another person, an opinion that he promptly wired back to his superiors. Surely other British networks were short staffed and more in need of manpower than Johnny's. "Use him, already on his way," came the reply. Annoyance overcame de Graaf. "It just didn't make sense. Something was wrong," he thought. London's insistence was perplexing. Somehow he would get to the bottom of this; and he would start by keeping a very close eye on this new recruit.

A week later the new agent arrived and made contact. His name is still guarded under lock and key in MI6's files. Part of the reason for the secrecy was his royal bloodline. Johnny always called him "the Aristocrat."[10] He was a presentable, bright Oxford man of ramrod slender build, with a boyish face crested with a crew cut. Despite his alert, personable ways and favorable first impression, Johnny continued to have an anxious feeling about him. The really perplexing thing was that he could not put his finger on what caused his uneasiness, which was more disturbing than anything.

De Graaf was aware that the man had attained officer rank while serving with the British guards in the Far East. But his field intelligence work consisted of little more than being on post before SIS sent him to Argentina. Guardedly, Johnny revealed very little to him about the Argentina network, mentioning no agent numbers or present and past jobs done by the unit. De Graaf normally chose his words carefully anyway. Now, he doubled his reserve. The Aristocrat soon left to his remote posting, a zone that was not considered important enough to require an agent up until that time. Once he was set up, he would only report to Johnny when Johnny requested a meeting.

The entire network was far too important to take chances with an unknown until de Graaf had time to assess him more fully. Perhaps de Graaf's intuition was correct, or perhaps he had been in intelligence work too long to trust anyone completely.

For a period of a month, both the Soviet and British undertakings continued to run smoothly. Johnny met his agents separately in their assigned zones, and by invitation in small selected groups of no more than five men outside their sectors of operation. These meetings at prearranged rendezvous were always a closely guarded secret. Locations were carefully checked out prior to, and rigorously protected during, each get-together. It was a system of communicating information that had never failed.

Then, out of the blue, there was a problem. Prior to one encounter, the police were seen lying in wait for the group to convene. Luckily, there were no arrests. All of Johnny's operatives got away safely, but it was apparent that their security had been compromised. Johnny was convinced that the incident suggested a traitor within the gates. Someone had tipped off the police. Whoever he or she was, de Graaf had to find out quickly. Otherwise the entire network, and everyone's life, was at risk.

Finding the culprit, however, was not easy. The process continued for days, making sleep difficult. For several nights Johnny tossed and turned, rolling the faces of all his people back and forth, over and over in his mind. Lying in bed, he went over each agent's past, looking for an odd word, an expression, or a clue that would provide the link he was searching for. He still mistrusted the new man, but it was a feeling without foundation, just a hunch. The Aristocrat was performing well, and despite his arrival and the present crisis there was no proof he was the wrongdoer. De Graaf had known well-seasoned veterans to suddenly roll over for a few extra pieces of gold or a cause. Everyone was under suspicion until such time that each was proved otherwise.

Finally Johnny came up with a plan that he hoped would ensnare the traitor. He recalled his two agents from Chile and separately gave them the same message. It was not really an important memo, but in a remote way a necessary one. They left separately, the same way they had arrived. When the message they were carrying was delivered, it was clear that neither individual was a double agent. There had been no tipoff, no police waiting in the shadows. De Graaf then had a base of two clean agents. Days later he did the same thing with three more agents, and again there was no leak. Over a period of thirty-five days he recalled every individual, checking each one out in this way, until only three men, including the Aristocrat, remained to be tested. These remaining three he called in individually on the same day, giving them identical messages. After they left, he hit pay dirt! The police were predictably informed. Johnny called in two of the already cleared agents and told them to be ready for an impending surveillance assignment. An hour later he gave two of the men still under suspicion a rendezvous message. The Aristocrat was not one of those chosen for this task. As they departed, the two clean agents shadowed the selected operatives. They soon reported back that both their men were okay and 100 percent trustworthy.

This left only the Aristocrat. Johnny arranged a meeting with him and a clean agent. Both were given an urgent directive. As prearranged, the blueblood departed, but unbeknownst to him a companion was on his tail. The trustworthy agent gave his account within an hour. He had followed the Aristocrat for a few streets, whereupon he watched him get into a waiting car and speed off. Hailing a cab himself, he followed the Aristocrat straight to Calle Moreno 1550, the entrance to a building taking up an entire city block, the Departmento Central de Policía (or Central Police Station). That was it; Johnny had his man.

London was cabled with all the facts for the intelligence chiefs to digest. He hoped they would follow his suggestion of recalling the Aristocrat to Britain and dealing with him there. De Graaf's wire ended with "Await your instructions."

Within the hour he had their answer. "Do what you find necessary, Johnny." In espionage circles that reply meant only one thing, a "disposal." They wanted him killed.

The brilliant sun, just rising, found Johnny on the road to the Aristocrat's distant assignment in one of the northern provinces.[11] Soothing rays of warmth began to glisten as his little car sped down the roads of the Argentine Pampas. Had his thoughts been as pleasant as the grasslands flashing by, he would have been invigorated. However, they were not and he was not. It was the pressing need to save lives of valuable agents that occupied Johnny's mind that day. By nightfall he had reached the lush terrain in a mantle of bluish mist, when at last he pulled the car off the side of the deeply rutted road. Twinkling stars pulsated like flashing beacons, but he was only vaguely aware of their presence from the backseat, as exhausting sleep closed in around him.

At 5:00 A.M. he was digesting a hurried breakfast from the burlap food pack he had brought along. Back on the road, a high noon sun beamed down when he ultimately reached his destination. The Aristocrat greeted his boss warmly, surprised by Johnny's unexpected appearance. Following some superficial small talk, de Graaf lulled his host into relaxing by telling him he was off to do some hunting and asked him to join. While readily agreeing, the Aristocrat explained that he did not have a rifle. "Then act as my guide," Johnny responded, "and we'll both use mine." Johnny had selected a specific forested area for the hunt, one he was acquainted with, but unknown to the Aristocrat. Jovial conversation followed as they drove back into the dusty one-lane trails that slashed through the bush.

They soon arrived at a small clearing, well away from the seldom-used path. The Aristocrat agreed to take the point while Johnny followed him twenty paces back with his loaded Winchester. Birds of vivid colors chattered and flew from limb to limb as the two men penetrated the foliage. The sun disappeared as vegetation shut out much of the blinding brightness. A monkey scampered across a snakelike vine high above, as they followed the small trail deeper into the crowded undergrowth.

Abruptly, at a jagged bend in the path, the jungle floor gave way under the Aristocrat's boots, plunging him into a sucking bog. "Help, help, my God, Johnny, I'm caught in quicksand!" he screamed. His face was ashen, his hands outstretched, ghostly in their pleading. "Caught in your own deception, you black-hearted British traitor!" Johnny coldly replied, grateful for the solid ground beneath him. In seconds, the muck sucked in its violently thrashing victim up to his armpits. Johnny raised his rifle as his target struggled in panic. Aiming carefully, Johnny fired a round at the Aristocrat's head. His tossing form, now four-fifths submerged, ceased its struggle. A deathly stillness enveloped the jungle and the parting sands received their newfound fatality. The ooze closed over the last of him, followed by a few small bubbles burping to the surface. Then there was nothing.

Johnny turned, rifle in hand, and made his way back through the jungle to the car sitting in the sunlit clearing. "If I had not done in this man, I could have been lying dead out there," he thought. As de Graaf drove away, the jungle came to life once again. Birds flew from branch to branch, singing amid the sounds of other animals. "London, damn you! It's done! Now I'm the one who has to live with it, not you. Damn the world! Damn London!"

In the next decade, one of the hardest things Johnny ever had to do was visit the Aristocrat's socially prominent parents. As their son's commanding officer, he was instructed to tell them that during a crucial assignment their boy had died bravely in the service of king and country. He was ordered to give them an inscribed serving tray. London insisted it was necessary, but Johnny knew he had to lie and not tell the sad but proud parents that their son was a turncoat and that it was he who had killed him. With this pretense at morality, De Graaf had learned the hard way that Britain's intelligence services were second to none in outright viciousness.[12]

Johnny asked the SIS what kind of clues they had that this man was not trustworthy. They said they were suspicious in a way from his boasting of family wealth and personal income during his short intelligence stint. But they had to be totally sure he was a double agent, so they sent him on to Argentina. Vivian said, "We chose you to check him out, Johnny. For you are an enormously patient spymaster, who would eventually find out what was what and warn us."

"Great!" de Graaf shot back. "So I was the guinea pig. You didn't count the sleepless nights I endured because of all this, did you?"

"We'll give you a few bottles of champagne and you can catch up on your rest now," they replied, chuckling heartily. Johnny could not see anything humorous in the entire episode. All he knew was that a damnably cruel deception had been played on him that could have resulted in thirty-one deaths, not just the Aristocrat's. He told them that had he followed his intuition, he would have sent the new man back the day he arrived.

"We needed more proof than that Johnny," they replied.

Days later, Johnny was back in Buenos Aires when he received a cable, on November 22, 1936, recalling both himself and Helena to Moscow.[13] The telegram did not come as a surprise, because four months earlier Stuchevski and his wife had been ordered to return. Over the course of the next eleven days, Johnny and Helena discussed what awaited them in the USSR. In early December, on the last day of Franklin D. Roosevelt's visit to Buenos Aires, as Argentine and American officials were busy down in the harbor on the heavy cruiser USS *Indianapolis,* ready to carry Roosevelt to Uruguay, things between Johnny and Helena came to a head. Helena had again cultivated a number of romantic interests during Johnny's absences. One was apparently with a physician. The man may have been an officer in the Argentine army. There is an army facility not far from the Calle Florida house. Johnny later reported that the man lived just six houses away.[14] Whoever he was, or whether he even existed, at 3:00 P.M. on a showery Thursday, December 3, 1936, Helena's life came to an abrupt and dramatic end.[15]

Helena Krüger had left school in 1931 to work at home in the Krügers' Papelallee 32 apartment for a construction company, doing some of the firm's paperwork. Once Johnny found out what she was up to, however, he got angry, and Helena's employment was cut short. She quit the job and returned to her studies. Late the following year, Johnny stayed with the Krügers while on his way to England. Helena was fourteen and a half years old at the time. When Johnny left Berlin by train for London via Denmark, Helena was at his side and on her life's first great journey.

One should be careful about accusing Johnny de Graaf of being a child molester. Besides, his first and last wives were closer to his own age. In the Krügers' case, the economic situation became desperate when Gustav Krüger was fired and blacklisted from any employment after Hitler came to power. Ernst went to work, and Johnny was encouraged to send what he could. His money usually came with the postman in the form of a *Geldbriefträger* (actual cash or a check).[16] He sent about two hundred marks (then about US$50), and it arrived every month until April 1937. Johnny also sent funds to his son, Oscar de Graaf, across the country in Ahlen. The Gestapo confiscated Oscar's *Geldbriefträger* money, a check for US$800, at least once.[17] What he sent the Krügers was supposed to go for Helena's education. Some did, and some went for her clothes. She always wore nice things throughout those difficult years. Johnny attempted to persuade her to study rather than work. Helena placated him by concentrating on languages at a boarding school in the Neukölln section of Berlin. She did not reside at the school but took the streetcar to class each day. It also pleased Johnny that Ernst was briefly a member of the Young Communists. Helena, on the other hand, never joined any political organization either as a simple volunteer or as a regular member.[18]

At the conclusion of his first mission to England, de Graaf had left Helena in London when he returned to Moscow. On his next trip to the UK, in January 1932, he rejoined her, but according to what he told the FBI twenty years later, she was difficult to deal with and had neurotic tendencies.[19] No doubt her idiosyncrasies became more prominent on being returned to her parents' home in Berlin, and on begging in tears to be taken back in Prague. Being left again, when de Graaf traveled first to Manchuria and then to China, did not help either. The fact that Helena was good looking and involved in a string of affairs shows that she was searching for the love that Johnny did not give her. The couple clearly did not mesh well.

After they reached Buenos Aires, Johnny discovered the affair with the physician and told her to end it or he would cut off her funds. Following the November 22 telegram, Helena must have become noticeably depressed, and she told Johnny she did not wish to leave Argentina. On December 3 he told her he was a double agent and perhaps that the British would protect them, but that they still would have to leave Argentina. His frankness did not help. Helena still wanted to stay. Johnny then suggested that she get a little apartment in town, which he would pay for. She refused and insisted that he move out instead. But de Graaf saw no reason to move, as they were not married and he was paying all the bills. Words became heated, whereupon Helena admitted that she did not want to leave because of her lover. At that point, Johnny maintains, he slapped her and walked out.[20] He insisted that he left the Calle Florida house and that when he returned that evening, he discovered that she had taken her own life with his Winchester rifle. "She left letters on the table to her parents so they would understand."[21] Another version of what happened holds that he did not merely slap her but was afraid of what she might have told and would tell her new love interest about his affairs. He questioned not only her loyalty to him but also her potential loyalty to her new benefactors in London. At this point Johnny may well have shot Helena in the smaller of two upstairs bedrooms.[22] The bullet struck the area between her stomach and heart. Her death was probably not instantaneous.

However it happened, Johnny assisted the San Martín police investigation of what he claimed was his wife's tragic suicide. Curiously, though, he told the authorities that she was twenty-four, when her real age was nineteen years, five months, and fourteen days.[23] It was likewise strange that no notification of the death was ever published in the *porteño* (persons from Buenos Aires) press or anyplace else, and all police records of the case were burned.[24]

So too was Helena's body. Johnny had it cremated, and he sent her clothes to his half-sister, who was living in Bremen with his father. Wilhelm de Graaf had remarried and moved to Bremen from Hamburg. Johnny never notified his Soviet contacts in Buenos Aires about the death of Helena. Lending support to his culpability was the fact that he almost never talked about her again. Why would he build this wall of silence around the topic if he were not somehow involved in her death? He repeatedly told one of his Canadian case handlers, later on, that the physician and Helena had entered into a murder-suicide pact. De Graaf maintained this story for the rest of his life. There are, however, two items that seem odd indeed in this kind of scenario. First is the point that two persons were not killed in the same place. Obituary records show only one death in the house on Calle Florida for December 3, 1936, or at any other time in that period. Indeed, the death records immediately before and after Helena Krüger's are for individuals in different residences. Both were males, and both died of natural causes.[25] Second, Johnny told his de facto brother-in-law, Ernst Krüger, that after Helena's demise he killed her lover in a duel.[26]

Despite cooperating with the authorities in the matter of Helena's death,[27] while conceivably trying to avoid the spotlight over the passing of her suitor, the government of General Agustín P. Justo decided that it had had enough of Francisco Gruber and asked him to leave the country. The Argentines likewise decided at some point to refuse to tell what they know about Gruber.[28] As he had been called back to the USSR anyway, all that was really left for Johnny to do was quietly get rid of his home and furnishings and book passage. The voyage had to be to Paris, France, because a visa for the Soviet Union awaited him in Paris. The telegram recalling Johnny and Helena had said as much and was signed by Manuilski.

On December 21, 1936, Johnny left Buenos Aires and traveled up to Rio de Janeiro, carrying with him the urn containing Helena's ashes. The reason for going first to Brazil is unknown. Perhaps a clue to this journey can be found in the fact that he telegraphed Inspector Francisco Julien before stopping in Brazil. He then left Rio, on January 7, 1937, in Julien's company, traveling by car to Santos to catch the Blue Star Line's SS *Avila Star*. The vessel's destination was Cherbourg. Johnny cabled Foley of his departure, ship's name, arrival date, and port. "Will contact you from there," Johnny ended. Foley replied, "We expect you Hôtel Haussmann, near Opera House." Arriving in Cherbourg, he stayed on the ship until it reached port in Boulogne on January 28, 1937.[29] Then he wired Gertrude and her mother sufficient funds for a trip to Paris. There was some degree of apprehension between the Krüger family and Johnny over Helena's death. They thought that Johnny and Helena had actually been married. Even so, Emily Krüger brought her seventeen-year-old daughter to Paris, where de Graaf put them up in a hotel. His reason for requesting the meeting was simple; he had learned that one of Gerti's suitors was a German soldier who had asked for her hand in marriage. For the next two days, before seeing Foley and Vivian, he wined and dined the two women. Gerti was the Krüger sister he really wanted, and, like the soldier, he too proposed.[30]

But it was an awkward time for wedding plans. Because of the failure in Brazil, Johnny did not know what lay ahead in Moscow. Gertrude told him that she would give him her answer the next time he came out of the Soviet Union.[31] It was thus a tender parting at the Paris train station as Gerti and her mother caught the express back to Berlin. Johnny recalled her shiny, beautiful face pressed against the compartment window, blowing him kisses as the train eased away.

An hour later de Graaf was waiting at the Hôtel Haussmann when the Englishmen arrived. They greeted each other and immediately began a lengthy discussion. Vivian was very soft spoken and put people at ease at once. His darting eyes, however, missed little. Certainly he would not be taken as one of the top men in counterespionage at British intelligence. He looked more like a retired schoolteacher one might encounter feeding pigeons from a park bench on a lazy afternoon.

Johnny filled in Vee-Vee and Foley on his Brazilian and Argentine assignments, along with the awkward recall to Moscow. They were very concerned about his return to the Soviet Union and tried to talk him out of it. "You're gambling with your life, Johnny, in going back in this time," Frank stated. Deep concern furrowed in his brow. Vivian agreed.

"But Frank, I have always been a bit of a gambler. In fact, it is my way of life! So what else is new?" Johnny answered. "I'm under orders of the General Staff, M4, and not the Comintern, which is a good deal safer than the other way around," Johnny went on. Besides, had he bolted from the Soviet Union at that moment, they would suspect that he was a double agent, or that he had had a hand in the disappointing effort in Brazil. Moscow would then dispatch assassins to hunt him down. Vee-Vee and Foley were still set against it. They argued, but Johnny's mind was made up. So they left it at that, telling him to make contact if he ever came out alive. Johann de Graaf was a man with nerves of steel.[32] This would certainly be the ultimate test.

The Soviet Embassy in Paris was slow in issuing a visa to reenter the USSR. It took four weeks for them to finally stamp the necessary approval in Johnny's Franz Gruber passport. The next problem was getting to Moscow. In May 1933 the Nazis had placed a hundred-thousand-mark reward on Johnny's head. On the other hand, the Gestapo did not really know what he looked like.[33]

DESPS chief Miranda Corrêa went to Berlin in March 1937 to study Nazi efforts at dealing with communism. He brought with him a dossier on suspected European leftists. Among those in the file was Franz Gruber, along with Gruber's Brazilian driver's license photograph.[34] The Germans promptly catalogued the image and placed Franz Gruber's name on their list of wanted individuals. But by the time that happened, de Graaf was already on his way to Moscow. Before Miranda Corrêa arrived, the picture the Gestapo thought was Johnny de Graaf was actually a photo of someone else.[35] The mistake of attaching an incorrect name to a photograph was a common Gestapo error,[36] causing an inexplicable number of innocent persons to be picked up, tortured, and even executed.

On Monday, March 1, 1937, Johnny knocked on the door of the Krügers' apartment at Sonnenburger Straße 22. Once inside, he presented the family with the vase containing Helena's ashes. Johnny stayed with Gustav, Emilie, Ernst, and Gertrude Krüger until that Wednesday. At one point, he and Gerti went to a restaurant to dine. The establishment had tables for the guests with telephones on them. This was quite the thing in Berlin in the 1920s and '30s. The idea was for interested patrons to be able to get up their courage from the safety of their own table to flirtatiously telephone someone of the opposite sex sitting at another table. As Johnny was sipping a beer, the phone on the table he shared with Gerti rang. It was a uniformed SS officer wanting to dance with her. His uniform allowed him the irritating privilege of butting in on the lives of otherwise involved couples. Rather than cause questions by refusing, Gerti danced with the man.[37]

They made it back to the Krügers' apartment safely that evening, though all too soon it was time for his ordeal, the long train ride to Moscow and his waiting Soviet superiors. The journey gave him time to reflect and rehearse what to say. Was it foolhardy to return? Perhaps. Could the NKVD really find him if he just disappeared? Maybe. Only time would tell if the balloon was up, he kept telling himself.[38] Only time would tell if he would be found out.

14

THE RETURN TO MOSCOW

By the time Johnny's train rolled to a stop at Moscow's Belorusskaya Station on March 5, 1937, he had already decided on a bold, three-part defense of his actions in South America. He felt it was a strategy that would keep him both alive and maybe even financially secure. De Graaf was met at the station by a Fourth Department chauffeur and driven to the Hotel Novo Moskovskaya, where he was given room 670. The following day, he went to the Comintern's new headquarters on the outskirts of the capital and was ushered through the elaborate security system. Alfred Langner met him and walked him to his own office. Alexander Abramov from the Communication Department (formerly OMS) soon arrived to pick up the Franz Gruber passport and request that Johnny submit an account of his expenses.[1]

When Abramov left, Langner asked Johnny what had happened in Brazil. De Graaf stated that what they attempted to do had failed because the Brazilian Communist Party was not properly organized or ready to conduct a revolution. He then mentioned, confidentially, that Manuilski's directive that everyone had to safeguard the life of Luís Carlos Prestes above all else was an unwise order. Langner agreed.[2]

Also on March 6, the first of what would be several meetings took place between de Graaf and the ИККИ. Gevork Alikhanov, of the IKKI Cadres Department, Moisei Chernomordik, deputy head of IKKI, and Stella Blagoeva, an analyst, sat across from Johnny at this first debriefing. In later meetings it would be just Blagoeva and de Graaf. Blagoeva was arguably the most feared woman in the Comintern. A widow and former history teacher from Bulgaria, she was brought to Moscow by the general secretary of the Comintern, Georgi Dimitrov, in 1931. Comrade Blagoeva reported to Dimitrov, to Manuilski, and to the NKVD.[3]

Before her interrogation really got under way, Johnny waited for the opportunity to speak privately with Alikhanov. Getting Gevork alone, Johnny told him that he had run across an inventor in Argentina who had perfected an electric, smokeless, and noiseless cannon. All the inventor wanted was free passage and asylum for himself and his family in the USSR. He would then turn his miracle weapon over to the Soviet Union. Or the Soviets could purchase the invention outright. Johnny said that he had personally test-fired a prototype and that he had supported the inventor with his own money, aware of the value of such a device to the USSR. De Graaf also mentioned the electric cannon later to Comrade Müller of OMS.[4]

The actual meetings between Blagoeva and Johnny continued for hours at a time for fifteen days until March 21, 1937.[5] Besides some parenthetical questions about the assignment in China, what happened in South America, especially Brazil, was the main topic of interest. Blagoeva wanted to know everything and anything. Johnny told her what he remembered, always careful to cover himself. He explained how he, Antônio Bonfim, and Prestes had developed a plan to bring northeasterners to Rio for training, how there had been disagreements with Prestes, and how their meetings stopped taking place. He mentioned Helena's becoming Prestes's driver; rigging the bombs at Prestes's apartment; the failure of the revolution owing to poor planning; the arrests of the conspirators; how he managed to slip through the net; and Helena's suicide. Johnny even revealed that Helena had had an affair with Carlos da Costa Leite,[6] one of Prestes's confidants from their days as cadets at the Realengo Military Academy in Rio de Janeiro.[7]

De Graaf was told to return to his hotel room and put everything down on paper, including the mission to China. His undated report comprised twenty-four typed pages, including charts and a graph with the names of eight central persons, together with whom they knew, from the events in Rio.[8] His comments included his *pièce de résistance.* If the Comintern would give him a free hand and enough money, he could return to Brazil and, through his contacts among the Brazilian upper classes, arrange for the release of Ewert and Ghioldi. His chances of succeeding, he said, were about 90 percent. Prestes would have to wait until his case could be carefully studied. Evidently the US$1 million might still be put to use if the right terms could be reached. Finally, Johnny offered to continue the valuable work he had had to abandon in Buenos Aires in order to return to Moscow—preparing South American terrorists and infiltrating them back into the Argentine army and navy.[9]

Stella Blagoeva too deliberated about what she knew from all the sources at her disposal, not just from what Johnny was telling her. From the reports she had read, she thought that Ewert acted suspiciously in Brazil. The discussion Johnny and Helena had at the Hotel Passage in 1933 and the accusations against Gekker were similarly pointed out to her. Then there were Johnny's missions to Romania and China. Each was looked into again, and the results made their way into her growing file on de Graaf. She was even told of Vasiliev's statement regarding Johnny's being a natural-born terrorist. From his Franz Gruber passport, Blagoeva determined the general course of his movements from the time he left the USSR for Brazil in November 1934 until passing through Poland on his way back to the USSR in March 1937. This included both trips to Brazil. She was curious about the lack of an exit stamp from Argentina in his fake passport. Finally, the KPD had informed Moscow that during his journey to the Soviet Union in 1937, Johnny had gone to Berlin for three days to give Helena's ashes to her parents, and that he had later bragged about his bravery in disregarding the Nazis and their reward for his capture.[10]

Among the things in de Graaf's favor was Amleto Locatelli. In July 1936 the Italian became the first important member from the debacle in Brazil to return to Moscow. He was on Johnny's side because he was convinced that the Communists in Brazil were ill prepared for an uprising in November 1935. His long report of July 20, 1936, was impressive, if only because he was naive in ignoring what it would do. Locatelli's accusations against those responsible in Brazil for not being ready, and for essentially being poor revolutionaries, reflected badly on Luís Carlos Prestes. More dangerously, by implication, it brought in Prestes's protector and sponsor, Dmitri Manuilski. Besides the descriptions of Prestes as stubborn and not security conscious, Olga was said to have overstepped her authority and tried to keep Prestes inaccessible. Ewert was overbearing, hasty, and also not concerned sufficiently with security. He too attempted to keep Prestes isolated. Like her husband, Ewert's wife, Sabo, was reported to have been indifferent to the group's security. Rudolfo Ghioldi was seen as weak, and Baron may well have given up Prestes to the police. Locatelli mentioned that Johnny, Helena, and the Stuchevskis had been taken into custody but let go because the authorities could not find anything against them.[11] In addition, Locatelli pointed out that (1) the members of the party in Brazil were small in number, (2) the unions were not in Communist hands, (3) the organization of the ANL was bad, both while it existed and after it was outlawed, (4) there was no military committee within the Brazilian Communist Party, (5) General Miguel Costa (Prestes's de facto superior in the Coluna Prestes) wavered in São Paulo about the uprising when he should have supported it, and (6) Prestes put a stop to Johnny's suggestion that small military units be formed to accomplish specific tasks as the revolution got under way, such as neutralizing the Polícia Militar base in Botafogo.[12]

Manuilski did not like Locatelli's original statement. The Italian had written an account that could put Manuilski's career on the line. Thus it was that Comrade Dmitri requested that Comrade Amleto come to his office for a little chat.

In 1935 Dmitri Manuilski had been promoted to the position of the Central Committee's representative on the IKKI, and also as the IKKI's secretary in charge of cadres.[13] Locatelli was a simple field agent. The meeting was a mismatch. Amleto Locatelli was accused of being a homosexual, a dangerous charge in the USSR of the 1930s. He was said to have had a brief affair with a Canadian in Paris on the way back to Moscow. The charge may have been true, as Manuilski had the reports in his hands to show the Italian. The documents may also have been fabricated. Whatever the case, Locatelli decided to rewrite and resubmit his version of what had transpired in South America. His finished eighteen-page document was a piece of self-criticism in which he admitted errors of judgment and perhaps even the endangerment of the entire operation in Brazil. He never directly answered the charge of homosexuality. Instead of being arrested and executed, Locatelli, through the intercession of Palmiro Togliatti, the important Italian Communist and leader of the Comintern's efforts in Spain, was allowed to leave the country and join the International Brigades in the Spanish Civil War (1936–39). It is presumed that he was killed in action in March 1937, although there is a report that he may have deserted and in so doing escaped the USSR's watchful eyes forever.[14]

Unfortunately for de Graaf, the Stuchevskis had preceded him to Moscow. In late October or early November 1936, Pavel and Sofia arrived without singing Johnny's praises. They were trying to save their own skins by blaming others for the failed revolution. For four months, beginning on November 14, 1936, the couple produced approximately a hundred pages of material on what had happened in South America. Their comments contained nine main accusations against Johnny. Some of the claims were true—but no one in Moscow knew it—some were untrue, and some were ridiculous. Each was given as a fact. They began with the charge that Bonfim had written to Prestes, both before and after his own arrest, stating that Johnny was a provoker. Bonfim was arrested on January 13, 1936, and Johnny left Brazil on January 21, 1936. Why, they asked, was Johnny given a visa for exit and reentry, once he was arrested? This seemed suspicious to Prestes, since it occurred during the state of siege following the attempted coup. The newspapers in Rio stated that de Graaf was arrested as Berger's secretary on January 5, 1936. Olga said that she knew Gruber was "nakhalni" (a very brazen and forward person) and could get himself out any situation. Baron said on January 25, 1936, that Johnny obtained an exit and reentry visa. He learned this from Helena when he drove her someplace. Pavel Stuchevski claimed that de Graaf told him in Buenos Aires that neither he nor Helena used Baron's car. Baron said that he gave Johnny a thousand pesos because Johnny mentioned he did not have enough money for the trip to Argentina. Baron also knew that de Graaf had sold his car, they said. In Buenos Aires, Johnny did not want to answer any queries about the sale of the vehicle and tried to avoid answering such questions. Stuchevski did not insist, he claimed, because Johnny did not have to report to him. As Prestes's chauffeur, Helena knew everyone of importance in the attempted revolution. Finally, the Stuchevskis claimed, Johnny turned in Baron. And Johnny was, in fact, a spy for the White Russians.[15]

Aware of what Locatelli and the Stuchevskis were saying, Johnny's old instructor Pavel Vasiliev did not believe the two Russians. He wrote that if nothing could be found against Johnny, he should not remain in the Soviet Union but should be sent abroad for other jobs in terrorism, among other things. Vasiliev's suggestion, however, did come with a self-serving qualification. He recommended that anything new the investigators turned up regarding Johnny's Brazilian work should be sent to the NKVD.[16]

Gevork Alikhanov felt that there was sufficient material for the NKVD to become involved. In addition to the claims by the Stuchevskis, in a preliminary draft dated April 10, 1937, Alikhanov added the following "inconsistencies": (1) Johnny and Helena were apprehended on the night of January 5, 1936, and released the next morning. Johnny "behaved badly" while in police custody. (2) On the night of de Graaf's apprehension, his landlord, a German Nazi and the director of the Transatlantic Cable Company, was called by the police. He vouched for Johnny. After de Graaf's release, this man and a host of additional acquaintances, including an Austrian major, kept in close contact with Johnny, even after his departure. (3) Elza Fernandes, the companion of Antônio Bonfim, was picked up by the police and held in custody for eighteen days. She was tortured during that period. She also knew who Helena was. It seemed questionable to Moscow that Elza had not revealed at least something she knew about the woman who knew everyone. (4) De Graaf used the Franz Gruber passport even in Argentina despite knowledge of the close cooperation between the Argentine and Brazilian police. (5) He carried out the special education of undercover party members even though he was aware of this same police cooperation. (6) De Graaf announced that his wife committed suicide in Buenos Aires on December 3, 1936, after he returned to Moscow. Her death took place on the day before their planned departure from Argentina for Europe and Moscow. He failed to report Helena's suicide to anyone (not to the Communist Party of Argentina, not to OMS). The local police did not report the event, either. Gruber concluded the police investigation himself, without encountering any obstacles, regardless of the fact that he lived in Buenos Aires with the same passport he had used in Brazil. (7) The police had not issued a stamp in his passport allowing him to leave Argentina. He claimed that he traveled on a British ship and got off in Boulogne. However, the mark in the passport indicates that he got off in Dunkirk. (8) De Graaf spent three days in Berlin on his way to Moscow, even though the Gestapo was looking for him. (9) During his first conversation with the Human Resources Department of IKKI, he expressed a desire to return to Brazil immediately to bring about the release of Ghioldi and Evert. Yet, during his one year in Argentina, he never brought up this topic in spite of being connected to the IKKI apparatus in Buenos Aires. (10) Vasiliev had spoken out in Johnny's defense, if nothing could be uncovered against him. In what appears to be the version he actually sent to the NKVD, dated April 11, 1937, the reference that Vasiliev had sided with Johnny was deleted. There was a recommendation that the NKVD "should take a close look at Gruber."[17]

The NKVD did examine de Graaf very carefully. A barrage of paperwork and comments made their way from one agency to the NKVD and back again, for months. Johnny, too, sent letters. He wrote Manuilski on April 3 complaining that he had not been able to meet with him since returning to Moscow and pleaded for an appointment. The issue of Prestes, Ewert, and Ghioldi needed to be discussed urgently. He pointed out that he would wait in his room at the Hotel Novo Moskovskaya until noon each day for Manuilski's phone call.[18] The following month, on the fifteenth, he wrote to Alikhanov about the conclusion of the trials of Prestes, Ewert, and Ghioldi. He could not understand why Alikhanov had tentatively rejected an earlier proposal. This was probably in reference to the electric cannon. Johnny ended by pointing out that Brazil and Argentina would be the next places of fascist adventurism.[19] The final letter in this series, on June 20, went to the chairman of the International Control Commission, Comrade Anwält. It was a restatement of the electric cannon offer, along with a reminder that he had by then been waiting three months for a reply.[20] There is no record that Manuilski, Alikhanov, or Anwält ever answered any of these communications. Indeed, they probably wanted nothing to do with de Graaf until his future was decided.

In unconfirmed material from Johnny's testimony to the FBI, he stated that around May 1937, five plainclothes NKVD agents grilled him at the Comintern offices for seven hours about the Brazilian events.[21] He mentioned that he refused to talk to them until Vasiliev told him on the telephone that it was okay to do so. At the finish of the long cross-examination, he was sent back to his hotel and told to work on a report of the Brazilian uprising, and to be ready in the early evening or the next morning in case the NKVD wanted to speak with him again. Four days later, he was called to the NKVD office at the Comintern and subjected to another lengthy interrogation. He was asked to sign a Russian translation of his earlier remarks but refused to do so until a German version was produced. While de Graaf could speak Russian, he was not totally fluent in the language.

In November he was brought before the Central Committee of the VKP(b) in the Kremlin. The purpose of this meeting was to determine the responsibility for the failed attempt to overthrow Getúlio Vargas. The heavyweight representatives of the CC consisted of the minister of defense, Marshal Kliment Voroshilov, commissars of heavy industry Anastas Mikoyan and Lazar Kaganovich, foreign secretary Vyacheslav Molotov, and the new chief of the NKVD, Nikolai Yezhov.[22]

Johnny was asked to tell his life history and give his opinion on the catastrophe in Brazil. Comrade Waldemar, who knew Johnny from Germany in 1923, and Langner both spoke in favorable terms about de Graaf. When the last question had been asked, Johnny was told to return to his hotel and write out a third report on the Brazilian proceedings. There would be one more session, again before the Central Committee, in which they wanted to know if Johnny had forced his military views on Luís Carlos Prestes. The only people at this second meeting with the CC were a general who served as an aide to Marshal Voroshilov, Voroshilov himself, Kaganovich, and Molotov. The general who assisted Voroshilov stated that Prestes's tactics had been useless and that de Graaf's guerrilla plans were better. Voroshilov was one of the leaders of the purges and his aide dared not make such a comment without the marshal's blessing and the concurrence of Molotov. Johnny would later tell one of his sons that this was the turning point.[23]

He was then ordered back to his hotel to await further instructions. Passing time at the Novo Moskovskaya between these interrogation sessions, however, proved to be the most nerve-wracking period of de Graaf's life. He ate compulsively and ballooned up to about 230 pounds (around 105 kg).[24] He was in a state of hidden panic, and with good reason. From the assassination of the Leningrad party leader and Stalin rival Sergei Kirov in early December 1934, until the removal of NKVD head Yezhov in December 1938, the Soviet Union and Moscow labored under the effects of the Great Terror. The most terrible years were 1937 and '38, as all segments of Soviet society fell victim to the paranoia of mass purges and liquidations. Pavel Stuchevski and his wife, Sofia Stuchevskaya, were among the executed. So too were Alexander Abramov, his replacement, Müller, whose real name was Boris Melnikov, along with two of Johnny's cross-examiners, Gevork Alikhanov and Moisei Chernomordik. Even his ultimate protectors Ian Berzin and Pavel Vasiliev would walk their last miles.

It was definitely a precarious time. The capital of world communism was undergoing a period of instability just long enough for someone like Johnny de Graaf to bluff his way through it all. It was Olga Bernário who first called Johnny brazen, and brazen he would have had to be. During the Terror, Stalin approved 383 lists with the names of condemned persons. On some days the lists of those to be executed were short; on other days they were long. But the arrests in the middle of the night went on everywhere.[25] How could this have been a benefit to de Graaf? Rather than being a committed Communist attempting to please superiors within the Stalinist orbit, Johnny was on the outside looking in. He could tell any lie, any truth, or anything in between to obtain what he wanted. Those doing the evaluation of Franz Gruber did not want to step on the toes of persons who might in turn do them harm. A mistake by anyone, not just by de Graaf, could spell doom. On August 27, 1937, Blagoeva appears to have issued her final pronouncement on Gruber. Writing to an unnamed individual, she requested them to "translate this and the previous documents regarding Gruber's connections with the arrested and send them to the NKVD."[26]

General Berzin finally summoned his agent to his office and said, "Take a good long rest now, Johnny," after praising de Graaf's efforts during the Brazilian episode. Johnny was to endure many more months of "rest" before he would learn what would happen. As he made his way back to the Novo Moskovskaya, he hummed a pleasurable tune as the scant downtown traffic flashed by. De Graaf felt that his bluff might have succeeded. It allowed him to look forward to a vacation far from the twists and turns of espionage anxiety. The trips away from Moscow, the wining and dining, and the visiting of new sights, in contrast, soon became boring. Night after night, Johnny returned to the bleakness of hotel room 670 to be greeted with deathly solitude and no messages to report for a briefing. This monotony was broken only by some minor surgery and a two-week stay at a local military hospital. There, anything Johnny wanted was brought to him during his convalescence, from wages to hard-to-get foods. Associates sent flowers; even General Berzin and some M4 comrades stopped by for a visit.

Once released from the hospital, de Graaf yearned to begin work either at headquarters in Moscow or with another mission, but no order came, despite his subtle prodding. He felt safe in the General Staff's hands but forever apprehensive that the truth concerning the Brazilian mission would surface in some small way. It was a test of nerves, and Johnny could only reason that if they had him nailed he would have been arrested, tortured, and then dispatched with a bullet to the brain by some NKVD stooge. As he was alive and free to roam, his suspicions always awaited the never-arriving proof. Time the healer could save him. Time the eventual claimant could also destroy him. Time was the game. He took an oath to himself that as long as it took, he would not be his own undoing.

As more weeks turned into months, Johnny was never aware that his excursions were being watched. Yet the unknown shadows on his tail probably became as fed up as he was with the aimless walks and repetitive visits to redundant places. Half a year plodded by in this manner, Johnny playing the daily game through his well-practiced pleasant exterior. The NKVD learned that on April 7, 1937, he had slept with a female in his hotel room who had signed the downstairs register as Comrade Soltz. Johnny had a revolver in his hotel room, safely hidden, he believed. It was not. The authorities discovered it in mid-May 1937. What they never realized was that five of the revolver's six bullets were to be used against the NKVD if they ever had come for him. The last cartridge was to take his own life.[27]

After convincing himself that the black gadget called a telephone in his room could not ring, it was an unexpected surprise when it did emit the unfamiliar sound late one evening. Berzin wanted to see him the next day. Joy and the release of tension should have been his reaction, and it was, too, but only momentarily. Within seconds Johnny's mood became cloaked in suspicion and doubt. What did this appointment with General Berzin mean? Had they yielded, or was this to test his reactions in hopes of an awaited slipup under the prolonged pressure? Or was it that he was now cleared of suspicions and about to be assigned a new mission?

The next morning Johnny donned a garb of self-innocence as he entered General Berzin's office. The general greeted de Graaf warmly. Then came the news. "Johnny," he exclaimed in uncontrollable delight, "I have something wonderful to tell you. Your son, Johnny Junior, is here in Moscow. He came on his own!" De Graaf stared at him briefly. "It's true! It's true, Johnny! And he's here, right here waiting for his dad!" Light-headedness stunned de Graaf as he listened to Berzin's shimmering details. He was happy that Maria had let him come.

When thirteen-year-old Johnny Junior visited KPD headquarters in Berlin, he had simply told the officials that his father was in the Soviet Union and that he wanted to go to Moscow to join him. His statement was quickly verified through the Comintern, and soon the young man was on his way to the USSR. Once he got there, he was placed in a home for the offspring of approved political immigrants. It was an Austrian children's home, a special institution set up to accept orphans and the descendants of largely German and Austrian agents. Johnny Junior was admitted to its confines as one more faceless student. De Graaf would not be told of his son's arrival for nearly five years.[28]

The Soviet Union was only too pleased to take in Johnny's firstborn and arrange for his transportation to Moscow. It meant they had secured a family hostage, a guarantee that would keep the boy's father from deserting and underwrite his return following international assignments. Since de Graaf had already performed several missions to their liking, he need not be told where his son was unless doubts were ever raised about his loyalty. He could then be better controlled through a simple reminder. De Graaf knew that the system bred such state security principles. He thanked Berzin profusely and sped to the school's address, which the general had jotted on a slip of paper: "Калашы переулок, д.12." It was Kalashny Alley 12, the location of Kinderheim No. 6, or Children's Home No. 6.[29]

Tree-shrouded grounds with stately buildings greeted de Graaf's curious gaze at his son's home in the western part of Moscow near the Arbat. Here youngsters of various ages received care, food, and schooling. They were assigned pleasant rooms and given clothing and even a few rubles for pocket money. Everything was provided for, all nice and neat, compliments of the state. The director, a bright young man in his early thirties, Ivan Semjonov,[30] himself once a homeless soul, gave Johnny the grand tour. Outside, on the ball courts crowded with pockets of assorted schoolboys, they found him. The director called out Johnny Junior's name, and one lad stopped throwing a ball, turned their way, and cautiously walked to within a short distance of the two men.

With a lump in his throat, the senior de Graaf gazed at this gangling dark-haired youth. He had his father's frame, although at five foot seven (170 cm) he was shorter than his father, with hard-packed muscles showing beneath his sweat-stained jersey. Their eyes locked on each other as Johnny took in his handsome features, soft brown eyes, and tasseled, windblown hair. With one great lunge, Johnny Junior threw himself into his dad's open arms, sobbing with joy. Tears sprang from Johnny's eyes and began running down his cheeks as he held his favorite child in a bearlike grip.[31] Radiating his own emotions, the director displayed a satisfied smile. The elder de Graaf nodded his thanks, softly turned and walked away, clinging to Johnny Junior.

Rain, hail, and thunder could have gushed from the heavens that day and they would not have noticed. The two strolled along the wooded paths talking about whatever, the proud father with his arm over his boy's shoulder. De Graaf learned from his youthful companion that his other two children both were well and in school in the Ruhr. Their aunt Emma had been like a mother and saw to them to the best of her ability. Hours passed as Johnny and his son wandered under the trees of this parklike setting, chatting nonstop. The only topic not explored was Johnny's work for the Soviet Union. Johnny Junior knew that his father was a Red Army officer, and that is all he would ever know.

A late school bell rudely interrupted their conversation. With an embrace and a feigned punch to his son's jaw, and a promise to return in a few days, Johnny left his son and returned to his hotel. Johnny Junior wanted to leave with his father, and it took some explaining to convince him that military regulations made it impossible. Tender and convincing was Johnny's tone as he outlined for his son that he was all set where he was, with friendships, good food, and, most important, excellent schooling at the Karl Liebknecht Middle School. Johnny Junior had a situation better than many Muscovites.[32] Still, he was sad and could only be gladdened by his father's promise to visit him often so they could spend more time together.

Moscow's lights could not have generated the warm, happy feeling that now enveloped Johann de Graaf. Months of solitude and uneasiness vanished with the feeling that the world's greatest blessing had come his way. M4 continued its policy of no assignment and forced leisure, but now he did not care that more months were slipping by. Each time Johnny visited Kinderheim No. 6, he thought he could see that his son had grown a little more, nearing his first steps of manhood. When they could, they went places together. At each meeting, the younger de Graaf continued to badger his father with requests to take him away from school. He wanted to stay with the person he had come so far to find, until at last he reluctantly understood and accepted his lot. He realized that his dad was involved in important government work and could be called on to travel at a moment's notice. But the frustration was there. Ignoring what was evident, Johnny convinced himself that everything was fine in the relationship with his son.

One day, de Graaf received a note at the Hotel Novo Moskovskaya forwarded to him from the offices of M4. It was brief and in no way enlightening. The Karl Liebknecht school headmaster, Comrade Zhelasko,[33] requested that Johnny pay him a visit. De Graaf went directly to Zhelasko's residence on the school grounds, where the headmaster was grateful and full of praise for his promptness. Following the formalities, Zhelasko got down to his reason for calling the meeting. "Your son is a smart little devil," he began. "I guess all of us were the same at his age." Johnny could only guess what he had on his mind. Zhelasko stated that Johnny Junior dressed better than his fellow students (his clothes were from Germany) and had bragged about it to his fellow students. The school administrators took his fine attire away and gave him ordinary Russian clothes to wear.[34] Zhelasko pointed out that Johnny Junior also thought it clever to repeat rumors. Each day he had some gossip to pass on to the school staff that he had picked up who knows where. The lad was becoming a pest with chitchat, and the school was not prepared to put up with such nonsense. "Realize he seeks attention. That is why he does this, expecting goodwill and favor from his mentors. But he has to understand that this is not the way to accomplish his aims or fulfill his needs. To be blunt and to the point, if he does not behave, he will have to leave the school."

Embarrassed, Johnny thanked Zhelasko for his candor and told him he would take the matter in hand. Zhelasko arranged for Johnny Junior to leave his classes and go with his father for the day. The two left school and went straight to de Graaf's hotel, where Johnny brought his son up to his room for a man-to-man talk. When the two were seated, Johnny related what had been brought to his attention. Johnny Junior sat silently, listening intently to each word. His gaze never left his father's despite the restless stir of his hands. "Listen, son, I am here for only a little while. You have all you could wish for at that school. You know I have and I will visit you as often as can. Now, I want you to stop this tattling and bothering the director and his staff with tales that will only lose you all the friends and supporters you should have. No one likes a squealer and you will find, if you haven't already, that when people discover you betray their confidence, they will avoid you like the plague. Now, I am telling you for your own good, behave yourself, stay out of trouble, and keep your nose clean! Do you understand?"

Johnny Junior nodded, hung his head, and said he was sorry. Then he added that it was hard growing up. "I know that, son. We have all stumbled along the way," Johnny continued. "But that's what growing up, living life, is all about.

Each one of us does crazy things at times; yet we learn from them, the rights and the wrongs, and once we know our failings we try to change so we will be profitable for having experienced them. Only those who have learned nothing from their first mistakes repeat them again. You are a bright young man; don't you see you hurt others and yourself the most, when you do not use common sense?"

He said he understood. They talked on the way back to school, but despite his words of assurance and understanding, de Graaf felt concerned about this new problem. He felt that this new crisis could sneak up on him because there was no warning of what lay in hiding. Johnny Junior gave his father his promise that he would buckle down and cut out the smart guy stuff as they parted late that day at the school gates. Johnny knew he had been a big part of his son's troubles, since he was often gone during his childhood.

Another month passed, and from the school reports and occasional meetings with his son, de Graaf felt that the education by stumbling was taking hold. His son appeared open and happy. There were no more notes of new incidents or old ones still lingering. Johnny began to believe that the episode was behind them. A lesson had been learned, new knowledge and insights had unfolded for both Johnnys. But the real problem was still there under the surface. Johnny Junior craved his father's attention and Johnny Senior had little time to give such things. At one point following his return to the Soviet Union in 1933, Johnny Junior complained to the family back in Ahlen that he had only seen his father eight times.[35]

Out of the blue, de Graaf was forced to swing his thoughts in another direction. The long-awaited call came on a cold day in late January 1938. Berzin wanted him to report the next day. As he made his way to M4's headquarters the following morning, de Graaf felt no qualms or apprehension this time. He was now convinced they had cleared him and that he would finally get back to work.

Berzin greeted Johnny with a firm handshake and a warm, cordial manner. Indeed, he had been let off the hook. Ian gave Johnny a drink and toasted his good work. Manuilski had told Johnny during the interrogation process that he was probably the only true Leninist in Brazil. Manuilski may have been only parroting an accolade given by Molotov during the Central Committee's questioning. Now Berzin repeated the compliment. Then he read Johnny the statements of Stuchevski and Locatelli, prefaced by remarks that they had been wrong and he had been right.[36]

He asked about Johnny Junior, apparently interested in his progress at school. They soon made themselves comfortable, and Berzin explained the assignment. "Johnny, the mission is to Japan first and then on to Brazil," he began. "We have great need for military intelligence from Brazil. The country is overflowing with pro-German elements, and it is vital we know what the Brazilian government, and also this powerful faction, are up to." De Graaf nodded in agreement, following Berzin's every word as his superior went on about the growing might of Hitler's Germany. "The USSR has to have agents in key trouble spots where support for the Nazis is strong, such as Brazil. There, as in many other countries, covert agents are forever being arrested."

To try to avoid his being taken into custody, the Soviets decided to provide de Graaf with a cover story that would allow him to move freely and gather intelligence without arousing suspicion. They settled on a small import-export business. Such firms were considered secure in those days because they had legitimate reasons to send telegrams back and forth.[37] Of course, the real meaning of their communications would be in code. Johnny was to be given a largely free hand in setting this up, first in Tokyo, where he was to be connected with the group run by an old acquaintance, Richard Sorge, and then in Rio de Janeiro, where he was to tie in the other end.[38] The arrangement would allow him to travel periodically from Japan to Brazil and back again without causing undue notice.

Johnny listened closely, slowly weighing the various points. Berzin explained that in Tokyo he was to make contact with a German who was a golf club manager. They would meet near a particular putting green. Each day at a specific time he was to be there until they met. The contact would appear by taking notice of Johnny's putting practice and begin a golf discussion with him. During the conversation, he would identify himself by examining one club and saying, "This is very poorly made, isn't it." That would be the signal. No doubt he would have an advance description of Johnny, while Johnny would recognize him only through the expression.[39] Once a connection was established, the German would assist de Graaf in obtaining the information he needed to set up the import-extort business. As soon as the Tokyo office was up and running, Johnny would proceed to Rio de Janeiro, launch the other agency, and use a radio operator, Hans Wilhelm, who would arrive later from Moscow.

There was also an alternative to the plan, Berzin explained. He could go to Brazil first and start an office there. Once arranged, he would then proceed to Japan, make contact, and tie the two strings together at that end. Until the Tokyo enterprise was open for business and receiving messages, Brazilian intelligence information would be telegraphed to a Communist front operation in Brussels.

The decision was de Graaf's. He could make his own way, so long as the mission and wireless network between these countries were established. To the outside world, the business would be 100 percent legal. He would deal in sporting goods, cotton, and scrap iron for Japan, and in porcelain, silk, and china imports for Brazil. As for the real reason for setting all this up, de Graaf was told he was to gather as much information as possible on shipbuilding and armament factories in Japan. His targets of interest included the naval yards northwest of Tokyo. This would be a particularly difficult facility to crack, as it was totally sealed off, and workers could not leave. Johnny was to rely on help from the Japanese Communist Party to get in, or to get someone in. He was also to try to obtain intelligence on steel manufacturing in Osaka, the metal works in Kobe, and the naval yards in Nagasaki. Moscow also wanted him to assess the will of the Japanese people to fight. His initial funds would amount to US$60,000 (US$890,000 in 2009 dollars).[40] He would take US$30,000 with him and the balance would be sent when called for.[41]

Johnny thought it all out carefully while Berzin sat in silence, awaiting his response. Frank Foley and British intelligence had to know about this and fast, which meant making contact with Foley as soon as he left the Soviet Union. It would prove more difficult to get in touch with him while en route to Japan, since that journey might well be made via the Trans-Siberian Railway. Then too, Japan was a country that treated all foreigners with suspicion, which would make setting up the front at that end far more difficult than in Brazil. His seafaring days as a youth had taught him as much.

"Brazil would be the best course first," Johnny at last told Berzin. As he saw it, it would be vital for the USSR to know more about the political and military climate in Brazil, since it was a country that seemed to be in flux. And by going there to begin with, he and Hans Wilhelm would be able to assemble and transmit information back to the center in Brussels sooner. Johnny could then go on to Tokyo and complete the circuit. Finally, he would concentrate on the other tasks and eventually drop Brussels as the radio relay point.

General Berzin agreed to this approach. He too felt it would be the quickest and most secure way of starting the mission. Both men were of the opinion that either Rio de Janeiro or São Paulo would be an ideal city in which to locate the business office. Johnny would enter Brazil using an Austrian passport under his former alias, Franz Gruber.[42] It would be the safest way, as he had already made many contacts using that name. Two emergency addresses in the United States, both in California, were provided in case of major problems: a Mr. David, at 228 Broadway in San Diego, and Mrs. Rose Tollins, at 2566 Pine Street in San Francisco.[43] Hans Wilhelm, using the name Harry, would travel to Brazil separately a few weeks later and meet Johnny at a prearranged time in a Rio de Janeiro restaurant.

Berzin assured Johnny that he could continue to meet with his son until he departed, and that in his absence the boy would be well taken care of. The general then wanted to know if they should supply him with a wife for the trip to improve his cover. Johnny answered that this would not be necessary, as he hoped to marry Gertrude Krüger on his way to Rio de Janeiro, if it was okay. He then quickly added that perhaps it would be a good idea to bring along her parents too, so they could operate the Brazil end of the import-export business when he was in Japan. Johnny mentioned that both Gustav and Emilie Krüger had been Social Democrats sympathetic to communism. Gustav had even once been a member of the KPD.[44]

Berzin told him, "It's your neck. Make your own travel plans," he added, as de Graaf was about to leave. "The document section will have your papers and passport for you shortly. The funds will be delivered to your hotel just before you leave. Good luck, Johnny!" They shook hands and Johnny left Berzin's office feeling elated. At last the long wait was over. He was free of apparent suspicion by M4. Making his way back to the Novo Moskovskaya, he told himself that one day he would be released forever from this hated Communist system.[45] He sang the praises of Locatelli, who had unwittingly covered for him in the Brazilian disaster. De Graaf had passed the test in Moscow and survived with his life; the possible leak never came.[46]

From the beginning of April until the first days of May 1938, Johnny spent a lot of time in an apartment in Moscow arranged by M4. Berzin wanted him to become familiar with a number of books and classified documents about Japan. M4 did not want these items to be kept in a hotel. At night, Johnny would walk back to his room at the Moskovskaya.[47] Returning one evening, the receptionist gave him a postcard from Gerti in Berlin. It stated simply, "Dear Johnny, how long does a girl have to wait to say yes? Love my dearest, your Gerti." Johnny read the card over several times. His growing affection for this young woman began to well up in his eyes. He whispered out loud to himself while holding the card, "Not long now, Gerti, not long, my love." That night he slept like a newborn babe, at peace and full of happiness and great expectations.

A few days before his departure for Brazil, Johnny's tranquil state of mind was shattered. While walking in Moscow, a friend of his son stopped him and said, "Comrade, your boy is in prison." Dumbfounded, de Graaf said, "What?"

"Yes," he repeated. "He's in prison on military orders."

"How do you know?" Johnny demanded.

"I was there when they arrested him," the youth stammered nervously.

Johnny was speechless. "This could not be. There had to be some mistake." Quickly, he visited General Berzin and reported the incident. "I have been told on the street that my son was arrested and is now in prison," he began.

"What's the rascal done?" Berzin inquired.

"I don't know," Johnny replied. "That's all I know about it. The lad who told me is from the children's home, and all he knew was that my son and three or four others had been arrested."

"Don't worry, Johnny," his superior smiled. "We'll find out what it's all about." The head of M4 then picked up the phone and called the chief of the NKVD, Nikolai Yezhov. Berzin told Yezhov what he could, laughing all the while, and then he raised the receiver so de Graaf could hear Yezhov's words. "We'll send him home within minutes, right away." After hanging up, General

Berzin said, "Johnny Junior and four pals had committed some petty thievery and thrown rocks at the windows of abandoned buildings. Quite a commotion," he laughed.[48] "Unfortunately, young people always get out of control," Berzin remarked with amusement. "Go to the children's home and see him, for they will take him there. He should be back before you arrive."

Johnny went to the Kinderheim No. 6 as fast as he could, and as Berzin had said, Johnny Junior had already been checked in. He went to his son's room, entered, and shut the door. Eighteen-year-old Johann sat on his bed with his head down. "My boy, you have done many childish and stupid things, but this time you have hurt your father deeply!" Johnny began, forcing back his anger. Johnny Junior looked up, tears in his eyes.

"I didn't want to hurt you, Dad, but I just hate being here!" He was as outspoken as Johnny had been at his age, but they both knew the answer beforehand.

"No, to get you out of Soviet Union at this time is impossible."

"Can I take you to the station when you go, Father?" he finally asked.

"I will have to ask permission for that," Johnny replied. Johnny Junior looked disappointed. So de Graaf tried to explain to him that those were the regulations, which could not be changed without permission. He then made a phone call to M4 and received authorization for his son to meet him at the train station in two days' time. Johnny Junior son was happy with the small victory and happier still when his father informed him that he was to be moved out of Kinderheim No. 6 and into a small hostel room at the work-occupational school connected to the Stalin Auto Works, where he was to be taught a trade.[49]

"Look!" de Graaf said. "You will get your own room, completely furnished with all the belongings you can use, and you'll live away from the school. Learn, study, as you have the brains for it, and with a place of your own off the school grounds, you can have a little more independence and still have responsibility."

On that evening in May 1938, de Graaf returned to his hotel, deeply worried that his son would get into trouble again during his absence, despite the promises to behave. He hoped he had learned his lesson. Perhaps now that he was more on his own, he would start to show some maturity. Johnny's thoughts were interrupted by a call instructing him to meet his traveling companion, the wireless operator, at 7:00 P.M. in a Moscow park.

Hans Wilhelm arrived promptly, and the two men strolled into a deserted area of the grounds and talked. General Berzin had assured Johnny that Hans Wilhelm was one of the best from M4's wireless school. Johnny hoped he was, since he would hold their very lives and the success of the undertaking in his nimble fingers. Hans Wilhelm was about thirty years of age, five eight or nine (172.7 to 175.3 cm) in height, and weighed in at some 150 lbs. (or just over 68 kg). His hair was dark brown and fine. De Graaf sized him up at their first meeting as being of Czech origin, with rather noticeable Slavic cheekbones. Perhaps Wilhelm's most striking feature was his sloping face, which terminated in a somewhat pointed chin. The man spoke Czech, German, English, and perhaps Russian. He was single and very much a skirt chaser. Johnny was not satisfied. He told the major who introduced them that he did not want Hans Wilhelm, but the officer seemed adamant. So de Graaf bluntly laid down the law. He informed his assigned radioman that if he spent money wildly or messed with women, he would shoot him.[50]

Continuing with his hard-line approach, Johnny mentioned that this would not be a glamorous job, and that he would have lots of work to do, with no time for foolishness. Should he prove unreliable, the mission would fail, maybe doing both of them harm in the process. This seemed to sink in, and Hans Wilhelm assured Johnny that he could be counted on. They went over their plans to travel separately, and to meet in Rio on a given day and time in a restaurant familiar to Johnny. Hans Wilhelm assured de Graaf of his best intentions, and they parted and went their separate ways.

A friend of Johnny's from the Ruhr, M4 officer Karl Franserra, also lived in the Novo Moskovskaya. He was a general instructor under the chief of communications of the Red Army. He was an expert on sending and receiving and all that it involved, and Johnny decided to pay Karl a visit. He went to his accommodations on a floor below. "Karl, by any chance do you know a man by the name of Hans Wilhelm?" de Graaf asked.

"Oh yes," he answered. "He's one of our students."

"Was he born a Czech, but became an Australian?" Johnny inquired.

"Yes, that's him all right," Franserra offered, smiling in recognition.

"Karl, we are good friends, and I value your opinion, so please answer me this. How do you rate this man's knowledge in the area of communication technology?"

Franserra put his chin in his hand, and minutes passed before he spoke. At last he informed de Graaf that Hans Wilhelm had been only a fair student, and that he had heard rumors that was a playboy. He gambled, drank, and chased women. He was boastful to the other students about his sexual exploits. He spent money too easily and owed debts to several classmates. He was reprimanded by the school administration, and that seemed to calm him down for a while. Karl added that if Hans Wilhelm had concentrated more on his studies than on being a stud, he would have passed his courses with much better marks than he did. He concluded by assessing Hans Wilhelm as a high-risk individual.

De Graaf nodded in agreement. They had only one drink together, as the time was getting late and Johnny had things to do. He thanked Karl and told him to forget about the inquiry. The next step to be taken would be between Johnny and the General Staff. Johnny headed upstairs to his room and placed an urgent call to Berzin's office to arrange a meeting that night.

A reply came back shortly; Berzin would see him. Their conference was brief, as Johnny explained to Ian Berzin his doubts about Hans Wilhelm and what he had learned of him. "Berzin, I don't trust this man." The general listened, but as the hour was late, he ended the get-together by saying, "Johnny, it's a command decision that neither you nor I can change. We cannot question those on top. Let's hope you're wrong and all will turn out for the best." With that, he shook de Graaf's hand and wished him success in the new mission. Johnny left his office for the hotel, very worried indeed.

Sleep eluded him that night as he tossed and turned, thinking about what Karl had said, which concurred with his own first impression of Hans Wilhelm. "Well, there was no going back now." M4 had made the decision, and de Graaf could not question it. Time would tell, but he worried that this weak link could cause his downfall.

Early dawn broke with overcast skies on May 18, 1938, as Johnny arrived at the train station and saw his firstborn. He stood there smiling, all decked out in very fine, expensive clothes. When Johnny asked where his son had gotten such a grand suit, he reminded his father of his earlier petty crimes. Johnny did not want to know more, told his son to behave himself, and gave him some money. They embraced, and then Johnny turned and walked with a lump in his throat to board his train. He did not look back, for he knew his boy's sad gaze followed him. Little did de Graaf know that it would be the last hug he would ever give his namesake.

Johann de Graaf II had been picked up on January 11, 1938. Despite what Berzin later told his father, he was immediately under suspicion of being involved in the Hitler Jugend (Hitler Youth) affair, a case that resulted in eighty to ninety arrests. Once the German dictator came to power in January 1933, all German-speaking political immigrants to the Soviet Union were suspected of being fascists or counterrevolutionaries. More than eight hundred Germans were deported. Beginning in 1937, a majority of those apprehended were either shot or sentenced to the gulag. In July 1937 Stalin ordered the seizure of the remaining Germans and Austrians.

Early the following year, the NKVD in Moscow invented a fictional conspiracy and began a sweep of German-speaking teenagers in the capital. Guilt by association was the watchword. The largest number of arrests came among those studying at the various institutes of learning in the capital. This included the Karl Liebknecht School and those working as apprentices at the Stalin Auto Works. Many were taken to the NKVD's Lubianka center and imprisoned in the building's infamous cellar dungeons. Around forty were shot, and twenty or so were sent to the work camps. Johnny Junior was extremely fortunate. He had been troublesome at both the Kinderheim and the Auto Works but was one of six to be released. He walked out of captivity on May 14, 1938, in time to see his father off.[51] He was arrested again sometime later and was reportedly at the

Taganka Prison in Moscow on September 11, 1941. Between the two incarcerations he married a Russian named Sarah, with whom he had a son. He became a Soviet citizen. The last word to his sister in Ahlen came during the war, along with his photograph.[52]

From this point on, Johnny Junior's life may have taken several turns. His brother believed that he was killed by the Soviets when they discovered later that their father was an MI6 agent.[53] Johnny heard that Johnny Junior worked as an aeronautical engineer in Moscow, and that he died in an air crash while fighting the Nazi army invading from the west.[54] Ironically, his brother, Oscar, had joined the Wehrmacht (the Third Reich's army) and at age eighteen became a decorated member of that invading army as part of a tank crew. Oscar de Graaf suffered a severe wound at the Battle of Stalingrad that required the amputation of his left leg above the knee. He was placed on one of the last flights out of the city and von Paulus's encircled Sixth Army.[55]

De Graaf never obtained any real proof that Johnny Junior died in the Soviet Union during the war. He tried everything he could think of to determine what happened to his son. He even attempted to convince himself that if he were still alive, a family member would have heard from him. Johnny checked with the Red Cross, which had no information on his son. He asked London to find out, but the war was raging and they too could not uncover anything. After V-E Day de Graaf wrote the Red Cross again, but no details were ever available. Despite the end of the Soviet Union several decades later and the opening of some archives, the authorities in Moscow continue to maintain their silence on this youth, whose destiny was sealed when he traveled alone across Europe to look for his father.[56]

FIG. 39 Johnny de Graaf Jr. as an adult.

FIG. 40 Oscar de Graaf in his Wehrmacht uniform on October 28, 1940.

FIG. 41 Marianne Oberschild (née de Graaf).

FIG. 42 Johnny de Graaf in 1938.

FIG. 43 Gertrude Krüger in 1938.

FIG. 44 DESPS in Rio de Janeiro in the late 1930s. Standing (third from left) is Francisco Julien. Miranda Corrêa is seated on the left. Seated on the right is Emílio Romano.

FIG. 45 The house at Avenida Rainha Elisabeth 219.

FIG. 46 To the right of Johnny and Gerti are her parents, Emilie and Gustav Krüger, in 1938 or 1939. Gerti is wearing the same dress as Helena in figure 31. This was done to help convince the Brazilian authorities that she was Helena.

FIG. 47 Johnny's 1937 Ford, before it was wrecked, in a photo taken by Ernst Krüger.

FIG. 48 Ernst Krüger in the Spreewald Forest, south of Berlin, after returning from Brazil.

FIG. 49 The scuttling of the *Graf Spee*.

FIG. 50 Franz Gruber's DESPS archive photo. "I.S." stood for Britain's Intelligence Service. The photograph actually came from de Graaf's 1935 Brazilian driver's license. Miranda Corrêa gave a copy of the picture to the Gestapo on his visit to Germany in 1937.

FIG. 51 De Graaf relaxing on the back veranda at Rainha Elisabeth.

FIG. 52 Cecil Borer in 1939.

FIG. 53 The Polícia Central in the 1930s.

FIG. 54 The Fortress of Santa Cruz.

FIG. 55   Cliff Harvison.

FIG. 56   Palmerston Avenue 49 in Montreal's Mount Royal suburb. One of the basement window slats can be seen to the left of the garage door.

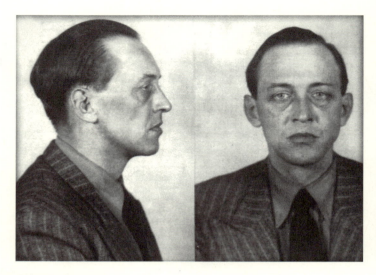

FIG. 57 Werner von Janowski's RCMP mug shot.

FIG. 58 Adrien Arcand in 1933.

FIG. 59 Tim Buck.

FIG. 60 The Wilberforce apartments in London.

FIG. 61 Johnny at the end of the war in 1945.

FIG. 62 De Graff in the uniform of a British Army officer. The inscription, from Goethe, reads, "Nur der verdient sich Freiheit wie das Leben, der täglich sie erobern muß" [Freedom and life itself are deserved only by those who have to win them each day]. Jonny, England, August 12, 1946 [the 6 is overwritten with 7]."

FIG. 63 The boardinghouse at 1863 Dorchester Street West (now called Boulevard René-Lévesque Ouest) in Montreal.

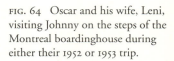

FIG. 64 Oscar and his wife, Leni, visiting Johnny on the steps of the Montreal boardinghouse during either their 1952 or 1953 trip.

FIG. 65 Wedding day. Sári and Johnny on June 14, 1952.

FIG. 66 Going swimming during the visit of Oscar and his wife, Leni (taking the picture), to Montreal in 1953. From right to left, Oscar, Johnny, and Sári. The others are unidentified residents of the boardinghouse.

FIG. 67 At the wheel of his car.

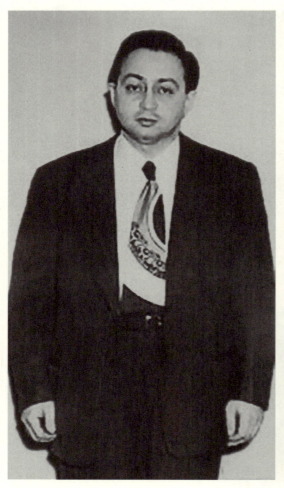 

FIG. 68 Harry Gold.

FIG. 69 Thomas L. Black on July 14, 1950.

FIG. 70 The main house at Horningtoft.

FIG. 71 Tourist cabin proprietor.

FIG. 72 In old age.

FIG. 73   All that remained of Horningtoft when visited by one of the authors in 1995.

15

BRAZIL TWO

Using a Belgian passport, Johnny watched the Soviet capital disappear from view as his train left for the Finnish border. In Helsinki, he sent Gerti two hundred marks. Her family had moved to Gleim Straße 10^{IV}. The relocation took place because Johnny stopped sending money while he was in Moscow. Two hundred marks was more than enough for train passage for Gertrude and her mother to Copenhagen, where they would meet up with Johnny. De Graaf sent another wire to Frank Foley in Berlin from a steamer on its way to Stockholm. It read, "Dear Friend, I am on a long trip and look forward to seeing you in Copenhagen." On May 21, 1938, Johnny's train from Sweden pulled to a stop on the subterranean tracks at København H, and he checked into a hotel. He had mentioned to Gerti that he wanted to get married in Copenhagen, but if she was opposed to the idea she should come anyway to say goodbye.[1]

The next day, Gertie and Emilie Krüger arrived and were relaxing in the room Johnny had reserved for them. The reunion was truly wonderful. Emilie Krüger was happy to see the love Gerti and Johnny had for each other. He explained the purpose of their get-together, which met with everyone's immediate and joyous approval. Gerti had her German passport with her and seemed more radiant than ever. De Graaf already had picked up his Franz Gruber passport from an M4 operative in Copenhagen. So as to avoid raising suspicions in Brazil, and because Gerti resembled her sister, she agreed to assume Helena's identity, and her passport was altered to read Erna Krüger. Since Helena was already known in Brazil, Johnny was probably just trying to add some insurance.[2] No need to have the authorities in Rio snooping around into what had happened to Helena.

On May 22, Frank Foley arrived on an evening train and went directly to de Graaf's hotel, where Johnny waited for him alone. "What's cooking, Johnny?" Frank asked as he vigorously pumped his agent's hand. He made no bones about the fact that he and Vivian believed Johnny would never get out of the Soviet Union alive. For the next two hours, de Graaf filled Foley in on what had taken place and on what the Soviets were planning on this new project. Before Johnny finished his comments, he picked up the phone and called for Gerti. Foley was more than surprised to learn that she was in Copenhagen, and more baffled still when she joined them. Later that evening, after Gerti had left, Johnny told Frank that they were going to get married during this operation. "I know British officers have to ask permission to marry, so I trust you will concur, for we plan to wed with or without MI6's permission," Johnny told him.

"That's great, Johnny!" Foley replied. "I think you have chosen a wonderful girl, but you know you will have to have Vivian's permission first."

"What?" de Graaf shouted. "To hell with Vivian!"

"Hold on, Johnny!" Foley cut in. "Let's not get our backs up. I'll contact the chief in London and tell them to expect us. This will only be a slight detour to your Brazilian journey. I'll arrange ship's accommodations for all of us for the trip. This will also give Vivian, you, and me a chance to discuss your Soviet assignment in greater detail and work out our requirements prior to your making for Brazil."

Johnny agreed and Frank hastily left to advise London of their plans and arrange accommodations on the next ship sailing from Esbjerg to Britain. Foley was never a man of indecision, so Johnny was not surprised the following evening when they boarded the train for the west coast and were soon at sea. Gerti and her mother had said their goodbyes at the station in Copenhagen before Emilie Krüger returned to Berlin.[3] Foley disappointed de Graaf en route by saying, "I don't think Vivian will give you permission to marry, Johnny."

"Fine, then tell him I quit, for Gerti and I will be married whether you fellows like it or not. So that's that!" Johnny retorted angrily.

When their ship docked in Harwich, England, there was an immediate problem. The English customs authorities discovered US$20,000 that Johnny had hidden in his belt. The money was to be used to buy the Argentine smokeless electric cannon. The authorities, probably including Foley, were surprised that the Soviets had so many genuine American dollars at the time.[4] Foley obviously took care of this matter, because Johnny and Gerti made their way to the Imperial Hotel in London and checked into separate single rooms. Sharply at 9:00 the following morning, Vee-Vee arrived, greeting Johnny pleasantly while carefully scanning his bedroom. "Are you looking for my bride to be?" Johnny asked.

Vivian was embarrassed but covered it up by saying, "You're too good for that, Johnny. Please forgive me, but sometimes we British are a bit crooked. I just naturally wanted to see if one or two rooms were used last night." De Graaf was livid.

"Had you found Gerti in my bedroom, you would no doubt not give your permission for our wedding!" Johnny snapped.

"Oh no, Johnny," he calmly replied. "I know you both too well, through Frank Foley." Leaving Johnny's door ajar, he then strode down the hall to Gerti's room and knocked. "Come out, Gerti," he commanded. Gerti opened the door and greeted him, fully dressed, with a bright, cheery smile. His warm grin was returned, as Vivian extended his hand to her and in a booming voice for all to hear said, "Congratulations Gerti; anyone Johnny brings us is welcome!"

Although he told the British that they were married on May 21, 1931 (when he was actually in the Soviet Union and she was in Germany), the Canadians that they married on May 21, 1938 (the date on which his train arrived in Copenhagen), and the Americans that they wed on June 6, 7, and 8, there is no record that any marriage ever took place. It is of course a possibility that the registration and other documents pertaining to their union were removed. Johnny claimed to various parties that he and Gerti were married in Berlin, in a small town outside Edinburgh, and to others that they married in London.[5] Nonetheless, Johnny and Gerti soon boarded the Royal Mail Lines steamship SS *Almanzora* in Southampton. Johnny saw that Gerti was safely settled before proceeding to another stateroom to speak with Vivian and Foley. For several hours Johnny again went over their questions concerning his new M4 assignment. Finally, as it was getting late, and because Johnny had left Gerti alone in their stateroom, they agreed to break off the discussion and continue the following morning.

The next day Foley and Vivian returned and began the conversation with the topic of Hans Wilhelm. Once Johnny's Soviet wireless man joined him in Rio de Janeiro, the two would carry out Moscow's wish to establish radio contact with the Brussels receiving station until the Tokyo connection was up and running. In the meantime, Johnny would send letters and telegrams in business doublespeak from Rio to "Mary" at "Tecbrevet" (really M4) in Brussels.[6]

Incoming and outgoing Soviet exchanges would be copied and passed on to London via Alfred Hutt, the Light Company executive they had used before. Hutt would send everything to Britain by the telegraphers at the embassy. De Graaf's British orders would come from the MI6 chief in Montevideo, an individual using the pseudonym "Williams," with the telegraphic address "Canalise—Montevideo."[7] Williams's instructions would be sent to the embassy in Rio and delivered to Johnny's residence by messenger. Codes were explained and memorized prior to the *Almanzora*'s departure that evening. Vivian's parting words in wishing his operative success were, "Be damn careful down there. The Brazilian scene is a hotbed of unrest and just crawling with pro-Nazi spies in the upper echelons. Extreme caution is the word, for you could be a sitting duck from many sides." His comments were certainly not encouraging, but after what Johnny had just been through in the USSR, they could not have been taken too seriously. Johnny was glad when the two men left, just before the gangplanks went up and the big ship slipped her moorings, late on Saturday, June 25, 1938.[8]

What lay ahead was anyone's guess, and now that Gerti was along, there was added concern.

They enjoyed a very smooth sea voyage that seemed all too brief, once the *Almanzora* tied up on July 10 at Praça Mauá, and Johnny and Gerti walked down the passageway to Rio de Janeiro. Among the officials dealing with arriving passengers was Antonio Emílio Romano, chief of the political section at DESPS.[9] Romano remembered Johnny from January 1936. He wanted to know what he was doing back in the country. Romano confiscated the Franz Gruber passport but let them land.

The couple took a cab to the Hotel Atlântico in Copacabana, where Johnny telephoned Inspector Francisco Julien. Julien saw to it that Johnny's phony passport was returned.[10] Johnny also learned that Filinto Müller was still chief of the capital's Polícia Civil, and still head of DESPS. Müller was a good salesman. He had convinced de Graaf that he was a staunchly pro-government supporter and Nazi hater. Johnny had believed this from his first mission to Brazil. De Graaf felt that Filinto Müller was a good policeman.

Soon after arriving, de Graaf paid Müller a visit at his home in Copacabana. Filinto showed great delight at finding Johnny active in Brazil again. Müller was a tall military man with a rather narrow head and a stylish thin black moustache. He knew Johnny as Franz Gruber, a British SIS agent. Over steaming *cafezinhos* (demitasse-size cups of coffee) provided by Müller's wife, Consuelo, Johnny explained London's concern about Nazi infiltration in Brazil. Filinto listened intently to Johnny's proposal to combine Rio's aims with London's, providing mutual benefit to both countries. He enthusiastically agreed to work together, pooling resources and intelligence information. To ease his movement within Brazil, Filinto stated that he would see to it that Johnny was given a Brazilian passport. Not only would de Graaf continue to have direct contact with him through Francisco Julien, but he would also assist Johnny's manpower needs whenever necessary. De Graaf did not know it then, but Julien's job at DESPS, and within the Quadro Movel, was foreign intelligence.[11] He, too, was evidently a good actor, with different political preferences than Johnny's.

At Filinto's urging, his new ally would travel to Santa Catarina and assist the commanding general of Brazil's Fifth Military District, in all probability João Marcellino Ferreira e Silva,[12] in his efforts at getting eligible males to sign up for their obligatory military service. All previous recruitment efforts had been for naught, as the locals had let it be known that they were more German than Brazilian. De Graaf felt that helping with this task could only support his real reason for accepting Müller's invitation: the establishment of a spy network up and down the coast favorable to His Majesty's intelligence services.

Traveling by steamer down the coast to Florianópolis, Johnny made his way to the military base and was given a briefing on the situation. General Ferreira e

Silva then had as many of the potential recruits as could be rounded up taken to a large field at the garrison. The general gave the young men a patriotic speech, urging each to cooperate for the glory of Brazil, but his words fell on deaf ears. The inductees continued to disobey their officers' orders. Watching all of this, Johnny took Ferreira e Silva aside, explained what might work, and urged him to offer the inductees a second option. Watched over by armed soldiers, the group was made to stay out in the open, directly under the blaze of an intense sun, without water or food, until they agreed to begin their military training. It took two days, and they did not know how lucky they really were. De Graaf had actually persuaded the general to let them die under the unforgiving rays if necessary.

At the end of July the Grubers found a house that suited them perfectly. For 150:000$000 (150 *contos de reis,* or US$8,670, US$131,363 in 2009 dollars), they were able to purchase a furnished twelve-room, three-story home at Avenida Rainha Elisabeth 219 in Copacabana.[13] There was a lovely backyard with a commanding view of the sea from the rear balcony, rich wood paneling in the interior, and even a music salon with a large white piano. De Graaf had his own study in the basement with a lock on the door that no one, not even the maid, was allowed to enter. Gerti reveled in puttering around in the garden, enjoying the warm climate and constant bright sunshine amid the new sights. Johnny was able to purchase a black 1937 Ford, and in short order the Grubers blended comfortably into *carioca* life.[14]

Four blocks to the east, down the slight hill on Avenida Rainha Elisabeth and perpendicular to it, is Avenida Atlântica. Facing the ocean, at Avenida Atlântica 1046, sits the Hotel Riviera (now renamed the Orla Hotel). In those days the Riviera was one of the biggest buildings at that end of the beach in Copacabana. Johnny made the acquaintance of Aldo Rosso, the owner of the Riviera, and soon the two men were discussing a possible business relationship. Although Rosso's daughter later claimed it was a deception, on September 17, 1938, a deal was signed whereby de Graaf became a 25 percent partner in the hotel for another 150:000$000.[15]

Some three weeks earlier, on August 25, 1938, and on each day with a "5" in it thereafter, until October 5, Johnny was in place at 4:00 P.M. sharp at the Bar Alpino. A German eatery, the Alpino overlooked the sea just outside the city. There Johnny waited for his wireless agent from Moscow to make an appearance. When Hans Wilhelm did not show up, de Graaf went to the planned second option, the Casino de Copacabana, in the Copacabana Palace Hotel, at 10:00 P.M. and waited at a specific table, to the right on the second floor. Both attempts on August 25 did not pan out, because Hans Wilhelm failed to appear at either location. Johnny reasoned that Wilhelm could have been delayed, so he was not too concerned. But when September 5 also resulted in no-shows for Wilhelm, despite Johnny's early arrivals and late departures, he became uneasy. Had Johnny's radio operator been found out and arrested? Johnny's mind raced, wondering anxiously if he would be next. For a number of weeks he continued to frequent the Alpino and then the casino. Beginning in November, he began to go only on the fifteenth of each month.[16]

There was a back-up plan. Should Hans Wilhelm's absence continue, M4 would send another agent. The recognition sign between the two was for the replacement to enter either establishment holding a white handkerchief. Johnny was to speak first, asking, "Are you Henry?" The answer would be, "No, I'm not, but I know you. Don't you remember?"[17]

Back in Germany, things had not gone well for Gerti's parents. Gustav Krüger's political views were out of place in the new Germany. He had been on the left fringe of the SPD before joining the KPD. His beliefs cost him not only his administrative position with the government gas company in 1933; they caused him to be blacklisted from any type of employment. Thereafter, Ernst Krüger struggled as a machinist to support the family. Almost every month a check arrived from Johnny to help out. The money came with letters from Johnny and Gerti, warning about what was happening in Germany. Before long, Johnny helped again, this time arranging in advance all the paperwork with the Brazilian Embassy in Berlin and paying for their steamship tickets. On September 21, 1938, Gustav, Emilie, and Ernst Krüger all disembarked from the SS *Monte Rosa* and set foot on Brazilian soil.

As they came down the gangplank, Gerti was there waiting for the family at dockside with one of her small dogs and an unnamed individual, most likely Francisco Julien. The Brazilian customs officials were cranky and slow, even more so with the Krügers because of their excessive baggage, until the stranger with Gerti stepped forward. When he displayed his credentials the officials instantly changed their demeanor, petted Gerti's dog in a self-reproaching manner, and let the Krügers pass without even opening a suitcase. Everyone then climbed into Johnny's Ford for the ride to Rainha Elisabeth 219.[18]

And what a ride it was. Johnny and Gertie's house was on the *carioca* social circuit in 1938–39. Ernst remarked that there was always a crowd of important Brazilians there. High-ranking military personnel—one of whom Johnny had saved from an assassination attempt at a party—the interventor of Rio de Janeiro, Ernani do Amaral Peixoto,[19] and many wealthy and influential citizens regularly met at the Grubers' residence. Ernst was a reticent observer of much of what went on when he was not out walking his sister's pair of German Shepherds, washing the Ford, or at the beach. Johnny made all of the Krügers call him Franz.[20] Gustav and Emilie occupied their own rooms in the house for a while. Johnny had loads of money, money enough to pay for everything, including a private language teacher, Hans Lessing, for Gerti and Ernst. Gerti used her real first name with Lessing and was studying English, while her brother was learning Portuguese.

There was also a piano instructor for Gerti, operations for her, Ernst, and Emilie, and, as an extra show of appreciation for the surgeon and family physician, Dr. Luiz Guimarães Dahlheim, a new car. Tecbrevet funds were even available for a fledgling perfume business, skin ointment research, and an assistant, Dr. Otto Willi Ullrich, plus a down payment on a parcel of real estate on Rua Saint Romain in Copacabana. There were also periodic loans to Inspector Julien totaling 35:000$000 (or just over US$1,842), another car, a Packard, when the Ford was wrecked in 1939,[21] and a ticket back to Hamburg for Ernst (following an argument with his sister he expressed a rash desire to return to Germany). Ernst left Rio at 6:00 P.M. on December 30, 1938, aboard the SS *Santa Eugenio,* despite Johnny's warnings that Hitler was planning a war. Johnny had arranged a job for Ernst with Condor, the German airline, if he could learn Portuguese. But Ernst felt his sister treated him like a servant. Emilie was ready to return with Ernst until Gustav grumbled, "Are you married to me or to your son?"[22] Later, Johnny moved his in-laws to an apartment at Barão da Torre 33, in Ipanema, where he paid the rent.[23] Clearly, de Graaf was spending Soviet money in a different way than they had intended. He was definitely putting down a lot of smoke to hide his activities in the tropics.

Johnny was picked up by the police in October 1938 and held briefly. Section 4, or S/4,[24] at DESPS was responsible for his apprehension. This was the Control of Explosives, Arms, and Ammunition Unit. It is not known why S/4 was interested in Johnny. Possibly it had something to do with his earlier role as an instructor in bomb making and terrorism prior to the ill-fated Communist revolution of 1935. For whatever reason, he was not held for long.

Both Johnny and Gerti applied for permanent residence visas on November 26, 1938, which were granted on February 9, 1939.[25] In addition, at some point during Johnny's second trip to Brazil, Johnny was invited to meet privately with Getúlio Vargas. Brazil's leader displayed his gratitude for de Graaf's work in thwarting the attempt to overthrow him in 1935 by presenting the MI6 agent with an engraved silver cigarette case. As near as one family member could recall, the inscription read, "Thanks for keeping the Communist Revolution from succeeding." It was signed "Getúlio Vargas."[26]

In the same month that they applied for permanent residence, Johnny and Gerti went shopping in the center of Rio. They stopped for a while at Rua Uruguaiana 47 and looked through the windows of the Atelier Vienense, a store that specialized in women's clothing imported mainly from the United States. A second visit resulted in a conversation with Josef Bunzlau, the husband of the owner, Czechoslovakian immigrant Helena Benkendorf, who was interested in expanding her business. She liked Johnny's idea of importing silk from and exporting cotton to Japan. She said she would think about it. A few days later a shipment of clothes from the Charles Berenheim Company in San Francisco arrived, and Bunzlau went to the Rainha Elisabeth house to see if Johnny was interested in buying into a portion of the merchandise. He was, and he gave Bunzlau a US$500 banknote on the spot.

Following some negotiating, Johnny bought a quarter-interest in the Atelier Vienense for 120:000$000 (or US$6,928), although, as in the case of the Hotel Riviera, Helena Benkendorf's daughter later said this was a deception. Johnny likewise agreed to help finance the importation of garments from the United States. To that effect, de Graaf and Benkendorf gave 15:000$000 (US$877) each to an American, Leopold Missiduschinck, an acquaintance of Johnny's, to take a shipment of Brazilian shoes to New York. The idea was that he would return with trousers to sell in Brazil. Since Johnny was soon to leave for Japan, his business dealings with Benkendorf required someone with his best interests at heart. De Graaf consequently took his father-in-law to the Atelier Vienense to meet Benkendorf. It was okay with her for Gustav Krüger to represent Johnny. Gustav, whom Johnny privately called Papa, could stand in for him when his de facto son-in-law was out of the country.[27]

In April 1939 Johnny received a letter from Mary in Brussels, dated March 15, informing him that US$4,620 of the US$10,000 he would receive from Moscow had been deposited in his account with the London South America Bank. Another letter from Tecbrevet and M4, dated March 31, arrived in April. It mentioned that in respect to his "invention," nothing could be done without first consulting Senhor Heinrich Gruber, someone Johnny had never heard of. De Graaf took this to mean that future payments would continue only after meeting this individual, whose alias made him appear to be a relative of Franz Gruber.[28]

On September 1, 1939, Johnny heard the news that the Nazis had invaded Poland as he drove home from lunch at the Alpino. He had long since given up trying to meet up with Hans Wilhelm and was aghast to hear on his car radio that World War II had broken out. Thank heavens the Alpino was a German-run restaurant that accepted him without reservations.

On September 2 Johnny mailed a communication by air to Mary, requesting that the Soviets send an emissary to New York in order to normalize payments to him. If dispatching someone to New York was not feasible, he requested that the bureau in New York pay him an additional US$24,000 (US$369,230 in 2009 dollars).[29] He would then journey to New York to meet with their representative. To that end, Johnny got busy preparing a set of false books, complete with bogus debit and credit entries to take with him if need be. The purpose was to have something on paper to show the Soviets that would justify his request for more money.[30]

On September 3 Brussels wired in code that Hans Wilhelm was last seen in Paris and must now be in Brazil. Johnny telegraphed back that he was not there and asked for instructions. He received a reply the following day, instructing him to proceed to Paris and meet Helen at the Hotel Lutecia. Evidently, Helen was a new M4 radio operator sent to accompany him to Japan. That voyage would now begin from Europe. Johnny was to take the Krügers with him to the Orient. He would be paid US$250 a month, US$300 a month for Emilie and Gustav Krüger, and US$2,000 for travel money to Tokyo. But traveling first to Europe was impractical because de Graaf had an Austrian passport. As soon as he sat foot in France, he would be taken into custody as possibly pro-German. Much later, Tecbrevet answered that it could only accede to his request to send an agent to New York with the agreement of M4. At the moment, however, that was impossible because of the war in Europe. De Graaf suspected that the Soviets had found him out.[31]

At the end of September Johnny was telephoned by someone calling himself Franz Gruber. As this was de Graaf's alias in Brazil, he was surprised, to say the least. The caller said that he was also a relative of an older Franz Gruber. He wanted to speak with Johnny, and they agreed to an 8:00 P.M. meeting at Rainha Elisabeth. When the man appeared at the front door, he said his real name was Heinrich Simone and that he was a machinist off a Belgian freighter anchored in Guanabara Bay. He had tried to find de Graaf in Rio at the Hotel Riviera. When Johnny asked him why he had gone to the Riviera looking for him, Simone answered that "our people" had arranged it. Tecbrevet did not know Johnny's home address—they sent everything to the hotel. At that moment de Graaf's suspicions were confirmed. The man was from Moscow.

Simone then inquired when and where they could meet in private, as there was money coming from Europe for Johnny. Johnny suggested the Bar Alpino the following night at 9:30. Simone agreed, but he did not show up at the Alpino for their appointment. Johnny may not have wanted to meet at the Hotel Riviera because there was at least one SIS operative staying there. Edith Jarminski, known in the profession as "English Edith," took up residence in the Riviera at about this time. She tried to keep a low profile, but her lavish ways, particularly in spending money and carousing, gave her away to DESPS.[32]

At 3:00 in the afternoon, the day following Simone's no-show, he telephoned, saying that he had to see Johnny at once. They met in the Bar Lido, where Johnny was informed that Simone had missed his boat, which had steamed down the coast to Santos. He needed money to get to Santos by automobile in order to catch the ship. De Graaf gave him all the cash he was carrying, a little more than 1:000$000 (or a bit more than US$58). A few days passed before Johnny was phoned by the man who had driven Simone to Santos. He too said that he had to meet Johnny immediately. They decided on the Bar Lido, where the chauffeur gave Johnny a note alleging that Simone wanted an additional 500$000 (500 *mil reis* or US$29 and change). He was to give the money to the driver, and then Simone would tell him "something new." It is unclear whether Johnny paid the money, but the chauffeur later contacted de Graaf a second time, asking for more money. That request was refused.[33]

A new venture unfolded in October 1939 when a top-priority cable from London arrived at Johnny's door. It read, "Note, order, information. A German battleship is supposed to be somewhere in the South Atlantic, find that ship." There were no more details, but within hours Johnny had alerted the entire counterespionage network along the Brazilian coast to peak observation status. Additional men were mobilized in the search.

De Graaf became anxious when a German passenger liner stopped in Rio sometime after the cable from London. The vessel held a party, which Johnny attended, posing as a local Nazi well-wisher. Snooping around the ship, he found a very large lifeboat covered with a tarpaulin that looked like some kind of torpedo boat. Unfortunately, he did not get a chance to pull back the covering, so he bought a ticket on the passenger vessel for a trip to Santos. The night the ship put to sea, it stopped dead in the water and began lowering the now uncovered lifeboat into the ocean. Later, de Graaf had some of his people rummage around the same area in daylight. They uncovered torpedo dumps, gas and oil drums, and ammunition. In São Paulo they uncovered arms at a reserve water facility in the southern part of the state. The information was turned over to Müller, who had everything removed. To be sure that later discoveries would not reach the Nazis, the coastal watchers learned to skip the part about informing DESPS and simply blow everything up.[34]

On December 2, 1939, de Graaf sent Mary a cable explaining that he could not travel to Paris using his existing documents. He requested that the Soviets arrange a new passport for him, one he could use for travel to Europe. This request met with complete silence. No doubt his Moscow superiors had decided they could not get their operative out, and that, as a free agent, he would somehow make his own way back. In effect, Johnny was cut loose and was left to handle the mess as best he could. De Graaf's follow-up cables to Brussels also went unanswered. Brussels had gone dead.

Through Hunt, Johnny cabled SIS in London that his wireless man had not shown up, adding the details on the severed contact with the Soviet Union. "What now?" Johnny asked.

"Cancel all current activity," came the decoded reply from London. "Establish closer liaison with Brazil secret police to apply all knowledge and experience against Nazi factions. Use coastal surveillance for German attempted landings and activities. Advise daily progress." He was already doing much of what they wanted.

A day later de Graaf received a wire from the MI6 chief in Montevideo, instructing him to set up a wireless station using the discarded Soviet plan of the import-export business. "Williams" was really Dr. Sil Milo, a former university professor. How he was ever chosen as a station chief was beyond Johnny. Milo's background was not in intelligence but in chemistry, which added greatly to his incompetence. Johnny would argue with Montevideo from that day forward, and find himself slowly going his own way despite his directives.

De Graaf telegraphed Milo back saying that he would not use or establish the same cover to develop a sending and receiving center. This idea had a high risk factor, as who knew which, if any, Soviet agents were watching in Rio de Janeiro? Besides, it would serve no purpose whatsoever. Communications to and from London were already secure. The SIS was receiving all the information it required by the current method. Johnny refused to entertain the plan, despite Milo's follow-up wires. What point would it serve to man, staff, and equip an additional unit to accomplish the same thing? To use the Soviet import-export front as cover for a new group would also expose his dual role to Moscow if the Soviets suddenly came back on the air. Johnny reasoned that Montevideo did not know what it was doing. He decided to wait them out instead.

Vivian had informed Johnny before he arrived in the country that London wanted him to watch more than four thousand miles (more than 6,400 km) of Brazilian coastline. Fortunately, he had been able to hire a pair of former Austrian army officers, both of whom had fine intelligence backgrounds and were fluent in several languages. They were 100 percent pro-British and anti-Nazi and knew many others who felt the same way. Starting with these two, more agents had been recruited, until they had a trained nucleus of thirty-six operatives. Each individual was strategically stationed along the coast. Once in the field, they recruited additional watchers from large stretches on both sides of their stations of operation.

Who were these agents? As of this writing, the English intelligence community declines to comment on any of its people in Brazil in the 1930s and '40s. Müller's DESPS, however, managed to put together a list of English operatives and sympathizers for this general time frame.[35] Some of the names given below were certainly associated with de Graaf's coastal watchers. To the right of each entry is a brief note on the agent's function and the month and year of first mention in DESPS documents.

Name	Notes
Abbott, Arthur	Press aide at English Embassy—December 1940
Anderson, Lindsey	Chief of SIS in São Paulo—January 1940
Archer, Humphrey Edward	Agent in Recife—December 1940
Arnon, Frank	Agent in Rio de Janeiro—September 1941

Barallo, Waldemar — Collaborator in Rio de Janeiro—n.d.
Barão — Collaborator in Rio de Janeiro—January 1941
Bazin, Jean — Agent in Fortaleza—January 1941
Bercuó, Urbano — Collaborator in Rio de Janeiro—December 1940
Berger, Peter — Agent in Rio de Janeiro—January 1941
Blake, Arthur Thomas — Agent in Rio de Janeiro—December 1940
Buckley, Clifford William — Agent in Bahia—December 1940
Burrous, Donald — Collaborator in Rio de Janeiro—February 1941
Cabral — Handled in Rio Grande do Sul by Mace—December 1940
Carr, Philip Alfred Vansittart — Official at English Embassy—December 1940
Carvalho, Reis de — Collaborator in Rio de Janeiro—December 1940
Castro Junior, José Leite de — Collaborator in Rio de Janeiro—n.d.
Caswell — Chief of SIS in Curitíba—January 1941
Colson — Handled in Rio by D. S. MacGrath [or McGrath]—January 1941
Corrêa, Ismael José — Handled in Rio by William Shaw—January 1941
Corrêa, Olavo — Policia Civil investigator in Rio—January 1941
Costa, Amaro — Collaborator in Rio de Janeiro—December 1940
Cross, David — Handled in Rio de Janeiro by Franz Gruber—January 1941
Dalbos, Ivonne — Collaborator in Rio de Janeiro—December 1940
Davis, Donovan Thomas — Collaborator in Rio de Janeiro—December 1940
Dodd, Frank L. — Collaborator in Rio de Janeiro—December 1940
Ehrenberg, J. — Agent in Porto Alegre—January 1941
Einstein, Alfred — Agent in Blumenau—January 1941
Eisler, Pauline — Collaborator in Rio de Janeiro—September 1941
Epstein, Jacob Jacques — Agent in São Paulo—December 1940
Ferreira, Manuel — Collaborator in Rio de Janeiro—n.d.

Fisher	Handled in Rio de Janeiro by Lourenço da Silva, Freelander, and Ruffier—January 1941
Fothergill, Henry McLean	Agent in Bahia—December 1940
Franco, Ernesto Vitor	Collaborator in Rio de Janeiro—n.d.
Freelander, Arthur	Collaborator in Rio de Janeiro—December 1940
Freeman, Mike	Handled in São Paulo by J. J. Epstein—December 1940
Freeman, William Philippe	Subchief of SIS in Rio—September 1940
Frisbee, Albert Henry	Collaborator in Rio de Janeiro—December 1940
Gordon, R. W.	Collaborator in Rio de Janeiro—December 1940
Gordon, Vencil	Subchief of SIS in Rio—September 1941
Greenwood	?—January 1941
Gruber, Franz (Johnny de Graaf)	Agent in Rio de Janeiro—1935–36, 1938–40
Hamilton, Christopher G. W.	Handled in Rio by Franz Gruber—December 1940
Harcourt-Rivington, Seaward H.	Agent in Rio de Janeiro—October 1940
Hess, Erich Joachim	Collaborator in Rio de Janeiro—September 1941
Huetter, Helmut	Agent in Rio de Janeiro—n.d.
Hulton, Edward	Agent in Rio de Janeiro—September 1941
Hutt, Alfred	Second in command of SIS in Rio de Janeiro—December 1940
Hutte, Charles	Agent in Rio de Janeiro—January 1941
Jany, Joseph	Agent in São Paulo—January 1941
Jarminsky, Edith	Agent in Rio de Janeiro—December 1940
Jordão, Alexis de Miranda	Handled in São Paulo by J. J. Epstein—December 1940
Julien, Francisco de Menezes	DESPS investigator and collaborator in Rio—December 1939
Kiessewetter, Werner	Agent in Montevideo, Uruguay—January 1941
Klerekoper, Jaques	Collaborator in São Paulo—n.d.
Knox, Geoffrey George	English Ambassador, head of SIS in Brazil—July 1940
Ladisch, Paul Alois	Agent in Rio de Janeiro—December 1940
Lee, Ambrose Northorp[a]	Naval aide in Rio de Janeiro—January 1941

Lima, Rodolfo Mota	Collaborator in Rio de Janeiro—December 1941
Lygia	Handled in Rio by D. S. MacGrath [or McGrath]—January 1941
Mace	Agent in Rio Grande do Sul—December 1940
McCall, Henry William Urquart	Naval attaché in Rio de Janeiro—May 1940
McCrimmon, Kenneth Howard	Press chief in Brazil—December 1940
McGrath [or MacGrath], Donald Scott	Naval attaché and subchief of SIS in Rio de Janeiro—December 1940
Megan, Norton	?—February 1941
Melo, Tancredo de	Collaborator in Rio de Janeiro—n.d.
Miller	Chief of commercial maritime espionage—December 1940
Murphy, Cornelius James	Collaborator in Rio de Janeiro—September 1941
Oliva, Nestôr Gomes	Collaborator in Rio de Janeiro—January 1941
Olsburgh, Ralf	Collaborator in Rio de Janeiro—December 1940
Page, Ethel	Collaborator in Rio de Janeiro—September 1941
Paine, Walter	Agent in Rio de Janeiro—December 1940
Patterson, Robert R.	Agent in Recife—October 1939
Phillimore, John G.	Suspected agent in Rio de Janeiro—December 1940
Pinha, José	Collaborator in Rio de Janeiro—January 1941
Pinto, Diogenes	Collaborator in Niterói—n.d.
Pullen, Charles[b]	Collaborator in Rio de Janeiro—December 1940
Pullen, Edward[b]	Collaborator in Rio de Janeiro—January 1941
Pullen Junior	Agent in Bahia and Ceará—January 1941
Rand, B. R.	Collaborator in Rio de Janeiro—January 1941
Roussel, Silva Araújo	Collaborator in ?—December 1940
Ruffier	Agent in Rio de Janeiro—January 1941
Saboya	Handled in Rio Grande do Sul by Mace—December 1940

Schoenfeld, Humberto Conde de	Agent in Rio de Janeiro—January 1941
Shaw, William	Collaborator in Rio de Janeiro—December 1940
Silva, Lourenço da	Handled in Rio de Janeiro by Arthur Abbott—July 1940
Souza, João Joaquim de	Collaborator in Rio de Janeiro—n.d.
Stemmer, Karl	Agent in Montevideo/Porto Alegre—January 1941
Tuerkel, Herbert Ralf	Agent in Rio de Janeiro—January 1941
von Minkewitz, Hubert	Agent in Rio de Janeiro—January 1941
Walden, Helmuth	Collaborator in Rio de Janeiro—January 1941
Wilcox	Handled in Rio by D. S. MacGrath [or McGrath]—December 1940
Wilson, Robert Amcotts	Naval attaché in Rio de Janeiro—March 1941
Wood, William Eric	Agent in Recife—December 1940
Yong, Parry[b]	Collaborator in Rio de Janeiro—February 1941
Yong, Wilson[b]	Collaborator in Rio de Janeiro—February 1941

[a] Tentative.
[b] Possibly the same person.
n.d. No date.

Eventually the group fanned out in both directions to form a solid network covering most of the Brazilian eastern seaboard. Using US$30,000 of saved Soviet funds, Johnny and his men had local observers, from fishermen to plantation workers, on the payroll. In time they used two planes to make daily overhead patrols. Ground stations kept in touch with adjoining units, tying in all sea, land, and air reports by telegraph.

Filinto Müller and Johnny, by way of his ostensible agent, Julien, kept each other posted and at times met at Müller's home to compare their intelligence. Johnny's coastal reports kept him aware of both external and sometimes internal infiltration. Müller openly displayed his concern over the many German sympathizers among the officers in Brazil's armed forces. In so doing, the pro-Nazi police chief played Johnny like a fiddle. De Graaf never saw Filinto's duplicity.

Britain's Brazilian network was running efficiently, but it placed ever greater demands on Johnny. For days at a time he would be up the coast, and then return home to countless British cables waiting for decoding. In addition, all the gathered intelligence had to be coded and sent out. Always concerned about

Johnny's health, and watching him grow more and more exhausted, Gerti finally put her foot down. By this time Johnny had told her about the nature of his work. "Johnny, you cannot go on like this," she told him. "You look like death, and no wonder. You aren't getting any rest. Do you want to die?"

"Mutzi [German slang for "kitty," Johnny's pet name for her], I have to go on. I have to get these wires answered and my reports sent. I have no choice, for only I can do the coding and decoding," Johnny answered.

"Then let me help, Johnny, let me decode and code for you, show me how, and then you can get your sleep and we can cut this workload in half."

"I cannot do that, Gerti. The codes have to die with the man. I have been entrusted with them and they are to remain with me."

Gerti looked at Johnny and accused him of being too stubborn for his own good. She pointed out that he needed to sleep regularly and take better care of his health. If he wanted to die for his precious codes, okay, then go ahead. But as the person who loved him, come what may, she found it a little strange that he did not trust her entirely.

Hours later, and dog-tired, Johnny finally broke down and agreed to let her be his assistant. There was really no choice; he could not handle the entire load himself. One slip, one letter coded the wrong way, meant that a complete rewrite was necessary, as any mistake affected the following letters as well. Gerti had to be exceedingly careful. If the SIS in London ever found out that she was handling the work, Johnny had no doubt of the outcome.

Gerti learned quickly and in fact came to code and decode faster than Johnny. From then on, when he returned home, she would read him the cables and he would dictate the replies. Each morning the outgoing messages would be dropped off at the Light Company for Hutt to pass on to the embassy clerks. Naturally, they had no idea what messages to London or Montevideo ticked away under their fingers. A messenger delivered the incoming cables in the morning to the Rainha Elisabeth address, much to Johnny's disapproval. Each envelope was stamped "The British Government." Unbelievable as it sounds, the system was not changed despite de Graaf's objections. It was equivalent to receiving a ready-to-explode box of dynamite in the mailbox each morning. Johnny's full name, address, and c/o the import-export company, were plainly visible through the envelope window. "A real gem in the wrong hands!" he thought. But then again, for about a month, beginning on May 30, 1939, Hutt lived at Avenida Atlântica 790, apartment 32, only three blocks from the Hotel Riviera. On June 27 he moved to an apartment on the other side of Rainha Elisabeth, at Rua Alberto de Campos 84 in Ipanema. It would have been easy for Johnny or Gerti or both to walk the short distance between the residences, or to call first and arrange a meeting somewhere in between when necessary.[36]

Montevideo wired that they were sending Johnny a German, Dr. Werner Kiessewetter, whom they had met and felt could assist the cause. He claimed to have maps of all the Wehrmacht's hidden underground installations in Germany. This mystified Johnny. A day passed, and Werner arrived in Rio. At their first get-together, Johnny was suspicious of this small, gray-haired, wizened man with a prominent nose and darting eyes. As with other assessments in the past, his reservations might have simply been symptomatic of working in the spy game. Johnny asked Kiessewetter to bring proof of the German army's underground tunnels, for he too knew such things existed.

Werner returned a week later with small, handmade maps of some installations. A few of these were known to Johnny as being in southern Germany. There were also some Brazilian maps that he could have copied. De Graaf passed the lot on to London and thought that would be the end of it. But soon Williams in Montevideo began insisting that Johnny take Werner into his spy network. Johnny protested, asking, "How do we know he is not on the German payroll and on a mission as a sleeper agent sent to penetrate our organization?" Their wire came back reading, "This is an order. Werner is absolutely trustworthy." A gut feeling told Johnny otherwise, but he followed the directive and let the new man handle small tasks that were not vital. What also bothered Johnny was that Werner rented a home on the same street where he and Gerti lived. And Montevideo's badgering never let up. They soon became irritated at Johnny's keeping Werner occupied with trivial things.

This bickering eventually prompted a visit by the chief himself. Sil Milo was a bald, red-faced, tubby man who left Johnny flabbergasted after he had spoken a few words. The squat professor and regional MI6 chief was a complete dreamer. He had all kinds of wild ideas about what the Brazilian network should be doing and harped on again about the import-export telegraph idea. Johnny told him off and, after hearing more irrational ideas, sent him packing back to Uruguay in anger. The last thing he needed was a foolish teacher for a boss. He brought all of this to Hutt's attention when calling on him at the power company.

When Milo and Hutt reported what had happened to London, Vivian flew down to Rio to see Johnny. He checked into the Copacabana Palace and met with de Graaf after freshening up. Vee-Vee was delighted with the progress to date and with the valuable information he had been receiving. Much to Johnny's surprise, he also raised the import-export scheme, and it took Johnny an hour to convince him that it was unwise. Besides, they did not have the professional operator that it would require. Vivian finally concurred that the plan held many grave risks that Johnny and his group could ill afford. Back to London he went, a little more aware of the operations and necessities in Brazil.

Montevideo next referred Karl Stemmer to Johnny, and he at once recognized the name. Stemmer, like de Graaf, had originally been sentenced to death for his part in the August 1917 naval mutiny in Wilhelmshaven.[37] He later fought against the Kapp Putsch. A fine officer, Stemmer moved to Brazil in 1921 and was selling semiprecious stones for a living. When they met again in Rio de Janeiro, he had developed excellent contacts among the pro-Germans in the south of the country, who believed him to be on their side. Actually, Stemmer's hatred for Nazi Germany was equal to Johnny's. De Graaf wanted him on the team, but Montevideo was only willing to pay £25 a month, which was not enough to provide for Stemmer and his family. Fortunately, Johnny was able to double this amount from his own wages. Stemmer agreed and lived for a week at the Rainha Elisabeth house until he found a place of his own.

De Graaf's group continued its scrutiny of the coast, and if anything increased it as the war consumed more victims. Karl Stemmer worked into ever widening circles of German supporters in the state of Santa Catarina. Later, Johnny sent him down to Uruguay, where he did excellent work. It was good to have someone he could trust in Sil Milo's backyard, someone willing to risk his life for Britain's intelligence services. De Graaf was soon to be reminded, however, that the service placed little value on its agents' personal safety because it mistrusted the relaying of pertinent information that could save lives. Unknown to Johnny, he was to be the first victim in Brazil.

The unpleasant episode began on a serene night with a pleasant breeze off the sea, as de Graaf made his way back to Rainha Elisabeth. Somehow the evening drive along the highway to Copacabana always relaxed him, as traffic was noticeably light at this hour. The day's fieldwork was done, and the liaison with Filinto Müller's DESPS was working well. The police chief seemed very enthusiastic about the joint operation, and well he should, since Johnny's group had already supplied DESPS with intelligence, some of it about Nazi agents.[38]

Between Rio and Copacabana, in the suburb of Botafogo, the highway terminated into a risky junction at a point where a hillside street into Copacabana converged with the surrounding thoroughfares. During daylight hours, this spot was hazardous, and one had to approach it with caution. At night it was a breeze, however, for lighter traffic and shining car lights actually diminished the danger. Driving along slowly, Johnny's thoughts drifted to Gerti and a waiting dinner. As he came to the difficult intersection, without warning he saw a large truck, with its lights out, careening down the hill road and swerving straight toward him. In a desperate effort he yanked the steering wheel, but the truck lunged across the highway, ramming de Graaf's Ford broadside, spinning it across the pavement and into a ditch. Johnny was thrown out of the vehicle on impact and landed in a trench next to his car. He sustained a few bruises and cuts, but no broken bones.

Lying prone, he raised his head just high enough to see two men in the truck cab some thirty feet (9.14 m) away. He caught a glimpse of the license plate as the driver and his companion stopped, got out, and looked at the upside-down Ford in the ditch. Apparently they did not see him. In seconds, they hopped back in their cab, threw the truck briefly into reverse, and with the lights now on, sped off down the highway. As de Graaf stood gazing at his automobile, he could see it was a total write-off. One front wheel was still slowly spinning on its twisted axel. "This was no accident!" he thought to himself. There was little question that the truck had lain in wait with its lights out, only to swerve down the hill to try to kill him as he drove along. Someone wanted de Graaf dead, and he knew he had to locate the would-be assassin before he could try again. Killers could be hired to do such dirty work for 20$000 apiece, or a little over US$4 each, anywhere in Brazil at that time.[39] These two inexperienced men were certainly paid something for their night's work.

Conveniently a passing motorist stopped, picked Johnny up, and drove him to within a few blocks of his doorstep. Gerti, shocked at his appearance, wasted no time in bathing his scratches and cuts without asking questions. A tow truck was dispatched to retrieve the smashed car and complete the police report. In the morning, despite the odd throb and ache, Johnny got through to Müller and asked him to trace the license number. The only explanation Johnny gave Vargas's chief of police was that he had some moving to do and wanted to hire these particular men and their truck. A short while later, Filinto called back with the name and address of the trucking firm plus the names and home addresses of the two men who drove the truck.

That night, Johnny paid them a visit. Both individuals were at a house in a run-down area north of Rio de Janeiro. Since they did not know what Johnny looked like, only his wrecked Ford, he was able to worm a few details out of them about the job they had just carried out. Giving them more money for their troubles than the 20$000 their previous employer had paid, he knew they would not say a word about the conversation. The cash, plus the promise of an impending job, bought their silence. Even in parting they still had no idea who de Graaf was, but they were hopeful he would hire them as promised.

With the facts the two truck drivers provided, Johnny was able to pin down his would-be killer. The assassin was connected to the German legation in Rio de Janeiro. His name was probably Heinz Harold Schmutter.[40] By working with some of the pro-Nazi supporters at DESPS, Schmutter had directed the operation with their support so that it would appear that the secret police had set up the whole thing.

Johnny had no idea how Schmutter was familiar with him. If Dr. Werner was working with the Nazis, he knew very little of the group's operations, since he was purposely kept far away from anything of importance. If he was a spy for the Germans, they would keep him in place as a sleeper until he edged in deeper and could expose the entire organization. At that point, Werner knew little more about Johnny's group than the local paperboy. It had to be someone else, someone from the outside who knew Johnny. Much later, de Graaf would learn the whole story, when the British informed him about his missing Soviet radio operator.

Hans Wilhelm had arrived in Brazil on schedule, but penniless. He quickly left Rio and made for Belo Horizonte, where he contacted the British consul. He told his story and asked for asylum. En route to Brazil, he had blown all his money, US$5,000, on high times and women in Paris. Broke, with only his boat ticket remaining, he had sailed for Brazil and arrived two days after Johnny and Gerti. He told the consul in Belo Horizonte that all he wanted was a paid position and a safe haven. "Why didn't you report to the man you were supposed to work with and tell him what had happened?" the consul asked.

"Oh no, I couldn't do that," Hans replied in terror. "He would have killed me!" Hans Wilhelm remembered Johnny's threat in Moscow.

The British consul turned him down, gave him a little cash, and sent him on his way. When Hans Wilhelm was out the door, the consul informed London of the interview. British intelligence knew then that he was Johnny's lost wireless man, because while still in London de Graaf had mentioned that he was suspicious of him to Vivian and Foley. MI6 failed to contact Johnny to say he had been found. Instead, he was on the loose, available to the highest bidder.

Still in search of funds and back in Rio, Hans Wilhelm approached a pro-Nazi officer at DESPS, who sent the Moscow-trained wireless operator to the Germen Embassy, where Hans Wilhelm ended his travels of many months. Once he walked into the Deutsche Botschaft at Rua Paissandu 93, he disappeared. It was as if he had never existed.[41] He knew Johnny only as a Soviet spy in explaining the Moscow-sponsored mission to the Germans. It would be enough to put the Germans on their guard and plot de Graaf's demise. If Werner worked for them too, the tie-in would be complete.

What had happened to his radio operator was unknown to Johnny as he decided to put a stop to Herr Schmutter. After having him shadowed to determine his habits, late one overcast afternoon de Graaf stepped up to Schmutter on a sidewalk in downtown Rio. The Nazi froze when he felt the prod of a revolver in his back through Johnny's coat pocket. Schmutter was forced into the backseat of a waiting car that immediately screeched away from the curb. Sitting next to the man who had tried to kill him, Johnny spun the Nazi to one side, forced his hands behind his back, and handcuffed him. Little beads of sweat appeared on Schmutter's face. They headed south, then through Jardim Botânico, before turning onto Estrada Dona Castorina. The car proceeded up into the hills past the Chinese Vista, where the road becomes the Estrada da Vista Chinesa. At last they stopped near the summit, just as the receding clouds were producing another postcard sunset. Flinging the door open, Johnny grabbed the man and forced him out. He then poked him with his gun back toward the edge of a cliff.

Shaking and pleading for his life and garbling something about his mother, he stepped backward one foot at a time as Johnny approached. "Jump, you snake! I do not want to shoot you for all to hear," de Graaf spat out. Schmutter begged for his life until he was at the precipice's edge. Johnny continued toward him and struck him with his fist full in the face, forcing him to fall over the side with a scream of terror. No report of Schmutter's death ever made the papers, radio newscasts, or obituary records.

On another trip to Santos, Johnny joined the two Austrian officers whose knowledge of the sea was limited. Walking along the docks, de Graaf noticed two German freighters in port—but with full steam up. One of the vessels, the *Altmark,* had the word *NORGE* painted in big block letters on identical flaps along her sides (the word means Norway in Norwegian). While Johnny understood the language, he did not know at the time that the *Altmark* was only making a pretense at neutrality. If she was challenged, the flaps could be lowered to reveal two large guns.[42] The other vessel was the *Tacoma.* Both ships seemed curiously heavy with radio antennas, which struck Johnny as very odd.

Dressed to blend in with the stevedores, he watched the comings and goings of the crews of the two ships from separate vantage points. He paid particular attention to the sailors who frequented the various restaurants and bars on the docks. There was no doubt in his mind that the ships were tenders outfitted as merchantmen. Leaving the two craft under the surveillance of the Austrians, Johnny strolled along to what appeared to be the restaurant most frequented by the crews. In no time, he was seated among the ratings he knew so well, praising the Fatherland and buying rounds of drinks for his former countrymen. Gradually, he edged the sailors into loose conversation, proclaiming in anger that as a German he too would like to be active in the war but was stuck in Brazil.

Following a few more rounds of beer, Johnny turned to a boatswain beside him and asked, "What are the chances of my getting on your ship and going home, so I can do my duty for my country?"

"Oh, no," he slurred. "We can't do that, it is not permitted."

"Then why are your ships in port?" Johnny inquired.

"We are standing by for orders."

"Orders to go to sea?"

"Yes, we have to be careful, for we don't want them to catch us." He then let it slip that they were supply vessels to a battleship. Johnny had no idea until then that they were connected to such a large warship. But he could not get the name of the battleship out of them.

Soon after the outbreak of hostilities in 1939, the pocket battleships KMS *Admiral Graf Spee* and KMS *Deutschland* slid into the Atlantic. Their task was to sink enemy and neutral merchantmen with cargoes bound for English ports. Posted to the Southern Hemisphere, the *Graf Spee* would catch its victims off guard by hoisting French colors as it came in for the kill. On September 30 de Graaf received word that the SS *Clement* had been sent to the bottom off the northeast coast of Pernambuco.[43] Farther out to sea, another cargo ship escaped.

The *Graf Spee* let it go and in so doing made a fatal mistake. The moment the crew of the spared freighter hit shore, in Recife, out came the story, but they got the name of the ship wrong. They thought it was the KMS *Admiral Scheer*. Johnny had the agent in Recife, Robert R. Patterson, hasten to the port and question the crew, who could really only confirm that the attacking ship was massive. There was no doubt she was a battleship, and probably the one they sought. Had Hans Langsdorff, the *Graf Spee*'s captain, followed up his attack and given chase to the second freighter, Johnny's hunt might have been less successful. De Graaf reported to London that they had found, "a battleship or large, armed freighter that has been lying around for years."

To the south, in the port of Santos, the two German vessels were being watched around the clock. De Graaf instructed a pair of Müller's police who had joined Johnny's group to travel down the coast in opposite directions on horseback and report anything they saw using small radios that sent signals back up the beach. For two more days Johnny remained in Santos, observing the ships and casually talking with the crews until the *Altmark* slipped her lines and headed out to sea. As soon as she cleared port, he cabled London. "*Altmark*, to best of group's knowledge, supply vessel to pocket battleship *Graf Spee*."

Two light cruisers, the HMS *Ajax* and the HMNZS *Achilles*, together with the cruiser HMS *Exeter*, were ordered into the hunt, patrolling from Santos to the southern coast, where the Río de la Plata joins the sea between Argentina and Uruguay. By tracking the *Altmark*, the British fleet finally located their quarry near Montevideo. The *Graf Spee* swung away from the coast and plunged into the open to attack the three enemy warships. A fierce sea battle ensued on December 13, 1939. The *Exeter* was put out of action and made for the Falkland (or Malvinas) Islands. The *Ajax*, the *Achilles*, and the *Graf Spee* were all damaged in the fighting. The German warship broke off the engagement and made for Montevideo for superficial but necessary repairs.

By international sea law, during times of war a belligerent vessel could remain in a neutral port for only twenty-four hours before having to return to sea. Captain Langsdorff was in immediate contact with the German legation about his predicament, while the British and French protested to the Uruguayan government. Actually, they did not complain too loudly, for they wanted time for a reinforcement squadron to arrive. As the conclusion of the diplomatic maneuverings in Montevideo, the *Graf Spee* was told she could stay seventy-two hours to conclude the necessary repairs. All the while, the *Ajax* and *Achilles* stood by ready and waiting miles offshore. They were joined on December 14 by the cruiser HMS *Cumberland*, which had steamed at full speed up from the Falklands. Langsdorff believed that there was a much larger flotilla of Allied warships just over the horizon. After being informed that the repairs could not be made in the time allotted by the Uruguayans, he wired Berlin that there were but three options: to be interned, to scuttle the ship, or to try to fight his way through the Río de la Plata estuary to Buenos Aires. Argentina was largely pro-German. Hitler and his chief of naval operations, Admiral Eric Raeder, urged that the pocket battleship first try to fight its way to Argentina. Otherwise, they were to scuttle the vessel. The *Graf Spee* was not to be interned.

Hans Langsdorff had sunk nine freighters in the Atlantic and Indian Oceans totaling some fifty thousand tons. Not one member of the nine ships had lost his life. The *Graf Spee* always gave warning for steamers to stop and then removed the crews before sinking the vessels. Langsdorff was an officer from another era and was not a Nazi. As his seventy-two-hour respite was running out, he contacted the governments of Argentina and Uruguay and arranged for his crew and seconds in command to receive safe internments in prisoner-of-war camps for the duration of the war.

On December 17, 1939, taking a handful of men and engineers, Langsdorff sailed the *Graf Spee* just past the territorial limits of Uruguayan waters. The vessel then stopped and dropped anchor, and a tug came alongside to take all hands back to port. Minutes later the *Graf Spee,* timed with massive charges, tore herself apart with mighty explosions. She settled into a sea of mud and was still visible, burning, for days. Langsdorff committed suicide in a Buenos Aries hotel on December 20, wrapped in the *Graf Spee*'s battle ensign.[44] The British government never acknowledged Johnny de Graaf's role in the end of the German raider. This was, however, not the final word on the subject. It was later claimed, although by a suspect source, that Filinto Müller was already supplying crewmen off of the *Graf Spree* with Brazilian passports so that they could travel back to Germany and fight again.[45]

With Gerti three months pregnant, DESPS picked up Johnny while he was in Praça Mauá on December 14, 1939. It was the day after the sea battle started off the Uruguayan coast.[46] He was first taken to the sala de detenção (detention room) at the Polícia Central and then whisked across Guanabara Bay and imprisoned in the infamous stronghold that had held so many before, the Fortress of Santa Cruz.[47] Johnny's stay in this reinforced concrete structure, located on the other side of the bay from Sugar Loaf, was ordered, so he was told, following Dr. Werner's arrest. The good doctor was supposed to have blabbed instantly to the police that Franz Gruber was the head of all British agents in Brazil.

Placed in a gray cell on the third tier, about an hour after he arrived a soldier opened his cell door and handed him a large basket of flowers and assorted fruits, including bananas and oranges.[48] "You must be his friend, for he arrested you first and then sent you this gift," the guard smirked, slamming the solid black steel door behind him. The card read, "From a friend," no signature. Johnny pondered this new twist and wondered what was going on now. No explanation was given for his imprisonment, and other than the guards, no one interrogated him. Soon he learned that Dr. Werner had been detained first and confined to a cell on the floor below. Filinto Müller's Quadro Movel agent, Francisco Julien, followed, and was placed in a cell three down from de Graaf's. He had been picked up on orders from Müller or someone close to him.[49] Johnny asked Julien if Müller was aware of their arrests, to which he replied that he was not. Julien explained that the day before, Müller had been forced to leave the country for a six-week vacation. His temporary replacement was Captain Miranda Corrêa. This was a lie. Müller was neither out of the country nor on vacation.[50] He was still pulling the strings through the anti-Communist section of DESPS, run by another pro-Nazi, Captain Felisberto Batista Teixeira. On December 11, 1939, Batista (Müller) contacted the U.S. Embassy in Rio de Janeiro to see what information the Americans had on Franz Gruber's connection with American Communists. The answer was none.[51]

Captain Batista Teixeira had a reputation with the prisoners that preceded him. He liked to pretend that he was dozing as a suspect was hustled into his office for questioning. When the individual resisted or did not answer the way he wanted, he would suddenly come to life and start beating the captive.[52] All of this would surprise de Graaf in the coming days. For the moment, he still thought that there had been some mistake. He hoped that whoever was in charge would straighten things out. De Graaf may have known that Hans Lessing had been apprehended earlier, on December 9. His crime was writing to a relative in Finland. Lessing was released the same day.[53] Aldo Rosso was likewise taken in and held for twenty days by DESPS, but never tortured. He was let go after his wife went to Filinto Müller's home. She got in feigning that she was a seamstress, then convinced Senhora Müller of her husband's innocence.[54] Karl Stemmer's spouse did not need the opportunity to plead her case with Consuelo Müller. Julien pointed him out as someone of interest who might be able to give information on Franz Gruber's Communist activities. It was a good thing he was in Uruguay. The information Julien provided his police superiors about Stemmer was augmented by Gestapo agent no. 5, who worked the Brazilian capital.[55] Josef Bunzlau and Helena Benkendorf were only called in to DESPS on December 8 to give their sworn statements.[56] Gustav Karl Krüger was merely questioned later.

During the first few days, Johnny saw no one, but each night he was taken upstairs to a gray, bare interrogation room and asked about his espionage activities. He told his interrogators to contact Filinto Müller, because everything had been done with his knowledge for the benefit of Brazil. De Graaf was told that Müller had been sent on vacation. Most of the guards were pro-Nazi. One who was not told him that it cost the German Embassy US$300 to have him arrested.[57] This was his payback for the scuttling of the *Graf Spee*.[58] The paltry amount probably only reflected the apprehension about de Graaf in government circles in the first place.

Johnny's main questioner was a tall individual with a neatly trimmed moustache, and one very smooth customer, DESPS/Quadro Movel detective Cecil de Macedo Borer.[59] Borer was advised that de Graaf knew too much for his own good, and perhaps that he was even in Brazil to attempt another revolution.[60] De Graaf refused to tell Borer anything really important. He was prepared to follow the intelligence credo and commit suicide before giving up his nation or associates. Borer, however, was too experienced to give in to a prisoner who refused to talk. Johnny was questioned three times in December 1939 and three times in January 1940. One of the things Batista Teixeira wanted was a confirmed list of coastal watcher names,[61] but Johnny would not budge on that. He never turned in a single colleague. Writing all of Borer's questions for him in advance, Batista Teixeira began to include other items. There are two surviving sets of queries from this latter group. The one from December 21, 1939, went as follows:

1. Ask if he knows a machinist off of a Belgian freighter named Simon Heinrich [sic].
2. Ask if he recently had an encounter with this man.
3. What was the reason for his meeting[?] (If he says there wasn't a meeting, tell him he is lying because there was a note in his own papers from Heinrich about the meeting).
4. Ask to whom he planned to present the statement of debits and credits for the money received.
5. Ask how he explains that he had an espionage mission in Japan and came to Brazil where he lived for more than a year. How does he account for the use of money here[?] How does he explain that he did not fulfill the espionage mission to Japan, but continues to enjoy the confidence [of Moscow] to the point of recently receiving US$10,000, and still is to be sent US$15,000 later.
6. Ask him how he explains being arrested in 1935, turning in various leaders of the PCB, and continuing to receive the support of his government [the USSR].
7. With whom has he made appointments to meet here in Rio?
8. What was the purpose of these meetings?
9. Ask who is "K" on his balance sheet that receives payments of US$400.
10. Does not "K" mean your wife, Gertrude Krüger, who entered Brazil using the name of her disappeared sister, Erna Krüger[?]
11. Is not "Mary" really a synonym for Tecbrevet, which itself is actually the Comintern[?][62]

Each night, as he was returned to his bleak cell, Johnny could hear the screams of other inmates being tortured reverberate down the halls. On the third night, the jailers came at midnight and hauled de Graaf off to a barren room. There, Borer and two burly assistants began the interrogation again. This time, when he did not reply, the guards stripped him and began bashing him with a hard wooden club laced with small holes called a *palmatória*. The holes were to let the air escape without splitting the skin. They swung at him from both sides as Johnny struggled in chains to avoid the blows. The pain was unbearable. In short order, his body was covered with deep bruises of yellow, blue, and green hues.

On January 3, 1940, besides the names of the coastal watchers, Batista Teixeira wanted to know:

1. Do you know Ullrich?
2. What is your relationship with him?
3. Ullrich accuses you of controlling the finances of the PCB. [Is that true?]
4. What did you do to the profits from the Hotel Riviera to make them look like losses?
5. Aldo Rosso confessed that the profits from the Hotel Riviera were much more [than the reported amount]. They were close to 500:000$000. [Is that true?]
6. Do you know the language teacher Hans Lessing[?] How did you meet him?
7. What kind of relationship did you have with him?
8. Why did you have such an interest in employing him at the Hotel Riviera?[63]

Johnny explained that Dr. Otto Ullrich was, in fact, a chemist he employed to work on perfume and ointment research. He said that he had never controlled the PCB's purse strings and that Aldo Rosso was lying. In fact, Johnny cried out, Rosso was simply trying to rob him of his investment! All the police had to do was get the account ledgers at Avenida Rainha Elisabeth. As for Hans Lessing, Johnny answered that he first met him in July 1938, and that he had taught his family Portuguese and English until January 1939. He arranged a job for Lessing as the in-house English teacher at the Hotel Riviera after the former teacher had been fired for dishonesty, plus he knew Lessing needed the work. Lessing lasted only about three months, however, owing to his distaste for the job, coupled with his stinginess. In respect to the cash from the Hotel Riviera that he turned into losses, de Graaf answered that he had hidden them in personal expenditures.[64]

Staggering under the blows, and at times half-unconscious from the pain and shock, he tried to answer as little as possible. When his replies came, they came in bursts. If unsatisfied, the police would spin him around and hit him in the kidneys. Early in the morning, Johnny was thrown back in his cell, following, at times, up to three hours of torture. Left to recuperate during the day, as night approached he prepared himself with a good deal of self-discipline, limping back and forth from wall to wall. He kept thinking over and over, "Hold on! Hold on! Be ready for the worst and you will survive!" In this way he was able to take the coming evening's nightmare without breaking.

Julien was released after two days and Dr. Werner five days later. Neither was tortured but only experienced a barrage of questions. De Graaf wondered about their sudden departures. He felt certain that Werner was a Nazi agent (this was later confirmed by London, which knew he was but never mentioned it). He also began to have serious doubts about Julien, who continued to ask for his "loan" even following Johnny's release.[65] Johnny would learn afterward that Francisco Julien was in fact a Nazi supporter in the pay of the German Embassy.[66]

De Graaf was transported back across the bay to the headquarters of the Polícia Especial, up on now removed Santo Antônio Hill. Called "Tomato Heads" because of their khaki uniforms and red caps, and led by a reputed sadist, Lieutenant Euzébio de Queiroz Filho, they were the most horrific police Brazil had to offer.[67] In their custody, Johnny was subjected at least once to the torture known as the *pau-de-arara,* or "Parrot's Perch."[68] It is chilling to note that while at the Polícia Especial's headquarters, Johnny may have walked up and down the same stairs, driving his nemesis insane, the man he had informed on in 1935, Arthur Ernst Ewert.

Though they were finished with Harry Berger, the authorities had not yet decided what to do with de Graaf. At times he was taken the short distance to the Polícia Central for his nightly anguish sessions. It was there, early one evening, that he hailed a passing guard by knocking on the cell door as he heard the man's footsteps approaching. The jailer stopped, slid open the metal slot, and looked in. Johnny asked him for a razor blade. The guard shook his head, but asked why Johnny wanted it. "I want to die my way, if it gets so bad that I can't stand the torture anymore," Johnny whispered. He nodded and returned a few minutes later with a razor blade, which he threw quickly through the slot. De Graaf grabbed it as it hit the floor and hid it in a crack in the wall. "I was now ready in the event the time arrived. Should I feel that I was about to break, I would take it with me and slash my wrists or throat before they could stop me. They would be welcome to what remained."

When the guard returned, Johnny asked to talk with him. The man was not the kind of power-hungry jailer that one so often finds in such places, but actually a decent person. De Graaf took a chance and asked him to contact Gerti when off duty. To his amazement, the man agreed. Johnny warned him to be very careful approaching his house because it might be under observation. He then gave the jailer a letter for Gerti, after translating what was in it. He told the guard to approach the residence on Rainha Elisabeth as if he were a salesman. Johnny told the man that he would reimburse him if he ever got out of jail alive. The short note told Gerti to call Hutt. He knew Hutt would immediately contact the British ambassador, Geoffrey George Knox, chief of the SIS in Brazil.[69] He could only hope that the ambassador would work quickly for his release.

He was left to wonder whether the guard had actually contacted Gerti until a note from her was slid under Johnny's cell door. The friendly jailer had done it. Gerti wrote that the ambassador was trying to arrange a diplomatic solution.[70] But day after day no word came, as his frustration mounted with the slow Brazilian and British diplomatic machinery. He began to wonder if it moved at all on his behalf. Then again, this was wartime, so it was bound to take a while. Finally, one midnight came and went, then 1:00 A.M., then 2:00 A.M., and still no one appeared to take him from his cell. All he could hear were the screams of the tormented ones in other parts of the fortress. As time passed, he began to get nervous, thinking that this was the day. "Johnny, be brave and stand," he kept telling himself over and over. Yet the hours ticked by, and none of the dreaded footsteps approached his door.

In a rear corner of his Polícia Especial cubicle, on the ceiling, a small air vent curled up then down to the floor below, above a guard station. Suddenly Johnny heard a voice say, "No more beating Senhor Gruber, for the British ship *Ajax* is in port." De Graaf stared at the vent above his head in disbelief, but the order was repeated as a new guard joined the group. "No more torture for Gruber, Tôni," came the muffled command.

After that, he could not sleep. Until morning he sat on the edge of his steel bed, staring at the walls. At last his cell door clanged open and the prison doctor came in; the very man who had once interrupted a torture session checked de Graaf over and then told Borer that he could take more. On that occasion, the police set to with great vigor, and knocked Johnny senseless to his knees. But this time the physician took Johnny to the infirmary for what became daily applications of cold compresses, massages, and other procedures that attempted to bring life back into his battered body. After each treatment, he was carried back to his cell.

Late that night, as Johnny tossed to and fro on his bed, a guard came to the cell door. "Senhor Gruber," he whispered, "the chief of police is back now."

"Would you give him a message for me?" Johnny pleaded.

"I don't know if I can," replied the frightened guard. He listened to Johnny's words anyway and departed in silence.

Johnny thought he knew Müller well enough to know that once Filinto became aware of where he was, he would do all in his power to effect his release. All day Johnny waited in anticipation. Early the following morning, the torture detail opened his cell, and he thought the end had finally arrived. Johnny had heard of people committing suicide by jumping over the tier rails to the concrete floor below.[71] On being visited by the thug squad this time, he braced himself against the back wall, thinking, "If they come in to get me, I'll plunge through them, taking a few with me as I dive over the outside rail."

But de Graaf's suicide plan was unnecessary. A mulatto policeman, described by Johnny as "the biggest, cruelest son of a bitch I ever knew,"[72] took him the few blocks to the Polícia Central and to the office of Filinto Müller on the second floor. It was a nobly adorned, lengthy, semirectangular room with thick red carpeting and black furniture trimmed in red. At the far end, on the right, Müller sat behind a large polished black desk. Johnny took a chair at the opposite side of the room, the bullying guard rigidly alert at his side. Müller called Johnny by name, but he was in a painful daze and thought he was dreaming. He called again, his voice booming down the length of the large room. "Filinto, please give me a second to get my bearings and get used to this light," Johnny replied. The red and black decor and bright sunlight streaming in through the draped windows hurt his eyes after so much time in dark cells. Müller called de Graaf forward. "Would you remove this bastard goon from here first?" Johnny asked, gesturing to the tormentor beside him.

"Saí!" (Get out!), Müller shouted, and the guard beat a hasty retreat, closing the door behind him. "Please come here, Johnny," Filinto said in a pleasant tone. But Johnny was bitter and told him to come to where he sat, turning around to show Müller that the guards had bound his hands behind his back.

"Please, Johnny, you know Brazil as well as I do, come forward and sit here beside my desk," he implored. De Graaf got up and went forward. Müller stood up, untied Johnny's hands, and helped him into a chair. He then told Johnny the story of how they had sent him off on a holiday, telling him not to talk to anyone or he would lose his life. An army officer took over his duties, a tool of the pro-Nazi group. Filinto had returned earlier than expected and was appalled by what had taken place, and that Johnny had been picked up and tortured.

"What now?" de Graaf questioned, noting that Müller's gaze was taking in each bruise on his exposed and battered body.

"I can't let you go out the condition you're in," he finally replied, shaking his head. "It is too obvious you've been beaten and tortured. But I promise you this: I will do everything possible to bring you back to good health. You will have the best doctors, food, and medicines I can get. I have given orders already," he continued. "The guards will have nothing to do with that section anymore and your cell will have a special lock that will take a special key to open, so no one can get at you." He assured Johnny that he would get word to Gerti that her husband was alive and would be home soon.

A program was quickly started to help de Graaf regain his vigor. Day after day, for five days in succession, the doctor who had aided in his torture tried to bring him back to a semblance of himself. Special foods were sent in, warm baths followed vitamin injections, rubdowns, compresses, and rest. Every attention was given to him. Finally Johnny demanded to see Filinto, and an hour later entered his office. "Filinto, I appreciate what you have done and I do feel better for it, but I ask you politely to please release me and let me go home."

"Johnny," Filinto said sympathetically, "give me two more days." He did not explain why. Unbeknownst to Johnny until he arrived, Müller had called in a prominent specialist from São Paulo, who worked miracles on Johnny that week. A few days later Filinto summoned de Graaf again to say that the new doctor still needed a few more days to get him well. "This man, Johnny, is the best in Brazil, and wouldn't ask for more time if he felt it was not necessary," Filinto expounded. Johnny agreed.

"Can I call Gerti?" Johnny asked.

"Yes," Müller smiled. "You can use my phone right here on the desk." Excitedly, Johnny dialed his home number, 27–6909, despite the hour being 2:00 A.M.[73] It rang twice. Gerti answered and, on hearing Johnny's voice, collapsed. When Johnny told Filinto that she had fainted, he immediately dispatched a car and an ambulance to the de Graaf home. Gerti was rushed to the hospital. Johnny stood by helplessly, the connected phone still in his hand, as Müller contacted a physician and had him follow the ambulance. The result of Gerti's fall was that she had a miscarriage.[74] Johnny was assured the next morning that she was well but very weak and should remain in the hospital for a time. He wanted to be at her side; however, the doctor insisted that he remain at the prison for another day, as the shock of seeing him could have been too much for her.

Filinto subsequently informed Johnny that he was being deported to Britain on the SS *Monarch,* sailing in two days from the port of Santos. He told Johnny on numerous occasions that he had been ordered to have him arrested but had consistently refused. "I could use you working for me, Johnny, if you care to remain in Brazil," he remarked, his eyes hopeful of a favorable response.

"That would be impossible, Filinto, although I appreciate the offer," Johnny replied. The working class in Brazil was democratically minded, but the upper class, including high-ranking officers and even the commanders of two of Brazil's battleships, were solidly behind the Nazi effort. How President Vargas held on to his power Johnny did not know, except for men like Filinto Müller. There was no way he could abandon the British to work in that morass. Filinto understood and did not press the matter further.

Müller arranged for Johnny's release the following day, January 16, 1940,[75] and on parting warmly shook his hand. "I am terribly sorry this ever happened, Johnny," he said with regret in his voice. "I just wish I had been able to prevent it. I just wish I had known."

"Don't trouble yourself," Johnny replied with a smile. "You saved my life and Gerti's, and for that I will always be in your debt." Müller shrugged this off, patted Johnny on the back, and wished him good luck.

At the hospital, Gerti was sitting up in bed and burst into tears on seeing Johnny. He held her tenderly in his arms, whispering how much he loved her. He told her about leaving Brazil as soon as she was stronger. Gerti liked the idea. They spoke little of their lost baby, a twist of fate that touched both of them deeply, with no one to blame but life itself.

Because of her condition, the doctors recommended that Gerti not travel for at least ten days. Since Johnny had to be out of the country within forty-eight hours and did not want his wife to have to travel alone, he again contacted Filinto, who promised to pull a few strings. Owing to medical complications from the miscarriage, she did not leave the hospital until February 26. Johnny was allowed one day beyond Gerti's release to leave the country. During the wait he sold the car, their home, and all the household possessions. He did not get much, only 30:000$000 (US$1,818, or only US$27,969 in 2009 dollars).[76] But within the twenty-four-hour window, on February 27, 1940, they boarded the 8,712-ton Royal Mail Lines ship, SS *Highland Chieftain,* in Santos and sailed for London in a first-class cabin.[77] Her parents stayed in Rio and eventually died there of old age. Moscow would write their agent off as having been killed in Brazil.

16

THE WAR'S FIRST YEARS

The English capital, its spiraling towers, Georgian buildings, and throngs of busy people, looked great to the two refugees. The journey from Brazil had been slow but serenely peaceful, in spite of the threat from German sub packs while en route. On April 5, 1940, Johnny and Gerti landed and once again checked into the Imperial Hotel in Russell Square.[1] They were grateful indeed to be in Britain after the nightmare they had just experienced in Brazil.

Vee-Vee made his appearance after they returned to their room from a leisurely meal in the hotel restaurant. "So glad to see you both," he began. Vivian shook Johnny's hand profusely and gave Gerti a peck on the cheek. Seated comfortably, they told Vivian what had happened in Rio de Janeiro. He questioned; they answered, elaborating on the details of the brief wires he had received. "How did you keep up with all the coding and decoding Johnny?" he finally inquired, a puzzled look on his face. "Don't know how one man could do it all, but you did."

Johnny felt the time was ripe to tell him. Gesturing toward Gerti, he said, "A short while ago you just kissed my helper. I was aware I was breaking an oath, but there was no other way, for as you acknowledge, it was an impossible task for one person to accomplish alone." Vivian glanced over toward Gerti, who displayed a glowing smile. His face showed no surprise or anger.

"Thanks, Gerti," he remarked softly. "Let's say we just keep this little revelation between the three of us. I can appreciate there was no alternative, but those above me may not be as tolerant and understanding." Johnny knew the matter would go no further. A short time later, Gerti excused herself, leaving the two men to venture into topics that she felt best left between them. Late that evening Vivian departed, but not before assigning Johnny to six weeks of debriefing and report writing at MI6 Section V nerve center in the Broadway buildings, 54

Broadway in Westminster, not far from the houses of Parliament.[2] "Quite a clever wee gal you have there, Johnny," he remarked casually before heading for the lobby. Johnny could not have agreed more.

One thing that was suggested at headquarters was that Johnny change his name. Anyone looking for him would have it all the harder. De Graaf, on the other hand, was a proud man and prouder still of his family name. Modifying "De Graaf" to "De Graff," together with anglicizing "Johann Heinrich" to "John Henry," was the compromise finally agreed upon. It was the tactic again of hiding in plain sight.[3]

The weeks dragged on slowly. With or without his new name, John H. de Graff still hated writing reports and sitting through conference after lengthy conference. He and Gerti had been staying briefly in a flat owned by Kim Philby. This was probably the basement apartment at Grove Court, Holly Mews.[4] Philby was the *Times* correspondent in Arrais, France, at the time. Before Philby returned to London in June 1940,[5] Johnny obtained a bottom-floor apartment at 25 Jermyn Street, much to Gerti's delight.[6] She treasured the new surroundings, quickly demonstrating a nice touch for furnishings, with pictures, flowers, and numerous decorative delights. Had Philby ever discovered that Johnny had been living in his apartment—apparently his mother, Doris, still lived there—De Graff's new cover would have been blown. He always worried that the Soviets might have killed him, and maybe Gerti, too, had Philby found out. But Johnny's superiors never told Philby the true identity of his mystery lodgers.[7]

Later, the blackouts, curfews, the evening drone of bombers and bombs would be barely acknowledged, as Gerti fixed their evening meals by when Johnny was home. She shopped daily, showing an uncanny shrewdness in every small purchase. She and Johnny were elated to be in London, a city they both loved, despite the nightly marauders that would drop their cargo of death from the heavens.

"How would you like to have an internment mission?" Vivian asked Johnny one morning after six tiresome weeks had evaporated.

"What kind of mission?" Johnny queried, puzzled by Vivian's terminology.

"Would you be willing to go undercover in a German internment camp, here in London, for, say, a month or so?" he replied, his soft stare penetrating Johnny to the core.

"What's up? Explain the details and I'll tell you," Johnny responded.

With the outbreak of the war, Britain, like many other countries, had rounded up all known German citizens and Nazi sympathizers. The arrests continued throughout the war, as intelligence sources discovered more and more suspects. Any German national was considered a potential threat until proved otherwise. MI6 wanted de Graff to pose as a Nazi sympathizer. He would be apprehended and processed in the normal way and interned in a London camp in order to ferret out the true Nazi spies among the prisoners. Simply put, his job would be to grade the herd. Once the incarcerated Germans had accepted him, he would make daily and weekly reports to MI6 via the camp commander, an army officer who was in fact with MI6. To him and him alone would Johnny reveal his true identity. De Graff agreed to the mission only because it got him away from the depressing desk routine.

That evening Johnny informed Gerti that he would be gone for a few weeks while interned in London for the SIS. The facility for his undercover assignment was not far from the Clapham South tube station. The Oak Lodge School for Deaf Girls and the Jewish School for Deaf Children, at 101 Nightingale Lane, London SW12, had been appropriated for the duration of the war.[8] They were used as a single internment camp for suspect foreigners, one of many such sites in the British Isles. Gerti accepted the mission with good humor, knowing full well that Johnny was anxious to be active. At no time did she ever show her apprehension, always backing her husband despite the anxieties she undoubtedly felt.

Vee-Vee and Johnny spent the following two days in Vivian's office poring over the details of the assignment until all was set and Johnny was ready for action. Late that week, while strolling down an East End side street, he was picked up by Scotland Yard, arrested, and bundled off, according to plan. At police headquarters he identified himself as one Karl Grubnick, enduring hours of interrogation. Fingerprinting, photos, and mounds of forms followed. Grubnick was processed as just another German national, a potential Nazi spy.

The next day, along with other captives and a dossier for each, Johnny's group of prisoners awaited transportation to the gates of their respective confinement centers. SIS officials had arranged for his arrest, false ID, and past history. To the most thorough investigator, a check on Grubnick would provide no loopholes and only reveal a well-documented class "A" German. Individuals so adjudicated by a magistrate were interned for the duration of the war.

Screeching to a jarring halt, the prison lorry braked before the large gray-stone school at 101 Nightingale Lane, surrounded by a high stone wall strung with barbed wire and dotted with spotlights. Like a herd of oxen going to slaughter, the prisoners fell out and lined up. They were promptly escorted by six armed soldiers through the checkpoint, the gatehouse, and across the courtyard into the administration building. Inside, busy military clerks checked the prisoners' files, typed up more documents, issued khaki outfits, and, an hour later, called each new inmate one by one into the office of the camp commandant, Captain Courtney.

When it was Johnny's turn, this crew-cut officer dismissed the guard and, once the door had closed, told de Graff to be seated. Facing Johnny was a tall, medium-weight military-type individual with a ruddy complexion on a small oval face. Johnny judged him to be in his thirties, but his blond brush cut was deceptive. According to plan, Johnny knew his true identity. Until this meeting, however, he did not know Johnny's.

Courtney listened intently as Johnny exposed his cover, and without comment or show of surprise picked up the desk phone. He confirmed everything in seconds. In the interim, Johnny surveyed his small office, its pale white walls broken only by a wide barred and screened window that overlooked the west courtyard. The captain's scratched and dented brown desk, a row of filing cabinets, and two hard-backed chairs completed the office's interior.

His call completed, Courtney rose and came forward, extending a broad smile and his open hand. "Please be seated, Johnny, and let's get down to business," he suggested. Courtney informed de Graff that the camp contained about two hundred inmates. Prisoner Grubnick's entrance into the detainment center would proceed according to regular routine. They agreed that Johnny could ask to see him anytime he had information to be relayed back to MI6. Captain Sykes, Courtney's subordinate, was a career military man who would be kept in the dark concerning Grubnick's real identity and purpose. The senior captain would get word to Sykes in a few days that he did not trust this Karl Grubnick fellow. And anytime Grubnick sought out Sykes for a chat, he was to report the entire conversation to him, even if the prisoner's words made little sense.

This method of communication was foolproof. Sykes was an officer who followed orders to the letter and would undoubtedly repeat what he had heard word for word, no matter how senseless it seemed. Courtney would then pass the text on to MI6 at 54 Broadway. By using the two officers, the senior only for top priorities, the junior for the balance, the cover of communication was beyond any inmate's suspicion. No special privileges were extended to de Graff in such contact.

Finalizing the instructions, Johnny was marched under guard up two flights of stairs to a floor where the former classrooms had been converted into dormitories. Passing along the corridors, he witnessed detainees mopping and scrubbing floors, while others whiled away their time on the outside courts in sporting activities. He could feel their gaze as he passed. No doubt a fresh arrival broke the monotony.

Johnny's new quarters contained twenty metal cots, gray army blankets on each bed neatly folded, and a wooden footlocker. His entrance caused only a few turned heads, reposing or reading from their prone positions. As soon as his escort departed, several inmates made their introductions, showing interest without suspicion in the new roommate. Within a week, de Graff was part of the drab routine. He made friends but kept them at a distance by letting them make the first overtures. His aloofness and private counsel, all part of the plan, attracted the interest of the other prisoners. Had he sought out companionship, he felt, he would have brought notice to himself and created misgivings within the group.

The daily routine began with the wake up call at 6:00 A.M. Next came breakfast in the basement cafeteria at 7:00. After dormitory inspection, the men began their chores of washing, cleaning, and painting until noon. An hour's free time, and then outdoor sports and exercise followed, until supper at 5:00 P.M. This was followed by the evening inspection and more leisure time until lights out at 9:00 P.M. The British, with their strict discipline and regimentation, ordered that everything run according to the clock.

By the end of the second week, de Graff had a fair impression of his fellow prisoners, recognizing the leaders, the followers, and those with no alignment. One day he was surprised to recognize two bearded men, one a little shorter than the other, whom he had met ten years earlier while on assignment for Moscow in Romania. Fortunately they did not recognize him. Johnny's acquaintance with the pair dated back to Bucharest, when the Romanian Communist Party had asked him to look the two up to obtain financial aid. Both men were very wealthy and lived in spacious homes up in the hills opposite one another. Using their money and influence, they worked against Communist propaganda by supporting the Iron Guards, the notorious pro-Nazi organization living underground in Romania. Johnny had paid them a visit at their hillside retreats, imploring each for economic assistance to improve the conditions of local Jews—without success. Even though they too were Jews, they were avid fascists, and under no circumstances would they consider switching to the Socialist camp. The encounter was brief and frank on that day. Months later, the Communist Party was able to kidnap one of the leading Iron Guard officers and ship him to Moscow for questioning. The Romanian Communist Party and the Iron Guards were bitter enemies even in those prewar years.

Johnny felt strongly that the two men were still pro-Nazi. The fact that they were there in the Nightingale Lane camp posed a further question. Were the British aware whom they had trapped in their net? He had to find out. By provoking a brief tussle with one of the guards, Johnny was taken to the commandant's office. Captain Courtney asked the soldiers who brought him to wait outside. After the door closed, he asked Johnny to explain. "I think Vivian should know he has two pro-Nazi gems in here," he began. "They're real sweethearts from my Romanian experience." Courtney listened intently as Johnny explained his past knowledge of the two Romanians. Once made aware of their possible relationship with the Iron Guards, he assured de Graff that he would convey the information to headquarters without delay. "I have not been here that long to have spooked out the total population. However, these two are prime Nazi spy material without a doubt!" Johnny informed him emphatically. Courtney hastened to a bank of filing cabinets and within seconds retrieved two files.

"Let's see who we have, Johnny," he mused as he spread out both manila folders on his desk. Together they glanced over the brief material, labeled "Potential."

Both men had come to Britain two years earlier, using French passports. They had opened a transfer agent's office dealing in imported perfumes. Their inactivity in trade, frequenting of known German haunts, and numerous trips had eventually caught the attention of the SIS. Unconfirmed suspicion was enough to cause their arrests. Fifty thousand unaccountable pounds found in their possession cinched their internment. Remaining mute during interrogation, they shed no light on their financial assets or mysterious backgrounds. Their passports were cleverly executed forgeries that had escaped initial detection. Beyond that, nothing more was known.

"Did they recognize you, Johnny?" Courtney asked, with a look of concern.

"No, they do not know me and showed no signs of recognition, which figures, for the brief encounter we had was some time ago," Johnny replied firmly. "We're safe on that score and safe to get to know them better."

Courtney smiled, giving a deep sigh of relief. "What's next?" he asked.

Johnny thought the best plan would be for him to continue to play it cool. From what he could see, the two men were looking for supporters. They had coffee parties in their room every second day or so for a select few. No doubt they were curious about Johnny, since he had not made an effort to speak to them. De Graff felt that his self-imposed isolation would soon bring the two Romanians to him. When that happened, he felt he could talk his way into the group, but the overture would be entirely on their part. He did not plan to seek them out and blow the whole deal. Captain Courtney nodded in agreement.

"Once contact is made, things may move fast," Johnny continued. "So, should headquarters want to speak to me in progress, we'll need a signal other than a call to your office. Too many visits with you will soon be noticed, and I have no intention of bashing guards around to get hauled in here."

"I agree," Courtney replied.

Across the street there were many vacant Georgian apartments. Johnny could see the upper windows from the exercise yard. He told Courtney to tell Vivian to have MI6 occupy a vacant bedroom in one of the buildings. On the windowsill they were to set three flowering pots of different colors. De Graff would periodically look at the window, and should the color arrangement or number of pots vary, he would know they wanted him to get in touch. If he had information to report, he would jumble it up and give it to Courtney's second in command, Captain Sykes.

"Excellent plan. Which house and which window is best?" Courtney prodded enthusiastically.

"Third house on the left, second floor," de Graff responded.

"Good as done, Johnny," he answered with delight. "Guard!" The door opened. "Get this man out of here! And if he assaults another of our men, let me know at once, do you hear? At once!" The soldier snapped to attention and saluted.

Four days passed, and out in the exercise yard the curious Romanians approached Johnny. One of the bearded men inquired, "You always walk around very preoccupied in thought and keep to yourself, friend. What is it?"

"Nothing too much to it," Johnny replied passively. "If you wait for the eventual sentence of death for high treason, you live with the man who will face you." They made no reply as Johnny kept walking, but they followed alongside.

"Why do you sometimes stop and gaze over the wall?" one asked. "The people who live over there raise lovely flowers in their windows, and I'm a lover of flowers," Johnny replied. Without a further word they moved on. Promptly at 1:00 P.M. the following day, he received an invitation to join their coffee get-together. "Now they are on the hook," Johnny thought. Three other prisoners joined them. The conversation was kept light and jovial. De Graff did not say much, acting like a man in depression, and all went well.

"You come to tell me you like our coffee?" the camp's second officer inquired the following morning, when Johnny paid him a visit.

"Yes, it's excellent, but the tenth dormitory needs a new broom and more blankets," Johnny continued. Sykes showed his annoyance.

"Always complaints, you blokes always have complaints!" MI6 would get word that he had made contact, as Sykes would pass on both his compliment and his complaint to the commandant, word for word, unknowingly in code.

Two weeks of casual chats over coffee followed, as Johnny gradually opened up, revealing his distaste for Britain and his lot, much to the restrained delight of his two bearded hosts. Others showing up for the free coffee were not pro-Nazi or pro-German, as Johnny soon found out. They were dropped from the guest list and replaced by new potential recruits. Meanwhile, having spent almost a month in captivity, Johnny had had ample time to screen all the inmates. He came to the conclusion that the only spies incarcerated there were himself and his two slick friends.

"Everyone is nuts here but me and the two beards," Johnny told Sykes one day.

"We're all nuts, you say," Sykes repeated, visibly irritated at being interrupted in his office during a phone call. "You're bloody nuts—that's for sure," he retorted, briskly calling a guard to get de Graff out of his way. "He's balmy," he later told Captain Courtney, "quite off his stick. He flings open my door and yells we're all nuts except him and his two beards. He's flipped, sir."

"Keep a close watch on him, and night or day relay whatever he says to me," his superior reiterated. "No doubt he's under strain."

"If he gets any worse, he'll strain us or hang himself, sir," the shaken officer replied. Courtney smiled.

Glancing out the window the following day, Johnny saw that the floral presentation had been rearranged. The pink bloom previously on the left was now in the center, the purple bloom in its place. "What's up?" Johnny inquired of Courtney as soon as they met.

"They want you to plan an escape with your two friends. Sound them out. You can't take confinement anymore, and only the gallows await you. You know how to get them interested." De Graff agreed. "Here's your stumbling block; you have a great plan for escape, but no funds for use on the outside. See if they'll bite."

The next afternoon, as Johnny paraded back and forth along the courtyard walls, the Romanians joined him. "You are restless, friend," the tall one whispered.

"I have to get out of here, I have to escape," Johnny responded.

"Yes, why don't you do it," the man remarked. "Haven't you formulated a plan yet?"

"Yes, I have a plan, a foolproof plan," Johnny answered, "but there's one slight problem and that is that I have no money." They hung on his words intently. A silence followed.

"Money does not play any role on our side," one finally said. "If you take us into your plan, you will see," the tall man boasted with pride.

"When I am ready and you come up with a large amount of cash, I can pay off some people so we'll be overlooked. I'll let you know," Johnny informed them. They agreed to tell Johnny when they had the money. The clang of the dinner bell ended further discussion.

"Only you and me on this. With more than three it is too dangerous and I'll drop the whole idea," Johnny whispered before breaking away. The two Romanians concurred.

That week the flowerpots virtually bounced off the sill. Soon everything was organized. MI6, through the commandant, had arranged for guards to be absent from certain posts and for a series of wall lights to malfunction. Military orders were subtly changed without question or suspicion to allow a safe, undetected escape. Johnny's two companions would believe that the right guards had been paid off. The Romanian Iron Guard supporters came through right on time with an abundance of cash. De Graff's stay in the camp had now reached seven weeks. He was anxious to get out and get back to Gerti.

Early one evening, before blackout, the three men were marched in front of two soldiers to the small barbershop and shower building perched higher than the outside wall a short distance away. Once inside the structure, with the guards at the outer door, they continued into the bathing area. But glancing through a small window overlooking the wall that took in some of the buildings across the street, Johnny almost suffered heart failure. There in the window, off to his left and well lit, stood one lone flowerpot. The other two were missing. He wondered if it was a signal or a startling change of plans. Pretending that he needed to talk to the sentries to confirm that the side door was unlocked and that a rope hidden at the foot of the wall was in place, Johnny told the Romanians to stay put until he returned.

Outside the building, he asked a guard to take him to Captain Courtney, saying that he was suddenly ill. The guard hesitated but then agreed, leaving his companion in place next to the building. As they left, Johnny noticed that the spotlights on the wall close to the bathhouse were still burning brightly. This was according to plan. They were to be turned off in ten minutes. The sudden darkness would allow the three men to escape through an unlocked side door. They were then to fling the rope and grappling hook over the wall in the shadows, climb to the top, and flee. All three escapees, of course, would be under continuous SIS surveillance.

"Something changed?" Johnny inquired of Captain Courtney. "I saw the signal." Courtney came forward from behind his desk, looking like a cat that had caught a mouse. "The escape is off," he explained with a smile and look of smug satisfaction. "MI6 now has sufficient proof that your pals are Gestapo agents, and they have rounded up their banker plus four more members of the group." Johnny sighed with relief and satisfaction.

While he changed into his civilian clothes in the adjoining room, his two companions were retrieved from the bathhouse, quite provoked by the wait. Not long thereafter, de Graff entered the captain's office and faced them. At seeing the man they thought would take them to freedom in street clothes, a look of complete bewilderment flashed across their faces. Before they could recoil from the surprise, Johnny began. "You don't remember me from Romania, when I visited you at your homes in the hills seeking aid from you for your Jewish brethren?" They were perplexed. "You both laughed, sent me away, and gave your financial help to the Nazi Iron Guards." A lightning flash of recognition dawned on their faces. "Both of you are Nazi agents. Aren't you glad that we meet again?" Johnny demanded. They froze in brooding silence, both somewhat pale. It was all over in twenty minutes. The two men were handcuffed and led away to prison and weeks of heavy interrogation.

To preserve his cover, Johnny was marched out of the camp under guard and then whisked away to MI6 headquarters. Vivian was delighted with the mission's success, Gerti was overjoyed to see her husband safe and sound, and Johnny was glad that his confinement was over, after almost two months as Karl Grubnick.

Every night the ominous threat of the London Blitz took on graver tones. The bombing, the mounting toll of death and destruction grew to new heights. By early September 1940, terror filled the air throughout the city. Hitler had underestimated the British will to survive, and the pendulum swung the other way in time, but until it did, for several hours a week Britain was held captive from the air. On December 29, 1940, the great London fire took place, yet the British, soiled and maimed, threw off the wreckage and fought on. De Graff was on reserve status during this time, which meant that he ventured out each day to scout around, keeping his eyes and ears open in that most English of institutions, the public house. One could learn a great deal just by quietly sitting in a London pub for an hour or two, watching the people and eavesdropping on their conversations. His job was to report any suspicious findings or encounters.

"Could you find your way to Colombia in South America?" Vivian asked unexpectedly in his office one morning after Johnny had spent six weeks with his pub-crawl duties.

"I have no doubt I can, but by devious routes," Johnny confirmed. "What do you have in mind?"

"A little security work is needed down there, the full details of which you will be given en route," he stated in his quiet way. Johnny smiled in agreement, knowing not to press Vee-Vee for more information.

The itinerary was as follows. They would sail from Liverpool on a fast-moving, unarmed, unescorted freighter to Canada. Using British passports, they would apply to the U.S. consul in Montreal for American visas under the names William John[9] and Gertrude Graff, then enter the United States and go on to New York, where they would sail to Colombia using the names John and Gerti Graffnor.

Two nights later they boarded the SS *Glenorchy* in Liverpool and were again on the high seas. The *Glenorchy* was a specially designed speedy freighter that had twelve passenger cabins besides the officers' quarters. No one, including the friendly, overweight captain, had any idea of William and Gertrude's true identities or purpose. All meals were served at the captain's table, together with the chief officer. Both men were very pleasant, showing no sign of concern with the fact that their ship was an unarmed sitting duck as it moved across the Atlantic.

Despite rough seas, some of it caused by a storm that in fact provided protection from roving U-boats, they made excellent time to Canada. The *Glenorchy* reached St. John, New Brunswick, on January 19, 1941. The couple's nonimmigrant visas were for a two-week stay, with their final destination listed as the residence of E. G. Howard, 6 West 52nd Street, New York, New York. The next step was the train up to Montreal and the Hotel Windsor on Peel Street, where a reserved room was waiting.[10] After checking in, the de Graffs did a little sightseeing. They walked to the top of Mount Royal hill overlooking the city. Skaters of all sizes and ages crowded in a frozen pond called Beaver Lake, while slightly below the rim, toboggan slides and a ski jump off Côte de Neiges Road drew even more spectators. A magnificent meal at Chez Ernest on Drummond Street, made romantic with candlelight and fine music, completed their first day in Canada.

After breakfast the next morning they paid a call on the U.S. consul in downtown Montreal. It was not a pleasant visit. Johnny and a rather belligerent official, who obviously did not care for their German accents and even less for the names on their passports, haggled for about an hour. The de Graffs departed, certain they would have a rough time obtaining the necessary permission to enter the United States.

Late that afternoon, still fuming at the American consular officers, they received some unexpected company at their hotel room. It was in the form of a tall, solidly built man bundled up in a smart gray overcoat. He introduced himself as Corporal Noel of the Royal Canadian Mounted Police. His manner and appearance were both impressive as he inquired about their trip and explained that his superior, Inspector Clifford W. Harvison, would be pleased if Johnny could pay him a visit at the RCMP's downtown office.

"When would he like to see me?" Johnny inquired.

"Now, if you are free to do so," the Mountie replied. "I have a car waiting downstairs." Gerti remained at the hotel while Johnny went to meet the inspector. The drive to the RCMP's Montreal headquarters was brief, and in no time Johnny found himself seated before a plainclothes officer. The man greeted de Graff warmly as Johnny surveyed him and the sparse furnishings in his orderly office. Preferring Cliff to his associates, he was a slender, wiry type, not as tall as some officers Johnny had seen passing through the corridors, but a good five foot eight (1.73 m) or more. A warm, easy expression showed on his narrow, creased face, which was set off by a prominent nose and large drooping ears. His eyes were friendly. Johnny took an immediate linking to Harvison, who no doubt possessed great intensity under his cloak of calmness.

"MI6 has advised us of your coming," he began, "and I wanted to meet you to see if we could assist you in any way. We maintain a close relationship with Vivian and his group." Johnny was not surprised at this piece of information. He was well aware that Canada was part of the British Commonwealth. Harvison appeared to know a fair amount about Johnny, too, and de Graff was happy to fill him in on the areas where he was lacking.

"Your agent name is Petersen when outside the London office," he remarked.

"Yes, for mail, home address, et cetera," Johnny replied. "The usual protective routine."

"We'll use the same, while you're here and in the U.S.," Harvison answered. Over a cup of coffee, they chatted, as Johnny informed him of his visa problem. "Let me see what we can do about it. We'll contact Washington and pull a few strings," he responded warmly. Johnny thanked him, hoping he would be able to do something.

On February 6 Inspector Harvison phoned "Petersen" at his hotel. "Johnny, this is Cliff. I think everything should be in order now. Pay the consul a visit tomorrow morning, and good luck." The following day, two immigration officials at the U.S. consulate told William John de Graff and his wife that they were being denied visas on the grounds that they might become public charges and because they did not have valid Canadian visas for their return. It was also pointed out to Johnny that he had dyed his hair since the first meeting. Johnny told them emphatically that he had done this to please his much younger wife. But the two bureaucrats were unmoved and probably felt that this was an attempt to disguise his appearance.[11]

Cliff Harvison managed to get the de Graffs' two-week Canadian visas extended. Johnny and Gerti then appealed the American consul's decision. Harvison pulled more strings, including having a letter of assurance sent from someone of prominence[12] at the Canadian Pacific Railway to the U.S. consul. On March 7, 1941, the special assistant to the attorney general of the United States notified the Immigration and Naturalization Service that the de Graffs' appeal had been sustained and that they could travel to the United States, remaining in the country for six months as nonimmigrants. They had to deposit $1,000 in the form of a U.S. guaranteed security bond within two days. Through Harvison, Johnny learned how this was accomplished. An operative in New York using the name John Gray put up the required money in the form of collateral with the U.S. Fidelity and Guarantee Company. Meanwhile, Johnny and Gerti moved out of the Windsor and into the Homeville Rooming House at 1126 Sherbrooke Street West. On May 15, four days after Johnny's forty-seventh birthday, the $1,000 was posted and they obtained their visas. Five days later they left for New York City by train. The de Graffs told the Americans back at the consulate in Montreal that they would stay initially at the Commodore Hotel while looking for a small apartment to rent for the duration of their stay. Their train crossed into New York at Rouses Point on May 20, 1941.[13]

Arriving at Penn Station the following morning, Johnny and Gerti checked into the Commodore, across the street from the Chrysler Building. Once unpacked, Johnny planned to visit the British consulate to obtain his sealed mission orders and other papers for the Colombian assignment. However, a phone call from His Majesty's consulate to come right over interrupted their first hour at the Commodore, and Johnny left immediately. The caller was George Renwick, a short, stocky man of pale complexion. He was a former British army captain at the New York consulate. Amid Renwick's colorful office, he looked like a typical first secretary.

"I have your entire life in front of me," Renwick proclaimed, opening a bulging dossier. Johnny knew then that Renwick was an SIS officer and that the consulate post was only his cover. At no time did Renwick let on who he was, but his statement left little doubt in Johnny's mind. "They say you are an expert on Nazism, communism, and foreign intelligence," he said, looking up.

"If that's what they tell you, they should know," Johnny replied, with growing annoyance. Renwick's cocky attitude began to provoke him.

"What are your views on the Soviet Union?"

"What do you want to know?" Johnny answered.

"In your opinion, when will the battle with Russia and Germany against us begin?"

De Graff laughed. "Captain, who told you such silly nonsense about the Soviets and Nazis joining forces?"

"This information was provided to us by a very high-ranking officer in the German army. He should know," Renwick snapped.

"It's also possible they may have put sand in your ears," Johnny responded. "For your information, Captain, in less than four weeks Germany will attack Russia. Have you not learned anything from 1914 until now?" Johnny lashed out, his face colored in anger.

"Oh, you'll see," Renwick shouted.

"Yes, I'll see, all right," Johnny replied. "I'll bet you a bottle of champagne that Germany invades Russia within a month."

"You're on," said Renwick, shaking Johnny's hand on the bet. As it turned out, de Graff would have lost, as Germany invaded the Soviet Union on June 22, 1941, one day after the one-month time limit.

May 22, 1941, found Johnny back at the consulate to pick up the visas for Colombia. During his discussion there, two men with Canadian accents entered the office to inform Johnny that the South American assignment was off. A cable minutes later confirmed this change. "Journey cancelled," it read; "you are ordered to proceed to Montreal and report to RCMP." He never found out what he was to do in Colombia, as everything about the mission ground to a halt. De Graff could only surmise that it involved arranging security protection for UK industries doing business there vital to the war effort.

Johnny and Gerti did not immediately return to Canada. There is very little documentation on where they spent the next five months, until October 29, 1941, when they finally showed up in Montreal.[14] It may be that Gerti had decided to undergo an operation while in New York. If so, the nature of this surgery could have been related to her unending desire for children and a physical condition that made pregnancy dangerous. She had consulted specialists before, and Johnny mentioned that she did so again. This was her only trip to the United States.

Eleven years later Johnny told the FBI that they had stayed in New York and rented a one-room apartment on the ground floor of a numbered cross street between 5th and Madison Avenues near the Central Park Zoo. They resided there while Gerti had surgery at a hospital near the northern edge of Central Park. In 1952 this sent the FBI scurrying about the area seeking confirmation. But no matter who they interviewed or how many questions they asked, they could find nothing to verify that William and Gertrude de Graff had ever sat foot in the city. The hunt to find John Gray likewise proved to be a dead end. It was pointed out to the FBI again and again that records pertaining to all three persons could well have been destroyed during the preceding years.[15]

Wherever Johnny and Gerti had gone, even before they finally left the United States, it produced an internal squabble in the RCMP.[16] Britain's National Archives (formerly the Public Record Office) contains material that conceivably relates to Johnny's activities during this period but stubbornly refuses to disclose it.[17] The currently available documents indicating the de Graffs' possible destination consist of three letters exchanged between the RCMP in Ottawa and Montreal before and during the phase of bickering, that is, from May 3 to October 29, 1941. In the RCMP communications dated April 19, September 11, and October 23, the couple was either in or on their way to Halifax, Nova Scotia.[18]

Among a series of interviews with Johnny's second son, Oscar, it was pointed out that there was a German spy operating in Montreal whose operative name was "Kaiser." This individual ran a group of agents between Montreal and Halifax watching Allied ship movements. The port of Halifax was crucial to the war effort, as it was the starting point for the supply vessels heading for Britain. U-boats roamed the cold waters off the shore of Newfoundland and Nova Scotia, sending ships destined for the United Kingdom to the bottom. Kaiser's group kept in contact with German submarines by signals and walkie-talkies.

No one knew what Kaiser looked like, only that he had a scar from a knife or sword wound on his back. The authorities were tipped off that he would be staying at a particular hotel. Going to his room, they made him remove his pajama top to confirm that he was the individual. Kaiser was then offered a choice: either work for the Canadians by giving false information to the U-boats, or face execution. Kaiser stated, "No, I will not work for you." He thereupon shot himself in the head with a hidden pistol. De Graff's superior in this operation was Colonel T. E. "Ted" Ryder, on whose farm, near Hampton, New Brunswick, Johnny and Gerti spent four weeks during or around the time of the episode. An admirer of Johnny's efforts, Ryder told him, "This was your masterpiece, your nicest bit of work."[19]

At some point before their return to Montreal, Inspector Harvison was put in charge of the de Graffs and just who would find out what about them. When they arrived back in the city, they were driven directly to Harvison's home, located in an attractive area on the fringe of Mount Royal, near Côte de Neiges. Cliff came to the door as they drove up. It was his first meeting with Gerti, and once he had made the couple at home in his living room, Harvison enlightened his guests. "Well, are you surprised to be back with us?" he inquired with a knowing smile.

"We certainly are," Johnny replied.

"We have received special orders from your Valentine Vivian of MI6 to accept you on temporary loan for major intelligence work needed here. In this assignment, which will be undercover, we will respect his request to allow you to make your own way as a free agent. He say's you don't like to be hamstrung."

"What is it the RCMP wants me to do?" Johnny asked.

"Simply put, Johnny, we want you to pose as a German spymaster to penetrate and infiltrate the Nazi spy and sympathizer movement in Canada." Gerti looked over at her husband and forced a smile. Looking across to Cliff, Johnny said, "Okay, when do I start?"

"Right now," Harvison replied.

17

THE MONTREAL NESTS

The Canadian fascist movement was born under the leadership of a Québécois named Adrien Arcand. His longwinded speeches and sometimes open, sometimes clandestine assemblies did not escape the notice of the RCMP. Anti-English, anti-Semitic, and pro-German, Arcand and his top lieutenants had been under surveillance for years. Following Canada's declaration of war on Germany on September 10, 1939, Arcand was allowed to linger for a number of months but was then picked up with several of his blue-shirt colleagues and interned. Inspector Cliff Harvison was in charge of the arrests.[1] A large number of Québécois, however, staunchly came out against conscription and were sympathetic to the Vichy government once Hitler overran France in June 1940.[2]

As in Britain, when war came, Canadian security forces consulted previously compiled lists of known German sympathizers and suspects. Over a matter of days, hundreds were detained or questioned. In smashing the backbone of Arcand's organization, the RCMP action forced the lower fringe and other sympathizers into hiding. Still at large, these individuals posed a collective threat of unknown potential. They had to be brought to the surface whenever and wherever possible. In the weeks that followed, Cliff and Johnny worked long hours studying suspect files and known Nazi haunts. Johnny was given a Canadian agent number, S.A. 235, with S.A. standing for secret agent.[3] That the Canadians issued Johnny such a number was indicative of the large job the Mounties envisioned ahead of them in bringing in the fascist stragglers.

By 1942, knowing they could remain in Canada for some time, Gerti and Johnny began to think of buying a home rather than renting one, with the risk of a prying landlord questioning their activities. They had enough personal savings to afford a car, with something left over for a down payment on a small house.

Johnny's salary was doubled when residing in countries considered hostile, but not in a friendly nation such as Canada. There, it was back to the original base pay. For much of the war, and still being called William John Graff, S.A. 235 was paid in U.S. funds out of New York. The British came up with half and the Canadians the other half. Together it amounted to US$211.25 per month, or US$2,780 in 2009 dollars.[4] In Montreal they could thus afford a comfortable but not extravagant existence.

When Johnny got away from the office one Saturday afternoon, he and Gerti set out for a few hours of house hunting. They eventually wound up once again in the suburb of Mount Royal, then an upper-income community of mainly English-speaking residents. Their car traveled along avenues and down crescents, allowing them to view new and old homes. Stopping at one site, Johnny approached two carpenters who were working on a nearly finished house. They looked up and smiled as Gerti and Johnny entered the recently painted hallway. The two workers answered perfunctory questions about the structure politely, but with noticeable German accents. Much to their surprise, Johnny began speaking in German. They responded likewise.

While Gerti toured the house and eventually went back to the car, Johnny chatted with the two men, leaving the subject of home construction and prices to ask about common interests in the Fatherland. Gradually he moved the conversation along, praising Hitler's efforts and denouncing the politics of the West. The workmen took the cue enthusiastically, soon revealing their pro-German views. Unlike others, however, they acknowledged that they did not put their opinions into action. The name Adrien Arcand was mentioned with praise, even though by then he was sitting in a camp for detained rightists in Fredericton, New Brunswick. Arcand would be released only in July 1945.[5]

Following some closing comments, Johnny bid his new acquaintances farewell and joined Gerti, who waited patiently at curbside. She noticed his excitement and asked him to explain. As they pulled away, Johnny told her about the two German workers. Once drawn out, they had unknowingly provided him with a couple of names of Germans who they felt shared his fervor. In their eagerness to please a fellow countryman, they had likewise painted a picture of the scattered Canadian Nazi movement as disorganized but still alive and functioning.

Late that afternoon, on quiet, winding Palmerston Avenue, Gerti and Johnny fell in love with a small house at number 49, one month away from completion.[6] It had an attached garage and a walk-in vestibule leading to an L-shaped living room and dining room. The kitchen was bright and cheery, with lots of cupboard space, which pleased Gerti. Upstairs there was a large master bedroom and a small second bedroom, which could be used as a den. The bathroom faced a good-sized backyard, a field, and the rear of the homes on Debbie Avenue.

One could enter the house from the garage via a side door that opened to a semilanding and the choice of eight steps down into the basement or three steps up to the kitchen. The basement ran the full length and breadth of the house and contained only a compact furnace and sinks. A large dwelling on a raised level was positioned to their right, another on the left. Standing on the newly laid front lawn, they liked the soon-to-be-finished home and the very clean and tidy community of which it was a part. They agreed that this was it and wasted no time in contacting the agent to make a deposit. While at the building site, Johnny and Gerti met Ward and Violet Scott, became friends, and lived with them a short time until their new home was ready. The Scotts resided a short walk away on Appin Avenue.[7] Once the last coat of paint was dry and the paperwork completed, the de Graffs moved into their first permanent address since leaving London.[8]

In the meantime, Johnny had met with Cliff and begun the laborious combing of files for the names the two laborers had given him. By chance, they found them. The suspects had the surnames Klein and Seigmire. Both had been picked up for questioning but were later released when no grounds were found for holding them. "We're in luck, Johnny!" Cliff exclaimed on locating the two dossiers. "These are our boys!" Harvison and de Graff read over the Klein file, absorbing the details. Hans Klein had come to Canada from Germany in the late 1930s, just before the outbreak of the war. With a chemical engineer's degree, he was gainfully employed with a small company, and was married to a Canadian and had a young son. Although not in the Adrien Arcand group, he was certainly a peripheral member, having demonstrated Nazi leanings on several occasions.

Rudolph Seigmire, or "Rudy," had come to Canada from Germany as a lad when his parents immigrated. By 1942, a resident for twenty years, he had successfully obtained an electrical engineering degree. Since graduating, Seigmire had been employed with Quebec Hydro. He was unmarried and lived alone in a small downtown apartment. Like Klein, he was regarded as a fringe Nazi.

"What are you thinking, Johnny?" Cliff inquired as de Graff mused over the folder. "The same thoughts I have?"

"Prime candidates in very key positions," Johnny replied.

"My views exactly," Cliff said grimly. "They sure could raise hell in those plants if they choose to. It's like having a robbery suspect in a bullion room." Johnny smiled in agreement. The hours passed as they spent most of the day and into the evening working out a course of action. It would be Johnny's initial plunge into the gray world of undercover activity in Montreal. Their first choice was Herr Seigmire, who appeared to be the more active of the two. For a week they kept him under surveillance until they were familiar with his main habits.

A fortnight later de Graff began visiting Seigmire's regular eating establishment. The man loved German dishes. Besides grabbing the odd meal at a corner diner across from his office, he spent the balance of his eating hours at a small, secluded German restaurant off busy St. Lawrence Boulevard. Johnny began frequenting the place at different times and days. His visits were purposely set up this way to avoid being considered someone only interested in eating when Seigmire was in the restaurant. He knew that at some point they would meet. It was enjoyable as well to relax and view the customers while absorbing their conversations. A word or phrase signaling pro-Nazi sentiments was likewise noted in Johnny's mind and passed on to Cliff, along with the appropriate description and infrequently overheard name of the narrator. Rudy Seigmire came by himself or with a small group or acquaintances. Sometimes other people joined him. There was no doubt that he began to notice Johnny's presence as one of the restaurant's German-speaking patrons.

"I'm ready to make contact," Johnny informed Cliff late one summer evening by phone in 1942.

"How do you plan to swing it, Johnny?" he cautiously inquired.

"Raise a stink," Johnny told him firmly. "I'm quite good at that, you know." Harvison laughed, agreed, and asked de Graff to phone him with what happened.

Late that night, before falling asleep, Gerti turned to Johnny and said, "I love Canada, Johnny, and our little home here. Wouldn't it be nice to settle down and raise a family?" Johnny had an answer ready for this question. Ever since the miscarriage in Rio, he had been worried about her unending desire to become a mother. He started out slowly, telling her that he too liked Canada and Montreal. However, he was opposed to taking the chance of another pregnancy and risk losing the woman he loved. Sure, there was a chance that she could have a normal pregnancy, but it was not a large possibility. It just was not worth the risk. He wanted her in good health. Perhaps they should face the fact that she was not strong enough to have a child.

"But I am, Johnny," Gerti insisted. "I went to another doctor today, and he says I'm fine and should have no problems whatsoever."

"Let's talk it over tomorrow, Mutzi," Johnny replied softly. "We have lots of time yet to make a sound decision." She smiled, but that twinkle in her eye meant that she had planned the outcome already.

The next evening found Johnny entering the German restaurant. With a quick glance around, he located Seigmire alone and about to order. He hung up his coat, took out and placed a cigarette in its holder, then lit it before proceeding toward an empty table on the far side of the room. Timing his walk across the floor to parallel a waitress carrying a hot plate of beef stew, Johnny swung into her path, jarring her abruptly. The plate slipped from her grasp and fell to the floor, spreading the steaming substance in a wide arc. Bellowing at her for her carelessness, Johnny exploded in German for all to hear, "Hitler would not tolerate such incompetence in the new Germany!"

The poor girl turned a noticeable shade of red as a hush fell over the dining room. The stunned guests gawked in their direction. Mumbling an apology and joined by her manager, both placated the patrons at nearby tables. The hum of conversation slowly returned. Johnny secured an empty table and sat down, enduring furtive glances in his direction, when an up-thrust hand caught his eye. Seigmire, as unobtrusively as possible, was trying to attract Johnny's attention. De Graff pretended to ignore him, feigning anger at what had just taken place. Rudy finally got up and walked to Johnny's table.

"It's unfortunate the silly girl did not keep out of your way, sir," he began. "Such stupidity! Did you have anything spilled on your clothes?"

"No," Johnny growled back. "But that was just lucky." They smiled.

"I am eating alone, and, as you are also, would you care to join me at my table?" he asked very pleasantly. Johnny nodded in agreement.

Seigmire was a short, stocky man of about five foot five (165 cm), slightly bald with wisps of fair hair complementing his deep-set blue eyes. His facial features were so distinct that from forehead to jaw bone they appeared chipped out of stone. A flashing smile of white pearly teeth was his only softening feature. Once seated, both men introduced themselves and shook hands across the table the German way, with a single up and down motion. Johnny used the name Captain Burger. He never gave his first name, thereby forcing Seigmire to use the military rank—with the corresponding respect.

"Captain Burger," he inquired, "you were a military man, perhaps a sea captain?"

"Oh, I sailed the seas, but my rank is from the military, and I'm proud of it," Johnny answered.

"Yes, yes, of course," Rudy stammered. "Germany has made many men of courage from her youth," Johnny nodded. They ordered their meals. They had a long and leisurely discussion on many things, from his job to the war effort and events back in Germany. Seigmire related that he had visited his birthplace before the war, and went on to describe in glowing terms the progress and wonders of the Fatherland. Johnny let him continue. Rudy wanted to talk. He used fast-flowing words with flashing eyes, caught up in emotion. At no time did he ask Johnny's business, so determined was he to express his own views. "I have seen you here before," he finally purred.

"Yes, I drop in once in a while when I am down this way," Johnny calmly replied. The conversation progressed, as Johnny appraised the man before him. There was no doubt that he was pro-Nazi, with a fervor that left one breathless. He had nervous energy in abundance, as well as intelligence bent only by fanatical dedication. After their congenial evening, they shook hands on parting, agreeing to meet in four days for another round of food and chat. As Johnny drove home, taking a devious route for protection, he felt pleased that the first plateau had been reached.

"Great, Johnny!" Cliff expounded enthusiastically later that night when de Graff phoned him at home. "Tell Gerti to put on the coffee pot," he instructed. "I'll be over in ten minutes." Cliff was only a short drive away, over on Graham Boulevard. Gerti had coffee ready when he arrived and gently knocked at the door. The two men promptly began discussing what Rudy could be up to. They continued talking into the early morning hours, well after Gerti had retired. A seed had been planted. In time, they expected it to grow and bloom in their infiltration operation. It was just a matter of water and proper care.

Friday evening came, and Johnny deliberately turned up late for his restaurant appointment with Seigmire. Apologizing, he explained that he had been out of town and had just arrived back in Montreal an hour earlier. Seigmire barely heard Johnny's words, so anxious was he to talk about Germany. He explained his theory of Hitler's success as Johnny listened intently. "Not only do I feel this way," he proclaimed with pride, "but several of my friends do also."

"The world is small," Johnny stated, drawing him out. "I was beginning to believe Montreal had few true patriots to the Führer's cause."

"Not so!" Seigmire said defiantly. "The police had arrested some of the big people, but there were still pockets of believers in Montreal. These groups shared their thinking, and would rise again to carry on despite the RCMP. The Mounties only arrested those they knew. It was just the tip of an iceberg that was taken in," Seigmire concluded, his face flushed with pride.

"Men cannot accomplish much singly. With the core gone, those remaining need to unite in order to survive and carry out a solid collective effort," Johnny stated coldly.

"True," said Seigmire, "but it will come, that I am sure of, for already small groups are regrouping and have meetings. My friends and I have heard of one such group and in time there will be hundreds," Seigmire added.

"You and your friends do not belong?" Johnny questioned.

"No, they are not for us, for we are mostly businessmen. It would be awkward, for their ways undoubtedly would not be ours. We have heard mention of some, but do not care to find out who they are or where they meet. We have our own group." With that, the two men agreed to get together again a week later, when Seigmire would bring some of his associates. "It will be a stimulating evening," he boasted, "good food, good company, and then we can go over to my apartment for a fine talk." De Graff told him he would look forward to it.

Cliff and Johnny conferred the next day in Harvison's office. They agreed that the plot was thickening. The following week, Johnny was again tardy when he met with Seigmire. As at the restaurant, he did not want to appear overly eager for the meeting. This time it was at the suspect's compact flat off Sherbrooke Street. Rudy's home was smartly decorated with floral drapes against ivory walls, colorful pictures, assorted chairs, and two blue Chesterfields that pressed the wall-to-wall crammed bookcase almost out of existence. "Captain, I would like you to meet my friends," Seigmire announced, gesturing with a flourish toward the assembled group seated around a table. A maze of four additional beaming faces greeted Johnny. Miller Smitz, the first newcomer Johnny acknowledged, was a short, plump man with a round, glistening face and thick fat hands. He was an accountant. Fritz Hummer was next. He was conservative looking, of medium height and weight, immaculately dressed, and displayed the wealth of his profession as a fur merchant. Hummer had shiny black hair, carefully parted, overshadowing his pasty white face and high forehead. Numerous gold fillings glittered in his restricted, thin-lipped smile.

Martin Monger, the night watchman, was built like a thin reed, topped with a flat nose and horn-rimmed glasses. Chestnut hair gave way to dark, hollow sockets of brown eyes, darkly circled with thick black creases. High cheekbones did nothing for his pockmarked complexion. Finally, Johnny met Hans Klein, the chemical engineer, with whom he was well acquainted after reading Harvison's files. Klein was a large man, six foot four (1.93 m), and well built. Slightly bald, Klein flaunted a wide smile on his half-moon face of docile inactivity.

Amid a meal of homeland dishes, they bantered for a while before gorging on their recollections of Deutschland in vivid, colorful tales. Johnny volunteered little but noted everything. Several hours later, they were toasting Germany-this and Germany-that with wine glasses held aloft. Feeling the effects of heavy food, and now the ample wine, the conversation swung into a channel that de Graff was anticipating. Each in his own way praised Hitler's efforts and glories. Then they took turns damning the Canadians and the Western world to a complete downfall, and ended by puffing up their own personal plans for action. The wilder the plan, the more stimulated the others became, caught up in and aided by the bobbing nods of assent. Johnny listened with rapt attention, remaining silent in order to appear to be the deep thinking man of wisdom.

Ideas ranged from a bomb attack on the large Saint Hubert Air Force Base near Montreal, to setting fire to the Canadian Industries munitions plant just outside Montreal in Sainte-Thérèse, to the assassination of key Montreal officials.[9] Each sympathizer craved action, from his dismal comments to his mesmerized outbursts. Johnny smiled inwardly at their wild jabber and complete lack of caution in front of a newcomer. Arguments and loud discussions ensued as freely as running water, without regard to or awareness of de Graff's quiet presence and lack of participation. They carried on like this for several minutes, as Johnny knew they had in each of their previous meetings. People can sometimes be harmless in what they say or proclaim, but de Graff knew full well that anger and frustration could burp up an "I'll-show-you type" who would be uncontrollable.

Johnny waited for the pause that comes when the wind is spent and the sailor becomes aware once more of his tranquil surroundings. He was ready. It came! "Captain Burger," Fritz Hummer, the fur man, began, swinging all heads in his direction, "you sit back and say little. What are your views, may I ask?" Only the ticking of a mantel clock broke the stillness as every pair of flashing eyes centered on Johnny. He felt totally safe and certain in what he was going to say, as he waited for the long, silent, thoughtful pause to take effect and prepare the stage.

"Gentlemen, you are all of my devotion, but you rant and rave in circles with your poppycock plans and disorganization!" They dropped their smiles in quick succession, their expressions turning from dismay to affront. "You babble on like old ladies without purpose of thought or sense of direction!" Johnny fired off both barrels in a booming, authoritative, arrogant shout. Astonishment held them transfixed. "You call yourselves Nazis, but I can assure you Hitler would have the lot of you shot as bloody incompetents!

"Arcand has been arrested," Johnny went on, "while you whine, wobble, and puke around like aimless children with big plans, big mouths, and no brains! None of you deserve to lick the Führer's boots, let alone plan his conquest of Canada!"

Not a muscle, not an expression, changed as they sat spellbound. De Graff lunged in for the kill. "Not one of you has military training. Not one of you soft-handed swine has known the true cause, purpose, training, plotting, and the power of ultimate overthrow and success!" Two nodded; he had them. The others sat staring in stupefaction. Then Johnny berated them for failing to ask him who he was, what he did, or where he came from. Because he spoke German, they had accepted him without question. "I could be an RCMP man, or an FBI agent, or all kinds of things, but your plans are so loose that your security is nonexistent. You'd let any stray cat or dog into your fold without question!"

Their faces went pale and they began to tremble in fear. Johnny paused now, waiting for the aggressor. "Who are you?" demanded the bolstered but uncertain voice of their host, Rudolph Seigmire, uncertainly. The others, uncomprehending, looked on.

"I am Captain Burger, Hitler's spy leader for Canadian espionage!" Johnny thundered. Before they could catch their breath, he soared on, "I was landed here by submarine to seek out and enlist Nazi supporters and coordinate all Canadian spy activities in the name of the Führer. Any true German who fails to follow my orders can be shot as a traitor to our cause. Heil Hitler!"

They rose en masse and raised their arms in the Nazi salute. Johnny's vehement bombast left them no choice. They returned to their places, rigid, attentive, and still in a thunderstruck daze, but now beaming with pride and admiration. De Graff grumbled on that he now had to supervise another group of misfits, and that he had other groups in the city and across Canada. That was why he had no time to waste on misguided fools who thought they could operate on their own without experienced control and direction from Berlin. "I have been in this business too long to be fooled," he concluded.

A long pause followed, as each in his own way recovered from the criticism. But Johnny continued the attack, roaring, "Do you claim allegiance to Hitler and the Fatherland?"

"Heil Hitler!" they shouted in unison.

"Do you wish to serve the Führer and the German victory?"

"Ja!" they thundered.

"Do you realize, as humble little men, that you can damage the German cause with your ill-conceived and ill-coordinated plans not approved by Berlin?"

"Ja!" they shouted.

"Are you willing to follow my orders and commands or be shot if not obeyed, in the Führer's name?" Johnny thundered.

"Ja!" they proclaimed in regimental unison.

"Good," Johnny said softly as he withdrew his automatic pistol from the back of his belt and carefully laid it on the coffee table in front of him. All eyes in his audience were instantly glued to the cold black steel.

"Now," he said abruptly, "I will explain how I operate, how you operate, and how it is going to be." They nodded agreeably. "First of all," Johnny continued, "all your plans, all your ideas, come to me first, understood?" They moved their heads up and down in agreement. "Then and only then do we discuss them. If I deem they are feasible, only then will I send them on to Berlin for approval. We may wait months, or even years for an approval, but when they say go—only then and not sooner—will we take action, understood?" Without waiting for an answer he emphasized that any independent sabotage could result in a tightening of Canadian laws, which would make it much more difficult to gather information. And information was what Berlin wanted.[10] De Graff went on, explaining that each of them was an expert in his field, which was exactly what was needed. No one was to know of their meetings without Johnny's advance approval. Total security was of the utmost importance. Each man could meet other members, outside of their collective meetings, only at prearranged and preapproved times and places. All other gatherings were forbidden.

"Do any of you know if you were watched going into the restaurant tonight or in nights past?" They shook their heads. "See what I mean, no security? Why, the whole force of the RCMP could have been waiting, and you would not have known. Know why I was late?" Johnny demanded.

"Nein!" they replied firmly.

"For the simple reason that I checked the place out for any signs of surveillance, to protect us, before I even walked down the street."

They mumbled praise for Johnny's ingenuity. He had them in his hand. He let them speak, showing great allegiance and respect for their new leader. They covered in detail the rules and aims of their unit, until each understood with pride and quiet fervor his personal membership in such an elite group. The net was cast. Each man was told to obtain specific information from his place of work, which would test their allegiance, devotion, and skill. They could not count on Captain Burger for funds, as there was little money around since Brazil declared war on the Fatherland on August 22. Money for the Canadian operation had come via Brazil.[11] With this, he had said enough for the moment. Johnny agreed to meet them in a week's time at a prearranged place. They were given explicit instructions for getting there and were ordered to travel alone. Separately, at ten-minute intervals, everyone left, taking the numerous exits the building afforded.

When S.A. 235 arrived home, Gerti made him a bite to eat and he phoned Harvison to tell him the news. Cliff was so taken with the names and descriptions of the newcomers de Graff had brought him that he worked very late that evening at headquarters, updating and researching his ever-expanding files. Cliff and Johnny conferred the next morning in his parked car off Park Avenue. "They accepted you last night, Johnny?" Harvison asked after his agent had related the details.

"No question there. Yes, I believe I'm in, and the next meeting should solidify it," de Graff explained. He told Cliff that he had given them some basic assignments in order to find out just what information was available to each at their places of employment. The Hydro engineer appeared impatient to get started. The furrier, by contrast, was perhaps the rebel in the group, so Johnny planned to watch these two closely. Of the three remaining individuals, he pegged them as follower types who would not ask many questions.

"Good," Cliff smiled. "Now we're getting somewhere. I'll check out these new ones and get more background on each. I'll give you a call on what we find out. Meanwhile, watch your step and keep us posted." As they parted, Johnny knew he had a lot of checking up to do on his own.

The group's second meeting took place on the sloping hillside overlooking Park Avenue and the wide open spaces of Fletcher's Field. A ballgame was in progress below that had drawn a good-sized crowd. Seated on the grass slope, the members addressed Johnny with respect, as one by one they related their findings.

Martin Monger explained his rotating shift as night watchman, sometimes working a 4:00 P.M. to midnight week, followed by a graveyard shift and a midnight to 8 A.M. tour the following week. The warehouse was a bonded dockside building used for international trade in all manner of things, from machinery to tobacco. Monger doubted that he could carry any item out of the warehouse undetected, as port security was tight. But he could advise Johnny on all the ships in the harbor and obtain copies of their cargo lists. "A ship carrying munitions?" Johnny asked.

"Oh yes, I am sure I can get the details without much trouble," he proudly replied.

"Do so," Johnny commanded. "And bring a copy of the ship's manifest to the next meeting." Monger was pleased with the assignment.

Fritz Hummer knew of a black-market contact who claimed he could supply anything requested. He hesitated about giving the man's name and location, but fortunately the others turned on him before Johnny did and he relinquished that tidbit. Johnny told him to keep his eyes and ears open for additional contacts they could use.

Miller Smitz, the accountant, was familiar with various business assets, cash pickups, and deposits in his roving occupation. He was willing to expertly cook any set of books and by so doing steal funds to support the cause. Dates, times, and places of Brinks armored car collections and deliveries also formed part of his knowledge. Johnny asked him to put everything down on paper for their next rendezvous.

Hans Klein, the chemical engineer, was certain that he could obtain any ingredients they might need for explosives and volunteered to bring along small samples of each. Seigmire could hardly wait for his turn. Almost cutting Klein off, he finally stammered in excitement, "I have access to every blueprint for all Hydro installations in Montreal and throughout the province of Quebec," he began. This would have a direct bearing on practically all places that depended on electric power in the province, and not just private homes. Places that were vital to the war effort would be affected, such as the Arvida aluminum factory, near Jonquière and the Saguenay River. The Arvida was one of the biggest aluminum plants in the world. Since the manufacture of aluminum requires lots of electricity, the factory was built in such a place as to be able to use the rushing waters of the Saguenay.[12] Johnny could only imagine what would happen if power was turned off in the province.

"If Hitler wants this part of Canada blown up or propelled into total darkness with a complete electrical shutdown, I can do it," Seigmire said, with eyes that were almost glassy. "Adrien Arcand would have seen to this, had he and his men not been arrested," he lamented.

"Can you copy some of these blueprints?" Johnny asked.

"Oh yes!" he expounded. "I deal with all of them daily, and we have a copier right in our engineering office. No trouble at all." He agreed to obtain the greater Montreal layout, including all stations, transformers, and key diagrams. "Montreal in blackness!" he laughingly exclaimed.

"Remember," Johnny commanded them, "you are to do nothing on your own. The material and plans you provide will be forwarded on to Berlin." They and only they would get back to Captain Burger with the green light. He underlined that he took orders just as they did. The higher-ups in Berlin would give the timing, date, and go-ahead. Johnny stated that no one in the room could proceed with any sabotage without Berlin's sanction. They knew what was best. They were the only ones in command of the total world picture. He asked if everyone understood this key point of the "leadership principle." They nodded their assent. The group separated, agreeing to meet again when Johnny phoned Seigmire with the time and place. Rudy would relay the message to the others by phone. Klein walked down the slope with Johnny, planning to go in opposite directions once they reached the sidewalk.

"I guess you are very busy with all your responsibilities," Klein remarked.

"No time for myself, I can tell you," Johnny replied firmly.

"You handle the group near here, too," he stated as a fact.

"I head up hundreds," Johnny returned. "Which one are you referring to?"

"Oh, I overheard a brief conversation the other day on a street corner," he replied. Two men were talking in German, and although he only caught a bit of what they were saying, they mentioned that a meeting would be held on Friday night at the stone house near Fletcher's Field. One man was giving the other directions to a location below the hill's rim. Klein felt he should mention it because these men were certainly not following the orders for tight security.

Johnny's mind flashed quickly, startled by this gem of a disclosure. "The bloody fools," he steamed. "I will fix them for their stupidity. Not only do they have the meeting place wrong, but the date. God, it's like bringing up a bunch of children!

"Thank you Klein," Johnny smiled at him. "I'm grateful to you and will take the matter in hand." Hans Klein shone like a beacon. "Tell no one of what you have just said to me," Johnny commanded.

"Not a word," Klein responded promptly. "I have no intention of being shot. Heil Hitler!" He spun around and walked briskly away. Johnny later made a call to Cliff from a corner drugstore. Fortunately, he was there. "My home in half an hour," Johnny stated.

"Agreed," he replied. They hung up.

"Good God! You had yourself a night of it, Johnny," Cliff remarked after hearing the evening's details seated at Johnny and Gerti's kitchen table. "The boys and I will have our work cut out for us, sifting through all of this fresh material," he proclaimed.

"Did you get the photos of our meeting?" Johnny asked.

"Yes, they should turn out well with that night camera," Cliff replied. "The lab is developing them now. My fellow wasn't spotted?" he asked.

"Not a glimpse of him," Johnny remarked. "He was too far away to be noticed; thank heaven for the telephoto lens and your lab specialist."

"Amen!" Harvison sighed.

"The Hydro man is a fanatic who poses a real threat in his position," Johnny related. "We'll see what he brings in, but I know from what he said, it will be a real eye opener."

"As soon as you get those blueprints, pass them on for our evaluation," Cliff replied. Then they discussed Klein's revelations about the conversation he had overheard. Cliff phoned downtown to have the house plotted and identified and the background material on its ownership unearthed.

"We have two days to find out all we can about the place and put it under surveillance," Johnny told him.

"Why just two days?" Harvison asked. "Good surveillance is time consuming if you want all the facts."

"Two days only, Cliff, for I plan to walk into that meeting," Johnny informed him, much to Cliff's surprise. Staring at de Graff incredulously, he soon recovered.

"That's suicide, Johnny—you don't know who they are, and they don't know who you are. Good grief, you can't just show up and take over!" he exclaimed.

"I can and I will, Cliff," Johnny told him flatly. "I know how these birds operate. They are uncontrolled at present, and if they are Nazi plotters, they are very untrained. For all we know, they may just be German Canadians having an innocent party. Your men should find that out before I attend the meeting." They argued back and forth, but Cliff had learned about Johnny's mind and when it was set. He eventually agreed, once de Graff had explained his plan. He left to follow up on the research needed in the short amount of time available. Johnny tiptoed into the bedroom, crawled into bed beside his Gerti, and fell asleep.

Cliff phoned late the next evening. "We pinpointed the house and the owners," he related. "A German couple, no record on them to date. They have a German boarder living upstairs, and every week, either on a Wednesday, Thursday, or Friday night, they have several guests over for a get-together in their front living room. Certainly looks as if it has potential. We are having the house watched and should have more for you later."

Harvison called again the following afternoon with more details and arrangements for that evening. Nine o'clock that night found Johnny waiting inside a phone booth down the street from the stone house. Ten minutes passed before the phone rang. A voice at the other end said, "There are five men in there with their cars parked outside."

"Thanks," de Graff replied. "Inform Inspector Harvison I'm on my way." Five minutes later Johnny was standing before a thick wooden front door. He rang the bell.

Seconds passed and then the barrier swung open to reveal a short, gray-haired woman who looked at Johnny curiously. "Sorry to be late," Johnny apologized in German. "I hope I am not the last to arrive." She seemed perplexed, but had no time for hesitation as Johnny was now in the entrance hall and in the process of taking off a light raincoat. Taking the garment from him, she hung it up, gestured for him to follow, and proceeded to lead her guest down the short hallway to a wood-framed glass door that led into the living room. As they approached, the mumble of conversation within grew louder. "They're all in there," she said softly. "They have just begun." She disappeared down the hallway into the rear of the house. Johnny opened the door and entered.

Six men, sitting around in a circle, abruptly ceased talking and looked up as Johnny approached and took an empty chair beside them. They stared in disbelief at this bold, unknown addition. One man turned to another and whispered in German, "Who is he?" The other shrugged, "I don't know!" A fragile, gray-haired little man, whom Johnny took to be the host, stared at him, puzzlement on his tiny face. "Sir, who are you?" he demanded in the polished German of the well educated. "I think you have walked into the wrong home."

"Are you all from the Fatherland?" Johnny demanded. Cautiously they acknowledged that they were. "Like me, do you support the German state and her cause in time of war?" Johnny asked emphatically. Fascinated, they nodded in agreement.

"Then, gentlemen," Johnny assured them, "I do not have the wrong house. For your information, I am Captain Burger, German spy leader for Canada and under direct orders from Berlin. I am in charge of all Nazi groups in Montreal and in Canada." He told them that the purpose of his visit was to inform them that they were under his command from that moment on and would operate only on his explicit directions, like all the other Nazi groups in Canada. No further independent operations would be taken unless Berlin told him to initiate such actions.

An hour later, they sat spellbound. As Johnny finished his authoritative speech of directives, threats, and commands, they were left limply nodding in agreement, capable of only one-word answers to his questions. Like the other group, they ate up the military harangue and succumbed to de Graff's role of deception. Pointing his finger at the two men who had had the conversation on the street, Johnny lit into them unmercifully for their carelessness. They shrank under the attack, frustrated and puzzled as to how he knew.

Seated in the dark wood–paneled English-style living room, they became united in the cause of National Socialism over the course of the evening. Kris Volter, the host, was captivated and set the tone of support. The rest of the group was a motley pack, but they had three things in common. First, all were blue-collar workers: two brothers were in construction; another individual was a mechanic; there was also an electrician and a railroad-yard worker. Second, they all lived in the same apartment building, off St. Lawrence Boulevard. Finally, they knew they were disorganized and were anxious to be led. To a man, they were devout Nazis. They broke up late that evening and, like the other group, walked away with a head full of rules and regulations for the glory of the Third Reich. Johnny said he would contact them about their next meeting and was the last to depart. Cliff's men had their license numbers and names to begin developing new dossiers.

The files became even fatter at the next gathering of the first group, when Seigmire proudly remarked that he had brought Johnny the blueprints of part of the Greater Montreal Hydro circuits. While the cold winds of early November 1942 whipped around outside, he claimed that he would have the rest within the month. He had already assembled and copied them over the years in hopes that Germany could use them.

Johnny praised his efforts and those of the group and said that their hard work would be forwarded to Berlin. Later that night they scheduled their next meeting, and then one by one each man departed with renewed dedication to the cause. Johnny lingered until just Seigmire and he remained. Seated together, enjoying a midnight cup of coffee, de Graff began to look more deeply into Rudolph Seigmire's mind and dreams. Seigmire showed no hesitation in sharing his innermost thoughts. Prodded on by Johnny's questions, he confided that over the past twenty years he had saved up the tidy sum of Can$20,000 with which he hoped someday to purchase a small farm. This was the dream for which he had cut so many corners, his boyhood ambition of being closer to nature. De Graff wished him success in attaining this goal, praised his efforts in the group, and expressed the hope that he would succeed in their missions to come. The dazzling flakes of the first snow had replaced the wind as Johnny left the warm apartment and confronted the night's cold.

Cliff was overwhelmed when S.A. 235 presented him with his report of the evening's undertaking. The sample packets of various chemicals donated by Klein, shipping manifests, long sheets of dates, times, and figures from the accountant, added to Seigmire's Hydro contribution, created a windfall for Cliff and his men. The rebel and furrier, Fritz Hummer, was the only one who arrived empty-handed with not a scrap to report. He had remained silent during the meeting. His reticence was ignored by the others, but not by Johnny. He felt more and more that the furrier offered an internal threat in the subtle things he said and did not say.

A visit to Johnny's Fletcher's Field group later that week again proved worthwhile, except that the two brothers in home construction craved immediate action. They wanted the green light to blow up the Canadian Marconi Company at one end of Thornton Avenue in Mount Royal. Johnny held them in check despite the small cluster of supporters they seemed to have influenced. By demanding plans of their proposal in three weeks' time, which Johnny yet again said would be sent on to Germany for approval, he was able to calm them down. In so doing, he saw that it might eventually take a little more to control the two brothers. They did not care for Johnny's instructions but finally acknowledged that each person must follow orders.

"My God!" Johnny mused as he drove home after the encounter. "Blow up the Marconi factory! Good grief! That operation is located a few blocks from my home!" The Marconi Company produced telephones, switching equipment, wireless radio components, early TVs, and radar. It was both a civilian and a military contractor. It was also adjacent to the Montreal train tunnel. There was a busy railroad spur right behind the plant and over the tunnel during the war. Many of the long trains that rambled down this line carried tanks, trucks, planes, and other armaments, and had onboard guards manning aircraft guns. De Graff phoned Cliff to suggest that he advise the electrical plant's security staff to continually check their grounds and yard area. "Also," he added, "I think you had better advise the army guards at all railroad tunnels to check out their areas carefully. I have no idea what these extremists will do on their own." Cliff's men did check the local tunnels and in one of them discovered a crudely made bomb that was poorly wired. Once it was defused they rested easier. Johnny thanked his lucky stars for their fast action and training. The pattern unfolding before them looked like it would take all their efforts to contain. Had the RCMP not had an inside man to assist them in supervision and control, Nazi espionage might well have run rampant in Montreal.

18

A MAN FROM THE SEA

On November 10, 1942, a day to remember for the gusting early snow and sleet that had increased with the week, Gerti called her husband to the phone to say that Cliff was on the line. "Johnny, can you be ready in a half-hour for a trip up to New Carlisle on the Chaleur Bay in the Gaspé area?" he asked.

"Sure, are we flying or going by train?" Johnny inquired.

"By car," came the reply. "No trains are running because of the weather, and the airports are all closed."

"Okay, so we go by car," Johnny confirmed. "Now, what do you plan to do way up there?" The trip was more than four hundred miles (643-plus kilometers).

Harvison informed Johnny that, together with Sergeant J. R. W. "Pete" Bordeleau, they were going to pay the New Carlisle detachment of the Quebec Provincial Police (or QPP) a visit.[1] The QPP had just phoned to say they had apprehended a freshly landed German spy. Johnny quickly packed a small overnight bag, and within the hour the three men were on the road out of Montreal.

The weather had other ideas about a journey, however, as their vehicle plowed ahead in a freezing rainstorm on its way to the community at the eastern edge of the Gaspé Peninsula. Angry squalls buffeted the car, demanding all of Bordeleau's skill as a driver to keep them on an icy highway that could barely be made out. The road conditions slowed their progress to a snail's pace. While Pete twisted and turned the steering wheel, Cliff shouted the background details to Johnny over the howling wind.

On the morning of November 10, Werner Alfred Waldemar von Janowski, a suspect of medium height and average build, walked into the Carlisle Hotel, owned by Earle J. Annett Sr.[2] Slightly disheveled and carrying two battered suitcases, he asked in French for a room so that he could bathe and have a shave before lunch. New Carlisle, a small town that thrived on summer tourist traffic but died during the fall and winter months, was not used to strangers at that time of year. Annett was also aware that during wartime his isolated town, amid a cove-dotted and secluded shoreline, offered an ideal refuge for spy landings from submarines. He asked the visitor if he had arrived by bus, to which the man replied that he had, despite the fact there had been no bus arrivals for hours. The proprietor became aware of a peculiar odor that accompanied the guest; he could not place it, but it was later determined to be an oily aroma that permeates the clothes of persons who have spent long periods under water in submarines.

Assigned to a room, the guest bathed and shaved and soon appeared downstairs for a meal. Suspicions bothered Annett as he checked the man's room, passing up the two locked suitcases but retrieving from the wastebasket a discarded matchbox from Belgium, long unavailable in Canada.[3] Once informed that the visitor intended to take the afternoon train to Montreal, Annett dispatched his son, a taxi driver, to the police office to relate the details. He later returned to drive the guest to the station. With this forewarning, the QPP was able to have a plainclothes corporal, Alphonse Duchesneau,[4] among the passengers on the platform when von Janowski arrived at the station.

Boarding the same train as the stranger, Duchesneau purposely took a seat next to him. A conversation ensued in which the suspect, with a touch of a German accent, claimed to be a radio salesman from Toronto. Together with this and the background information from Annett, the policeman decided to confront von Janowski directly before the train moved. He identified himself, much to the man's surprise. Claiming that there must be a misunderstanding, the German produced a Canadian registration certificate from province of Ontario, in English and French, in the name of Braulter, with a Toronto address.[5] The policeman noted that such forms issued in Quebec were in both English and French, whereas all other provinces issued them to residents in English only. This proved to be a fatal error in the fake documentation given him back in Germany.

With the QPP corporal intent on inspecting the man's bags, the suspect admitted that he was a lieutenant in the German navy who had landed by U-boat 518 the previous night. He claimed that he had decided to bury his uniform in the sand, switch to civilian garb, and desert his mission. He insisted that he be allowed to retrieve his buried military apparel and be accorded prisoner-of-war status under the Geneva Convention. The suitcases he had with him on the train contained a radio transmitter-receiver, more civilian clothing, a loaded revolver, nearly Can$5,000 in old currency, and US$1,000 in American twenty-dollar gold coins.[6] He was permitted to retrieve and don his uniform, then kept under close guard at Annett's hotel while awaiting the men from Montreal. The Quebec Provincial Police's original call to the RCMP contained only the briefest details, as Cliff explained. Even on that basis, the RCMP had immediately imposed a total news blackout of the incident.

After breakfast on November 11, Johnny entered the hotel in New Carlisle by a side door and stood unnoticed behind von Janowski as he sat in the lounge talking to his guards. Cliff got word to the QPP officer in charge to have the man locked up in the local jail in his civilian clothes. In the short space of time it took for the officers to carry out these instructions, Johnny was able to learn enough from the conversation to form some preliminary opinions.

The prisoner was soon safe in a cell under the close eye of a veteran World War I warden, who pursued his job with soldierly dedication. Up to this point, von Janowski had not seen Johnny, Cliff, or Pete. Using the convenience of the warden's office, they asked that the prisoner be brought before them. While waiting, Johnny told Cliff that from what he had overheard of the suspect's use of French at the hotel, he had been in the French Foreign Legion, an observation Johnny based on two uncommon words in his French.[7] Furthermore, Johnny felt strongly, this was not his first visit to Canada, a conclusion Johnny reached after hearing that some of his words combined English and French Canadian phraseology.

On entering the room, the man clicked his heels in true German style and gave Cliff a sharp bow. He immediately demanded in English to be allowed to wear his uniform and be accorded treatment as an officer and a gentleman. Cliff responded, "Nuts, I believe you are a spy! So sit down and shut up until I speak to you!" It was crucial that they establish at once whether he was put ashore alone or as part of a group. There was also the possibility of turning him, that is, compelling von Janowski to work for Canada as a double agent.

Executed spies are without value. Following a capture, all intelligence services first attempt to open up the prisoner, thereby assessing his value and mission. Once this is accomplished, the possibility of conversion to a double-agent role is usually considered. Von Janowski's true story and assignment had to be assessed before the RCMP could begin to consider the alternative to executing him as a captured spy. Had he been in uniform when arrested, he could have been classified only as a prisoner of war and put in confinement. As he had been caught in civilian clothes, however, and confirmed as a German officer, his deception afforded him no protection from the death penalty.

He began by saying he was to meet a Frenchman in Montreal and pass on the two suitcases to him. Cliff asked his contact's name, but von Janowski did not know it. He was supposed to begin the conversation by asking "Parlez-vous français?"[8] It was explained to him that all the people in this town were French, so he had better begin again. Annoyed, von Janowski then repeated the story of deserting his mission in hopes of obtaining prisoner-of-war status. To his claim that he was an officer in the German navy, Johnny had an answer. He told the prisoner that he was a navy man himself, adding, "You may have seen a ship once in awhile, but you're not a navy man. You wear the stripes of a senior lieutenant of the German navy, and you say you are only a lieutenant. You're the dumbest devil I have ever seen in my life."[9]

All agents were given two or more cover stories to memorize in the event of capture. Now, with von Janowski's first attempts laid bare, he grabbed for his final alternative. Abruptly he stated that he was not a naval officer but a captain in the German army. While stationed in Brussels, months earlier, he had been exposed by the Gestapo for living with a girl who was one-quarter Jewish. Because of this crime, he was propelled into the espionage service, agreeing to this mission to Canada rather than face imprisonment at home. He swore that his role had been forced upon him. Once in Canada and safely secluded in Montreal, he planned to abort the mission and passively sit out the remainder of the war. This reasoning fell apart when Cliff reminded him that he had been apprehended with the two-way telegraph set in his possession on the train. Was this not unnecessary luggage under such circumstances? Von Janowski realized that he had run out of explanations.

Cliff and his two assistants then began to plant seeds of conversion and mistrust. "How come German intelligence, so skilled and so clever, would hand you two dead giveaways?" they asked. He looked confused. "The large, obsolete Canadian bank notes you had were discontinued here over five years ago and are totally out of circulation," they continued. "Also, the blatant blunder with your registration certificate in two languages, but issued from Ontario."

Johnny was likewise puzzled over these two points, since he was knowledgeable of von Janowski's superior, Admiral Wilhelm Canaris, head of the Abwehr, or German military intelligence. Canaris was an extremely capable man who would not have allowed such obvious blunders had he not personally wanted the mission to fail. If this was the case, he had set up von Janowski to be apprehended. In fact, Canaris was one of those already plotting against Hitler.[10] A year later, in 1943, the Führer would have Canaris arrested. The admiral was executed for treason near the war's end.

While de Graff claimed that there were four, officially, only two German spies ever landed in Canada.[11] Werner von Janowski was the second. Marius Alfred Langbein, the first, came ashore in New Brunswick on May 14, 1942.[12] His assignment was to watch the Allied ships leaving Halifax. Langbein resided in Canada for a time before the war. He buried his gear east of Saint John in the region of St. Martins and managed to report ship movements back to Germany for a couple of months before changing his mind. He deserted and went to Montreal, where he was soon arrested in a brothel. The stationhouse sergeant hinted that if he gave a false name for the arrest form and posted Can$25 in bail, he would be let go until his trial. This break allowed Langbein to walk out of the police station.[13] He promptly moved to Ottawa and began calling himself Alfred Haskins. Thanks to Abwehr money, Langbein lived in cheap hotels until December 1944, when his funds ran out. He then turned himself in to Canadian authorities.

Werner von Janowski's case was different, for he had been caught red-handed. But the easy apprehension appeared strange to Johnny, because back in Berlin Admiral Canaris formulated each mission with competence. Thrusting his probe deeper, Cliff confused von Janowski with the gold coins. The old currency would have made it difficult to use, thereby creating suspicion in those approached by the Abwehr agent. It was frankly pointed out to the German that such basic errors by a competent organization showed either no concern for his safety or that the mistakes were made on purpose. Noticeably shaken by the conversation, von Janowski sank into thought. Finally he sighed, got up, and walked to the window.

In a square across the street, a group of medal-strewn World War I veterans had assembled to celebrate November 11, Canadian Armistice Day. They were paying their silent respects together with fellow townspeople, a ceremony that further shook von Janowski. Much later, he related that he had been informed that the people in Quebec were in revolt. Winking, Cliff handed Pete and Johnny each a large, obsolete Canadian bank note. Pete held his up to the sunlit window, examined it, and, shaking his head, returned it to Cliff. De Graff did the same without comment. The spy was captivated and confused, and then became angry when Harvison, deceiving him, stated that the bills he had been supplied with were counterfeit. That did it. Von Janowski smashed his fist on the table, cursing the Abwehr and the Gestapo, which he now saw as working together to plan his operation's failure and resulting execution.

He babbled rapidly that he had been landed by sub and that until his arrest he had every intention of fulfilling his assignment. During the heavy rainstorm the previous night, he had paddled alone from the submarine in a collapsible one-man rubber lifeboat. Once he reached Montreal, he was to set up his radio and contact his superiors in Hamburg twice a day. Germany would advise him of their information needs, which he would seek out and report back to them. So obsolete were their directions that they had told him to establish contact with Adrien Arcand and his group, the Nationalist Party. Unknown to von Janowski, by that time Arcand had been in jail for more than a year. Even so, the incarcerated head of the NP still claimed that the party had fifteen thousand members in the province of Quebec alone.[14]

As part of von Janowski's orders, he was to arrange for the arrival of future agents classed as low-level expendable saboteurs. He was informed that Arcand's party was devoted and extremely well organized. They were to provide help in obtaining vital information and resources. He acknowledged that when in Marseille he had joined the French Foreign Legion—within whose ranks no French-born national was allowed. After he had given five years of service to his unit, at the outbreak of the war he returned to Germany, where he was jailed because of his Foreign Legion affiliation. His father, an influential Nazi Party member, was able to arrange for his release and conscription into the German army. He also married at that time.

Special schooling in sabotage in Brandenburg, west of Berlin, followed, along with an eventual assignment to villages near the border with Holland. Wearing Dutch winter clothing over their German uniforms, they entered the Netherlands ahead of the Nazi invasion and initiated covert acts of sabotage. After completing their assignments they left Holland and entered Belgium wearing Belgian military uniforms. They committed similar acts of espionage there, again in advance of the German forces.

Following the defeat of the Low Countries, the group was posted along the English Channel as one of the advance destruction units for Germany's planned invasion of Britain. When the landing in Britain was called off, in mid-September 1940, von Janowski was returned to Brandenburg for additional instruction. His subsequent assignment was to Brussels, where he established counterespionage groups made up of civilians. Von Janowski was promoted to the rank of captain and was decorated with the Iron Cross. The Gestapo then stumbled onto the relationship with von Janowski's quarter-Jewish girlfriend, arrested him, and placed him in a concentration camp. There he endured hardship and brutality until he finally volunteered for foreign intelligence missions. Several weeks of intense preparation in Hamburg followed. This education was very basic and did not include instruction in how to make explosives from local materials in Canada. He concluded his story with a sigh and then demanded again that he be allowed to put on his uniform—but this time he added the request to be tried and executed without delay. Cliff told him that because he was a spy apprehended in civilian clothes he could not be accorded the protection afforded by the Geneva Convention. Von Janowski thereupon clammed up.

Signing for his release and change of custody to the RCMP from the QPP, they bundled von Janowski and his belongings into the car and set out on the long trip back to Montreal. Pete drove, with Cliff sitting in the front passenger seat. Johnny sat in the back with the handcuffed prisoner. Lieutenant Wilfred S. Samuel of naval intelligence, another German speaker, sat on the other side of von Janowski.[15]

From the start of the trip, the prisoner kept going in circles about his rights, a trial, and an execution by firing squad. Everyone in the vehicle got so fed up with this blabbering that von Janowski was told in no uncertain terms to shut up or he would be gagged. Unknown to Cliff, Johnny took out a small length of string he had in his pocket, fashioned it into a hangman's noose, complete with thirteen rings, and played with it before the curious eyes of his backseat companion. Von Janowski's gaze never left Johnny's hands as de Graff placed a finger in the little noose and drew the loop tight, ever so slowly. Von Janowski watched intently for twenty minutes without a word and then, with terror in his voice, demanded to be shot.

Gazing at him wistfully, Johnny calmly replied that no one captured in Canada was ever shot. "I demand to be shot!" he shouted again. Cliff turned around, not noticing the toy noose at first, and gave the man a stern look.

"We shoot no one in Canada," Johnny stated softly to the pale man, gawking at the miniature noose. "Spies are hanged here."

"That is not so!" he retorted. Von Janowski began to cry, pleading, "You have to execute me by firing squad, that is the law!"[16]

"No," Johnny soothed, "we hang spies, slow and easy, for bullets are costly and needed in the war effort. Once spent, they cannot he used again. A hangman's noose, however, is silent, inexpensive, simple to set up anywhere, and can be used again and again for hundreds of hangings, without replacement."

Johnny thought Cliff would have a heart attack on hearing the deception. Such remarks were not in accordance with RCMP regulations. Then again, Johnny was not governed by them, as were Cliff and Pete. De Graff was a free agent on loan to the Mounties and thereby able to say and do more without serious repercussions. Harvison looked angry and shook his head, indicating that Johnny was not allowed to threaten the spy in this way. Pete coughed—Johnny was sure to cover up a chuckle.

"You cannot hang me, spies are not hanged!" the frightened man shrieked.

"We can, and we will!" Johnny stormed, fed up with his nonsense. "Unless by the time we reach the towers of Quebec City, before Montreal, you come clean and agree to save your neck from the noose, by cooperating with us."

"I won't do that, you have to shoot me by law!" he pouted now, with far less conviction.

"Make up your mind, friend," Johnny snapped. "We do not shoot; we hang here, a long, slow, twisting end." Johnny thrust a finger into the little noose again and spun it ever so slowly after pulling it tight. De Graff had von Janowski terrified. Cliff turned away to face the front. Von Janowski sank into his own black thoughts.

The battlements and spires of Quebec City soon appeared on the horizon. Johnny pointed them out to the trembling man. "Time's up. What is your decision?"

Shaking like a leaf von Janowski stammered, "Don't hang me; I'll tell you all and do what you want!"

"Okay," Johnny answered. "We guarantee your life as far as Canada is concerned, and Great Britain, [but] if you have any death on you from [the] occupation forces of Denmark or of Sweden or Norway or of Holland or of Belgium, we will hand you over to these governments after the war is over."[17] The rest of the men in the car smiled in quiet satisfaction.

The Royal Canadian Mounted Police's "C" Division (the Quebec branch of the RCMP), headquartered in Montreal, must have appeared huge to the captive off the submarine. Booked, fingerprinted, and photographed, Werner von Janowski was registered as dark blond with blue eyes, five foot eight (1.73m), and thirty-eight years of age. He was finally led down long halls to be lodged in a closely supervised cell in the Atwater Street building. Following a brief stop at a small Quebec City restaurant on their return trip, von Janowski had satisfied his appetite, which seemed to pacify him into somewhat of a state of resigned calm. Quietly he had revealed that he was Polish born and provided other tidbits of his past. Much more information would come to light in the weeks that followed.

Gathered in Cliff's office, with their man secure floors below, they began to go through von Janowski's luggage and personal effects. Sewn into the lining of his thick topcoat, they retrieved his telegraph code and decoding books. German-made VD pills, foreign matches, a candy bar, an attractive photo of a woman he had claimed was his German wife, along with other items, were all placed on a table. After they were registered, Harvison's next problem was to turn the spy around completely, so that he would have no doubt whatsoever that von Janowski was cooperating honestly and fully. Cliff had to make sure, as well, that they did not have a triple agent on their hands.

If they could be certain of his leanings, the next issue was where to keep him, since he could not serve Canadian plans confined to a cell. They needed a preferably central location that was not suspicious looking. It needed to be safe and escape proof. It also needed to be a place where a guarded von Janowski could be kept twenty-four hours a day while transmitting the RCMP's prepared messages to Hamburg. The magnitude of the situation was discussed for several hours. Suddenly Johnny startled Cliff by saying, "If you can get Ottawa to approve the expenditure, I will convert the basement of my home into such a setup, and our man can work from there."

"Great idea, Johnny, but would you and Gerti really be willing to have Werner living under you?" Cliff asked.

"Sure, if Ottawa will agree to pay for the material required and the additional food, for Gerti will have to make all his meals and likely feed his guards as well," Johnny added. Cliff quickly arranged to have the proposal dispatched to Ottawa. Both men hoped for a positive reply and a minimum amount of red tape. Johnny volunteered to do all the labor himself without charge, so that it would be done to his specifications and so that the odd renovation would be safeguarded by having no other laborers involved who could talk about what was going on at the Palmerston Avenue address.

Once Johnny informed Gerti of the proposal, she embraced the idea wholeheartedly. Ottawa fumed and fussed over the plan for a while but finally gave in, no doubt under strong RCMP pressure. They would finance the project. Days later, surrounded by two-by-fours, wood panels, water pipes, vents, and bags of concrete, de Graff began work. Gradually a compact subterranean apartment took shape. In two weeks it was complete.[18] The RCMP paid Johnny Can$514.61 for the work plus Can$135.61 each month for room and board for the prisoner, food for the guards, and gasoline for his car.[19] Von Janowski would have a large bed–sitting room, containing shower, toilet, and sink. Adjoining his room was a good-sized guardroom with the only door into an enclosed hallway. Off to one side of the restricted passageway, across from the furnace room, was the telegraph alcove. A small kitchenette flanked it. A solid door in the vestibule, at the base of the stairs leading up and out, made the total package a completely self-sufficient unit. Midway up the stairs was a second locked door to the garage and another to the kitchen, from which Gerti passed the meals down to the guards below.

The small, ground-level basement windows were covered with a thick grill and solid steel bars cemented into their casings. Fastened into the ceiling above the bedroom and guard's quarters were air ducts that eventually merged. Johnny extended the fused duct to his and Gerti's bedroom in such a way that he could hear what was being said below, without being heard by von Janowski in the basement.

The spy had no means of escape from his room without passing through the always-occupied guardroom and opening the far door to enter the hall. Even then, at the end of the passage, he would be faced with the locked door at the base of the stairs, then the locked door into the garage, followed by the locked door leading to the floor above. Cliff confirmed that Werner had no chance of escape, once he had inspected the newly completed quarters.

Two plainclothes armed RCMP police would be with von Janowski around the clock on eight-hour shifts. Over a period of twenty-four hours, that meant stints of three two-man guard teams. When von Janowski was not occupied with the twice-daily job of sending or receiving messages, the sentries would take their prisoner out for exercise and activity. Over the year that followed, Werner von Janowski was accompanied to movies, sports events, walks, and even downtown shopping, always under the watchful eye of his armed and physically powerful escorts.

An RCMP specialist in telegraphy and electronics, W. Gordon Southam,[20] appeared at all scheduled broadcast times. He also checked and maintained the equipment, including the fifty-foot mast Johnny put up in the backyard.[21] RCMP code experts made up the messages to be sent to Germany and decoded them upon arrival. In Ottawa, RCMP commissioner Stewart Taylor Wood felt that the situation called for expert advice. Von Janowski represented the biggest catch of his career. Wood contacted Sir David Petrie, the head of MI5 in London. Petrie agreed with Wood and sent Cyril Mills across the Atlantic to act as supervisor during the initial stages of von Janowski's conversion. Mills was one of the more knowledgeable case officers of the "Twenty Committee." This was the famous XX or "double-cross" unit of interdepartmental experts who specialized in the tactical deception of Nazis. The effectiveness of this group allowed Britain to control a large number of German spies in the United Kingdom by turning them into double agents. In the spring of 1942, Frank Foley took over the XX operation.[22]

Almost as soon as Mills arrived in Montreal, he and Harvison were arguing. Perhaps it was a question of how von Janowski would be interviewed and treated, perhaps posturing over who would be in charge down in the trenches, perhaps a little of both, but the two men quickly got into a simmering dispute that continued for the entire period of von Janowski's Canadian stay. The controversy began with Mills's changing the name of the case from "Braulter et al." to "Operation Watchdog." "Watchdog" became the code name applied to von Janowski.[23] The RCMP was slow to adopt the new label. Then, too, Mills's interrogation techniques were much more unyielding than Harvison's. Without intending it, a good-cop, bad-cop scenario came into play, using a host of angles in the battle to force von Janowski's cooperation.[24]

Besides the RCMP and MI5, representatives from the Canadian government and the intelligence services of the army, navy, and air force all contributed to the team that dealt with the captured German. This select group evaluated Nazi requests sent to their prisoner for every shred of military information connected with Canada and the Allies. They determined details to be sent back and those to be ignored. However, if all the information conveyed to Germany via telegraph was false, this would eventually be spotted; the Abwehr would know it had been fooled and would cease contact. It was therefore vital that some truth be included with the falsehood. This was no easy task, as all such replies were screened and agonized over for their desired result. De Graff's function was to keep the security tight on their apparent dual agent while he remained on his premises. Beyond that, the RCMP took over all other items and overall unit control. Gerti would cook for the men, while Johnny pursued his activities with his two clandestine Nazi groups. Still, Johnny never slept without a loaded revolver under his pillow in case von Janowski tried to escape.

Werner von Janowski's role in all of this was vitally important. His finger had to be on the telegraph key to tap out the Canadian messages. Like fingerprints, no two ways of using the telegraph key are alike. Werner's touch was recorded by a machine and known to his German receivers. His personal tap had to correspond to his impulse chart, established before he left Germany. Otherwise the Nazis would smell a phony from the differing readings on the meter-style recorder.[25]

The team encountered a problem when several attempts to raise Hamburg and Berlin, using the transmitter-receiver von Janowski had with him, all ended in failure. The apparatus was just not powerful enough, even during ideal weather conditions. Southam then arranged for a much larger unit to be sent over with a massive fifty-foot outside aerial, replacing the one on the roof. After it was installed in the backyard, secured with strong wires and hooked up to the new transmitter, this soaring monster solved the crisis—too well.

So powerful was the new equipment that the first test broadcasts could have tipped off the Germans. A number of adjustments were quickly made, and the device was tuned to the correct strength. Once Southam's adjustments were complete the deception began, and Hamburg and Berlin began rejoicing straightaway over the first contact from Montreal and the spy they called "Bobbi." Everything was off and running. Beginning on November 28, and for some eight months thereafter,[26] the coordinated deception proved invaluable in providing Canada and her allies with numerous insights into Germany's plans and actions.

The Nazis' thirst for details on Canada's war effort was wide, varied, and revealing. Arranging replies involved the input of the entire group in a mammoth task. It was fortunate that Berlin called for only two transmissions daily; otherwise the timing would have been impossible. Initially Hamburg displayed great interest in the transmissions. They asked for information on the strength of military units stationed in and around Montreal and Quebec City. They suggested that Bobbi visit Quebec to report on the kinds and types of vessels in the harbor. Hamburg was also very keen on knowing the location of submarine nets in the St. Lawrence River. Demands regarding paper types, weights, inks, and dyes used in Canada's national registration certificates and ration coupons presented an ideal opportunity for trickery. This knowledge was beyond an agent's expertise, since it was of a highly technical nature and difficult for anyone to obtain.

Cliff determined to draw Hamburg out by having von Janowski inform the Nazis that he had actual copies of these documents. At first, it was considered following this up by requesting the forwarding procedure. But this idea was discarded because of the possibility that the Germans might get suspicious. The first statement was transmitted without the instruction request, in the hope that Hamburg would provide such details. This would enable the Canadians to learn the telegraph style and address of Nazi agents both at home and in neutral countries. Unfortunately, no word of any document routing was mentioned by Hamburg. It soon became very evident that the Germans wanted everything but planned to reveal nothing. It was either a one-way street or they had in fact been tipped off that von Janowski was in custody.

Conversely, what the Abwehr requested gave everyone a probable picture of what the Nazis knew and did not know, as well as an indication of some of their weaknesses. Hamburg requested information on the Mosquito bomber, which at that time was on the secret list. But it was due to be unveiled and released to the Canadian public the very week of the German query. Ottawa agreed to delay revealing the aircraft for two months, so that when von Janowski transmitted the Mosquito's specifications back to Hamburg, the Nazis would feel that they had obtained a real windfall. Hamburg was elated with the transmission and proud of their spy. Cliff, Johnny, and the rest of the team all chuckled heartily at his greatly enhanced value.

The remainder of Johnny's time continued to be taken up with his Nazi groups in Montreal. Captain Burger initiated all contact; at no time were the fascist sympathizers remotely aware of where he lived or how to reach him by phone. Such were the orders of their superior. They had accepted Johnny's periodic visits and weeks of absence as part of his responsibilities of handling like units all across Canada. During this period, de Graff would often visit the Montreal suspects individually in their homes.

One evening the two brothers in construction from the Fletcher's Field group handed de Graff a large box of dynamite and another box of caps they had stolen from work over the previous weeks. The containers had been hidden near Sainte-Anne de Bellevue following a building job.[27] The two men literally itched to blow something up, even after Johnny again told them that Berlin had to approve everything first. The brothers seemed upset at Johnny's inaction and the constant waiting for word from Germany. De Graff left with the highly volatile wooden boxes after browbeating the two terrorists into submission with heavy talk. Arriving home, he phoned Cliff and told him of his new possessions. Harvison asked Johnny to take them off somewhere and destroy them before they blew up his street. The Mounties dispatched a pickup team, who carted the containers away and rendered them useless.

Seigmire, the Hydro engineer, had gotten hold of a mound of blueprints. His rabid manner and insistence on action posed a frightening problem. Running on his own, there was no telling what he could or would do. He was too restless and too eager to accept control much longer. Rudy's desire to eliminate all Hydro installations in the province was paramount in his mind. He had plotted and worked on it on his own for years. Cliff and Johnny decided that it was time to take him out of circulation once and for all. The key leaders of Quebec Hydro were brought in for a conference with Cliff. Pertinent but limited details were provided, only enough to enable them to follow their part of the plan to neutralize Seigmire. They departed united in the overall strategy.

The executives were to start a rumor in the plant to the effect that Seigmire was a Nazi. They began the story quietly, and it spread around until Seigmire's co-workers picked it up. Despite his repeated denials, weeks of taunts and isolation followed. Everywhere he went at work, the words "Stinking Nazi!" or some such insult greeted him. Deprived of sleep from this new worry, and somewhat manic anyway, he soon became a nervous wreck. By the time Johnny next paid him a visit, Rudy was a wreck as he recounted his sorry plight. De Graff, in his role as Captain Burger, got angry and told him he did not have to take that kind of garbage from anyone. "Quit them!" Johnny told him.

"What will I do without a job?" Seigmire asked, more worried than ever.

"I recall you told me you had $20,000 put away for a farm someday," Johnny replied. "I know that is your dream. I also know of a good farm close to the American border that you likely could buy and enjoy life. You'll not attend any more meetings, but you and Berlin know you have done your part." He brightened at the thought of a farm and was most anxious that Johnny let him know if it was still for sale. Johnny assured him that he would.

Cliff and Johnny soon found a suitable farm location within Seigmire's means but well isolated. Seigmire became ecstatic when Johnny showed him the land and buildings. He immediately quit his job, bought the property, and moved in. His settling down took him out of the picture and made him harmless. Seigmire's departure was explained to the other members of his group as a special assignment directive from Berlin. He had to leave Montreal and pursue more important matters. "Berlin received his Hydro blueprints and liked them," one remarked with group pride. "They sure did," Johnny told them. Well after the war was over, however, Seigmire could be found working his little farm south of Montreal with absolute delight and devotion.

Returning home each night, Johnny would slip down to the basement to chat with the Mounties and von Janowski for a few minutes. On one occasion, Johnny was in the cellar rooms standing beside one of the prisoner's suitcases. At the time, Werner was occupied with Gordon Southam in the telegraph room. Something caught Johnny's eye. Stooping down to examine the female photo inside the lid, de Graff discovered it was not the original picture they had seen of his wife, but one of a quite different woman. Examining it more closely, it revealed faint lettering on its lower corner, which read, "Queen Lingerie Shop, Queen Street, Toronto."

In a call to Harvison, it was agreed that Johnny would drive to Toronto and follow everything up. How this photo had escaped their earlier inspection Johnny did not know, unless von Janowski had it well hidden and brought it out when he felt safe. The shop in Toronto was not hard to locate, and a pleasant, overweight woman greeted Johnny as he entered. Her name was Olive Blanche Quance. To her inquiry if she could be of assistance, Johnny explained that he was looking for a friend named Werner von Janowski, and asked if she knew where he could reach him. Immediately the woman colored with anger, shouting that she knew the bum because she had married him many years earlier. She lived with him for two years, during which time he drained her of her assets. The woman had a fair amount of money before running into Werner. One night he took what was left of her savings and vanished. The last she heard, he was somewhere in Germany, and if she ever caught up with him she said she would kill him. "The dirty swine!"[28]

"That's none of my business," said Johnny. "I only want to find out where he is."[29] He thanked her and departed.

De Graff was right. The man the Abwehr called Bobbi had been in Canada before. He landed in Quebec City aboard the SS *Crefeld* on May 19, 1930. On December 20, 1931, he married Olive Quance, a woman sixteen years his senior. In August or September 1933, von Janowski allegedly left Canada for France aboard the SS *Ascania*.[30] Upon learning of Werner's first wife in Toronto, Cliff said he would dig up more and then sit down with their prisoner again for an enlightening talk.

De Graff beat his boss to it. "Greetings from your first wife!" he announced when he visited von Janowski in the basement the next evening.[31] "You're not only a spy but a bigamist! You're married to two women right now, one in Toronto and another in Berlin," Johnny shouted. Werner's face whitened, knowing that the RCMP had found out a few more facts. "Had we not picked you up for spying, we could have picked you up for bigamy!" Johnny stormed, leaving the unsteady prisoner in his wake. From the time they arrested this man, Johnny could not stand him. In de Graff's view, von Janowski was a weak coward and a poor excuse for a man.

Needless to say, the coming and going of cars and men, as well as the massive fifty-foot broadcasting aerial, aroused the suspicions of the neighbors. Coupled with their apprehension was the knowledge that the de Graffs spoke German. Cliff phoned one night to say that the RCMP had received numerous telephone reports from their Palmerston Avenue neighbors concerning the odd carryings-on at the de Graff home.

George Elliott, the chief of police in Mount Royal, had also gotten calls. Not knowing what they were all about but certain they should be directed to government authorities, he passed the details on to the "C" Division command center. A cover was needed for these activities that would pacify the concerned residents. Cliff came up with an idea in this regard that resulted in a gradual end to the crisis. Paying a visit to Elliott, he explained that Johnny was engaged in highly technical research on war equipment. No other statement or details were given. The police chief, being most cooperative and anxious to do his part, assured Harvison of his full cooperation in mollifying the curious and making outside patrol protection available for the research installation. Thereafter, Elliott cut off inquiries by informing those who phoned that he was well aware of what was going on at 49 Palmerston Avenue. It was government research work and their mystery neighbor was patriotically serving Canada.

Werner von Janowski played his double-agent telegrapher role well—under close supervision. Yet, through his subtle words to the guards and other minute clues, the RCMP and Johnny knew that they could not let their vigilance down for an instant. He would turn around again if presented with an opportunity.

Often, while remaining quiet in his bedroom, Johnny would listen through his air duct to the captive chatting with the guards below, totally unaware he was being heard upstairs. Werner would switch from sounding out his captors to baiting them with taunts and threats. Finally tired of his own games, Watchdog would hush up and sit in scheming silence.

As for the two pro-Nazi groups Johnny was monitoring, both were attracting others to join. Purposely, de Graff kept each original nucleus to its initial size by insisting that all newcomers remain in the field. In this way they would report to members of the team, who in turn would keep S.A. 235 informed. They respected this method of security, which resulted in the RCMP's uncovering more names and material in ever-increasing quantities.

One evening, during a gathering of the Fletcher's Field faction, the situation Johnny had been expecting arrived. He endured heavy verbal crossfire for the group's inactivity. With fanatical unity they demanded to take the initiative in implementing some of their many plans. Doubt had started to circulate among them about the long delays in Nazi approval. This obstacle in Berlin caused them to doubt Johnny. Captain Burger was really the one who was stalling the operations, they proclaimed. "What guarantee do we have that you really are Captain Burger?" a spokesman for the assembled group demanded. "You have stated so from the beginning, which we accepted. Now we want proof."

"Thanks for asking," Johnny replied firmly. "I was waiting for this moment and wondering why it took you so long to ask the question. I am grateful you ask, and by so doing, it indicates to me you are alert," Johnny added. In this game, one always had to be several steps ahead and well prepared for such queries. At times, an individual's ingenuity could be sorely put to the test.

"You must have direct contact with our Fatherland?" one member stated, more as a question than a fact.

"I do," Johnny replied, glancing at each man's reaction. He noticed in their faces that the confrontation was a total expression of their thinking. It was planned by them rather than some individual spur-of-the-moment inquiry.

Oddly, the subject was dropped as suddenly as it appeared, which surprised de Graff, since they did not complete their attack. No more was said that night, but Johnny knew it was not the end of the scrutiny. Sure enough, two weeks later, the blade of the sword appeared. This time another member took on the role as spokesman-interrogator. Johnny was now well aware that they had held get-togethers in between the scheduled meetings. "You say you have contact by telegraph with Berlin?" the questioner asked.

"I told you before that I do," de Graff retorted. "Not one, but many telegraph stations are under my supervision."

"Would you then ask your headquarters and Deutschland center in Berlin to air the soldier's song 'Laura, Laura, Laura' on a given day?"

"Sure," Johnny answered. "Name the day."

"Please ask Berlin to play this song next Wednesday."

"It will be a pleasure," Johnny slammed back with full confidence. "Do you want the short version of the song? No, wait, in fact, I will choose and it will be the full song as played to our troops." The men looked at each other, quite bewildered. "Okay, listen to your radios next Wednesday, Thursday, and Friday nights," Johnny commanded. "I cannot say that the station will play it right away, for I do not control their airtime bookings. As to date and time, I must leave it to them. It is quite possible that they can play it on Wednesday night, but if not, then the other two evenings are open to them. I will see you Thursday night, the same time next week. Listen to your radios and I will do likewise, so we'll all be certain of our facts," de Graff said, calling the meeting to an end. At home later that evening, Johnny phoned Cliff about the test. The following day, they had von Janowski send the request out on the telegraph under Gordon's supervision. The song was played on Berlin radio the following Wednesday night, as directed. Cliff, Johnny, and the rest of their team were delighted and relieved.

The night after the broadcast, as Johnny entered the room at the Fletcher's Field meeting house, his doubters all clicked their heels and snapped to rigid attention, with arms raised. "Heil Hitler!" they barked in unison, all smiles and full of beaming praise for their leader. Johnny's accusers now became his most loyal and devoted supporters. He had been tried and found "not guilty."

That evening they asked again if they could enlarge the central group, for there were many recruits asking to be accepted into the inner circle. "No, that is impossible, for we have to work only with a small inside body for security purposes. This was for our own good and for theirs, too. Meanwhile, we should consider ourselves the privileged ones." They strongly agreed.

Johnny also announced that he could not see everyone when they wanted to see him, but only on scheduled nights. "I am not responsible for you alone," he informed them. "I have hundreds and hundreds of agents all over that fall under my command." Using this method and their awe of what they thought was Captain Burger's vast power and network, Johnny got them to accept his rules. It provided Johnny with having them adjust to his schedule and thereby excuse any absences he may have from time to time. Aware that he had each of their phone numbers and addresses, they likewise expected and received Johnny's irregular night calls and personal visits as part of their life.

Despite the established convention, de Graff became more and more aware that the furrier, Fritz Hummer, was slowly becoming estranged from his group. Cliff and Johnny were positive that he was a troublemaker. Hummer was far from passive, despite his silence. The man had two loves, his fur business and his burning dedication to the Nazi cause. Yet Fritz's obvious displeasure with the group's inaction was quite plain. Johnny knew that his way out would be to go it alone or start his own personal band, which could cause uncontrolled havoc.

They decided to disrupt Hummer's first love. Cliff made the arrangements. At their next meeting, the furrier, pale and nervous, stated with tired voice that he would have to give up his participation in the group. Questioned as to why, he explained with tear-filled eyes that he was experiencing great business problems. His suppliers were raising his wholesale prices; payments, once due in ninety days, were now due in thirty. In addition, his bank had refused a loan he was certain he would receive. He explained that he could be bankrupt soon if he did not find a solution to his sudden difficulties. The group allowed him to sever his relationship and concentrate full time on his business. That is, this was permitted under threat of death if he ever revealed what he knew. He agreed with a shaky "Heil Hitler" that he would remain silent. No one ever saw Fritz Hummer again. For the rest of the war he struggled just to stay above water financially. From time to time his debtors would slacken their grip, but never enough to allow him any participation in the group's activities.

In the meantime, 1943 had arrived for Watchdog, his handlers, and his guards. They continued to work in the Palmerston Avenue basement. All was proceeding as planned despite the now and again unexpected episode. One matter concerned the guards. Johnny felt that they were largely draft dodgers who had joined the RCMP to avoid the military. Regardless of his requests, they persisted in parking their police vehicles outside his residence instead of around the corner. They were also very lax on the way they let the prisoner do things, and von Janowski took advantage of this by having sex with one guard's wife. When Johnny reported this to Cliff, an investigation was begun that resulted in a guard change and the dismissal of a sergeant safeguarding the German. Only twice did Johnny strike von Janowski, and one of these altercations took place at this time. Werner had previously been smacked in the face for twice ignoring Johnny's order to do something. That cooled the Nazi for a while. But when he started up with the sergeant's wife, Johnny found out about it and told him to leave her alone.[32] Von Janowski answered, "Oh, she's just a fat old bitch, and anyway it's none of your business!"[33] De Graff instantly punched the German in the mouth and began choking him, saying, "No Canadian woman is a fat old bitch!"[34]

The most serious issue, however, had nothing to do with the amorous adventures of the man in the basement. There had been a number of leaks or near leaks in the press, beginning a little more than a week after von Janowski's capture with a report in a Memphis, Tennessee, tabloid that was picked up by *Newsweek* and published as a snippet on November 23, 1942.[35] Despite the best efforts of the RCMP and the Canadian Directorate of Censorship, small journalistic disclosures continued every so often for months to come.

Likewise part of these more somber events was an amusing occurrence one night late in the fall, when de Graff noticed something near the outside wall beside the basement windows. There was no snow as yet, and the ground cushioned his footsteps as he quietly approached the left side of the house, where he could discern the dark outline of a person's backside. The intruder was on his hands and knees, gazing past the bars into the spy's bedroom. Like lightning, Johnny lunged forward, grabbing the peeper by his jacket collar and lifting him roughly off the ground.

The man was surprised and scared as Johnny spun him around. It was a petrified neighbor. "What are you up to?" Johnny gruffly demanded, still retaining a firm grasp on his neck. The man fumbled for words, finally spluttering out, "There is something funny going on here, and I made it my business to find out what!"

"Have you seen what you wanted to see down there?" Johnny demanded angrily.

"I didn't see anything!" the frightened man stuttered. "There are thick curtains on the windows and I couldn't see through."

Johnny jammed his face into the trespasser's and seethed, "Then get the hell out of here! Go home and mind your own business or you'll really be in trouble, not just from me but with the police! Now get!" Johnny shoved him backward into a dark cedar hedge, where he tumbled head over heels, hastily picked himself up, and ran off.

Two weeks passed, and just as Johnny arrived home one evening, Gerti had a miscarriage. This was her second month of pregnancy. Fortunately her doctor arrived quickly and no complications arose. Gerti was back on her feet in a day, smiling brightly, but Johnny knew that she was crying inside at the loss of her second child. He knew how she longed for a baby of her own, but he hoped that she now understood, despite both of them wanting a child, that it was impossible. While they did consider adoption briefly,[36] Gerti had her mind made up that she would have Johnny's child.

Beyond this tragedy at home, de Graff and Harvison were soon uncovering new pastures that needed attention. "Johnny, there is a Canadian-German club on St. Lawrence Boulevard above a Greek restaurant," Harvison mentioned one evening in a parked car rendezvous on a secluded abutment to Pine Avenue off Côte des Neiges Road. "We have information it's a Nazi hangout, and, although small in size, could be influential in the local Nazi movement."

"Gee, Cliff, I have worked night and day up to my eyeballs trying to control and keep up with all these birds and their plots," Johnny responded. "Don't you have someone else you can send in?" he queried.

"No, no one but you, Johnny," Cliff stated, his face showing concern, not only for the additional burden he knew he was placing on his colleague, but aware that he and his men were spread very thin. Knowing Harvison's position and the long hours he devoted to his responsibilities, Johnny agreed to take on the additional load. He admired this slim cop so much that he felt he could never let him down, no matter what demands came their way. It pleased Johnny to please Cliff, and he knew the Mountie would appreciate it.

Seated at their kitchen table that night, Johnny told Gerti about it. "You can do it, Johnny. I know you are dog tired, but you can do it; get some rest, and in the morning you'll be right back into the swing of it, and there will be no stopping you." Gerti was right. As she had predicted, the following evening he was on St. Lawrence Boulevard, mounting the dark wooden stairs to the second-floor club. Heinrich Fellor, the Canadian-German club president, greeted de Graff as he opened the dented wooden door and entered a long dingy room, poorly lit and smelling of stale cigarette smoke.

Fellor was a medium-height, thick-boned individual who was seriously overweight, which his smiling, bloated face revealed. A brown belt stretched to its last hole still could not contain the rolling fat of his overhanging belly. He greeted Johnny in German without suspicion or caution, just the warmth of homeland hospitality for a fellow countryman. Through a smoky haze de Graff could see that the rectangular room was about fifteen feet wide and sixty or more feet long (4.57×18.29 m). Several men were seated at a round wooden table playing poker, leaving ten or more vacant tables with their empty chairs. Close to the entrance stood an unattended beat-up bar. Its back wall displayed not bottles but a large plate-glass mirror surrounded on both sides with bags of chips and peanuts. A solid red Coca-Cola cooler stood at the bar's end across from a back wall ledge. On the sill he could see a dark brown cash register of rare vintage.

Herr Fellor, whose extended hand plunged forward for Johnny's grasp, proceeded to take Johnny on an abbreviated tour of the club. The toilets were located off the main room, and at the hall's rear wall there was a door to a small office where they eventually sat and talked. The little room could not have been more than eight by eight feet (2.44 m^2), and accommodated a scarred wooden desk, two chairs, and a rusty, three-drawer, legal-size filing cabinet. Soiled walls radiated in the yellow brightness of a lone sixty-watt bulb suspended from the ceiling.

Fellor offered the German newcomer, William John Graff, an amateurish application form and a request for the Can$10 dollar membership fee, should he and his wife decide to join. De Graff gave him the money and completed the paperwork with his false name and address, which Fellor barely glanced at prior to filing it away in a wooden box. Explaining that the membership was small, only twenty couples, he began elaborating on the planned social activities, which included bridge contests, dances, and stag evenings. No liquor was sold on the premises. They only had bagged snacks and assorted soft drinks from the bar cooler. Fellor and Johnny then joined the four at the poker table. The men playing cards hardly looked up as they bantered back and forth in German. Johnny bought a bottle of pop, sucked on it for some time, and watched the card game in progress, appraising the players.

When the game finally broke up and the members departed, Johnny also left but promised to return that Friday evening for the club dance. Cliff was informed later that night that contact had been made. Johnny related that the club president was a German who worked for a Montreal newspaper. At heart he was a not a Nazi but a Communist, and he worked with Rebecca Buhay, secretary of the Canadian Communist Party.[37]

Johnny took Gerti to the dance that week, which claimed the distinction of having four couples on the dance floor, enjoying the recorded German tunes. Eight others attended, including six Jewish men, who sat on the sidelines talking vigorously without accompaniment. A few brave souls cut in to dance with the four wives, but apart from that the evening was a poorly attended affair. Over the weeks that followed, Gerti and Johnny attended more couples' nights, until they became so bored they began speaking about holding a total membership dance. For their enthusiasm in presenting the idea, they were elected to organize the festivities.

Updating Cliff on his intentions to get some pep as well as attract the membership to these dismal affairs, Johnny obtained permission to purchase beer for resale without a license. The de Graffs and one volunteer decorated the hall with colorful party streamers and bunting, and stocked the Coke cooler with grocery-store beer for the night's event. Johnny probably put some Pepsi in for himself, as he tried to avoid drinking Coca-Cola for political reasons. He felt Coke supported American big business too much.[38] The week prior to the big event, Johnny and Gerti went over the membership list, giving Cliff a copy, and sent invitations to each couple and unattached affiliate. On dance night, amid the blaring of sentimental tunes from the record player, the crowd danced, chatted, and drank away in honor of the finest event held in the club's history.

Gerti and Johnny got to be known as the top organizers of the association. It was maybe inevitable that Johnny replaced Fellor as president, only to inherit his red-figured balance sheets. Later, through more participation in the social events, the books swung into the black. By this time the membership had multiplied. Johnny came to know each member and enrolled the new pro-Nazis, Canadian Germans, and Communists alike.

By then Harvison's files were flourishing, as the new names, addresses, and descriptions were screened, checked, and recorded by the RCMP. There was surely a mixed bag in this net. Johnny continued holding the Canadian-German club meetings, the gatherings with his pro-Nazi groups, and the individual visits with the latter's members. He instructed these friends of the new Germany that should they see him in anyone's company—Communist, Canadian, or Nazi—he was to be ignored. They were to avoid the Canadian-German club, since his tasks for Germany demanded high skill, odd contacts, and no interference. They agreed, and Johnny never had occasion to scold them for breach of this rule.

One evening, prearranged through the contacts in the field, Johnny met an assistant of Adrien Arcand in a downtown alley. De Graff went well armed to this secret rendezvous. Amid the refuse containers and trash, he identified himself to Arcand's waiting companion. They had a brief chat and left as discreetly as they had come. It was a short meeting, but it was enough. Arcand's man walked away convinced that Johnny was the Berlin spymaster they had been promised. Once visiting his jailed leader, Johnny was certain he would say the battle was continuing, eventually providing him with valuable information to be passed on to the RCMP. This thinking proved to be correct. The Arcand remnants sent along their plans and the names and particulars of members.

The von Janowski affair took a different course. It began coming apart on March 5, 1943, when mainly the French-language press reported that a "Quebec member of legislature demands to know the whereabouts of German spy caught off the Gaspé. Is he dead or alive?" The representative, Onésime Gagnon, of the Union Nationale Party, had shocked Parliament by announcing that a German spy had been arrested in New Carlisle. The Canadian authorities managed to muzzle the papers where this brief passage had been printed. This included one journal from Ottawa, *Le Droit,* two from Montreal, *La Presse* and *La Patrie,* and three tabloids from Quebec City, *L'Action Catholique, L'Evémement-Journal,* and the *Chronicle-Telegraph.* Radio censors practiced more self-restraint and only broadcast those parts of M.P. Gagnon's speech dealing with the sinking of Nazi shipping in the St. Lawrence estuary. German shortwave transmissions the next day mentioned just the latter event. The newspapers received telephone warnings to watch what they printed in the future. The Canadian government avoided written admonitions to keep unnecessary documents on Operation Watchdog from circulating.[39]

Von Janowski's residence in the de Graff basement continued for another five months. The disputes between Harvison and Mills continued as well. There were arguments over all kinds of things, from clothing allotments for the prisoner to whether he should ask Hamburg station for more money to buy a car. Harvison thought the request would show that von Janowski wanted to get out and do some real spying—as they had asked. Mills felt that Bobbi had already been supplied with enough cash, and that asking for more would alert his Nazi superiors.

Assistant RCMP commissioner Frederick Mead, who drifted into an alliance with Mills, branded Harvison an amateur, a renegade, and a risk taker in the matter of what was being sent over the airwaves to Germany. Indeed, if Harvison had really handled the case so badly, why was he not removed? During the incessant bickering between Harvison and his team and Mills and his followers, what does seem clear is that von Janowski found enough space to inform Hamburg that he had been compromised. Werner von Janowski was a triple agent. The problem in understanding this for both the Canadians and the British was threefold. First, von Janowski was a manipulator. A better word might be a chameleon. He had a self-serving story for every occasion. He tried several times, for example, to convince his captors that he wished to switch his allegiance to the Allies, not just follow their orders as a POW. Second, he had to send his own messages, as those back in Hamburg knew his "fist," or precisely the way he sent Morse code. And third, the press in Canada could not be shut down on the story as efficiently as it could be in England, much to Mills's chagrin.[40]

On the morning of July 29, 1943, the *Montreal Daily Star* reported that at a meeting of the Quebec police and fire chiefs, the assistant director of the QPP, Léon Lambert, mentioned that individual members of the QPP had helped to capture more than just one spy in Canada. It was innocent enough until one considered that the Nazis had probably not landed more than just a very small number of spies in Canada off submarines.[41] Realizing this one morning at the breakfast table, Johnny telephoned an astonished Harvison.

"God, this is dynamite, Johnny!" he exploded. "Those damned fools have now blown our undertaking! I guess we only have about a month left with Werner before Germany realizes our ploy."

"No, we only have a week, Cliff," de Graff explained dejectedly. "Within a week, once the other papers pick up the story, it will be in German intelligence hands in Lisbon. After that, it's all finished," Johnny added. Cliff sadly agreed.

Seven days later, to the day, they all gathered downstairs for the final transmission to Hamburg. There was no question that they did not have the press clipping. The Canadians' last message read, "You've been had." Minutes later, the dots and dashes of the Germans' reply arrived: "We know. Goodnight."

The telegraph operation was quickly dismantled, and on August 24, 1943, Bobbi was whisked away to Britain for use by MI5.[42] Cliff escorted him to London and remained there for two months studying British intelligence operations before returning to Canada. At the war's end, von Janowski was released by the English and returned to Germany. Some time later, Cliff passed on a letter he had received from von Janowski, addressed to Johnny in care of the RCMP. Werner explained how valuable he had been to Canada during the war and asked Johnny to send him some food, "as life in Germany was very, very bitter."[43] De Graff still despised this man he called a snake. Six cans of dog food, with the labels removed, were packaged and sent to von Janowski with Johnny's compliments. After about a month, he wrote again to say the food tasted great and could de Graff send more.[44] The second parcel contained another six cans of dog food, but this time with the labels were left intact. Johnny never heard from Werner von Janowski again.

19

TO CATCH A SUBMARINE

By 1944, Quebec's pro-fascist groups had become restless again. Over a period of time, Johnny cut contact with the straggler Nazis who filtered their information to the blocs he was stewarding. He did not wish to prompt them into active roles in any way. The word had gone out, telling the fringe to lie low until contacted. This put potentially dangerous people on ice. Others were taken care of in a different way. The RCMP, for example, saw to it that the two construction workers who stole the dynamite and detonators were drafted into the Canadian army.[1]

The revelations about Werner von Janowski did not mention his role as a double agent. But, of course, the publication of his capture and imprisonment, brief as they were journalistically, caused a stir among the pro-Nazi groups and again placed Johnny under a cloud of suspicion. Members probed and prodded, asking if he was aware of the spy's landing and the press account of his unsuccessful mission. Johnny told them forcefully that he certainly was aware of the German's coming, ensuing arrest, and imprisonment. After all, de Graff went on, he communicated daily with Berlin. Before von Janowski left the Fatherland, they had advised Johnny of his assignment.

These sessions were so vocal with all of their demands for espionage that Johnny knew he would again have to prove himself. The members were tired of counting service badges on the street, ships in port, and lists of war materials from passing trains. They demanded results and finally stated they would not carry out any further mundane assignments. With Berlin and Captain Burger or without them, they clamored for action. Johnny had kept them in check for almost two years. Now, in early 1944, they were again biting at the bit.

Informed of the disorder, Cliff Harvison decided on a plan of action that would strengthen Johnny's hand. Fortunately, the police had in custody at their "O"

Division (Ontario branch of the RCMP) main facility in Toronto a previously captured German agent who was most willing to cooperate with the Canadian authorities. This tall, blond, autocratic individual had held an important rank in the Nazi Party in Germany. He was an ideal choice to play the role of a Nazi leader. Through the commissioner and headquarters intelligence chiefs, a meeting was arranged with Assistant Commissioner V. A. M. Kemp, the officer commanding "O" Division, and his Criminal Investigation Bureau colleague, Inspector George B. McClelland. They agreed to have the German brought briefly to Montreal so that Cliff could make use of his services.

Johnny thereupon made an important announcement to the members of his Nazi sympathizers. The top spy leader for North America would be visiting Montreal and had consented to meet with three representatives, one from each of the respective groups. They were all impressed, even more so when Johnny enlarged on the story, with fictitious details of the spy's highly successful and interesting exploits. He told them that Hitler himself had personally picked Johnny's immediate boss for the North American position. Fascinated and greatly uplifted, a clamor ensued as to who would be picked to meet the great man. Finally someone from each group, including the Arcand segment, was selected. A date was then given to the three chosen men, along with orders for each to wait by his phone on the appointed day for further instructions.

In early 1944 de Graff reserved a small suite in Montreal's Windsor Hotel for the planned rendezvous.[2] When the agent was ready, and under supervision in a room down the hall, Johnny phoned the three representatives and told them to make for the reserved hotel room immediately. They arrived quickly but were purposely kept waiting for an hour in the suite. At last the agent walked briskly down the hall and knocked on the door, whereupon Johnny admitted him. After a round of "Heil Hitler!" Johnny introduced him to the men, who were enthralled. He curtly thanked each for their work on behalf of the Fatherland, about which he stated Captain Burger had reported to him and to Germany. Then, shifting into an authoritative voice, he started settling accounts. Johnny left the room at this point.

"I am told that you and your associates are eager to get on with the business of sabotage. This is nonsense! We are not playing a game of fireworks! We are fighting a war, and you will follow orders just as soldiers in the field follow orders! I want no more of your idiotic talk of sabotage! When the time comes, you will get your orders. Until then there must be no more nonsense! Through the incredible stupidity of Adrien Arcand and a number of other local Nazis, plus some of those the Fatherland had sent to Canada, the apparatus was wrecked. Captain Burger and I are trying to bring it up from destruction to [become] a highly efficient operative network. Our task is not easy, but is crucial to Germany."

He then had them in his grasp. Continuing, the Nazi leader for North America said that the Canadian police had been lulled by their past successes and had fallen asleep. One single unauthorized act of sabotage would awaken them, and all the months and years of planning would be upset—again! When the day came, acts of sabotage would occur across Canada and the United States simultaneously. Until then, only fools and idiots would think of sabotage; and such fools and idiots would answer for their actions after victory.

He clicked his heels when he received no questions and gushed a "Heil Hitler!" After telling them not to leave for another half-hour, he departed as abruptly as he had entered. His performance, which the RCMP taped, had been literally spellbinding. The delegated men were awed by the phony Führer for North America and remained spellbound. They left thirty minutes later, fully convinced and determined to persuade the other members that they had seen the light. Once leaving the room, the RCMP's German agent haughtily strolled down the hall and around the corner to his waiting guards. Within the hour he was on his way back to "O" Division in Toronto. Thereafter there was no more talk of sabotage from Montreal's Nazi groups. Johnny's role had been well supported and solidified as a result of the bogus appearance. Indeed, from that point "until the end of the war, the RCMP, through Johnny, controlled the activities of the Fascist party in the Province of Quebec."[3]

As for the members of the Canadian-German club, S.A. 235 split them into political groups. Some, like the German Social Democrats, were usually trustworthy Canadians and wanted no part of fascism or communism. But the other Germans, along with members from Czechoslovakia and the Communists from Britain, were likewise a part of this soup bowl. Gradually, Johnny gave seven staunch Communists more and more attention and prominence. He bought extra dance prizes so that the Reds would be certain of winning something. In the limelight, they reveled much about themselves, to the disgust and annoyance of some of the Social Democrats, who finally quit. "The wheat and the chaff have begun separating," Johnny thought. One evening, during a club meeting, he made a suggestion. "We enjoy ourselves here, dancing and drinking while the war goes on. You know what we should do, take political training."

"Good idea," they all replied enthusiastically, especially the six Jewish men, who were staunch Communists.

"Well," de Graff continued, "if everyone agrees, here is what we will do. We are all united; even our Czech members are Social Democrats, with the majority of us being Communists. I have a book here, just arrived from Europe, entitled *The New Germany*." This was a chance to find out how strongly the club members felt about the opinions and philosophy of Karl Marx and others like him.

At once the Nazi-leaning and Social Democratic members took offense. "We're sorry, but we are not really interested in such readings," a spokesman for their circle remarked. "We'll still come to the club for dances and such activities, but not as study members." Agreeing among themselves, they left.

The departure of this segment delighted the Communists, who soon asked

Johnny if they could use the club for their party meetings. "No," he stated firmly, much to their surprise.

"Are you a Communist?" they asked.

"Yes," he lied, "but the club is still too open to other elements in our club membership to be a safe place to hold regular meetings." They relented, informing William John de Graff where they were holding their gatherings and extending to him an invitation to attend. Johnny did show up for a meeting, and he learned that they called themselves the German-Canadian Federation. He began attending their various functions and some discussion groups. They had branches in Montreal and Toronto. To provide as much cover as possible, Johnny joined the Labor-Progressive Party. The LPP was formerly known as the Communist Party of Canada, which had been outlawed and forced underground beginning with the implementation of the War Measures Act on June 6, 1940.[4]

The German-Canadian Federation funneled some of its money, obtained through social events and dues, into its newspaper, the *Volksstimme* (People's Voice). Johnny proved to be a very popular member, and on November 19, 1944, he was elected president of the group. Under his leadership the number of adherents grew from twenty-five to forty-five, all soon registered in the RCMP's files. De Graff evidently tapped a source of new members when he persuaded many wives of the existing group to join the federation.[5]

Fred Rose[6] dropped into the club on several occasions. A member of Parliament, Rose was later proved to be a covert Communist and jailed through the revelations made by the code clerk of the Soviet Embassy in Ottawa, Igor Gouzenko, who had defected to Canadian authorities. Twice in one week, Rose showed up at the club to invite members to a picnic to be held outside Montreal. He made many contacts, and a good number of associates from the club attended the outdoor affair, including Johnny.

Rose began the picnic with a strong pitch for donations for Yugoslavia relief. A witty speaker with wide experience in public life, he asked the crowd, "Who gives Can$100?" A few raised their hands. Johnny gave five dollars. By the end of the afternoon, Fred Rose had been reasonably successful. De Graff felt then that Rose was a Communist. He was smooth and never unethical in his public pronouncements. He stood for Yugoslavia against the Nazis, but he was so clever that it would be hard to say he was not also a Nazi.

"Cliff, keep your eye on that snake," Johnny told him. "Something stinks! He's trouble if I ever saw it, and not to be trusted." In addition to relaying his feelings about the man to the RCMP, Johnny also told MI6 when he was back in Britain. The hundred or so copies of intelligence materials that Gouzenko secured from the Soviet Embassy revealed that Fred Rose was a top Communist operative. It led to Rose's arrest by the RCMP. Also exposed was the existence of an active Soviet spy network operating in Canada and the United States.

To cover his trail, Johnny's part in these affairs was explained away to the Nazi groups prior to his joining the Canadian-German club. "When we win the battle for Germany," he had told them in imposing tones, "the next battle they would face would be a political one with the Communists." They had to do the job in Europe first, then the work in North America, and then proceed south, which should be easy enough to crack. The Communists were smart, Johnny told the would-be Nazis. "They use the best-trained men and the biggest arsenal to accomplish their aims. Only when they rule the Communists can they control them and have them in check," he repeatedly told the men. To conquer one's enemy, one has to know one's enemy. "So, if you see me with them, you don't know me." But if they heard something about their members and operations, they were to pass the information on to him. It was thus not difficult for de Graff to use the Nazis to get into the Communist organizations and at the same time keep his eyes on both factions. Later on, he later gave up his elected position in the club, which shortly went back to its original low membership and red balance sheets.

In addition to his Nazi meetings and Communist delving, one day Harvison passed on to de Graff an additional assignment. Cliff informed him of a German Canadian, Rolf von Linter,[7] whom the RCMP had under investigation. Von Linter ran a medical instrument and equipment sales office and showroom near Dominion Square in downtown Montreal, close to the hotels. Handing Johnny the thin file the RCMP had on the fellow, Cliff stated, "We have our suspicions he is a German spy, but have not as yet been able to prove it. I would like you to take him off our hands and see what you can come up with."

De Graff snooped around, making inquiries about von Linter and his business around Dominion Square, the hotels, and the various stores, including Eaton's on St. Catherine's Street. The man's entire business was the sale of medical equipment. Besides paying high rent for his office and large showroom, he maintained a very well-to-do standard of living. His expensive home in Westmount, an upper-class area of Montreal, had been bought for cash weeks after his arrival in Canada. Added to the list of peculiarities was the fact that his firm could not actually sell anything, since it could not obtain anything to put on the market. Such imports were not available during the war. A note in his file stated that no record had been obtained of his invested funds. The RCMP had every bank in Canada run a check to see if he had any accounts with them anywhere. It was a mammoth job that took three months, but no one had any record of an account in his name. Finally, since the name Rolf von Linter, or anything close to it, does not appear in *Lovell's Montreal Directory* for the years 1943 and 1944,[8] it must be assumed that it was an alias and that the residence he occupied in Westmount was in another person's name, or that the name was garbled in Gordon Scott's interviews of de Graff.

While the banks were being queried, Johnny continued his investigation and eventually met three Germans who frequently played a German card game called skat with the suspect. They accepted de Graff as part of the group, and even allowed him to participate in several games, but he could not come by any additional information on von Linter.

Then, out of the blue, Johnny learned that von Linter regularly flew to New York on weekends, returning every Sunday night. Also odd was the fact that he paid all his personal and business expenses in cash. Johnny could only surmise that his funds came through the underground, since there were no longer any German businesses operating in Canada. Tailing von Linter to the United States would have meant obtaining a visa that, even with Cliff's assistance, translated into delay, red tape, and questions.

The RCMP, through Superintendent Henri Gagnon,[9] told Johnny from the start to respect Canadian laws. Yet de Graff could see no way to get Rolf von Linter without reverting to the familiar guerrilla tactics he knew so well. Cliff and Henri had both harped on about Johnny not taking things into his own hands, despite the fact that his actions might produce results.

Johnny waited until he was certain the suspect's wife was away on vacation and that von Linter was off playing cards. Then, undetected, he broke into his Westmount home and carefully searched the house from stem to stern. He explored every drawer, nook, and cranny with gloved hands and flashlight but came away with nothing. Letters, papers, documents, all minutely studied and carefully replaced, failed to reveal any hint of a dual life.

Fed up and frustrated, Johnny returned von Linter's file to Cliff with a note stating that since he could not use a stick in this investigation, he would devise other methods on his own. The next day Johnny drove to the U.S. border in Plattsburg, New York, only sixty miles (96.6 km) from Montreal. He asked to be presented to an agent of the FBI on duty at the international boundary. Ushered into a room with a representative, he explained the details of the case and all he had learned about von Linter. "By Canadian law I cannot touch the fellow," Johnny informed the FBI agent. Following a phone call to Washington, D.C., the American said that the FBI would be interested in having a long talk with the suspect if he could be handed over to them unharmed. Johnny agreed, arranged a group of dates for delivery, and drove back to Montreal feeling much relieved. De Graff did not inform Cliff about these plans, since he knew his superior would hit the roof and stop everything cold.

Johnny cased the von Linter residence during the day and learned only a few more details about his habits. He had enough information and set the moment for action. It would be the following Saturday around bedtime. When the chosen day arrived, Johnny was lying safely in wait for von Linter under his bed in the dark-paneled, thick-draped master bedroom. Rolf's wife was still away. De Graff had tailed him to the evening skat game, making sure he was in attendance. After seeing him sitting at a table with the others, he doubled back to the suspect's home and let himself in by the side door off the driveway with a slim skeleton key. Johnny then had a three-hour wait for von Linter's return, if he followed his usual habits.

Johnny was nearly asleep when he heard a key in the front door, followed by the sound of someone entering. Rolf von Linter walked into the bedroom, flicked on the light, undressed, put on his pajamas, and went into the adjoining bathroom. Johnny listened while he brushed his teeth and gargled. The bathroom light went out, succeeded by the one in the bedroom. Creaking bedsprings told Johnny that he was at last under the covers. De Graff silently waited until von Linter's deep snoring resounded throughout the room. Carefully, Johnny slid out from under the bed, stood up, and gazed down at the exposed face slumbering before him. He uncorked a small bottle of chloroform and poured it onto a gauze handkerchief. Slowly he placed the soaked fabric over von Linter's nose and then gently pressed it down with fingertip lightness.

The initial whiff of the liquid caused him to mumble and toss slightly to one side in unconscious escape. Johnny pressed the handkerchief more firmly over the man's nose. As he inhaled the drug he shuddered, made an attempt to wake, but quickly succumbed to the strong sedative. Von Linter's head flopped limply to one side and his hands dropped away, indicating that he was out cold. Johnny immediately went outside to his nearby car and slowly backed it up the driveway to the dark side entrance, well screened from the street. He unlocked and opened the trunk before heading back into the house to gather up the man's clothes and then the subject himself. Von Linter was a tall, slender man, and there was no difficulty in carrying his limp body over one shoulder, wrapped in a blanket, to the waiting car. Johnny gently deposited him and his attire in the trunk and quietly closed the lid.

Returning to the bedroom, Johnny made the bed, tidied the room and bathroom, put out the lights, and locked the side door after checking the front. Minutes later Johnny drove down the driveway and headed out of Montreal for the Plattsburg border. The trip took an hour. When he arrived, there was little conversation. He transferred the slumbering von Linter to a waiting FBI car and sped back to Canada. Six months later von Linter was tried in the United States and given a fifteen-year prison sentence for spying against the United States for Germany.

The week after his little border trip, Superintendent Gagnon asked de Graff where von Linter was. The RCMP had not seen or heard anything from Johnny and was concerned. Johnny told Harvison what he had done, and Harvison proceeded to rip into de Graff like a bombshell. Afterward, he smiled and said in earnest, "Johnny, it's a good thing we did not know of this caper of yours. If we had, you would have been jailed for breaking the law. All I can say is it was damn lucky for you we didn't know about it." Johnny returned his smile.

Late one summer day found de Graff seated in Cliff's office, having quickly responded to an urgent summons. "I have a story you won't believe at first," he began. "But I can assure you it is true, Johnny. At its conclusion, I have a question to pose to you, that if answered in the affirmative could mean great risk to you and very likely your death." De Graff sat in thoughtful silence as Harvison revealed the details. Canada maintained twenty-four army-administered prisoner-of-war camps, set up purposely to receive enemy combatants captured overseas. Mainly scattered through the provinces of Alberta, Ontario, and Quebec, many of these camps were located in isolated areas, where wild terrain and the natural elements blended in such a way to make escape virtually impossible. Those camps not so situated were centered near highways on the outskirts on sprawling cities, like the prominent Camp 30 in Bowmanville, east of Toronto on Lake Ontario.[10]

Feller, at Grand Ligne in Quebec, was one of the second varieties of internment center. It was located some twenty-two miles (about thirty-five km) southeast of Montreal and about eleven miles (nearly eighteen km) from the U.S. border. Known as Camp 44, the principal building was four stories tall and contained a maximum of 750 German officers and prisoners considered by their records and character to be troublesome and potential escapees.[11] These men were classified as "black" owing to the threat they posed. Under the capable administration of army major Ray Fairweather, Feller earned the reputation of being the best-guarded camp in Canada. The complex had formerly been an agricultural school, but after being turned into a POW facility it was swallowed up by parallel rows of barbed wire and guard towers with searchlights. At one end of Camp 44 a bridge ran over the security fencing. During the day this arrangement let cooperative prisoners walk out of camp and go over to the Feller farm, where they worked in agriculture and the care of livestock. Strictly an honor setup, all well-behaved prisoners who wanted to were allowed access to the farm. There was never an escape attempt from the facility, since to do so would have immediately cancelled the rights of all prisoners to work on the farm.[12]

Incarcerated in Camp 44 were seven of Germany's leading experts in submarine technology. During the testing of a newly designed German submarine in the North Sea, the craft had to be abandoned. The British plucked the crew, including the seven experts, from the water after they had spent hours floating around in life jackets. The Reich wanted these key individuals back and tried a host of things to arrange their escape. Canadian naval intelligence made a startling discovery after examining a load of German Red Cross books destined for Camp 44. Hidden in the volume's bindings were coded messages, maps, Canadian registration certificates, and Canadian and U.S. currency.

Partially decoded, the messages were addressed to the prisoners' leadership and revealed an escape plan to be carried out by the seven Nazi specialists. They were to be assisted by twelve other detainees, who would play the role of decoys, running interference and causing confusion. Once free of the camp, the experts were to make for a specific place in New Brunswick, which could not be decoded. On reaching the assembly point, a special signal would be sent out to sea that would be answered by a submarine. The U-boat was then to surface and approach the shore to pick up the escapees. Where the sub would lie in wait was also unknown.

Naval intelligence had approached the commissioner of the RCMP about this discovery and had asked for police aid in allowing the prison escape to take place under controlled observation. When the escapees reached the place of rescue, an attempt would be made to capture the submarine. The Canadians knew from the decoded parts of the messages that it would be a newly designed snorkel type of vessel. This unique U-boat was still a mystery to Canada and her allies and it could produce a windfall of information if taken intact.

RCMP specialists and naval intelligence concluded that earlier messages to the prisoners, which had not been intercepted, probably held the key to the meeting point and submarine location. Shadowing the escapees for six hundred miles (more than 965 km) to an unknown site would almost certainly be impossible. Code experts then agreed to reexamine the donated books, particularly their bindings, as well as having another go at the monitored messages. All of this was in the hope of locating and decoding the two geographical coordinates vital to the plan. If the latitude and longitude could be found, the documents and messages would be replaced in the bindings and the books could enter the detention center in the normal manner.

Meanwhile, Cliff Harvison started at square one, Camp 44 itself, to see if an escape tunnel was in progress and, if so, to determine its path. Using blueprints, he studied the Feller's layout with Major Fairweather and concluded that such a tunnel would have to begin at a central building before heading out at least to the parallel ditch beyond the security fence.

Late one evening, well after lights out, Harvison and an RCMP technician crawled along between the fence and the ditch. Using a sensitive microphone attached to a long metal probe, they pushed it into the soft soil every few yards. It allowed them to determine that a tunnel was definitely in progress. Through earphones, they could hear the sounds of digging and soil removal, as well as the muffled tones of conversation. The authorities then took more accurate readings and realized that a tunnel was only months away from completion. They felt certain this was the right tunnel, for it was more than three hundred feet in length (91 m). Such a major undertaking would command a top priority in manpower over any other tunnel less demanding and adventurous.

Corporal C. Bayfield of the Ottawa RCMP Intelligence Branch provoked a cheer when he announced that, while naval intelligence was still unable to locate the submarine's position, the key to the pickup point had been discovered through decoding. On the basis of this breakthrough, the RCMP revised its plan. The prisoners would be allowed to escape from the tunnel. Groups of police, connected by walkie-talkies, would form at Feller's farm each evening after nightfall. Lying in wait nearly half a mile away (eight hundred m), opposite the camp's front gate and bordering the deep ditch, the Mounties' job would be to recapture the escapees one by one. This was to be done without alerting the next prisoner in line, since everyone would come out of the ground in timed intervals. When the last fugitive had been apprehended, they would all be shipped to another camp, leaving those left behind at Feller with the idea that the breakout had been a success.

The press and radio would be advised of a major escape but not informed that the prisoners were back in custody. Any German submarine located in the St. Lawrence or off Canada's eastern coast would try to monitor Canadian radio broadcasts and would be pleased to learn the POWs were on the loose. Arranged also were additional radio bulletins, prepared by the RCMP, that would be released periodically as the imaginary group of fugitives got nearer to the coast. The broadcasts would give the names and descriptions of some of the actual men in the German escape group, advising the public of their recapture. The seven experts' names would not be mentioned, allowing the officers on board the submarine to believe that the valued specialists were still at large and on their way.

The plan would become very risky at this point because the supposed band of escapees nearing the rendezvous point would not be Germans but a group of Canadian police and military personnel. They would give the correct recognition signal and board the incoming submarine. At that point, they would commandeer the vessel and crew at gunpoint. As soon as the takeover began, Fairmile-D speedboats concealed along the shoreline would rush out to provide armed assistance and reinforcements for the U-boat's potential captors.

"Well, Johnny, quite an undertaking, isn't it?" Cliff finally asked. De Graff nodded, amazed at the magnitude of the plot. "Would you, knowledgeable in submarines, German speaking, and experienced in such work, be willing to volunteer to head up the group who'll hijack the submarine?" Cliff inquired, looking at Johnny intently. De Graff paused briefly and then agreed.

"Okay, Cliff, I'll do it. When do you want me to begin? I can be away from the Nazi groups without causing suspicion anytime you say." Cliff peered at Johnny intently.

"Do you fully realize, Johnny, as much as we need you for this, your chances of surviving once you and your group draw your guns on board the sub and force the takeover are almost nil?"

"Yes, I know that, Cliff," de Graff replied. "It's vital to Canada to capture the snorkel, so that's really all there is to it. I have no wish to die, but if that has to be the case during a war, I would only be one of millions who won't be around after the smoke and dust clear."

"Have you thought of Gerti? What will she do without you if you are killed?" Cliff added. "She would have to get some menial job. Did you think of that? I know for a fact in your present line of work, MI6 does not offer pensions to the widows of their agents who die in missions not commanded by them." Suddenly what Cliff was saying hit a nerve that Johnny foolishly had never considered. Enlightened and embarrassed, de Graff knew that his wife was not a strong woman and would die from such taxing labor. Looking at Johnny with concern, Harvison witnessed the shock his statement had caused. He added that it was different for members of the armed forces and the RCMP, who had pensions for their dependants. The RCMP could not give Johnny such a pension since he was not a member of the force, and although he worked for Canada, he was only on loan from Britain. The British were his real employers, and they provided no such coverage when he acted under the orders of others. They would say that it was up to Canada to give de Graff a pension. If Johnny's death occurred during a Canadian operation in Canada, while being paid and employed by Canada, a real battle would ensue. Cliff asked if Johnny understood. "The end result would be that Gerti would be the victim," he said.

"I see what you mean, Cliff. Someone has to see to Gerti's welfare, and it has to be Canada," Johnny stated emphatically. "I had, up to now, assumed the MI6 pension would be in effect."

"Okay, here's what I suggest," Cliff began. "I will inform Ottawa that a condition of your acceptance is that there be a survivor's pension. You'll have to go up to Ottawa and see the navy people. Make sure you tell them that if you die for Canada, the Canadian government agrees that a pension will be given to Gerti."

"Quite a democracy, isn't it, Cliff?" Johnny asked. "Britain drops all my coverage benefits because I'm on loan, and I have to beg Canada to provide for my wife." Exasperated, Harvison pointed out that he knew Johnny did not give a damn about himself when it came to service for an Allied country. So, yes, it was begging; but for Gerti's sake he would not have brought it up.

Cliff contacted Ottawa, while Johnny awaited a call to attend a meeting on the topic with the military authorities. While Johnny waited for an answer from Ottawa, he and a group of ten German Canadian military volunteers were assembled and sent to an east coast submarine base for training. Only Johnny, among the men, was familiar with such a craft. They took part in a crash course that provided the novices with a basic knowledge of submarine layout. Those in charge of the operation were the only ones aware of the exact rendezvous date the sub was to appear. It meant that a call to the men in training to gather at the appointed spot in twenty-four hours was the only notice they would be given.

Each man knew that the operation might well prove fatal. Each participant in this high-risk squad was chosen for his military knowledge, blue eyes, fair hair, solid build, and ability to speak at least some German. Johnny did not divulge any details to Gerti that would cause her to worry. He reasoned that, should he die, her financial fears would at least be greatly eased once she recovered from the emotional loss.

At last, a hasty call summoned Johnny to Ottawa. Arriving in the scenic capital, he was taken to a building not far from Parliament and seated on a hard wooden bench outside a closed-door conference room. De Graff awaited the verdict. Cliff told him to get it down in black-and-white, in writing, and he promised he would see to it that if the worst were to occur, the provisos for Gerti's well-being would be honored to the letter.

The door of the conference room eventually opened and a naval captain, sent out by the assembled board of admirals, approached Johnny. "We find it impossible to give you a position of petty officer military rank for this mission," he rigidly stated.

"Did I ask for a petty-officer rank?" Johnny demanded. "We don't work for ranks, we work for the benefit of the country and have faith the country will look after us." The young officer was silent, then turned and went back into the conference room, closing the door behind him. Minutes later he returned.

"You don't demand officer rank in the Canadian navy, then?" he inquired with some surprise.

"Do I have to say the same thing twice?" Johnny bellowed, now well irritated with this diddling around and red tape. "Sir, I'm here to serve Canada, and stripes don't mean a bloody thing to me!" The captain turned red and went back into the room. Ten minutes later, he was out again.

"Would a pension of the army rank of sergeant major be high enough?" he asked sheepishly.

"I don't know. How much does he get?" Johnny asked, still annoyed.

"About $300 a month," came the reply. This was fine now, Johnny thought, but what about in the future? Back in again went the captain.

Finally Johnny had had enough. He got up, opened the doors, and said to the surprised high-ranking board assembled inside, "Gentlemen, you work it out. I don't care about the uniform, the rank, and all that garbage. If you can give me a good, reasonable, guaranteed pension in writing for my wife, now and in years to come, I will accept this mission—otherwise not." A few sharp glances and mumblings were exchanged, which finally ended in a satisfactory arrangement for both parties—in writing. Johnny thereupon boarded his train back to Montreal, feeling quite relieved.

That evening, Cliff phoned Johnny at home to say that the entire operation had been cancelled. De Graff wondered at first if it was something he had done or said while in Ottawa, but it wasn't. For more than two months the RCMP surveillance team of fifty policemen, mostly regulars and a few reservists, had assembled each night before dark in the main building of a rented farm they named Bleak House. A cook had been added to their ranks to feed the constables prior to their taking up positions in the fields around Camp 44. They stayed in place until sunrise, sometimes enduring rain and swarms of mosquitoes.

During this period the tunnel moved ahead, the work commencing each night after lights out and lasting until the following morning's wake-up call. Each night, underground sounds were heard by the microphone probe detachment. They reported to the watchers outside, who logged in the hole's progress at specific times. Stationed near the breakout point, yet well hidden, a solitary observer was in place to flash signals to the capture squads at any sign of a breakout.

The day prior to Johnny's Ottawa trip, a Camp 44 guard stumbled on a prisoner hidden in the foliage outside the prison compound. Cliff and the facility's commander were at the major's home, close to the camp's front gate, when the incident was reported. They hurried to the area and flushed out two more prisoners from the undergrowth, who stopped running only when the major fired a shot in the air. They reacted by hitting the ground and not moving. After their capture, it was supposed that the long tunnel was ready. A close check of this passageway, however, proved that the tunnel still had a long way to go. It was then brought to light that the newly captured men had escaped through their own tunnel, which was unknown and unauthorized by the Germans' escape committee.

For two subsequent nights no sounds were heard from the first tunnel. It was evident that all work had ceased, stopped by the revelations brought back into camp by the three recaptured prisoners. They had reported that even in daytime the outside was too well guarded. No more escape attempts were made, and all activity on the main tunnel halted. Submarine commanders are basically wary men, and the Grand Ligne center contained many of them. They may also have sensed a setup and aborted the planned escape. A wireless radio, discovered hidden in a building wall much later, could have consequently given them new orders unknown to Cliff and his cohorts. It was capable of sending and receiving to plane and submarine alike. After three nights of inaction the prisoners filled in their tunnel, burying both their plans and those of the Canadian authorities in the process. Had the breakout actually been tried, it would have been recorded in history books as one of World War II's great adventures and potentially one of its greatest accomplishments.

The Canadians did not know it, but a calamity was in the planning stage by a number of uncompromising Germans at Camp 44. It centered around the so-called Hara-Kiri Club. In November 1944, Camp 44 was one of several sites chosen to carry out a collective mass suicide in an attack on the prison guards. The idea was inspired by the German legend of Ragnarök. The term comes from Old Norse *ragna rök* and means "doom of the reign," that is, the inevitable finale of a culture's gods.[13] It was taken to indicate that true Nazis should go down fighting to forestall the unavoidable end of their world and its conquest by the forces of evil. The catalyst would be the impending negative outcome of the war for the Germans. If it appeared that Hitler would lose, they were to strike in an orgy of blood. Nonsympathizers among their ranks would have been the first to die. Next would be the guards. Concern for their own lives was not to be considered. In human waves, they were to overpower their captors and head for key installations, such as power plants, airports, factories, and the like, and cause as much damage and loss of life as possible. Thanks to informers among the internees, this operation was never carried out. The Allies can be thankful for the few brave German prisoners who saw the lunacy of such schemes.[14]

Time sped by, and soon 1945 arrived with a blizzard and a cable from London requesting de Graff's return. Johnny had actually mentioned to Cliff several times, beginning in 1944, that he would like to return to Germany after the war. He felt he could do something good for the Allies in postwar Europe.[15] When the order finally came, in early April, he told the German-Canadian Federation that his firm had transferred him back to England.[16] Of course, Captain Burger twisted the story to his Nazi supporters in the Canadian-German club. He told them that he had been recalled to Berlin on short notice. "Split up, lie low, and do nothing against Canada," Johnny ordered the latter group, explaining, "Germany looks like she will lose this war. The victors, Canada, the United States, and all the others, will hunt Axis sympathizers down like dogs." He told them to keep their noses clean and stay out of trouble. In this way they would be able to survive without being molested or imprisoned by the country in which they lived.

And, like good little Nazis, they did as they were told. The RCMP had no cause to worry about these souls any longer. Some embraced Canada to such an extent that they became solid citizens and active in many Canadian groups and charities. In 1946 Johnny bumped into one of the Nazi group members working at the Bell Telephone Company in downtown Montreal.

"Captain Burger," he exclaimed in delighted surprise. "Am I ever glad to see you back in Canada."

"I'm glad to be back here," Johnny informed him. "It was a real hell I walked into when I returned to Germany."

"I guess so," the man said glumly. "But you got out alive, thank heaven! We were all worried for you during those bad times when Hitler was defeated. Canada really is a great country, isn't it?" he beamed with pride.

"It sure is!" Johnny answered. "The only place to be at peace."

De Graff's recall to London prior to the war's end disappointed Gerti greatly, since she loved Canada. Both hated to sell their cozy home on Palmerston Avenue, together with all their possessions and their car, once more. They applied for Canadian citizenship to make their return easier, but at that time Canada had a waiting period of one year after filing, and their application was turned down.[17] It was thus a sad moment when Cliff kissed Gerti tenderly and shook Johnny's hand vigorously prior to their April 27, 1945, flight to London.[18]

"Thanks, Johnny! Thanks for myself, my men, the force, and Canada for all your efforts!" Harvison said with emotion.

"God bless you, Cliff, Gagnon, Corporal Noel, and all the boys who helped us, and who opened your warm hearts to two strangers!" Johnny replied. "We'll be back, Cliff, just you wait and see!"

"I hope so, Johnny!" Cliff replied, with tears in his eyes.

20

THE CONTROL COMMISSION

London, once an exquisite lady, was now exposed in the gaping wounds of her struggle to survive. The Blitz had reduced many stately buildings to piles of rubble. A high death toll had been paid, but the British spirit of defiance, steeped in tradition and dedication, was strong. Valentine Vivian welcomed Johnny and Gerti back with great warmth and sincerity. Shortly assigned to headquarters, Johnny made the best of the desk work he never enjoyed.

In a spirit of victorious jubilance, the British celebrated Hitler's downfall and the surrender of Nazi Germany on May 7, 1945. The day the war ended, rejoicing throngs jammed London's already crowded streets. Giant parades and well-earned celebrations echoed in new hopes and new lives for all who had survived the hell of war. For defeated Germany, it meant four-power occupation and an administration split into clearly defined sectors. A major adjustment in rebuilding life from the dust lay ahead for the German people.

On May 17, 1945, Gerti and Johnny moved into a quaint apartment on the outskirts of London. It was a pleasant top-floor flat at 4 Wilberforce House, North Side, Clapham Common, London SW4.[1] The building sits across the large common from Nightingale Lane and the schools used as internment camps in 1940. Johnny and Gerti remembered his days there as Karl Grubnick. Otherwise, Gerti busied herself with a small, hedged garden, which proved to be her delight and challenge. She was fond of London, but she longed to be back in Canada.

"MI5 has asked for you again, Johnny," Vivian related one afternoon. "I know your feelings, so I turned their request down." He then explained that a certain group had advocated Johnny's internment during the war but that he had fought them off. De Graff knew he was referring to a group of officials in MI5. Johnny had purposely avoided transferring to that unit because they were too political for his tastes. On several occasions his path overlapped MI5 missions, forcing a few toes to be stepped on in carrying out assignments. Wartime rivalries mixed with petty jealousies in Britain's two major intelligence services. At times they became odd bedfellows. No doubt MI5 felt it should have had Johnny's services from the start, but Frank Foley was with MI6, and had been there in Berlin to take him in when he needed a hand. MI5 and MI6 often carried out joint projects, even to the extent of lending each other agents, but always present were the undercurrents of one-upmanship and point scoring.

At the close of the war, Allied control commissions eventually occupied all of the former Axis powers in Europe. This included Austria, Bulgaria, Finland, Germany, Hungary, Italy, and Romania. While their stay in some countries was short, this was not the case in Germany. The control commissions there were composed of all manner of administrative entities and were molded along the lines of the victorious powers. Among the more important of the contingents from the United Kingdom were units that contained advisors in trade and industry, military services, human resources, food and agriculture, transport, finance, law, politics, and intelligence.[2] The main job of the final three groups was to govern in the name of the Allies and de-Nazify their respective zones of responsibility. The largest and most important slice of the pie for Britain was responsibility for the northwestern section of the conquered nation.

Eighteen men from SIS were assembled to maintain a security-intelligence unit at Bad Oeynhausen,[3] about forty miles (sixty-five km) southwest of Hannover under the command of Major General J. S. Lethbridge of the control commission for the British sector.[4] Their task was overseen by the British military government in Düsseldorf and was to handle all security aspects of civil, criminal, and military law.

Although flattened and in a state of chaos, Germany was still a boiling pot in early 1946. Acts of sabotage and opposition played havoc with the occupation forces. The MI5 unit landing that May included de Graff and was considered to be a large one. But Johnny and some of his colleagues continued to have reservations about the officialdom being sent to Germany. They felt that the work to be carried out would be difficult owing to the group's own bureaucracy. It was as if not enough prior planning had been carried out. Johnny was likewise grateful that Gerti remained in London during this period of their lives. Defeated Germany was not a place that offered safety for anyone's dependants, especially if they were attractive German females.

Frank Foley and Vivian informed Johnny that the detachment would work under military law with numerous other government bodies and agencies. Jealousies would be a way of life. Lieutenant Colonel Felix Cowgill headed up the special SIS group that would work out of the same building as the British military government. He had been the former head of Section V in MI6 before resigning in 1944.[5] Frank also mentioned to Johnny that Cowgill was a close friend and asked if he knew him. Johnny had heard his name but had never met him.

Still, de Graff did not care for the undertaking. He saw it as a probable paperwork nightmare with various government fiefdoms in overlapping confusion. "I'm telling you right now," Johnny informed Foley and Vivian, "I don't like it, for one cannot serve the three different sectors of military forces, MI6, the control commission, and the military government at the same time."

Frank spoke up. "I wouldn't like to say whether or not you are right or wrong, Johnny. I guess we'll soon find out. See Lieutenant Colonel Cowgill as soon as you arrive in Bad Oeynhausen, and give him my best wishes. He'll direct you to the control commission and will see you get all the equipment you need. By the time you arrive there, I'll have reached another area."

"Frank, Goddamn it! You aren't giving me the true picture there," Johnny lashed out. He suspected that Foley was not leveling with him since he did not say much that made sense. "Be honest with me. Can I get in touch with you and possibly situate myself in an area under your supervision?" Johnny asked.

"No, Johnny, sorry," Frank said sternly. "But Cowgill knows of you and has full background knowledge of how you operate. So I am sure you two will get along and you will give him your best. He'll be in touch with me so I'll be kept well informed. Take it easy, do your duty, and be damn careful right from the start."

That ended the conversation. De Graff saw black clouds on the horizon even before he went to Germany. He knew Vivian would be sure that Gerti was looked after during his absence. She smiled bravely and kissed her common-law husband deeply as he bid her farewell and hurried to the airport to join the others.

Arriving in Bad Oeynhausen, the group was introduced to Lieutenant Colonel Cowgill, a slender, somewhat shy, but rigid officer with a pleasant face, who saw that everyone was quickly quartered in a fancy downtown hotel. The structure had been conscripted as an officers' barracks for various men in the services. Sleeping quarters were spacious and grand, but all furniture and movable objects had long since disappeared, to be replaced with steel cots, military mattresses, and the odd footlocker. On the street level was a restaurant still in its full splendor. It was much like a fine dining room, but open only from 8:00 A.M. until 6:00 P.M. German nationals worked at the hotel and restaurant under the direction of an officer from the control commission and a few noncommissioned aides.

After unpacking, Johnny and some of the others went to the administration headquarters, a confiscated four-story office building a few miles away. The MI6 section was located on the second floor in a large room with endless rows of wooden desks and chairs. The only color, apart from the lime-green walls, was provided by the assorted maps that covered the walls. Two members of the London police department were already there, trying to look busy. They wore military-issue uniforms. Welcoming the newcomers, the Bobbies plied Johnny and the others with questions of home and made the new unit feel welcome with their hospitality. Together with Johnny, there were a total of nineteen men, all with SIS and all eager to get started.

The first couple of days were a disappointment. They had expected to be occupied and contributing to the de-Nazification effort. Instead, they sat around doing nothing. The third day finally brought something to do when they received completed application forms for travel, aid, and work histories to be checked. Under the military government, all German citizens seeking public employment had to be de-Nazified. This translated into filling out a form detailing past employment and income. Additionally, they had to list all political parties, clubs, unions, and other groups to which they belonged after Hitler took office. Thousands and thousands of these de-Nazification forms were filled out all over Germany, and the control commission was responsible for scrutinizing the completed forms. They would haphazardly examine each form, call the individual in for an interview, and then decide whether he or she could be pronounced de-Nazified. Speaking to the applicant was often difficult, because members of His Majesty's control commission were frequently not the best-equipped people for the job. Many could not speak German, and many were ill suited in other ways for the work, by either profession or training.

Like those few of his colleagues who could read the de-Nazification forms in the host language, Johnny was bored with the work within a week. He tried to trudge on, but he finally stopped and went to his superior to make a complaint. The second officer in charge of de Graff's section was a former salesman for a firm in South Africa. Contacts in high places must have landed the man his job, since he had no intelligence experience or military background whatsoever. Energetically protesting the kind of tasks he had been given, tasks that could be handled by a layman, Johnny asked the junior officer for an activity commensurate with his experience.

As an example of what he had in mind, Johnny informed the South African that he was aware of a sabotage report filed by Major Edgar, the British officer overseeing the vast Krupp steel works in Essen. The superior gave Johnny a dirty look. Their conversation quickly escalated to the point where the two men exchanged pointed comments, resulting in Johnny's being assigned to handle an investigation into the affair at Krupp. The once massive armament factory, formerly employing more than 160,000 workers, was now in ruins. Britain was trying to rebuild the facilities and maintain production by keeping a workforce of six thousand on the assembly lines, producing mainly railroad equipment. A little more than twenty-five miles away (forty km) was the Möhne Dam, which had been rebuilt after being partially destroyed in 1943 by the dam-busting Lancaster bombers of the Royal Air Force. Despite the attacks, the Möhne had endured in a greatly reduced but still working capacity.

Major Edgar and his female secretary greeted Johnny as he introduced himself at the Krupp office the following morning. Though a veteran military officer, Edgar freely admitted to Johnny that he had no experience in security, intelligence, or espionage. Regardless of his lack of training in these areas, Edgar and his assistant would come to assist de Graff far more than Johnny's own superiors in Germany.

Nights of worry showed on the major's face as he ran his large hands through his bushy black hair, recounting to Johnny the plant's difficulties. Constantly plagued by threats of explosion and collapse, Krupp's workers reacted with frequent wildcat strikes. This played havoc with the production schedules and left locomotives standing unfinished. The previous day had begun with a rumor that the Möhne Dam was about to collapse. Someone had rung the alarm and all hands had fled to higher ground, fearing for their lives. Only a handful of the brave returned when nothing happened.

Once the major had finished, Johnny began. "First, I need a large hall where we can speak to all your employees," he said. "Does this town have such an auditorium still standing?" Major Edgar confirmed that it did and directed Johnny to the person to see. Johnny visited the hall owner, who not only offered the building for the evening free of charge but also asked if he could attend the gathering. Quickly, word went out to the employees at Krupp to be present at a giant meeting that night.

Promptly at 8:00 P.M., standing before the packed hall with Major Edgar and his secretary seated beside him on the stage, Johnny got to his feet, held up his hands, and began speaking in his native German. He warned the crowd that bogus threats of sabotage were no joking matter, for they stopped work and caused loss of income. "Those among you who cause such disruptions know who you are, just as the innocent also know you. By creating these rumors—and those who believe and follow them—you are only hurting yourselves, your families, and your friends. Without production, you receive no wages, without money you have nothing to eat. If you wish to starve, then go away by yourselves and starve to death, but do not take food out of the mouths of your families, the loved ones who depend on you to feed, house, and clothe them. You all knew hunger during the war. The war is over. Do you now wish to go hungry again, at a time when you can rebuild your lives, your hopes, and dreams without fear and in peace?"

Mumbling, turned heads, and nods of acceptance told Johnny that his comments had made sense. Silence returned. "Do you have any complaints against the military administration?" Johnny demanded to know, gesturing to Major Edgar. "If so, let's hear them. Let's clear the air and get these things out in the open." A man who appeared to be something of a leader got to his feet.

"The British major is a nice fellow, but he doesn't know what he's doing. No one has any axe to grind with him." He returned to his seat as the assembly applauded. Johnny felt the major's secretary staring at him, even though his back was to her. Johnny turned, glanced at her, and whispered, "There'll be many more meetings. Please bear with me; I'm not here to punish you." Her face of gloom turned to a smile.

"We are here to help you repair your war-torn country, so that you will be able to stand again as free men without Adolf Hitler!" The hall reverberated with thunderous applause. Someone shouted, "There are a hell of a lot of scalawags running around here!"

"Are you sure about that?" Johnny asked.

"Yes!" came the answer.

"Are you willing to tell me, privately, some of their names?" retorted Johnny.

"Yes!" again was the reply.

"Are you a Communist?" Johnny asked.

"Yes!" stated the man.

"Well, that's fine. That'll be enough out of you, or I'll send a personal letter to Stalin telling him of your complaint," Johnny quipped. The man sheepishly sat down with a flushed face amid a storm of laughter. Later, he did come forward and volunteer valuable information about several of the workshop's troublemakers.

Just before the meeting adjourned, with the promise of another the following night, a poorly clad man rose and brought silence.

"There is a meeting tonight for young Communists called *Edelweiss* [Hitler's favorite flower]. It will be held in a restaurant not far from the plant."

"Will you tell me privately exactly where this place is?" Johnny asked.

"Yes, I will," the man replied.

"Odd name for a Communist group. Do you believe they are Communists?" Johnny demanded.

"No, they aren't. They're all Nazis!" he shouted.

"Are you a Communist?"

"Yes," was the man's reply.

"Thank you, everyone," Johnny said loudly to the crowd. "We'll see you all tomorrow." They smiled back and hurriedly exited the hall. The shabbily dressed worker came forward and quickly gave de Graff the directions to the restaurant. Before Johnny could thank him, he melted into the exiting throng. Johnny immediately phoned control and had another MI6 officer join him. The two then went to the local police station and got a policeman to assist them. They drove to the restaurant and burst through the shaded, unlocked front door. Those inside froze as soon as they took in the British and Polizei uniforms. Groups of young teenage boys and girls were clustered around tables containing mounds of pamphlets and books. The proprietor soon arrived, having been summoned by a call from the police.

"Please sit down and join us," de Graff told the frightened restaurant owner. "We don't plan to eat you; all we want to do is talk to you." The owner slumped into a chair and began a dialogue with a policeman while Johnny and his companion walked to the one of the tables, gazing at the group of adolescents. Scattered about were pornographic letters and books. Johnny picked up one titled *The Wedding Night*.

"Is this what you people study?" he asked the nervous spectators.

A hush and red flushes of embarrassment sprouted in profusion. Watching the boys closely, Johnny said, "Girls, you stand to one side." A sudden move of protest in a facial expression signaled out the instigator of the group. He came forward slowly, his face now rigid and defiant. Being the leader, he had no intention of being shown up as a coward before his peers. "You study this dirty garbage?" Johnny asked him, thrusting the book in his direction.

"Yes, all we are doing is having a little fun!" he shot back.

"You call yourself a culture organization," Johnny barked. "Is this an example of culture?" The leader now burned from ear to ear before everyone's gaze. He did not reply.

"Would you be kind enough to read this out loud?" de Graff asked, turning to the nearest girl. She went beet red and tears came to her eyes. "No need to blush, little one," Johnny said soothingly. "We were all young once, and all made our mistakes. Who gave you this material?" he asked. More silence. One looked to the other, hoping someone would take the initiative. Finally, a girl in the rear said in a barely audible voice, "The leader of the group." The lad gave her a searing look of contempt. Seals were put on the literature and the teenagers were led off to the police station, where they were again lectured. Their parents were called to come and take them home. Only the youthful leader and the restaurant owner were held and charged.

A day later, Johnny visited Major Edgar at the plant. He learned through his secretary that the officer did understand a lot of German and could speak it, despite his words' being a bit muddled at times. Johnny harped on the value of holding meetings with the workers in order to get to know the people, their lives, and their concerns. Using this method they could create a peaceful atmosphere in the plant and better morale among the workers, eliminating threats and costly production delays. Edgar agreed with the approach and assured Johnny that he would take over for Johnny on the stage once the ball was rolling.

That evening the assembly hall was packed again. After Johnny's initial speech, a man and his wife stood up. "Thank you, Captain. You sure straightened out many of our children last night." The hall resounded with applause.

"Don't you think you all should keep a closer eye on them from now on?" de

Graff asked. Suddenly, someone in the rear of the hall shouted, "You fellows with your fine-sounding words still protect all the big sons of bitches running around here!"

"You sure do!" another spectator echoed.

"Would you then tell me the names of these sons of bitches, so that you, the major here, and I can pay them a visit?" Johnny inquired. He said he would, and when the meeting ended he supplied the British with the names and addresses of several top Nazis. From this tip, an investigation was started, which ended weeks later with the arrest of the men in question.

The next assembly produced even more people who spoke about their fears and preoccupations. On the way out, a member of the audience in his thirties stopped Johnny and addressed him as Herr, to which Johnny told him he would prefer that his military rank be used. De Graff did not care for the respect that Herr implies in German. The man corrected himself and went on, "Captain, I believe your security system protects the big ones and also the small ones." Johnny looked at him quizzically. Without pausing for breath, the man said that he could take Johnny and Major Edgar to a house where a widow lived with a son who was a vicious bandit. The poor woman was frightened and beside herself with worry. "Most people know he's a thief and a grave robber, but everyone's afraid to turn him in for fear of retaliation. I cannot say more, other than his name and address, since I too am afraid." Johnny convinced his informant that he would be safe, at which point the man reluctantly agreed to show Major Edgar and Johnny the way.

A frail, elderly woman, who showed surprise at the late callers, answered the knock on the door of her two-story brick home on a side street in the city center. She was acquainted with their escort, so she showed the major and his companions into her living room. There they stated the purpose of the visit and asked the lady if the tales about her son were true. "Yes, yes they are," she responded with a quivering voice. "I don't know what to do. If he were aware I was telling you this, he would kill me!"

"When do you expect your son home?" Johnny inquired.

"Oh, he'll not return until one or two in the morning," she replied, trembling. Johnny instructed the man who had taken them to the house to take the woman to his home and stay there with her so she would feel safe. The rest would be left to the two visitors. He helped her on with her coat and they departed.

Major Edgar and Johnny went upstairs to the son's room. It was a good-sized area, but more like a museum than a bedroom. The walls were adorned with Nazi flags, swords, swastika armbands, and photos. In the cupboard they located several radios, phonographs, fur coats, and men's suits. The dresser drawers were like a jewelry store, laden with watches, rings, bracelets, and necklaces of various sizes, shapes, and styles. Binoculars, guns, wallets, and purses were beneath his bed in boxes. Under his pillow they found a loaded German Luger. The room was a warehouse, containing a fortune in stolen booty.

The major left to bring back reinforcements. A half-hour later he returned with four well-armed police and MI6 agents to aid in the stakeout. Carefully placed in strategic locations, they awaited the return of the suspect. At 2:00 A.M. a key rattled in the darkened home's front door and a muscular man entered. When the door closed and the hall light flicked on, Johnny emerged from a nearby closet, grabbed the thief from behind, spun him around, and belted him in the jaw with one cleanly delivered punch. The thief's hands flew up, releasing the valise he was carrying. Before he could do anything to defend himself, Johnny's fist thudded into his solar plexus, forcing a swoosh of air from his open mouth. His knees buckled, collapsing him in a heap.

The others appeared with drawn revolvers as the man hit the floor. Johnny told him he would have no qualms about killing him if he moved. The suspect lay still, grimacing in pain. Not one of the MI6 agents had any sympathy for this individual, who disrespected the dead and kept a town in terror. The thief and his accumulated mounds of loot were promptly turned over to the local police. Major Edgar and Johnny did not have time to complete the investigation, but the police chief would see that identifiable items were returned to their rightful owners. No doubt the other goods the thief had taken from the community's various shops would also close a lot of unsolved crimes.

Thereafter, plant meetings and arrests continued on a larger scale. Espionage threats and work stoppages ceased. Laborers were happy to finally see concrete action. They appeared in throngs to deliver their complaints as news of the cleanup spread through the plant like wildfire, growing bigger with each retelling. The major gained enough experience by watching Johnny in action to eventually release him from his job. During a final assembly, the workers rose en masse to applaud the efforts made on their behalf.

De Graff had led a successful operation, enabling SIS to do intelligence work and assist in the rebuilding of the German nation at the same time. Johnny knew that Major Edgar, a bright, likeable man, would continue the job they had started. He returned to Bad Oeynhausen.

On his first day back at the control commission's office, a few bumbling officials asked him what he had been doing. Johnny told them it was none of their business; it was a criminal matter that would not interest them. One officer replied gruffly that Johnny should have reported to him. "I did not, sir, and I will not, sir, for my group's head is Felix Cowgill and no one else," de Graff frankly informed him. Before the man could reply, Johnny walked out of the building. Every official was out to make his mark, whether in his area of responsibility or not. Sections overlapped sections and agencies extended beyond agencies. Just as he knew they would be, the bureaucracies set up to de-Nazify Germany were a frustrating quagmire of confusion and officialdom at its worst.

Johnny had served in the morass for more than three months. In the end, he told the control commission that he would pick up his papers and return to London. Their reply was a resounding no.

"I better have them by tomorrow morning or else!" Johnny threatened.

"Oh, you bloody devils of the SIS think you can do anything and go anywhere, whenever you please!" the commission officer sputtered.

"Yes, that's the way it is!" Johnny retorted. A real clamor over a furlough followed. It would take two weeks of pestering delays before de Graff arrived back in London.

During the wait, he went shopping in the local jewelry stores to find a necklace to give to Gerti. Not seeing one he liked, he happened to mention the fact to a control commission supply officer. The officer and a few colleagues said they would do a little nosing around, and to pay them a visit in a week. One week later Johnny contacted the officer, who spread out a large bag of assorted jewelry on a table. "Take your pick and I'll give you a good price," he stated. Johnny selected a gold brooch and necklace, which were quoted at a reasonable price— too reasonable! Johnny thought. When the individual insisted that he did not want to be paid in cash but by check, it was a red flag. Germany was overflowing with forged currency; there were even bogus pound sterling notes in circulation. The seller's adamancy about receiving a check, which he knew would be good, coupled to the amount of merchandise for sale, convinced de Graff that the supply officer was running an illegal venture. Accordingly, he made a special mark on the check so that it could be used later as evidence.

A day passed. Visiting a small café run by a German couple Johnny had gotten to know, they mentioned that coffee was hard to obtain, unless it was bought at the high prices in the barrack's restaurant below the hotel after closing hours. Johnny looked into this and learned that the control commission's supply branch, which gave orders to German factories for almost every commodity they produced, sold the goods back to the Germans on the black market, instead of distributing the merchandise free to the needy. Supplies of food, shoes, and clothing, paid for by the British government and ultimately the British taxpayer, were finding their way into German hands for a price.

Many scum servicemen and pen pushers made fortunes in this way, tolerated or unnoticed by more responsible administrators. Johnny had witnessed a German being turned away when he asked a British sergeant for shoes. The man was informed that there were none, yet behind the sergeant in a large locked room were literally thousands of pairs. All could be had after hours for an inflated amount. Bribes and corruption, even to the point that British officers could "buy" things in a local store without being asked to pay, were commonplace. Gifts, luggage, and all kinds of merchandise were available to the occupying forces for little or no charge—particularly if they paid by check—and to the German populace at exorbitant rates in the evening if they paid by cash or with other valuables.

Then there was the case of a Jewish physician, Dr. Philip Aureba,[6] who had been in Buchenwald. Two Jewish bodyguards assisted the doctor. The trio traveled around in a jeep with the word "Buchenwald" painted on it. They stole whatever they could, while a commanding officer whom Johnny admired evidently winked at the operation. De Graff left this last part out of his initial report, but he called the physician a criminal. The officer tried to manipulate the statement by watering down the accusations against the doctor. Johnny refused to accept this and rewrote the report with the original charges against all concerned, including the officer.[7]

The final straw came when a Canadian called Nottingham, a control commission overseer in the British district, called everyone in Johnny's unit into his office and announced that from then on they would work under him and follow his instructions. "Where is Lieutenant Colonel Cowgill?" the men asked. "He is our superior." It was then revealed that "Mr." Cowgill—the replacement referred to him as "Mr."—had been fired and returned to civilian life.[8] The assembled group was dumbfounded; Cowgill was an honest, hardworking officer whom they all respected. He also had a good command of military knowledge despite his lack of an intelligence background. Nottingham, in de Graff's view, was "a brash fellow." He was a civilian and former member of the Ontario legislature who had no military or intelligence experience at all. To Johnny, Nottingham was not qualified to take over. The fuse was lit.

"Gentlemen, now that Lieutenant Colonel Cowgill is gone, you are my boys," stated the pink-cheeked Canadian.

"I am not one of your boys," Johnny shouted out in a fury, "and never will be!" This momentarily shook Nottingham from his smugness, and before he could recover himself, de Graff grabbed a nearby chair and flung it across the room, dashing a table lamp to pieces. "Count me out!" Johnny stormed at the officer as he thundered out of the room. His behavior left all aghast. Two hours later, he jumped on a plane and flew back to London.[9]

In London Johnny went straight to MI6's Section V in Westminster to see Vivian.[10] Johnny did not wait to be announced but strode briskly into his office, surprising Vee-Vee at work, and told him that he was quitting. "Do you want me to fight against nothing over there?" Johnny demanded. "You received my reports. You know what I have done." De Graff argued that an experienced intelligence man was not needed in Germany. "Those in charge do everything in their power to give such men flunkey tasks led by nitwits." Persons there to render aid, in Johnny's judgment, were selling it to the highest bidder. "It's a real performance, Vee-Vee, a real performance! If the British public only knew the bloody farce and rip-off for which their hard-earned money is being spent. Certainly there are good men over there, but they are rendered ineffective in short order by the interwoven echelon of stacked bureaucracy, fat-cat appointments. I quit!"

Vivian, taken aback by Johnny's outburst, sat calmly and listened without interruption to his harsh words. Finally he spoke up. "Damn it, Johnny! I sure admire your fighting spirit," he stated. He then pointed out that he knew Germany far better than Johnny thought he did. Many agents had returned, fed up with several of the same things that infuriated de Graff. Vivian did not condone or disagree with the man standing before him. Rather, he pointed out that they were not the ones who gave the orders. If he were in control of intelligence, the story would be otherwise. He then urged Johnny to take a few weeks off. After a rest and some recreation, he felt, Johnny might see things differently. "You have an excellent record of service with us, a pension, and everything. Don't let this fracas spoil a fine performance and a future in work you do so well."

Johnny agreed to take a break and return to see him in a fortnight. Gerti was happy with the brooch and necklace, but he told her they might have to be turned back in as evidence during his next visit to headquarters. Johnny hoped to retrieve the money he had paid for them. She understood.

Two weeks later Johnny reported in again at 54 Broadway. Vivian was friendly and pleasant as de Graff took a seat before him. "After this short furlough, would you go back to Germany, Johnny?" he inquired, his eyes fastened on Johnny's.

"No, never to that same setup, to do those assignments," Johnny replied firmly.

"I thought not," Vivian replied. "You are a very stubborn fellow, you know." He paused. "Okay, there is another mission we have in mind for you, as station chief in Cairo. This is a vital intelligence area for us and our top man has just been transferred. You will find all excellent agents there, fully trained and capable. How would you like to take over?"

"That all depends," Johnny replied. "Tell me how many men we have lost over there who have died through the Arabs?" Vivian paused, thought a minute, and then spoke up.

"Five in the last few years, I believe."

"Were their deaths avenged?" Johnny asked, staring at him intently.

"No," he responded. "It's very ticklish there, for we cannot afford to start a bloodbath when we lose an agent or two. The main thing is we still operate, despite our losses."

"I will take on the job," Johnny told him. "But I want carte blanche."

"Can't be done, Johnny!" said Vivian, his voice rising in annoyance. "I can't give you any authorization to avenge any deaths that your men may incur. That's impossible and cannot be granted on any level of the British government."

"Vivian, there is no way that I would stand by and see any of my men killed in service by the Arabs, without dishing out the same to them," Johnny answered. He pointed out that to stand at the grave of a dead operative and say a few words about how he died bravely for his country, throw a few flowers on the coffin, and walk away was not enough. Johnny remarked that Arab terrorists thought nothing of slitting a man's throat, with or without cause, and then walking away whistling. His men would need to know that they would get protection. Anything short of full authority would not do.

"Johnny, I can't give it to you!" Vivian stated emphatically. "The mission has to be on these terms or not at all."

"So it will be not at all!" Johnny stated angrily. Vivian slumped into his chair.

"You refuse Germany, you refuse Cairo. There is no other mission open at present, other than here at headquarters for a spell, until a spot comes up," he said dejectedly.

"Vivian, I quit!" Johnny shot out, much to his boss's surprise. "Pay Gerti's and my way back to Canada and I will resign from MI6 right now."

A long discussion ensued, but Johnny's decision was firm. He would leave the service. All of Vivian's arguments about his value to SIS, the future, the loss of his pension, made no impression. Upset at Johnny's decision, and with reluctance, he accepted de Graff's revolver. Johnny had brought it along but left it downstairs. He turned in all his identification papers, passports, and service items he had accumulated over the years. Each article contained many memories.

The de Graffs put everything up for sale once again. It would net them £3,000.[11] Along with the money, the SIS gave Johnny an Irish decanter. It was a duplicate of the one given to Lord Nelson.[12] They likewise provided two first-class tickets for ship's passage back to Canada and held a farewell party in London in mid-August 1946, attended by Vivian, Frank Foley, and many associates. Champagne corks popped; there were many speeches and warm embraces. Months later, Frank would mail Johnny a letter of recommendation. It read:

<u>TO WHOM IT MAY CONCERN.</u>
I wish to testify that I have known
MR JOHN de GRAFF
For many years.

He is a man of outstanding honesty and straightforwardness, who has never been known to go back on his pledged word which is his bond. He is capable, intelligent and immensely hard working—under a rough exterior he hides great benevolence and kindness which he extends to all men of good will, and which he lavishes on his friends. I can speak from knowledge because I am honoured to be able to count myself among his best friends.

I feel certain that no man will regret having placed trust in him, either in business or in private life.

Frank Foley [by hand]
Berlin in January 1947 [by hand]

At present: Assistant Inspector General.
Public Safety Branch,
I.A. & C. Division,
Headquarters,
Control Commission Germany (BE)
BERLIN, B.O.A.R.[13]

Before the retirement party ended, Frank presented Johnny with a new billfold on behalf of the SIS. Inside were four crisp Canadian thousand-dollar bills, then worth a total of £1,000 and change.[14] "We know you leave without a pension," Frank said with deep feeling in his voice. "So this is just a little something from the outfit for all the work you have rendered this service." It made Johnny so choked up that he could not reply. He could only extend his hand to all of those who were his friends and colleagues. Gerti was showered with gifts and a dozen red roses, which brought tears streaming down her shiny cheeks. The men and the service had been good to him, and he departed with no ill will whatsoever. He held them in high regard for the rest of his life. The British further requested that the immigration officials in Canada, at the de Graffs' port of landing, not be informed of Johnny's background, only that he would have an amount equaling £4,000.[15] It was likewise emphasized that Johnny was not to be confused with the pro-Nazi Canadian Johannes de Graff.[16]

Johnny and Gerti traveled by train to Liverpool and embarked for Montreal on the four-thousand-ton SS *Cavina*.[17] A silver moon glistened on the tranquil sea that Wednesday evening, August 21, 1946. When the vessel left the harbor, its engines pulsated in a dull, constant rhythm as Johnny and Gerti hugged each other at the bow. He was fifty-two years old and she was twenty-six.[18] For a long time they looked out over the water in great relief and happiness. "Johnny, I'm so glad we're going back to Canada to lead a peaceful normal life as simple people," she whispered.

"I am too, Mutzi. It's been quite an adventure, quite a struggle, but never dull," Johnny replied. "Over there, Gerti, a few thousand miles away, lie our new hopes, our new dreams, and our new home in Canada. We will become Canadians, settle down quietly, and enjoy many fond memories and new experiences as civilians."

"I'll love that," Gerti cooed. She nestled closer to her man, as the soft night wind ruffled her hair. They clung close together, staring out to sea. As the ocean rose from its tranquil depths and the salt breeze filled their nostrils, they smiled and kissed.

21

HOME

Cliff Harvison met Johnny and Gerti when the *Cavina* reached Montreal on August 31, 1946.[1] "What are your plans, now you've left the intelligence service?" Cliff asked, as the three greeted each other.

"Just snoop around, learn something of the business world, so we can stand on our two feet," Johnny replied with conviction.

They checked into the familiar Hotel Windsor, next to Dominion Square, and resided there until September 13. During the intervening two weeks, de Graff purchased a rundown rooming house located at 1863 Dorchester Street West.[2] During Quebec's "French only" movement in the 1970s, the street was renamed boulevard René-Lévesque Ouest. They moved in on September 14, 1946, and Johnny was quick to begin dismantling the building's interior. Using his knowledge of carpentry and plumbing, he turned the structure into a first-rate accommodation. Almost naturally, while he was tearing down walls, pounding nails, and painting, his mind often drifted back to his former missions. It was really hard to completely give up thinking about the old trade, much less adjust to the way civilians saw the world. Once the renovation was complete, including a pleasant apartment for himself and Gerti, and the rest of the rooms rented out, he became restless.

He needed a new cause, and one was about to explode across the world arena. With the start of the Korean War at the end of June 1950, Johnny's universe was again aflame with the Red menace. Winston Churchill had given his famous "Iron Curtain" speech just four years earlier. It was a time of "them versus us" paranoia, signaling the start of the cold war. In the nearby United States, the specter of McCarthyism began grabbing the headlines. A distinction should be made, however, in what followed. Johnny was not, nor did he ever become, a Canadian version of U.S. senator Joseph McCarthy. De Graff said he did not believe in what McCarthy's practiced.[3] The senator from Wisconsin was out to promote himself and wreck lives. De Graff felt that his job, his only job, was to inform Canadians of Moscow's plans. He deemed Communist infiltration to be taking place in Canada and believed that many Canadians were unaware of what this would mean to them and their country. After Gerti, this inform-the-public operation became Johnny's new raison d'être.

To the consternation of the RCMP, the SIS, and later the FBI, and despite the danger, Johnny set out on a one-man journey to expose the Communist threat. These intelligence organizations doubtlessly wished he would have grown old gracefully—in silence. Instead, he hit the lecture trail. During much of this segment of his life, for safety's sake de Graff used the cover name "Captain Johnny X." Aided by demonstrating explosives and his vast knowledge of Communist methods, he revealed what he knew to often mesmerized audiences. Invitations to speak were soon coming in from various points across Quebec, Ontario, and the Canadian east coast. He refused guest fees, asking only that his transportation and lodging expenses be paid. At his zenith, de Graff delivered six or seven lectures a week.[4] Many of these talks made the newspapers. Others irritated the public and for that reason also made the newspapers.[5]

Before a group at the Rotary Club in Montreal on September 10, 1951, he told his audience that, in Stalin's words, "as long as capitalism and communism exist, one must go, one must conquer." He also warned that Canadian Communist legions numbered more than half a million. He berated the RCMP for not taking the Communist threat seriously enough.[6] Gerti, ever fearful for Johnny's life, could not persuade him to give up these antagonizing speeches. She accepted them with a heavy heart and lived in constant worry for his personal safety. "I have to do this," he told her one evening. "Canadians have to face a reality, which until now they had no idea existed, and defend themselves against it." She stopped trying to convince him.

It was inevitable that the Communist Party of Canada (or CPC) sought to slam a lid on this turncoat tormentor. Cliff Harvison phoned one evening to deliver the first news. "Johnny, you've made some big enemies. Today Tim Buck placed your name high on the CPC's assassination list." Buck was the CPC general secretary. Johnny was not surprised. "Our informer is in reality one of our people working undercover," Cliff related. "The list crossed his desk today and he advised us." Thereafter, the RCMP had someone in plain clothes in Johnny's audiences. Reserve constables also volunteered in assisting in de Graff's circle of protection. It was later revealed that about half the CPC membership viewed Johnny as an impediment to their plans and existence, demanding that he be killed.

Tim Buck and others agreed, but they felt that owing to Johnny's growing notoriety, his execution at that time would unleash an intense probe into CPC activities. It could even cause serious repercussions for the very existence of the party in Canada. Soviet and Canadian diplomatic relations were under severe strain already because of the Igor Gouzenko affair, and Johnny's murder would have had somber consequences in Ottawa and Moscow. Buck's faction won the day, much to the frustration of the opposition, some of whom quit the CPC in protest.

No attempts were made on Johnny's life, but occasional verbal and written threats were made. One such incident arose at the conclusion of an assembly held in a church hall in a small farming town in Ontario. A crude note, written in cut-out lettering pasted to thick brown paper, was left obtrusively on the demonstration table as the audience departed. "'X,' you're a dead man!" it stated. The RCMP laboratory determined that the wrapping paper was of European make and was not available in Canada. Johnny likewise received phone calls from persons who said they would "fry" or kill him.[7]

After Johnny began his campaign, the CPC obviously informed Moscow. The Soviets were no doubt taken aback at discovering that their agent, who they had assumed had died in Brazil in 1939 or 1940, was very much alive and wreaking havoc on their Canadian objectives—and that he had been a traitor working with MI6 for years. To kill him in early 1950s, while he basked in the glare of publicity, despite his double cross, would not be in their best interest. They would not forget him, but they would wait.

In the meantime, the RCMP, the military, and other security groups asked Johnny to give demonstrations of his knowledge of simple bomb making in their training courses. During these presentations, Johnny discovered that a key ingredient of his powerful explosive was readily obtainable at any Canadian drugstore, and in bulk. He informed Harvison, who saw to it that the over-the-counter availability suddenly dried up.

During his appearance in Halifax, Johnny cautioned a belligerent doubter in the audience to keep a good distance away from his small primed charge. Unexpectedly, the man forced his way forward, knocking Johnny back against the metal lid of the explosive. At nearly the same moment the modest bomb went off, tearing into Johnny's arm. With blood dripping down his side from the injury, Johnny rebuked the man before the packed hail, and then carried on with his demonstration and comments.

The version Johnny told has it that at the conclusion of another assembly, held in Knox Presbyterian Church in downtown Montreal, he was approached by a needy-looking woman who volunteered her services in his mêlée with the Communists. Charlotte, or Sári (pronounced Char-ree), Akontz was a newly arrived refugee from Hungary who had endured imprisonment and great hardship during the war. He felt an affinity with her, remembering his own tribulations at Osowiec. She impressed him with her honesty and desire. Another version, by two independent sources, claims that they knew each other from the Hungarian Embassy in Vienna, where she had worked.[8] What is not contested is that Sári entered Canada on a sponsored program and worked for the Children's Welfare Institute in Montreal's Westmount area. For a time she also held a job in a bank. Once Sári demonstrated her typing ability and was run through a security check by the RCMP, Johnny virtually adopted her as an office assistant and companion to Gerti, who was once again expecting.

Gertrude had never given up on her goal of motherhood. She had made her mind up long before, and nothing Johnny ever said could change it. During a theater performance the couple attended one evening in the spring of 1950, she collapsed in the ladies' room. Gerti was into the fifth month of her pregnancy by then and very much looking forward to the new addition to the family. Rushed to the Royal Victoria Hospital in Montreal, she went into a coma in the intensive care unit. She miscarried, and despite the attention of her specialist, Dr. Scott,[9] she lay in a state of unconsciousness for five days. Johnny was beside himself with worry. Late one evening the doctor phoned to give him the prognosis. "I know of your effort and courage in speaking as you do against communism," he began. The physician urged Johnny to summon the same courage, perhaps even more than in the past, as he would surely need it in the months ahead. "I deeply regret to say there is no hope for your wife. She has a grave kidney and liver disorder. She was not a strong woman and should never have been advised to have children. Her system cannot take it. She will regain consciousness, and could return home under strict bed rest, observation, and medication. But even with all our facilities, knowledge, and skill, she only has months to live at best."

Johnny was shattered. Once Gerti returned home, Sári waited on her every need. Johnny cut out his lectures so he could remain at her side. Gerti, now frail and weak, insisted one evening that Johnny attend a large meeting as guest speaker since it had been previously arranged. He tried to refuse, but she insisted. That night, before a packed hall, he faltered in his speech and had to stop in front of the audience. He could think of little more than Gerti dying at home. He exited the stage and his host took over. "Here you have a man who is fighting for your freedom, despite the fact that his wife is deathly ill," the host informed the silent hall. Johnny reappeared, more composed, and in his forceful way stunned his listeners with his revelations on communism, without further pauses in the delivery.

At age thirty-one, Gerti passed away on September 23, 1951, despite all medical efforts to save her.[10] Her final words to Johnny, in a whispered voice, were a request that he marry again as their union had been so wonderful. A smile, a kiss, and she died in his arms.

Gerti never became a Canadian, as Johnny had, but remained a British subject until the end.[11] It was an unimportant detail, because flowers and letters of sympathy from individuals and groups in many parts of Canada and abroad flooded the funeral home. Only a youth at the time, Gordon Scott attended the funeral, along with his parents, brother, and sister. Even in death, beautiful Gerti looked angelic. Standing next to her coffin, her companion's viselike handshake contained his strength and determination not to break down in public. To those few who knew Johnny well, however, a deep glaze could be seen on his face.

Cliff Harvison, who had been transferred to RCMP operations in British Columbia, wired a floral bouquet of a dozen red roses and a personal note to Johnny. Members of the force acquainted with Johnny and Gerti attended the funeral. Cliff, greatly concerned that Johnny might attempt suicide over his loss, sent a detail of officers to watch over him. When Johnny heard of this, he telegraphed Cliff his thanks and dismissed the guards with deep appreciation for their kind thoughts. He had to carry on for his and Gerti's sake, he informed them.

A Can$600 dollar fee was due Dr. Scott, which Johnny sent on to him a day later. The physician promptly returned his check, with a note stating that fifty dollars was sufficient payment for a brave man who had endured so much in his lifetime, one who had gained wisdom and knowledge that he was now trying to communicate to others.

For a while, Johnny's speaking efforts tapered off after Gerti's death. He tried finding solace in other work and concentrated on his rooming house, yet he remained deeply tormented. He was very different following her passing. He stopped caring about a lot of things and about a lot people close to him. He passed through an intense and agonizing mental crisis. Those who have never met the love of their life, but settled for something less, might not understand what he was going through. At one point he walked in front of a tram on St. Catherine's Street in Montreal. Was it an accident or on purpose? No official incident report was ever recorded by the police, so one answer is as good as another. Luckily, a passerby pulled him from harm's way at the last moment.[12]

Perhaps it was his unshakable desire to warn Canadians that really saved him. He again began to give speeches, but this time they were often animated deliveries, as if he "were on some kind of mission."[13] On November 28, 1951, he spoke before the Boy Scouts in Montreal.[14] On April 12, 1952, he appeared at a meeting of the Canadian Legion across town. He formed an organization called "Crusaders Against Communism," but it appears to have floundered rather quickly. Two and a half years later, he started the Canadian Crusaders, which probably suffered the same end.[15]

His new lecture series was bound to produce problems for two reasons. After Gerti's death he began to embellish some of his stories, and he sometimes spoke as if he was speaking for the RCMP, when he was not berating it.[16] Being mentioned in these two opposing ways so irritated the Royal Canadian Mounted

Police that they had Cliff Harvison return from clear across the country to give Johnny a talking-to. In Harvison's description of the encounter, he expressed his belief that Johnny's words were largely used to satisfy his vanity rather than cause any damage to the celebrated police force. He likewise wrote that de Graff saw his role as trying to unite public opinion and that of law enforcement if ever Canada stood a chance of defeating Moscow. But then Harvison added, "At the end of the war he suddenly found himself without employment and without connection with any official body or government. It is, I suggest, understandable that a man with his background would find it extremely difficult to make the required transition from his previous activities to a position of landlord of a middle-class boardinghouse, particularly at a time such as the present when the Communist threat, which he has fought for a lifetime, is becoming increasingly great. His present platform appearances are a very natural result of his background plus a feeling on his part that he has been neglected and cast aside."[17] Indeed, part of Johnny's tirade was a reaction to the belief that he had been treated shabbily by the RCMP once ending the arrangement he had with it as Secret Agent 235. When he returned to Montreal after leaving MI6, the Canadians put him out to pasture without a pension. That was too much for an individual who had given so much and always spoken his mind. Following Harvison's visit, the man Johnny thought was the best policeman he ever knew, de Graff toned down his rhetoric.[18]

Before Gerti's death, Johnny had mailed J. Edgar Hoover a letter offering his services in the fight against communism. Dated February 6, 1950, and signed "Paul Petersen," the letter gave an outline of Johnny's Soviet activities and stated that he had become disillusioned with communism, that he had worked as a double agent for a European country until retiring, and that he could be contacted by someone Hoover trusted explicitly. He ended by giving his Dorchester Street address.[19] The communication set off a flurry of interbureau memos and letters. Part of the FBI's interest revolved around the name Paul Petersen. Petersen had been the Soviet agent who ran the spy Thomas L. Black in the United States in the 1930s, while "Paul" had been the name used by the Soviet superior of Harry Gold, who was then incarcerated in the United States. Johnny chose the name because he knew it would get Hoover's attention. It did.

Cliff phoned one evening in late February 1952, just as de Graff was about to turn in after a hectic day. "Johnny," he said, "I'm expecting a couple of visitors early tomorrow morning. They have asked expressly to see you. They want your assistance."

"Who are they, Cliff?" Johnny inquired. "Intelligence people?"

"Yes, the FBI. They asked to see you in Montreal and we agreed, just to view a few mug shots." Setting all this up may have been the event that triggered

Hoover's dislike of Harvison. In the view of the notorious FBI director, Harvison had had the temerity to talk back to him not once but a couple of times.[20]

The next morning de Graff was seated in Harvison's office plowing through a pair of large books of photographs of Communists, while the two Americans, FBI special agents Silverthorn and Plantz, watched attentively.[21] Out of the hundreds of snapshots, Johnny identified twenty-five Soviet officers. Suddenly he recognized a photo of Manfred Stern, his military school instructor and friend from M4 in China.

"Do you know him?" inquired one of the FBI men, noticing Johnny's lengthy pause.

"Yes, that is Fred Stern, a general in the Red Army, but certainly not a Communist Party member," Johnny stated emphatically. "He is not the type of fry you're seeking."

"You sound like a Communist sympathizer yourself," the leaner of the two men stated.

"You bloody fool!" Johnny angrily retorted. They did not have the faintest idea what communism was, much less why people joined its ranks. "I had followed communism, true, as an alternative to German political dictatorship and suppression of the working people who were starving. Yes, I embraced communism in those days, but I was not a loyal party member. There was a difference. Few choose communism and its politics for world domination. Most followed it unknowingly, because in their local situations it posed an alternative to another system and power they could not tolerate." He had seen, known, and been involved in both sides, and knew far more about it than a group of smartly dressed novice agents.

At this point, Cliff held up his hand to indicate that his former colleague had said enough. He then lit into the two Americans in a more diplomatic way. Both Silverthorn and Plantz looked pretty foolish afterward and offered their apologies, which de Graff accepted. Johnny handed them back their books, saying those were all he could recognize. In so doing, he felt proud that he had not classed Stern with the others. He glanced at the ceiling above, with its long-stemmed globe of light. Inwardly he told himself, "Dear Fred, I hope when your day comes, you will die at peace in your bed." Years later, he learned that his friend had met a very different and horrible end.

Silverthorn and Plantz talked with de Graff over several days between February 24 and March 11, 1952. Their written interview, which Johnny signed, was ninety-four pages long and covered much of de Graff's life up to leaving Rio de Janeiro for London near the end of February 1940. Besides his lengthy commentary and the identities of the twenty-five Soviet agents, he provided the operatives' backgrounds, what intelligence branch they worked for, and some of their missions. The consequences of their foreign assignments were not something he could supply, since those results were never openly discussed.[22] Even so, the FBI agents seem to have returned to the United States much pleased with the information they were given.

Knowing that Johnny sought solitude, Sári left to work in a small Ontario town after Gertrude died. Of the thousands of memories floating through his head, Johnny kept remembering Gerti's last wish. To honor her, he began to think seriously of asking Sári to marry him. He knew and trusted Sári, and she had looked after Gerti with great dedication. Yet, as with Maria, his first wife, he was unsure of his feelings. He sought the advice of his neighbors from Montreal, Violet and Ward Scott. He asked them several times if they thought he should marry Sári. They always advised strongly against it. Sári was not an easily likable person. She had odd mannerisms, and already a past with some mental problems, and was much less of a catch than Gerti.[23] In spite of their counsel, Johnny contacted Sári and asked her to become his bride. They signed a prenuptial agreement and were wed in a simple ceremony on June 14, 1952.[24] But, as the Scotts had foreseen, the union was not a happy one. Johnny's pain was still too fresh. Gerti's presence was still everywhere. He would later call his marriage to Sári the biggest mistake of his life.[25] His behavior soon became much more physical, and he often used foul language, something he had rarely done around Gerti.[26]

During the FBI interviews in Montreal earlier in the year, Silverthorn and Plantz had mentioned that Thomas L. Black, an admitted Soviet agent, and Harry Gold, a convicted Soviet agent, had fingered him as their superior in the United States in the 1930s. At least Gold was connected with the Klaus Fuchs spy case and the resulting theft of America's secret research on the atomic bomb. Johnny denied that he ever acted as a Soviet agent in the United States. Moreover, he volunteered to come to the United States to confront anyone who said he had worked under Johnny's command there. Thus it was that the FBI paid his way with a check for US$150, and at 10:30 A.M. on December 4, 1952, Johnny stepped off train no. 169 in Philadelphia's 30th Street Station for a face-to-face showdown.[27]

The confrontation with Thomas L. Black took place in the Philadelphia office of the FBI in the presence of three FBI agents. Johnny was asked a series of questions about his contacts in the National Oil Products Company of Harrison, New Jersey, about how he instructed students, how he submitted and received reports, if he had ever given those under him gifts, whether he had ever requested that a student or source have his photograph taken, if he had ever eaten at Gafantti's or Luchow's restaurants in New York City, what he knew about the Trotskyites, and whether he had ever heard of the California Institute of Technology. Johnny answered all of these questions with ease, affirming that he had never set foot in the United States in the 1930s. He stated that he had heard of the

Westinghouse Electric Company but had no knowledge of its ultraviolet light, known as the Westinghouse black lamp.[28]

Thomas L. Black had ample time to observe Johnny talking, walking, and gesturing. At the conclusion of the two-and-a-half-hour meeting, he was almost certain that Johnny was not the Soviet agent who had run him. He said that there were some resemblances, but the only one he could point out was that Petersen and de Graff smiled in a similar way. Black was contacted again, on December 11, 1952, and asked whether his opinion had changed. He stated that one of the 1930 photographs he was given to study, specifically the one of Johnny wearing a hat in 1932,[29] had prompted him to think that Johnny was Petersen. But after meeting Johnny in Philadelphia, he had changed his mind.[30]

The FBI then took de Graff to the U.S. Federal Penitentiary in Lewisburg, Pennsylvania, 156 miles (251 km) away, to meet with Harry Gold on December 5, 1952. The encounter began at 9:45 A.M., when the FBI placed four photographs of Johnny, taken in 1929, 1932, 1934, and 1945, on a table in front of a seated Gold. Choosing the 1932 picture of Johnny wearing a hat, Harry Gold said, "This photograph is a photograph of a person who introduced me to Soviet espionage in October or November 1935, in New York City, and that person is you."[31] Johnny vigorously denied this and asked why Gold thought he was "Paul." Gold replied that Johnny had the same voice, facial contour, and smile as Paul. Johnny answered that he was in Brazil in October and November 1935, planning with other conspirators to overthrow the government of Getúlio Vargas. He pointed out that this could be confirmed by interviewing persons in Brazil. Although he did not mention it, Harvison and Foley could have easily stepped in to substantiate his story as well. Following this exchange the meeting turned into a rehashing of benign questions and recollections. Gold persisted in maintaining that Johnny was Paul, except for one detail; Paul was shorter by about three inches (about 7.6 cm). Two weeks later, on December 18, 1952, Gold asked to see an FBI agent and admitted that he had changed his mind. Johnny was not Paul. He based his decision on the height of the two men and on Johnny's hands, which were much larger and rougher than he remembered Paul's hands as being.[32]

The FBI was convinced that Johnny was not the person they were looking for and let him return to Canada. Back in Montreal, on February 16, 1953, de Graff requested written clearance of his name from the Americans. The FBI refused but had their Ottawa liaison contact Johnny on March 19 to express verbally that he was no longer the subject of any FBI investigation and to thank him for cooperating in the matter.[33] Satisfied, and no doubt invigorated, Johnny went back to the anti-Communist lectern.

In late May 1953 Johnny traveled to Saint John, New Brunswick, and spoke before the United Services Institute on March 25 using his real name for the first time. His one-time mission chief, Colonel T. E. Ryder, introduced him to the audience. During his remarks, Johnny called the Labor Progressive Party of Tim Buck a bunch of "lousy rattlesnakes."[34] The RCMP found this bothersome, if only because of the enemies Johnny was making among Canada's Communists. The Mounties wanted de Graff out of Montreal, both for his safety and for theirs.[35] They approached Blake Clarke up the St. Lawrence River in Brockville, Ontario. He had a tourist lodge called Horningtoft up for sale.[36] The complex was made up of a main house, with up to nine rooms for guests, lots of interesting antiques, plus twelve small outside cabins. It was situated just steps to the river among a cluster of peaceful trees. The price was Can$90,000. De Graff agreed to relocate there and put together part of the cost on October 7, 1953, by selling his Montreal boardinghouse, an adjoining lot, and other possessions for Can$33,000 to Marie Antoinette David. Some of the money (Can$13,000) was loaned to her by Ted Ryder.[37] Blake Clarke financed the remainder that Johnny needed. Even before the paperwork was ready, on October 1, 1953, Johnny left Montreal for good and moved into Horningtoft.[38]

Blake Clarke and Johnny got along well enough at first, and once again de Graff set to work turning his new venture into a viable enterprise. Horningtoft thrived for several years, as Johnny took care of every detail of the property's upkeep. But when motels began to appear up and down the St. Lawrence, on the Canadian side of the river, they took the foundation out of his business. Blake Clarke, however, still had to be paid his mortgage. Evidently Clarke made Johnny's life unpleasant about the payments. From that moment on, the two men did not see eye to eye. One year, Johnny had so few guests that he could not make the mortgage payments at all. He had to sell a piece of the land to be able to pay Clarke. Clarke at first opposed this sale but finally gave in, realizing that this was the only way he could get his money.[39] Until then, there had been accommodations for about seventy-five guests.[40]

While Johnny was leery of Jews, he probably ended up renting his cabins to them just as he had the rooms back at his Montreal boardinghouse.[41] De Graff's bias apparently did not extend to blacks. Once, when some African Americans rented a bungalow at Horningtoft, they told him that they would swim in the waters of the St. Lawrence only at night. Johnny replied, "You can go swimming anytime you feel like it." Later, a neighbor telephoned and asked if he knew that non-whites were using the beach and swimming in the water. Johnny replied, "What's wrong, is the water turning black?"[42]

Colleagues in the RCMP kept in touch for a while. The FBI also paid Johnny another visit. The Mounties first approved the Americans' request, and then Johnny was phoned to secure his consent for another identification session. This time, at Horningtoft, he identified fifteen more mug shots. It must have been humorous for the FBI and RCMP to witness this process. Looking through the catalogues of agents, Johnny would suddenly stop and say, "Well, well, look who we have here, a new coat and smile, but the same rat!" Or, "Well, this is interesting, wonder what this little weasel is up to? The last I heard of him was . . ."

Captain Johnny X was unremitting in his speeches at local forums. He even traveled to New York State to speak, and he appeared back in Canada on a CBC Television program.[43] An onlooker at one live talk, D. W. Sherman, remarked that Johnny told the audience not only of the bomb-making ability of Soviet agents but about how they used poisonous cigarettes that could be passed to unsuspecting targets for instant elimination.[44] One of the main attractions at these gatherings was his demonstration of how a mixture of rat poison, pepper, and salt could be used as a bomb.[45]

Johnny's biggest eye-opener on the lecture circuit came on January 11, 1954, when he claimed at the Brockville Home and School Association that there were some three thousand Soviet-trained agents living undetected in Canada. He said that he had observed Communists all over the country. They were taxi drivers, sailors, bus drivers, pilots, and factory workers. Even the Canadian armed forces had Communist infiltrators. To use an expression Johnny liked, these "pinkies" were passing information to Toronto or to North America's headquarters in Chicago. When the meeting and accusations were reported on the front page of one of Ottawa's leading newspapers, not only was Parliament buzzing but the American press picked up the story.[46] The next day, the *Chicago Daily Tribune* published an article repeating Johnny's charge of three thousand Red spies and mentioned that he "would be glad to testify before Senate investigators in Washington on his knowledge of the interconnection of Communists in Canada and the United States."[47] These American meetings were the infamous Army-McCarthy hearings. Johnny's willingness to be a witness made the Canadian government nervous.[48] Indeed, there were some in the administration who considered him "a confounded nuisance."[49]

Others felt differently. An account in the *Syracuse Post Standard* on January 22, nine days later, pointed out that in the opinion of Canadian authorities de Graff was the greatest counterintelligence agent in modern history.[50] This could have been journalistic hyperbole, but there was a grain of truth in it all. *Time* magazine smelled a story and put out feelers to the FBI. They were stonewalled by Hoover's agency and told that "requests to interview de Graff are being held in abeyance pending receipt of the current RCMP attitude toward future contacts with him."[51]

Indeed, the whole question of Johnny de Graff's place in the history of espionage in Argentina, Brazil, Canada, China, Germany, Manchuria, Romania, the United Kingdom, the United States, and the former Soviet Union is bizarre. If he was not the greatest counterintelligence agent in modern history, he was certainly one of the luckiest counterintelligence agents in modern history. In that respect, the British sent an operative from London to Brockville in an effort to learn why Johnny was never found out by the Soviets. The man spent several days talking to de Graff and taping everything. Johnny's RCMP handler, Neil Pollock, sat in on some of these interviews. In the end, the representative of Her Majesty's intelligence services returned to London. No one knows what conclusions were reached, and the British, as is their custom, refuse all comment.[52]

Along with his good fortune, Johnny was generous to a fault. Following the Hungarian uprising in October and November 1956, many Hungarian refugees came through Horningtoft, and Johnny put many of them up.[53] Some probably stayed without charge, since he saw these anti-Communists as natural allies. Others were given a free bunk, as few political immigrants got out of Europe with much money. He also felt that he had a talent for sizing people up. He respected honesty, and his admiration for truthfulness extended to everyone. But woe be it to those who were dishonest with him, be they businessmen, private persons, or refugees to Canada.

On October 1, 1960, Cliff Harvison was appointed commissioner of the Royal Canadian Mounted Police and assigned to the country's top police post in Ottawa. Since joining the force in 1919, when it was known as the Royal Northwest Mounted Police, Cliff had left the service briefly, then rejoined and moved up through the ranks to the most senior position through hard work and dedication. One of the first notes of congratulation Harvison received was from an old friend in Brockville. It read, "Congratulations Cliff on your well deserved promotion. You're in the driver's seat, remembering how it was in the ranks below. You can now call the shots and tangle with the top politicians in the capital you used to curse. Good Luck!" It was signed "Petersen." Harvison chuckled heartily.

Johnny's son Oscar and his wife, Leni (short for Helena), came to visit Johnny in 1952 for six weeks. Oscar was in Montreal in 1952 when the FBI was there to interview his father. Oscar and Leni were considering immigrating to Canada and came again the following year in March. They returned to Ahlen on August 15, 1953, deciding not to stay after all, in part because of Leni's growing worry that her father-in-law would never stop his sermonizing against the Communists. She was afraid that the CPC would discover where Johnny was and actually harm him, Oscar, or herself. While in Montreal, Oscar saw a certificate signed by Queen Elizabeth The Queen Mother, which read, "Dear Johnny X, thank you for your service to the British Empire." There was another royal memento of which Johnny was very proud. One of the former heads of the Canadian Security Intelligence Service, or CSIS,[54] Jim Warren, remembers seeing a photograph of Johnny in a borrowed British naval uniform that was signed by King George VI. Johnny was extremely proud of the photograph.[55]

Even though she felt that her father was part of the reason for her mother's early death, Marianne went to see Johnny in Canada in 1979. De Graff traveled back to Germany to see his children in 1968 and again in 1976. In 1978 he again flew to Germany, but on a business trip to another part of the country. He tried to set up a meeting with Ahlen's Red Youth in 1972, saying, "When you hear what I have to say, you will give up being Communists." At first they said fine, come on, but later changed their minds, telling him that he need not travel to the Ruhr to see them.[56]

Of the many problems that came between Johnny and Sári, two of the main ones, in his opinion, were her laziness and her desire to somehow get his money. He was not happy with her.[57] But she did contribute to their income and for a time went back to work in a Brockville bank.[58] Sári was not a stupid woman. She could speak and write several languages. There were even stories that she too had been involved in intelligence during World War II, although Johnny always avoided discussing the topic.[59] In 1967, while back in Hungary, Sári began to write letters to all of the world's major leaders protesting the killing of humans and animals. She was starting to act strangely again.[60]

Unbeknownst to her family in Budapest, Sári had been treated five times over a period of thirty years at the Brockville Psychiatric Hospital. She usually stayed a couple of months. Her first admission was on June 7, 1954. On that occasion she remained in the facility for seven months and was released on January 5, 1955. At each hospitalization she displayed the same problem, a manic-depressive reaction.[61] She would get grandiose ideas, make lists of persons to have over for a "Rigoletto," as she called her parties, and then fantasize about what would happen at these affairs. These persons were often close Canadians or family members. At other times she would telephone various countries and try to get through to people in positions of power. Even royalty was not immune. Johnny said that the reasons for her calls were often the same: politics, war, and human misery.[62] Sári learned to telephone at night, when her husband was asleep. A man with a short fuse anyway, Johnny exploded when the phone bills came with outlandish long-distance charges.

Johnny virtually hated his wife during his final years. She began starving him. When Neil Pollock came to visit, he always stopped at a Kentucky Fried Chicken outlet and picked up a bucket for de Graff, who would devour the stuff. He also brought along a bottle of sherry wine, which Johnny liked. Pollock quit the case in 1978 when Johnny told him that he had finally figured out what he was going to do: shoot Sári, commit suicide, and leave all his possessions to Neil. Pollock went back to headquarters and wrote a memo, just in case it really happened. He did not want to have anything to do with that chain of events. Neil Pollock had been Johnny's case officer for ten years. He informed his RCMP superior, Gus Begalki, and took himself off the assignment. Begalki then contacted Johnny to say that Pollock had been sent on a secret mission, and that he, Begalki, had been delegated to be Johnny's new handler from that point forward.[63]

Before Neil quit, he and Johnny attended a dinner party in the latter half of 1972 at the home of Ron Stewart in Washington, D.C. Stewart worked in the criminal division of Canadian intelligence in Washington. The reason for the get-together was for the British to present an award to Johnny. As the evening progressed, de Graff and Stewart found time for a private conversation. Johnny went over the killing of "the Aristocrat" in Argentina. Then they touched on the subject of Helena Krüger in Argentina. Johnny admitted killing her because he had questioned her loyalty to the British Crown.[64]

All through his years in Brockville, neighbors and those who knew Johnny thought he was making things up. The locals tended to write him off as a harmless crank who kept pretty much to himself.[65] Disheartened, he felt that after all he had done to try to improve the world, after all that he had suffered, nothing had really changed. The twilight of Johnny's life was full of dejection.[66] People had forgotten him. The publication of Harvison's autobiography, *The Horsemen,* in 1967, and a couple of magazine articles, rekindled a short interest in "Johnny," as Harvison referred to him in the book, still thinking of protecting his former agent. In this regard, de Graff was interviewed in the local Brockville paper under the caption "Counter Spy 'Johnny' Living Quietly in City."[67]

In Johnny's old age, Sári dominated the relationship. He usually just sat around listening.[68] She continued to neglect him; his health continued to decline. In 1967 he had surgery for an ulcer and in 1974 suffered a heart attack. Gradually, he started to forget things. A two-handed walker became part of his daily routine following a fall that broke his right hip in February 1979. It was particularly annoying when his eyesight began going bad and his weight dropped to some 130 pounds (nearly 59 kg).[69] His once vigorous body was in the last round of its last fight. On December 2, 1980, at 11:20 A.M., John Henry de Graff passed away of acute myocardial ischemia, advanced coronary heart disease, and an old arterial wall infarction, at the St. Vincent de Paul Hospital in Brockville.[70] Amazingly, he had lived to be eighty-six years of age. In the room where he died there is a window through which one can see the beautiful and eloquent waters of the St. Lawrence River on its way to the Gulf of St. Lawrence and eventually the Atlantic Ocean.

EPILOGUE

Just as Johnny had done with Gerti, Sári had her husband's remains cremated. When he was alive, Johnny kept the urn containing Gerti's ashes and their rings together on a piece of red velvet. Whenever he was sad, he would go to the vase and talk softly to what was left of her.[1] With Sári, there was no such sentimentality. She kept Johnny's ashes in Horningtoft somewhere. No one is aware of what happened to Gerti's remains once he passed away.

Soon Horningtoft began to run down. Sári sold off much of the big house's antique furniture to pay bills. She reduced the rents because of the type of clientele that had started staying in the cabins. Many were drunks and lowlifes. There was even a killing at Horningtoft between a couple of the alcoholics. The perpetrator was caught and sent to prison.[2]

Sári often gave blank checks to the wino tenants of the cabins so looked after by her deceased husband. The checks usually bounced, and the gas and electricity ended up being cut off for lack of payment. Ultimately, a naturalized Canadian named Andy Kovács got involved. Originally from Hungary too, his ex-wife had told him that there was a Hungarian woman living in dreadful conditions at Horningtoft. He went there, introduced himself to Sári, and offered his help. Sári was usually happy to have him around. He doubtlessly hoped to cash in on his new friendship at some point in the future. To get the utilities turned back on, Kovács maintained that he paid Can$6,000 out of his own pocket. He never did get the gas working again, although he paid the bill. The gas company said he would have to repair the various buildings' heaters first. Kovács also had to come up with the back taxes and insurance premiums.[3]

Sári was admitted to the Brockville Psychiatric Hospital again in July 1984, where she quickly became a pest who acted out her aggression on other patients. She was released that winter and at times walked around outside in the snow and ice in just her housecoat and slippers. Kovács noticed that she smoked three packs of cigarettes a day—in bed. He could not dissuade her from smoking that way. A friend got him some flameproof material, which he put between her and the mattress. Even if she preferred to live in squalor, Andy insisted that she bathe at least twice a week. On the appointed days, it was a big fight to get her into and out of the tub. She really left her bed only to go to the toilet, get something to eat, or fetch some alcoholic beverage to drink. Then it was back to bed to watch TV and smoke cigarettes. When her weight started to increase, Kovács put a padlock on the refrigerator. Sári never talked about missing the man she had married.[4]

She traveled back to Budapest in 1964 and stayed with relatives, the Fegyvernekys, in their flat at Szilágyi Erzsébet Fasor 103. There, too, Sári stayed in bed nearly all day watching television. Children's programs were the main diet; they fascinated her.[5]

Andy Kovács paid for another trip to Hungary in 1985. But by then Sári was obese from adult-onset diabetes. She died on July 8, 1985, at age sixty-four, while eating dinner with her niece, Maria "Marika" Harsanyi.[6] When the report of Sári's death reached Brockville, a number of her boozer tenants ransacked Horningtoft, taking whatever of value they could find. Kovács managed to recover Johnny's ashes. He gave them to the Barclay Funeral Home, without any kind of payment for their internment or safekeeping.[7] Despite the main house's historical importance, the structure was built in the nineteenth century, everything was bulldozed by the city in 1988 to make way for a supposed housing development. Weeds took over the premises for years.[8]

. . . AND THE OTHERS

George Aitken died in the United Kingdom in 1979.
Adrien Arcand passed away in 1967, convinced that Canada would eventually embrace his views.
Ian Berzin was executed in the purges of 1938.
Stella Blagoeva died in Bulgaria in 1954.
Eugene Dennis passed away in New York City in 1961.
Frank Foley succumbed to a heart attack at home in Stourbridge, West Midlands, in 1958.
Rodolfo Ghioldi died Buenos Aires in 1985, still honored by his countrymen despite having turned in several comrades to the police in Brazil in 1935.
Amanda de Graaf passed away in Hamm in 1951. Amanda remarried in 1941. Her last name at the time of her death was Rüschenschmidt.
Marianne de Graaf is still alive and living in Ahlen.
Oscar de Graaf, Johnny's second child, passed away in 1998. His wife, Leni, and their son, Johnny de Graaf III, reside in Ahlen.
Sophie and **Paula de Graaf**, Johnny's two sisters, died in Germany before the FBI's Montreal interview on March 10, 1952.
Waldemar de Graaf was sentenced to prison for skirmishing with Nazis. He died in the Ravensbrück Concentration Camp in 1943.
Walter de Graaf was arrested and forced to join the Wehrmacht because he was a Communist. He was killed during World War II.
Wilhelm de Graaf passed away in Bremen in 1956.
Willy de Graaf was sentenced to two years and four months' imprisonment for fighting with Nazis. He ended up becoming a Nazi and living with his father. At the time of the FBI's Montreal interview, Johnny had had no contact with his brother for about thirty years. Johnny threatened to kill Willy for joining the Nazis if the two ever met again.
Cliff Harvison retired from the RCMP in 1963 and passed away in Ottawa in 1968.
Ernst Krüger returned to Brazil after the war with his German wife, Waltraud, and their two children. Two more young ones were born in Brazil. He died in 1998 in Rio de Janeiro. Waltraud, her children, and her grandchildren are still alive and living in Brazil.
Alfred Langner fought for two years in the Spanish Civil War. He returned to

academic life in the USSR but eventually went back to Finland in 1946. He died there in 1976.

Dmitri Manuilski passed on in 1959.

Filinto Müller died in a mysterious fire when the commercial jet he was in made an unsuccessful emergency landing in a field near Paris's Orly Airport in 1973.

Harry Pollitt succumbed onboard the P&O liner SS *Orion* following a speaking tour in Australia in 1960.

Luís Carlos Prestes passed away in Rio de Janeiro in 1990. He was greatly respected and remained politically active to the end.

Manfred Stern was removed from his command of the International Brigades fighting Francisco Franco in 1937. He did return to Spain despite Johnny's warning. Stern died a broken man in a Far East gulag near Magadan in 1954.

Getúlio Vargas was removed from power by a military coup in 1945 but was elected president in 1950. He refused to hand over the reins of government to the military in 1954 and may have been connected to the botched assassination attempt of a rival. He committed suicide in office on August 24, 1954.

Valentine Vivian died of cancer in a London hospital in 1948.

Werner von Janowski's destiny is unknown.

KNOWN OR SUSPECTED ALIASES OF JOHANN HEINRICH AMADEUS DE GRAAF

Hans Alfred
August
Willen Bosma
Captain Burger
Captain Johnny X
Comrade August
Comrade Chung
Comrade Harry
Comrade Jan
Comrade John
Comrade Julius
Comrade Matern
Comrade Mattern
Jonny de Graaf
Johnny de Graf
J. H. de Graff
John Henry de Graff
Johnny de Graff
William de Graff
William John de Graff
Ludwig Dinkelmeyer
Graf
Jonny Graf
John Graff
John William Graff
William John Graff
John Graffnor
John[a] Gries
Gruber
Francisco Gruber
Franz Gruber
Franz Paul Gruber
Paul Gruber
Karl Grubnick

Hans
Iedko
Ioni
Johanssen
Jonnie
Jonny X
Julius
Kraff
Kraft
Júlio Krebs
Joseph Martel
Mattern
Alfred Mattern
Mr. X
Alfred Neinhartz
Otto
Pedro
Petersen
Paul Petersen
Professor
Richard
Rihard
S. A. 235
Herman Schneider
Gottfried[b] Treviranus
Valter
Jan Valtin
Herman van Heussen
Wagner
Walter
Richard M. Walter
Harry Wickman
William
X-502
Bruno Zimmerman

[a] Probably used in Canada at least during the von Janowski case.
[b] Almost certainly incorrect. It was first reported in Juan Pujol, with Nigel West, *Garbo* (London: Weidenfeld and Nicolson, 1985), p. 104.

NOTES

Unless otherwise noted, all interviews were conducted by R. S. Rose; all letters and e-mail messages were addressed to R. S. Rose.

INTRODUCTION

1. M. T. Murray (United Kingdom, Foreign and Commonwealth Office, hereafter UKFCO), letter, August 17, 1994.

CHAPTER 1. WILHELMSHAVEN

1. Neil Pollock, interview, Calgary, Alberta, September 16, 1996. Pollock was one of Johnny's RCMP case officers after de Graaf retired.
2. De Graaf originally told Gordon Scott that he was born in Hamburg. If this was done because he thought Scott would understand German geography better if he chose a big city close to his actual place of birth, if he misunderstood the question, or if it was done for some other reason, is not known. It is possible that he meant to say "near Hamburg." Verification that Johnny was born in Nordenham is in Rudolf de Graaf, letter, June 30, 1994, as well as documents at Российский государственный архив социально-политической истории (Rossiiskii gosudarstvennyi arkhiv sotsial'no-politicheskoi istorii—Russian State Archive of Sociopolitical History) (hereafter РГАСПИ). Note that this archive changed its name to the present form in 1999. It was formerly known as РЦХИДНИ, the Modern Russian History Document Conservation and Research Center.
3. Jonny in German.
4. Germany, Staatsarchiv Hamburg (hereafter GSH), document, "Meldekartei der von 1892–1925 verstorbenen oder aus Hamburg verzogenen Personen" (hereafter "Meldekartei der von 1892–1925"), Blatt 1A, Bestand 332–38, Meldewesen A30, film K6145.
5. The problem of where Wilhelm was born comes from his Hamburg police registration documents, in which he stated that his birthplace was Geestemünde (ibid.), and the registration of his death material in Bremen, which gives his place of birth in Geestendorf, not far away. Wilhelm Mensing, e-mail, August 18, 2006.
6. GSH, "Meldekartei der von 1892–1925."
7. Ibid.; U.S. Federal Bureau of Investigation (FBI), document, "Re: John Henry de Graaf, was," June 13, 1952, file HQ100–342513–49; and Rudolf de Graaf, letter, June 30, 1994.
8. Jens Graul, interview, Wilhelmshaven, August 3, 2006. Graul is one of the Wilhelmshaven city administrators.
9. GSH, "Meldekartei der von 1892–1925," Blätter 1A–2A; and Peter Gabrielsson, interview, Hamburg, July 28, 2006. Gabrielsson is one of the directors at the Staatsarchiv Hamburg.
10. Heinz-Dieter Ströhla, e-mail, July 9, 2004. Ströhla is the assistant archivist for the City of Wilhelmshaven.
11. Wilhelm Knöß, interview, Wilhelmshaven, August 1, 2006. Knöß is the deputy chief of the archives of the Deutsches Marinemuseum in Wilhelmshaven.
12. Ibid.
13. "Register of Ships N," http://www.webruler.com/gprovost/ShipsN.htm (accessed August 2, 2003).

14. This did not mean taking a bath. Not even the houses of the gentry had permanent warm water at that time. Taking a bath then meant to get the hot water heater going, wait an hour until there was enough warm water, and then take a bath, which normally was a family procedure—one after the other taking their turn in the dirtier-by-the-person bath water. Wilhelm Mensing, e-mail, August 11, 2006.

15. Heinz-Dieter Ströhla, telephone interview by Stefan Antheck, Wilhelmshaven, August 2, 2006. Antheck is a city functionary.

16. "Deutschland, Deutschland über Alles" (Germany, Germany over All) would not become the national anthem until 1922. Mensing, e-mail, August 11, 2006.

17. The family name is tentative.

18. Germans did not use Santa Claus until the 1950s. Instead, they had Nikolaus, who brought small gifts such as an orange or a piece of chocolate on December 6, and Christkind, who brought presents on Christmas Day. Mensing, e-mail, August 11, 2006.

19. РГАСПИ, document, "Lebenslauf des Parteigenosse Jonny de Graaf: Deutsche Partei Ruhrgebiet; z. Z. Russland," фонд 495, опись 205, дело 6385, лист 137; and *Ottawa Journal,* January 12, 1954, p. 12.

20. Ströhla, e-mail, July 9, 2004.

CHAPTER 2. MERCHANT MARINE

1. Written on the back of a stereoscopic card of Leopoldville was the following: "If you wish to visit the most important town of Congo Free State, Leopoldville, an ocean steamer will carry you up the broad seven-mile mouth of the Congo to Matadi, then a ride of 240 miles [386.3 km] on the Congo Railway, built in 1898, will bring you to Stanley Pool." "Stereoscopic Visions of War and Empire," http://www.boondocksnet.com/stereo/sv289f.html (accessed March 19, 2003).

2. The Congo Free State was annexed by Belgium in 1908 to become the Belgian Congo. When it was in 1908 that the *Niobie* dropped anchor there is unclear.

3. Many of these slavers were Arabs from Morocco. Pierre Wautier, e-mail to Christine Preston, March 22, 2003, and Christine Preston, e-mails, March 19 and April 4, 2003. See also Preston's "Scramble for Katanga," http://216.239.33.100/search?q=cache:nrHxq6W1to4C:kolwezikat.fr ee.fr/Publications/Kat2.rtf+slavery+%22Belgian+Africa%22&hl=en&ie=UT F-8 (accessed March 15, 2003).

4. R. S. Rose, "Slavery in Brazil: Does It Still Exist?" *Review of Latin American Studies* vol. 4, no. 1 (1991), p. 97.

5. Pollock, interview, September 16, 1996.

6. Selena Williams (State Records of New South Wales, Western Sydney Records Centre, Australia), e-mail, July 30, 2003. The *Tübingen* made three trips to Port Jackson in 1912, arriving on June 2, November 28, and December 22. It is unknown on which of the corresponding voyages de Graaf signed on.

7. РГАСПИ, document, "Betr. Jonny de Graaf," фонд 495, опись 205, дело 6385, лист 117.

8. The North German Lloyd docks were destroyed in the Great Hoboken Pier Fire of June 30, 1900. Robert Gordon, "The Great Harbor Fire: The North German Lloyd Disaster of 1900," *New Jersey History* (Fall–Winter 1982), pp. 1–13.

9. Robert Foster, interview, Hoboken, N.J., June 20, 2006. Foster is the executive director of the Hoboken Historical Museum.

10. *Union City (N.J.) Hudson Dispatch,* October 2, 1917, p. 1.

11. Foster, interview; and Reinhard Böhme, ed., *Rückblicke Deutscher Club von Hoboken 1857 a 1907* (Hoboken, N.J., 1907), p. 5.

12. United Kingdom, National Archives (hereafter UKNA), document, "Metropolitan Police," HO 405/17786, unpaginated [p. 2]; "Register of Ships Car-Cey," http://www.webruler.com/gprovost/ShipsC1.htm (accessed August 2, 2003).

13. *New York Times,* December 29, 1913, p. 8.

14. GSH, "Meldekartei der von 1892–1925," Blatt 1B.

15. Oscar de Graaf, interview, Ahlen, July 26, 1996. Oscar was the second son of Johnny and Maria. For more on this union, see chapter 5, "Germany in Chaos."

16. The authors are grateful to Oscar de Graaf for the information on two of the tattoos. Ibid.

17. Michael C. Meyer, *Huerta: A Political Portrait* (Lincoln: University of Nebraska Press, 1972), pp. 193–97.

18. The following month, the *Barbarossa* was granted safe haven in New York but was seized in April 1917 when the United States declared war on the Central Powers. She was renamed the SS *Mercury* in 1919 and used by the U.S. Navy as a troop carrier across the Atlantic. The *Mercury* was scrapped in 1924. N. R. P. Bonsor, *North Atlantic Seaway: An Illustrated History of the Passenger Services Linking the Old World with the New in Four Volumes*, vol. 2 (Cambridge: P. S. L. Patrick Stephens, 1978), p. 559.

19. FBI, document, "FBI, Montreal interview of John Henry de Graaf" (hereafter FBI, "Montreal interview of de Graaf"), March 10, 1952, pp. 3–4, file HQ 100–342513, NY65–15945.

20. Some of this is confirmed in ibid., p. 4.

21. Ibid., p. 119; *Kingston (Ontario) Whig-Standard*, October 13, 1954; p. [4]; Ernst Krüger, interviews, Praia de Mauá, RJ, Brazil, August 12 and September 19, 1994, and Rio de Janeiro, December 3, 1994; and Audrey Armitage, interview, Brockville, Ontario, July 14, 1995. Ernst Krüger was the brother of two of Johnny's common-law wives. Audrey and Jack Armitage were Johnny's neighbors in Brockville on the east side of Horningtoft.

CHAPTER 3. CONSCRIPTED

1. РГАСПИ, "Lebenslauf des Parteigenosse Jonny de Graaf"; and FBI, letter, "SAC Washington Field (65–5504), to Director, FBI (65–59191)," May 3, 1952, file HQ 100–342513.

2. Torsten Palmér and Hendrik Neubauer, *The Weimar Republic: Through the Lens of the Press*, trans. Maike Dörries, Peter Barton, Mark Cole and Susan Cox (Cologne: Könemann, 2000), pp. 49, 392–93.

3. Johnny told the FBI on two different occasions that he was actually arrested for speaking against German imperialism at a street rally in Rotterdam. Neither report appears to have been generated from the other. FBI, Liaison Office, Ottawa, "[unknown] to Director, FBI," February 27, 1952, p. 1, file HQ100–342513; and FBI, "Montreal interview of de Graaf."

4. Johnny often referred to someone he did not trust as a snake.

5. FBI, "Montreal interview of de Graaf."

6. F. A. Krummacher and Albert Wucher, *Die Weimarer Republik: Ihre Geschichte in Texten, Bildern und Dokumenten* (Wiesbaden: Löwit, 1965), p. 36; John R. P. McKenzie, *Weimar Germany: 1918–1933* (London: Blandford, 1971), p. 11; and David Childs, *Germany Since 1918* (New York: St. Martin's Press, 1980), p. 11.

7. РГАСПИ, document, "СПРАВКА (на основании автобиографии)," (hereafter "СПРАВКА"), фонд 495, опись 184, дело 6, лист 35. Observe that , "Betr. Jonny de Graaf," lists 1916 as the year Johnny became a member of the USPD. While he could have sided with it in spirit, the USPD was not formed until the following year.

8. A view of this base entrance can be seen in *Wilhelmshaven: Ein Führer für Fremde und Einheimische* (Wilhelmshaven: C. Lohse, 1899), unnumbered plate between pp. 92 and 93. It still exists as of this writing.

9. In some parts of the English-speaking world, the nickname would indicate a person who likes to drink beer. Whether this Scoopies had the often-accompanying beer gut is unknown. As these inductees were from the merchant marine, they had ample opportunity to pick up slang from one another's languages.

10. "Imperial German Navy Capital Ship Captains," http://www.gwpda.org/naval/ hsfcpco.htm (accessed August 23, 2003). SMS stood for *Seiner Majestät Schiff*, or His Majesty's ship.

11. Fitzhugh Green and Holloway Frost, *Some Famous Sea Fights* (Freeport, N.Y.: Books for Libraries Press, 1968), p. 283. The encounter is known as the Battle of Skagerrak in Germany.

12. Ibid., pp. 326–29.

13. Ibid., pp. 323–24; and Oscar de Graaf, interviews, July 26, 1996, and August 16, 1997.

14. Oscar de Graaf, interviews, July 26, 1996, and August 16, 1997; Pollock, interview, September 16, 1996; and FBI, "Montreal interview of de Graaf," pp. 4–5. He eventually gave the medal to his

daughter, Marianne, and the picture to his son, Oscar. Oscar later sold the rendition to a policeman who was also on the *Westfalen* but was too sick to man his station. Oscar de Graaf, interview, July 26, 1996. The authors are aware of the two Iron Crosses mentioned in the Canadian Security Intelligence Service (hereafter CSIS), Royal Canadian Mounted Police (hereafter RCMP) document, "[anonymous] interview with John Henry de Graff," Brockville, Ontario, May 22, 1968 (hereafter "1968 Brockville interview of John Henry de Graff"), pp. 5–6, file, John de Graaf, vol. TS. Oscar de Graaf, however, only remembered his father speaking about a single Iron Cross first class awarded after the Battle of Jutland. The authors are aware that few first-class Iron Crosses were given out to ordinary seamen.

15. FBI, "Montreal interview of de Graaf," p. 47.

16. Wilhelm Dittmann, *Die Marine-Justizmorde von 1917 und die Admirals-Rebellion von 1918* (Berlin: J. H. W. Dietz, 1926), pp. 48–52. Dittmann was the same individual mentioned in chapters 5 and 10. His report was part of a government investigation into victims among the sailors involved in the 1917 mutiny.

17. Daniel Horn, ed. and trans., *War, Mutiny, and Revolution in the German Navy: The World War I Diary of Seaman Richard Stumpf* (New Brunswick: Rutgers University Press, 1967), pp. 354–55, 373–77; Daniel Horn, *The German Naval Mutinies of World War I* (New Brunswick: Rutgers University Press, 1969), pp. 135, 148–55; and CSIS, RCMP, "1968 Brockville interview of John Henry de Graff," p. 4.

18. CSIS, RCMP, "1968 Brockville interview of John Henry de Graff," p. 5.

19. Germany, Bundesarchiv—Militärarchiv Freiburg (hereafter GBF), court transcript, "Abschrift zu J.I.429.Go., Der Chef des Admiralstabes der Marine, Nr.G.19775I4," PH2/478, Blätter [1]–2. Note that de Graaf later told the Soviets he had been sentenced to two years' imprisonment on January 12, 1931 (РГАСПИ, "Lebenslauf des Parteigenosse Jonny de Graaf," фонд 495, опись 205, дело 6385, лист 138), and to five years' incarceration on April 10, 1937 (РГАСПИ, "СПРАВКА"). De Graaf told the FBI that he had been sentenced to death but had his sentence reduced to five years owing to a court technicality. FBI, "Montreal interview of de Graaf," p. 5, and letter, "[unknown] to Director, FBI," February 27, 1952, p. 1, file HO 100–342513. Johnny also confided to at least one other source, his own son Oscar, that he was sentenced to death but that the penalty was changed to a life sentence. Uwe Rennspieß, *Jenseits der Bahn: Geschichte der Ahlener Bergarbeiterkolonie und der Zeche Westfalen* (Essen: Klartext, 1989), p. 251; and Oscar de Graaf, interview, August 16, 1997. He likewise admitted to two separate reporters on two different occasions that he had received a death sentence. *Brockville (Ontario) Recorder and Times,* January 13, 1967, p. 3; and *Ottawa Citizen,* January 12, 1954, p. 13. Johnny was called "Otto" in the latter newspaper article.

20. CSIS, RCMP, "1968 Brockville interview of John Henry de Graff," p. 4.

21. РГАСПИ, "Lebenslauf des Parteigenosse Jonny de Graaf."

CHAPTER 4. OSOWIEC

1. CSIS, RCMP, "1968 Brockville interview of John Henry de Graff," p. 8.

2. FBI, "Montreal interview of de Graaf." In another source, Johnny states that the temperature was minus 37 degrees Centigrade (minus 34.6 Fahrenheit). CSIS, RCMP, "1968 Brockville interview of John Henry de Graff," p. 8.

3. Tadeusz Krawczak, letter, January 23, 1997; and Artur Wiśniewski, manuscript, n.d., p. 1.

4. This was part of the administration complex that was later destroyed. It is probably located, unexcavated, to the northeast of the present commandant's office. Bogdan Oźlański, interview, Osowiec, August 9, 2002. Ozlanski was the commanding oficer of the Osowiec complex at the time of the interview.

5. Wilmont Young, interview, Brockville, Ontario, July 12, 1995. Young was the police chief in Brockville from 1938 to 1968.

6. Artur Wiśniewski, interview, Osowiec, August 9, 2002.

7. GBF, "Frhr. v. Liliencron," 17 Sg 109; and Reinhard Montag, "Das Lexikon der Deutschen Generale," http://www.lexikon-deutschegenerale.de/l_pr2.html (accessed September 3, 2003). Von

Liliencron was made a provisional major general on May 27, 1918, the GBF material points out, but continued to be paid the salary of a colonel.

8. РГАСПИ, "Lebenslauf des Parteigenosse Jonny de Graaf."
9. GSH, "Meldekarteí der von 1892–1925," Blatt 2A.

CHAPTER 5. GERMANY IN CHAOS

1. "Rosa Luxemburg (1871–1919)," http://www.kirjasto.sci.fi/luxembur.htm (accessed August 13, 2003).
2. Pollock, interview, September 16, 1996.
3. This new endeavor was to be composed of 22 capital ships, 12 light cruisers, and 72 destroyers. At Jutland the Germans mustered 20 capital ships, 9 light cruisers, and 62 destroyers. "The Scuttling of the German High Seas Fleet at Scapa Flow on the 21st of June 1919," http://www.ahoy.tk-jk.net/macslog/TheScuttlingoftheGermanHi.html (accessed September 5, 2003); and "Battle of Jutland—Order of Battle," http://www.gwpda.org/naval/jutob.htm (accessed September 5, 2003).
4. РГАСПИ, "Lebenslauf des Parteigenosse Jonny de Graaf."
5. Wilhelm Mensing, e-mail, August 8, 2006.
6. Germany, Stadt Ahlen (hereafter GSA), document, Der Bürgermeister, Einwohnermeldeabteilung, "Johann de Graaf," July 25, 2000. This copy, typed later, of an official document states that Johnny arrived in Ahlen from Münster on November 11, 1918. The day could be correct, but the month is wrong. The month was probably December.
7. Johnny de Graaf III, e-mail, April 18, 2006.
8. Ibid.
9. CSIS, RCMP, document, "Interview of Johnny de Graff by Sgt. [censored] and Cpl. [censored] in Brockville, Ontario," February 20, 1969 (hereafter "1969 Brockville interview of John Henry de Graff"), file, John de Graff, vol. 5, p. 12.
10. РГАСПИ, "Betr. Jonny de Graaf"; РГАСПИ, "Lebenslauf des Parteigenosse Jonny de Graaf"; and FBI, "Montreal interview of de Graaf," p. 6.
11. Palmér and Neubauer, p. 59.
12. William K. Klingaman, *The Year Our World Began, 1919* (New York: Harper and Row, 1987), pp. 35–37, 162–63, 475; and Nigel Jones, *A Brief History of the Birth of the Nazis* (New York: Carroll and Graf, 2004), p. 73.
13. "Militärische Intervention und das Ende," http://www.bikonline.de/histo/interv.html (accessed March 18, 2003).
14. РГАСПИ, "СПРАВКА."
15. Oscar de Graaf, letter postmarked February 5, 1997.
16. Oscar de Graaf, interview, Ahlen, August 31, 1996.
17. Jürgen Lange, *Die Schlacht bei Pelkum im März 1920: Legenden und Dokumente* (Essen: Klartext, 1994), p. 214.
18. GSA, Der Bürgermeister, Einwohnermeldeabteilung, "Johann de Graaf [Jr.]," July 25, 2000.
19. Johnny's role in one of these strikes, a later one on April 4, 1926, is discussed in Lange, p. 214.
20. For more on this topic, see Bernd Kaufmann et al., *Der Nachrichtendienst der KPD, 1919–1937* (Berlin: Dietz, 1993); and Wilhelm Mensing, "Gestapo V-Leute kommunistischer Herkunft—auch ein Strukturproblem der KPD?" *Mitteilungsblatt des Instituts für soziale Bewegungen,* vol. 34 (2005), p. 37 and passim.
21. Johnny told the FBI that he obtained the coal scar on his face from a small mine explosion. FBI, "Philadelphia interview of John Henry de Graaf," December 29, 1952, p. 16, file HQ 100-342513, PH65-4336.
22. John Maynard Keynes, *The Economic Consequences of the Peace* (New York: Harcourt Brace Jovanovich, 1920), pp. 211–16.
23. Frank P. Chambers, *This Age of Conflict: The Western World, 1914 to the Present,* 3d ed. (New York: Harcourt, Brace & World, 1962), pp. 136–37; Raymond J. Sontag, *A Broken World, 1919–1939* (New York: Harper and Row, 1971), pp. 54–57; Henry T. Allen, *The Rhineland Occupation* (Indianapolis: Bobbs-Merrill, 1927), pp. 159–61; Palmér and Neubauer, pp. 49, 392–93; and Jones, pp. 167–81.

24. Chambers, p. 139.

25. FBI, "Montreal interview of de Graaf," p. 7; and Werner T. Angress, "Weimar Coalition and Ruhr Insurrection, March–April 1920: A Study of Government Policy," *Journal of Modern History,* vol. 29, no. 1 (1957), pp. 2, 4–5.

26. Jones, p. 194.

27. Angress, p. 7.

28. Jones, p. 199.

29. Ibid.

30. Pollock, interview, September 16, 1996.

31. Angress, pp. 13–16. As to the growing carnage, Angress reports, "When the order to advance was finally given, the occupying troops showed no mercy but gave free rein to their accumulated hatreds. The arbitrary death sentences by drumhead court-martial, the display of monarchist flags and insignia, and the mass murders of prisoners seemed to confirm the suspicions of the insurgents, and of German labor at large, that the government had betrayed them to the Kappists" (p. 18).

32. Despite the comments in Angress (p. 7n), de Graaf's remarks support the views expressed by Erwin Brauer, in *Der Ruhraufstand von 1920* (Berlin: International Arbeiter, 1930), pp. 83–85.

33. FBI, "Montreal interview of de Graaf."

34. Ibid., pp. 7–8.

CHAPTER 6. *DIE* KPD

1. Oscar de Graaf, interview, July 26, 1996; РГАСПИ, documents, "[untitled handwritten notes in Russian by Stella Blagoeva]" (hereafter РГАСПИ, "Blagoeva notes"), фонд 495, опись 205, дело 6385, лист 79; "Biographie des Genossen Jonny de Graaf, Buchnummer 2173673 W.K.P.b," фонд 495, опись 205, дело 6385, лист 136; and "СПРАВКА."

2. РГАСПИ, "Blagoeva notes."

3. Ibid., лист 79 оборот; and РГАСПИ, "Biographie des Genossen Jonny de Graaf."

4. РГАСПИ, "Blagoeva notes."

5. David P. Hornstein, *Arthur Ewert: A Life for the Comintern* (Lanham, Md.: University Press of America, 1993), p. 37.

6. Hermann Weber, *Die Wandlung des deutschen Kommunismus: Die Stalinisierung der KPD in der Weimarer Republik,* vol. 1 (Frankfurt am Main: Europische 1969), p. 47.

7. Weber (ibid.) lists as his source Otto Wenzel, "Die kommunistische Partei Deutschlands im Jahre 1923" (PhD diss., Department of Philosophy, Freie Universität Berlin, 1955). The work by Wenzel, however, does not mention de Graaf as being at the Essen meeting. Neither does Wenzel's more heavily documented book, *1923—Die gescheiterte deutsche Oktoberrevolution* (Münster: Lit, 2003).

8. Palmér and Neubauer, p. 405.

9. РГАСПИ, "Blagoeva notes," лист 81. After Lenin's death, the Soviet Union found itself in a power struggle between three factions. On one side was the leftist opposition, headed by Leon Trotsky. This group claimed to represent proletarian aspirations of world revolution. In the center were Stalin and the other state bureaucrats who would seek to build socialism in one country. The right-wing opposition, led primarily by Nikolai Bukharin, was ultimately thought to represent interests that could promote a possible capitalist resurgence.

10. An idea of Leon Trotsky, founded in Moscow in March 1919, the Comintern was established to promote world revolution. Its two principal efforts took place in China and Brazil in the 1930s. The organization functioned until 1943, when Stalin dissolved it to mollify his American and British allies in World War II.

11. William J. Chase, *Enemies Within the Gates: The Comintern and the Stalinist Repression, 1934–1939* (New Haven: Yale University Press, 2001), p. 491.

12. "Stahlhelm," http://en.wikipedia.org/wiki/Stahlhelm%2C_Bund_der_Frontsol daten (accessed September 28, 2003).

13. GSA, Der Bürgermeister, Einwohnermeldeabteilung, "Oscar de Graaf," July 25, 2000.

14. Pollock, interview, September 16, 1996.

15. Frank Foley, letter [to John de Graff], January 1947. The date "in January" is on the original.

16. A. M. Prokhorov, ed., *Great Soviet Encyclopedia*, 3d ed., vol. 3 (New York: Macmillan, 1973), pp. 226–27. Berzin, a Latvian, took an active part in the Russian Revolution of 1917. His photograph can be seen in figure 14.

17. FBI, "Montreal interview of de Graaf," p. 15; РГАСПИ, "СПРАВКА," and "Blagoeva notes," лист 79 оборот; Adrian Klose (Dortmund Police Department, Dortmund, Germany), e-mail, July 22, 2005; and Steinwache Memorial Centre, http://www.ns-gedenkstaetten.net/nrw/en/dortmund/beschreibung/ (accessed July 22, 2005).

18. РГАСПИ, "Blagoeva notes" and "СПРАВКА"; Oscar de Graaf, interview, August 31, 1996.

19. CSIS, RCMP, document, "Copy of Montreal FBI interview of John Henry de Graaf," March 10, 1952, file, John de Graff (hereafter CSIS, RCMP, "Copy of Montreal FBI interview of de Graaf"), vol. 4, p. 8; and W. G. Krivitsky, *In Stalin's Secret Service: An Exposé of Russia's Secret Policies by the Former Chief of the Soviet Intelligence in Western Europe* (New York: Harper, 1939), p. 46.

20. GSA, Der Bürgermeister, Einwohnermeldeabteilung, "Johann de Graaf," July 25, 2000; and РГАСПИ, "СПРАВКА."

21. FBI, "Montreal interview of de Graaf," p. 17.

22. Ibid., pp. 15–17, 19; РГАСПИ, "Blagoeva notes," лист 80; and Lange, p. 214.

23. РГАСПИ, "Blagoeva notes," "СПРАВКА," and "Biographie des Genossen Jonny de Graaf." These three autobiographical РГАСПИ sources give sentences of twenty-one months. РГАСПИ, "Lebenslauf des Parteigenosse Jonny de Graaf," however, says the sentence was one year.

24. GSA, Der Bürgermeister, Einwohnermeldeabteilung, "Marianne de Graaf," July 25, 2000.

25. РГАСПИ, "Blagoeva notes."

26. CSIS, RCMP, "Copy of Montreal FBI interview of de Graaf," vol. 4, p. 16.

27. On March 3, 1933, little more than a month after Hitler became chancellor, the Gestapo arrested Thälmann. He was executed at Buchenwald concentration camp in 1944. Palmér and Neubauer, p. 402.

28. РГАСПИ, "Blagoeva notes," листов 79 оборот, 80–81, "СПРАВКА," and "Lebenslauf des Parteigenosse Jonny de Graaf." De Graaf informed the FBI that the newspaper delivery activity took place from the end of 1924 to the end of 1925. The reports made to the Soviets, since they were closer in time to the events and because de Graaf could have been executed in 1937 for giving a wrong answer to Stella Blagoeva, are taken here as accurate.

29. Ernst Krüger, interviews, September 19, October 17, and December 3, 1994. Helena was born in the German capital on June 19, 1917. Gustav Ernst Karl Krüger and Pauline Emilie Krüger, "Familien Stammbuch der Familie Krüger" (family album of photos and clippings), p. 14.

30. Krüger, interview, August 12, 1994.

31. РГАСПИ, "Blagoeva notes," лист 80. De Graaf stated to the FBI that he became subdistrict party secretary in 1925 (FBI, "Montreal interview of de Graaf"). Since Blagoeva could have easily confirmed the date of his appointment, and since his life hung in the balance, the РГАСПИ version will be considered more plausible.

32. РГАСПИ, "Blagoeva notes" and "СПРАВКА."

33. Johnny told the FBI years later, "The plainclothesman came to my office where I was working and found some of the papers [antimilitaristic propaganda] in my office. I readily admitted possessing these papers." FBI, "Montreal interview of de Graaf," p. 18.

34. De Graaf mentioned to the FBI that the arrest scenario was a bit different. In this FBI version, he arranged for a group of leftists to capture and turn in to the police several Nazis who had fought with six Ahlen comrades. Instead of the police arresting the Nazis, they picked up de Graaf. All of this took place after he had been informed by the local prosecuter that he was to be charged with high treason following his arrest for disturbing the peace. Ibid. It seems unlikely that someone about to be charged with high treason would be released when in police custody.

35. Ibid., and РГАСПИ, "Biographie des Genossen Jonny de Graaf."

36. CSIS, RCMP, "Copy of Montreal FBI interview of de Graaf."

37. FBI, "Montreal interview of de Graaf"; РГАСПИ, "Blagoeva notes"; and Oscar de Graaf, interview, July 26, 1996.

38. Krüger, interview, August 12, 1994.

39. Ernst Krüger, interview, Rio de Janeiro, December 14, 1994.

40. Michael Burleigh, *The Third Reich: A New History* (New York: Hill and Wang, 2000), pp. 118–19, 129. It is sometimes claimed that both Wessel and Höhler dabbled in pimping.

41. Ernst Krüger, interviews, September 19, December 3, December 14, and December 17, 1994, and letter, December 10, 1994.

42. CSIS, RCMP, "Copy of Montreal FBI interview of de Graaf," vol. 4, p. 19.

CHAPTER 7. THE MOSCOW STUDENT

1. Johnny told the FBI that he went to Berlin and not to Bern. In Berlin he met Langner and then traveled to Moscow. FBI, "Montreal interview of de Graaf."

2. Yrjö Hakanen (Communist Party of Finland), e-mail, March 14, 2005; and K. M. Anderson, e-mail, August 16, 2004. Anderson is the director of РГАСПИ in Moscow. The CIA had at least Langner's real name wrong. They called him "Alfred Langer," alias "Tuuri Lehti." CIA, report, "The Third (Communist International) Structure and Functions," November 1, 1947, RDP78-02646R000600130001-7, pp. 49–50. During the interviews the FBI made with de Graaf in Montreal, he consistently told the FBI that the last name of Lehén's principal alias was spelled Langner. De Graaf's version is used here.

3. CIA, "Third (Communist International) Structure and Functions," pp. 49–50.

4. FBI, "Montreal interview of de Graaf," pp. 18, 28.

5. РГАСПИ, document, "An die Int. Rote Hilfe, Politemigrantenabt. Moskau," фонд 495, опись 205, дело 6385, лист 36.

6. CSIS, RCMP, "Copy of Montreal FBI interview of de Graaf."

7. FBI, "Montreal interview of de Graaf," p. 119.

8. Ibid., pp. 19–20.

9. Pavel Vasiliev may be an alias. There are no records in the archives at РГАСПИ on anyone with that name. K. M. Anderson, e-mail, March 30, 2005.

10. FBI, "Montreal interview of de Graaf," p. 28; and РГАСПИ, document, "С. Секретно—-Тов. Апресну," фонд 495, опись 205, дело 6385, лист 34.

11. Montgomery M. Green, "Russia's Super-Secret Weapon Revealed!" *Plain Truth: A Magazine of Understanding*, January 1956, pp. 2–3. The Christian Media Centre in England published this report. Green is reported to have been a U.S. naval intelligence officer. It is one of the few accounts of life at Lenin University and in fact corroborates some of Johnny's own statements.

12. CSIS, RCMP, letter, "Memo for File [dated Ottawa, 15-11-68]," file, John de Graaf, vol. 5.

13. FBI, "Montreal interview of de Graaf," p. 22.

14. Stern was likewise known to the FBI as General Moische Stern and as General Gomez. At one point, early in the coming Spanish Civil War, and known as General Emilio Kléber, he would have command over the entire Republican army. Ibid., pp. 23–24. But he was perhaps best known to the world for his defense of Madrid. Krivitsky, p. 97. Stern would have missions not just in Spain but also in China and the United States. John Costello and Oleg Tsarev, *Deadly Illusions: The KGB Orlov Dossier Reveals Stalin's Master Spy* (New York: Crown, 1993), p. 255.

15. FBI, "Montreal interview of de Graaf," pp. 21–28.

16. Ibid., p. 31. Johnny told the FBI that Karl Franserra's name was spelled Carl Fromferra and that he was a student of sabotage attached to M4.

17. Germany, Hauptstaatsarchiv Düsseldorf (hereafter GHD), document, "Statement to the Gestapo by Karl Szymczak," May 7, 1938, Blatt 7, RW58-39516.

18. CSIS, RCMP, "Copy of Montreal FBI interview of de Graaf," vol. 4, p. 34.

19. The acronym stood for Народный комиссариат внутренних дел (People's Commissariat of Internal Affairs). The NKVD was the Soviet secret police from 1934 to 1946.

20. CSIS, RCMP, "Copy of Montreal FBI interview of de Graaf," and "1968 Brockville interview of John Henry de Graaf," p. 4.

21. GHD, "Statement to the Gestapo by Karl Szymczak," p. 6.

22. CSIS, RCMP, "Copy of Montreal FBI interview of de Graaf," vol. 4, p. 50.

23. Wilhelm Mensing, interview, Bonn, July 3, 2002.

24. Ibid.

25. РГАСПИ, "Biographie des Genossen Jonny de Graaf."
26. Wilhelm Mensing, *Von der Ruhr in den GULag: Opfer des Stalinschen Massenterrors aus dem Ruhrgebiet* (Essen: Klartext, 2001), pp. 17, 223; and Mensing, interview, July 3, 2002.
27. Mensing, *Von der Ruhr in den GULag*, p. 28; and Rennspieß, p. 249.
28. GHD, "Statement to the Gestapo by Karl Szymczak," p. 1; and Oscar de Graaf, interview, August 31, 1996.
29. Mensing, *Von der Ruhr in den GULag*, p. 27.
30. Rennspieß, p. 249.
31. GHD, "Statement to the Gestapo by Karl Szymczak"; and Mensing, *Von der Ruhr in den GULag*, pp. 27, 222.
32. Rennspieß, p. 250.
33. Oscar de Graaf, interview, August 31, 1996.
34. GHD, "Statement to the Gestapo by Karl Szymczak," p. 5.
35. Mensing, interview, July 3, 2002.
36. Oscar de Graaf, interview, August 16, 1997; and GSA, Der Bürgermeister, Einwohnermeldeabteilung, "Oscar de Graaf," July 25, 2000.
37. РГАСПИ, document, "Ueberführungskommission beim ZK de WKP(b)," February 21, 1931, фонд 495, опись 205, дело 6385, лист 116.
38. РГАСПИ, "Blagoeva notes"; and Costello and Tsarev, p. 45. Together with Stalin, Zinoviev and Kamenev briefly ruled the Soviet Union following Lenin's death. Both men were accused of being Trotskyites and were liquidated in 1936. It was the first of the great show trials. Cosetllo and Tsarev, pp. 251–52.
39. РГАСПИ, letter, "Jonny de Graaf to die Kaderabteilung der Komintern Moscow!" September 10, 1933, фонд 495, опись 205, дело 6385, лист 134; and "Ueberführungskommission beim ZK de WKP(b)."

CHAPTER 8. ASSIGNMENT ROMANIA

1. Johnny told the FBI that his initial mission was to Romania and Bulgaria. No confirmation that he went to Bulgaria, however, can be found in the РГАСПИ documents or in any of the interviews with de Graaf by Gordon Scott. FBI, "Montreal interview of de Graaf," pp. 33, 37–38; and РГАСПИ, "СПРАВКА," фонд 495, опись 184, дело 6, лист 144.
2. Robert C. Sahr, "Consumer Price Index (CPI) Conversion Factors 1800 to Estimated 2015 to Convert to Dollars of 2005," http://oregonstate.edu/Dept/pol_sci/fac/sahr/cv2005.pdf (accessed February 27, 2006), hereafter Sahr, Conversion Table.
3. FBI, "Montreal interview of de Graaf," pp. 32–34. At some time during the Romanian trip, Johnny used the name Wagner, either in travel documents or as an alias. Oscar de Graaf, interview, Ahlen, July 26, 1996.
4. РГАСПИ, "Blagoeva notes," лист 81; and Pollock, interview, September 16, 1996.
5. РГАСПИ, documents, "Meldung betreffs Verhaftung des Gen. Wilhelm, Lux, Zimmer 210, sowie Verhaftung des Arbeiters: Hans Luns, Bleistiftfabril Krassin," August 13, 1937, фонд 495, опись 184, дело 6, лист 17; "Gruber," фонд 495, опись 184, дело 6, лист 152; and "СПРАВКА."
6. FBI, "Montreal interview of de Graaf," p. 34.
7. Cișmigiu Gardens is the oldest park in Bucharest, celebrated for its classical English landscaping. It is often referred to as "Lover's Park."
8. CSIS, RCMP, "Copy of Montreal FBI interview of de Graaf," vol. 4, p. 37; and Vladimir Tismaneanu, e-mail, August 4, 2005.
9. FBI, "Montreal interview of de Graaf."
10. Pollock, interview, September 16, 1996.
11. CSIS, RCMP, "Copy of Montreal FBI interview of de Graaf"; and РГАСПИ, "Blagoeva notes," лист 80.
12. Béla Kun's real name was Aaron Cohen. "Bela Kun: The 133 Days," http://www.vanguardnewsnetwork.com/temp/TerrorTimeline/1919_BelaKunThe133Days.htm (accessed March 26, 2003).
13. CSIS, RCMP, "Copy of Montreal FBI interview of de Graaf."

14. Ibid., pp. 35–37.

15. "Great Romania (1919–1940)," http://66.102.7.104/search?q=cache:-zY1V3dIRyYJ:media.ici.ro/history/eng08.h tm+%22Romanian+Communist+Party%22+1930&hl=en (accessed July 24, 2005).

16. РГАСПИ, "Blagoeva notes."

17. Ibid.

18. Oscar de Graaf, interview, July 26, 1996.

19. FBI, "Montreal interview of de Graaf," pp. 38, 116. The FBI called this second hotel the Passaga. Someone made a typo with the last letter; it was the Passage. РГАСПИ, "Jonny de Graaf to die Kaderabteilung der Komintern Moscow!" The MOPR (International Red Aid), the Profintern (Red International Labor Unions), and the Comintern likewise used this hotel, according to de Graaf.

20. CSIS, RCMP, "1968 Brockville interview of John Henry de Graff," p. 21.

21. Ibid.

22. Chase, pp. 326–27, 340, 484–85.

CHAPTER 9. BRITISH MISSIONS

1. CSIS, RCMP, "Copy of Montreal FBI interview of de Graaf," vol. 4, p. 41.

2. Alan Ereira, *The Invergordon Mutiny: A Narrative History of the Last Great Mutiny in the Royal Navy and How It Forced Britain Off the Gold Standard in 1931* (London: Routledge and Kegan Paul, 1981), pp. 30–37, 42, 44.

3. Ibid., pp. 31–33; and Noreen Branson, *History of the Communist Party of Great Britain, 1927–1941* (London: Lawrence and Wishart, 1985), p. 68.

4. CSIS, RCMP, "Copy of Montreal FBI interview of de Graaf," vol. 4, p. 42.

5. FBI, documents, "Director, FBI (65–57843) SAC, New York (100–88095)," April 22, 1952, p. [1], file HQ 100-342513; and "Montreal interview of de Graaf," pp. 38–39.

6. CSIS, RCMP, "Copy of Montreal FBI interview of de Graaf," vol. 4, p. 41.

7. Ibid., p. 42; and РГАСПИ, document, "An den Verbindungsdienst des Sekretariats des EKKI," фонд 495, опись 205, дело 6385, лист 16. Following praxis in British English, "МАТЕРН" is translated as "Mattern." The American English spelling, with one "t," was sometimes found in the sources consulted. As the British translation is the most common, it will be used here.

8. FBI, "Montreal interview of de Graaf," pp. 38, 40; and letter, "SAC, Philadelphia, to Director, FBI," April 14, 1953, p. 2, file HQ 100-342513.

9. Ernst Krüger, letter, December 10, 1994.

10. CSIS, RCMP, "Copy of Montreal FBI interview of de Graaf," vol. 4, p. 37; and РГАСПИ, "Blagoeva notes."

11. FBI, "Montreal interview of de Graaf," p. 39.

12. *Times* (London), May 25, 1926, p. 2, and May 10, 1936, p. 2.

13. CSIS, RCMP, "Copy of Montreal FBI interview of de Graaf," vol. 4, pp. 42, 46.

14. Ibid., pp. 43–44.

15. Ibid., p. 44. Johnny mistakenly thought the cobbler's shop was in Tottenham Hale.

16. Ibid., and Branson, p. 64.

17. In another source, Johnny called the first two of these small journals the *Red Signal* and the *Red Fleet*. CSIS, RCMP, "1968 Brockville interview of John Henry de Graff," p. 24.

18. James Jupp, *The Radical Left in Britain, 1931–1941* (London: Frank Cass, 1982), p. 141; and John Curry, *The Security Service, 1908–1945: The Official Story* (Kew, Australia: Public Record Office, 1999), p. 107.

19. CSIS, RCMP, "Copy of Montreal FBI interview of de Graaf," vol. 4, p. 45; and GHD, "Statement to the Gestapo by [Margarete Rattai]," April 13, 1938, p. 7, RW58-39516. Wilhelm Mensing (e-mails, July 15 and 20, 2002) kindly provided the correct name of the above Gestapo informant. She was the wife of KPD member Karl Rattai.

20. Keith Laybourn and Dylan Murphy, *Under the Red Flag: A History of Communism in Britain, c. 1849–1991* (Phoenix Mill, Gloucestershire: Sutton, 1999), p. 69. Of the forty-five hundred, only about thirty-two hundred had paid their dues (p. 70).

21. Branson, p. 315.

22. "Invergordon Mutiny," http://www.masterliness.com/a/Invergordon.Mutiny.htm (accessed July 28, 2005).

23. Kenneth Edwards, *The Mutiny at Invergordon* (London: Putnam, 1937), pp. 359–60.

24. Branson, pp. 70–71.

25. Ereira, p. 35.

26. Michael Stenton, Peterhouse Cambridge, and Steven Lees, eds., *Who's Who of British Members of Parliament: A Biographical Dictionary of the House of Commons Based on Annual Volumes of Dod's Parliamentary Companion and Other Sources*, vol. 3 (Hassocks, Sussex: Harvester; Atlantic Highlands, N.J.: Humanities Press, 1979), p. 208. A check of all the remarks made in Parliament during this period reveals that Liddall's observation was not made in that body. United Kingdom, House of Commons and House of Lords, *Parliamentary Debates (Hansard)*, January 1, 1931, to December 21, 1934, vols. 247–76.

27. FBI, "Montreal interview of de Graaf," p. 42. From this point until leaving Moscow again for England, the story de Graaf told the FBI differs from that related to Gordon Scott. This may have been done to conceal how he came to be a double agent working for MI6. This transformation is not mentioned in the FBI material.

28. Krüger and Krüger, "Familien Stammbuch der Familie Krüger."

29. РГАСПИ, documents, "Gruber, Franz," фонд 495, опись 205, дело 6385, лист 69; "СПРАВКА," лист 35; and "Biographie des Genossen Jonny de Graaf."

30. CSIS, RCMP, "Copy of Montreal FBI interview of de Graaf," vol. 4, pp. 47–48.

31. Ibid., p. 48.

32. Ibid., pp. 48–49.

33. De Graaf recounted to the FBI that he did not go directly back to Moscow but that in Berlin he was ordered to Brussels and then to Rotterdam. At the first stop he trained thirty-two Belgian soldiers in "antimilitaristic matters." In Rotterdam he instructed eighteen members of the Dutch army and six sailors from the navy on the same topic. Following this last course, he returned to England in January 1932. Compared to the РГАСПИ material ("СПРАВКА"), the dates of this portion of the FBI version ("Montreal interview of de Graaf," pp. 43–46) appear to be incorrect. There is likewise no mention of stops in Brussels or Rotterdam in any documents at РГАСПИ.

34. FBI, "Montreal interview of de Graaf," pp. 42–43.

35. РГАСПИ, "СПРАВКА."

36. FBI, "Montreal interview of de Graaf," p. 43.

CHAPTER 10. BERLIN AND PRAGUE

1. FBI, "Montreal interview of de Graaf," pp. 47–48.

2. Ibid., pp. 48–49.

3. Ibid., p. 48.

4. Ibid., p. 49; and Pollock, interview, September 16, 1996.

5. Friedrich Ebert Stiftung, Regine Schoch, e-mail to Wilhelm Mensing, November 1, 2005. Stampfer had also been a member of the Reichstag from 1920 to 1933. He was on the SPD's central policymaking committee from 1925 to 1933. Thus Stampfer not only wrote about SPD policies but was engaged in making them as well. Ibid.

6. CSIS, RCMP, "Copy of Montreal FBI interview of de Graaf," vol. 4, pp. 52–54.

7. FBI, "Montreal interview of de Graaf," p. 51.

8. РГАСПИ, "Blagoeva notes," лист 81.

9. CSIS, RCMP, "Copy of Montreal FBI interview of de Graaf," vol. 4, p. 55; "1969 Brockville interview of John Henry de Graff," p. 11; and Pollock, interview, September 16, 1996.

10. РГАСПИ, document, "In Sachen de Graaf, Mitglied der KPD," фонд 495, опись 205, дело 6385, лист 114; William Waack, *Camaradas: Nos arquivos de Moscou; a histórias secreta da revolução brasileira de 1935* (São Paulo: Companhia das Letras, 1993), p. 82; and Max Hoelz, *Ich grüß und küsse Dich—Rot Front! Tagebücher und Briefe, Maskau 1929 bis 1933* (Berlin: Dietz, 2005), p. 42.

11. A photograph of Foley is presented here as figure 23.

12. Richard Aldrich, "Britain's Secret Intelligence Service in Asia During the Second World War," *Modern Asian Studies*, vol. 27, no. 1 (1998), p. 181. See also Christopher M. Andrew, *Secret Service: The Making of the British Intelligence Community* (London: Heinemann, 1985), pp. 339–447.

13. Michael Smith, whose few pages on Johnny contain several errors, writes that "it was some time before Frank sent a message to Head Office, saying; 'I am in touch with Johann who is Comintern and can supply full breakdown of British and other communist parties.'" Michael Smith, *The Spying Game: The Secret History of British Espionage* (London: Politico, 1996), p. 83. Johnny, of course, told Foley that he was attached to M4, not in the Comintern. It seems likely that Foley reported this to Valentine Vivian in London.

14. РГАСПИ, document, "Материал ИКК, Леов [untitled handwritten notes in Russian by Stella Blagoeva]," November 20, 1933, фонд 495, опись 205, дело 6385, лист 50.

15. CSIS, RCMP, "Copy of Montreal FBI interview of de Graaf," vol. 4, p. 56.

16. Johnny de Graaf is the source of this comment.

17. Krüger, letter, December 10, 1994.

18. FBI, "Montreal interview of de Graaf," pp. 51–52; and РГАСПИ, letter, "Jonny de Graaf to Hans [family name not given]," June 28, 1933, фонд 495, опись 184, дело 6, лист 139. This letter gives a date on which de Graaf was in Prague.

19. Oscar de Graaf, interviews, July 26 and August 31, 1996, and September 1, 1996; GSA, Der Bürgermeister: Einwohnermeldeabteilung, "Oscar de Graaf," July 25, 2000; Einwohnermeldeabteilung, "Johann de Graaf [Jr.]," July 25, 2000; and Mensing, *Von der Ruhr in den GULag*, p. 222. One of the surviving pictures Helena had made for Johnny, depicting Marianne, Oscar, and herself, is presented here as figure 22.

20. FBI, "Montreal interview of de Graaf," p. 98; РГАСПИ, "Blagoeva notes," лист 80 оборот; "Jonny de Graaf to Hans [family name not given]"; and "Biographie des Genossen Jonny de Graaf."

21. De Graaf told the FBI that he was ordered to Paris for four weeks of antimilitaristic propaganda in addition to the training of persons to start Communist cells in the military. He stated that the conditions of the party in Paris were sufficiently advanced that he only had to modernize the organization. He further mentioned to the FBI that he returned to Moscow via Switzerland. FBI, "Montreal interview of de Graaf," pp. 52–53. This account is not borne out by the documents at РГАСПИ.

22. РГАСПИ, "Biographie des Genossen Jonny de Graaf." Note that this document puts de Graaf back in Moscow in October 1933. On the other hand (РГАСПИ, "Jonny de Graaf to die Kaderabteilung der Komintern Moscow!") is a handwritten letter by Johnny to the Cadre Department of the Comintern dated September 10, 1933. He apparently wrote this letter from his Moscow hotel room.

23. РГАСПИ, "Jonny de Graaf to die Kaderabteilung der Komintern Moscow!"

24. GSA, Der Bürgermeister, Einwohnermeldeabteilung, "Maria de Graaf," July 25, 2000; and Wilhelm Mensing, e-mail, July 18, 2004.

25. Oscar de Graaf, interviews, July 26 and August 31, 1996.

CHAPTER 11. MANCHURIA AND CHINA

1. FBI, "Montreal interview of de Graaf," p. 53; and Ulla Plener, "Auskünfte einer NKWD-Akte über letzten Weg und Tod deutscher Kommunisten in der Sowjetunion (1936–1939): Willy Leow-Hofmann, Hans Rogalla, Josef Schneider, Paul Scholze, Harry Wilde," *UTOPIEkreativ*, vol. 39–40 (January–February 1994), p. 131. Plener points out (p. 132n3) that such executions were carried out immediately after sentencing.

2. РГАСПИ, "Blagoeva notes," лист 50 оборот, and "Jonny de Graaf to die Kaderabteilung der Komintern Moscow!"

3. РГАСПИ, "Blagoeva notes."

4. Ibid., лист 51; and Miin-ling Yu, "Introduction to Materials in Russia on the Relations Between the KMT, CCP, and Comintern, 1920s–1940s," http://216.239.63.104/search?q=cache:v7eL-BrjiDgAJ:ccs.ncl.edu.tw/Newsletter_79/P008_015.pdf+%22gekker%22+comintern&hl=en (accessed

March 20, 2005). The document by Blagoeva also states that someone is not a fugitive. It is not clear, however, to whom the observation pertains, Johnny, Gekker, or Rogalla.

5. Plener, pp. 131–32.
6. FBI, "Montreal interview of de Graaf."
7. Ibid., pp. 53–54.
8. FBI, letter, "John Edgar Hoover to [censored]," October 12, 1951, p. 3, file HQ 100-342513.
9. Stella Dong, *Shanghai: The Rise and Fall of a Decadent City* (New York: Harper Collins, 2000), p. 212.
10. FBI, "Montreal interview of de Graaf," pp. 53–54.
11. CSIS, RCMP, "1968 Brockville interview of John Henry de Graff," p. 32; and Cerys Hearsey (UKFCO Library), e-mail, August 10, 2005. Johnny referred to Kitson as "Mr. Squire." This could have been a subterfuge for safety reasons, or de Graaf simply forgot the correct name, perhaps confusing it in his narrative with the ship captain Marquis Square. The name of the English consul general in Shanghai at the time, John Fitzgerald Brenan, does not match either. Lorna Patterson (UKFCO Library), e-mail, October 27, 2003.
12. FBI, "Montreal interview of de Graaf," p. 54.
13. РГАСПИ, "СПРАВКА."
14. Walerij Brun-Zechowoj, *Manfred Stern—General Kleber: Die tragische Biographie eines Berufsrevolutionärs, 1896–1954* (Berlin: Trafo/Weist, 2000), p. 62.
15. Frederick S. Litten, "The Noulens Affair," *China Quarterly*, vol. 138 (June 1994), pp. 492–97, 502–3; Richard C. Thornton, *China, the Struggle for Power 1917–1972* (Bloomington: Indiana University Press, 1973), pp. 50–51; Cynthia Caughey Weber, "A Political Furor in Shanghai: The Case of Hilaire Noulens, 1931–1932" (master's thesis, Department of History, Arizona State University, 1995), p. 28; and Alexander Millar, "British Intelligence and the Comintern in Asia: The Noulens Case" (master's thesis, Department of History, Cambridge University, 2006), pp. 3–4.
16. CSIS, RCMP, "Copy of Montreal FBI interview of de Graaf," vol. 4, p. 60.
17. Ibid., p. 64.
18. FBI, report, "Unknown Subject, was: [censored]," New York, September 25, 1952, p. 6, file HQ 100-342513/NY 65-15334; FBI, letter, "John Edgar Hoover to [censored]," September 23, 1952, ibid.; FBI, "Montreal interview of de Graaf," pp. 55–56; and Charles A. Willoughby, *Shanghai Conspiracy: The Sorge Spy Ring, Moscow—Shanghai—Tokyo—San Francisco—New York* (New York: E. P. Dutton, 1952), pp. 281–84.
19. Arquivo Público do Estado do Rio de Janeiro (hereafter APERJ), Delegacia Especial de Segurança Política e Social (hereafter DESPS), document, "Application for Renewal of Passport of Machla Lenczycki [Sabo] at American Consulate," in file, "Arthur Ernst Ewert ou Harry Berger," prontuário 1721.
20. APERJ, DESPS, counterfeit passport, "Harry Berger," no. 542115, "Arthur Ernst Ewert ou Harry Berger," p. 3, prontuário 1721.
21. APERJ, DESPS, booklet, "Stammbuch der Familie Ewert," "Arthur Ernst Ewert ou Harry Berger," p. 6, prontuário 1721.
22. Ibid.
23. Ibid., p. 7.
24. Hornstein, pp. 4–12, 17, 80–81, 127–28; Leôncio Basbaum, interview by John W. F. Dulles, São Paulo, November 9, 1967; Chapman Pincher, *Too Secret Too Long* (New York: St. Martin's Press, 1984), p. 22; and José Joffily, *Harry Berger* (Rio de Janeiro: Paz e Terra; Curitiba: Universidade Federal do Paraná, 1987), p. 113.
25. Fernando Morais, *Olga*, 3d ed. (São Paulo: Alfa-Omega, 1985), pp. 59, 69.
26. FBI, "Montreal interview of de Graaf," p. 59.
27. Andreu Castells, *Las Brigadas Internacionales en la Guerra de España* (Barcelona: Ariel, 1974), p. 73n; and Antony Beevor, *Spanska inbördeskriget*, trans. Kjell Waltman (Lund: Historiska Media, 2006), p. 197.
28. U.S. National Archives (hereafter USNA), Shanghai Municipal Police Files, "Gen. von Seeckt Going Home," *North-China Daily News*, March 6, 1935, D 5697. Pincher (pp. 432–33) reports that the Shanghai Municipal Police Files have been "very thoroughly 'weeded' twice," once by the Soviets and a second time by the British. This seems credible, as nothing could be found in them relating to Arthur

Ewert or any of his aliases. Additionally, perhaps 10 percent of the files are missing. Some were lost at sea.

29. Frederick S. Litten, "The CCP and the Fujian Rebellion," *Republican China,* vol. 14, no. 1 (1988), p. 62.

30. Germany, Bundesarchiv Berlin (hereafter GBB), Bundesbeauftragte für die Unterlagen des Staatssicherheitsdienst der ehemaligen Deutsche Demokratischer Republik, document, "Zusammengefasste Notizen Betr: Olga Benario," BStU 000149, MfS-HA IX/11, SV 1/81, Blatt 254. Note that this was a Gestapo-generated document in the files of the Ministerium für Staatssicherheit, or Ministry for State Security, commonly known as "Stasi."

31. РГАСПИ, document, "Kurzer Spezialbericht über China, Shanghai Januar bis August 1934," фонд 495, опись 184, дело 6, листов 108–9; Litten, "Noulens Affair," p. 497; Stanley E. Hilton, *Brazil and the Soviet Challenge, 1917–1947* (Austin: University of Texas Press, 1991), p. 233n2; Morais, p. 37; and FBI, "Montreal interview of de Graaf," pp. 26, 61.

32. Dong, pp. 106, 192; and РГАСПИ, "Kurzer Spezialbericht über China," лист 108.

33. РГАСПИ, "Kurzer Spezialbericht über China"; FBI, "Montreal interview of de Graaf," p. 56; and APERJ, DESPS, "Harry Berger," no. 542115, "Arthur Ernst Ewert ou Harry Berger," prontuário 1721.

34. РГАСПИ, "Kurzer Spezialbericht über China"; and CSIS, RCMP, "1969 Brockville interview of John Henry de Graff," p. 9.

35. CSIS, RCMP, "Copy of Montreal FBI interview of de Graaf," vol. 4, pp. 60, 66; Joachim Krüger and Lieselotte Krüger (no relation to Gustav Ernst Karl or Pauline Emilie Krüger), e-mails, August 4 and 5, 2005; and "Eugene Dennis" http://en.wikipedia.org/wiki/Eugene_Dennis (accessed August 5, 2005).

36. Thornton, p. 55.

37. Edgar Snow, *Red Star over China* (New York: Random House, 1938), p. 353.

38. Ibid., p. 355.

39. Oscar de Graaf, interview, September 1, 1996.

40. *China Forum* (Shanghai), November 30, 1933, pp. 1–2.

41. РГАСПИ, "Kurzer Spezialbericht über China."

42. Ibid., лист 109. In the 1950s he was quoted as saying that "with six untrained helpers and $5 worth of explosives, I blew up a Japanese airfield. We destroyed 36 planes and killed 700 japs." *Chicago Daily Tribune,* January 13, 1954, p. 5.

43. APERJ, DESPS, "Franz Gruber ou Jonny de Graaf," p. 26, prontuário 33989; Agnes Smedley, *The Great Road: The Life and Times of Chu Teh* (New York: Monthly Review Press, 1956), pp. xiv–xv; Thornton, pp. 69–73; and J. A. G. Roberts, *The Complete History of China* (Phoenix Mill, Gloucestershire: Sutton, 2003), p. 388. Roberts adds that about twenty thousand wounded, the sick, and nearly all of the children were left behind. A note on the numeration of the above "Franz Gruber ou Jonny de Graaf" items: there are two different page numbers on the originals. The page number stamped in the lower right-hand corner of each page is the one being used here.

44. Bernard Wasserstein, *Secret War in Shanghai: An Untold Story of Espionage, Intrigue, and Treason in World War II* (Boston: Houghton Mifflin, 1999), p. 84.

45. РГАСПИ, "Kurzer Spezialbericht über China"; and APERJ, DESPS, "Harry Berger," "Application for Renewal of Passport of Machla Lenczycki [Sabo] at American Consulate."

46. РГАСПИ, document, "Session of the Politcommission of the Politsecretariat," фонд 495, опись 4, дело 286, лист 3; and Joachim and Lieselotte Krüger, e-mails, August 4 and 5, 2005.

47. Michael Smith, *Foley: The Spy Who Saved Ten Thousand Jews* (London: Hodder and Stoughton, 1999), p. 57; Aldrich, pp. 184–85; and Millar, p. 9.

48. РГАСПИ, "Kurzer Spezialbericht über China"; and USNA, Shanghai Municipal Police Files, "Gen. von Seeckt Going Home." Johnny recounted to the FBI that the group left together on a British vessel "about the end of October 1934." FBI, "Montreal interview of de Graaf," pp. 61–62. The month of October is not corroborated by РГАСПИ documents. Willoughby (p. 284), Morais (p. 73), and Hornstein (p. 167), evidently all citing Willoughby's unconfirmable source in the Shanghai Municipal Police Files, place the date of the Ewerts' departure for Vladivostok as July 19, 1934, aboard the SS *Yingchow.*

49. CSIS, RCMP, "1968 Brockville interview of John Henry de Graff," p. 37.

CHAPTER 12. BRAZIL ONE

1. FBI, "Montreal interview of de Graaf," p. 62; Waack, p. 22; and РГАСПИ, "Blagoeva notes," лист 60. Johnny told the Brazilians in 1939 that it was Vasiliev and not Langner who offered him the choice of countries. APERJ, DESPS, "Franz Gruber ou Jonny de Graaf," p. 14.

2. РГАСПИ, "Blagoeva notes."

3. Waack, pp. 32–33; and Hilton, pp. 22–23.

4. There is any number of possible candidates for these two individuals, including Esteban Peano and the secretary to Ghioldi and Ewert, known only as "Margarita" or "Marga." Peano was sent to São Paulo from Argentina to help organize the party. He could have traveled occasionally to Rio de Janeiro. Marga is discussed later in this chapter. РГАСПИ, documents, "Из сообщения Валтера (Эцьо, Локателли)" (title by hand in Russian), фонд 495, опись 205, дело 6385, лист 110; and "Verbindungen der einzelnen Genossen in Rio de Janeiro," фонд 495, опись 205, дело 6385, лист 86.

5. FBI, "SAC, Philadelphia, to Director, FBI," April 14, 1953; FBI, "Montreal interview of de Graaf," p. 99; and Krüger, interview, August 12, 1994.

6. Waack, pp. 99–100; and Yuri Ribeiro, interview, Rio de Janeiro, December 16, 1994. Ribeiro is one of the sons of Luís Carlos Prestes.

7. GBB, "Zusammengefasste Notizen Betr: Olga Benario," BStU 000152; and Wilhelm Mensing, e-mail, November 29, 2003. Grybowski was originally from the Ruhr.

8. GBB, "Zusammengefasste Notizen Betr: Olga Benario," BStU 000153.

9. Luís Carlos Prestes, letter, November 19, 1987; and Morais, pp. 15–16. Waack (p. 97) claims that Olga was not that conversant with Marx, Engels, Lenin, and Stalin. Morais (p. 49) disagrees.

10. Morais, pp. 49–62; and Cecil Borer, interview, Rio de Janeiro, May 13, 1998.

11. Prestes, letter, November 19, 1987; APERJ, DESPS, file, "Maria Prestes, Olga Benario," pp. 7, 7a, prontuário 1675; Cecil Borer, interviews, May 13, 1998, and Rio de Janeiro, May 28, 1998; Jorge Amado, *A vida de Luís Carlos Prestes: O cavaleiro da esperança*, 4th ed. (São Paulo: Martins, 1945), p. 98; Boris Fausto, *A revolução de 1930, historiografia e história*, 9th ed. (São Paulo: Brasiliense, 1983), p. 61; Waack, pp. 95, 99; and Israel Beloch and Alzira Alves de Abreu, coords., *Dicionário histórico-biográfico brasileiro, 1930–1983* (Rio de Janeiro: Forense-Universitária, 1984), pp. 2817–18.

12. APERJ, DESPS, file, "Rodolfo Ghioldi," prontuário 5878; newspaper article, *A Offensiva*, March 21, 1936, p. 1 (in APERJ, DESPS, "Carmen Alfaza [sic] Ghioldi," prontuário 21409); Brazil, Arquivo Nacional (hereafter BAN), passenger list, SS *Florida*, RV 367; Hornstein, pp. 205–6; Waack, pp. 105–7, 171, 173–74, 206, 300; and Harold Barron, interview, Hayward, Calif., January 15, 1994. Harold was Victor's brother.

13. РГАСПИ, "Blagoeva notes," листов 56, 80 оборот; Stephen Dorril, *MI6: Inside the Covert World of Her Majesty's Secret Intelligence Service* (New York: Touchstone, 2000), p. 7; *Svenska Dagbladet* (Stockholm), October 10, 1933, p. 21, and November 16, 1934, p. 25. The *Svea* and the *Primula* competed with each other for passenger traffic at this time. Knut Sveri, interview, Stockholm, July 25, 2006.

14. APERJ, DESPS, "Franz Gruber ou Jonny de Graaf," pp. 15, 25; and Curry, p. 7. Vivian was later made deputy chief of SIS in January 1940 (Curry, p. 7). This was not the first time that Foley had been in contact with Vivian regarding de Graaf. Foley had undoubtedly communicated with him ever since de Graaf had first come to him in Berlin seeking political asylum.

15. Cerys Hearsey (UKFCO Library), e-mail, January 5, 2005; and APERJ, DESPS, document, "Comunicação—Inv. 804 [Cecil Borer] to [Seraphim Braga], S-2," February 6, 1941, p. 4, inglês/pasta 3.

16. Neil Pollock, telephone interview, February 9, 1997.

17. Anthony Cave Brown, *Treason in the Blood: H. St. John Philby, Kim Philby, and the Spy Case of the Century* (Boston: Houghton Mifflin, 1994), p. 258. An example of Vivian's knowledge of the Comintern, at least as it related to Asia, can be seen in the thesis by Millar.

18. Costello and Tsarev, pp. 235–36. The opinion that Vivian was a fragile man is from Guy Burgess, who includes an unflattering sketch of the man among the drawings in ibid. (unnumbered figures between pp. 414 and 431). The picture of Vivian, presented here as figure 24, was taken four years and eight months earlier and does not reveal this state of weakness.

19. РГАСПИ, "Blagoeva notes," лист 56; BAN, "Florida," RV 367; APERJ, DESPS, "Franz Gruber ou Jonny de Graaf"; and FBI, "Montreal interview of de Graaf," p. 64.

20. John W.F. Dulles, *Anarchists and Communists in Brazil, 1900–1935* (Austin: University of Texas Press, 1973), p. 515; and APERJ, DESPS, "Franz Gruber ou Jonny de Graaf," pp. 25–26.

21. APERJ, DESPS, "Franz Gruber ou Jonny de Graaf."

22. Ibid., p. 25.

23. РГАСПИ, document, "Bericht über die Ereignisse im Brasilien vom 5 Januar 1935 bis 21. Januar 1936," лист 101.

24. APERJ, DESPS, "Franz Gruber ou Jonny de Graaf," pp. 24–25; and CSIS, RCMP, "1968 Brockville interview of John Henry de Graff," p. 39. Probably in jest, Johnny later referred to Ewert as "Apple Head" (p. 69).

25. APERJ, DESPS, "Franz Gruber ou Jonny de Graaf"; Marly de Almeida Gomes Vianna, *Revolucionários de 35: Sonho e realidade* (São Paulo: Companhia das Letras, 1992), pp. 138–39, unnumbered plate (2) between pp. 301 and 303; and Morais, pp. 77–82.

26. APERJ, DESPS, "Franz Gruber ou Jonny de Graaf."

27. Johnny mistakenly called Sabo "Ewert's girlfriend, Hilda," probably for security reasons even among the core revolutionaries. Another Communist likewise called Sabo "Berger's girlfriend." Cristiano Cordeiro, interview by John W. F. Dulles, Recife, PE, Brazil, October 11, 1968.

28. R. S. Rose, *One of the Forgotten Things: Getúlio Vargas and Brazilian Social Control, 1930–1954* (Westport, Conn.: Greenwood Press, 2000), pp. 22–32, 39–41. Comments by the press and its call for action on the part of the government are discussed in Hilton, pp. 50, 59, 63.

29. The Polícia Militar is still in existence today. It is not directly connected with the military. The name implies only that the polícia wear uniforms and usually live in barracks. They are supposed to provide the services of a regular uniformed police force protecting the civilian population.

30. FBI, "Montreal interview of de Graaf," p. 66; CSIS, RCMP, "1968 Brockville interview of John Henry de Graff," p. 42; РГАСПИ, "Из сообщения Валтера (Эцьо, Локателли)," лист 111; and Waack, p. 173.

31. FBI, "Montreal interview of de Graaf"; and APERJ, DESPS, "Franz Gruber ou Jonny de Graaf," p. 23.

32. РГАСПИ, "Bericht über die Ereignisse im Brasilien vom 5 Januar 1935 bis 21. Januar 1936," лист 98; Arquivo Histórico do Itamarati, Itamarati, Brazil (hereafter AHI), telegram, "Souza Leão to Itamaraty," January 9, 1940, and document, "Regis de Oliveira to Oswaldo Aranha," December 20, 1939, no. 477; and APERJ, DESPS, "Franz Gruber ou Jonny de Graaf." DESPS functioned as the political police from January 10, 1933, to March 28, 1944. Eliana Rezende Furtado de Mendonça, ed., *Os arquivos das polícias políticas: Reflexos de nossa história contemporânea* (Rio de Janeiro: FAPERJ, 1994), pp. 12, 16.

33. APERJ, DESPS, "Franz Gruber ou Jonny de Graaf," pp. 21, 23.

34. FBI, "Montreal interview of de Graaf," pp. 67; CSIS, RCMP, "1968 Brockville interview of John Henry de Graff," p. 40; Pollock, interview, September 16, 1996; and Vianna, p. 284.

35. "Amleto Locatelli" and "Jonny de Graaf" (computer files from РГАСПИ and other Moscow sources translated into Portuguese by Yuri Ribeiro); and Hilton, p. 55.

36. AHI, telegram, "Souza Leão to Itamaraty," January 9, 1940; FBI, "Montreal interview of de Graaf," pp. 66–68; and letter, "[censored] to Director, FBI," March 6, 1952, p. 1, file HQ 100–342513. Johnny told the FBI that Prestes ordered him to Bahia. There is, however, no record of his ever having disembarked from a ship in the state. Brazil, Arquivo Público do Estado da Bahia, Inspectoria da Polícia do Porto, Salvador, "Registro de entradas de passageiros" (n.p., n.d.), vol. 33. No record of aircraft passengers is available.

37. Paulo Cavalcanti, *O caso eu conto como o caso foi: Da Coluna Prestes à queda de Arraes,* 3d ed. (Recife: Guararapes, 1980), p. 142; and Severino Theodoro de Melo, interview, Rio de Janeiro, February 14, 2006. A corporal at the time, de Melo was one of the rebel soldiers at the Vila Militar complex. He denies Antonio Natanael Sarmento's statement (Sarmento, telephone interview, January 31, 2006) that the Twenty-Ninth Battalion was also the best equipped in the northeast. De Melo stated, "we only had World War I rifles."

38. Antonio Natanael Martins Sarmento, "Os abalos de sabado à noite: Do governo popular e revoloucionário em Natal à guerra do Largo da Paz em Recife, 1935" (master's thesis, Department of

History, Universidade Federal de Pernambuco, 1994), p. 92; and Severino Theodoro de Melo, interview, Rio de Janeiro, February 15, 2006.

39. *Jornal do Commercio* (Recife), November 27, 1935, p. 3.

40. РГАСПИ, telegram, "Commission Politique to Куда," July 31, 1935, фонд 495, опись 184, дело 54, листов 17–18.

41. Ibid.

42. APERJ, DESPS, "Franz Gruber ou Jonny de Graaf," p. 22; and FBI, "Montreal interview of de Graaf," pp. 68–69.

43. FBI, "Montreal interview of de Graaf," p. 69.

44. Julio José Chiavenato, *Cangaço: A força do coronel* (São Paulo: Brasiliense, 1990), pp. 35, 43; Fernando Portela and Cláudio Bojunga, *Lampião: O cangaceiro e o outro* (São Paulo: Traço, 1982), p. 73; and *O Globo* (Rio de Janeiro), February 24, 1985, p. 8.

45. Robert M. Levine, *The Vargas Regime: The Critical Years, 1934–1938* (New York: Columbia University Press, 1970), pp. 43–48, 104; Hilton, pp. 65–66; and Vianna, pp. 185–86.

46. See, for example, Hilton, pp. 66–67; Waack, pp. 216–18; Cavalcanti, pp. 139–42; Levine, pp. 43–48, 104; Vianna, pp. 186–97; Homero Costa, *A insurreição comunista de 1935: Natal—o primeiro ato da tragédia* (São Paulo: Ensaio, 1995), pp. 137–48; and Paulo Sérgio Pinheiro, *Estratégias da ilusão: A revolução mundial e o Brasil, 1922–1935* (São Paulo: Companhia das Letras, 1991), pp. 297–300.

47. Costa, pp. 138–39, 141–43.

48. Ibid., p. 85.

49. Frederico Mindêllo Carneiro Monteiro, *Depoimentos biográficos* (Rio de Janeiro: Gráfica Olímpica, 1977), p. 109; and Wandenkolk Wanderley, interview by John W. F. Dulles, Recife, October 17, 1968.

50. De Melo, interviews, February 14 and 15, 2006; and Malvino Reis Neto, interview by John W. F. Dulles, September 2, 1963. *Diario de Pernambuco* (Recife), November 28, 1935, p. 8, states that the fighting began at around 9:00 A.M., while the *Jornal do Commercio,* November 27, 1935, p. 3, comments that the hostilities started a little after 8:00 A.M. De Melo insists, however, that 9:00 A.M. was the correct hour (interview, February 14, 2006).

51. Pollock, interview, September 16, 1996; and Jailson Sena, interview, Socorro, PE, Brazil, January 12, 2006. Sena is the sergeant in charge of the base museum at the Vila Militar in Socorro.

52. Pedro Vilela Cid, interview by John W. F. Dulles, Natal, October 18, 1968.

53. APERJ, DESPS, "Álbum do Delegacia Especial de Seguança Politica e Social," 1940, Rio Grande do Norte; Hilton, pp. 69, 71; and R. S. Rose, "Johnny's Two Trips to Brazil," *Luso-Brazilian Review,* vol. 38, no. 1 (2001), p. 4. Although things were put down in short order, the government's troops were insufficient in Pernambuco and Rio Grande do Norte. They had to be helped out there by the forces of local *fazendeiros*. Nelson Werneck Sodré, *História militar do Brasil* (Rio de Janeiro: Civilização Brasileira, 1965), p. 256; and APERJ, DESPS, document, "A revolução comunista no Brasil e os commentarios da 'internacional communista,'" n.d., comunismo/pasta 9. The two names for the event likewise depend on one's political point of view. Leftists prefer Prestes's title of "Revolução Social," while those of a more conservative stripe like "Intentona Comunista." Luís Carlos Prestes, interview, Rio de Janeiro, August 13, 1987.

54. Prestes's daughter, Anita Leocadia Prestes, and his sister, Lygia Prestes, claim that this accounting of their father/brother in a panic was obviously false. Anyone who knew Prestes, they stated, would know that such behavior was totally out of character for him. Anita Leocadia Prestes and Lygia Prestes, interview, Rio de Janeiro, April 17, 2004.

55. APERJ, DESPS, "Franz Gruber ou Jonny de Graaf," p. 22.

56. Antonio Augusto Faria and Edgard Luiz de Barros, *Getúlio Vargas e sua época,* 2d ed. (São Paulo: Global, 1983), p. 38; Beloch and Abreu, p. 2932; Paulo Brandi, *Vargas: Da vida para a história,* 2d ed., rev. (Rio de Janeiro: Zahar, 1985), p. 102; John W. F. Dulles, *Vargas of Brazil: A Political Biography* (Austin: University of Texas Press, 1967), pp. 150, 152; *International Press Correspondence* (London), May 16, 1936, p. 632; and APERJ, DESPS, document, "Ao povo e ás classes armadas do Brasil," November 27, 1936, comunismo/pasta 20.

57. Cavalcanti, p. 144.

58. Levine (p. 130) commented on the question as follows: "The domestic communist press claimed that 20,000 Brazilians had been imprisoned . . . [while] the French communist journal,

L'Humanité, offered the figure of 17,000. In October 1937, the New York *Times* [*sic*] claimed that Filinto Müller had acknowledged 7,000 arrests by federal authorities, not counting those carried out on state and local levels." To these accounts, one reporter, Herondino Pereira Pinto (*Nos subterraneos do Estado Novo* [Rio de Janeiro: Germinal, 1950], p. 62), was taken captive himself and was able to give an accounting from the other side of the bars. He places the total number of detainees at more than thirty-five thousand by the end of 1936. In support of this final statistic, leftists arriving back in Moscow put the number at thirty thousand. РГАСПИ, letter, "Frederic to Fernando Morales," December 4, 1936, general file, "Ъразили," фонд 495, опись 29, дело 98, лист 18.

59. U.S. Department of State (hereafter USDS), report, "Sackville to G-2," December 24, 1935, no. 3600, MID 2657-K-70/22; Waack, pp. 252–53; and Vianna, p. 184. A picture of some of this stash of weapons can be found among the unnumbered plates in Vianna.

60. Morais, p. 110.

61. "Amleto Locatelli"; Antony Beevor, *Berlin: The Downfall, 1945* (London: Viking Penguin, 2002), p. 363; Rose, *One of the Forgotten Things,* pp. 44–53, 55, 69, 74–75; and Waack, p. 346.

62. Borer, interview, May 13, 1998. Borer's comments are supported in part in APERJ, DESPS, "Franz Gruber ou Jonny de Graaf," p. 21.

63. Cecil Borer, interview, Rio de Janeiro, May 29, 1998; APERJ, DESPS, "Franz Gruber ou Jonny de Graaf"; and Waack, p. 254.

64. Waack, p. 276.

65. APERJ, DESPS, "Franz Gruber ou Jonny de Graaf."

66. РГАСПИ, "Bericht über die Ereignisse im Brasilien vom 5 Januar 1935 bis 21. Januar 1936," листов 100–102; and APERJ, DESPS, "Franz Gruber ou Jonny de Graaf," p. 21.

67. РГАСПИ, "Bericht über die Ereignisse im Brasilien vom 5 Januar 1935 bis 21. Januar 1936," лист 102; and FBI, "Montreal interview of de Graaf," p. 71.

68. РГАСПИ, "Blagoeva notes," лист 56 оборот; "Bericht über die Ereignisse im Brasilien vom 5 Januar 1935 bis 21. Januar 1936"; and FBI, "Philadelphia interview of John Henry de Graaf," p. 4.

CHAPTER 13. ARGENTINA

1. РГАСПИ, "Blagoeva notes," листов 48, 63 оборот; and CSIS, RCMP, "Copy of Montreal FBI interview of de Graaf," vol. 4, p. 77.

2. CSIS, RCMP, "Copy of Montreal FBI interview of de Graaf," vol. 4, p. 78.

3. FBI, "Montreal interview of de Graaf," pp. 71–72.

4. Waack, p. 282. Johnny mentioned to the FBI ("Montreal interview of de Graaf," p. 72) that Locatelli got out by going to Chile, then crossing the Andes to Argentina, before traveling on to Buenos Aires. The version he told the Soviets (Waack, p. 282) is deemed more creditable.

5. FBI, "Montreal interview of de Graaf"; and Waack, pp. 302–21.

6. Comisión del Comité Central del Partido Comunista, ed., *Esboro de historia del Partido Comunista de la Argentina: Origen y desarrollo del Partido Comunista y del movimiento obrero y popular argentino* (Buenos Aires: Anteo, 1947), p. 88n; and РГАСПИ, "Bericht über die Ereignisse im Brasilien vom 5 Januar 1935 bis 21. Januar 1936," лист 103.

7. РГАСПИ, telegram, "René to [Moscow]," June 26, 1936, фонд 495, опись 184, дело 6, лист 21; and *New York Times,* June 27, 1936.

8. РГАСПИ, telegrams, "[Moscow] to René," July 8, 1936, фонд 495, опись 184, дело 4, лист 21; "[Moscow] to René," July 26, 1936, фонд 495, опись 184, дело 4, лист 21; and Waack, p. 308. The Stuchevskis were probably liquadated toward the end of 1938. Waack, p. 342.

9. FBI, "Montreal interview of de Graaf," p. 73.

10. Pollock, interview, September 16, 1996.

11. Although de Graaf never mentioned where he drove, the most likely destination is either the province of Formosa or Misiones.

12. Ron Stewart, telephone interviews, January 8 and December 14, 1997. Stewart, a longtime member of the RCMP stationed in Washington, D.C., mentioned that during his years on the force,

people often thought the CIA was the bearer of this ignoble title of cruelty. But from his perspective, he knew that British intelligence led the pack in its cruelty and seriousness.

13. Waack, p. 321. On October 21, 1937, the Soviets had already prepared visas for them both. РГАСПИ, "An den Verbindungsdienst des Sekretariats des EKKI." One of those signing the visa approval was Manuilski.

14. FBI, "Montreal interview of de Graaf," p. 98; CSIS, RCMP, "1969 Brockville interview of John Henry de Graff," p. 15; Waltraud Krüger, interview, Rio de Janeiro, December 14, 1994; and Ernst Krüger, interviews, August 12 and December 14, 1994. Ernst Krüger's wife, Waltraud Krüger, heard from her husband's cousin, Elisabet Kalmeier, in Berlin, that the lover was a physician. Ernst Krüger, however, insists that the other male was an officer in the Argentine army. Elisabet Kalmeier could not be located in Berlin for her statement.

15. Krüger, interviews, August 12, October 17, and December 14, 1994; *La Nacion* (Buenos Aires), November 30, 1936, p. 1, and December 3, 1936, pp. 1, 12; and Neil Pollock, e-mail, June 25, 2004.

16. Ernst Krüger, letter, June 8, 1997. This type of letter carrier, with money for person-to-person payments, no longer exists in Germany. Wilhelm Mensing, e-mails, September 14 and 15, 2004.

17. Krüger, interviews, August 12, September 19, and December 8, 1994, and letter, December 10, 1994; and Oscar de Graaf, interview, August 16, 1997.

18. Krüger, interviews, September 19 and December 3, 1994, and letter, December 10, 1994. Her brother considered Helena a "very silly girl." Waack claims that she was a member of the KPD's Young Communists and Department of Sports (p. 82), while later saying that he could not find any evidence from the KPD's records that Helena was involved with either of these groups (p. 325). There is no record in Johnny's РГАСПИ file that mentions anything on this topic.

19. FBI, "Montreal interview of de Graaf," pp. 97–98.

20. CSIS, RCMP, "1969 Brockville interview of John Henry de Graff."

21. Ibid.

22. Pollock, interview, September 16, 1996; Krüger, interview, August 12, 1994; and CSIS, RCMP, letter, "[censored] to L. H. Nicholson," February 19, 1952, pp. 1–2, file, John de Graff, vol. 3. The author-censored letter to Commissioner Nicholson was apparently from a listener at a McGill University alumni meeting at which Johnny spoke and openly admitted killing a wife who was provided by Moscow to spy on him. The implication was that the murder occurred in South America.

23. Archivo Histórico de la Provincia de Buenos Aires, La Plata, Argentina (hereafter AHPBA), documents, "Libro de defunciones—General San Martín, 1936," La Plata (for Helena Krüger), fol. 31, "Libro de defunciones—General San Martín, 1936," Provincia de Buenos Aires (for Helena Krüger), fol. 31 (a copy of the original document by another functionary); FBI, "SAC, Philadelphia, to Director, FBI," April 14, 1953; Krüger and Krüger, "Familien Stammbuch der Familie Krüger"; Norberto Manzi, interview, San Martín, Argentina, February 13, 2000; and Pollock, interview, September 16, 1996, and telephone interview, December 21, 1997. Norberto Manzi and family are the current occupants of the calle Florida residence.

24. Carlos Americo Gallardo, interview, San Martín, Argentina, June 4, 1998. At the time of this interview, Gallardo was the chief of police in San Martín.

25. AHPBA, "Libro de defunciones—General San Martín, 1936," La Plata (for Pedro Menini), fol. 30, and ibid. (for Vicente Bastianelli), fol. 32.

26. Oscar de Graaf, interviews, July 26, 1996, and August 16, 1997; Pollock, interview, September 16, 1996; and Krüger, interview, August 12, 1994. When two FBI agents traveled to Montreal and questioned him in 1952, Johnny initially withheld all mention of Helena. He was probably startled when asked about her out of the blue, and if she had committed suicide. "De Graaf stated he did not furnish this information at first because it was intensely distasteful to him and was a memory he would like to forget. He was emotionally upset during this part of the interview. He later reiterated several times that this was the only information he had withheld from the agents." FBI, letter, "SAC, New York (65-15945), to Director, FBI (100-342513)," p. 2, file HQ 100-342513. Note that in the interviews of Johnny made by Gordon Scott, used in much of this biography, de Graaf likewise left out all mention of Helena.

27. FBI, "Philadelphia interview of John Henry de Graaf," p. 26.

28. The Argentine government routinely turns down all requests to open the Policía Federal Argentina files on Francisco Gruber, citing Ley no. 23.326 and Decreto-Ley no. 6580/58, artículo 76.

Juan Carlos Severi (secretaria de seguridade interior, Argentina), letter, September 2, 2004, Ref. Exp. SSI no. 9152/04, Nota DNAP y FFSS, no. 2446/04.

29. APERJ, DESPS, "Franz Gruber ou Jonny de Graaf," pp. 21, 46–47, and document, "Franz Gruber (Jonny de Graaf), termo de declarações e resposta aos quisitos formulados pelo Sr. Cap. Delegado Especial—20-XII-1939 a 3-1-1940, Secção de Segurança Social," p. 19, prontuário 33989; РГАСПИ, "СПРАВКА," лист 144; *La Nacion*, January 6, 1937, p. 12; and Waack, pp. 22, 321, 325–26.

30. Krüger and Krüger, "Familien Stammbuch der Familie Krüger"; FBI, "Montreal interview of de Graaf," pp. 75, 97; "Philadelphia interview of John Henry de Graaf," p. 26; Krüger, interview, August 12, 1994, and letter, December 10, 1994. In an interview with Gordon Scott, Johnny gave Gerti's age as twenty. This would have been nearly Helena's age. The reason for this error is unknown.

31. FBI, "Montreal interview of de Graaf," p. 74.

32. Krüger, interview, September 19, 1994.

33. GHD, document, "Essen Krim. Ass. II A. to Staatspolizeistelle in Düsseldorf," March 4, 1937, p. 1, RW58–50684. This document ends with the observation that a photo of de Graaf was not available.

34. Rose, *One of the Forgotten Things*, p. 46. The driver's license photo is reproduced here as figure 50.

35. GBB, document, Zentrales Parteiarchiv der SED, Reichssicherheitshauptamt, Geheime Staatspolizei, "Namensverzeichnis zu Aufstellung von Lichtbildern flüchtiger Kommunisten und Marxisten," May 1939, p. 7 [8], and "Zusammenstellung von Lichtbildern flüchtiger Kommunisten und Marxisten," Verzeichnis no. 196, May 1939, p. 55, R58/2308. Ernst Krüger guaranteed that the figure third from the end in the first group of photos in Waack's book *Camaradas*, with number 0243 stamped on it by the Gestapo, is *not* a snapshot of Johnny de Graaf. Krüger, interview, December 3, 1994.

36. Two additional examples: the Gestapo had incorrect pictures for Luís Carlos Prestes and Olga Bernário. GBB, document, Reichssicherheitshauptamt, Geheime Staatspolizei, "International Tätige Kommunisten!" pp. 9, 73, R58/3201.

37. Oscar de Graaf, interview, September 1, 1996. Pictures of such a chat, albeit not of Gerti and the SS officer, are presented in Palmér and Neubauer, pp. 272–73.

38. The expression "The balloon was up!" meant "Bang, you've been caught!" Johnny was preoccupied by the haunting possibility that one little slip, a single word or phrase, could trip him up.

CHAPTER 14. THE RETURN TO MOSCOW

1. FBI, "Montreal interview of de Graaf," p. 75.
2. CSIS, RCMP, "Copy of Montreal interview of John Henry de Graaf," vol. 4, p. 82.
3. Chase, pp. 477–78; Waack, p. 319.
4. РГАСПИ, letter, "Franz Gruber to Vorsitzenden der Internationalen Kontrollkommission Ekki," June 20, 1937, фонд 495, опись 205, дело 6385, листов 175–76.
5. РГАСПИ, "Blagoeva notes," листов 57, 60.
6. Ibid., лист 70.
7. Fundação Getúlio Vargas, "Prestes, Luís Carlos," http://www.cpdoc.fgv.br/dhbb/verbetes_htm/4366_1.asp (accessed March 12, 2005).
8. РГАСПИ, "Verbindungen der einzelnen Genossen in Rio de Janeiro"; "Bericht über die Ereignisse im Brasilien vom 5 Januar 1935 bis 21. Januar 1936," листов 87–103; "Nachtrag zum Bericht über Brasilien 1935: Möglichkeiten der Verhaftung des Gen. Evert u.s.w.," фонд 495, опись 184, дело 6, листов 104–7; and "Kurzer Spezialbericht über China."
9. РГАСПИ, "Nachtrag zum Bericht über Brasilien 1935," листов 106–7.
10. РГАСПИ, "Blagoeva notes," литов 45, 53, 56–56 оборот.
11. Waack, pp. 308–9. Observe that it was Johnny who told Locatelli that Olga and Ewert attempted to keep Prestes isolated. РГАСПИ, "Из сообщения Валтера (Эцьо, Локателли)."
12. Amleto Locatelli, "Relatorio sobre minhas atividades no Brasil," July 20, 1936, manuscript (translated into Portuguese by Yuri Ribeiro). Yuri is one of the sons of Luís Carlos Prestes. This partial

copy of Locatelli's long initial report was obtained by Ribeiro through an anonymous source and given to R. S. Rose.

13. Chase, p. 487.

14. Waack, pp. 310–14, 317–18, 342. A report signed by someone named Locatelli, stating that he was a deserter from the International Brigades, was published in the French journal *L'Emancipation Nationale*. Waack points out that it was never confirmed that Amelto was the author.

15. РГАСПИ, "Blagoeva notes," листов 72–74; and Waack, pp. 318, 321.

16. РГАСПИ, letter, "[unknown] to тов. Апресяну," April 10, 1937, фонд 495, опись 205, дело 6385, лист 34.

17. Ibid., листов 33–34; and РГАСПИ, letter, "Алиханов to тов. Апресяну," April 11, 1937, фонд 495, опись 205, дело 6385, листов 31–32.

18. РГАСПИ, letter, "Franz Gruber to [Dmitri] Manuilski," April 3, 1937, фонд 495, опись 184, дело 6, лист 24.

19. РГАСПИ, letter, "Franz Gruber to [Gevork] Alikhanov," May 15, 1937, фонд 495, опись 184, дело 6, лист 20.

20. РГАСПИ, letter, "Franz Gruber to Anwält," June 20, 1937, фонд 495, опись 184, дело 6, листов 175–76.

21. FBI, "Montreal interview of de Graaf," p. 77. A communication from the embassy of the Russian Federation states that there are no records of this interrogation in the archives of the Federal Security Service (the successor of the NKVD). Boris Marchuk (Russian Federal Security Service), letter, August 7, 2001.

22. CSIS, RCMP, "Copy of Montreal FBI interview of de Graaf," vol. 4, p. 87.

23. Ibid., pp. 83–88; Oscar de Graaf, interview, September 1, 1996; and Yuri Modin, *My Five Cambridge Friends: Philby, Burgess, Maclean, Blunt, and Cairncross, by Their KGB Controller*, trans. Anthony Roberts (Toronto: Knopf, 1995), p. 29.

24. FBI, "Montreal interview of de Graaf," p. 81.

25. Chase, pp. 5–6, 237, 473, 477; Waack, pp. 287, 330–32, 342; FBI, "Montreal interview of de Graaf," p. 79; and Prokhorov, *Great Soviet Encyclopedia*.

26. РГАСПИ, letter, "Stella Blagoeva to [unnamed]," August 27, 1937, фонд 495, опись 205, дело 6385, лист 15; and CSIS, RCMP, "1969 Brockville interview of John Henry de Graff," p. 12.

27. РГАСПИ, letters, "Дьков to Черномордику и Цируль" (June 7, 1937), фонд 495, опись 205, дело 6385, лист 40; and "Белов to Полячек" (June 8, 1937), фонд 495, опись 205, дело 6385, лист 39.

28. РГАСПИ, document, "Политэмигранты, прибывшие из Германии через негорелое с июля 1933 г. до февраля 1934 года," фонд 495, опись 175, дело 86, лист 251. This is the only available document showing when Johnny Jr. arrived in the USSR. It was sometime between July 1933 and February 1934.

29. Hans Schafranek, with Natalja Mussijenko, *Kinderheim Nr. 6: Österreichische und deutsche Kinder im sowjetischen Exil* (Vienna: Döcker, 1989), pp. 48, 71–72.

30. Ibid., pp. 55–56.

31. Wilhelm Mensing, interview, Bonn, July 4, 2002.

32. Mensing, *Von der Ruhr in den GULag*, p. 223.

33. Wolfgang Leonhard, *Child of the Revolution*, trans. C. M. Woodhouse (London: Ink Links, 1979), pp. 23, 44.

34. Oscar de Graaf, interview, July 26, 1996.

35. Ibid.

36. CSIS, RCMP, "Copy of Montreal FBI interview of de Graaf," vol. 4, pp. 82–83, 88–89, and "1968 Brockville interview of John Henry de Graff," p. 44.

37. Amtorg in New York was used for just this purpose from the 1930s until the United States entered World War II. Unfortunately for them, however, some of their people defected or became double agents, and then went before the House Un-American Activities Committee. Pollock, interview, September 16, 1996.

38. Ibid.; Oscar de Graaf, interviews, July 26 and September 1, 1996; and Smith, *Foley*, pp. 54–55. For more on Sorge, see Robert Whymant, *Stalin's Spy: Richard Sorge and the Tokyo Espionage Ring* (New York: St. Martin's Press, 1998).

39. De Graaf mentioned to the FBI that it was not at a golf club but at a sporting goods store in Tokyo that he would meet the contact. Johnny was to go there exactly two weeks after arrival and look at the hockey sticks. He would be approached by another patron, who would ask, "Are you interested in hockey?" De Graaf was to answer, "Yes." The other customer would then say, "You shouldn't buy hockey sticks here; they are no good. I will take you to an American shop where you can get them and they are of a much better quality." FBI, "Montreal interview of de Graaf," p. 84.

40. Sahr, Conversion Table.

41. FBI, "Montreal interview of de Graaf," pp. 82–83.

42. APERJ, DESPS, "Franz Gruber ou Jonny de Graaf," pp. 46–47. Although the number of Johnny's phony passport was the same, 500042, its date of issue was different from the one used during his first trip, December 6, 1934 (versus March 12, 1934). The Soviets simply issued Johnny another passport with blank pages so as not to show visas and entrance and exit stamps.

43. APERJ, DESPS, document, "Camada sensível" (heading in top left corner), Anexo Franz Gruber, March 30, 1939 [sic; 1940] (hereafter Anexo Franz Gruber), prontuário 33989.

44. FBI, "Montreal interview of de Graaf," p. 87.

45. Which of the political extremes he hated more is a moot point. But he did say that "the communism in Russia is more rotten than the Nazism in Germany." Oscar de Graaf, interview, July 26, 1996.

46. FBI, "Montreal interview of de Graaf," p. 83.

47. Ibid., pp. 83, 85.

48. Oscar de Graaf, interview, July 26, 1996.

49. Mensing, *Von der Ruhr in den GULag*, p. 222.

50. FBI, "Montreal interview of de Graaf," p. 86; and CSIS, RCMP, "1968 Brockville interview of John Henry de Graff," p. 49.

51. Wilhelm Mensing, e-mails, May 5, 2002, and July 18, 2004, and interview, July 4, 2004; Oleg Dehl, with Natalja Mussienko [Mussijenko], *Verratene Ideale: Zur Geschichte deutscher Emigranten in der Sowjetunion in der 30er Jahren* (Berlin: Trafo, 2000), pp. 251–56; and Barry McLoughlin, *Stalin's Terror: High Politics and Mass Repression in the Soviet Union* (London: Palgrave Macmillan, 2003), pp. 208–21.

52. Henry Ralph Lewenstein, *Die Karl Liebknecht Schule in Moskau, 1932–1937: Erinnerungen eines Schülers* (Lüneburg: Nordostdeutsches Kulturwerk, 1991), p. 68; Mensing, *Von der Ruhr in den GULag*, pp. 222–23; and Oscar de Graaf, interviews, August 16, 1996, and August 31, 1997. The final photograph is reproduced here as figure 39.

53. Oscar de Graaf, interview, July 26, 1996.

54. Marianne Oberschild (Marianne de Graaf's married name), telephone interview by Wilhelm Mensing, November 2000.

55. Oscar de Graaf, interview, July 26, 1996.

56. R. S. Rose asked the Federal Security Service in 2001 to provide any information it had on Johnny de Graaf II, without success. R. S. Rose, letter to ФСБРФ, November 6, 2001. Wilhelm Mensing asked the German Embassy in Moscow to inquire if the Federal Security Service or the Historic Center of the Ministry of the Interior had any information on the legal proceedings against Johnny de Graaf Jr., or if they knew where such documents might be stored. The answer was negative. Wilhelm Mensing, e-mail, May 5, 2002.

CHAPTER 15. BRAZIL TWO

1. FBI, "Unknown Subject, was: [censored]," p. 4, and "Montreal interview of de Graaf," pp. 86–87; and Krüger, interviews, August 12, September 19, and December 3, 1994.

2. FBI, "Montreal interview of de Graaf," pp. 87–88, and "Philadelphia interview of John Henry de Graaf," p. 27; CSIS, RCMP, "1969 Brockville interview of John Henry de Graff," p. 15; and Ernst Krüger, interview, December 14, 1994.

3. FBI, "Montreal interview of de Graaf," p. 88.

4. Oscar de Graaf, interview, July 26, 1996.

5. UKNA, document, "Application for a Certificate of Naturalization," HO 405/17786, p. 2

(hereafter "Application for a Certificate of Naturalization"); Canadian Department of the Secretary of State, document, "Naturalization" (de Graff, John Henry), June 4, 1945, file 3498, pp. 2R, 28R (hereafter "Naturalization [de Graff, John Henry]"); FBI, "Unknown Subject, was: [censored]"; and "Montreal interview of de Graaf," p. 88. A search of the official records in Edinburgh and London using their real names and all known aliases produced no confirmation of marriage between Johnny and either Gertrude or Helena Krüger. Ernst Krüger (letter, October 10, 1996) was also of the opinion that de Graaf never married either of his sisters.

6. APERJ, DESPS, "Das declarações de Jonny de Graaf, prestadas ao Exmo. Sr. Delagado Especial de Segurança Politica e Social, referentea ás atividades de espionagem da Tecbrevet, coligimos os seguintes dados informativos," Anexo Franz Gruber, pp. 1, 3.

7. Ibid., p. 2.

8. BAN, passenger list, SS *Almanzora,* RV 409; and *Times* (London), June 27, 1938, p. 23.

9. Romano also functioned as a DESPS torturer. David Nasser, *Falta alguém em Nuremberg: Torturas da polícia de Filinto Strubling Müller,* 4th ed. (Rio de Janeiro: O Cruzeiro, 1966), p. 63; and Thomé Amado, interview, Rio de Janeiro, September 28, 1994. Amado was one of Romano's victims.

10. FBI, "Montreal Interview of de Graaf." Julien had been a university professor before working at DESPS. CSIS, RCMP, "1969 Brockville interview of John Henry de Graff," p. 6.

11. Borer, interviews, May 28 and 29, 1998.

12. Brazil, Estado-Maior do Exercito, *Almanak: Ministerio da Guerra para o anno de 1938* (Rio de Janeiro: Estado-Maior do Exercito, 1938), p. 19.

13. Brazil, Rio de Janeiro, 2 Cartorio, bill of sale, "Escriptura de venda do predio e respectivo terreno á avenida Rainha Elisabeth n°. 219, que fazem o dr. José Cesario de Mello e sua mulher a Franz Gruber, com quitação," July 30, 1938; FBI, "Montreal Interview of de Graaf," pp. 88–89; APERJ, DESPS, "Franz Gruber ou Jonny de Graaf," p. 10; *Jornal do Brasil,* July 30, 1938, p. 16; and Sahr, Conversion Table. The street name Elisabeth is spelled with a "z" in some documents.

14. BAN, file, "Gustav Ernst Karl Krüger," no. 172219, pp. 1–3; Krüger, interviews, August 12 and October 17, 1994. A person or thing from the city of Rio de Janeiro is called a *carioca* in honor of an indigenous tribe that once lived in the area.

15. Brazil, Rio de Janeiro, 2nd Registry Office, "Certidão—L° 964 fls. 52-v-," September 17, 1938; APERJ, DESPS, "Franz Gruber ou Jonny de Graaf," pp. 13, 31. Emilia Rosso, the daughter of Aldo Rosso, claimed that Johnny did not own any piece of the hotel. Rather, it was an arrangement done by Rosso in order to give Johnny the cover of looking like a respectable businessman. This seems an unlikely story in view of the hotel's books, which Johnny described for DESPS following his arrest in late 1939. Emilia also claimed that her father lent Johnny his car. Again, this is improbable, since Johnny had a driver's license with the number of his Ford on it. Nonetheless, the point here would be that Aldo Rosso did all of this for Johnny so that he could get a "permanencia," or permanent residence permit. Emilia Rosso, telephone interview, July 24, 1994.

16. APERJ, DESPS, "Riasento. (Intraduzivel)" (heading in top left corner), Anexo Franz Gruber, and "Franz Gruber ou Jonny de Graaf," p. 32. Rio de Janeiro was full of casinos at this time, of which the Copacabana was one. They were officially closed following World War II, during the government of Eurico Gaspar Dutra.

17. APERJ, DESPS, "Franz Gruber ou Jonny de Graaf."

18. Rose, "Johnny's Two Trips to Brazil," p. 8; Krüger, interviews, August 12, September 19, and December 14, 1994. Ernst had to get special permission to leave Germany in 1938. He did so through a Nazi contact who told the authorities, falsely, that Ernst would propagandize for the Third Reich in Brazil. Because of the employer, Ernst was a forced to become a member of the Hitler Youth. The Nazi official thought it would be a good idea. The German War Ministry put a stamp in Ernst's passport allowing him to leave. Krüger, interviews, September 19 and December 14, 1994.

19. Rose, "Johnny's Two Trips to Brazil." Ernani married Alzira Vargas, the daughter of President Getúlio Vargas.

20. Krüger, interview, August 12, 1994. The fact that Gerti used her real name, not Erna Gruber, with Hans Lessing might explain how the authorities got onto the fact that she had assumed her dead sister's identity once Lessing had been picked up by DESPS in December 1939.

21. APERJ, DESPS, "Franz Gruber ou Jonny de Graaf," pp. 10, 16–17; and Krüger, interview, December 3, 1994. The surgeries were for an unspecified procedure at the São Cristovam Maternity

Hospital, probably for Gertrude, a hernia operation for Ernst at the German Hospital, and a hysterectomy for Emilie. The fragrance and ointment research was done at a room turned into a makeshift laboratory in the Rainha Elisabeth house.

22. Ernst Krüger, interview, December 14, 1994. On reaching Hamburg, Ernst was immediately drafted into a Nazi work brigade and later into the Wehrmacht. Sent to France, he saw little active duty as a result of five self-induced hernias to avoid combat. He was never in agreement with German war aims.

23. Krüger, interviews, August 12 and September 19, 1994. Gustav Krüger worked at home in Ipanema as a watch repairman. He had many customers, one of whom was one of Getúlio Vargas's two sons. Ernst Krüger, interview, December 14, 1994.

24. APERJ, DESPS, "Franz Gruber ou Jonny de Graaf," p. 41.

25. BAN, documents, "Franz Gruber to Senhores Membros da Comissão de Permanência de Estrangeiros," "Erna Gruber to Senhores Membros da Comissão de Permanência de Estrangeiros," and "Franz Gruber e esposa," CE/1525, CE/1526, February 9, 1939, November 26, 1938, file, "Franz Gruber e esposa," IJJ⁷ 89 M.J.N.I. 1938, no. 8818.

26. Oscar de Graaf, interview, July 26, 1996.

27. APERJ, DESPS, "Franz Gruber ou Jonny de Graaf," pp. 10–14, and document, "Termo de declarações [Josef Bunzlau]," in Anexo Franz Gruber, pp. 1–5; Ernst Krüger, interview, December 14, 1994; and CSIS, RCMP, "Copy of Montreal FBI interview of de Graaf," vol. 4, p. 96. In the FBI material, de Graaf mentioned that he paid US$10,000 to Helena Benkendorf. Rosa Benkendorf stated that Johnny's business relationship with her mother was another sham arrangement. Rosa Benkendorf, telephone interview, July 31, 1994. It is interesting to note, however, that Helena did not mention this in her December 8, 1939, police statement about the business dealings she had with Franz Gruber.

28. APERJ, DESPS, "Franz Gruber ou Jonny de Graaf," p. 34.

29. Sahr, Conversion Table.

30. Copies of these fictitious accounts can be seen in APERJ, DESPS, "Franz Gruber ou Jonny de Graaf," pp. 11–13.

31. Ibid., pp. 33–34, 36; and USDS, report, "John W. Ford to Jefferson Caffery," June 9, 1940. Johnny told the FBI that Brussels urged him to go to Paris in a letter he received in mid-July 1938. FBI, "Montreal interview of de Graaf," p. 91.

32. APERJ, DESPS, document, "Inteligence [sic] Service," D-11, December 3, 1940, p. 1, inglês/pasta 3.

33. APERJ, DESPS, "Franz Gruber ou Jonny de Graaf," pp. 29–30.

34. RCMP, "1968 Brockville interview of John Henry de Graff," p. 51, and "1969 Brockville interview of John Henry de Graff," pp. 5–6.

35. APERJ, DESPS, documents, "Intelligence Service—Serviço secréto inglês," December 17, 1940, inglês/pasta 3; "Serviço secréto inglez," SSI boletim 257, September 18, 1940, pp. xi–xiv, inglês/pasta 3; "Politica externa britanica com o Brasil," July 11, 1940, inglês/pasta 3; "Serviço secréto inglês," K-48, May 6, 1940, inglês/pasta 3; "Inteligence [sic] Service," D-11, October 2, 1940, inglês/pasta 3; "Inteligence [sic] Service," D-11, December 3, 1940, inglês/pasta 3; "Inteligence [sic] Service," SSI boletim 14, January 15, 1941, p. vi, inglês/pasta 3; "Inteligence [sic] Service," n.d., inglês/pasta 3; "Inteligence [sic] Service," D-11, July 4, 1940, inglês/pasta 3; "Serviço secreto inglês," K-48, June 1, 1940, inglês/pasta 3; "Inteligence [sic] Service," SSI boletim 347, December 17, 1940, pp. viii, ix, inglês/pasta 3; "Serviço de propaganda," December 17, 1940, inglês/pasta 3; "Inteligence [sic] Service," D-7, December 12, 1940, inglês/pasta 3; "Serviço secreto inglês," D-19, December 19, 1940, inglês/pasta 3; "Inteligence [sic] Service," SSI boletim 357, December 27, 1940, p. iii, inglês/pasta 3; "Inteligence [sic] Service," D-11, December 27, 1940, inglês/pasta 3; "Inteligence [sic] Service," SSI boletim 360, December 30, 1940, pp. viii, ix, inglês/pasta 3; "Inteligence [sic] Service," D-11, January 1, 1941, inglês/pasta 3; "Inteligence [sic] Service," S-1, January 11–12, 14, 1941, inglês/pasta 3; "Inteligence [sic] Service," S-1, boletim 11, January 13, 1941, p. x, inglês/pasta 3; "Inteligence [sic] Service," S-1, boletim 15, January 15, 1941, p. x, inglês/pasta 3; "Inteligence [sic] Service," S-2, January 25, 1941, inglês/pasta 3; "Inteligence [sic] Service no Rio de Janeiro," K-66, January 15, 1941, inglês/pasta 3; "Inteligence [sic] Service," D-11, January 26, 1941, inglês/pasta 3; "Inteligence [sic] Service," D-11, January 29, 1941, inglês/pasta 3; "Inteligence [sic] Service," S-2, January 31, 1941, inglês/pasta 3; letters, "Seraphim Braga to Cap. Delegado Especial," January 16, 1941, inglês/pasta 3; "Seraphim Braga to Cap. Delegado Especial," February

6, 1941, inglês/pasta 3; flow chart, "Constitução do serviço de informações (parte) a E. B. (HMS *Britain*)," February 11, 1941, inglês/pasta 3; "Inteligence [*sic*] Service," D-11, March 31, 1941, inglês/pasta 3; M. P. Coombes (Association of Royal Navy Officers), e-mail, September 17, 2003; and David Ashby (UK Ministry of Defense, Naval Historical Branch), letter, October 3, 2003.

36. BAN, letter, "[illegible] to Ilmo. Sr. Diretor do Instituto de Identificação," June 7, 1939, file, "Alfred Hutt," SPMAF/RJ, no. 8579; and Light, personnel file, "Alfred Hutt," fol. 2643.

37. APERJ, DESPS, letter, "[illegible] to Insp.-Chiefe da S.O.P to Delegado da O.P.E Social," December 14, 1939, file, "Carlos Stemmer," prontuário 1394.

38. APERJ, DESPS, driver's license, "Franz Gruber," p. 2. Note the comments written in red in between the lines of the driver's license.

39. The conversion of 4$937 per U.S. dollar is the official rate. *New York Times,* November 21, 1939, p. L41, and November 30, 1939, p. L35.

40. No official corroboration of Schmutter's existence in Brazil is currently available. Part of the problem is due to the fact that the comings and goings of foreigners were not regulated until 1938. Schmutter's entry into Brazil before such legislation took effect would account for the lack of material on him. His name could also have been an alias or the result of a misunderstood pronunciation between Johnny and Gordon Scott.

41. APERJ, DESPS, "Franz Gruber ou Jonny de Graaf," p. 8; and Fritz Berber, ed., *Jahrbuch für Auswärtige Politik, 1940* (Berlin: Aug. Gross, 1940), p. 303.

42. UKNA, letter, "H. W. U. McCall to HM Ambassador, Buenos Aires," December 21 1939, p. 7, war dispatch no. 4, serial no. 45/74/39, ADM 223/69; and Willi Frischauer and Robert Jackson, *The Altmark Affair* (New York: Macmillan, 1955), p. 114.

43. S. W. Roskill, *The War at Sea, 1939–1945* (London: H. M. Stationery Office, 1954), pp. 113–15, 120–21.

44. Ibid., 115–21; and S. W. Roskill, *White Ensign: The British Navy at War, 1939–1945* (Annapolis: U.S. Naval Academy, 1966), p. 56.

45. Nasser, p. 92. Nasser is said to have written his book on orders from his boss, Assis Chateaubriand, who was out to get Müller.

46. APERJ, DESPS, "Franz Gruber ou Jonny de Graaf," front matter, "Anotações diversas," December 14, 1939 (hereafter "Anotações diversas"). The Americans said the arresting group was from the Polícia Especial. USDS, letter, "Pawley to Secretary of State [George C. Marshall]," June 10, 1947, p. 2. Ernst Krüger claimed it was the navy that apprehended Johnny (interview, December 14, 1994). Carlos Lacerda, in his *Depoimento,* 2d ed. (Rio de Janeiro: Nova Fronteira, 1977), p. 53, stated it was the army. Johnny likewise believed it to be the army. CSIS, RCMP, "1969 Brockville interview of John Henry de Graff," p. 5.

47. APERJ, DESPS, "Franz Gruber ou Jonny de Graaf," p. 8. Note the handwritten comment on this letter from the commander of the Santa Cruz Fortress to Filinto Müller by Felisberto Batista Teixeira, "Recalha-se à Sala de Detidos, passando pela L4."

48. CSIS, RCMP, "1968 Brockville interview of John Henry de Graff," p. 53.

49. Borer, interview, May 28, 1998.

50. Ibid.; CSIS, RCMP, "1968 Brockville interview of John Henry de Graff," p. 52; and APERJ, DESPS, "Franz Gruber ou Jonny de Graaf," p. 7. This item on page 7 in Johnny's APERJ, DESPS file is a letter dated December 14, 1939, from the minister of war, Eurico Gaspar Dutra, to Filinto Müller ordering the arrest of Franz Gruber. Police chief Müller personally signed off on the top of the letter and wrote the word "urgent" on it before transferring it to DESPS to be carried out. It reached DESPS at 12:39 P.M. on December 14. In addition, newspapers would have revealed a foreign vacation by the chief of the Polícia Civil. No such news article was found. As for Miranda Corrêa, in March 1937 he traveled to Germany to study Nazi efforts to suppress communism. There, he personally met with Heinrich Himmler. Beloch and Abreu, p. 2344.

51. USDS, letters, "William C. Burdett to Secretary of State [Cordell Hull]," December 12, 1939, p. 1, decimal file 832.00B/121, despatch 2206, and "A[dolf] A. Berle, Jr. to Jefferson Caffery," March 11, 1940, decimal file 832.00B/121, despatch 621; and APERJ, DESPS, document, "Inteligence [*sic*] Service," SSI boletim 31 (I, II, III, IV e V), January 31, 1942, inglês/pasta 3.

52. Thomé Amado, interview, September 28, 1994. Amado was incarcerated for his political beliefs during these years and learned of Batista's behavior from firsthand sources.

53. APERJ, DESPS, document, "D.P.S., Serviço de Informações, setor arquivo, no. 16628, ref:-prot:- 20.952/48"; APERJ, file, "Hans Lessing," prontuário 1358, and letter, "Chefe do Setor to D.P.S, Serviço de Informações," December 13, 1939 [p. 25], file, "Hans Lessing," prontuário 1358.

54. Rosso, interview.

55. APERJ, DESPS, "[signature illegible] Insp.-Chefe da S.O.P to delegado da O.P.E Social," file "Carlos Stemmer"; "Franz Gruber ou Jonny de Graaf," p. 5; and document, "Inteligence [sic] Service," S-2, January 31, 1941, inglês/pasta 3.

56. APERJ, DESPS, "Termo de declarações [Josef Bunzlau]," in Anexo Franz Gruber, pp. 1–5.

57. CSIS, RCMP, "1969 Brockville interview of John Henry de Graff," p. 5.

58. Pollock, interview, September 16, 1996.

59. Borer, interview, May 28, 1998.

60. Borer, interview, May 13, 1998.

61. *Brockville Recorder and Times,* January 13, 1967, p. 3.

62. APERJ, DESPS, document, "[untitled handwritten notes in Portuguese by Felisberto Batista Teixeira]," December 21, 1939, Anexo Franz Gruber.

63. APERJ, DESPS, document, "Janeiro de 1940," January 2–3, 15, 1940, mapas de presos detidos de janeiro a dezembro 1940/pasta 1; "Franz Gruber ou Jonny de Graaf," p. 17; and "[untitled handwritten notes in Portuguese by Felisberto Batista Teixeira]," [January 3, 1940], Anexo Franz Gruber.

64. APERJ, DESPS, "Franz Gruber ou Jonny de Graaf," p. 16.

65. CSIS, RCMP, "1969 Brockville interview of John Henry de Graff," p. 6.

66. CSIS, RCMP, "1968 Brockville interview of John Henry de Graff," p. 51.

67. Ibid.; Robson Gracie, interview, Rio de Janeiro, August 6, 1991; and Sodré, p. 278.

68. Borer, interview, May 28, 1998. The *pau-de-arara* is a form of torture in which the victim is forced to sit on the floor with his knees drawn in toward his chest. The wrists are bound together on each side of the subject's legs and in front of his knees. An iron pole is slid through the gap just behind the bent knees and on top of the individual's elbows. Thus constrained, the iron pole and attached victim are lifted off the ground. Both ends of the pole are placed on two independent but secure positions, such as on two stacks of tires. While dangling, sufferers are raped, beaten, burned with cigarettes, soaked with water, or shocked. The *pau-de-arara* is still used in Brazil.

69. CSIS, RCMP, "1968 Brockville interview of John Henry de Graff," pp. 53–54; Hearsey, e-mail, January 5, 2005; and APERJ, DESPS, "Comunicação—Inv. 804 [Cecil Borer] to [Seraphim Braga], S-2," February 6, 1941, ingles/pasta 3.

70. AHI, "Souza Leão to Itamaraty," January 9, 1940, and "Regis de Oliveira to Oswaldo Aranha," December 20, 1939.

71. It could be that Johnny knew about the faked suicide of the only American from the attempted Communist revolution of 1935—the revolution he helped to thwart. Victor Allen Barron was actually thrown off the second story of the interior courtyard at the Polícia Central in 1936. Rose, *One of the Forgotten Things,* p. 52.

72. CSIS, RCMP, "1969 Brockville interview of John Henry de Graff," p. 7.

73. *Livro vermelho dos telefones, 1939,* 15th ed. (Rio de Janeiro, 1940).

74. Krüger, interview, September 19, 1994. The authors are aware of the slightly different version that Johnny returned home first and Gerti had her miscarrage, in CSIS, RCMP, "1968 Brockville interview of John Henry de Graff," p. 54. Johnny told the account used here to Gordon Scott.

75. APERJ, DESPS, "Anotações diversas."

76. Krüger, interview, August 12, 1994; *New York Times,* February 28, 1940, p. L34; and Sahr, Conversion Table.

77. UKNA, Passenger Manifest of SS *Highland Chieftain,* BT 26/1191/38, and document, "Conditional Landing," HO 405/17786.

CHAPTER 16. THE WAR'S FIRST YEARS

1. Passenger Manifest of SS *Highland Chieftain;* "Conditional Landing"; and document, "Regional Advisory Committee," HO 405/17786, p. [2], all in UKNA.

2. Roy Berkeley, *A Spy's London,* foreword by Nigel West [Rupert Allason] (London: Cooper, 1994), pp. 7–8. Some of Johnny's desk time could also have been spent at the MI6 Section V facility at St. Albans, north of London.

3. Oscar de Graaf, interview, July 26, 1996. In UKNA, "Application for a Certificate of Naturalization," p. 1, Johnny states that this name change took place in 1941. While this is possible, it seems doubtful that it occurred after he arrived in Canada. It was probably done earlier, while he was in London, to offer both him and Gerti cover while in the UK. Oscar de Graaf agreed with this version of events. The praxis of using his new name, John Henry de Graff, will be followed in the remainder of this volume. Note that the FBI continued to use "De Graaf" in its documents.

4. Berkeley, pp. 91, 94.

5. Ibid.; and Kim Philby, *My Silent War* (New York: Grove, 1968), p. 260.

6. UKNA, "Application for a Certificate of Naturalization." The authors are aware of the address de Graff provided the Americans (FBI, report, "Secret, SY—Mr. John W. Ford, SY—Omar Henry," July 17, 1952, pp. 1–2, file HQ 100–342513–53) of 29 St. James's, London SW1, which is not confirmed in UKNA, "Application for a Certificate of Naturalization."

7. Pollock, interview, September 16, 1996.

8. UKNA, miscellaneous documents, "Furnishing of GPO with camp addresses," HO 215/293; and Peter Merrifield, interview, London, June 1, 2004. Merrifield is the headmaster of the Oak Lodge School.

9. Some records transposed the first two names.

10. Canada, Citizenship and Immigration Canada—Citoyenneté et Immigration Canada (hereafter CIC), "Naturalization [John Henry de Graff]," p. R2, file 3498; Department of Mines and Resources, Commission of Immigration, letter, "R. N. [illegible] to the Commissioner RCMP," February 20, 1941, no. 707615; and CSIS, RCMP, letter, "E. H. Perlson to the O.C. 'C' Division RCMP," February 24, 1941, file, John de Graff, vol. 1.

11. FBI, "Unknown Subject, was: [censored]."

12. The FBI has removed this individual's name from the released document. Ibid.

13. Ibid., p. 10; and CSIS, RCMP, letter, "A. Drysdale to the O.C. 'C' Division RCMP," February 10, 1941, Report D.D. 28-2-41.

14. CSIS, RCMP, letter, "H. A. R. Gagnon to R. R. Tait," October 29, 1941, file, John de Graff, vol. 1. There is no mention in any of the RCMP communication during this period on how the de Graffs returned to Montreal.

15. FBI, "Unknown Subject, was: [censored]," pp. 10–11, 13.

16. The RCMP assistant commissioner in Ottawa, R. R. Tait, wrote to the RCMP in Montreal at least six times from May 3 to October 23, 1941, trying to find out what was happening with the de Graffs. His requests were disregarded. In Tait's last communication, he threatened disciplinary action if ignored again. Harvison then telephoned Tait and explained that the RCMP had been waiting for a report from Johnny to be translated from German into English. The translated report had nothing to do with his trip to the United States. Tait's letters to the O.C. "C" Division of the RCMP, dated May 3, July 31, August 12, and August 22, can be found in CSIS, RCMP, file, John de Graff, vol. 1. See also "R. R. Tait to H. A. R. Gagnon," October 23, 1941; "H. A. R. Gagnon to R. R. Tait," October 29, 1941; "C. W. Harvison and H. A. R. Gagnon to the O.C. 'C' Division," November 7, 1941, all in ibid.; and [John H. de Graff], "Informations Material zum Kampf gegen Kommunismuss [*sic*]," n.d., and "Information Material Relating to the fight of Communism," n.d., ibid.

17. The file in question, HO 405/17786, covers Johnny's life from January 1, 1940, to December 31, 1946. Despite the fact that fourteen pages were released to one of the authors, the bulk of the file is exempt from release under the Freedom of Information Act, 2000. The reason for this exception is contained in the catchall provision known as Section 24, which allows items to be retained to "protect national security." Lale Ozdemir (UKNA), e-mail, October 27, 2005.

18. CSIS, RCMP, "R. R. Tait to the O.C. 'C' Division RCMP," April 19, 1941, "R. L. Cadiz to the Officer Commanding 'C' Division RCMP," September 11, 1941, and "R. R. Tait to H. A. R. Gagnon," October 23, 1941, all in file, John de Graff, vol. 1.

19. Oscar de Graaf, interviews, July 26 and September 1, 1996.

CHAPTER 17. THE MONTREAL NESTS

1. Lita-Rose Betcherman, *The Swastika and the Maple Leaf* (Toronto: Fitzhenry and Whiteside, 1973), p. 146.
2. Jack Armitage, interview, Brockville, Ontario, July 14, 1995.
3. CSIS, RCMP, document, "Classification Sheet—Feuille de classement," file, John de Graff, vol. TS, and letter, "V. A. M. Kemp to the O.C. 'C' Div., RCMP," August 21, 1944, file, John de Graff, vol. 2.
4. CSIS, RCMP, letters, "J. Leopold to the Intelligence Officer," November 22, 1941, and "H. A. R. Gagnon to the Commissioner RCMP," July 6, 1942, both in file, John de Graff, vol. 1; and Sahr, Conversion Table.
5. Betcherman, p. 146.
6. Canada, "Naturalization [de Graff, John Henry]," p. 2R.
7. Ward and Violet Scott are the parents of one of the authors.
8. In UKNA, "Application for a Certificate of Naturalization," Johnny incorrectly gives the date of his landing in Canada, January 19, 1941, as the date he and Gerti moved into the Palmerston Avenue home.
9. CSIS, RCMP, report, "Summary of Activities of Agent 235, up to October 6, 1942," pp. 1, 5, file, John de Graff, vol. TS.
10. CSIS, RCMP, letter, "H. A. R. Gagnon to the Commissioner RCMP," September 28, 1942, pp. 1–2, file, John de Graff, vol. 1.
11. Ibid., p. 2.
12. Jack Armitage, interview.

CHAPTER 18. A MAN FROM THE SEA

1. Clifford W. Harvison, "The Spy Who Came Out of the Sea," *Brockville Recorder and Times*, January 7, 1967, p. 9. The RCMP account changed Johnny's name to "John Gries." Canada, National Archives (hereafter CNA), RCMP, report, "Memorandum to D.N.I., Interrogation of Werner Janowski, lieutenant, German Army," November 14, 1942, RG 24, Acc. 1983–84/167, vol. 306, S-1487-J-2.
2. CNA, RCMP, reports, "A. Drysdale to Departmental Secretary," March 23, 1943, file, Werner von Janowski, doc. 54, vol. 3, 1464; and "[C. W. Harvison] to O.C. 'C' Division, RCMP, re: Werner von Janowski," November 13, 1942, ibid., vol. 1, 063.
3. Annett's son, Earl Annett Jr., claimed that the matches fell out of von Janowski's pocket when he reached for a handkerchief to wipe his hands. From that point, the version by Harvison until von Janowski was transported to Montreal is different in some details from the one recounted by Johnny. Harvison's version, however, includes some discrepancies. See Harvison, "Spy Who Came Out of the Sea," pp. 9–12, and Clifford W. Harvison, *The Horsemen* (Toronto: McClelland and Stewart, 1967), pp. 106–13.
4. CNA, RCMP, report, "A. Drysdale to Departmental Secretary," March 23, 1943, file, Werner von Janowski, doc. 54, vol. 3, 1464–65. Duchesneau's name is spelled "Duschene" in CNA, RCMP, report, "G. H. Archer Re: Werner S. W. Janowski to Werner Alfred Waldemar von Janowsky—Enemy Agent," ibid., vol. 1, 215.
5. Harvison spells von Janowski's cover name "Brauntner" in "The Spy Who Came Out of the Sea" (p. 9) and "Braunter" in *The Horsemen* (p. 107). The spelling used here is from official RCMP documents.
6. CNA, RCMP, report, "[C. W. Harvison] Re: Werner von Janowski," file, Werner von Janowski, doc. 54, vol. 1, 271–72, 274; and Dean Beeby, *Cargo of Lies: The True Story of a Nazi Double Agent in Canada* (Toronto: University of Toronto Press, 1996), p. 138.
7. CNA, RCMP, "[C. W. Harvison] Re: Werner von Janowski," 273; letters, "C. W. Harvison to H. A. R. Gagnon," February 12, 1943, file, Werner von Janowski, doc. 54, vol. 2, 1004–6; "S. T. Wood to [censored]," February 15, 1943, ibid., 1002–3; and "F. J. Mead to [censored]," February 13, 1943, ibid., 1001. These sources offer no additional information regarding the two speech peculiarities.
8. Johnny de Graff, interview by Nancy Duffy, tape recording, Brockville, Ontario, Fall 1971.

This is the only known recording of Johnny de Graff's voice that still survives. Nancy Duffy was the school-age daughter of Ed Duffy of the RCMP. She conducted the interview with Johnny as background for a school project.

9. Ibid.
10. Fleming, pp. 176–78; and Pincher, p. 297.
11. De Graff, interview by Duffy.
12. Beeby, caption on final unnumbered photo between pp. xi and 1.
13. Harvison, "Spy Who Came Out of the Sea," p. 12, and *Horsemen*, pp. 120–21.
14. Harvison, "Spy Who Came Out of the Sea," p. 12.
15. CNA, RCMP, reports, "[W. S. Samuel] Naval Service, Memorandum to D.N.I., Interrogation of Werner Janowski, Lieutenant, German Army," November 14, 1942, file, Werner von Janowski, doc. 54, vol. 1, 124–30, and "A. Drysdale to Departmental Secretary," March 23, 1943, ibid., vol. 3, 1463; and Beeby, p. 53.
16. De Graff, interview by Duffy.
17. Ibid. The Germans, of course, never occupied Sweden during World War II.
18. Ibid.
19. CNA, RCMP, letter, "F. J. Mead to H. A. R. Gagnon," February 16, 1943, file, Werner von Janowski, doc. 54, vol. 2, 988–89.
20. CNA, RCMP, letter, "C. W. Harvison to H. A. R. Gagnon," January 12, 1943, ibid., 755–56, and report, "H. A. R. Gagnon to the O.C.—'C' Div., RCMP—MTL," December 2, 1942, ibid., vol. 1, 410.
21. Harvison, "Spy Who Came Out of the Sea," p. 12, and *Horsemen*, p. 113.
22. Beeby, pp. 90–91; J. C. Masterman, *The Double Cross System in the War of 1939–1945* (London: Sphere, 1973), pp. 58, 190; and Smith, *Foley*, p. 243.
23. See, for example, the way the von Janowski case name is used in Juan Pujol, with Nigel West [Rupert Allason], *Garbo* (London: Weidenfeld and Nicolson, 1985), pp. 104–5; and Masterman, p. 121. Pujol's work also gave rise to a new alias for Johnny, Gottfried Treviranus.
24. Beeby, p. 98.
25. There is the view that von Janowski fooled both the Canadians and the British. This position holds that he actually let his handlers in Hamburg know through a coded signal during a transmission that he had been captured. David Stafford, *Camp X* (New York: Dodd, Mead, 1986), p. 260.
26. CNA, RCMP, document, "Royal Canadian Mounted Police [receipt]," August 30, 1943, file, Werner von Janowski, doc. 54, vol. 4, 2179. Note that the nine months referred to in the *Ottawa Citizen*, January 12, 1954, p. 13, is incorrect. Johnny probably meant von Janowski's total time in Canadian captivity and not the time spent in his basement.
27. CSIS, RCMP, "Summary of Activities of Agent 235, up to October 6, 1942," p. 1.
28. De Graff, interview by Duffy.
29. Ibid.
30. CNA, RCMP, "[C. W. Harvison] Re: Werner von Janowski," 273; report, "[C. W. Harvison] to O.C. 'C' Division, RCMP, re: Werner von Janowski," file, Werner von Janowski, doc. 54, vol. 1, 062; and Beeby, p. 54. CNA, RCMP, letter, "S. T. Wood to Louis S. St. Laurent," September 21, 1945, file, Werner von Janowski, doc. 54, vol. 4, 2568, gives the date of the marriage as December 5, 1931.
31. De Graff, interview by Duffy.
32. CSIS, RCMP, report, "Johnny de Graff, Montreal, P.Q.," March 17, 1951, pp. 4–5, file, John de Graff, vol. 3.
33. Ibid., p. 5.
34. Ibid.
35. CNA, RCMP, letter, "R. W. Baldwin to Bavin," November 21, 1942, file, Werner von Janowski, doc. 54, vol. 1, 224–25; and Beeby, pp. 70–71. In part incorrect, the *Newsweek* blurb went, "Watch for an announcement revealing the capture of a German submarine commander near New Carlisle, Quebec." *Newsweek*, November 23, 1942, p. 14.
36. CSIS, RCMP, "[censored] to [censored]," October 29, 1943, file, John de Graff, vol. 2. This document also contains a handwritten reference to Inspector Leopold of the RCMP dated March 11, 1940, conceivably touching on the same subject.

37. Ivan Avakumovic, *The Communist Party of Canada: A History* (Toronto: McClelland and Stewart, 1975), pp. 11, 247. Buhay was of eastern_European extraction and had been involved in radical politics in New York and Montreal during World War I as an opponent of conscription.

38. Pollock, interview, September 16, 1996.

39. CNA, RCMP, letter, "S. T. Wood to [Louis S.] St. Laurent," March 8, 1943, file, Werner von Janowski, doc. 54, vol. 3, 1346, and "R. W. Baldwin to F. J. Mead," March 8, 1943, ibid., 1362–63.

40. Beeby, pp. 114–17, 122–23, 126–30, 135–36; and CNA, RCMP, letter, "Werner [Billy] Branton [Werner von Janowski] to [unknown]," November 1, 1947, file, Werner von Janowski, doc. 54, vol. 4, 2612.

41. Beeby, p. 133. The Canadian government imposed a news blackout on all Axis attacks against Allied shipping in Canadian waters "to avoid demoralizing the population and informing the enemy." *Times Colonist* (Victoria, British Columbia), October 13, 2005, p. B8. It is conceivable that the ban applied to the individuals landed off submarines as well.

42. CNA, RCMP, document, "[untitled]," file, Werner von Janowski, doc. 54, vol. 4, 2217, p. 31; letter, "A. Drysdale to C. H. Little," September 3, 1943, RG 24, Acc. 1983–84/167, vol. 306, S-1487-J-2; and Beeby, pp. 137–38.

43. De Graff, interview by Duffy.

44. Ibid.

CHAPTER 19. TO CATCH A SUBMARINE

1. *Brockville Recorder and Times,* January 13, 1967, p. 5.

2. Harvison, *Horsemen,* p. 119.

3. Harvison, "Spy Who Came Out of the Sea," p. 13.

4. Communist Party of Canada, *Canada's Party of Socialism: History of the Communist Party of Canada, 1921–1976* (Toronto: Progress, 1982), pp. 137–38.

5. CSIS, RCMP, letters, "C. W. Harvison to the Commissioner RCMP," September 2, 1944, "C. W. Harvison to 'C' Division RCMP," December 15, 1944, and "J. J. Granner to 'O' Division RCMP," August 2, 1945, all in file, John de Graff, vol. 2.

6. No relation to one of the authors.

7. The last name could also have been spelled "von Lenter," or it could even have been an alias. For the sake of consistency, we will use "von Linter" here.

8. John Lovell, *Lovell's Montreal Directory, Containing Alphabetical and Street Directories of Greater Montreal* (Montreal: Lovell, 1952), lists structures by street address in numerical order together with the building's occupants.

9. Beeby, p. 32.

10. Yves Bernard and Caroline Bergeron, *Trop loin de Berlin: Des prisonniers allemands au Canada, 1939–1946* (Montreal: Septentrion, 1995), pp. 17–22, 216–20.

11. Ibid., p. 305.

12. "German Prisoners of War at Feller During WW II," http://www3.sympatico.ca/relger/POW-camp.html (accessed April 19, 2003).

13. "The Native (Heathen) Religion," http://66.102.7.104/search?q = cache:SyqFoApEohQJ:www .geocities.com/reginheim/religion.html + %22Dusk + of + the + Gods%22 + German + legend&hl = en (accessed September 5, 2005).

14. Bernard and Bergeron, pp. 294–96.

15. CSIS, RCMP, letter, "C. W. Harvison to the Commissioner RCMP," November 27, 1944, file, John de Graff, vol. 2.

16. CSIS, RCMP, letter, "C. W. Harvison to the Commissioner RCMP," April 12, 1945, ibid., and document, "Extract RCMP Toronto," June 18, 1945, ibid.

17. Canadian Department of the Secretary of State, letter, "Oscar Coderre to V. A. M. Kemp," April 27, 1945, ibid.

18. CSIS, RCMP, telegram, "S. T. Wood to the Officer Commanding RCMP," April 28, 1945, ibid.

CHAPTER 20. THE CONTROL COMMISSION

1. UKNA, documents, "Certificate of Naturalization [John Henry de Graff]," HO 334/161, AZ17678, and "Application for a Certificate of Naturalization."
2. United Kingdom, Control Commission for Germany (British Element) (hereafter UKCC), *Report for the Month of June 1946,* vol. 1, no. 1, inside front cover; *Report for the Month of July 1946,* vol. 1, no. 2, inside front cover; and *Report for the Month of August 1946,* vol. 1, no. 3, inside front cover.
3. Oscar de Graaf, interview, July 26, 1996.
4. UKCC, *Report for the Month of June 1946; Report for the Month of July 1946;* and *Report for the Month of August 1946,* inside front covers.
5. Curry, p. 23.
6. CSIS, RCMP, "1968 Brockville interview of John Henry de Graff," p. 60. The physician's family name was sounded out in the Canadian document. It may actually have a different spelling.
7. Ibid., pp. 60–61.
8. Ibid., p. 60.
9. The version in ibid. (pp. 60–61) has this differently. There, Johnny claimed that Nottingham sent him "on a mission to find out the difference between two colonels in charge of the labor crews in a chemical plant. I solved that problem my way, not his way, by bringing these two colonels together instead of splitting them apart." Following this came the episode with Dr. Aureba, and then de Graff resigned and flew to London. The description used here is the one given to Gordon Scott.
10. Section V of MI6 had moved out of London in 1940 to St. Albans, then back again. At war's end, it was once more in the Broadway buildings. In between was a stay at 14 Ryder Street, also in Westminster. Berkeley, pp. 295–96; and Smith, *Spying Game,* p. 99.
11. CSIS, RCMP, letters, "J. W. Holmes to F. B. Cotsworth," August 15, 1946; "E. Blake Budden to John Holmes," August 16, 1946; and document, "John W. Holmes to file," August 21, 1946, all in file, de Graff, J. H., RG 25, vol. 2121 f. AR 1115/1–3.
12. Pollock, interviews, September 16, 1996, and December 21, 1997.
13. Frank Foley, letter to John de Graff, January 1947.
14. The conversion rate is taken from the *Times* (London), August 16, 1946, p. 7.
15. CSIS, RCMP, "E. Blake Budden to John Holmes," August 16, 1946; and "John W. Holmes to file," August 21, 1946, as cited in note 11 above.
16. Johannes de Graaf, an apparent Nazi agent in prison in the United Kingdom, was trying to return to Canada at about the same time. Johannes had told the Canadian authorities in London that he was born in Canada (Saskatoon) but moved with a family member back to Holland. CNA, RCMP, file, "De Graaf, J," file, Johannes de Graaf, RG 25, vol. 2120 f. AR 1052/1. Britain's version of this material is in UKNA, file, "Johannes de Graaf," KV2/125.
17. UKNA, Passenger Manifest of SS *Cavina,* BT 27/1586.
18. Ibid.

CHAPTER 21. HOME

1. CIC, "Naturalization [John Henry de Graff]," pp. R20, R26, file 3498. They had actually been processed into Canada at Quebec City. CSIS, RCMP, letter, "J. Leopold to J. E. Duggan," March 20, 1952, file, John de Graff, vol. 4.
2. Canada, document, "Petition for a Certificate of Canadian Citizenship by a British Subject," John Henry de Graff (petitioner), March 7, 1952, p. 2. This document is taken as proof of the hotel Johnny and Gerti used, in spite of the Mount Royal Hotel stationery on which Johnny wrote the RCMP in Ottawa. CSIS, RCMP, letter, "J. H. de Graff to [C. E.] Rivett-Carnac," September 12, 1946, file, John de Graff, vol. 3.
3. *Kingston Whig-Standard,* October 13, 1954, p. [4].
4. *Brockville Recorder and Times,* January 13, 1967, p. 5.
5. For but one example, see the *Kingston Whig-Standard,* October 13, 1954, p. [4].
6. *Montreal Gazette,* September 11, 1951, p. 17.
7. *Brockville Recorder and Times,* January 13, 1967, p. 5.

8. Andy Kovács, interview, Brockville, Ontario, July 17, 1995; and Angela Fegyverneky, telephone interview, July 10, 2002.

9. No relation to one of the authors.

10. There are two official dates for Gerti's death. The one given here is from her death certificate. Province of Quebec, Ministry of Health, document, "Registration of Death [for] Gertrude Erica Kruger [sic]," no. 123677. The second date, one day earlier on September 22, 1951, is from the mortuary that cremated her remains. Province of Quebec, Ministère de la Justice, Direction de l'état civil de Montréal, document, "Death Registration [for] Mrs. John Henry de Graff," September 25, 1951.

11. Quebec Ministry of Health, "Registration of Death [for] Gertrude Erica Kruger [sic]"; Quebec Ministère de la Justice, "Death Registration [for] Mrs. John Henry de Graff"; and CIC, letter, "Irena K. Lang to Ernst Kruger [sic]," May 12, 1997.

12. Violet Scott, interview, Oshawa, Ontario, July 20, 1996.

13. George Headry, telephone interview, August 9, 1995. Headry attended one speech.

14. *Montreal Gazette,* September 11, 1951, p. 9.

15. Ibid., April 12, 1952, p. 3; CSIS, RCMP, letters, "J. A. A. Thivierge to the Commissioner RCMP," April 16, 1952, file, John de Graff, vol. 4; "The Commissioner RCMP to [censored]," October 6, 1954, file, John de Graff, vol. 5; and Ted Bargiello, telephone interview, July 16, 1995.

16. CSIS, RCMP, report, "Johnny de Graff, Montreal, P.Q.," March 31, 1951, pp. 1–2, file, John de Graff, vol. 3. Note the added comments on this document, written by J. R. Lemieux to RCMP superintendent G. B. McClellan[d] and dated April 2, 1951; and letter, "Geo. B. McClellan[d] to the O.C. 'E' Division RCMP," April 4, 1951, ibid.

17. "C. W. Harvison to the Commissioner RCMP," May 12, 1951, ibid., pp. 1–3; and "Geo. B. McClelland to the O.C. 'E' Division RCMP," October 5, 1951, ibid.

18. "Johnny de Graff, Montreal, P.Q.," March 17, 1951, pp. 6–7, ibid.; and letter, "C. W. Harvison to the Officer Commanding 'E' Division RCMP," April 6, 1951, p. 1, ibid. Some of those outside the force who knew him confirmed Johnny's opinion that he felt abandoned. Jack Armitage, interview.

19. FBI, letter, "Paul Petersen [de Graff] to J. Edgar Hoover," February 6, 1950, pp. 1–2, file HQ 100–342513.

20. William C. Sullivan, with Bill Brown, *The Bureau: My Thirty Years in Hoover's FBI* (New York: W. W. Norton, 1979), p. 184.

21. CSIS, RCMP, "1969 Brockville interview of John Henry de Graff," p. 25. The uncensored FBI interview did not mention their first names.

22. FBI, letter, "[unknown] to Director, FBI (65–43302)," May 5, 1952, pp. 1, 4, file HQ 100–342513.

23. Scott, interview.

24. Quebec Ministry of Health, document, "Registration of Marriage [for] John Henry de Graff and Charlotte Akontz," no. 108020; and Ministère de la Justice, Bureau de la publicité des droits de Montréal, document, "Marriage Contract no. 236," May 17, 1952, pp. 1–3, 954464.

25. Pollock, interview, September 16, 1996.

26. Scott, interview. Ross Fenemore corroborates the bad humor story. Ross Fenemore, interview, Brockville, Ontario, July 15, 1995.

27. FBI, letter, "Director [J. Edgar Hoover] to [censored]," December 2, 1952, file HQ 100–342513; and "Philadelphia interview of John Henry de Graaf," p. 8.

28. FBI, "Philadelphia interview of John Henry de Graaf," pp. 8–10. Johnny was also asked about two individuals. The FBI has censored their identities in the released documents. Johnny said that one of these persons worked at the Comintern's library in Moscow. The other was a member of the KPD in the Ruhr in 1927 or 1928.

29. The photograph is shown here as figure 18.

30. FBI, "Philadelphia interview of John Henry de Graaf," pp. 10–11.

31. Ibid., p. 16.

32. Ibid., pp. 17–19, 27.

33. FBI, letter, "Johnny de Graff to Dear Friend," February 16, 1953, file HQ 100–342513; and "Liaison Representative to Director [J. Edgar Hoover]," April 4, 1953, ibid.

34. *Saint John (New Brunswick) Telegraph-Journal,* May 26, 1953, p. 1.

35. Kovács, interview.

36. The name derives from that of a small community in Norfolk County, England, where a previous owner was born in 1802. *Brockville Recorder and Times,* May 11, 1988, p. 3.

37. Gouvernement du Québec, Ministère de la Justice, Bureau de la publicité des droits de Montréal, documents, "Transfer no. 10,042," October 7, 1953, pp. 1–7, 1040801; "Transfer no. 10,043," October 7, 1953, pp. 1–5, 1040802; "Transfer no. 10,044," October 7, 1953, pp. 1–5, 1040803; and Province of Ontario, Land Registry Office, document, "Abstract Index," lot 17, concession 1, p. 197.

38. CSIS, RCMP, letter, "J. A. A. Thivierge to the Commissioner RCMP," October 1, 1953, file, John de Graff, vol. 5; and Blake Clarke, interview, Brockville, Ontario, July 12, 1995.

39. Jack Armitage, interview.

40. Clarke, interview; and *Brockville Recorder and Times,* May 11, 1988, p. 3.

41. Neil Pollock claims that Johnny would not rent his Horningtoft cabins to Jews (interview, September 16, 1996). This seems dubious, however, in light of the fact that a person named Kazimierowicz, apparently Jewish, was one of six long-term tenants in the Montreal boardinghouse in 1952. Another Montreal lodger, Eddy Fish, may likewise have been Jewish. Lovell, *Lovell's Montreal Directory,* p. 946.

42. Pollock, interview, September 16, 1996.

43. *Ottawa Citizen,* February 4, 1954, p. 21.

44. D. W. Sherman, letter postmarked August 15, 1995.

45. *Ottawa Citizen,* January 16, 1954, p. 5.

46. *Ottawa Journal,* January 12, 1954, p. 1.

47. *Chicago Daily Tribune,* January 13, 1954, p. 6.

48. Canadian Department of External Affairs, letter, "George P. [illegible] to the Commissioner RCMP," January 21, 1954, file 42340.

49. CSIS, RCMP, letter, "M. W. M to [Minister of Justice Stuart S.] Garson," January 29, 1954, file, John de Graff, vol. 5. This view was reaffirmed in letter, "L. H. Nicholson to Minister of Justice Stuart S. Garson," February 2, 1954, ibid.

50. *Syracuse (N.Y.) Post Standard,* January 22, 1954, p. 1.

51. FBI, letter, "[censored] to A. H. Belmont," January 28, 1954, pp. 1–2, file HQ 100-342513.

52. Pollock, interview, September 16, 1996.

53. Jack Armitage, interview.

54. CSIS was formed in 1984 and assumed many of the functions of the RCMP Security Service. Canadian Office Consolidation/Codification Administrative, *Canadian Security Intelligence Service Act/ Loi sur le Service canadien du renseignement de sécurité,* R.S. 1985, c. C-23/L.R. (1985), ch. C-23, 2000, p. 1.

55. Jim Warren, telephone interview, February 17, 2001; and Neil Pollock, telephone interview, February 28, 2001. The photograph is identical to the one shown here (figure 62), but without the German inscription. Warren goes on to say, "Whether it was actually presented by the King, or Johnny was simply told that the King had taken a special interest in him, it could well have been either. I suspect the same principle lay behind the British naval officer uniform. I know that we in Canada used the same sorts of 'flattery' tools in regard to valued agents." Jim Warren, e-mail, February 19, 2001.

56. Oscar de Graaf, interviews, July 26 and September 1, 1996, August 16, 1997; and Johnny de Graaf III, e-mail, August 15, 2004.

57. Oscar de Graaf, interview, August 16, 1997.

58. Eva Szabo, interview, Brockville, Ontario, July 17, 1995.

59. Although it was unsubstantiated, Angela Fegyverneky, the wife of one of Sári's only living relatives, Sándor Fegyverneky, believed that Sári worked for French intelligence in some capacity. Angela Fegyverneky, telephone interview, August 12, 2002.

60. Ibid.; and Sándor Fegyverneky, interview, Zánka, Hungary, August 12, 2002.

61. Anonymous-1, telephone interview, July 18, 1995. This individual worked at the Brockville Psychiatric Hospital and feared the loss of this position for revealing this information.

62. Sándor Fegyverneky, documents, "[untitled notes in English, French, Hungarian, and German by Charlotte de Graff]," n.d.; and Sándor Fegyverneky, letter, "Johnny de Graff to Sándor and family," November 14, 1967, both in Sándor Fegyverneky's personal papers.

63. Pollock, interview, September 16, 1996.

64. Stewart, interviews, January 8 and December 14, 1997; Pollock, interview, December 21, 1997, and Pollock, letter, December 21, 1997.

65. Young, interview.

66. Jack Armitage, interview; and Don Swayne, interview, Brockville, Ontario, July 15, 1995. At the time of the interview, Swayne was the city editor of the *Brockville Recorder and Times*. He interviewed Johnny for the piece that appeared in the paper on January 13, 1967, pp. 3, 5.

67. *Brockville Recorder and Times,* January 13, 1967, pp. 3, 5.

68. Steven Szabo, interview, Brockville, Ontario, July 17, 1995.

69. CSIS, RCMP, document, "Featherbed," May 31, 1968, file, John de Graff, vol. 5; report, "John Henry de Graff," September 3, 1976, ibid.; letter, "[censored] to Memo for File," April 25, 1979, ibid.; Oscar de Graaf, interview, July 26, 1996.

70. Ruth Kitson, letter, April 24, 1996. At the time of her letter, Ruth Kitson was the director of patient care services at the St. Vincent de Paul Hospital. A quarter-page obituary was published in the local paper. *Brockville Recorder and Times,* December 3, 1980, p. 20.

EPILOGUE

1. Oscar de Graaf, interview, August 16, 1997.

2. N. Leslie Sterritt, interview, Brockville, Ontario, July 14, 1995. Sterritt was the former Brockville police chief who succeeded Wilmont Young.

3. Kovács, interview.

4. Ibid.

5. Sándor Fegyverneky, interview.

6. Ibid.; Angela Fegyverneky, interview; Kovács, interview; *Brockville Recorder and Times,* August 9, 1985, p. 5; and Province of Ontario, Brockville Office of the Sheriff, document, "Surrogate Court Letters Probate [Last Will and Testament of Charlotte de Graff]," September 18, 1985, Surr. 3389/85, p. 2. Maria visited Johnny and Sári in Brockville several times.

7. James O. Barclay, interview, Brockville, Ontario, July 17, 1995.

8. *Brockville Recorder and Times,* May 11, 1988, p. 3.

BIBLIOGRAPHY

ARGENTINA

Archivo Histórico de la Provincia de Buenos Aires (AHPBA). La Plata.
Brazil
    Arquivo Histórico do Itamarati (AHI). Itamarati.
    Arquivo Nacional (BAN). Rio de Janeiro.
    Arquivo Público do Estado da Bahia. Inspectoria da Polícia do Porto. Salvador.
    Arquivo Público do Estado do Rio de Janeiro (APERJ). Rio de Janeiro.
Canada
    Canadian Security Intelligence Service (CSIS)
    Citizenship and Immigration Canada/Citoyenneté et Immigration Canada (CIC).
    Department of External Affairs.
    National Archives of Canada (CNA), Royal Canadian Mounted Police (RCMP)
Germany
    Bundesarchiv Berlin (GBB), Bundesbeauftragte für die Unterlagen des Staatssicherheitsdienst der ehemaligen Deutsche Demokratischer Republik, Zentrales Parteiarchiv der SED, Berlin
    Bundesarchiv—Militärarchiv Freiburg (GBF)
    Hauptstaatsarchiv Düsseldorf (GHD)
    Stadt Ahlen (GSA)
    Staatsarchiv Hamburg (GSH)
Russia
    Российский государственный архив социально-политической истории (РГАСПИ)
United Kingdom
    National Archives (UKNA)
United States
    National Archives, Washington, D.C. Shanghai Municipal Police Files

PUBLISHED SOURCES

Aldrich, Richard. "Britain's Secret Intelligence Service in Asia During the Second World War." *Modern Asian Studies,* vol. 32, no. 1 (1998).

Allen, Henry T. *The Rhineland Occupation.* Indianapolis: Bobbs-Merrill, 1927.

Amado, Jorge. *A vida de Luís Carlos Prestes: O cavaleiro da esperança.* 4th ed. São Paulo: Martins, 1945.

Andrew, Christopher M. *Secret Service: The Making of the British Intelligence Community.* London: Heineman, 1985.

Angress, Werner T. "Weimar Coalition and Ruhr Insurrection, March–April 1920: A Study of Government Policy." *Journal of Modern History,* vol. 29, no. 1 (1957).

Avakumovic, Ivan. *The Communist Party of Canada: A History.* Toronto: McClelland and Stewart, 1975.

"Battle of Jutland—Order of Battle." http://www.gwpda.org/naval/jutob.htm (accessed September 5, 2003).
Beeby, Dean. *Cargo of Lies: The True Story of a Nazi Double Agent in Canada*. Toronto: University of Toronto Press, 1996.
Beevor, Antony. *Berlin: The Downfall, 1945*. London: Viking Penguin, 2002.
———. *Spanska inbördeskriget*. Trans. Kjell Waltman. Lund: Historiska Media, 2006.
"Bela Kun: The 133 Days." http://www.vanguardnewsnetwork.com/temp/TerrorTimeline/1919_BelaKunThe133Days.htm (accessed March 26, 2003).
Beloch, Israel, and Alzira Alves de Abreu, coords. *Dicionário histórico-biográfico brasileiro, 1930–1983*. Rio de Janeiro: Forense-Universitária, 1984.
Berber, Fritz, ed. *Jahrbuch für Auswärtige Politik, 1940*. Berlin: Aug. Gross, 1940.
Berkeley, Roy. *A Spy's London*. With a foreword by Nigel West [Rupert Allason]. London: Cooper, 1994.
Bernard, Yves, and Caroline Bergeron. *Trop loin de Berlin: Des prisonniers allemands au Canada, 1939–1946*. Montreal: Septentrion, 1995.
Betcherman, Lita-Rose. *The Swastika and the Maple Leaf*. Toronto: Fitzhenry and Whiteside, 1973.
Böhme, Reinhard, ed. *Rückblicke Deutscher Club von Hoboken 1857 a 1907*. Hoboken, N.J., 1907.
Bonsor, N. R. P. *North Atlantic Seaway: An Illustrated History of the Passenger Services Linking the Old World with the New in Four Volumes*. Vol. 2. Cambridge: P. S. L. Patrick Stephens, 1978.
Brandi, Paulo. *Vargas: Da vida para a história*. 2d ed., rev. Rio de Janeiro: Zahar, 1985.
Branson, Noreen. *History of the Communist Party of Great Britain, 1927–1941*. London: Lawrence and Wishart, 1985.
Brauer, Erwin. *Der Ruhraufstand von 1920*. Berlin: International Arbeiter, 1930.
Brown, Anthony Cave. *Treason in the Blood: H. St. John Philby, Kim Philby, and the Spy Case of the Century*. Boston: Houghton Mifflin, 1994.
Brun-Zechowoj, Walerij. *Manfred Stern—General Kleber: Die tragische Biographie eines Berufsrevolutionärs, 1896–1954*. Berlin: Trafo/Weist, 2000.
Burleigh, Michael. *The Third Reich: A New History*. New York: Hill and Wang, 2000.
Castells, Andreu. *Las Brigadas Internacionales en la Guerra de España*. Barcelona: Ariel, 1974.
Cavalcanti, Paulo. *O caso eu conto como o caso foi: Da Coluna Prestes à queda de Arraes*. 3d ed. Recife: Guararapes, 1980.
Chambers, Frank P. *This Age of Conflict: The Western World, 1914 to the Present*. 3d ed. New York: Harcourt, Brace & World, 1962.
Chase, William J. *Enemies Within The Gates: The Comintern and the Stalinist Repression, 1934–1939*. New Haven: Yale University Press, 2001.
Chiavenato, Julio José. *Cangaço: A força do coronel*. São Paulo: Brasiliense, 1990.
Childs, David. *Germany Since 1918*. New York: St. Martin's Press, 1980.
Comisión del Comité Central del Partido Comunista, ed. *Esboro de historia del Partido Comunista de la Argentina: Origen y desarrollo del Partido Comunista y del movimiento obrero y popular argentino*. Buenos Aires: Anteo, 1947.
Communist Party of Canada. *Canada's Party of Socialism: History of the Communist Party of Canada, 1921–1976*. Toronto: Progress, 1982.
Costa, Homero. *A insurreição comunista de 1935: Natal—o primeiro ato da tragédia*. São Paulo: Ensaio, 1995.
Costello, John, and Oleg Tsarev. *Deadly Illusions: The KGB Orlov Dossier Reveals Stalin's Master Spy*. New York: Crown, 1993.
Curry, John. *The Security Service, 1908–1945: The Official Story*. Kew, Australia: Public Record Office, 1999.

Dehl, Oleg, with Natalja Mussienko [Mussijenko]. *Verratene Ideale: Zur Geschichte deutscher Emigranten in der Sowjetunion in der 30er Jahren.* Berlin: Trafo, 2000.

Dittmann, Wilhelm. *Die Marine-Justizmorde von 1917 und die Admirals-Rebellion von 1918.* Berlin: J. H. W. Dietz, 1926.

Dong, Stella. *Shanghai: The Rise and Fall of a Decadent City.* New York: Harper Collins, 2000.

Dorril, Stephen. *MI6: Inside the Covert World of Her Majesty's Secret Intelligence Service.* New York: Touchstone, 2000.

Dulles, John W. F. *Anarchists and Communists in Brazil, 1900–1935.* Austin: University of Texas Press, 1973.

——. *Vargas of Brazil: A Political Biography.* Austin: University of Texas Press, 1967.

Edwards, Kenneth. *The Mutiny at Invergordon.* London: Putnam, 1937.

Ereira, Alan. *The Invergordon Mutiny: A Narrative History of the Last Great Mutiny in the Royal Navy and How It Forced Britain Off the Gold Standard in 1931.* London: Routledge and Kegan Paul, 1981.

"Eugene Dennis." http://en.wikipedia.org/wiki/Eugene_Dennis (accessed August 5, 2005).

Faria, Antonio Augusto, and Edgard Luiz de Barros. *Getúlio Vargas e sua época.* 2d ed. São Paulo: Global, 1983.

Fausto, Boris. *A revolução de 1930, historiografia e história.* 9th ed. São Paulo: Brasiliense, 1983.

Frischauer, Willi, and Robert Jackson. *The Altmark Affair.* New York: Macmillan, 1955.

Fundação Getúlio Vargas. "Prestes, Luís Carlos." http://www.cpdoc.fgv.br/dhbb/verbetes_htm/4366_1.asp (accessed March 12, 2005).

"German Prisoners of War at Feller During WW II." http://www3.sympatico.ca/relger/POWcamp.html (accessed April 19, 2003).

Gordon, Robert. "The Great Harbor Fire: The North German Lloyd Disaster of 1900." *New Jersey History* (Fall–Winter 1982).

Green, Fitzhugh, and Holloway Frost. *Some Famous Sea Fights.* Freeport, N.Y.: Books for Libraries Press, 1968.

Green, Montgomery M. "Russia's Super-Secret Weapon Revealed!" *Plain Truth: A Magazine of Understanding,* January 1956.

Harvison, Clifford W. *The Horsemen.* Toronto: McClelland and Stewart, 1967.

——. "The Spy Who Came Out of the Sea." *Brockville (Ontario) Recorder and Times,* January 7, 1967.

Hilton, Stanley E. *Brazil and the Soviet Challenge, 1917–1947.* Austin: University of Texas Press, 1991.

Hoelz, Max. *Ich grüß und küsse Dich—Rot Front! Tagebücher und Briefe, Maskau 1929 bis 1933.* Berlin: Dietz, 2005.

Horn, Daniel. *The German Naval Mutinies of World War I.* New Brunswick: Rutgers University Press, 1969.

——, ed. and trans. *War, Mutiny, and Revolution in the German Navy: The World War I Diary of Seaman Richard Stumpf.* New Brunswick: Rutgers University Press, 1967.

Hornstein, David P. *Arthur Ewert: A Life for the Comintern.* Lanham, Md.: University Press of America, 1993.

"Imperial German Navy Capital Ship Captains." http://www.gwpda.org/naval/hsfcpco.htm (accessed August 23, 2003).

"Invergordon Mutiny." http://www.masterliness.com/a/Invergordon.Mutiny.htm (accessed July 28, 2005).

Joffily, José. *Harry Berger.* Rio de Janeiro: Paz e Terra; Curitiba: Universidade Federal do Paraná, 1987.

Jones, Nigel. *A Brief History of the Birth of the Nazis.* New York: Carroll and Graf, 2004.

Jupp, James. *The Radical Left in Britain, 1931–1941.* London: Frank Cass, 1982.

Kaufmann, Bernd, et al. *Der Nachrichtendienst der KPD, 1919–1937.* Berlin: Dietz, 1993.

Keynes, John Maynard. *The Economic Consequences of the Peace.* New York: Harcourt Brace Jovanovich, 1920.
Klingaman, William K. *The Year Our World Began, 1919.* New York: Harper and Row, 1987.
Krivitsky, W. G. *In Stalin's Secret Service: An Exposé of Russia's Secret Policies by the Former Chief of the Soviet Intelligence in Western Europe.* New York: Harper, 1939.
Krummacher, F. A., and Albert Wucher. *Die Weimarer Republik: Ihre Geschichte in Texten, Bildern und Dokumenten.* Wiesbaden: Löwit, 1965.
Lacerda, Carlos. *Depoimento.* 2d ed. Rio de Janeiro: Nova Fronteira, 1977.
Lange, Jürgen. *Die Schlacht bei Pelkum im März 1920: Legenden und Dokumente.* Essen: Klartext, 1994.
Laybourn, Keith, and Dylan Murphy. *Under the Red Flag: A History of Communism in Britain, c. 1849–1991.* Phoenix Mill, Gloucestershire: Sutton, 1999.
Leonhard, Wolfgang. *Child of the Revolution.* Trans. C. M. Woodhouse. London: Ink Links, 1979.
Levine, Robert M. *The Vargas Regime: The Critical Years, 1934–1938.* New York: Columbia University Press, 1970.
Lewenstein, Henry Ralph. *Die Karl Liebknecht Schule in Moskau, 1932–1937: Erinnerungen eines Schülers.* Lüneburg: Nordostdeutsches Kulturwerk, 1991.
Litten, Frederick S. "The CCP and the Fujian Rebellion." *Republican China,* vol. 14, no. 1 (1988).
———. "The Noulens Affair," *China Quarterly,* vol. 138 (June 1994).
Livro vermelho dos telefones, 1939. 15th ed. Rio de Janeiro, 1940.
Locatelli, Amelto. "Relatorio sobre minhas atividades no Brasil." Manuscript, July 20, 1936, translated into Portuguese by Yuri Ribeiro.
Lovell, John. *Lovell's Montreal Directory, Containing Alphabetical and Street Directories of Greater Montreal.* Montreal: Lovell, 1952.
Masterman, J. C. *The Double Cross System in the War of 1939–1945.* London: Sphere, 1973.
McKenzie, John R. P. *Weimar Germany: 1918–1933.* London: Blandford, 1971.
McLoughlin, Barry. *Stalin's Terror: High Politics and Mass Repression in the Soviet Union.* London: Palgrave Macmillan, 2003.
Mederios Filho, João. *82 horas de subversão: Intentona Comunista de 1935 no Rio Grande do Norte.* Natal, 1980.
———. *Meu depoimento.* Natal: Oficial, 1937.
Mendonça, Eliana Rezende Furtado de, ed. *Os arquivos das polícias políticas: Reflexos de nossa história contemporânea.* Rio de Janeiro: FAPERJ, 1994.
Mensing, Wilhelm. "Gestapo V-Leute kommunistischer Herkunft—auch ein Strukturproblem der KPD?" *Mitteilungsblatt des Instituts für soziale Bewegungen,*" vol. 34 (2005).
———. *Von der Ruhr in den GULag: Opfer des Stalinschen Massenterrors aus dem Ruhrgebiet.* Essen: Klartext, 2001.
Meyer, Michael C. *Huerta: A Political Portrait.* Lincoln: University of Nebraska Press, 1972.
"Militärische Intervention und das Ende." http://www.bikonline.de/histo/interv.html (accessed March 18, 2003).
Millar, Alexander. "British Intelligence and the Comintern in Asia: The Noulens Case." Master's thesis, Department of History, Cambridge University, 2006.
Modin, Yuri. *My Five Cambridge Friends: Philby, Burgess, Maclean, Blunt, and Cairncross, by Their KGB Controller.* Trans. Anthony Roberts. Toronto: Knopf, 1995.
Montag, Reinhard. "Das Lexikon der Deutschen Generale." http://www.lexikon-deutschegenerale.de/l_pr2.html (accessed September 3, 2003).
Monteiro, Frederico Mindêllo Carneiro. *Depoimentos biográficos.* Rio de Janeiro: Gráfica Olímpica, 1977.
Morais, Fernando. *Olga.* 3d ed. São Paulo: Alfa-Omega, 1985.

Nasser, David. *Falta alguém em Nuremberg: Torturas da polícia de Filinto Strubling Müller*. 4th ed. Rio de Janeiro: O Cruzeiro, 1966.

"The Native (Heathen) Religion." http://66.102.7.104/search?q=cache:SyqF0ApE0hQJ:www.geocities.com/reginheim/religion.html+%22Dusk+of+the+Gods%22+German+legend&hl=en(accessed September 5, 2005).

Palmér, Torsten, and Hendrik Neubauer. *The Weimar Republic: Through the Lens of the Press*. Trans. Maike Dörries, Peter Barton, Mark Cole, and Susan Cox. Cologne: Könemann, 2000.

Philby, Kim. *My Silent War*. New York: Grove, 1968.

Pincher, Chapman. *Too Secret Too Long*. New York: St. Martin's Press, 1984.

Pinheiro, Paulo Sérgio. *Estratégias da ilusão: A revolução mundial e o Brasil, 1922–1935*. São Paulo: Companhia das Letras, 1991.

Pinto, Herondino Pereira. *Nos subterraneos do Estado Novo*. Rio de Janeiro: Germinal, 1950.

Plener, Ulla. "Auskünfte einer NKWD-Akte über letzten Weg und Tod deutscher Kommunisten in der Sowjetunion (1936–1939): Willy Leow-Hofmann, Hans Rogalla, Josef Schneider, Paul Scholze, Harry Wilde." *UTOPIEKreativ*, vol. 39–40 (January–February 1994).

Portela, Fernando, and Cláudio Bojunga. *Lampião: O cangaceiro e o outro*. São Paulo: Traço, 1982.

Preston, Christine. "Scramble for Katanga." http://216.239.33.100/search?q=cache:nrHxq6W-1t04C:kolwezikat.free.fr/Publications/Kat2.rtf+slavery+%22Belgian+Africa%22&hl=en&ie=UTF-8 (accessed March 15, 2003).

Prokhorov, A. M., ed. *Great Soviet Encyclopedia*. 3d ed., vol. 3. New York: Macmillan, 1973.

Pujol, Juan, with Nigel West [Rupert Allason]. *Garbo*. London: Weidenfeld and Nicolson, 1985.

"Register of Ships Car-Cey." http://www.webruler.com/gprovost/ShipsC1.htm (accessed August 2, 2003).

"Register of Ships N." http://www.webruler.com/gprovost/ShipsN.htm (accessed August 2, 2003).

Rennspieß, Uwe. *Jenseits der Bahn: Geschichte der Ahlener Bergarbeiterkolonie und der Zeche Westfalen*. Essen: Klartext, 1989.

Roberts, J. A. G. *The Complete History of China*. Phoenix Mill, Gloucestershire: Sutton, 2003.

"Rosa Luxemburg (1871–1919)." http://www.kirjasto.sci.fi/luxembur.htm (accessed August 13, 2003).

Rose, R. S. "Johnny's Two Trips to Brazil." *Luso-Brazilian Review*, vol. 38, no. 1 (2001).

———. *One of the Forgotten Things: Getúlio Vargas and Brazilian Social Control, 1930–1954*. Westport, Conn.: Greenwood Press, 2000.

———. "Slavery in Brazil: Does It Still Exist?" *Review of Latin American Studies*, vol. 4, no. 1 (1991).

Roskill, S. W. *The War at Sea, 1939–1945*. London: H. M. Stationery Office, 1954.

———. *White Ensign: The British Navy at War, 1939–1945*. Annapolis: U.S. Naval Academy, 1966.

Sahr, Robert C. "Consumer Price Index (CPI) Conversion Factors 1800 to Estimated 2015 to Convert to Dollars of 2005." http://72.14.2003.104/search?q=cache:cRO73Tw13wJ:oregonstate.edu/Dept/polesci/fac/sahr/cv2005.xls++2015+to+convert+to+dollars;plof+2005&hl=en&ct=clnk&cd=2 (accessed January 30, 2006).

Sarmento, Antonio Natanael Martins. "Os abalos de sabado à noite: Do governo popular e revoloucionário em Natal à guerra do Largo da Paz em Recife, 1935." Master's thesis, Department of History, Universidade Federal de Pernambuco, 1994.

Schafranek, Hans, with Natalja Mussijenko. *Kinderheim Nr. 6: Österreichische und deutsche Kinder im sowjetischen Exil*. Vienna: Döcker, 1989.

"The Scuttling of the German High Seas Fleet at Scapa Flow on the 21st of June 1919." http://

www.ahoy.tk-jk.net/macslog/The ScuttlingoftheGermanHi.html (accessed September 5, 2003).
Smedley, Agnes. *The Great Road: The Life and Times of Chu Teh*. New York: Monthly Review Press, 1956.
Smith, Michael. *Foley: The Spy Who Saved Ten Thousand Jews*. London: Hodder and Stoughton, 1999.
———. *The Spying Game: The Secret History of British Espionage*. London: Politico, 1996.
Snow, Edgar. *Red Star over China*. New York: Random House, 1938.
Sodré, Nelson Werneck. *História militar do Brasil*. Rio de Janeiro: Civilização Brasileira, 1965.
Sontag, Raymond J. *A Broken World, 1919–1939*. New York: Harper and Row, 1971.
Stafford, David. *Camp X*. New York: Dodd, Mead, 1986.
"Stahlhelm." http://en.wikipedia.org/wiki/Stahlhelm%2C_Bund_der_Frontsoldaten (accessed September 28, 2003).
"The Steinwache Memorial Centre." http://www.ns-gedenkstaetten.net/nrw/en/dortmund/beschreibung/ (accessed July 22, 2005).
Stenton, Michael, Peterhouse Cambridge, and Steven Lees, eds. *Who's Who of British Members of Parliament: A Biographical Dictionary of the House of Commons Based on Annual Volumes of Dod's Parliamentary Companion and Other Sources*. Vol. 3. Hassocks, Sussex: Harvester; Atlantic Highlands, N.J.: Humanities Press, 1979.
"Stereoscopic Visions of War and Empire." http://www.boondocksnet.com/stereo/sv289f.html (accessed March 19, 2003).
Sullivan, William C., with Bill Brown. *The Bureau: My Thirty Years in Hoover's FBI*. New York: W. W. Norton, 1979.
Thornton, Richard C. *China, the Struggle for Power, 1917–1972*. Bloomington: Indiana University Press, 1973.
United Kingdom, Control Commission for Germany (British Element). *Report for the Month of August 1946*, vol. 1, no. 3.
———. *Report for the Month of June 1946*, vol. 1, no. 1.
———. *Report for the Month of July 1946*, vol. 1, no. 2.
United Kingdom, House of Commons and House of Lords. *Parliamentary Debates (Hansard)*, January 1, 1931, to December 21, 1934, vols. 247–76.
U.S. Central Intelligence Agency. "The Third (Communist International) Structure and Functions," November 1, 1947, RDP78–02646R000600130001–7.
Vianna, Marly de Almeida Gomes. *Revolucionários de 35: Sonho e realidade*. São Paulo: Companhia das Letras, 1992.
Waack, William. *Camaradas: Nos arquivos de Moscou; a histórias secreta da revolução brasileira de 1935*. São Paulo: Companhia das Letras, 1993.
Wasserstein, Bernard. *Secret War in Shanghai: An Untold Story of Espionage, Intrigue, and Treason in World War II*. Boston: Houghton Mifflin, 1999.
Weber, Hermann. *Die Wandlung des deutschen Kommunismus: Die Stalinisierung der KPD in der Weimarer Republik*. Vol. 1. Frankfurt am Main: Europäische, 1969.
Wenzel, Otto. *1923—Die gescheiterte deutsche Oktoberrevolution*. Münster: Lit, 2003.
———. "Die kommunistische Partei Deutschlands im Jahre 1923." PhD diss., Department of Philosophy, Freie Universität Berlin, 1955.
Whymant, Robert. *Stalin's Spy: Richard Sorge and the Tokyo Espionage Ring*. New York: St. Martin's Press, 1998.
Wilhelmshaven: Ein Führer für Fremde und Einheimische. Wilhelmshaven: C. Lohse, 1899.
Willoughby, Charles A. *Shanghai Conspiracy: The Sorge Spy Ring, Moscow—Shanghai—Tokyo—San Francisco—New York*. New York: E. P. Dutton, 1952.
Yu, Miin-ling. "Introduction to Materials in Russia on the Relations Between the KMT, CCP, and Comintern, 1920s–1940s." http://216.239.63.104/search?q=cache:v7eLBrj1DgAJ:ccs.ncl

.edu.tw/Newsletter_79/P008_015.pdf+%22gekker%22+comintern&hl=en (accessed March 20, 2005).

INTERVIEWS

Unless otherwise noted, all interviews were conducted by R. S. Rose.

Amado, Thomé. Rio de Janeiro, September 28, 1994.
Anonymous-1. Telephone. July 18, 1995.
Armitage, Audrey. Brockville, Ontario, July 14, 1995.
Armitage, Jack. Brockville, Ontario, July 14, 1995.
Barclay, James O. Brockville, Ontario, July 17, 1995.
Bargiello, Ted. Telephone. July 16, 1995.
Barron, Harold. Hayward, Calif., January 15, 1994.
Basbaum, Leôncio. Interview by John W. F. Dulles. São Paulo, November 9, 1967.
Borer, Cecil. Rio de Janeiro, May 13, May 28, and May 29, 1998.
Cid, Pedro Vilela. Interview by John W. F. Dulles. Natal, Brazil, October 18, 1968.
Clarke, Blake. Brockville, Ontario, July 12, 1995.
Cordeiro, Cristiano. Interview by John W. F. Dulles. Recife, October 11, 1968.
De Graaf, Oscar. Ahlen, July 20, July 26, August 31, and September 1, 1996, and August 16, 1997.
De Graff, John Henry. Interviews by Gordon D. Scott. Brockville, Ontario, March 1975 to January 31, 1976.
———. Interview by Nancy Duffy. Tape recording. Brockville, Ontario, Fall 1971.
De Melo, Severino Theodoro. Rio de Janeiro, February 14 and 15, 2006.
Fegyverneky, Angela. Telephone. July 10 and August 12, 2002.
Fegyverneky, Sándor. Zánka, Hungary, August 12, 2002.
Fenemore, Ross. Brockville, Ontario, July 15, 1995.
Foster, Robert. Hoboken, N.J., June 20, 2006.
Gabrielsson, Peter. Hamburg, July 28, 2006.
Gallardo, Carlos Americo. San Martín, Argentina, June 4, 1998.
Gracie, Robson. Rio de Janeiro, August 6, 1991.
Graul, Jens. Wilhelmshaven, August 3, 2006.
Headry, George. Telephone. August 9, 1995.
Knöß, Wilhelm. Wilhelmshaven, August 1, 2006.
Kovács, Andy. Brockville, Ontario, July 17, 1995.
Krüger, Ernst. Praia de Mauá, Brazil, August 12, September 19, December 8, 1994; Rio de Janeiro, October 17, December 3, 14, and 17, 1994.
Krüger, Waltraud. Rio de Janeiro, December 14, 1994.
Manzi, Norberto. San Martín, Argentina, February 13, 2000.
Mensing, Wilhelm. Bonn, July 3 and 4, 2002.
Merrifield, Peter. London, June 1, 2004.
Oberschild, Marianne. Telephone interview by Wilhelm Mensing. November 2000.
Oźlanski, Bogdan. Osowiec, August 9, 2002.
Pollock, Neil. Calgary, Alberta, September 16, 1996; telephone, February 9 and December 21, 1997, and February 28, 2001.
Prestes, Anita Leocadia, and Lygia Prestes. Rio de Janeiro, April 17, 2004.
Prestes, Luís Carlos. Rio de Janeiro, August 13, 1987.
Reis Neto, Malvino. Interview by John W. F. Dulles. September 2, 1963.
Ribeiro, Yuri. Rio de Janeiro, December 16, 1994.
Rosso, Emilia. Telephone. July 24, 1994.

Sarmento, Antonio Natanael. Telephone. January 31, 2006.
Scott, Violet. Oshawa, Ontario, July 20, 1996.
Sena, Jailson. Socorro, PE, Brazil, January 12, 2006.
Sterritt, N. Leslie. Brockville, Ontario, July 14, 1995.
Stewart, Ron. Telephone. January 8 and December 14, 1997.
Ströhla, Heinz-Dieter. Telephone interview by Stefan Antheck. August 2, 2006.
Sveri, Knut. Stockholm, July 25, 2006.
Swayne, Don. Brockville, Ontario, July 15, 1995.
Szabo, Eva. Brockville, Ontario, July 17, 1995.
Szabo, Steven. Brockville, Ontario, July 17, 1995.
Wanderley, Wandenkolk. Interview by John W. F. Dulles. Recife, October 17, 1968.
Warren, Jim. Telephone. February 17, 2001.
Wisniewski, Artur. Osowiec, August 9, 2002.
Young, Wilmont. Brockville, Ontario, July 12, 1995.

PERSONAL COMMUNICATIONS

Unless otherwise noted, all letters and e-mail messages were addressed to R. S. Rose.

Anderson, K. M. E-mails, August 16, 2004, March 30, 2005.
Ashby, David (UK Ministry of Defense, Naval Historical Branch). Letter, October 3, 2003.
Coombes, M. P. (Association of Royal Navy Officers). E-mail, September 17, 2003.
De Graaf, Johnny, III. E-mails, August 15, 2004, April 18, 2006.
De Graaf, Oscar. Letter, postmarked February 5, 1997.
De Graaf, Rudolf. Letter, June 30, 1994.
Foley, Frank. Letter to John de Graff, January 1947.
Hakanen, Yrjö (Communist Party of Finland). E-mail, March 14, 2005.
Hearsey, Cerys (UK Foreign and Commonwealth Office Library). E-mails, January 5 and August 10, 2005.
Kitson, Ruth. Letter, April 24, 1996.
Klose, Adrian (Police Department, Dortmund, Germany). E-mail, July 22, 2005.
Krawczak, Tadeusz. Letter, January 23, 1997.
Krüger, Ernst. Letters, December 10, 1994, October 10, 1996, June 8, 1997.
Krüger, Joachim, and Lieselotte Krüger. E-mails, August 4 and 5, 2005.
Marchuk, Boris (Russian Federal Security Service). Letter, August 7, 2001.
Mensing, Wilhelm. E-mails, May 5, July 15, and July 20, 2002; November 29, 2003; July 18, September 14 and 15, 2004; August 8, 11, and 18, 2006.
Murray, M. T. (UK Foreign and Commonwealth Office). Letter, August 17, 1994.
Ozdemir, Lale (UK National Archives). E-mail, October 27, 2005.
Patterson, Lorna (UK Foreign and Commonwealth Office). E-mail, October 27, 2003.
Pollock, Neil. E-mail, June 25, 2004; letter, December 21, 1997.
Prestes, Luís Carlos. Letter, November 19, 1987.
Preston, Christine. E-mails, March 19 and April 4, 2003.
Rose, R. S. Letter to фСБРф, November 6, 2001.
Severi, Juan Carlos (Secretaria de Seguridade Interior, Argentina). Letter, September 2, 2004.
Sherman, D. W. Letter, postmarked August 15, 1995.
Stiftung, Friedrich Ebert, Regine Schoch. E-mail to Wilhelm Mensing, November 1, 2005.
Ströhla, Heinz-Dieter (Staatsarchiv, Wilhelmshaven, Germany). E-mail, July 9, 2004.
Tismaneanu, Vladimir. E-mail, August 4, 2005.
Warren, Jim. E-mail, February 19, 2001.
Wautier, Pierre. E-mail to Christine Preston, March 22, 2003.

Williams, Selena (State Records of New South Wales, Western Sydney Records Centre, Sydney, Australia). E-mail, July 30, 2003.

NEWSPAPERS AND PERIODICALS

Brockville (Ontario) Recorder and Times, 1967–88
Chicago Daily Tribune, 1954
China Forum (Shanghai), 1933
Diario de Pernambuco (Recife), 1935
O Globo (Rio de Janeiro), 1985
International Press Correspondence (London), 1936
Jornal do Brasil (Rio de Janeiro), 1938
Jornal do Commercio (Recife), 1935
Kingston (Ontario) Whig-Standard, 1954
La Nacion (Buenos Aires), 1936–37
Montreal Gazette, 1951–52
Newsweek magazine, 1942
New York Times, 1913–40
Ottawa Citizen, 1954
Ottawa Journal, 1954
Saint John (New Brunswick) Telegraph-Journal, 1953
Svenska Dagbladet (Stockholm), 1933–34
Syracuse (N.Y.) Post Standard, 1954
Times (London), 1926–46
Union City (N.J.) Hudson Dispatch, 1917
Victoria (B.C.) Times Colonist, 2005

INDEX

Abbott, Arthur, 269, 273
Abramov, Alexander Lazarovich, 103, 139, 159, 180, 225; liquidated, 231
Abwehr. *See* Germany, military intelligence
Achilles (light cruiser), 280
Admiral Graf Spee (pocket battleship): Figure 49, pages 279–82; British, French, and German diplomatic manuvering in Montevideo, 280–81; payback for Johnny, 281–83
Admiral Scheer (pocket battleship), 280
agent hotels, 114, 149–50, 160–61, 177, 179, 225
Agi-Prop. *See* Soviet Union
Agitation and Propaganda Department. *See* Soviet Union, Agi-Prop
Ahlen, 121, 161, 236, 243, 383, 399 n. 34; armies try to occupy, 73–74; coal mines, Figure 7, pages 70–72, 78, 87, 94; Johnny arrives in, 65, 87, 94, 397 n. 6; Johnny sends cash to son in, 220; train station renamed the Workers and Soldiers Commission, 78
Ahlen's Red Youth, 384
AIB. *See* Brazil
Aitken, George, Figure 21, pages 152–55, 157, 161, 389; helps publish and distribute propaganda, 154; International Brigade, 152; Johnny to assist, 152, 163; ordered to Moscow, 159; stevedores, 162
Ajax (light cruiser), 280, 286
Akontz, Charlotte, 374–75; background, 374–75; Children's Welfare Institute, 375; death of Gerti, 374–75, 379; marries Johnny. *See* Charlotte de Graaf; mental problems, 379; nickname, 374
Alberta, 350
Albuquerque, Afonso de, 206
Aldershot, 154
"Alemazinha." *See* Helena Krüger
Alex (Gen.), 103, 108, 110; advice from, 111, 139–40, 142, 148–49; dismissed, 150; gift to, 113; Johnny's graduation, 112–13; translator Maria, 108, 110
Algiers, 27
Alikhanov, Gevork, 225; "inconsistencies" in Johnny's account of the Brazilian failure, 229; Johnny tells of Argentine weapons inventor, 226; Johnny's unanswered letters to, 230; liquidated, 231; recommends NKVD, 229

Allied control commissions, 359; bribes and corruption, 367–69; de-Nazification, 359, 361; Nottingham (Canadian overseer), 368
Allies, 1, 76, 330, 342, 356, 359; military police, 92; Canadian news blackout, 341–42, 422 n. 41
Almanzora, 261–62
"Alois," 140
Alsace-Lorraine, 51
Altmark, 279–80
Amado, Thomé, 415 n. 9, 417 n. 52
American Concession. *See* Shanghai
American Consulate, Cologne, 157–58
American Consulate, Montreal, 299–301
American Embassy, Rio de Janeiro, 282
Amtorg, 153, 413 n. 37
Anahory, Israel Abrahão, 197
Anderson, K. M., 400 n. 2
Anderson, Lindsey, 269
ANL. *See* Brazil
Annett Jr., Earle J., 420 n. 3
Annett Sr., Earle J., 321–22, 420 n. 3
anti-Nazi propaganda, 169
Antwerp, 28–30
"Arabs," 370, 394 n. 3
Aranha, Oswaldo, 204
Arcand, Adrien, Figure 58, pages 305–7, 312, 315, 389; arrested by Cliff Harvison, 305; assistant meets Johnny, 340–41; Nationalist Party, 325
Arcand group: and Nazi leader for North America, 344; controlled, 345, 347, 352
Archer, Humphrey Edward, 269
Argentina, 197, 210, 212–24, 226–29, 382, 407 n. 4, 410 n. 4; *Admiral Graf Spee*, 281; army, 226, 411 n. 14; Communist Party (PCA), xvi; 196, 212–15, 221, 229; PCA Central Committee turned into the police, 215; Policía Federal Argentina, 214–17, 229, 411 n. 28; pro-German, 281; navy, 226
Argentine weapons inventor, 226, 230, 260
Armitage, Jack and Audrey, 395 n. 21
Arnon, Frank, 269
Arrais, 291
Arvida aluminum factory, 315
Ascania, 334
asphalt worker, 96
Atelier Vienense, 265–66; Charles Berenheim Co., 266; declaration by Rosa Benkendorf, 416 n.

Atelier Vienense (*continued*) 27; Gustav Krüger, 266; importing and exporting to/from Japan and the USA, 265–66; Johnny buys an interest in, 266

"August." *See* Johnny de Graaf

Aureba, Philip, 368, 423 nn. 6, 9

Australia, 16, 18–20, 22–25, 67, 241; English prisoners, 18–19; police racket, 19, 23

Austria, 102, 359; Hitler Youth affair, 242

Avenida Rainha Elisabeth 219, Figure 45, pages 263–64, 266, 284–85, 415 n. 13; arrival of the second "Franz Gruber," 267; assassination attempt, 264; *carioca* social circut, 264; call Johnny "Franz," 264; envelopes from "The British Government," 274; Ernani do Amaral Peixoto, 264; Karl Stemmer and family, 276; laboratory, 415 n. 21

Avila Star, 222

Axis, 356, 422 n. 41

Bad Oeynhausen, 359–60, 366

Bahia, 408 n. 36

Baltics, Imperial German army, 76

Barallo, Waldemar, 270

Bar Alpino, 263–64, 266–67

"Barão," 270

Barbarossa, 27, 29–30, 395 n. 18; mid-Atlantic meeting with *Cayo Manzanillo*, 29–30; renamed *Mercury*, 395 n. 18; stowaways, 27

Bar Lido, 267

Barron, Victor Allen, 228; American Embassy (Rio de Janeiro), 210; arrest, 210, 227; arrives in Rio de Janeiro, 198; Brazil mission, 198; Locatelli criticizes, 227; sicknesses, 198; torture and "suicide," 210, 418 n. 71

Basel, 200

Batista Teixeira, Felisberto, 282–84, 417 n. 52

Battle of Jutland, 46–47; a.k.a. Battle of Skagerrak, 395 n. 11, 397 n. 3

Battle of Pelkum, 80

Bauer, Gustav, 77

Bavaria, 64

Bayfield, C., 351

Bazin, Jean, 270

Begalki, Gus, 384–85

Belgian Congo, 394 n. 2; slavery in, 17–18

Belgium, 26, 30, 92, 267, 283, 322, 326–27, 394 n. 2, 430 n. 3; army, 82, 87, 403 n. 33; Versailles Treaty, 81–82

Bell Telephone Co., 356

Benário, Olga, 196, 203, 211, 228, 407 n. 9; alias Maria Bergner Vilar, 197; arrested in Brazil, 211; arrives in Rio de Janeiro, 197; background, 196–97; Bernburg, 211; Brazil mission, 203; calls Johnny brazen, 228, 231; deportation and death, 211; gives birth, 211; hiding in Rio, 210–11; Ian Berzin, 197; Johnny criticizes, 202; Locatelli criticizes, 227; M4, 197; picture in Gestapo files, 412 n. 36; Prestes's bodyguard, 197; Ravensbrück Concentration Camp, 211; religion, 197, 211; Rua Barão da Torre, 136, 201; saves Prestes's life, 211

Benkendorf, Helena, 265–66, 416 n. 27

Benkendorf, Rosa, 416 n. 27; question by DESPS, 282

Bercuó, Urbano, 270

Berger, Harry. *See* Arthur Ernst Ewert

Berger, Peter, 270

Berlin, 4, 9–10, 48, 53, 63, 77, 84, 97, 139, 148, 158, 166, 168, 187, 220, 260–61, 399 n. 29, 400 n. 1, 403 n. 33, 411 n. 14; *Admiral Graf Spee*, 280; Affonso Henrique de Miranda Corrêa visit, 223; American Embassy, 170; Brandenburg sabotage school, 326; Brazilian Embassy, 264; British Embassy, 170–71; Canadian Nazis and pro-Nazis, 312–13, 315, 318–19, 333, 356; Frank Foley, 170–71, 173–75, 180–82, 187, 199–200, 259, 359, 407 n. 14; Gerti and mother travel to and from Paris, 222; Gerti dances with Nazi, 223–24; Horst Wessel murder, 99–100; Johnny's cemetery press, 169; KPD, 72, 88–89, 93, 95–97, 99, 167, 179, 233; Krüger residences, 95, 99–100; Krügers, 182, 200; marriage of Johnny and Gerti, 261, 414 n. 5; Ravensbrück Concentration Camp, 211; Romania, 139; strikes, riots, and revolution, 68–69, 72–73, 93, 168; Werner von Janowski, 331, 335–36, 343; Whitsunday KPD rally, 95–96, 99

Bermann, Hoffman, 51, 57

Bernardes, Artur, 198

Bern, 101–2, 400 n. 1

Berzin, Ian Karlovich (Peteris Ķuzis), Figure 14, pages 92, 113, 165; Berlin and Prague, 174, 176; Brazil II mission, 236–39, 241–42; British missions, 159, 163–64; China mission, 181, 192; congratulates Johnny on being cleared, 236; Emilie Krüger, 238; following Johnny's return from South America, 232–33; Gertrude Krüger, 238; Gustav Krüger, 238–39; Hans Wilhelm, 241–42; Harry Pollitt, 161; Johnny Jr., 233, 238–40, 242; Johnny's graduation, 112; Johnny's superior, 113, 122; Latvian, 399 n. 16; liquidated, 231, 389; Manchuria mission, 179–81; Olga Benário, 197; Romanian mission, 147–50; Russian Revolution of 1917, 399 n. 16; Stuchevski and Locatelli's statements, 236; Willy Leow, 178

Bialystok, 102

Billy, 153

Black, Thomas L., Figure 69, pages 377, 379; face-to-face showdown with Johnny, 379–80

Blagoeva, Stella, Figure 36, pages 389, 399 nn. 28,

31; background, 225; interrogation of Johnny, 226–27; most feared woman in the Comintern, 225; other sources of information, 226–27; recommends NKVD, 231–32
Blake, Arthur Thomas, 270
Blücher, V. V. (Galem), 113
Bolsheviks. *See* Soviet Union
Bonfim, Antônio Maciel, 229; aliases, 200; Brazilian revolution, 200, 206; Johnny turns in, 210; Stella Blagoeva interrogation of Johnny and, 226
Bordeleau, J.R.W. "Pete," 321, 323, 326–27
Borer, Cecil, Figure 52; description 282–83; Johnny turned in everyone except Prestes, 211, 410 n. 62; sample questions asked Johnny, 283–84; torture, 286
boot camp, 39–43
Botafogo assassination attempt, 276–79
Boulogne, 222, 229
Bowmanville, Ontario, 350
Boy Scouts in Montreal, 376
Bracht, Franz, 168
Brandenburg, 326
Brandler, Heinrich, 89, 93, 95
"Braulter." *See* Werner von Janowski
Braun, Otto (Karl Wagner), 108, 186; Olga Benário, 197
Brazil, 260, 267–68, 283, 286, 380, 382, 415 n. 18, 418 nn. 68, 71; 5th Military District, 262; AIB, 201; ANL, xv, 201–2, 204, 227, 230; armed forces, 198; army, 202, 206, 208, 417 n. 46; arrests and killings following attempted Communist revolution, 209, 409 n. 58; attempted Communist revolution, 197–209, 409 n. 53; Brazil I mission assignment, 200, 213–14, 225, 407 n. 1; Brazil II mission assignment, 236–38; Brazil II mission—British supplement, 262, 269; Comintern, 398 n. 10; Communist Party (PCB), xvi, 200, 202–3, 205–8, 214, 225, 227, 283–84, 409 n. 58; DESPS, xv, 204–5, 210–12, 226–27, 262, 265, 267–69, 276–77, 281–83, 408 n. 32, 415 nn. 15, 20, 417 n. 50; Gestapo agent No. 5, 282; Japan, 237–38; navy, 417 n. 46; Nazis and pro-Nazis, 261–62, 268, 273, 276–78, 282, 285, 288; Old Republic, 198; Partido Popular, 207; police, 203, 208, 229; Polícia Civil, 204, 206, 210, 417 n. 50; Polícia Especial, 210, 215, 285–86, 417 n. 46; Polícia Militar, 202, 204, 206, 209, 408 n. 29; pro-German elements, 236; Quadro Movel, 211, 282–83; Realengo Military Academy, 226; registration of foreigners, 417 n. 40; unions, 227
Bremen, 3, 29, 37, 87, 393 n. 5; family moves to, 61; strikes, riots, and revolution, 63–64, 68–69; Wilhelm de Graaf remarries and resides in, 221

Bremerhaven, 3, 16; Gerkinses's home, 7, 14; sailors's home, 25–26
Bremerhaven, 25–26; unsafe conditions, 26
Brenan, John Fitzgerald, 405 n. 11
Britain. *See* United Kingdom
Britain's Intelligence Service. *See* United Kingdom, MI6
British Columbia, 376
British Commonwealth of Nations, 300
British Consulate, Belo Horizonte, 278
British Consulate, New York, 301
British Embassy, Berlin, 170–71
British Embassy, Prague, 175
Brockville Home and School Association, 382
Brockville, Ontario, 1, 381–85, 387, 395 n. 21
Brockville Psychiatric Hospital, 384, 386, 425 n. 61
Brownshirts. *See* Germany, SA
Brussels, 200, 324, 403 n. 33; contact point for USSR, 237–38, 416 n. 31; goes off the air, 268; "Mary" at "Tecbrevet," 261, 267; new plans for Johnny and the Krügers, 267
Bucharest, 139–43, 145, 147–48, 401 n. 7
Buchenwald, 368, 399 n. 27
Buck, Tim, Figure 59, pages 373–74, 381
Buckley, Clifford William, 270
Budapest, 384, 387
Budenny, Semyon Mikhailovich, 107
Buenos Aires, 2, 196, 210, 212; *Admiral Graf Spee*, 281; Communist Party. *See* Argentina; Johnny and Helena arrive, 213, 221; Johnny and Helena recalled to USSR, 219; Johnny leaves, 222; Locatelli, 210, 214, 410 n. 4; meets Pavel Stuchevski, 215; police, 215
Buhay, Rebecca, 340, 422 n. 37
Bukharin, Nikolai, 398 n. 9
Bulgaria, 225, 359, 401 n. 1
Bunzlau, Josef, 265–66, question by DESPS, 282
Burger (Capt.). *See* Johnny de Graaf
Burgess, Guy, 407 n. 18
Burrous, Donald, 270

"Cabral," 270
Cachin, Marcel, 161
Cai Tingkai, 189; Arthur Ewert, 189; 19th Route Army, 189
California Institute of Technology, 379
Calle Florida 246, San Martín, 215, 220–21, 411 nn. 23–24
Camp 44. *See* Canada
Canada, 1, 183, 261, 299–308, 321–22, 326–31, 333–37, 341–42, 346–50, 357–58, 370–72, 374, 376, 380, 382–84, 414 n. 54, 419 n. 3, 420 n. 8, 421 n. 25, 422 n. 7, 425 n. 55; air force intelligence, 330; army, 343; army intelligence, 330; Camp 30 (POW camp), 350; Camp 44 escape attempts, 350–56; Camp 44 (POW camp), 350;

Canada (*continued*)
   capture a U-boat mission, 350–55; "C" Division, xv, 328; Colombia mission, 299–302; Communist Party (CPC), xv, 340, 346, 373–74, 381, 383; CSIS, xv, xix, 383, 385, 425 n. 54; Directorate of Censorship, 337; Labor Progressive Party, 346–47, 381; Nationalist Party, 325; naval intelligence, 330, 350–52; navy, 353–54; Nazis and pro-Nazis, 303–43, 347, 356, 371, 423 n. 16; "O" Division, xvi, 344–45; POW camps, 350; press control, 342, 422 n. 41; QPP, xvi, 321–23, 326, 342; RCMP, xv–xvi, xix, 300, 302–5, 310, 312–13, 322–24, 326–30, 333–37, 340–41, 343–49, 351–53, 355–56, 373–77, 381–84, 410 n. 12, 419 nn. 14, 16, 420 nn. 1, 5, 8, 421 n. 36, 424 n. 18; RCMP Criminal Investigation Bureau, 344; RCMP intelligence, 351; RCMP Security Service, 425 n. 54; Soviet agents in, 382; U-boats and, 303, 312, 351–52, 421 n. 35, 422 n. 41; War Measures Act, 346
Canadian case handlers. *See* Gus Begalki and Neil Pollock; death of Helena Krüger, 221
Canadian Crusaders, 376
Canadian-German club, 340, 347; at end of war, 356; physical description of premises, 339; social events, 340; split into political groups, 345
Canadian Industries munitions plant: Nazis sympathizers proposal to set fire to, 311
Canadian Marconi Co.: Fletcher's Field group's desire to blow up, 319–20
Canadian Pacific Railway, 301
Canadian Security Intelligence Service. *See* Canada, CSIS
Canaris, Wilhelm, 324–25
cangaço, 207
Cape Horn, 16, 18
Cape Town, 18
"Captain Johnny X." *See* Johnny de Graff
Cario; Johnny offered station chief job but refuses over "carte blanche issue," 369–70
Carlisle Hotel (New Carlisle, Quebec), 321–23
Carr, Philip Alfred Vansittart, 270
Carvalho, Reis de, 270
Cascadura classes, 203
Casino Copacabana, 263–64
Castro Junior, José Leite de, 270
"Caswell," 270
Caterina Acalo, 20–22; cargo, 21
Catilina A. Walmen, 26–27; described, 26; Johnny leaves, 27; problems on board, 26–27
Cavalcante, Carlos Lima, 207
Cavina, 371–72
Cayo Manzanillo: McL. Hunter, 28, 30–31; cargo, 29; Mexico, 29; mid-Atlantic meeting with *Barbarossa*, 29–30
CBC Television, 382

CCP. *See* China, Communist Party
"C" Division. *See* Canada, RCMP
Central Committee (German). *See* Germany, Communist Party
Central Powers, 395 n. 18
Central Revolutionary Military Commission. *See* China
CIA. *See* United States
Chabarovsk, 180–81, 192
Charles Berenheim Co., 266
Chateaubriand, Assis, 417 n. 45
Chatham, 154
Cherbourg, 222
Chernomordik, Moisei, 225; liquidated, 231
Chiang Kai-shek, 181–82, 185, 187–90, 192
Chicago, 382
Chicago Daily Tribune, 382
Children's Home No. 6, 233–36, 239–40, 242
Chile, 18, 21, 197, 217, 410 n. 4
China, 174–76, 181–90, 192–96, 226, 378, 382, 400 n. 14; 8th Route Army, 184; 19th Route Army, 189; Central Revolutionary Military Commission, 188; Comintern, 181–82, 398 n. 10; Communist Chinese Army, 185, 188–89; Communist Party (CCP), 182, 184, 187, 189–90; China mission assignment, 176; Kuomintang Army, 181–82, 185, 187–89; M4, 181; port workers, 21–22
China Forum, 189
Chinese laundries, 190–92
Chinese Vista, road to, 278–79
Christian Media Center, 400 n. 11
Christkind, 13, 394 n. 18
Chronicle-Telegraph, 341
Churchill, Winston, 372
Cişmigiu Gardens, 141, 401 n. 7
Clarke, Blake, 381
Clement, 279
coal mines, 48, 65–68, 74–75, 87, 114–22, 139–41; Friedrich Ebert 72; *Hauer*, 66–67; Karl Haniel, 74–75; *Lore*, 75
coastal watchers, 268–73; Johnny questioned about by DESPS, 284
Coca-Cola, 339–40
Codreanu, Corneliu Zelea, 146
cold war, 372
Cologne, 82–84; U.S. Consulate, 157–58
Colombia, Colombia mission, 299, 301–2
"Colson," 270
Comintern. *See* Soviet Union
Comintern's Far Eastern Bureau. *See* Soviet Union
Comintern's South American Bureau. *See* Soviet Union
Comintern's West European Bureau. *See* Soviet Union
Commodore Hotel (New York), 301

Communist menace lectures, 373, 372–77, 380–82
Comrade Anwält, 230
Comrade August. *See* Johnny de Graaf
Comrade Chung. *See* Johnny de Graaf
Comrade Julius. *See* Johnny de Graaf
Comrade Mattern. *See* Johnny de Graaf
Comrade Milton. *See* Eugene Dennis
Comrade Müller. *See* Boris Melnikov
Comrade Soltz, 232
Comrade Waldemar, 231
Comrade Zhelasko, 235
Congo Free State, 394 nn. 1–2
Congo Russo, 182
conscription, 31, 34–49
Constanţa, 142–43
Copacabana, 200–201, 262–63, 265, 276
Copacabana Palace Hotel (Rio de Janeiro), 200, 275; Casino Copacabana, 263–64
Copenhagen, 4, 153, 164, 173, 199, 259–61
coronelismo, 207
Corrêa, Ismael José, 270
Corrêa, Olavo, 270
Costa, Amaro, 270
Costa, Miguel, 227
court-martials, 45, 48–49, 63
Courtney (Capt.), 292–98
Cowgill, Felix, 359–60, 366
CPC. *See* Canada, Communist Party
CPGB. *See* United Kingdom, Communist Party
CPUSA. *See* United States, Communist Party
Crefeld, 334
Cross, David, 270
Crusaders Against Communism, 376
CSIS. *See* Canada
Cuba, 197
Cumberland (cruiser), 280
Czechoslovakia, 102, 174, 241, 265; Social Democrats, 345

Dahlheim, Luiz Guimarães, 265
Daily Worker, 153–54
Dalbos, Ivonne, 270
Dalian. *See* Darien
Dallgow-Döberitz, 77
Darien (Dalian), 181
David, Marie Antoinette, 381
"David," Mr., 238
Davis, Donovan Thomas, 270
death and cremation, 385–86
De Graaf, Amanda, 14–15; and husband, 8–9; asks Johnny for money, 29; dies, 389; deceives in-laws, 5; described, 4; deserts family, 28–29; full name, 4; homelife, 4; Johnny's wish to go to sea, 14; rebukes Johnny, 4–6, 8–9, 12–14; remarries, 389; unfaithfulness, 7–8, 13
De Graaf, Johann Heinrich Amadeus (De Graaf, Johnny, De Graff, John, De Graff, Johnny), Figures 1, 3, 6, 16–18, 30, 42, 46, 50–51, 61–62, 64–67, 71–72, pages 1–49, 52, 54–76, 78–108, 110–96, 198–271, 273–321, 323–30, 332–50, 352–87, 393 nn. 1–2, 394 nn. 6, 15, 395 nn. 21, 3–4, 7, 14, 396 nn. 19, 2, 397 nn. 6, 19, 21, 398 nn. 32, 7, 399 nn. 28, 31, 33–34, 400 nn. 1–2, 11, 16, 401 nn. 1, 3, 402 nn. 19, 17, 403 nn. 27, 33, 404 nn. 13, 16, 18–19, 21–22, 405 n. 11, 406 nn. 42, 48, 407 n. 14, 408 nn. 24, 27, 36, 410 nn. 4, 11, 411 nn. 13, 18, 22, 26, 28, 412 nn. 30, 33, 35, 38, 414 nn. 39, 42, 45, 5, 415 n. 15, 416 nn. 27, 31, 417 nn. 40, 46, 418 n. 71, 418 n. 74, 419 nn. 2–3, 6, 14, 16, 420 nn. 8, 1, 3, 421 nn. 23, 26, 423 nn. 9, 2, 424 nn. 18, 28, 425 nn. 41, 55, 426 n. 66; 1st Naval Revolt, 48–49, 275; 2nd Naval Revolt, 59, 63; 3rd Infantry Regiment, 202, 206, 209; 8th Route Army, 184; 21st Infantry Battalion, 207–8; 49 Palmerston Avenue, 306, 328, 334, 337, 357; able-body seaman's papers, 24–25; abuse in Chinese ports, 20–21; accusations by the Stuchevskis for the failure in Brazil, 228–29; *Admiral Graf Spee*, 279–82; Adolf Hitler, 165–66, 168, 173, 177, 202, 220, 237, 242, 265, 281, 298, 305–6, 308, 312–13, 315, 324, 344, 356, 358, 361, 363; adoption, 338, 421 n. 36; Adrien Arcand, 305–6, 312, 315, 325, 344; Adrien Arcand's assistant, 340–41; Adrien Arcand group, 344–45, 347; Affonso Henrique de Miranda Corrêa, 212, 282; agent hotels, 114, 149; Ahlen, 65–66, 68, 70, 72–74, 78, 87, 90–91, 94–95, 121, 161, 169, 174, 177, 220, 236, 243, 383; A.I. Gekker, 179, 226; *Ajax*, 280, 286; Albert Giesler, 11–12; Albert Schmidt, 160–61; Aldo Rosso, 263, 282, 284; Alexander Abramov, 103, 139, 159, 180, 225; Alex (Gen.), 103–8, 112–13, 139–40, 142, 148–50, 181; Alfred Haskins, 324–25; Alfred Hutt, 199–200, 203–5, 211–12, 215, 261, 268, 271, 274–75, 285; Alfred Langner, 101–2, 104, 108, 114–15, 122, 149, 151–52, 161, 165, 179, 195, 225, 231; Alfred Mattern, 152, 391, 402 n. 7; aliases, 122, 139, 141, 152, 162, 192, 292, 391; Allied control commissions and de-Nazification, 359, 361, 365, 368; Allied control commissions, bribes and corruption, 367–69; Allies, 1, 76, 330, 342, 356, 359; *Almanzora*, 261–62; altercations with mother, 4–6, 8–9, 12–14, 19; *Altmark*, 279–80; Amleto Locatelli, 203, 205, 210, 214, 227–28, 236, 239; American Consulate, Cologne, 157–58; American Consulate, Montreal, 299–303, 306, 310–11; Andrei Milov, 116–20, 122; ANL, 201–2, 204, 207; Anton and Margarete Klutzka, 65–66, 70; Antônio Bonfim, 200, 206, 210, 226; "Arabs," 370, 394 n. 3; Argentina, 196, 210, 212, 230, 281, 382;

De Graaf, Johann Heinrich Amadeus (*continued*) Argentina mission, 212, 214, 223; Argentina operatives, 215–17; Argentine police, 215–17, 211; Argentine weapons inventor, 226, 230, 260; arrests following foiled Brazilian Communist uprising, 209–10; Arthur Abbott, 269, 273; Arthur Ewert, 89, 97, 167–68, 182–87, 189–90, 192, 195–96, 199–206, 210–12, 230, 285; ashes of, 387; Atelier Vienense, 265–66, 416 n. 27; "August," 174–75, 391; Australia, 16, 18, 22–25, 241; Austria, 102, 242, 359; Avenida Rainha Elisabeth 219, 263–64, 266, 274, 276, 284–85; awarded Iron Cross, 47–48, 395 n. 14; Bad Oeynhausen, 359–60, 366; Bar Alpino, 263–64, 266–67; *Barbarossa*, 27, 29–30; Battle of Jutland, 46–47; battleship *Westfalen*, 46–49, 394 n. 14; Béla Kun, 142–43, 146–47, 149–50, 195; Belgian Congo and slavery, 17–18; Belgium, 26, 30, 82, 87, 92, 322, 326–27; Berlin, 53, 63, 68–69, 72–73, 77, 84, 95–97, 99–100, 139, 148, 158, 166–71, 173–75, 179–81, 199–200, 220, 222–24, 233, 239, 259–61, 312–13, 315, 318–19, 326, 331, 333, 335–36, 343, 356, 359; boot camp, 39–43; born, 3, 393 n. 2; Botofogo assassination attempt, 276–79; Brazil, 195, 202, 222, 230, 260, 267, 278, 283, 286, 380, 382; Brazil I mission assignment, 196, 198–207, 213–15, 223, 226–27, 232; Brazil I mission skepticism, 196, 198–199, 202, 204–5, 214; Brazil I mission three-part defense, 225–26, 230–31; Brazil II mission assignment, 236–38; Brazil II mission—British supplement, 262, 269; Brazilian army, 202, 206, 208; Bremen, 29, 37, 61, 87, 221; Bremerhaven, 7, 14; *Bremerhaven*, 25–26; British businesses in Shanghai and industrial espionage, 190–92; British Consulate, New York, 301–2; British Embassy, Berlin, 170–71; British military, 81–85, 156; British mission, 151–52, 163, 165, 220; Brockville, 1, 381–85; Brockville Psychiatric Hospital, 384, 386; Bruno Zimmermann, 164, 391; Brussels, 200, 237–38, 261, 267–68, 324; Bucharest, 139–42; Budapest, 384, 387; Buenos Aires, 2, 196, 210, 212–13, 215, 219, 221–22, 281; Bulgaria, 225, 359; Calle Florida 246, 215, 220–21; Camp 44 escape attempts, 350–56; Canada, 261, 299–308, 311–14, 318, 322–24, 326–27, 331, 334, 342, 348–53, 356–58, 370–71, 373–77, 380, 382–84; Canadian-German club, 338–40, 345, 347, 356; Canadian Marconi Co., 319–20; Canadian naval intelligence, 330, 350–52; Captain Burger, 309, 311–12, 314–15, 318, 332, 335–36, 343–45, 356, 391; "Captain Johnny X," 373, 382, 391; capture U-boat mission, 350–55; Cario station chief job, 369–70; Carlisle Hotel, 321–23; Carmen Ghioldi, 198, 201, 210, 212; Casino Copacabana, 263–64; *Caterina Acalo*, 20–22; *Catilina A. Walmen*, 26–27; *Cavina*, 371–72; *Cayo Manzanillo*, 28–31; CCP, 184, 187, 189–90; Cecil Borer, 282–84, 286; Chabarovsk, 180–81, 192; Charlotte Akontz, 374–75, 379; Charlotte de Graff (nee: Akontz), 379, 384–85; Chiang Kai-shek, 181–82, 185, 187–90, 192; Children's Home No. 6, 233–34, 240, 242; Chile, 18, 21, 215, 217; China, 174, 175, 181–82, 185–87, 194–96, 210, 378, 382; China battle plan, redraws, 185–86, 192; China mission, 174–76, 181–82, 220, 226; Chinese army (unspecified), 185, 188; Chinese laundries, 190–92; Chinese port workers, 21–22; Chinese Vista, road to, 278–79; Christkind, 13, 394 n. 18; Clifford W. Harvison, 300–301, 303–5, 307–8, 310–11, 314, 316–17, 319–30, 332–34, 336–43, 347–57, 372–74, 376–78, 380, 383, 385; coal mines, 65–68, 72, 74–75, 94, 139–41, 144–45, 165; coal scar, 67, 141, 397 n. 21; coastal watchers, 268–73, 284; Coca-Cola, 339–40; Colombia mission, 299, 301–2; Comintern, 114–15, 119, 140–42, 147–49, 151–61, 163–65, 170, 173, 175, 178–83, 185–86, 195–96, 200, 213, 223, 225, 230, 233, 283; Comintern's West European Bureau, 148, 158–60, 164, 173–74; Communist Chinese Army, 185, 188–89; Communist infiltration in Canada, 373, 376–77, 382; Comrade August, 122, 391; Comrade Chung, 184, 391; Comrade Julius, 143, 391; Comrade Mattern, 162, 391; conscription, 31, 34–49; Constanța, 142–43; Consuelo Müller, 262, 282; Copacabana, 262–63, 265, 276; Copacabana Palace Hotel, 200, 263, 275; Copenhagen, 153, 164, 173, 199, 259–61; court-martialed, 45, 48–49; Courtney (Capt.), 292–98; CPC, 340, 346–47, 373–74, 381, 383; CPGB, 152–57, 159, 162–63, 345; Criminal Investigation Division, 344; CSIS, 383, 385; Cyril Mills, 329–30, 341–42; Czechoslovakia, 102, 174, 241, 265, 345; *Daily Worker*, 153–54; death and cremation, 385–86; decision/plans to leave USSR, 106–7, 115, 158, 173; "Della ligou," 205–6, 208; de-Nazification, 359, 361; Denmark, 7, 153, 327; DESPS, 204, 210–12, 262, 265, 267–69, 276–78, 281–83; Dietrich Gerkins, 7, 15–20, 22; Dimitri Manuilski, 114, 151, 161–63, 165, 169, 195–96, 219, 222, 225, 230, 236; dislikes injustice, 18–19; dislikes Kaiser Wilhelm II, 10, 34, 40–42, 71–72, 110; dislikes Ruth Fisher, 88–89; dislikes SPD, 64, 71, 166; distributes Communist propaganda, 95–96, 98; Donbass mission, 114–15; Donovan Thomas Davis, 270; D. S. MacGrath (or McGrath), 270, 272–73; Düsseldorf, 87, 359; Earle J.

Annett Sr., 321–22; Edgar (Maj.), 361–66; Edinburgh, 163, 261; Edith Jarminski, 267, 271; education as sailor, 7, 17–19, 24–25; Edward S. Parker, 157–58; Elsie Ewert, 183–84, 190, 192, 200–201, 210; Emilie Krüger, 95, 99, 121, 152, 158, 206–7, 222–23, 238, 259–60, 264–65, 267, 289; Emma Klutzka, 174, 177, 234; Emma Todicain, 12, 46; Ernst Krüger, 95, 99, 220, 222–23, 264–65; Ernst Thälmann, 95, 166–67; Esbjerg, 153, 260; estrangement from Maria, 72, 90, 94; Ethel Page, 272; Eugene Dennis, 183, 186–87, 190, 192; explosives: Figures 32–33; 80, 188, 203, 205, 209, 374, 212, 332; explosives classes, 188, 203, 205, 212; explosives lectures, 373–74; false passports, 100, 139, 148, 153, 158, 164, 166, 170, 180, 182, 225, 259, 262, 268, 295; FBI, 302, 312, 348–49, 373, 377–82; feelings for grandparents, 5, 9; Feilder (Herr), 11–12; Felisberto Batista Teixeira, 282–84; Felix Cowgill, 359–60, 366; fights, 11–12, 19–24, 26–27, 39–41, 44–45, 47, 58–59, 71, 83, 120–21; Filinto Müller, 204, 210–12, 262, 268–69, 273, 276, 280–82, 286–89; Finland, 101, 199, 282, 359; Fletcher's Field group, 316–20, 332, 335–36, 343, 347; *Florida*, 198, 200; fond of harbor as child, 5–6; Ford automobiles, 181, 204, 263–65, 276–77, 415 n. 15; Fortress of Santa Cruz, 281–82; France, 9–10, 21, 92, 94, 280, 305; Francisco Gruber, 2, 222, 391; Francisco Julien, 211, 222, 262, 264, 271, 273, 282, 285; Francisco Romero, 205, 209; Frank Foley, 170–76, 180–83, 187, 199–200, 222–23, 238, 259–61, 278, 330, 359–60, 370–71, 380; Franz Paul Gruber (Johnny de Graaf), 200, 211, 212, 215, 223, 225, 227, 229, 231–32, 238, 262, 266, 270–71, 282, 391, 416 n. 27, 417 n. 50; Free Corps, 34, 68, 77–80, 83, 85, 90, 94; French Communist Party, 161, 178; French Concession, 183, 187; French Foreign Legion, 323, 326; Frimmer (Herr), 10; Fritz Hummer, 311–15, 319, 336–37; Frunze Military Academy, 107–13, 179, 182, 200; Fujian, 185, 189; General Staff (German), 57, 77, 185; General Staff (Soviet), 107, 111, 113, 115, 144, 146, 149, 166, 179–80, 182–83, 185–86, 192, 196, 223, 232, 241; Geneva Convention, 322, 326; Genoa, 26–27, 200; Geoffrey Knox, 271, 285; Georg Ladebour, 38, 45, 64, 172; George Aitken, 152–55, 161–63; George Kitson, 181–82, 187, 189–92; George Renwick, 301–2; German-Canadian Federation, 346, 356; German Embassy, Rio de Janeiro, 277–78, 282, 285; German legend of Ragnarök, 355–56; German military intelligence (Abwehr), 324–25, 330–31, 334; German miners in USSR, 114–22, 165; German nationalism, 6, 9–10; German nationals and internment camps, 291–98; German naval police, 40, 45; German officer on train, 36–37, 39; German police, 14, 19, 71, 73–74, 78, 86–87, 92, 98, 153, 363; German POWs, 342, 344–45; German spymaster, 304, 341; German youth and pornography, 363–64; Germany, 10, 33–34, 36, 38, 41, 45–46, 48, 62, 72, 85, 91, 100–102, 111, 139–40, 152–53, 158, 160, 165, 168, 170, 173, 175, 183, 200, 207, 210, 242, 261, 264, 280–81, 302, 305, 307, 309, 313, 319, 325, 329, 331, 333, 340–42, 344–45, 349, 358–59, 361, 369, 382, 384; Gertrude as Helena, 259, 283; Gertrude Krüger, xiii–xiv, 2, 95, 158, 206–7, 222–24, 238–39, 259–65, 274, 277, 283, 285–86, 288–91, 297–308, 314, 317, 328–30, 338–40, 353–54, 357–60, 367, 370–73, 375–76, 379, 386; Gestapo, 168–70, 210, 220, 298, 324–26; Getúlio Vargas, 196, 200, 202, 204, 230, 265, 380; Gevork Alikhanov, 225–26, 230–31; given dog, 90–91; goes to sea, 14–15; goes to Shepetovka, 120–21; Gottfried Treviranus, 391, 421 n. 23; Grajaú "bomb factory," 205, 209; Grand Ligne, 350, 355; "Group of 42," 43, 45, 48–61, 63; Gus Begalki, 384–85; guerrilla-warfare classes, 184, 203, 205, 212, 214; Gustav Krüger, 95, 99–100, 121, 152, 158, 220, 223, 238, 264–67, 282; Halifax, 303, 324, 374; Hamburg, 4, 26, 36–37, 39, 61, 85–87, 95, 152–53, 221, 265, 289, 326, 328, 331–32, 341–42, 393 nn. 2, 5; Hampton, New Brunswick, 303; "hangman's noose trick," 326–27; Hans Klein, 307, 311–13, 315–16, 319, 325; Hans Langsdorff, 280–81; Hans Lessing, 264–65, 282, 284; Hans Rogalla, 169, 179; Hans von Seeckt, 77, 185; Hans Wilhelm, 237–38, 240–41, 261, 263–64, 266–67, 277–78; Hara-Kiri Club, 355–56; Harry Gold, 377, 379–80; Harry Pollitt, 152–55, 157, 159–63; Harry Wickman, 182, 391; Harwich, 153, 260; "Heil Dir im Siegerkranz," 9, 394 n. 16; Heinrich Fellor, 339–40; Heinrich Simone, 267–68, 283; Heinz Harold Schmutter, 277–79; Heinz Neumann, 167–68; Helena Benkendorf, 265–66, 282; Helena Krüger, 1–2, 95, 152–53, 157–58, 164, 174–77, 180, 182, 196, 198–200, 204–5, 207, 211–13, 219–22, 226, 259, 283, 385, 411 nn. 22, 26; Helena Krüger's ashes, 221–23; Helsinki, 164, 182, 259; Henri Gagnon, 348–49, 357; Herman Schneider, 153, 166, 391; Herman Schubert, 152–53; Herman van Heussen, 164, 391; *Highland Princess*, 212, 213; Hoboken, 27, 394 n. 8; Hoffmann Bermann, 51, 57; Holland. *See* The Netherlands; Hong Kong, 20–21, 180–81; Honório de Freitas Guimarães, 200, 203, 205; Horningtoft, 1, 381, 383; Horst Wessel, murder of, 99–100; Hotel Novo Moskovskaya, 149,

De Graaf, Johann Heinrich Amadeus (*continued*) 225, 230–32, 235, 239, 241; Hotel Passage, 149–50, 177, 179, 226; Hotel Riviera, 263, 415 n. 15, 267, 274, 284; Hotel Windsor, 299, 301, 344, 372; Hungary, 359, 374, 384, 386–87; Hugh Gurney, 199, 204; Hugo Haase, 38, 45, 48, 172; Hunedoara, 146–47; Ian Berzin, 92, 112–13, 122–39, 147–50, 159–61, 163–65, 174, 177–81, 192, 231–33, 236–42; identification left in/taken from USSR, 152–53, 165–66, 171; Igor, 118–19, 122; Igor Gouzenko, 346, 374; IKKI, 114, 161, 225; incarcerations, 41, 44–46, 62–63, 87, 92, 94, 98–99, 101, 146–47, 265, 281–88; Imperial German army, 5–6, 35, 51, 55–60, 69, 73–74, 76–77, 96, 98, 108, 172, 243, 324, 326; Imperial Hotel, 260, 290; importing and exporting to/from Japan and the USA, 265–66, 269; injuries/surgeries, 11–12, 41–42, 44–45, 55–56, 58–59, 155, 187, 232, 374; International Lenin University, 101–13; Iron Guards, 146, 294, 297–98; Italian Communist Party, 161; Italy, 27, 102, 200, 359; Itamarati, 204, 210; Ivan Semjonov, 233–34; Jacob Jacques Epstein, 270–71; Jakob Göbel, 166, 173; Jaques Klerekoper, 271; J. Ehrenberg, 270; Japan, 180, 236–39, 266–67, 283; Japanese agent, 190–92; Japanese army, 182, 185, 189; J. Edgar Hoover, 377–78; Jews, 1, 76, 91, 184, 197, 210–11, 292, 294, 298, 324, 326, 340, 345, 368, 381, 425 n. 41; Jiangxi, 185, 188–89; João Marcellino Ferreira e Silva, 262–63; Johanna Gerkins, 6–7, 14–15, 20, 22, 25; "Johanssen," 152–53, 391; John Graffnor, 299, 391; John Gray, 301–2; John Gries, 391, 420 n. 1; John Henry de Graff, 291, 419 n. 3; Johnny de Graaf Jr., 71–72, 90, 94–95, 99, 121, 161, 174–75, 233–36, 239–40, 242–43; Josef Bunzlau, 265–66, 282; Joseph McCarthy, 372–73; Joseph Stalin, 105, 112–13, 167, 201, 231, 363, 373; J. R. W. "Pete" Bordeleau, 321, 323, 326–27; "Julius," 141, 391; jumps ship, 23, 26, 30, 32, 36; "Junescu," 141, 143; Juny Commune's Camp No. 6, 115–22, 175; Kapp Putsch, 77, 275; Karl Franserra, 110, 241; Karl Grubnick, 292–93, 298, 358, 391; Karl Herltz, 160–61, 195; Karl Liebknecht Middle School, 234–35, 242; Karl Stemmer, 78, 273, 275–76, 282; Kinshasa (Leopoldville), 18, 394 n. 1; Kliment Voroshilov, 112, 230–31; KPD, 68–75, 79, 86–89, 92–99, 114, 122, 152, 161, 165–69, 175, 210, 227, 233, 239, 264, 345, 363; KPD Berlin rally, 95; KPD conferences, 87–91; Krenick (Capt.), 24–25; Krüger family, 2, 95–96, 99–100, 174–75, 182–83, 200, 222–23; Krupp steel works, 361–63; Kuomintang Army, 181–82, 185, 187–89; Labor Progressive Party, 346–47, 381; "Laura, Laura, Laura," 335–36;

Lazar Kaganovich, 230–31; Lenin, 110, 149, 167, 195, 205–6, 236; Liverpool, 299, 371; London, xiii, 2, 9, 19–20, 189, 199, 204–5, 210, 216–17, 219–21, 260–62, 268–69, 274–75, 285, 289–90, 299, 329, 342, 356–58, 367–68, 382–83; Lourenço da Silva, 270–71, 273; Ludwig Dinkelmeyer, 139–40, 144, 147–48, 391; Luís Carlos Prestes, 196, 198–99, 201–7, 209, 211; M4, 111, 113, 146, 148, 152, 157, 159–60, 163–64, 174–76, 179–81, 192, 195, 210–11, 215, 223, 225–26, 230–32, 234–36, 239–42, 259, 261, 264, 266–67, 378; Luiz Freiherr von Liliencron, 57–58; "Mace," 270, 272; Malvino Reis Neto, 206, 208; Manchuria mission, 174–76, 179–81, 220; Manfred Stern, 108, 111–12, 182–83, 185–90, 192–95, 378, 390; Mao Zedong, 188–89; Margarita (or Marga), 203, 210; Maria de Graaf (nee: Klutzka), 69–72, 90–91, 94–95, 121, 161, 169, 174–75, 177, 379, 384; Maria Klutzka, 66–67, 69–70; Marianne de Graaf, 94–95, 121, 161, 174, 234, 243, 384, 395 n. 14; Marius Alfred Langbein, 324–25; Marquis Square, 31–35; marriages, 69–70, 259–61, 379; Martin Monger, 311–15; "Mary," 261, 266, 268, 283; "Mattern," 179, 183, 391; Max (Maj.), 108–9, 111–13; McCarthyism, 372–73; McL. Hunter, 28, 30–31; merchant marine, 14–34, 82, 92–96; Mexico, 16, 18, 29; MI5, 171, 329–30, 342, 358–59; MI6, 2, 171–73, 189–90, 199–200, 210–12, 214, 216, 221, 243, 260–62, 265, 267–69, 274, 278, 285, 290–93, 295–98, 300–301, 303, 346, 353, 359–61, 363, 366–68, 370–71, 373–74, 377; Miller Smitz, 311–13, 315; minesweeper, 43–44; mining engineer, 139–40, 144–45; Möhne Dam, 361–62; Montevideo, 261, 268–69, 274–75, 280; Montreal, 299–304, 306, 310–11, 315, 318, 322–25, 327, 330, 332–33, 341, 343–50, 356–57, 371–72, 374–77, 379–81, 383, 419 n. 14; Montreal FBI interview, 378–79; Moscow, 80, 89, 93, 102–3, 106–8, 113–22, 139, 143–44, 147–49, 152, 154–55, 157–61, 164–65, 169–70, 173–81, 186–87, 190–93, 199, 203, 206–7, 214–15, 219, 222–25, 227, 232–34, 237, 239–40, 243, 259, 261, 266–67, 283, 289, 373–74, 377; Moscow student, 101–13, 200; Mosquito bomber, 331–32; mother's unfaithfulness, 7–8, 13; Mount Royal, 299, 303, 306, 319; murder-suicide plan, 384–85; name change, xix, 291; Natal, 207–8; Nazis and pro-Nazis, 165, 168–69, 172, 177, 183, 224, 227, 237, 261–62, 266, 268, 273, 276–78, 282, 288, 291–92, 294–96, 303–7, 309–12, 318, 320, 326, 331, 335, 337–38, 340–41, 344–45, 347, 352, 355–56, 358, 365, 371; Nazi army, 243, 324, 326; Nazi leader for North America, 344–45; Nazi reward for Johnny's capture, 223, 227; Nazi spies, 294, 298, 303, 330; Neil Pollock, 383–85; Netherlands, 3, 9, 326–27; New Brunswick, 324, 351; New Carlisle, 321, 323, 341; Newcastle, 23–24; New York, 27, 29–30, 266, 299, 301–2, 348–49, 379–80; Nightingale Lane Internment Camp, 292–98, 358; Nikolai Yezhov, 230–31, 239; *Niobe*, 7, 14–22, 25; NKVD, 179, 224–25, 230–32, 239, 242; NKVD interrogates Johnny on failure in Brazil, 230, 413 n. 21; Noel (Cpl.), 300, 357; Non-Aggression Pact, 201–2; Nordenham, 3–4, 393 n. 2; North German Lloyd, 27, 394 n. 8; Norway, 279, 327; Nose, 9, 12, 14; "O" Division, 344–45; OGPU, 104–7; Olga Benário, 196, 201–2, 204, 210–11, 231; Olive Quance, 333–34; OMS, 103, 139, 159, 215; *Onn 6*, 92–94; Ontario, 322, 350, 368, 373–74, 379, 381; Oscar de Graaf (Johnny's brother), 3, 28, 72, 75–76, 91; Oscar de Graaf (Johnny's son), 91, 94–95, 121, 161, 174, 220, 234, 243, 383, 395 n. 14; Osip Piatnitski, 161, 195; Osowiec, 49–62, 85–86, 102, 374; Ottawa, 303, 324, 328–29, 331, 341, 351, 353–55, 374, 380, 382; "Otto," 391, 396 n. 19; Otto Braun, 108, 186; Otto Klutzka and family, 47–49, 65–67, 70; Otto Ullrich, 265, 284; Paris, 157, 170, 178, 182–83, 200, 207, 214, 222, 267, 278; *pau-de-arara*, 285, 418 n. 68; Paula de Graaf, 3, 5; Paulina (Cornelia), 142–45, 147; Paul Petersen, 377, 380 391; Paul Wilhelm, 140, 174; Pavel Stuchevski, 196, 203–4, 210, 212, 214–15, 228–29, 236; Pavel Vasiliev, 104–7, 149, 151, 161, 227, 229–30; PCA, 196, 212–15, 221; PCA Central Committee turned into the police, 215; PCB, 200, 205–7; PCR, 141–43, 146–48; "Pedro," 201, 391; Pernambuco, 206, 279–80; "Petersen," 300, 383, 391; Philadelphia FBI appointment, 379–80; plans to free Luís Carlos Prestes, 215, 226; Plantz (FBI special agent), 378–79; Plattsburg, New York, 348–49; Ploeşti refinery, 139, 143–44; Plymouth, 19, 32, 154, 163; Poland, 49, 56, 60, 65, 86, 102, 139, 227, 266; police (in general), 22, 111, 177, 203; Polícia Central, 211–12, 281, 285, 287, 418 n. 71; Polícia Civil, 204, 210, 262; Polícia Especial, 210, 215, 285–86; Polícia Militar, 202, 204, 206; Polish Communists, 161, 175, 180; Polish miners, 165; Port of Jackson, 24, 394 n. 6; possible execution, 36, 49, 169; Prague, 173–76, 179, 220; prejudices, 1, 91, 381, 425 n. 41; promoted, 46; QPP, 321–22, 326, 342; Quebec, 315, 322, 325, 331, 341, 343, 345, 350, 372–73; Quebec City, 327, 331, 341; Quebec Hydro, 307, 332; Quebec Hydro blueprints, 307, 315–16, 319, 332–33; Queen Lingerie Shop, 333–34; RA, 45–49, 52; Ray Fairweather, 350–51; RCMP, 300, 302–5, 310, 312–13, 320, 322–24, 326–30, 333–35, 337–38, 341, 343–49, 351–53, 355–56, 373–77, 381–84; Rebecca Buhay, 340, 422 n. 37; Recife, 205–7, 280; Red Army, 103, 105–6, 111, 167, 234, 241, 378; Reichstag, 34, 88, 97, 99, 165, 172, 210; resigns, 369–70; return to Ahlen, 87, 94; return to London, xiii, 2, 19–20, 153, 163, 200, 261, 291, 357–58; return to Moscow, 122, 143, 147–49, 157–59, 164, 174–76, 181, 192; respect for father, 5, 8–9, 13–15; reunited with family, 37–38, 61; RFB, 94–95, 165–66, 168, 173; Richard Sorge, 186, 237; Rio de Janeiro, 196–201, 202, 204, 206–8, 210–12, 215, 222, 237–38, 241, 261–62, 267, 269, 275, 277–78, 290; Robert R. Patterson, 272, 280; Rodolfo Ghioldi, 196, 201, 203–4, 210, 212, 230; Rolf von Linter, 347–50; Romania, 139–50, 294, 359, 382; Romanian army, 139, 141, 143–44; Romanian mission, 147–50, 152, 226; Rosa Luxemburg Battalion, 78–84; Rotterdam, 20, 31–33; Rua Barão da Torre 33, 265; Rua Barão da Torre 636, 201, 204; Rudolph Seigmire, 307–16, 319, 332–33; "Ruffier," 271–72; Ruhr, 48, 65, 75, 82, 90, 101, 107, 153, 157, 384; Ruhr Communists, 68–70, 72–74, 77–79, 87, 110, 167–68, 241, 384; S.A., 235, 305, 314, 319, 335, 345; sailors's homes, 25–26; Santa Catarina, 262, 276; Santos, 214, 222, 267–68, 279–80, 288–89; São Paulo, 198, 201, 209, 238, 268, 288; school, 5–6, 8–14, 33; "Scoopies," 39–41, 47; Scott (Dr.), 375–76; Section V (MI6), 199, 359, 368; Shanghai, 21, 180, 182–84, 186–92, 203; *Siguranza*, 141, 144–46, 148; Sil Milo, 261, 269, 275–76; Silverthorn (FBI special agent), 378–79; Sofia Stuchevskaya, 198, 210, 214–15; *Soldier's Voice*, 153–54; Sophie de Graaf, 3–5, 8–9, 12, 28, 37–38, 61; sorrow following Gerti's death, 376–77; Soviet agents, 92, 176, 269, 377–80, 382; Soviet Embassy, Paris, 222–23; Soviet Embassy, Prague, 174–76; Soviet espionage network in Canada and the USA, 346, 373, 380; Soviet Union, xvi, 93, 102–3, 105–7, 110–11, 114, 148, 152, 157–58, 161, 164–65, 173, 180, 192, 196, 219, 222–23, 226–27, 229, 231, 233–34, 236, 238, 240, 242–43, 260–61, 268, 301–2, 382, 398 n. 9, 401 n. 38; Soviet Union, recalled to, 192, 219, 221–23; Spain, 194–95; Spartacus League, 64, 68–71; SPD, 10, 25, 38, 62, 64, 71, 77, 79, 88, 91, 99, 165–66, 170, 172, 197, 239, 264, 345; speeches, 72, 96–97; Stalin Auto Works, 240, 242; Stella Blagoeva, 225–27, 231–32; stevedores, 154, 162–64; Stockholm, 164, 259; Sweden, 31–32, 182, 199, 259, 327; Switzerland, 9, 100–101, 110, 200; Sykes, (Capt.), 293, 296; "Tecbrevet," 261, 265–67, 283; T. E. "Ted" Ryder, 303, 380–81; "The Aristocrat," 216–19, 385; The widow and her

De Graaf, Johann Heinrich Amadeus (*continued*) son, 365–66; Thomas L. Black, 377, 379–80; Tim Buck, 373–74, 381; Todicain (Herr), 12; Tokyo, 237–38, 261, 267; Tony (Gen.), 108; Toronto, 322, 333, 344–46, 350; tortured, 283–86; trains Romanians, 143, 145; Trans-Siberian Railway, 180–81, 192, 238; Trotskyites, 179, 379, 401 n. 38; *Tübingen*, 24–25, 394 n. 6; *Tutht*, 22–24; unemployed, 64, 87, 94; U-boats, 2, 303, 312, 321–22, 351, 421 n. 35; U-boat experts at Camp 44 and escape plans, 350–56; Ukraine, 114, 165, 194; United Kingdom, 2, 21, 30–32, 81–84 151–57, 163–64, 171–73, 260–62, 274, 277, 280, 286, 288, 294–95, 298, 306, 327, 330, 356, 382–83, 385; United States, 29–31, 158, 238, 261, 265–66, 299–303, 348–49, 356, 377–79, 382; Uruguay, 214–15, 276, 280–81; U.S. intention papers, 31–32, 35, 157–58; USPD, 34, 38, 45, 62, 64, 71, 172, 395 n. 7; Valentine Vivian, 199–200, 222–23, 260–61, 269, 275, 278, 290–91, 299–300, 303, 358–60, 368–70; Victor Allen Barron, 198, 210; Vienna, 139, 148; Vila Militar, 206, 208; VKP (b), xvii, 122, 140, 152, 162, 179, 230, 378; Vladivostok, 180–81, 192; vows to go to sea, 6, 13–14; Vyacheslav Molotov, 230, 236; "Wagner," 391, 401 n. 3; Waldemar de Graaf, 3, 12, 37; "Walter," 214, 391; Walter Gerkins, 7, 16–17, 19–20, 22, 25; Walter Ulbricht, 100, 166; wanted man, 85–87, 92, 94, 148, 169, 177, 223, 227; Ward and Violet Scott, xiii, 307, 379; warns Canadians of Moscow's plans, 372–73; Washington, D.C., 300, 348, 385; Weimar army, 69, 73–74; welcomes German families to USSR, 120–21; Werner (Capt.), 108, 179–81; Werner Kiessewetter, 271, 274–75, 277–78, 281–82, 285; Werner von Janowski, 321–37, 341–43; W. Gordan Southam, 329, 331, 333; Wilhelm Canaris, 324–25; Wilhelm de Graaf, 4–5, 8–9, 11, 13–15, 28, 36–38, 61, 221, 393 n. 5; Wilhelm Dittmann, 38, 45, 48, 64, 172; Wilhelm Florin, 167–68; Wilhelm Pieck, 100, 166; Wilhelmshaven, 4–7, 9, 12, 14, 25, 36, 39; William John de Graff, 346, 391; William John Graff (also John William Graff), 299, 306, 339, 391; William Rust, 153–54; 184, 197–98; William Shaw, 270, 273; Willy de Graaf, 3, 28; Willy Leow, 166, 169–70, 178–79; Wolf (Sgt.), 54–55, 57, 86–87; World War I, 34, 64, 76, 91, 108, 115, 141, 143, 151, 173, 323, 325; World War II, 2, 211, 266, 279–81, 355, 384, 413 n. 37; X-502, 192, 391; XX ("Twenty Committee"), 329–30; Young Communists, 220, 411 n. 18; Zhu De, 181–82, 186–89; Zhou Enlai, 188, 217; ZK, 88–90, 95, 101, 166–67

De Graaf, Johnny. *See* De Graaf, Johann Heinrich Amadeus

De Graaf Jr., Johnny, Figure 39, pages 95, 161; arrives at Shepetowka, 121; arrives in USSR looking for father, 233, 413 n. 28; at Children's Home No. 6, 233–36, 240; at father's departure from Moscow, 242; at Juny Commune's Camp No. 6, 121; becomes a Soviet citizen, 243; born, 71–72; Hitler Youth affair, 242; Ian Berzin, 233, 238–40, 242; incarcerated, 239, 242–43; Johnny tries to locate via Red Cross, 243; marries and has a son, 243, possible fate, 243, 414 n. 56; problems at Karl Liebknecht Middle School, 235–36; problems with police, 240; Stalin Auto Works, 240; wants more attention than Johnny can give, 234–36; wants to leave USSR, 240

De Graaf, Helena, Figure 64; afraid for Johnny, Oscar and herself, 383; nickname, 383

De Graaf, Maria (*See* also Klutzka, Maria), Figure 11, page 394 n. 15; arrives at Shepetowka, 121; death, 169, 177, 384; estrangement, 72, 90, 94–95; forced to give a son to the Soviets, 175; gives birth, 71, 91, 94; Johnny's mixed feelings toward, 67–69, 379; Juny Commune's Camp No. 6, 121; KPD assists, 161; lazy, 70, 72, 90, 94; marries Johnny, 69–70; not spoken of during Helena Krüger's visit, 174; police trap at burial, 177; refuses divorce, 161

De Graaf, Marianne, Figures 22, 41, pages 95, 161, 236, 389; arrives at Shepetowka, 121; at Juny Commune's Camp No. 6, 121; blames father for mother's early death, 384; born, 94; cared for by Emma Klutzka, 174, 234; Helena Krüger's visit, 174, 404 n. 19; last letter from Johnny Jr., 243; shunned, 177; visits Johnny in Canada, 384

De Graaf, Oscar (Johnny's brother), 3, 28, 72, 75, dies, 76

De Graaf, Oscar (Johnny's son), Figures 11, 22, 40, 64, 66, pages 95, 161, 236, 389, 394 n. 15, 395 n. 16, 396 n. 19; arrives at Shepetowka, 121; at Juny Commune's Camp No. 6, 121; born, 91; cared for by Emma Klutzka, 174, 234; Gestapo, 220; Helena Krüger's visit, 174, 404 n. 19; Johnny sends cash, 220; joins Wehrmacht, 243; looses leg at Stalingrad, 243; member of von Paulus's 6th Army, 243; named after uncle, 91; shunned, 177; travels to Berlin then to USSR, 174–75; visit Johnny in Canada, 383

De Graaf, Paula, 3, 5, 28, 389

De Graaf, Sarah, 243

De Graaf, Sophie, 3, 12, 28, 389; helps at home, 4–5; helps father after mother deserts family, 28; helps Johnny protect father, 5, 8; reunited with Johnny, 37–38, 61

De Graaf, Waldemar, 3, 12, 28, 37, 389

De Graaf, Walter, 3, 28, 389

De Graff, William John. *See* Johnny de Graaf

De Graaf, Wilhelm, 8–9, 11, 28, 36, 389; born, 3, 393 n. 5; described, 3; family's poverty, 4–5, 13; full name, 3; Johnny's wish to go to sea, and, 14; moves family, 4, 28; musician, 3–4, 9, 11, 13; origins, 3; reunited with Johnny, 37–38, 61; wife deserts family, 28; wife's unfaithfulness, 7–8, 13
De Graaf, Willy, Figure 6, pages 3, 28, 389
De Graff, Charlotte, Figures 65, 66; background, 374–75; cremates Johnny's remains, 386; death, 387; dominates relationship, 385; Johnny's mixed feelings toward, 379; Johnny's murder-suicide idea, 384–85; marries Johnny, 379; mental problems, 379, 384; possible intelligence background, 384, 425 n. 59; returns to Budapest, 384, 387; "Rigolettos," 384; "Sári," 374; Ward and Violet, 379; *See also* Charlotte Akontz
De Graff, Johnny. *See* De Graaf, Johann Heinrich Amadeus
De Graff, Johannes: pro-Nazi Canadian, 371, 423 n. 16
Departmento Central de Policía, 217
Delaware, 30, 32
Denmark, 7, 153, 199, 220, 327
Dennis, Eugene, Figure 26, pages 183, 389; alias Comrade Milton, 187, 190; Arthur Ewert, 187, 190; attempt to kill Johnny, 187; CPUSA general secretary and national chairman, 187; Profintern, 183; recalled to Moscow, 192; Shanghai, 186–87
DESPS. *See* Brazil
Deutschland (pocket battleship), 279
"Deutschland, Deutschland über Alles," 394 n. 16
Dimitrov, Georgi, 225
Dinkelmeyer, Ludwig. *See* Johnny de Graaf
Dittmann, Wilhelm, 38, 45, 48, 64, 396 n. 16; employed by British, 172
Dodd, Frank L., 270
Dodd, William Edward, 170
Donbass, 114–22
Dortmund, 71, 92; Rosa Luxemburg Battalion, 80; *Ruhr Echo*, 95
Dresden, 77; economics course, 94
Duchesneau, Alphonse, 322, 420 n. 4
Ducroux, Joseph, alias Serge Lefranc, "Dupont," 182
Duffy, Ed, 420–21 n. 8
Duffy, Nancy, 420–21 n. 8
Duisburg, 73, 87
Dunkirk, 229
Dupont. *See* Joseph Ducroux
Düsseldorf, 87, 359
Dutra, Eurico Gaspar, 415 n. 16, 417 n. 50

Ebert, Friedrich, 68; coal miners, 72
Ecuador, 197
Edelweiss, 363

Edgar (Maj.), 361–66
Edinburgh, 163; marriage, 261, 414 n. 5
Ehrenberg, J., 270
Ehrhardt, Hermann, 77
8th Route Army. *See* China
1863 Dorchester Street West (boulevard René-Lévesque Ouest) boarding house, Figures 63, 64, pages 372, 425 n. 41
Einstein, Alfred, 270
Eisler, Elfriede. *See* Ruth Fischer
Eisler, Gerhard, 93
Eisler, Pauline, 270
Elbrick (Col.), 83–84
Elliott, George, 334
Emmerich, 35
Engels, Friedrich, 407 n. 9
Engels/Pokrovsk, 179
England. *See* United Kingdom
"English Edith." *See* Edith Jarminski
Epstein, Jacob Jacques, 270–71
Erzberger, Matthias, 77
Esbjerg, 153, 260
Essen, 72–73, 78; coal mines, 87; German miners and families to USSR, 114–22; Johnny distributes propaganda, 98; KPD conference, 87, 398 n. 7; KPD headquarters, 96; Krupp steel works, 361–63; Rosa Luxemburg Battalion, 80–81; *Ruhr Echo*, 95
Ewert, Arthur Ernst, Figure 10, pages 2, 89, 93, 97, 168, 203, 228–30, 407 n. 4; alias Harry Berger, 187, 198; "Apple," 201, 203; "Apple Head," 408 n. 24; argument over tactics in Brazil, 202; argument over tactics in China, 186, 189, 405 n. 28; arrested in Brazil, 210–11, 226; arrives in Rio de Janeiro, 198; background, 183–84, 210; behind plan to kill Johnny, 187; Brazil mission, 195, 196, 198, 200; Brazilian press fabrication, 210; carelessness in Brazil, 198, 210, 226; carelessness in China, 186–87, 203, 210; Cai Tingkai, 189; *China Forum*, 189; Comrade Milton, 187, 190; death, 210; dislikes Johnny, 97, 187, 199; flies to Recife, 205; helps convert Prestes to communism, 196; Johnny dislikes, 89, 97, 167, 183, 187, 195–96, 199, 202–3; Johnny's booby trap offer, 203; KPD, 89, 97, 167–68, 183–84, 210; Locatelli criticizes, 227; Manfred Stern dislikes, 185, 189; "Negro" and Johnny, 210; party stooge, 167; planning in Brazil, 202, 204, 206; Polícia Especial, 210, 285; recalled to Moscow, 192, 406 n. 48; possible release, 226, 229–30; Reichstag, 184, 210; same language teacher in Brazil as Johnny, 212; SDP, 183; Shanghai, 182–83, 189–90, 192; tortured, 210
Ewert, Elise, 203; arrested in Brazil, 210–11, 226; arrives in Rio de Janeiro, 198; as Arthur's "girl-

Ewert, Elise (*continued*)
 friend," 408 n. 24; background, 182–83; Brazil mission, 198, 200; death, 210; deported to Germany, 210–11; Locatelli criticizes, 227; recalled to Moscow, 192, 406 n. 48; "Sabo," 183, 200–201, 210, 408 n. 24; Shanghai, 190; tortured, 210
Ewert, Minna, 183
Exeter (cruiser), 280

Fairmile-D speedboats, 352
Fairweather, Ray, 350–51
false passports, 100, 139, 148, 153, 158, 164, 166, 170, 180, 182, 225, 259, 262, 268, 295
Far Eastern Bureau. *See* Soviet Union
Far East command. *See* Soviet Union
FBI. *See* United States
Federal Bureau of Investigation. *See* United States, FBI
Federal Penitentiary in Lewisburg, Pennsylvania, 380
Federal Security Service (Russian Federation). *See* Soviet Union
Fegyverneky, Sándor and Angela, 425 n. 59
Feilder (Herr), 11–12
"Felix," 214
Feller POW camp. *See* Canada, Camp 44
Feller's farm. *See* Canada, Camp 44
Fellor, Heinrich, 339–40; description, 339
Fenemore, Ross, 424 n. 26
"Fernandes" *See* Antônio Maciel Bonfim
Fernandes, Elza, 229; executed, 210–11; Johnny turns in, 210
Fernandes, Rafael, 207
Ferreira, Manuel, 270
Ferreira e Silva, João Marcellino, 262–63
5th Military District. *See* Brazil
Finland, 101, 199, 282, 359
1st Naval Revolt (1917). *See* Germany
Fischer, Kurt, 108
Fischer, Ruth (Elfriede Eisler), Figure 8, pages 87–90, 93; Johnny dislikes, 88–90
Fish, Eddy, 425 n. 41
"Fisher," 270
"flattery" tools, 425 n. 55
Fletcher's Field group, 316–20; blue-collar composition, 318; controlled, 345, 347, 352; demand for proof, 335–36; desire to blow up Canadian Marconi Co., 319–20; dynamite and the two brothers in construction, 332, 343; Johnny's explanation and, 347; "Laura, Laura, Laura," 335–36
Florenty, 145
Florianópolis, 197, 262
Florida, 198, 200
Florin, Wilhelm, 95, 167–68

Foley, Frank, Figure 23, pages 170–71, 187, 359–60, 380, 389, 404 n. 13; "August," 174–75, 391; becomes chief of XX, 330; Brazil II mission, 238; British behind German naval mutiny, 172; China, 175–76, 181, 187; Copenhagen meetings, 199, 259–60; doubts Vivian's will allow marriage, 260; Johnny's resignation, 370–71; Krüger family, 182, 200; letter of recommendation, 370–71; London meetings, 261; Manchuria mission, 180–81; offers Johnny double-agent role, 172–73, 407 n. 14; Paris meeting, 182–83, 222–23; Prague meeting with Johnny, 175–76, 181; provides Johnny with funds, 173–74; position in MI6, 171; travels with Johnny and Gerti to London, 260–61
Fonseca, Wilson Sousa, 208
Ford automobiles, Figure 47; 181, 204, 263–65, 276–77, 415 n. 15
Fortress of Santa Cruz, Figure 54, pages 281–82; Francisco Julien, 282; Warner Kiessewetter, 281–82
49 Palmerston Avenue, Figure 56, pages 306, 328–30, 334, 337; moved in, 420 n. 8; sold, 357; the perified neighbor, 338
Fosterites. *See* William Z. Foster
Foster, Robert, 394 n. 9
Foster, William Z., 184
Fothergill, Henry McLean, 271
4 Wilberforce House, 358
France, 9–10; army, 82, 87, 92–94, 157, 197, 222, 267, 291, 334, 416 n. 22; Chinese port workers, 21; Communist cells in military, 404 n. 21; Communist Party, 161, 178, 409 n. 58; Communist sympathies in army, 92; Consul General, Rouen, 197; French Foreign Legion, 323, 326; intelligence service, 425 n. 59; slave trade, 18; Versailles Treaty, 81–82; Vichy government, 305
French. *See* France
French Concession. *See* Shanghai
Franco, Ernesto Vitor, 271
Franco, Francisco, 194
Franserra, Karl, 110, 241, 400 n. 16
Fredericton, New Brunswick, 306
Free Corps. *See* Germany
Freelander, Arthur, 271
Freeman, Mike, 271
Freeman, William Philippe, 271
Freikorp. *See* Germany, Free Corps
Friker (Capt.), 39
Frisbee, Albert Henry, 271
Frimmer, Fritz, 10
Frimmer (Herr), 10
Frunze Military Academy. *See* Soviet Union
Fuchs, Gerhard, 103
Fuchs, Klaus, 379

Fujian (Fukien), 185, 189
Funk, Albert, Figure 6, pages 70, 72, 87, 94

Gabrielsson, Peter, 393 n. 9
Gagnon, Henri, 348–49, 357
Gagnon, Onésime, 341
Gallardo, Carlos Americo, 411 n. 24
Geestemünde or Geestendorf, 3, 393 n. 5
Gekker, A. I., 179, 226
Geneva Convention, 322, 326
Genoa, 26–27, 200
Gerkins, Dietrich, 7, 15–22; dispute with son, 17, 20, 22; forgives Johnny, 22, 25; nickname, 17
Gerkins, Johanna, 6–7, 14–15, 20, 22, 25
Gerkins, Walter: becomes a problem, 17, 20; death, 20, 22, 25; education as sailor, 7, 16–17, 19; leaves *Niobe*, 20
German-Canadian Federation, 346, 356
German Embassy, Moscow, 414 n. 56
German Embassy, Rio de Janeiro, 277–78; pays US$300 to have Johnny arrested, 282
German Labor Party. *See* Germany, USPD
German Legation, Montevideo, 280
German legend of Ragnarök, 355–56
German miners and families to USSR, 114–22, 165; arrive at Shepetovka, 120–21
German nationals and internment camps, 291–92; *See also* Nightingale Lane Internment Camp
German passenger liner (unnamed), 268
German POWs, 342, 344–45; U-boat experts at Camp 44 and escape plans, 350–51
German Red Assistance. *See* Germany, Communist Party
German Soviet Republic, 64
German spies. *See* Germany, Nazi spies
German Steel Helmet. *See* Germany, Free Corps
German U-boats. *See* Canada and Germany, Nazi navy
German youth and pornography, 363–64
Germany, xiii, 3–4, 35–36, 43, 50, 64, 66, 76–77, 81–82, 100, 102, 139–40, 152–53, 157, 165, 170, 173, 183, 200, 207, 210–11, 223, 227, 242, 261, 264, 305–7, 309, 311–12, 319, 321–33, 340–42, 347–49, 358, 382, 384, 417 n. 50, 421 n. 17; 1st Naval Revolt (1917), 48–49, 275, 396 n. 16; 2nd Naval Revolt (1918), 59, 63; abdication of Kaiser, 59; abuse in Kiautschou (Qingdao), 21; *Admiral Graf Spee*, 279–82; Anarchists, 77; and Chinese port workers, 21; Battle of Skagerrak (Jutland), 46–47, 63, 397 n. 3; Catholic Center Party, 62, 64; Communist Party (KPD), xvi, 68–69, 72–75, 77, 79, 86–99, 110, 114, 122, 152–53, 156, 161, 165, 167–68, 175, 183–84, 197, 210, 227, 233, 239, 264, 345, 363, 402 n. 19, 424 n. 28; Control Commission and de-Nazification, 359, 361, 365, 369; Fatherland Party, 77; Free Corps, 34, 68, 77–80, 83, 85, 90, 94; General Staff, 57, 77, 185; German military intelligence, 324–25, 330–31, 334; Gestapo, 168–70, 197, 210, 220, 223, 282, 298, 324–26, 399 n. 27, 402 n. 19, 406 n. 30, 412 nn. 35–36; Gestapo agent No. 5, 282; Hitler Youth, 415 n. 18; Imperial German army, 5–6, 35, 51, 55–60, 69, 73–74, 76–77, 96, 98, 108, 172, 243, 324, 326; imperialism, 395 n. 3; invades USSR, 121, 302; Kapp Putsch, 77, 275, 398 n. 31; Marines, 77; merchant marine, 22–27, 93; militarism, 9, 30, 34, 38, 76, 416 n. 22; naval police, 40, 45; Imperial German navy, 5–6, 36–50, 62–64, 96, 141, 172; Nazis, 165, 167–69, 170, 172, 174, 177, 183, 211, 223–24, 227, 229, 237, 266, 268, 276, 306–7, 309, 312, 326, 330–31, 337, 344, 351, 358, 365, 399 n. 34, 414 n. 45, 415 n. 18; Nazi army, 243, 324, 326, 416 n. 22; Nazi navy, 2, 279–81, 303, 312, 321–24, 350–52, 421 n. 35; Nazi spies, 294, 298, 303, 330–31, 344–45, 423 n. 16; Osowiec, 49–61; police, 14, 21–22, 62, 64, 71, 73–74, 78, 83, 86–87, 92–94, 98–99, 111, 153, 168, 177, 197, 363, 399 n. 34; RA, xvi, 45–49, 52, 64; Reichstag, 34, 38, 62, 88, 97, 99, 165, 172, 184, 210, 403 n. 5; Revolution of 1923, 82–83, 93–94, 160; RFB, xvi, 88, 94–95, 165–68, 173; Ruhr Communists, 68–70, 72–74, 77–79, 87, 110, 167–68; strikes, riots, and revolution, 62–64, 68–69; SA, xvi, 90, 99; ships at Veracruz, 29; slave trade, 18; Spartacus League, 62, 64, 68–69, 75, 79, 81, 85, 183; SPD, xvii, 10, 25, 38, 62, 64, 71, 77, 79, 88, 91, 99, 165–66, 170, 172, 183, 197, 239, 264, 345, 403 n. 5; Stasi, 197, 406 n. 30; stevedores, 93; Syndicalists, 77; unions, 93; USPD, xvii, 34, 38, 45, 62, 64, 71, 77, 93, 172, 395 n. 7; Weimar army, 69, 73–74; Young Communists, 411 n. 18; ZK, xvii, 88–90, 95, 101, 166–67
Gerstenberg, Wilhelm, 69
Gestapo. *See* Germany
Ghioldi, Carmen de Alfaya: arrest, 212; arrives in Brazil, 198; Brazil mission, 198; remains level headed, 201; stays with Johnny and Helena, 203
Ghioldi, Rodolfo José, 196, 203, 229–30, 389, 407 n. 4; alias, 198; arrested, 212; arrives in Rio de Janeiro, 198; Brazil mission, 198; Locatelli criticizes, 227; possible release, 226, 229–30; secretary, 203; stays with Johnny and Helena, 203; turns in Victor Allen Barron, 210; viewed as weak, 227
Giesler, Albert, 11–12
Glasgow, 7
Glenorchy, 299
Göbel, Jakob, 166, 173
Goebbels, Joseph, 99
Gold, Harry, Figure 68, pages 377, 379; face-to-face showdown with Johnny, 379–80

Gomez (Gen.). *See* Manfred Stern, aliases
Gordon, R. W., 271
Gordon, Vencil, 271
Gouzenko, Igor, 346
Graf Spee. See *Admiral Graf Spee*
Graff, Gertrude. *See* Gertrude Krüger
Graff, William John (also John William). *See* Johnny de Graaf
Graffnor, Gertrude. *See* Gertrude Krüger
Graffnor, John. *See* Johnny de Graaf
Grajaú "bomb factory," 205, 209
Grajewo, 53
Grand Ligne, Quebec, 350, 355
Graul, Jens, 393 n. 8
Gray, John, 301–2
Great Depression, 152, 173
"greatest counterintelligence agent in modern history," 382
Green, Montgomery M., 400 n. 11
"Greenwood," 271
Grevenbroich, 83
Gronau: anti-war demonstration, 96; KPD district, 96
"Group of 42," 43, 45, 48–49
Gruber, Erna. *See* Helena Krüger
Gruber, Francisco. *See* Johnny de Graaf
"Gruber, Franz." *See* Heinrich Simone
Gruber, Franz Paul. *See* Johnny de Graaf
Gruber, Heinrich, 266
Grubnick, Karl. *See* Johnny de Graff
Grunewald Forest, 168
Grybowski, Franz, 197
Guimarães, Honório de Freitas: Brazil revolution, 200; "Martins," 200, 203
gulags. *See* Soviet Union
Guralski, Abraham (Boris Heifetz), 196; helps convert Prestes to communism, 196
Gurkhas, and Chinese port workers, 21
Gurney, Hugh, 199, 204; MI6, 199

Haase, Hugo, 38, 45, 48, 64; employed by British, 172
Halifax, 303; accident at lecture, 374; "Kaiser," 303; Marius Alfred Langbein, 324
Hamburg, 4, 36–37, 39, 85–87, 152–53, 393 nn. 2, 5; "Bobbi," 331, 334, 341–42, 421 n. 25; De Graaf family residences, 4, 28, 61 221; deportation of Olga and Sabo to, 211; Ernst Krüger returns, 265; KPD, 86–87, 152; Military Intelligence (Abwehr) transmission station, 325–26, 328, 330–32; Philharmonic Orchestra, 4; RFB leader Johnny, 95; strikes, riots, and revolution, 63–64, 69
Hamilton, Christopher G. W., 271
Hamm, 4, 72–73, 85; coal mines, 87; Free Corp occupation, 78–80; KPD leader Johnny, 96; RFB leader Johnny, 94; *Ruhr Echo*, 95
Hampton, New Brunswick, 303
Haniel, Karl, 74–75
Hannover, 359
Hara-Kiri Club, 355–56
Harcourt-Rivington, Seaward H., 271
"Harry." *See* Hans Wilhelm
Harsanyi, Maria "Marika," 387
Harvison, Clifford W., Figure 55, pages 300, 374, 380, 389; appointed RCMP commissioner, 383; arrests Adrien Arcand, 305; best policeman Johnny ever knew, 377; bickers with Cyril Mills, 330, 341; Canadian-German Club, 338–40; capture U-boat mission, 350–55; Columbia mission, 300–302; deals with Johnny and Gerti's visa problem, 300–301; described, 300; Frederick Mead, 341; Gerti's funeral, 376–77; Johnny and Gerti arrive in Montreal, 300, 303, 372; Johnny and Gerti leave Montreal, 357; Johnny hopes to help Allies in Germany after war, 356; Montreal's pro-Nazis, 304, 306–8, 310–11, 314, 316–17, 319–20, 332, 336–38, 343; Nazi leader for North America, 344–45; problem with J. Edgar Hoover, 377–78; publishes *The Horsemen*, 385; Rolf von Linter, 347–50; survivor's pension for Gerti, 353; Vivian, 303; warns Johnny about Tim Buck and the rest of the CPC, 373–74; Werner von Janowski, 321–30, 332–34, 337, 341–42, 420 n. 3; whereabouts of the de Graffs, 419 n. 16
Harwich, 153, 260
Haskins, Alfred. *See* Marius Alfred Langbein
Hattingen, Rosa Luxemburg Battalion, 80–81
Hazor, Willy, 86–87
Headry, George, 424 n. 13
Heckert, Fritz, 114
Heifetz, Boris. *See* Abraham Guralski
"Heil Dir im Siegerkranz," 9, 394 n. 16
"Helen," 267
Helgoland (battleship), 63
Helsinki, 164, 182, 259
Herltz, Karl, 160–61, 195; German Revolution of 1923, 160
Hess, Erich Joachim, 271
Highland Chieftain, 289
Highland Princess, 212
High Sea's Fleet. *See* Germany, navy
Hitler, Adolf, 121, 165–68, 173, 177, 220, 237, 242, 265, 298, 305–6, 308, 312–13, 315, 324, 356, 358, 361, 363, 399 n. 27; *Admiral Graf Spee*, 279; Nazi leader for North America, 344; Non-Aggression Pact, 201–2; Werner von Janowski, 321–37, 341–42
Hitler Youth affair, 242
Hoboken, 27–28; Great Hoboken Pier Fire, 394 n. 8; sailor's town, 27

Ho Chi Minh, 182
Hoek van Holland, 32
Höhler, Ali, 99, 400 n. 40
Holland. *See* The Netherlands
Hollenzollern, 62, 64, 69, 78
Homeville Rooming House (Montreal), 301
Hong Kong, 180–82; port workers, 20–21
Hoover, J. Edgar, 377–78
Horningtoft, Figures 70, 73, pages 1, 381, 383, 395 n. 21, 425 n. 41; Andy Kovács, 386–87; Blake Clarke, 381; bulldozed, 387; degenerates move in, 387; gas and electricity cut off, 386; Sári de Graff, 386–87
Horstman, Dr., 99
Hotel Atlântico (Rio de Janeiro), 262
Hotel Astor (Shanghai—now Hotel Pujiang), 183
Hotel Flamengo (Rio de Janeiro), 200
Hôtel Haussmann (Paris), 222
Hotel Lutecia (Paris), 267
Hotel Novo Moskovskaya (Moscow), 149, 225, 230–32, 235; hides gun in room, 232; Karl Franserra, 241; studies in Moscow apartment before returning to, 239
Hotel Passage (Moscow), 149–50, 177, 179, 226, 404 n. 22; also used by Comintern, MOPR, and Profintern, 402 n. 19; FBI misspells, 402 n. 19
Hotel Riviera (Rio de Janeiro—now Orla Hotel), 26, 274; Aldo Rosso, 263; "Franz Gruber," 267; Johnny buys an interest in, 263; Johnny questioned about by DESPS, 284; statement by Emilia Rosso, 415 n. 15
Hotel Windsor (Montreal), 299, 301, 344, 372, 423 n. 2
Howard, E. G., 299
Hsiang Chung-fa, 182
Huangshi, 188
Huerta, Victoriano, 29
Huetter, Helmut, 271
Hulton, Edward, 271
Hummer, Fritz, 314–15, 319; estranged and dangerous, 336; described, 311; nutralized, 337 profession, 311; pro-Nazi, 311
Hunedoara, 146
Hungarian Embassy, Vienna, 375
Hungary, 142–43, 146–47, 149, 359; refuges to Canada, 375, 383; uprising, 383
Hunter, McL., 28; ill will, 30–31; refuses to pay Johnny, 30
Hutt, Alfred, Figure 29, pages 199, 204, 271; addresses, 274; confirms Johnny's being MI6 to Filinto Müller, 212; contacted by Vargas, 208; contacts London, 208, 268, 285; continues to be used during Brazil II mission, 261; Filinto Müller knows of Johnny, 211; Johnny discusses Sil Milo's demands with, 275; MI6, 199–200, 203; provides Johnny list of Argentine contacts, 215; reply from London, 208; official at Light, 199, 203
Hutte, Charles, 271

Iacobovici, Eugen. *See* "Junescu"
"Igor": complains of German workers, 119; manager of Juny Commune's Camp No. 6, 118–19, 122
IKKI. *See* Soviet Union
Imperial Hotel (London), 260, 290
Independent German Social Democratic Party. *See* Germany, USPD
Indianapolis, 219
International Brigades, 228, 413 n. 14
International Control Commission. *See* Soviet Union
International Lenin University. *See* Soviet Union
interventor, 207
Invergordon Mutiny. *See* United Kingdom
Iron Guards. *See* Romania
Italy, 27, 102, 200, 359; Communist Party, 161
Itamarati, 204, 210

Jaenicke, Erna, 99
Jany, Joseph, 271
Japan, 186, 236–39, 283; agent in Shanghai, 190–92; army in China, 182, 185, 189; Brazil II mission, 237–39, 267; Communist Party, 238; Manchukuo, 180; navy, 237–38; reason for mission to, 237–38
Japanese Communist Party. *See* Japan, Communist Party
Jarminski, Edith, "English Edith," 267, 271
Jews, 1, 76, 91, 184, 197, 210–11, 292, 294, 298, 324, 326, 340, 345, 368, 381, 425 n. 41; cheated Johnny, 91
Jiangxi (Kiangsi), 184–85, 188; Johnny denounces Chinese Communists to London, 189; Long March, 189, 406 n. 43
Johansen, Wilhelm, 33–34
"Johanssen." *See* Johnny de Graaf
Jordão, Alexis de Miranda, 271
Julien, Francisco de Menezes, Figure 44; background, 415 n. 9; contact or probable contact by Johnny, 211, 222; DESPS/Quadro Movel, 211, 262, 271; imprisoned at Fortress Santa Cruz, 282; in pay of German Embassy, 285; Johnny loans money to, 265, 285; Johnny uses to contact Filinto Müller, 262, 273; Karl Stemmer as someone of interest, 282; pro-Nazi, 285; travels with Johnny to Santos, 222
"Julius." *See* Johnny de Graaf
"Junescu" (Eugen Iacobovici), 141, 143; Saul, 143
Juny Commune's Camp No. 6. *See* Kharkov: Juny Commune's Camp No. 6
Justo, Agustín P., 222

Kaganovich, Lazar, 230–31
"Kaiser," 303
Kaiserliche Marine. *See* Germany, Imperial navy
Kaiser Wilhelm II, 9–10, 38, 40–42, 45, 47–48, 51, 62–64, 78, 83, 107–8; abdicates, 59; birthday, 10, 69; effigy, 62; Johnny's hatred of, 34, 71–72
Kalmeier, Elisabet, 411 n. 14
Kamenev, Lev, 122, 401 n. 38
Kapp, Wolfgang, Kapp Putsch, 77, 275
Karl Liebknecht Middle School, 234–35; Hitler Youth affair, 242
Kazimierowicz, 425 n. 41
Kentucky Fried Chicken, 384
Keynes, John Maynard, 76
Kharkov, 175; Juny Commune's Camp No. 6, 115; Comintern, 117–19; Maria de Graaf leaves, 121, 175; personnel, 121; problems, 116–22; solutions, 118–19
Kiautschou (Qingdao), 21
Kiel, 49, 63, 86–87
Kiessewetter, Werner, 271, 274–75; arrested and taken to Fortress of Santa Cruz, 281–82; claims Johnny is head of all British agents in Brazil, 281; description, 275; Johnny's suspicions of, 275, 277–78; London fails to inform, 285; Nazi agent, 285
Kiev, 120
Kinderheim No. 6. *See* Children's Home No. 6
King Carol II, 143, 145
King George V, 156
King George VI, 383, 425 n. 55
Kinshasa (Leopoldville), 18, 394 n. 1
Kitson, George Vernon, 181–82, 187, 189–92, 405 n. 11
Kitson, Ruth, 426 n. 70
Kléber, Emilio. *See* Manfred Stern, aliases
Klein, Hans, 315–16; described, 311; German immigrant to Canada, 307; pro-Nazi, 307; shipping manifests, 319
Klerekoper, Jaques, 271
Klutzka, Anton and Margarete, 65–67; description of home, 66, 70
Klutzka, Anna, 66, 70
Klutzka, Dora, 66, 70
Klutzka, Emma, 66, 68, 70, 177; cares for Johnny's children, 174, 234, 236; Helena Krüger's visit, 174
Klutzka, Maria (*See* also De Graaf, Maria), 66–68; injured, 69; marries Johnny, 69–70; nicknames, 66
Klutzka, Otto, 47–49, 65–67, 70
Kemp, V.A.M., 244
"Knight of Hope." *See* Luís Carlos Prestes
Knöß, Wilhelm, 393 n. 11
Knox, Geoffrey George, British Ambassador and head of MI6 in Brazil, 271, 285

Kobe, 238
Köbis, Albin, 49
Korean War, 372
Kovács, Andy, 386–87; Johnny's ashes, 387
KPD. *See* Germany, Communist Party
Krenick (Capt.), 24–25
Kriegsmarine. *See* Germany, Nazi navy
Krüger, Emilie, Figure 46, pages 95, 99, 121, 152, 158, 223, 260, 265; brings Gerti to Copenhagen, 259; brings Gerti to Paris, 222; call Johnny "Franz," 264; death, 289; full name, 95; in Brazil, 264–65; Johnny arranges for visas and passage to Brazil, 264; *Monte Rosa*, 264; new orders from Brussels, 267; promotes daughter, 95–96, 207; Rua Barão da Torre 33, 265; surgery, 265, 415 n. 21; urges Johnny to take Helena back, 175
Krüger, Ernst, Figure 48, pages 95, 99, 223, 389, 395 n. 21; call Johnny "Franz," 264; considers Helena silly, 411 n. 18; drafted into Wehrmacht, 416 n. 22; Hans Lessing, 264–65; Helena's Argentine lovers, 411 n. 14; in Brazil, 264; job with Condor Airlines, 265; Johnny arranges for visas and passage to Brazil, 264; Johnny's 1939 arrest, 417 n. 46; joins Hitler Youth, 415 n. 18; joins Young Communists, 220; *Monte Rosa*, 264; reports Johnny was in a duel, 222; *Santa Eugenio*, 265; supports family, 220, 264; surgery, 265, 415 n. 21; ticket back to Hamburg, 265; wrong picture of Johnny in Gestapo files (and in Waack's *Os Camaradas*), 412 n. 35
Krüger family, 99–100, apprehensive over Helena's death, 222; Frank Foley, 182, 200; Johnny Jr., resides with, 99, 174–75; Johnny's family resides with/visits, 121, 152, 158, 174, 223–24; Johnny sends funds, 220, 259, 264
Krüger, Gertrude, Figures 43, 46, pages xiii, xiv, 95, 121, 152, 158, 223, 259, 261, 277, 367, 412 nn. 30, 37; accepts Johnny's proposal, 239; adoption, 338, 421 n. 36; altered passport to be Helena, 259, 283; and Johnny's 1939 arrest, 285–86, 288; arrives in Brazil, 261–62, 278; arrives in Canada, 299, 303, 372, 419 n. 3, 423 n. 2; Avenida Rainha Elisabeth, 219, 263; call Johnny "Franz," 264; Canadian-German club, 339–40; dances with Nazi, 223–24; citizenship, 357, 375–76; death, funeral, and cremation, 375–76, 386, 424 n. 10; early bond with Johnny, 95; Frank Foley, 260; Francisco Julien, 264; Gertrude Graff, 299; Gertrude Graffnor, 299; goes to Copenhagen with mother to meet Johnny, 259; goes to Paris with mother to meet Johnny, 222; Hampton, New Brunswick, 303; Hans Lessing, 264–65, 415 n. 20; hospitalized, 265, 288–89, 302, 415 n. 21; Johnny's coding assistant, 274, 290; Johnny's new calling in

Canada, 373; Johnny questioned about by DESPS, 283; leaves Brazil, 289; leaves London, 370–71; leaves Montreal, 301, 357; London, xiii, 2, 290–91, 297–98; loves Canada, 308, 357–58, 371; marriage with Johnny, 261, 414 n. 5; meets family, 264; miscarriages, 288, 338, 375, 418 n. 74; Montreal, 300, 303–6, 314, 317; 49 Palmerston Avenue, 306, 328–30, 334, 337, 357, 420 n. 8; new orders from Brussels, 267; New York, 301–2; nickname, 95; piano lessons, 265; returns to London, 289–90, 357–58; returns to Montreal, 303–4, 371–72, 377, 419 n. 14; survivor's pension, 353–54; stays in London, 359–60; Ward and Violet Scott, xiii, 307; will consider Johnny's marriage proposal, 222; Valentine Vivian, 260–61, 290, 358, 360; wedding plans, 260–61; writes Johnny, 206–7, 286; Werner von Janowski in the basement, 328–30; whereabouts, 419 n. 16

Krüger, Gustav, Figure 46, pages 95, 121, 152, 158, 223, 265; call Johnny "Franz," 264; death, 289; fired and blacklisted, 220, 264; full name, 95; Horst Wessel murder weapon (Johnny's revolver), 99–100; in Brazil, 264–65; job in Berlin, 158, 264; Johnny arranges for visas and passage to Brazil, 264; Johnny's nickname for, 266; *Monte Rosa*, 264; new orders from Brussels, 267; questioned by DESPS, 282; Rua Barão da Torre 33, 265; urges Johnny to take Helena back, 175; watch repairman, 416 n. 22; Vargas's son, 416 n. 23

Krüger, Helena, Figures 22, 31, 34–35, pages 95, 203, 228–29, 259, 283, 412 n. 30; affair with Carlos da Costa Leite, 226; "Alemazinha," 204; alias Erna Gruber, 200, 415 n. 20; argues with Johnny, 219–21; arrives in Buenos Aires, 213; arrives in London, 152–53; arrives in Moscow, 176; arrives in Prague, 175, 220; arrives in Rio de Janeiro, 198; at Polícia Central, 211–12; attends meetings (in place of Johnny), 204, 207; background, 220; born, 399 n. 29; Brazil mission, 196, 198–200; death and cremation, 1–2, 220–23, 226, 411 n. 22; described, 196, 220, 411 n. 18; dislikes Prestes, 204; French ability, 204; friendship with Olga, 204; Hotel Passage, 177, 179, 226; Johnny admits murdering her, 385, 411 n. 22; Johnny questioned about by DESPS, 283; knew all of the revolutionaries in Brazil, 204, 228–29; left in London, 157–58, 220; left in Moscow, 180, 182, 220; left with parents, 164; "Lena," 174, 204; lover said to have been killed by Johnny in a duel, 222; made aware of Johnny's MI6 connection, 221; marriage with Johnny, 222, 414 n. 5; membership in political groups, 220, 411 n. 18; Prestes's chauffeur, 204; recalled to Moscow,

219, 221, 411 n. 13; romantic interests, 196, 219–21, 226, 411 n. 14; travels to Ahlen, 174, 404 n. 19; travels with Johnny to USSR, 175–77; unaware of Johnny's MI6 connection, 205

Krüger, Waltraud, xvi, 389; Helena's Argentine lover, 411 n. 14

Krupp steel works, 361; worker unrest, 361–63

Kun, Béla, Figure 19, pages 142–43, 146–47, 195; accused, removed, arrested, executed, 149; Comintern money, 142–43; relationship with Johnny, 146, 149; unpopular with PCR, 142–43

Kuomintang Army. *See* China

Ķuzis, Peteris. *See* Ian Karlovich Berzin

Kuzbass, 121

Kuznetsk Basin, 115

Labor-Progressive Party. *See* Canada

Lacerda, Carlos, 417 n. 46

L'Action Catholique, 341

Ladebour, Georg, 38, 45, 64; employed by British, 172

Ladisch, Paul Alois, 271

Lambert, Léon, 342

Lampião (Virgulino Ferreira da Silva), 207

Langbein, Marius Alfred, 324–25; mission, 324

Langner, Alfred (Turre Lehén), Figure 12, pages 122, 389–90, 400 nn. 1–2; at Frunze, 108, 112; Berlin and Prague mission, 165; Brazil I mission, 195–96, 407 n. 1; British missions, 151–52; defends Johnny on return from Brazil, 231; Donbass assignment, 114–15; following Brazil and Argentina, 225; Harry Pollitt, 161; Luís Carlos Prestes, 225; Manchuria mission, 179; Manuilski, 225; PCB, 225; recruits Johnny, 101–2; Romanian mission, 139, 149; War and Anit-Militarism section of the Comintern, 101, 107

Langsdorff, Hans, 280–81; suicide, 281

La Patrie, 341

La Presse, 341

Latin America, 184

Latvia, 399 n. 16

"Laura, Laura, Laura," 335–36

Layman, Heinrich, 90–91; dog, 90–91; mother, 91

Le Droit, 341

Lee, Ambrose Northorp, 271

L'Evémement-Journal, 341

Lefranc, Serge. *See* Joseph Ducroux

Legionnaires. *See* Spain

Lehén, Turre. *See* Langner, Alfred

Leibovitch, Comrade, 103

Leipzig: KPD conference, 87–90

Leite, Carlos da Costa, 226

"Lena" *See* Helena Krüger

Lenin Mausoleum, 195

Lenin, Vladimir, 89, 110, 149, 195, 205–6, 236, 398 n. 9, 401 n. 38, 407 n. 9; Trotsky, 167
Leopold (Inspector), 421 n. 36
Leow, Willy, 89, 166, 169–70, 178; accuses Johnny, 179; dismissed, exiled, and executed, 179
Lessing, Hans: arrest, 282; Gerti, 264–65, 415 n. 20; Johnny questioned about by DESPS, 284
Liddall, Walter Sidney, 157, 403 n. 26
Liebknecht, Karl, 34, 62, 68–69
Lima, Rodolfo Mota, 272
Lisbon, 342
Liverpool, 299, 371
Locatelli, Amleto: accused of being gay, 228; arrives in Rio de Janeiro, 198; Brazil mission, 198, 203; described, 203; discusses what happened in Brazil with Johnny and Helena, 214; escapes from Rio to Buenos Aires, 210, 214, 410 n. 4; International Brigades, 228, 413 n. 14; Manuilski and, 227–28; Palmiro Togliatti and, 228; plans Recife trip, 205; praised by Johnny, 239; presumed death, 228; returns to Moscow, 203, 214; submits report on what happened in Brazil supporting Johnny, 227–28
London, xiii, 9, 19–20, 163, 290, 358, 367, 368; Johnny and Gerti, 2, 260–61, 289–90, 419 n. 3; Johnny and Helena, 153, 163, 202–11; marriage, 261, 414 n. 5; MI5. *See* United Kingdom; MI6. *See* United Kingdom; "The Aristocrat." *See* United Kingdom; Milly and Billy, 153; River Thames, 19; XX. *See* United Kingdom
London South America Bank, 266
Long March, 189, 406 n. 43
Lovell's Montreal Directory, 347
Lovestone, Jay, 184
LPP. *See* Canada
Lubianka Prison, 242
Ludendorff, Erich, 77
Lüttwitz, Walther Freiherr von, 77
Luxemburg, Rosa, 34, 62, 68–69
"Lygia," 272

M4. *See* Soviet Union
MacDonald, J. Ramsay, 151, 156
"Mace," 270, 272
Machado, José Caetano, 208
Madrid, 400 n. 14
Magadan gulag, 179, 390
Manchester Guardian, 141
Manchuria, 174–76, 179, 382; Manchuria mission assignment, 176, 179–80; Manchukuo, 180; Mukden, 180
Manchukuo. *See* Manchuria
Mannheim, 94
Manuilski, Dmitri, Figure 15, pages 114, 151, 165, 169, 390; Brazil I mission, 195–96; calls Johnny a true Leninist, 236; following Brazil and Argentina, 225; Harry Pollitt, 161–63; Johnny's confidential criticism, 225; Johnny's unanswered letters to, 230; Olga Benário, 197; recalls Johnny and Helena from Argentina, 219, 222, 411 n. 13; saves Johnny, 169, 236
Manzi, Norberto, 411 n. 23
Mao Zedong, 188–89; demoted, 189
Margarita (or Marga), 203, 210, 407 n. 4
Maria (Gen.), Alex's translator, 108, 110
"Martins." *See* Honório de Freitas Guimarães
Marxism, 200, 407 n. 9
Marx, Karl, 345
"Mary," 261, 268; Johnny questioned about by DESPS, 283
Marzili Park, 101–2
Maslow, Arkadi, 93
Matadi, 394 n. 1
"Mattern." *See* Johnny de Graaf
Mattern, Alfred. *See* Johnny de Graaf
Max (Maj.), 108–9, 111–13; gift to, 113
May, George, May Report, 151–52
May Report. *See* George May
McCall, Henry William Urquart, 272
McCarthy, Joseph, 372–73
McCarthyism, 372–73
McClelland, George B., 344
McCrimmon, Kenneth Howard, 272
McGrath (or MacGrath), Donald Scott, 270, 272–73
Megan, Norton, 272
Méier, 211
Meireles, Ilvo, 200
Meireles, Silo, 208
Melbourne, 18–19, 24
Melnikov, Boris: Johnny tells of Argentine weapons inventor, 226; liquidated, 231
Melo, Severino Theodoro de, 408 n. 37
Melo, Tancredo de, 272
Memphis, Tennessee, 337
Mercury, 395 n. 18
Merrifield, Peter, 419 n. 8
Metropole Hotel (Moscow), 160–61
Mexico, 16, 18, 29; Tampico Incident, 29
MI5. *See* United Kingdom
MI6. *See* United Kingdom
Miami, 197
Mikoyan, Anastas, 230
"Miller," 272
Mills, Cyril, 329–30, 342; bickers with Cliff Harvison, 330, 341; Frederick Mead, 341
Milly, 153
Milo, Sil ("Williams"), 269, 276; imprudent orders, 269, 275; insists Johnny take Kiessewetter, 275; sends Karl Stemmer, 275–76; visits Rio and argues with Johnny, 275
Milov, Andrei, 116–20, 122

Milton, Comrade. *See* Eugene Dennis
"Miranda." *See* Antônio Maciel Bonfim
Miranda Corrêa, Affonso Henrique de, Figure 44; learns that Johnny is an MI6 agent, 211; meets Heinrich Himmler, 417 n. 50; provides Johnny's photograph to Nazi, 223; takes over DESPS during Müller's "vacation," 282; visits Nazi Germany, 417 n. 50
Missiduschinck, Leopold, 266
Moabit Prison, 68; Otto Braun and Olga Benário, 197
Möhne Dam, 361, 362
Monarch, 288
Molotov, Vyacheslav, Figure 37, pages 230–31; saves Johnny, 236
Monger, Martin, 314–15; described, 311; profession, 311, 314; pro-Nazi, 311
Monteiro, Frederico Mindelo Carneiro, 208
Montevideo, 184, 197–98; *Admiral Graf Spee*, British, French, and German, diplomatic manuvering, 280–81; contact point for U.K., 268; sends Karl Stemmer, 275; sends Werner Kiessewetter, 274–75; Sil Milo ("Williams"), 261, 269
Montreal, xiii–xiv, 299–303, 306, 324, 350, 380–81, 422 n. 37; Bell Telephone Co., 356; Boy Scouts, 376; Communists and pro-Communists, 345–46, 356; German-speaking workers, 306; Johnny and Gerti return, 303–4, 371–72, 377, 419 n. 14; Johnny's FBI interview, 378–79, 400 n. 2, 411 n. 26; "Kaiser," 303; Nazis and pro-Nazis, 303–4, 306–20, 332–33, 335, 343–45, 347, 352, 356; Nazi leader for North America, 344–45; Rolf von Linter, 347–50; Rotary Club, 373; S.A. 235's salary, 306; Sári Akontz (later: de Graff), 374–75; visit by Oscar and Leni de Graaf, 383; Werner von Janowski, 322–25, 327, 330–34, 341, 420 n. 3; whereabouts of the de Graffs, 419 n. 16
Montreal Daily Star, 342
MOPR (International Red Aid). *See* Soviet Union
Morocco, 394 n. 3
Moscow, 106–8, 114, 120–21, 144, 155, 159, 161, 164, 176–78, 181, 192–93, 196–97, 199–200, 232–34, 237, 240, 243, 259, 398 n. 10, 400 n. 1, 403 n. 33, 411 n. 22, 424 n. 28; Comintern, M4, or other Soviet agency, 80, 89, 93, 113, 115–19, 143, 147, 151–52, 154–55, 157, 160, 165, 169–70, 173, 175, 179–82, 184, 186–87, 190–91, 203, 206–7, 212, 214–15, 222, 227–28, 232, 238–39, 242, 261, 266–67, 278, 289; Johnny's first arrival, 102–3; Johnny leaves, 115, 139, 152, 180, 199, 403 n. 27; Johnny questioned about by DESPS, 283; Johnny returns, 122, 143, 147–49, 157–59, 164, 174–76, 181, 192, 220, 222–25, 404 nn. 21–27
Mosquito bomber, 331–32

Mount Royal, 299, 303, 306, 319
Mount Royal Hotel, 423 n. 2
Mukden, 180
"Müller." *See* Boris Melnikov
Müller, Civis, 211; Quadro Movel, 211
Müller, Consuelo, 262, 282
Müller, Filinto, Figure 28, pages 204, 210, 282, 390, 417 n. 45; agrees to work with MI6, 262; allows Johnny and Helena to leave Polícia Central, 212; anti-Nazi claims, pro-Nazi realities, 210, 262, 273, 281; arms uncovered in São Paulo, 268; arrest of Ewerts, 210; arrest of Prestes and Olga, 211; arrests following attempted Communist revolution, 209, 409 n. 58; contact with Johnny via Julien, 262, 273; contacted directly by Johnny, 277; cooperates with foreign police, 210; December 1939 arrest of Johnny and, 282, 286–89, 417 n. 50; December 1939 "vacation," 282–86, 417 n. 50; description, 262; duplicity, 273, 286, 288; Getúlio Vargas and, 288; head of the Polícia Civil, DESPS, and the Quadro Movel, 204, 211, 262; informed that Johnny is an MI6 agent, 212; Johnny ordered to work closely with, 268; Johnny's evaluation of, 262; Johnny's release from the 1939 arrest, 287–89; knows of Johnny, 211; liaison with, 273, 276; meets Johnny, 212, 262; offers Johnny a job, 288; passports and Graf Spree crew, 281; potential coastal watchers, 269–73; provides Johnny with Brazilian passport, 262; provides Johnny with men, 262, 280; Quadro Movel, 211, 262; sends Johnny to Santa Catarina, 262; signs Johnny's exit and reentrance visas, 212
Munich, 63; Olga Benário, 197; strikes, riots, and revolution, 68–69
Münster, 397 n. 6; armies from 73–74, 78; KPD district, 96; prison, 98, 101
Murphy, Cornelius James, 272
Murray, M. T., 2

Nagasaki, 238
Nanchang, 185
Nanjing military airport, 189
Nasser, David, 417 n. 45
Natal, 207; 21st Infantry Battalion, 207–8; local PCB acts, 208; Vargas and, 207–8
National Oil Products Co., of Harrison New Jersey, 379
Nazi. *See* Germany
Nazi army. *See* Germany
Nazi leader for North America, 344–45
Nazi spies. *See* Germany
Netherlands, The, 3, 9, 326–27, 423 n. 16; army, 403 n. 33; navy, 403 n. 33
Neumann, Heinz, 167–68

New Brunswick, 324, 351
New Carlisle, Quebec, 321, 323, 341, 421 n. 35
Newcastle, 23–24, 67
Newfoundland, 303
Newsweek, 337, 421 n. 35
New York, 27, 29–30, 197, 266–67, 299, 301, 348–49, 379–80, 395 n. 18, 413 n. 37, 422 n. 37; S.A. 235's salary, 306
New York State, 382
Nicholson, L. H., 411 n. 22
Niederrhein, 74
Nightingale Lane Internment Camp (Oak Lodge School for Deaf Girls/Jewish School for Deaf Children), 292–98, 358; Escape attempt, 297–98; Nazi spies at, 294–98
Nikitin, B. P., 196
19th Route Army. *See* China
Niobe, Figure 2, pages 7, 14–22, 25, 394 n. 2; described, 7, 16; cargo, 18–19, 21–22; Johnny and Walter leave, 20; life aboard, 16–17
NKVD. *See* Soviet Union
Noel (Cpl.), 300, 357
Nordenham, 3–4, 393 n. 2
Norfolk Co., England, 425 n. 36
Northeastern Secretariat, 208
North German Lloyd, 27, 394 n. 8
Norway, 279, 327
Nose, 9, 12, 14
Noske, Gustav, 68, 77
Northeast of Brazil: *cangaço*, 207; *coronelismo*, 207; impoverishment, 207; Lampião, 207
Nottingham (Canadian overseer), 368, 423 n. 9
Noulens, Hilaire (Yakov [or Yacob] Rudnik), 182, 186, 190
Nova Scotia, 303

Obuch, Dr., 99
"O" Division. *See* Canada
OGPU. *See* Soviet Union
Oldenburg, 87
Oliva, Nestôr Gomes, 272
Olsburgh, Ralf, 272
OMS. *See* Soviet Union
Onn 6, 92
Ontario, 1, 322, 350, 368, 373–74, 379, 381
"Operation Watchdog." *See* Werner von Janowski
Orgotdel. *See* Soviet Union
Osaka, 238
Oslebshausen Prison, 64
Oslo, 28
Osowiec, Figure 5, pages 49, 62, 85, 102, 374, 396 n. 4; arrival, 50–51; deaths, 49, 52–55; description, 50–52; escape, 59–60; Hoffman Bermann, 51, 57; infirmary, 55–56; pact made, 52, 60–61; Polish peasants, 56; (Sgt.) Wolf, 54–56, 86–87; survivors, 49, 86; treatment at, 50–61; von Liliencron, 57–58; work on rail line, 53–55
Ottawa, 1, 303, 324, 351, 380, 382; broadcasts to Hamburg, 331; capture U-boat mission, 354–55; Igor Gouzenko affair, 346, 374; newspaper leaks, 341; pays to keep von Janowski in Johnny's basement, 328–29; survivor's pension for Gerti, 353–54; whereabouts of the de Graffs, 419 n. 16
Ottawa Citizen, 421 n. 26
Oźlański, Bogdan, 396 n. 4

Pabst, Waldemar, 68, 77
Packard automobile, 265
Page, Ethel, 272
Paine, Walter, 272
palmatória, 284
Panama, 197
Paraná, 197
Paris, 4, 170, 178, 200, 404 n. 21; contact point for USSR, 207, 214, 416 n. 31; Frank Foley, 182–83; Hans Wilhelm, 267; "Helen," 267; Soviet Embassy, 222–23; U.S. Embassy, 157; Valentine Vivian, 200
Parker, Edward S., 157
Partido Popular. *See* Brazil
Patterson, Robert R., 272, 280
pau-de-arara, 285; description 418 n. 68
Paulina (Cornelia), 142–45, 147; intellect, 143–44
PCA. *See* Argentina, Communist Party
PCB. *See* Brazil, Communist Party
PCR. *See* Romania, Communist Party
PCUSA. *See* United States, Communist Party
Peano, Esteban, 407 n. 4
Peixoto, Ernani do Amaral, 264
Pelkum, 79
Pepsi Cola, 340
Pernambuco: attempted Communist revolution, 205–6, 208, 409 n. 53; arrests and killings following attempted Communist revolution, 209; sinking of the *Clement*, 279
Peru, 18, 197
"Petersen." *See* Johnny de Graff
Petersen, Paul, 377, 380; *See also* Johnny de Graff
Petrie, David, 329
Petrov (Col.), 108
Philby, Doris, 291
Philby, Kim, 291
Philadelphia, 379–80
Phillimore, John G., 272
Piatnitski, Osip, 161; Brazil mission, 195
Pieck, Wilhelm, 93, 100, 166
"Pigeon Willy," 98, 399 n. 34
Pinha, José, 272
Pinto, Diogenes, 272
Plantz (FBI special agent), 378–79

Plymouth, 19, 32, 154, 163
Poland, 49, 56, 59, 60, 65, 86, 102, 115, 165, 121, 139, 227; army, 103; Communist Party, 161, 175, 180; Nazis invade and World War II begins, 266; police, 111, 142
Polícia Civil. *See* Brazil
Polícia Central, Figure 53, pages 211, 281, 285, 287, 418 n. 71
Polícia Federal Argentina. *See* Argentina
Polícia Militar. *See* Brazil
Port of Jackson, 24, 394 n. 6
Portsmouth, 154
Plattsburg, New York, 348–49
Ploești refinery, 139, 143–44
Pollitt, Harry, Figure 20, pages 152–55, 161, 390; CPGB economically dependent on Moscow, 155; fools Johnny into returning to Moscow, 157, 159–60; Invergordon Mutiny, 155–56, 162; lies, 152, 154–55, 162–63; ordered to Moscow, 159
Pollock, Neil, 383–85, 393 n. 1, 425 n. 41; resigns from case, 384
Portugal, slave trade, 18
Prague, 173–76, 179, 404 n. 18; British Embassy, 175; Frank Foley, 175–76, 181; Soviet Embassy, 174–76
Pravda, 89
Prestes, Anita Leocádia, 211, 409 n. 54
Prestes Column, 198
Prestes, Lydia, 409 n. 54
Prestes, Luís Carlos, Figure 27, pages 184, 196, 203, 228, 230–31, 390, 412 n. 12; alias Antonio Vilar, 197; Brazilian armed forces, 198; arrested 211, 226; arrives in Rio de Janeiro, 197; army, 197; background, 197–98; British inform Brazilian government on, 197; converted to communism, 196; Elza Fernandes, 211; in USSR, 196; issues impossible orders to Johnny, 209; Johnny criticizes, 202, 226; Johnny meets, 198; Johnny's booby-trap devices, 203, 226; Johnny's skepticism, 196, 198–99, 202, 204–5, 214; Helena becomes chauffer for, 204, 226; "Knight of Hope," 197; Locatelli criticizes, 227; Olga Benário and, 197, 211; orders Johnny to Bahia, 408 n. 36; orders Johnny to Recife, 205–6; panic claim, 209, 409 n. 54; picture in Gestapo files, 412 n. 36; plans to free, 215, 226, 230; Polícia Militar in Botafogo, 202, 204, 206, 209, 227; Praia Vermelha, 202, 206, 209; revolution planning, 201–7, 226; Rua Barão da Torre 636, 201; sentence, 211; start of revolution, 208–9; veracity of Johnny's statements on, 209; Stella Blagoeva's interrogation of Johnny about, 226
Primula, 199, 407 n. 13
Prisoner of War Camps. *See* Canada
Profintern (Red International Labor Unions). *See* Soviet Union

Prussia, 6, 51, 64, 74
Pujol, Juan, 421 n. 23
Pullen, Charles, 272
Pullen, Edward, 272
Pullen Junior, 272

QPP. *See* Canada
Quance, Olive Blanche, 333–34; married to Werner von Janowski, 334
Quebec, 315, 322, 325, 331, 341, 345, 350, 372; Johnny's lectures, 373; pro-fascist groups, 343
Quebec City, 327, 331, 334, 341
Quebec Hydro, 307, executives from, 332; Nazi sympathizer's proposal to cut power generated from, 315–16, 319, 332–33
Quebec's pro-fascists, 343, 345
Queen Elizabeth, the Queen Mother, 383
Queen Lingerie Shop, 333
Queiroz Filho, Euzébio de, 285

RA. *See* Germany
Radek, Karl, Figure 9, page 89
Raeder, Eric, 281
Ragnarök, German legend of, 355–56
Rand, B. R., 272
Rattai, Karl, 402 n. 19
Ravensbrück Concentration Camp, 211
RCMP. *See* Canada
Realengo Military Academy, 226
Recife: 29th Infantry Battalion, 206; Afonso de Albuquerque, 206; Carlos Lima Cavalcante, 207; "Della ligou," 205–6, 208; Frederico Mindelo, 208; Malvino Reis Neto, 206, 208; Robert R. Patterson, 280; Vila Militar, 206, 208, 409 n. 51; visits by Ewert, De Graaf, and Locatelli, 205–6; Wandenkolk Wanderley, 208
Red Army, 154; later called by Johnny *Red Signal*, 402 n. 17
Red Army. *See* Soviet Union, army
Red Army of the Ruhr, 78–79; headquarters, 79
Red Cross, 243
Red Gun, 154
Redlich, Johannes, 46
Red Soldier, 154; later called *Red Fleet* by Johnny, 402 n. 17
Renwick, George, 301–2; attempts to grill Johnny, 301–2; makes bet with Johnny, 302; MI6, 301
RFB. *See* Germany
Reichpietsch, Max, 49
Reichstag. *See* Germany
Reichswehr. *See* Germany, Weimar army
Reis Neto, Malvino, 206; orders preemptive actions, 208; sent "Della ligou" telegram, 208
Resnicek, Adolf, 175
Revolutionärer Ausschuß. *See* Germany, RA
Revolutionary Committee. *See* Germany, RA
RFB. *See* Germany

Rhine River, 74–75; *Onn 6*, 92–93
Ribeiro, Yuri, 412 n. 12
Rio de Janeiro, 196, 210, 215, 259, 269, 275, 290, 407 n. 4, 415 nn. 14, 16; 3rd Regiment, 202, 206, 209; arrival of "Franz Gruber," 267–68; arrival of Johnny and Gerti, 262; arrival of Johnny and Helena, 198; arrival of Prestes and Olga, 197; arrival of the other revolutionaries, 198; arrests and killings following attempted Communist revolution, 209; Brazil II mission, 237–38, 261; DESPS, 204; Filinto Müller, 208; Hans Wilhelm, 241; Johnny arrives from Buenos Aires, 222; Johnny and Francisco Julien travel from Rio to Santos, 222
Rio Grande do Norte, 207, 409 n. 53
Rogalla, Hans, 169, 179; arrested and found guilty, 179; executed, 179; sentenced to Magadan gulag, 179
Romania, 142–43, 226, 359, 382, 401 nn. 1, 3; army, 139, 141, 143–45, 147; Bucharest, 140–43; Communist Central Committee, 143, 146; Communist Party (PCR), xvi, 139, 141–44, 146–47, 148, 294; Communist fatalities, 144; General Staff, 144; Iron Guards, 146, 294, 297–98; Jews, 294; Nazis and pro-Nazis, 294; police, 142; Romanian mission assignment, 139, 143; *Siguranza*, 141, 144–46, 148
Romanian political police. *See* Romania, *Siguranza*
Romano, Antonio Emílio: Figure 44; 415 n. 9; confinscates Franz Gruber passport, 262
Romero, Francisco, 205, 209
Roosevelt, Franklin D., 219
Rosa Luxemburg Battalion, 78–85; defeats Weißenstein Free Corp, 78; exhausted, 81; fights to Pelkum, 79–80; fights with police, 83; Grevenbroich, 83; moves to Dortmund, 80; moves to Essen, 81; moves to Hattingen, 80–81; partial pardon, 84–85; refuses to fight for the British, 84; surrender to British, 81–83
Rose, Fred, 346
Rosso, Aldo, 263; arrest, 282; Johnny questioned about by DESPS, 284, 415 n. 15
Rosso, Emilia, 415 n. 15
Rotary Club in Montreal, 373
Rotterdam, 20, 31–36, 395 n. 3, 403 n. 33
Roussel, Silva Araújo, 272
Royal Canadian Mounted Police. *See* Canada, RCMP
Royal Navy. *See* United Kingdom, navy
Rua Barão da Torre 33, 265
Rua Barão da Torre 636, 201, 204
Rua Borda do Mato 187, 205
Rua Saint Romain real estate, 265
Rückert, Erwin, 99
"Ruffier," 271–72
Ruhr, 48, 65, 75, 82, 90, 101, 107, 153, 157, 384, 424 n. 28; Communists, 68–70, 72–74, 77–79, 87, 110, 167–68, 241, 384; victims march, 94
Ruhr Echo, 95
Rust, William, 153–54
Ryder, T. E. "Ted," 303, 380–81

SA. *See* Germany
S.A. 235. *See* Johnny de Graff
"Sabo." *See* Elise Ewert
"Saboya," 272
Sainte-Thésèse, 311
Salm (Frau), 99
Samuel, Wilfred S., 326
San Diego, 238
San Francisco, 238
San Martín, 215; police, 221
Santa Catarina, 262, 276
Santos, 214, 222, 267–68, 279–80, 288–89
São Paulo, 198, 209, 212, 227, 238, 268, 288, 407 n. 4
"Sári." *See* Charlotte Akontz or Charlotte de Graff
Sarmento, Antonio Natanael, 408 n. 37
Saskatoon, 423 n. 16
Saul, 143
Savannah, 30; Johnny jumps ship and takes train, 30
Saxony, 63
Schmidt, Albert, 160–61
Schmutter, Heinz Harold, 277–79, 417 n. 40; road to the Chinese View, 278–79
Schneider, Herman. *See* Johnny de Graaf
Schoenfeld, Humberto Conde de, 273
Schubert, Herman, 152–53
Schwan, Willy, 93
"Scoopies," 39–41, 47, 395 n. 9
Scott (Dr.), 375–76
Scott, Ward and Violet, xiii, 307, 379
Scurvy, 22
Seafarers's International Union, 33–34
2nd Naval Revolt (1918). *See* Germany
Secret Intelligence Service. *See* United Kingdom, MI6
Seigmire, Rudolph, 309, 311–12, 314; described, 309, 316; future plans, 319; German immigrant to Canada, 307; nickname, 307; pro-Nazi, 307–9, 332; Quebec Hydro blueprints, 307, 315–16, 319; put out of action, 333; rumor started, 332
Seiten, 40
Sena, Jailson, 409 n. 51
Semjonov, Ivan, 233–34
Severing, Carl, 74; pardons, 75, 84; Rosa Luxemburg Battalion, 80, 84
Shanghai, 180–83; American Concession, 190; Arthur Ewert, 182–83, 186–87, 405 n. 28, 406 n. 48; British consul, 181–82, 187, 189–92, 405 n. 11; *China Forum*, 189; Communist arrests,

182, 190; Comrade Milton's murder attempt, 187; French Concession, 183, 187; Hilaire Noulens, 182, 186; Johnny's activities in, 181–93; Johnny's gives courses, 184; Manfred Stern, 182–90, 192–93, 378; Municipal Police Files, 405 n. 28, 406 n. 48; OMS, 182; police, 187; port workers, 21; Richard Sorge, 186
Shaw, William, 270, 273
Sherman, D. W., 382
Siguranza. See Romania
Silesia, 63; strikes, riots, and revolution, 69 .
Silva, Lourenço da, 270–71, 273
Silverthorn (FBI special agent), 378–79
Simone, Heinrich ("Franz Gruber"), 267; Johnny questioned about by DESPS, 283
Singapore, 180
SIS. *See* United Kingdom, MI6
Smith, Michael, 404 n. 13
Smitz, Miller, 315; described, 311; profession, 311; pro-Nazi, 311
Social Democratic Party. *See* Germany, SPD
Soldiers of the Front Association. *See* Germany, Free Corps
Soldier's Voice, 153–54
Sondike, 32–33; Johnny jumps ship, 32; Marquis Square, 31–35
Soong Ching-ling, 187
Soraes, José Otaviano Pinto, 207–8
Sorge, Richard, 186, 237
South Africa, 361
South America, 226, 228–29
Southam, W. Gordon, 329, 331, 333
Southampton, 261
Souza, João Joaquim de, 273
Souza, Willi de, 212; scolded by Filinto Müller, 212
Soviet Embassy, Ottawa, 346
Soviet Embassy, Paris, 222–23
Soviet Embassy, Prague, 174–76
Soviet Trade Union International. *See* Soviet Union, Profintern
Soviet Union, xiii, 30, 49–51, 59–60, 75, 76–77, 80, 89, 92–93, 101–2, 110, 120–22, 139–40, 154–55, 157–58, 172–73, 182, 202, 214, 222–24, 226–29, 233, 236–38, 243, 260–61, 265–69, 273, 278, 289, 291, 302, 372–77, 382–83, 396 n. 19, 399 n. 28, 405 n. 28, 410 n. 4, 411 n. 13; agent hotels, 114, 149–50, 160–61, 177, 179, 225; agents, 92, 176, 269, 377–80, 382; Agi-Prop, 149; army, 103, 105–6, 111, 167, 234, 241, 378; army's Far East command, 113; Brazil efforts, 195–215, 225; Bolsheviks, 77, 110; China efforts, 181–93, 378; Comintern, xv–xvi, 89, 101, 103–4, 114–15, 117–19, 122, 140–43, 147–49, 157, 161, 163–65, 175, 178–86, 195–96, 200, 213, 223, 225, 228, 230, 283, 398 n. 10, 404 n. 13, 407 n. 17, 424 n. 28; Comintern's 6th Congress, 184; Comintern's Cadre Department, 404 n. 22; Comintern's Far Eastern Bureau, 182; Comintern's South American Bureau, 184; Comintern's West European Bureau, 148, 158–60, 164, 174; Communication Department (formerly OMS), 225; Communist, Party (VKP [b]), xvii, 122, 140, 152, 162, 179, 230, 378, 414 n. 45; CPGB, 155; Donbass coal mines, 114–22; espionage network in Canada and the USA, 346, 380; family hostages, 175, 233; Federal Security Service (Russian Federation), 413 n. 21, 414 n. 56; Frunze Military Academy, 107–13, 179, 181, 182, 200; General Staff, 107, 111, 113, 115, 144, 146, 149, 166, 179–80, 182–83, 185–86, 192, 196, 223, 232, 241; German Revolution of 1923, 92–93; gulags, 106, 179, 242, 390; IKKI, xv–xvi, 114, 161, 225, 227, 229; International Control Commission, 230; International Lenin University, 101–13, 400 n. 11; Hitler Youth affair, 242; M4, xvi, 92, 107, 110–11, 113, 146, 148, 152, 157, 159–60, 163–64, 174–76, 179–81, 192, 195, 197, 198, 215, 223, 225, 232, 234–36, 241–42, 259, 261, 264, 266–67, 378, 400 n. 16, 404 n. 13; MOPR, 402 n. 19; NKVD, xvi, 112, 121, 179, 196, 198, 224–25, 229–32, 239, 242; OGPU, xvi, 104–7, 114, 230; oil to Britain, 157; OMS, xvi, 103, 139, 159, 182, 198, 215, 226, 229; Orgotdel, 104; Osowiec, 56; prisons, 242–43; Profintern, 183, 402 n. 19; Revolution of 1917, 56, 110, 399 n. 16
Spain, 194; Civil War, 228, 400 n.14; International Brigades, 413 n. 14; Legionnaires, 194
Spartacus League. *See* Germany
SPD. *See* Germany
Square, Marquis, 31–35, 405 n. 11
Stalin Auto Works, 240; Hitler Youth affair, 242
Stalin, Joseph, 105, 107, 112–13, 122, 150, 363, 373, 398 nn. 9–10, 401 n. 38, 407 n. 9; Non-Aggression Pact, 201–2; rebukes Arthur Ewert, 184; Hitler Youth affair, 242; Sergei Kirov assassination, 231; shakes Johnny's hand, 112; Trotsky, 167
Stalingrad, 118, 243; Oscar de Graaf (Johnny's son), 243; von Paulus's 6th Army, 243
Stalinist Terror, 121, 231; show trials, 401 n. 38
Stampfer, Friedrich, 166, 403 n. 5
Stanley Pool, 394 n. 1
Stasi. *See* Germany
Stemmer, Karl, 78, 275; contacts in pro-German south of Brazil, 276; dislikes Nazis, 276; information on augmented by Gestapo agent No. 5, 282; when Johnny arrested in 1939, 282
Steptoe, Harry, 190
Stern, Manfred, Figure 25, pages 182, 390, 400 n. 14; alises, 400 n. 14; Cai Tingkai, 189; described, 108, 184; dislikes Arthur Ewert, 185,

Stern, Manfred (*continued*)
187, 195–96; friendship with Johnny, 111, 192–93, 378; Johnny identifies for FBI, 378; Johnny redraws China battle plan, 185–86, 192–93; Johnny's graduation, 112; Magadan gulag, 193, 378, 390; nickname, 185; Otto Braun, 186; recalled, 190; religion, 184; Shanghai, 182–90, 378; Spain, 194–95, 400 n. 14; urged not to return to Spain, 194–95
Stern, Moische. *See* Manfred Stern, aliases
Sterritt, N. Leslie, 426 n. 2
Stewart, Ron, 410 n. 12
St. Albans, England, 419 n. 2, 423 n. 10
St. Hubert Air Force Base, 311
St. John, New Brunswick, 299, 380
St. Martins, New Brunswick, 324
St. Vincent de Paul Hospital, 385, 426 n. 70
Stock Market Crash of 1929, 151
Stockholm, 164, 259
Storm Division. *See* Germany, SA
Strasbourg, 92
Ströhla, Heinz-Dieter, 393 n. 10
Stuchevskaya, Sofia Semionova, 198, 203; accusations for the failure in Brazil, 228–29; arrives in Buenos Aires, 214; arrives in Rio de Janeiro, 198; escapes to Buenos Aires, 210; M4, 198; liquidated, 231, 410 n. 8; returns to Moscow, 215
Stuchevski, Pavel Vladimirovich, 196, 203; accusations for the failure in Brazil, 228–29; agrees with Johnny on Brazil, 214; arrives in Buenos Aires, 214; arrives in Rio de Janeiro, 198; at Polícia Central, 212; claims Johnny is a spy for the White Russians, 214, 229; described, 203; escapes to Buenos Aires, 210; liquidated, 231, 410 n. 8; NKVD agent, 196, 198; OMS, 198; returns to Moscow, 203, 215; Soviet citizen, 196; suspicions in Buenos Aires, 214; warns Moscow, 215
Stuttgart, 77
Sun Yat-sen, 187
Svea, 199, 407 n. 13
Swansea, 26
Swayne, Don, 426 n. 66
Sweden, 31–32, 77, 182, 199, 259, 327, 421 n. 17
Switzerland, 9, 100–101, 110, 200, 404 n. 21
Sydney, 24–25
Sykes (Capt.), 293, 296
Syracuse Post Standard, 832
Szaborowski, Elise. *See* Elise Ewert

Tacoma, 279
Taganka Prison, 243
Tait, R. R., 419 n. 16
Tampico Incident, 29

"Tecbrevet," 261, 265, 267; Heinrich Gruber, 266; Johnny questioned about by DESPS, 283
Thalheimer, August, 88, 93
Thälmann, Ernst, 93, 95, 166–67, 399 n. 27; Stalin prefers over Arthur Ewert, 184; Trotsky, 167
"The Aristocrat": death, 218–19; description, 216; discusses in Washington, D.C., 385; Johnny order to eliminate, 218; Johnny confronts parents with the big lie, 219; spy, 217
The New Germany, 345
The Wedding Night, 364
The widow and her son, 365–66
3rd Regiment. *See* Rio de Janeiro
Thüringen (battleship), 63
Time, 382
Times, 291
Todicain, Emma, 12, 46
Todicain (Herr), 12
Tokyo, 237–38, 261, 267, 414 n. 39
Tollins, Rose, 238
Tony (Gen.), 108
Toronto, 183, 322, 333, 344, 350; Communists and pro-Communists, 345–46
torture, 283–86
Trans-Siberian Railway, 180–81, 192, 238
Treviranus, Gottfried. *See* Johnny de Graff
Trotskyites, 179, 379, 401 n. 38
Trotsky, Leon, 167, 398 nn. 9–10
Tübingen, 24–25, 394 n. 6; (Capt.) Krenick, 24–25; Johnny's able-bodied seaman's papers, 25; Johnny leaves ship, 25
Tuerkel, Herbert Ralf, 273
Turkey, 147
Tuth: life aboard, 22–23; officer fights with Johnny, 22–23; Johnny jumps ship, 23; Johnny leaves documents on board, 24; ship's nickname, 22
twenty-five Soviet agents, 378
25 Jermyn Street, 291
29 St. James's, London, 419 n. 6
29th Infantry Battalion. *See* Recife

U-boats. *See* Canada and Germany, Nazi navy
Ukraine, 114, 165, 194
Ulbricht, Walter, 93, 100, 166
Ullrich, Otto Willi, 265; Johnny questioned about by DESPS, 284
Undefeated Column, 198
Union Nationale Party, 341
United Kingdom, 2, 30–32, 81–84, 141, 153, 156, 163, 197, 216–21, 260–61, 277, 286, 289–90, 294–95, 298, 306, 326–27, 330, 341–42, 356, 382–83, 385, 403 nn. 27, 33, 405 n. 28, 414 n. 5, 419 n. 3, 421 n. 25; 1926 general strike, 155; army, 82–84, 92; Battle of the Atlantic, 303; Brazil II mission—British supplement, 262, 269; British mission

assignment, 151–52, 163, 165, 220; China efforts, 181–82; Chinese port workers, 21–22; class-based, 151; Comintern, 398 n. 10; Communist Party (CPGB), xv, 152–57, 159, 162–63, 345, 402 n. 20; Incitement to Disaffection Act of 1934, 154; Invergordon Mutiny, 155–56, 162; London Blitz, 298; losses at Battle of Jutland (Skagerrak), 46; MI5, xvi, 171, 329–30, 342, 358–59, 410 n. 12; MI6, xvi, 2, 171, 189–90, 199–200, 204, 210–12, 214, 216, 219, 221, 243, 260–62, 265, 267–69, 274–75, 288, 290–93, 295–98, 300, 303, 346, 353, 359–61, 363, 366–67, 370–71, 373–74, 377, 403 n. 27, 404 n. 13, 407 n. 14, 410 n. 12, 419 n. 2, 423 n. 10; military, 156; navy, 32, 151–56, 163, 280, 286; Nazis and pro-Nazis, 291–92, 294–96, 423 n. 16; operatives, 215; police, 363; Scotland Yard, 292; Section V (MI6), 199, 359, 368, 423 n. 10; Shanghai industrial espionage against, 190–92; slave trade, 18; Soviet oil to, 157; stevedores, 154, 162–64; Versailles Treaty, 81–82; viciousness and Britain's intelligence services, 219; XX ("Twenty Committee"), 329–30

United Services Institute, 380

United States, 30, 183–84, 261, 265–66, 303, 348–49, 378, 382, 400 n. 14, 413 n. 37, 414 n. 5, 417 n. 46, 418 n. 71, 419 n. 16, 422 n. 7; army, 92; American Workers Party, 184; Brazil II mission emergency addresses, 238; CIA, xv, 400 n. 2, 410 n. 12; Columbia mission, 299–302; Comintern, 398 n. 10; Communist agents, 378–79; Communist Party (CPUSA), 156, 184, 282; declares war on Central Powers, 395 n. 18; FBI, xv, xix, 302, 312, 348–49, 373, 377–82, 395 n. 3, 396 n. 19, 397 n. 21, 399 nn. 28, 31, 33–34, 400 nn. 1–2, 14, 401 n. 1, 402 n. 19, 403 nn. 17, 33, 404 n. 21, 406 n. 48, 408 n. 36, 411 n. 26, 416 n. 31, 419 nn. 3, 6, 12, 424 nn. 21, 28; FBI Montreal interview, 377–79; Federal Penitentiary in Lewisburg, Pennsylvania, 380; House Un-American Activities Committee, 413 n. 37; moral duplicity, 30; navy, 31, 395 n. 18; naval intelligence, 400 n. 11; Nazis and pro-Nazis, 348–49, 356

Unna, 70–71

Urals, 165

Uruguay, 184, 197, 214–15, 219, 276; *Admiral Graf Spee*, 280–81

U.S. Fidelity and Guarantee Co., 301

USPD. *See* Germany

USSR. *See* Soviet Union

Vallée, Alphonsine. *See* Sofia Semionova Stuchevskaya

Vallée, Leon Jules. *See* Pavel Vladimirovich Stuchevski

Valparaiso, 21

van Heussen, Herman. *See* Johnny de Graaf

Vargas, Getúlio, Figure 28, pages 196, 200, 202, 230, 380, 390; contacts Hutt who contacts Johnny, 208; deportation of Olga and Sabo, 211; Filinto Müller and, 288; gives engraved silver cigarette case to Johnny, 265; informed by British, 197, 204, 208; Natal, 207–8; one of his sons, 416 n. 23

Vasiliev, Pavel: accusations for the failure in Brazil, 229–30; Alikhanov's "inconsistencies" in Johnny's account of the failure in Brazil, 229; aware of Locatelli's comments regarding the failure in Brazil, 229; Béla Kun, 149, 400 n. 9; Brazil I mission, 195, 407 n. 1; British mission, 151–52, 161; Berlin and Prague, 165; China mission, 187; does not believe the accusations by the Stuchevskis, 229; Langner's superior, 104; liquidated, 231; makes recommendations regarding the failure in Brazil, 229; NKVD, 229–30; Orgotdel, 104–5; saves Johnny, 169; says Johnny is a natural-born terrorist, 227; sees that Johnny gets Soviet passport, 175

Venice, 182

Venezuela, 207

Veracruz, 29

Versailles Treaty, 76–77, 81–82; Woodrow Wilson's 14 Points, 76

Vichy government. *See* France

Vienna, 139, 148

Vila Militar. *See* Recife

Vilar, Antonio. *See* Luís Carlos Prestes

Vilar, Maria Bergner. *See* Olga Benário

Ville de Paris, 197

Vivian, Valentine, Figure 24, pages 199–200, 359–60, 390, 404 n. 13, 407 n. 14; Brazil II mission—British supplement, 269; Canada mission, 303; Colombia mission, 299–300; described, 200, 222–23, 407 n. 18; knowledge of the Comintern and Marxism, 200, 407 n. 17; meets Johnny and Gerti London, 290, 358; meets Johnny in Brazil, 200, 275; meets Johnny in Paris, 222–23; Johnny in London, 261, 291; Johnny resigns, 369–70; nickname, 199; Section V, 199, 359, 368, "The Aristocrat," 219

VKP(b). *See* Soviet Union, Communist Party

Vladivostok, 180–81, 192

Volksstimme, 346

Volter, Kris, 318

von Janowski, Werner, Figure 57, pages 321–25, 335–37, 343, 390, 421 n. 23; background, 323, 326; Berlin, 331; bigamist, 333–34; "Bobbi," 331, 334, 341; box of matches, 322, 420 n. 3; "Braulter et al." to "Operation Watchdog," 322, 330, 335, 337, 341; changes story, 323–24; decorated, 326; description, 328, 341–42; dog

von Janowski, Werner (*continued*)
    food, 342; "fist," 330, 342, 421 n. 25; Germans possibly tipped off, 331, 341; Hamburg, 331, 334, 341; in the basement, 329, 337, 421 n. 26; Johnny's "hangman's noose trick," 326–27; last messages, 342; marriage, 421 n. 30; Mosquito bomber, 331–32; out of the basement, 329, 331, 337; triple agent, 341–42; "turning him completely," 326; warned/struck, 327, 337
von Liliencron, Luiz Freiherr, 57–59, 396 n. 7
von Linter, Rolf, 347; FBI, 348–49; German spy, 347; kidnapped and taken to U.S. border, 349; name confirmation problem, 347, 422 n. 7; profession, 347; sentenced, 349
von Minkewitz, Hubert, 273
von Papen, Franz, 167
von Paulus, Friedrich: 6th Army, 243; Oscar de Graaf (Johnny's son), 243; Stalingrad, 180, 243
von Seeckt, Hans, 77, 185
von Watter, Oskar Baron, 77, 79–80
Voroshilov, Kliment, Figure 38, pages 112, 230–31
Vorwärts, 166

Wagner, Karl. *See* Otto Braun
Waldemar (Maj.), 108
Walden, Helmuth, 273
"Walter." *See* Johnny de Graaf
Walter (Frau), 183
Wanderley, Wandenkolk, 208
Warren, Jim, 383, 425 n. 55
Warsaw, 102
Washington, D.C., 300, 348, 410 n. 12
Wehrmacht. *See* Germany, Nazi army
Weimar, 68
Weimar Republic, 88, 90, 148; promoting daughters in, 95–96
Weißenstein Free Corp, 78
Werner (Capt.), 108, 179–81; Comintern, 180–81; excellent intelligence/espionage network, 180–81; Ford dealerships, 181; Ian Berzin, 181
Wesel, 35
Wessel, Horst, Figure 12, pages 99–100, 400 n. 40; Horst Wessel Song, 99; murder weapon, 99–100
Western World, 198
West European Bureau. *See* Soviet Union, Comintern's West European Bureau
Westfalen, 4; coal mines, 65, 75, 87; strikes, riots, and revolution, 77–78
Westfalen (battleship), Figure 4, pages 46–49, 395 n. 14
Westinghouse Electric Co., 380

Westminster, 154, 291, 368, 423 n. 10
White Russians, 214, 229
Wickman, Harry. *See* Johnny de Graaf
Wiescherhöfen, 94
Wilberforce apartments: Figure 60
"Wilcox," 273
Wilhelm, Hans, 237–38; alias "Harry," 238; approaches DESPS, 278; arrives in Rio de Janeiro, 278; asks for British asylum, 278; described, 240–41; discussions with Foley and Vivian, 261, 278; German Embassy, 278; high-risk individual, 241; Ian Berzin, 241–42; Johnny's warning, 241, 278; MI6 fail to notify Johnny, 278; Paris, 267, 278; planned meetings in Rio, 263–64, 266; replacement, 267; travels to Belo Horizonte, 278
Wilhelm, Paul, 140, 174
Wilhelmshaven, 4, 9, 14, 33, 36, 46, 52–53; De Graaf family residences, 4; harbor, 6–7; Jade Busen, 5–6; naval base, 5–6, 39, 47, 48–49, 64
"Williams," 261. *See* Sil Milo
Wilmington, 29–30, 32, 36
Wilson, Robert Amcotts, 273
Wilson, Woodrow: 14 Points, 76
Wisconsin, 373
Wolf (Lt. Comdr.), 47
Wolf (Sgt.), 54–55, 57, 86–87
Wollweber, Ernst Friedrich, 63–64
Wood, Stewart Taylor, 329
Wood, William Eric, 273
World War I, 34, 64, 76, 91, 108, 115, 141, 143, 151, 173, 323, 325, 422 n. 37
World War II, 2, 211, 266, 279–81, 355, 384, 398 n. 10, 413 n. 37, 415 n. 15, 421 n. 17

X-502. *See* Johnny de Graaf

Yagoda, Genrikh, 112
Yezhov, Nikolai, 230–31, 239
Yingchow, 406 n. 48
Yong, Parry (possibly Wilson Yong), 273
Yong, Wilson (possibly Parry Yong), 273
Young Wilmont, 426 n. 2
Yugoslavia, 346

Zentrum. *See* Germany, Catholic Center Party
Zerkin, Clara, 88
Zhejiang, 185
Zhou Enlai, 188
Zhu De, 181–82, 186–89; Otto Braun, 186
Zimmermann, Bruno. *See* Johnny de Graaf
Zinoviev, Gregory, 122, 401 n. 38
ZK. *See* Germany